Transcending the Boundaries of Law

Transcending the Bounda l be
central to future develc law.
In its pages, three gen have
become key feminist th acy,
and law and politics. very
first anthology in femi man
and N. Thomadsen, e iove
away from the study o The
scholars in *At the Boun* iing
law and legal instituti iety
tradition. This new an itors
to that volume with ider
theorists. It provides a age-
ment with issues relati for
future inquiry, includi eory
should move beyond ical,
political, and social im ner-
ability inherent in the

Martha Albertson l v at
Emory University and eory
Project.

Transcending the Boundaries of Law

Generations of feminism and legal theory

Edited by
Martha Albertson Fineman

Routledge
Taylor & Francis Group

a GlassHouse book

First published 2011
by Routledge
2 Park Square, Milton Park, Abingdon, Oxon, OX14 4RN

Simultaneously published in the USA and Canada
by Routledge
270 Madison Avenue, New York, NY 10016

A GlassHouse book

Routledge is an imprint of the Taylor & Francis Group, an informa business

© 2011 editorial matter and selection Martha Albertson Fineman, individual
chapters © the contributors

Typeset in Baskerville by
Taylor and Francis Books
Printed and bound in Great Britain by
CPI Antony Rowe Ltd, Chippenham, Wiltshire

British Library Cataloguing in Publication Data
A catalogue record for this book is available from the British Library

Library of Congress Cataloguing in Publication Data
Transcending the boundaries of law : generations of feminism and legal theory
/ edited by Martha Albertson Fineman.
    p. cm.
  ISBN 978-0-415-48138-0 – ISBN 978-0-415-48140-3 1. Feminist
jurisprudence. I. Fineman, Martha.
  K349.T73 2010
  346.01'34–dc22   2009053404

ISBN13: 978-0-415-48138-0 (hbk)
ISBN13: 978-0-415-48140-3 (pbk)
ISBN13: 978-0-203-84853-1 (ebk)

This book is dedicated to future generations of feminist students curious about the interweaving of gender, law, power, and society. It is hoped that they will be interested in learning the stories of those of us who went before them.

Contents

Illustrations

Graphs

Tables

Contributors

Michèle Alexandre is Associate Professor of Law at the University of Mississippi. Her teaching areas are constitutional law, critical race theory, civil rights, human rights, and feminist legal theory. She has been involved with the Feminism and Legal Theory Project for the past six years and has found it one of the most rewarding experiences of her career.

Mary Anne Case is an Arnold I. Shure Professor of Law at the University of Chicago Law School. She has presented more than a dozen papers and participated in several Uncomfortable Conversations at the Feminism and Legal Theory Workshop since 1994. She contributed chapters to two other collections developed from the Project: *Feminist and Queer Legal Theory: Intimate Encounters, Uncomfortable Conversations* (Martha Albertson Fineman, Jack E. Jackson, and Adam P. Romero, eds, Ashgate Press 2009) and *What's Right for Children?* (Martha Albertson Fineman and Karen Worthington, eds, Ashgate Press 2009).

Fiona de Londras is a lecturer in the School of Law, University College Dublin where she is also a member of the Institute of Criminology. She primarily researches international law's capacity to restrain repressive state action. While reading for her PhD in 2006, she spent three very happy months as a Visiting Scholar at the FLTP in Emory and visited once more in the spring of 2009.

Martha Albertson Fineman is a Robert W. Woodruff Professor of Law at Emory University and the Founding Director of the Feminism and Legal Theory Project.

Darren Lenard Hutchinson teaches constitutional law, equitable remedies, and seminars in critical race theory, law and social change, and equal protection theory at the American University, Washington College of Law. He writes extensively on issues related to constitutional law, critical race theory, law and sexuality, and social identity theory. He also authors *Dissenting Justice*—a blog related to law and politics.

Isabel Karpin is Professor in the Faculty of Law at the University of Technology, Sydney. She teaches and researches in feminist legal theory, health law, disability and the law, genetics and the law, reproduction and the law, law and culture, and constitutional law. She has been involved with the FLTP since 1992 when it was based at Columbia University.

Laura T. Kessler is Professor of Law at the University of Utah. Her main scholarly interest is discrimination and families. She began her academic career in 1993 through involvement in the FLTP. Her work appears in two other Project anthologies: *Feminism Confronts Homo Economicus* (Martha Fineman and Terence Dougherty, eds, Cornell University Press 2005) and *Feminist and Queer Legal Theory: Intimate Encounters, Uncomfortable Conversations* (Martha Albertson Fineman, Jack E. Jackson, and Adam P. Romero, eds, Ashgate Press 2009).

Holning Lau is Associate Professor of Law at the University of North Carolina School of Law. Lau thanks the Feminism and Legal Theory Project for being an invaluable forum for cultivating ideas and an extraordinary source of inspiration, camaraderie, and mentorship.

Linda C. McClain is Professor of Law and Paul M. Siskind Scholar of Law at Boston University School of Law. She is the author of *The Place of Families: Fostering Capacity, Equality, and Responsibility* (Harvard University Press, 2006), and co-editor (with Joanna L. Grossman) of *Gender Equality: Dimensions of Women's Equal Citizenship* (Cambridge University Press, 2009). As a new law professor, she made her first academic presentation at a workshop sponsored by the FLTP and continues to participate in the Project.

Martha T. McCluskey is Professor of Law and William J. Magavern Fellow, State University of New York at Buffalo. She contributed to several other FLTP collections, including *Feminism, Media, and the Law* (Martha Albertson Fineman and Martha T. McCluskey, eds, Oxford University Press 1997); *Feminism Confronts Homo Economicus: Gender, Law, and Society* (Martha Albertson Fineman and Terence Dougherty, eds, Cornell University Press 2005), and *Feminist and Queer Legal Theory: Intimate Encounters, Uncomfortable Conversations* (Martha Albertson Fineman, Jack E. Jackson, and Adam P. Romero, eds, Ashgate Press 2009).

Mary Jane Mossman is Professor of Law and University Professor at Osgoode Hall Law School, York University, in Toronto, Canada. She teaches courses in family law and property law and is involved in research relating to access to justice and the history of women in law. She considers it an honor to be included in this volume celebrating the FLPT's 25th anniversary, particularly because the Project has been so significant for Canadian feminist legal scholars.

Siobhán Mullally teaches at University College Cork, Ireland. She publishes widely in the field of gender, human rights, and migration law. She has visited the FLTP Project at Emory, as have her doctoral students. She has worked with international NGOs and UN bodies in Timor-Leste, Afghanistan, and Pakistan, and she previously served as Chairperson of the Irish Refugee Council (2006–8).

Roxanne Mykitiuk is Associate Professor of Law at Osgoode Hall Law School, York University, where she teaches health law and bioethics, law and disability, and family law. In 1991 she attended her first FLTP workshop at Columbia University and resolved to do graduate work there with Martha Fineman, which she did. She has been a participant in numerous Project workshops ever since.

Fionnuala Ní Aoláin is concurrently the Dorsey and Whitney Chair in Law at the University of Minnesota Law School and Professor of Law at the University of Ulster's Transitional Justice Institute in Belfast, Northern Ireland. She is co-founder and Director of the Institute and was nominated twice by the Irish government to the European Court of Human Rights in 2004 and 2007, the first woman and the first academic lawyer to be nominated. She was appointed by the Irish Minister of Justice to the Irish Human Rights Commission in 2000 and served until 2005. She began attending FLT Workshops while completing her J.S.D. at Columbia University.

Victoria F. Nourse is LQC Lamar Professor of Law at Emory University. She formerly served as Special Counsel to the Senate Judiciary Committee and to then-Senator, now Vice President Biden and as Assistant Counsel to the Senate Iran–Contra Committee.

Twila L. Perry is Professor of Law and the Alexander T. Waugh Sr. Scholar at Rutgers University School of Law, Newark. Her primary interest is in the intersection of feminist legal theory, critical race theory, and family law. She began attending FLTP conferences in the early 1990s.

Dorothy E. Roberts is the Kirkland and Ellis Professor at Northwestern University School of Law and a faculty fellow of the Institute for Policy Research. She is author of *Killing the Black Body: Race, Reproduction and the Meaning of Liberty*. She began participating in the FLTP, when it was located at Columbia, as soon as she became a professor in 1988. Her early engagement in the Project was pivotal to her development as a feminist legal scholar.

Adam P. Romero holds a J.D. from Yale Law School, and he served as a law clerk to Hon. M. Margaret McKeown of the US Court of Appeals for the Ninth Circuit. A regular participant in the Feminism and Legal Theory Project since 2002, he co-edited with Martha Fineman and Jack E. Jackson the FLTP volume, Feminist and Queer Legal Theories: Intimate Encounters, Uncomfortable Conversations (Ashgate Press 2009).

Laura Spitz is Associate Professor of Law at the University of Colorado, where she teaches contracts and commercial law. She has participated in FLTP workshops since September 2002, when she presented a paper at the Corporate Citizens in Corporate Cultures: Restructuring and Reform workshop in Toronto. She spent the 2008–9 academic year at Emory University as a Visiting Professor of Law.

Michael Thomson is Professor of Law, Culture, and Society at Keele University, UK. He is a health care lawyer with a particular interest in the regulation of reproduction, reproductive technologies, and masculinities. He has been involved with the FLTP since 2004 when he was a Visiting Scholar at Cornell Law School.

Margaret Thornton is Professor of Law and ARC Professorial Fellow at the Australian National University in Canberra. Her current research project, "EEO in a Culture of Uncertainty," examines the retreat from social justice within a neoliberal climate. She has taught and published in the area of feminist legal theory for 30 years.

Robin West is Research Dean and Professor at Georgetown University Law Center. She writes and teaches on law and humanities, feminist legal theory, general jurisprudence, and constitutional law. Her latest book is *Marriage, Sexuality and Gender* (Paradigm Press).

Patricia J. Williams is the James Dohr Professor of Law at Columbia University. She also writes the column, Diary of a Mad Law Professor, for *The Nation* magazine. Her books include *The Alchemy of Race and Rights, Seeing a Color-Blind Future, and Open House: On Family, Food, Piano Lessons and the Search for a Room of My Own.*

Acknowledgements

I would first like to thank the contributors to this Feminism and Legal Theory Project 25th anniversary collection for their intellectual companionship and the support I have received from them throughout the years. I appreciate their wonderful chapters and how patiently they have awaited the preparation of the final manuscript. But my debt goes beyond their contributions to this volume. I could not have maintained the energy and effort it has taken to build and nurture this on-going feminist feast called "the Feminism and Legal Theory Project" without the assistance, participation, and friendship they have consistently offered. In that regard, I must also recognize that a multitude of other scholars, not represented in this collection, have also made significant contributions to the FLT Project. I am equally indebted to and appreciative of them.

I also owe a debt to those dedicated souls who have helped to bring this book together in its final form. This book reflects the superlative editorial and copyediting work of assistant editor Melanie Mendenhall and Women's Studies graduate student, Celeste Bocchicchio. Corina Domozick, who recently joined the Feminism and Legal Theory Project as Project Associate, made significant contributions, particularly to amassing the bibliography.

Martha Albertson Fineman

Introduction

Martha Albertson Fineman

Twenty-five years ago, shortly after my own successful, but nonetheless harrowing bid for tenure, I began the Feminism and Legal Theory Project (FLT) at the University of Wisconsin. The explicit purpose was to provide a supportive and encouraging environment for scholars interested in doing feminist theory work. Early workshop sessions were in the summers, often lasting a week or more. They were organized around topics or themes, such as differences and motherhood.

The women and men who came to those early sessions were searching for a way to reconcile growing critical and feminist sensibilities with the study and teaching of law as we had experienced it as students and beginning professors. A handful of Women and the Law courses had been created and were being taught at that time, but there were very few women law professors and the word "feminist" was fairly new to law schools.

During those early sessions, we struggled in our presentations and discussions, often borrowing from feminist work in other disciplines, trying to push the language of feminism found in literature or history into a legal frame. The language found in other disciplines didn't always fit very well into the legal frame, particularly because the discipline of law had its own discourse and some rather inflexible standards that resisted new ways of approaching old problems.

In so far as feminist theory is critical theory, it faced a formidable subject in encountering the law. The law historically is conservative in nature. Concepts such as *stare decisis* and adherence to the idea of precedent controlling decisions make change difficult. In addition to valuing stability and continuity, law adhered (at least rhetorically) to principles of neutrality and objectivity. Teaching law was supposed to be a rational and logical exercise, not one that introduced particular perspectives or political positions. Feminism was seen as importing bias into teaching and scholarship, a form of special pleading in which women always came out on top.

Justice is, after all, blind, and we are a nation of laws, not men (sic) as the sayings go. Claims for reform based on the idea that a group (women) was not represented by the men who controlled law and its institutions and that the law was therefore biased were not well received. A large burden for as the first generation of feminist *legal* scholars was to convince our colleagues in the legal academy that feminism had its place and was as meritorious as its contemporaries: law and economics and critical legal studies. To some extent feminist legal theorists were able to build on the critiques of legal realists who challenged the objectivity of law during the 1930s and 1940s. Feminist legal theorists also benefited by inroads made at a number of law schools by the fleeting Critical Studies Movement during the 1970s and 1980s.

Law as a discipline remains a tough terrain for feminist thought, however. Even though most US law schools now have courses and seminars on feminist legal theory, many remain skeptical about its contributions, particularly those who have not educated themselves about feminist legal theory and the insights it can bring to their understanding of law and legal institutions. Increasingly feminists themselves raise questions about using the label "feminist," since it is seen as divisive or off-putting.

Some of our early efforts at feminist legal scholarship were published in 1991 in the first anthology of feminist legal theory, *At the Boundaries of Law: Feminism and Legal Theory*, which I edited along with Nancy Thomadsen. I selected the term "boundaries" for the title because while feminism had made its way into law, crossing some conceptual and intellectual boundaries, it had barely done so. Feminist legal theory clearly stood in law's margins—near the boundary that marked law off from other academic disciplines. The Introduction to this earlier collection is included as an appendix to this volume.

This new collection marks the passage of a quarter of a century of scholarship supported by the FLT Project. Its title connotes that the current position of feminist theory might be perceived as "transcending" law. This could mean two different things. The first is a mere celebratory claim that feminism is nearer the center than the periphery of law, having transcended or moved beyond law's boundary. However, some would argue that what has been transcended is not the boundary that marks off law, but law itself. This claim is more controversial, both within and without legal feminism because any claim that feminist theory has gone beyond or transcended law raises a fundamental question about the future of feminist *legal* theory: what will give focus and content to feminist legal theory if it has left law behind?

The chapters in this collection do not always agree on where feminism should be positioned in regard to law. Some proceed as though feminist insights were central to law and law reform (or at least in legal education). Others see little possibility for real feminist transformation in law, adhering to the notion that law is inherently male and impervious to feminist inroads. A few other authors in this collection seem to have transcended law in their own work. While they might focus on legal institutions and bring an understanding of how law interacts with society and positions of power, their concern is not with changing or reforming law but in better understanding how power is manifested. In that sense arriving at (or in) law is not the goal. In fact, law may be but an obstacle to be understood and ultimately transcended.

This book is divided into seven sections, beginning with reflections on the history of feminist theory and moving on to reflect on key themes in feminist legal theory: equality, bodies, universals and identities, intimacy and family, the state, and politics. These themes and some of the chapters reflect the fact that while much has changed since that first collection of essays, much remains the same. This new collection presents a range of feminist legal scholarship and a diversity of feminist legal scholars, including men, who were absent from the first FLT collection. Readers will encounter exciting and varied scholarship in the following pages that should leave them with a sense of the richness of feminist legal theory as it has developed over the last 25 years.

From women in the law to feminist legal theory

Introduction to Section One

This section reflects on some of the history of feminist legal theory from its beginnings as women in the law. The chapters include personal reflection and legal research, histories of professional women and of legal theories. They set the stage for the rest of the book by giving a background to the theoretical developments that follow.

Mary Jane Mossman's chapter addresses the tensions for early women lawyers between gender consciousness and the newly emerging norms of professionalism. She asks whether these women were feminist lawyers or more closely identified with norms of their profession. Mossman considers the French origins of the term "feminism" and its roots in the suffragette movement, highlighting the significance of being "woman identified" to feminism. Her chapter stresses the longstanding nature of the tensions generated by conflicting professional and personal challenges for women and demonstrates that bringing women into law does not necessarily mean feminist sensibilities will follow.

Margaret Thornton traces the history of feminist legal theory in Australian law schools in the changing political climate. This chapter shows how the fortunes of feminist legal theory are dependent largely on the state. She traces the trajectory of a discomfiting liaison between feminism and the legal academy over three decades, highlighting the contingent nature of feminist legal theory, particularly its sensitivity to the prevailing political climate. In Australia, the pendulum has swung from social liberalism to neoliberalism, which has induced uncertainty and instability. While under social liberalism, feminist legal theory received a modicum of acceptance within the legal academy, it contracted then withered with the onset of neoliberalism resulting in the academy's subtle remasculinization.

Patricia Williams takes us back to the struggles of women in and with law through a humorous but poignant account of the ways in which fashion intersects with power. She discusses the symbolic significance of the requirement that attorneys in the Solicitor General's Office wear traditional "morning coat" attire when arguing before the Supreme Court. Williams considers the complications this requirement has created for female attorneys and whether it reflects the persistence of law's failure to accept women into the profession. The chapter discusses how some fashions have restricted women's actions, even harmed their bodies (e.g. stiletto heels). However, fashions that constrict can also give women a sense of empowerment. Williams ends by recounting her experience at the 2008 Democratic Convention, where she wore a pair of heels that impeded her ability to move easily around the city of Denver. Even as she regretted her shoe choice, the shoes provided a sense of power or difference while navigating the chaos of the convention.

My chapter considers the legal concept of equality in the US from an historical and analytic perspective. Beginning with the establishment of Portia Law School for women and court decisions such as *Muller v. Oregon*, I discuss the tension between seeking equality as sameness of treatment and seeking positive improvements in women's lives. While women have officially attained legal equality with men, the benefits of citizenship are still distributed in highly unequal ways. In part this is because as a nation Americans value autonomy over equality, sacrificing substantive equality in the name of greater independence while ignoring the realities of our shared states of episodic dependency and constant vulnerability.

Chapter 1

"Le féminisme" and professionalism in law

Reflections on the history of women lawyers

Mary Jane Mossman

> [A] close examination of individual lives will reveal ... *a self-conscious feminist in virtually every early woman lawyer* ... They gained strength and purpose from the knowledge that they were working for a cause greater than themselves. At the same time that feminism ennobled their efforts, being female subjected them to discrimination.
>
> (Babcock 1998: 1699, emphasis added)

> Although the first women to enter male professions saw their attempts as part of "the cause of woman," *by the latter part of the nineteenth century professional ideology itself was increasingly magnetic.* There was a lively debate among the few women lawyers in the 1880s whether a woman should pursue her profession *because* of her sex ... or must *forget* her sex in order to pursue her profession.
>
> (Cott 1987: 232, first emphasis added)

These quotations reflect differing perspectives about the relative impact of ideas of "feminism" and "professionalism" for the women who first gained admission to the bar in the United States in the last decades of the nineteenth century. For legal academic Barbara Allen Babcock, early women lawyers were closely connected to feminism, although, as she also notes, they sometimes suffered discrimination on the basis of their sex. By contrast, as feminist historian Nancy Cott suggests in the second quotation, even though these early women lawyers were often engaged in lively debates about "the woman question," ideas about legal professionalism were becoming increasingly "magnetic" for them; indeed, her comment suggests that women lawyers had to eschew gender to pursue professional success. In the context of these divergent views, this chapter explores relationships between ideas about feminism and about professionalism in law in the experiences of some nineteenth-century women lawyers in the United States. In doing so, the chapter suggests that an assessment of how early women lawyers negotiated between the demands of gender and of professionalism requires a more nuanced account of their circumstances and their strategies. Indeed, in the efforts on the part of these early women lawyers to overcome traditional barriers and to seize opportunities, it is possible to see the beginnings of the dilemma facing modern women lawyers: the ongoing struggle to forge a "gendered professionalism."

As part of a larger project on the history of women lawyers (Mossman 2006, 2008, forthcoming), this chapter focuses on how ideas about gender and professionalism were manifested at different points in the twentieth century, how women lawyers negotiated these challenges in their work as lawyers, the extent to which gender shaped professional identities for women lawyers, and whether, if at all, women lawyers espoused ideas about "gendered professionalism." The chapter begins by highlighting a recurring historical debate about whether early women lawyers in the United States were "feminists," and it returns to the theme of my first presentation to the Feminism and Legal Theory Project more than 20 years ago (Mossman 1991). At that time, I focused on feminism and judicial decision making in *law* to reveal how "legal method" and legal reasoning may constrain or undermine the force of feminist arguments in the legal context.

Here I explore similar issues with respect to feminism in the context of the *legal profession*, using two examples. One example explores some aspects of the complicated relationships between women lawyers and suffrage activists in the United States in the late-nineteenth century; although individual women lawyers sometimes actively supported the suffrage cause, their legal arguments in cases about admission to the bar often tended to undermine suffrage goals. A second example focuses on the experiences of women lawyers who took part in the World's Columbian Exposition in Chicago in 1893; arguably, this event reveals how women lawyers were beginning to distance themselves from other women and to create a professional identity that reflected, at least to some extent, ideas about gendered professionalism. As both these examples reveal, the question whether women lawyers in the United States in the last decades of the nineteenth century were feminists presents important challenges for the history of women lawyers, as well as for our contemporary legal professions (Kay 2007).

Historical ideas about feminism and professionalism in law

> Here was the burden for the nineteenth-century woman lawyer. As a proper *lady* of her day, social etiquette required that she wear a hat in public. But as a *lawyer*, professional etiquette demanded that she remove her hat when she entered the courtroom. As a result, the question of the hat once again confronted women lawyers with the enduring challenge of reconciling their traditional role as *women* with their new professional identity as *lawyers*.
>
> (Drachman 1998: 95, emphasis added)

The starting point for this assessment of nineteenth-century women lawyers is the traditional male exclusivity of legal professions, a feature clearly identified in the "question of the hat" for early women lawyers. For example, "maleness" was a defining feature of nineteenth-century professions; indeed, an occupation could not traditionally be called a profession "if it was filled with women" (Gidney and Millar 1994: 239). The admission of women as lawyers inevitably created challenges at the intersection of ideas about gender and ideas about professionalism in law. As research on women in medicine has illustrated, women who sought admission to the bar faced different problems than women who wished to become doctors; women doctors could argue that they were simply extending women's nurturing and healing roles or that women doctors could protect women patients' modesty (Drachman 1984; Harris 1978). By contrast, women seeking admission to the bar were clearly "intruding on the public domain explicitly reserved to men" (Harris 1978: 112). In this context, as Virginia Drachman (1998: 2, emphasis added) argues, aspiring women lawyers were required to change the law itself: "women had to persuade male judges and legislatures to reinterpret the male-constructed jurisprudence that made their entry into the legal profession *not only unthinkable, but illegal.*"

In spite of these challenges, some women did begin to gain admission to the bar in the late-nineteenth century in the United States, often several decades before women succeeded in becoming lawyers in other jurisdictions. Some of these early women lawyers engaged in legal practice with at least some success (Mossman 2006). The first women lawyers benefited from legal reforms in family law and from societal changes that opened up access to higher education in the US in the late-nineteenth century. In this way, their achievements were connected to broader social changes concerning new roles for women. Indeed, reported decisions about women's claims for admission to the bar often reflected these new societal ideas about the woman question. Thus, ideas about gender and legal professionalism were issues both inside and outside the legal sphere of courtrooms, law firms, and law schools in the latter half of the nineteenth century (Bolt 1993; Hoff 1991). How individual women lawyers engaged with these ideas, and how they forged their way as a tiny minority of the legal profession, reveal some interesting patterns at the intersection of gender and legal professionalism.

At the same time, the issue of whether these early women lawyers were "feminists" presents a number of problems. As Karen Offen's research reveals, the word "*féminisme*" originated in France near the end of the nineteenth century:

> [T]he early history of the word *féminisme* ... [reveals that] it only began to be used widely in France in the early 1890s and then principally as a synonym for women's emancipation. The first self-proclaimed "feminist" in France was the women's suffrage advocate Hubertine Auclert, who from at least 1882 on used the term in her periodical, *La Citoyenne*, to describe herself and her associates.
>
> (Offen 1988: 126)

However, as Offen (1988: 126) also notes, by 1892, "le féminisme" had gained popular currency in the French press as a result of the first self-proclaimed "feminist congress" in Paris, sponsored by a woman's group, *Solidarité*. Although news of this congress was also reported in Britain in the *Englishwoman's Review* in 1892, the journal did not adopt the English word "feminism" until 1896. In addition to Britain, Offen locates usage of the word by the mid-1890s in Belgium, Spain, Italy, Germany, Greece, and Russia; indeed, by the time of the 1896 international women's congress in Berlin, it seemed that the word had achieved considerable prominence in Europe (Offen 1988: 126–27). Yet, Offen argued that the word "feminism" was not generally used in the United States until about 1910 (127).

Similarly, Nancy Cott (1987: 3) claims that "People [in America] in the nineteenth century did not say *feminism*," rather use of the word "feminism" in the early decades of the twentieth century coincided with the height of the suffrage campaign. Moreover, although feminism was vitally connected to the suffrage movement, its proponents tended to distinguish it from suffragism and from the woman's movement generally: feminism was both "broader in intent, proclaiming revolution in all the relations of the sexes, and narrower in the range of its willing adherents" (1987: 3). In this context, Cott (1987: 3–4) laments how "the vocabulary of feminism has been grafted onto the history of women's rights," suggesting that "historians' tendency to lump together the woman movement, the chronology of the suffrage movement, and the vocabulary of feminism has been misleading for our comprehension of the early twentieth century." Clearly, this research confirms that women lawyers in the decades before the end of the nineteenth century were unlikely to use the language of "feminism" in describing their goals and strategies as legal professionals. Thus, it seems clear that Babcock's assertion that an examination of the lives of early women lawyers would reveal most of them as "self-conscious feminists" does not reflect the appropriate historical and linguistic usage of this word.

Yet, it is arguable that Babcock intended to make a historical judgment about these women, based on their ideas and actions, rather than merely focusing on linguistic terminology in use in the late-nineteenth century. Yet, just as the features of contemporary feminism can be debated, the question of what ideas and/or actions constituted feminism historically is also highly contested (Cott 1989; Dubois 1989). For purposes of this assessment of early women lawyers, Cott's suggestion that "feminism" involves three elements provides a useful starting point. According to Cott (1987), feminism involves an opposition to sex hierarchy (the equality claim); a recognition that women's condition is socially constructed, and thus can be changed (the reform argument); and some level of identification with the group called women (the woman-identification argument). Many nineteenth-century women lawyers could meet the first two elements; as the historical account suggests, many of them consciously adopted equality goals and worked for legal and social reforms to benefit women (Mossman 2006). However, the question about whether they were "woman identified" presents a more complex challenge, necessitating an exploration of how ideas about gender intersected with ideas about professionalism in law to shape the identity and experiences of nineteenth-century women lawyers.

Significantly, the meaning of legal "professionalism" was also evolving in the late-nineteenth century in the United States and elsewhere (Bledstein 1976; Stevens 1983). As Robert Stevens (1983) noted, for example, new ideas regarding professional standards in law emerged after the Civil War. Thus, in the 1860s and 1870s, the "circuit-rider office lawyer" became less visible, and the new type of law firm, with several partners and assistants catering to the needs of developing corporations, emerged. As the numbers of lawyers also increased substantially, from 20,000 in 1850 to more than 60,000 in 1880, some members of the profession expressed concern about standards of practice; thus, when the American Bar Association was established in 1878, a prominent item on its agenda was practice standards (Stevens 1983). One response to these concerns was the establishment of professional law schools, in which the study of law was more rational and "scientific." Burton Bledstein (1976) reported that the number of professional law schools in the United States doubled between 1870 and 1890. In this same period, the case method of instruction, initially pioneered by Langdell at Harvard, became *the* innovation in legal education and confirmed Harvard's elite status. The popularity of the case method derived from its claims to "[s]cience, apparent practicality, elitism, financial success, and 'thinking like a lawyer' ... " (Stevens 1983: 63–64). Thus, although scholars have continued to debate a number of differing explanations for the rise of professionalism in law in the late-nineteenth century, there is general agreement that reforms in legal education and the establishment of professional organizations reflected a sense of increased professionalism in legal work (Freidson 1986; Geison 1983; Larson 1977).

In spite of increasing numbers of university law schools and innovations in methods of legal education, women were not welcome at some of the most prestigious law schools, including Yale, Harvard, and Columbia, until well into the twentieth century. As a result of their exclusion from these institutions, women were also excluded from elite law firms and opportunities. Both elite legal education and corporate law firms remained steadfastly defined by traditional ideas of white, Protestant masculinity (Auerbach 1976); for "legal science [epitomized by the case method] reinforced the idea of law as a hard, manly occupation grounded in seemingly objective, deducible rules" (Grossberg 1990: 143–44). In such a context, aspiring women lawyers "seemed to assume that any connection with feminism would prove detrimental to their professional progress" (Cott 1987: 231), and they increasingly internalized the professions' claims to objectivity, empiricism, rationality, impersonality, and collegially determined standards:

> The professional credo, that individual merit would be judged according to objective and verifiable standards, made a promise so potent to women professionals that they upheld the ideal even when they saw it travestied in

practice ... Women's lack of power and leverage in the male-dominated professions meant that, had they criticized the application of "objectivity" as male practice, they could easily have been dismissed entirely. An essential component of professional definition was the claim to self-regulation, an essential practice was the closing of ranks against outsiders, and *had women poised their strategy against rather than with the professions' objectivity they would have marked themselves as outsiders.*

(Cott 1987: 234–35, emphasis added)

One consequence of these ideas of legal professionalism was that early women lawyers began to see a community of interest between themselves and professional men, and by contrast, a gulf between themselves and nonprofessional women (Cott 1987). Thus, Cott's third element of the definition of "feminism," the need for "woman identification," needs careful exploration. This chapter suggests that women lawyers' relationships to the suffrage movement, and how they chose to participate in the World's Columbian Exposition in 1893, provide opportunities to assess some of the nuances at the intersection of ideas about gender and about legal professionalism for the first women lawyers in the United States.

Women lawyers and the suffrage movement

Although the women's rights movement reduced itself to a demand for the vote by 1900, in the pre-Civil War period its program was much broader. The Seneca Falls Declaration protested against the exclusion of women from the professions and trades and demanded equality in this area ... [In] the early years the right to work outside the home was a much more central concern than the right to vote. Furthermore, from the beginning there was a close connection between organized feminism and the victories of women trying to open the professions to themselves and their sex.

(Harris 1978: 86)

As Barbara Harris' comment suggests, the Seneca Falls Declaration in 1848 established a range of goals for the women's movement, based on women's equality with men. These goals included opening up the professions to women and the right to vote, as well as other reforms (Hoff 1991). Indeed, several of the first women lawyers were active in suffrage campaigns and in other activities of the women's movement. For example, Phoebe Couzins, one of the first women to graduate from Washington University Law School in 1871, devoted much of her life to the suffrage cause; and Ada Bittenbender, who gained admission to the bar in Nebraska in 1882, worked professionally as attorney for the National Women's Christian Temperance Union (Drachman 1993; Robinson 1890). However, some women lawyers received advice that it was inappropriate to practice law while engaging in activities concerned with women's rights.

In a letter to other women lawyers in 1889, Catharine Waugh reported that both lawyers and judges had warned her about the incongruity of working for women's rights while also practicing law. However, Waugh seems to have ignored much of this advice when she campaigned for Prohibition in the late 1880s. Furthermore, when she married, she arranged her honeymoon so that she could present a speech in the South Dakota suffrage campaign (Drachman 1993).

These examples reveal a number of different responses on the part of individual women lawyers to the women's rights movement in the late-nineteenth century. Taken together, they suggest that early women lawyers could choose whether, or to what extent, they wished to be involved in the women's movement, including suffrage. However, a series of cases in the 1870s and 1880s about women's right to practice law began to create *legal* barriers between suffrage activists and women lawyers. It seems that the reasoning in these cases tended to strengthen ideas about women's entitlement to practice law while, at the same time, eroding connections between women lawyers and the women's movement. As a result, while some women lawyers continued to take part in suffrage activities, many women lawyers increasingly responded to "magnetic" ideas about professionalism, responses which increasingly distanced them from other women activists.

The starting point for this legal reasoning was the 1873 *Bradwell v. Illinois* decision, in which a majority of the US Supreme Court held that the Privileges and Immunities Clause in the Constitution did not preclude Illinois from restricting Myra Bradwell's eligibility to practice law (Gilliam 1987). Although Bradwell had generally used arguments based on common law principles and on statutory interpretation in the Illinois courts, it seems that she appended constitutional arguments to her appeal to the Supreme Court *after* a meeting with Elizabeth Cady Stanton and Susan B. Anthony in late 1869 (Drachman 1998). Clearly, Bradwell's connection to Cady Stanton and Anthony suggests some congruence between suffrage goals and access to the legal profession among members of the women's movement, at least in the early 1870s. In this context, however, the outcome in *Bradwell* represented a significant defeat for a number of reasons. First, the case set a negative precedent with respect to the issue of women's entitlement to enter the legal profession, not only in the United States but in other jurisdictions, particularly Canada (*In re French* 1905); and, as a result, many aspiring women lawyers shifted their efforts from court applications to lobbying state legislatures for statutory amendments permitting women to practice law (Mossman 2006). Second, the concurring opinion of Justice Bradley in the Supreme Court decision confirmed, *as a matter of legal doctrine*, the concept of separate spheres for women and men, "founded in the divine ordinance, as well as in the nature of things" (*Bradwell* 1872: 141). Both these results represented significant setbacks for women who wished to gain access to the legal profession.

In addition, the case influenced the progress of suffrage claims in the courts because the narrow reading of the Privileges and Immunities Clause in *Bradwell* was adopted to uphold state legislation limiting women's right to vote. Susan Anthony apparently contacted Myra Bradwell after the Supreme Court decision, hoping to use the court's rejection of a woman of Bradwell's stature to derive political capital in upcoming suffrage conventions; Anthony reportedly promised to "pour hot shot into that old Court" (Friedman 1993: 27). However, just a few months after the *Bradwell* decision in 1873, its negative precedent was cited when Anthony herself was prosecuted for trying to vote in an election. *United States v. Anthony* (1873), relying on *Bradwell*, confirmed that women were not entitled to vote. Thus, it seems significant that even Bradwell's counsel in the Supreme Court had expressly acknowledged a concern that permitting women to practice law would lead to female suffrage, a situation that would "overthrow Christianity, defeat the ends of modern civilization, and upturn the world" (Hoff 1991). In this way, claims for women's access to the legal profession and claims for women's right to vote were clearly linked, both for judges who opposed them and for women activists who wished to achieve these goals.

However, these links began to fray in the 1880s and 1890s. Although courts respected the *Bradwell* precedent after 1873, so that most aspiring women lawyers sought statutory amendments permitting women's admission to the bar, some courts again began to respond to women lawyers' claims in the 1880s. For example, a Connecticut court granted Mary Hall's application for admission to the legal profession in 1882, characterizing the role of an attorney as a "lower" kind of public officer (Drachman 2001; *In re Hall* 1882). Moreover, by 1890, when Marilla Ricker sought admission to the bar in New Hampshire, the court held that women were entitled to practice law because the role of an attorney did not constitute a public office; *by so characterizing the practice of law, the court clearly distinguished an attorney's role from the right to hold public office and, more importantly, from the right to vote* (*In re Ricker* 1890). These judicial decisions occurred, of course, in a societal context in which some women had gained admission to the bar in a number of US states, and some of them were already practicing law with modest success. Indeed, Belva Lockwood had succeeded in gaining admission to the US Supreme Court in 1879 (Mossman 2006; Stern 1994). Thus, as the numbers of women lawyers increased, the views expressed by Justice Bradley about women's roles in *Bradwell* must have seemed increasingly outdated.

Nonetheless, because *Bradwell* was a Supreme Court precedent precluding women's right to enter the legal profession, state courts found it necessary to use new and different kinds of legal arguments to permit women's admission to the bar in the late-nineteenth century. Thus, the argument that an attorney's role did *not* constitute a public office created opportunities for women's claims for admission to the bar to succeed; yet, these same arguments often expressly distinguished claims about women's admission to the bar from claims for female suffrage. Moreover, some courts may have been persuaded to accept the claims of *the few* women who wished to practice law, while forestalling claims on the part of *the many* women for the vote. Virginia Drachman (1998: 36) reported that women lawyers consciously failed to respond to requests from some women activists to delay their efforts to gain admission to the bar until "women had gained equal citizenship with men." Although aspiring women lawyers may have seen themselves initially as part of a broader movement for women's equality, their goals and strategies seemed to diverge from the suffrage cause in the 1880s and 1890s, at least to some extent. Moreover, this result is consistent with Cott's argument (1987) that professional ideology was becoming increasingly magnetic for women professionals by the end of the nineteenth century.

More specifically, there is evidence that some women lawyers were consciously distancing themselves from the suffrage campaign in the 1890s. For example, Mary Greene, who had been admitted to the Massachusetts bar in 1888, explained her views on suffrage in a letter to the Belgian barrister, Louis Frank. Writing in 1895, her letter provided detailed information about the progress of women's rights in different parts of the United States, but also declared:

> I do not know enough about the methods of the woman suffragists in this country to tell you much about them. My views on the subject differ in so many ways from those of the leaders that I cannot work with them. I do not believe that the ballot will cure all ills, nor do I believe that women are powerless without the ballot. I prefer to teach women how to use the power and the rights they already possess (which here in America are many) in order that they may know how to ask intelligently for changes in the laws. I do not like the way in which these leaders persistently misrepresent the present laws ...
>
> (Greene 1895; see also Mossman 2006: 61)

Greene was equally unsympathetic to the efforts of Belva Lockwood, candidate for the Equal Rights Party in the US presidential elections in 1884 and 1888 (Norgren 2007). Greene tried to persuade Frank not to be impressed by Lockwood's candidacy, asserting that it was:

> most unfortunate both for herself and for the cause of her sex that Belva Lockwood allowed herself to pose as a candidate for the Presidency upon the nomination of a set of woman suffragists (*not* even a recognized political party) ... I am simply telling you what the general sentiment in the United States is, in order that the value of your writing may not be impaired by giving prominence to those women who are more or less laughed at at home ... I do think that you ought to know what public opinion is here whether it is just or unjust ...
>
> (Greene 1891; see also Mossman 2006: 62)

While Greene's comments suggest that Lockwood was somewhat sympathetic to the suffrage cause, Lockwood herself firmly declined to be described as "a New Woman;" as she asserted, "I do not believe in sex distinction in literature, law, politics, or trade; or that modesty and virtue are more becoming to women than to men; but wish we had more of it everywhere" (Stern 1994: 233).

These brief comments suggest that some women lawyers at the end of the nineteenth century were distancing themselves from the women's movement and espousing a commitment to gender neutrality. The extent of their "woman identification" was weak, or at least substantially submerged within a primary identity as members of the legal profession. Thus, the claim that nineteenth-century women lawyers were "feminists" may be difficult to sustain, not only by reason of the words of individual women lawyers who clearly distinguished themselves from suffrage activists and "new women," but also because legal claims by women lawyers tended to undermine claims to female suffrage. Therefore, Babcock's conclusion that there was a "self-conscious feminist in virtually every early woman lawyer" in the United States is highly questionable. At the same time, a more nuanced exploration of the relationship between feminism and these early women lawyers may offer useful insights about the intersection of late-nineteenth century ideas concerning gender and profession-alism in law. To examine these ideas in a different context, the chapter turns to the World's Columbian Exposition in 1893, and the experiences of women lawyers as they negotiated between the expectations of other women and of male lawyers at this event.

Women lawyers and the World's Columbian Exposition

In 1892, the United States planned to celebrate the 400th anniversary of Columbus's arrival in the Americas at a World's Columbian Exposition to be held in Chicago the following year. A Board of Lady Managers comprised of politically moderate, wealthy women decided the fair would emphasize women's domestic, philanthropic, and artistic activities as representative of women's role in the world. *Professional women who contested this portrayal formed the Queen Isabella Association in a united effort to include a tribute to Columbus's patron, Queen Isabella of Castile, at the upcoming fair. Denied space on the fair grounds by the Board of Lady Managers, the Association established its own club house two blocks away* ... In August 1893, over thirty women lawyers from across the country attended a conference with speeches given by leading women lawyers.

(McNamee 1998: 34, emphasis added)

As this report suggests, the World's Columbian Exposition in 1893 provided a catalyst for women lawyers to congregate in Chicago, where about eighty women had already gained admission to the Illinois bar (Drachman 1998). In addition, the Exposition offered concrete evidence of an increasing divergence of interests between women professionals on one hand and the women leaders designated to organize women's roles for the Exposition, the Board of Lady Managers, on the other. Both the Board's decision to exclude the women lawyers' meeting space from the fair grounds itself, and women lawyers' adoption of a name honoring Columbus's patron, Queen Isabella, underlined diverging interests between different groups of women. At the same time, however, the Exposition recognized women lawyers as members of the legal profession at the Congress on Jurisprudence and Law Reform, arguably the first time that women were included as legal professionals in a major public event of this kind. Nonetheless, it is possible that their acceptance as professionals was only partial, rendering their status ambiguous, both as women and as professionals in law. Thus, the World's Columbian Exposition provides an opportunity to examine how women lawyers established the seeds of "gendered professionalism" in the United States in 1893.

The organizers of the World's Columbian Exposition decided at an early point in the planning process to arrange for a series of congresses to take place during the Exposition. The plan included a variety of congresses, held at the Art Institute between 15 May and 28 October, on a wide variety of topics. A contemporary news report noted, the congresses would "consider and discuss appropriate themes in the domain of art, science, literature, education, government, jurisprudence, ethics, religion, reform, and other departments of intellectual activity and progress"(*Law Times* 1893: 330). However, one of the two most significant congresses was the World's Congress of Representative Women (Findling 1994), the first in the series. As a contemporary news report in March 1893 explained, the World's Congress of Representative Women was intended to provide a "presentation of the different fields of work in which women are now so extensively engaged ... representative women from all nations will be invited to take part ... " (Henrotin 1893: 627). However, a major schism developed early on in the planning process, with the result that permission to link women's work with a campaign for women's political rights was refused (Jordan 2004). It also seems likely that the women leaders of the Congress of Representative Women, who were often wealthy married women involved in a variety of philanthropic activities, may have had little in common with women working as lawyers, many of whom remained unmarried (McNamee 1998).

Significantly, some women lawyers had already been involved in correspondence as members of the Equity Club, an association that flourished for a few years in the late 1880s and early 1890s (Drachman 1998). While the Equity Club remained active, each woman lawyer submitted an annual letter about legal work and other activities and sometimes posed questions for each other about issues related to being a woman in law; the letters were then collected and circulated to members. Since some women lawyers had already become acquainted through the Equity Club by the time that organization began for the Chicago Exposition, they were well positioned to establish the Queen Isabella Association and to organize a conference of women lawyers.

However, women lawyers were eventually included as presenters at the Congress of Jurisprudence and Law Reform in the week of 7 August. As an enthusiastic publicity announcement explained, this Congress would hear papers "prepared by some of the most eminent jurists of the civilized nations of the world" on a variety of topics: "international law, the pressing demand of civilization for an international tribunal to adjust national controversies, the administration of civil and criminal justice under the laws of different nations ... and reforms which are now engaging the thoughtful attention of the Legal Profession throughout the world" (*Law Times* 1893: 330). Moreover, as a report of the Congress in August 1893 suggested, this Congress had a special historical significance for women lawyers:

> For the first time in the history of the world an international congress of lawyers has been held in which women lawyers have taken part. Nearly two years ago a men's committee on law reform was organized under the rules of the World's Congress Auxiliary. Later a woman's committee on law reform was added ... [A]fter mature deliberation, the woman's committee concluded that the interests of women in the profession of law would be best conserved by a joint congress.
>
> (*Chicago Legal News* 1893: 435)

Significantly, credit for this achievement was awarded to Myra Bradwell, who chaired the Woman's Branch of the World's Congress of Jurisprudence and Law Reform. She obtained recognition of women lawyers as speakers, "on the same platform with the male jurists, rather than, as was desired by many of the Committee, that the women jurists should hold a separate Congress of their own" (Greene 1896; see also Mossman 2006: 64).

Interestingly, Bradwell was already well known in Chicago, not only because of her unsuccessful appeal to the Supreme Court two decades earlier, but also as editor of the *Chicago Legal News* and wife of a prominent judge (Friedman 1993; McNamee 1998). Even though she had not succeeded in gaining admission to the bar herself, Bradwell's circumstances created this opportunity to support women lawyers, and her encouragement ensured that women lawyers were included as participants along with men at the Congress. As a result, two women lawyers from the United States, Mary Greene and Clara Foltz, presented papers at the Congress. In addition, Eliza Orme from Britain and Cornelia Sorabji from India were invited to participate and both sent papers to be read at the Congress. According to Louis Frank, women lawyers thus received official recognition from the most eminent jurists in the world in August 1893.

The participation of women lawyers in the Congress on Jurisprudence and Law Reform, albeit quite small in terms of numbers, clearly contrasted with their exclusion from the Congress on Representative Women. Moreover, "three months after the Congress of Representative Women concluded, the Law Department of the [Queen Isabella Association] commenced its international conference specifically for women lawyers" (Jordan 2004). The chair of the Isabella Society's law department was Ellen Martin, who had become the third woman admitted to the Illinois bar in 1876 and had established the firm of Perry and Martin with her friend, Mary Fredrika Perry (McNamee 1998). Martin and her colleagues organized a three-day meeting of women lawyers at the Isabella Clubhouse on 3–5 August 1893, with thirty women lawyers in attendance. The proceedings of the conference included recognition for some of the pioneers who had first gained admission to the bar in the United States, discussion of contemporary legal issues, and the formation of a National League of Women Lawyers (*Chicago Legal News* 1893). Since the *Chicago Legal News* reported quite fully on the proceedings, there is some evidence of how women lawyers themselves were negotiating their gender and professional identities in the 1890s.

The first session of the conference focused on the history of women in the legal profession, and included presentations by Arabella Mansfield, the first woman admitted to a state bar in 1869 in Iowa; Ada Kepley, the first woman to graduate from a law school in 1870 in Chicago; and Carrie Burnham Kilgore, the first woman admitted to the bar of Pennsylvania in 1883. At this session, Ellen Martin also delivered a paper about Myra Bradwell's case in the Supreme Court two decades earlier (*Chicago Legal News* 1893). Martin began her remarks by explaining that "women lawyers have no wrongs to right so far as the bench and bar are concerned, having been almost uniformly well treated by both everywhere" (*Chicago Legal News* 1893: 451). Similarly, Florence Cronise of Tiffin, Ohio, who presided for this meeting, "reviewed some of the experiences of women in the profession, called attention to the increase in numbers since the first admission in 1869, spoke of the pleasure of meeting other women in the profession, and exchanging views" (451). In conclusion, she stated:

> There is no profession or calling in life which has as liberalizing tendencies as the legal profession. It is impossible to practice law in its fullest sense and not have all your faculties strengthened, your love of humanity deepened and your charity for the shortcomings of human nature broadened. I do not believe that the petty envies and jealousies that seem to creep into other associations can ever disturb ours. We have come here to learn from each other, to bind ourselves more closely together, and to more fully realize that we are gaining numerical strength and to bid each other god-speed in the work.
>
> (451)

Cronise's comments suggest that women lawyers were beginning to identify themselves as legal professionals, emphasizing their acceptance within the legal profession, and perhaps further distancing themselves from other women's organizations (with their "petty envies and jealousies"). Their identity as women lawyers was also confirmed by their efforts to record the recent history and contributions of women lawyers more generally. Thus, the newly established National League of Women Lawyers identified four honorary members, pioneers among women in the legal profession: Myra Bradwell, whose case was the first to reach the US Supreme Court; Arabella Mansfield, who was the first to achieve admission to a state bar; Phoebe Couzins, the first to enter a program of law; and Ada Kepley, the first to graduate from an American law school (Mossman 2006). In addition, the group in Chicago decided that "all women who were known to those present to have the qualifications for active membership [would be] declared active members upon signing the membership roll" (*Chicago Legal News* 1893: 451). Poignantly, the conference also included memorial sketches of six women who had been admitted to the practice of law, who had already died: Lilly Peckham in Milwaukee, Lemma Barkaloo in St Louis, Alta Hulett in Illinois, Lavinia Goodell in Wisconsin, Mary Perry in Chicago, and Lelia Robinson in Boston (*Chicago Legal News* 1893). As these actions suggest, women lawyers were beginning to identify themselves collectively as professionals in law.

Yet, it is important to acknowledge that women's access to traditional professional organizations in the United States remained quite limited in the 1890s. For example, although women were welcomed at some bar associations, they were excluded from membership in the American Bar Association until 1918, and they were sometimes excluded from local associations, such as the Boston Bar Association, as well (Stevens 1983); indeed, it was in response to this exclusion that Lelia Robinson (1888) claimed to have created the Portia Club for dinner meetings of women lawyers. Furthermore, it seems that one obstacle to recognition for women lawyers in the Congress of Representative Women in Chicago may have been the absence of an organization. As Ellen Martin explained at the conference of women lawyers, there were two goals for the meeting of the law department of the Queen Isabella Association. One related to the need for "women lawyers [to] be better acquainted with one another." The second concerned the need to establish an organizational presence within the women's movement:

> As matters now stand we are sometimes well represented and sometimes very poorly; but (as the women say who control those organizations) we cannot complain when we have no organization to which they can refer for information. This meeting is for the purpose ... of enabling you to become better acquainted with one another, and steps have been taken toward the organization of a league ...
>
> (*Chicago Legal News* 1893: 451)

Thus, the Isabella Association meeting in Chicago in 1893 needs to be understood as part of an ongoing process of organization for women lawyers and the creation of a collective professional identity for them.

Reflections on the emergence of "gendered professionalism"

The meeting of women lawyers under the auspices of the Queen Isabella Association in 1893 reflected a significant historical moment for women in law in the United States: a recognition that they were members of the legal profession and, as a result, that they were quite distinct from other women and their interests. At the same time, however, the Queen Isabella Association demonstrated how women lawyers may have needed their own (gendered) professional association because they were not fully accepted in many of the (male-exclusive) professional organizations in law. Indeed, although women were included in the Congress on Jurisprudence and Law Reform, only four of them, after all, were formally invited to take part. In this way, this first meeting of the Queen Isabella Association created an opportunity for a larger group of women lawyers to establish a sense of collective identity as *women* who were *lawyers*. Completely excluded by the Women's Congress and recognized only in a limited way at the Congress on Jurisprudence and Law Reform, women lawyers established their own conference. Their optimistic comments at the meeting in Chicago suggest that they believed that full professional acceptance was imminent, so that they were increasingly unconcerned about the growing chasm between the leaders of the women's movement and their special place as women professionals. The Chicago meeting seems to confirm Cott's argument that women lawyers in the 1890s were becoming legal professionals, whose connections to "feminism" were becoming tenuous.

Although a number of individual women lawyers continued to support the suffrage cause and other aspects of women's equality, the use of legal arguments in the 1890s that differentiated women's right to practice law from women's access to suffrage created barriers between these different groups of women. Of course, these barriers also reflected differences in women's material circumstances. Many (although not all) women involved in suffrage and other causes, and particularly the women involved in the Women's Representative Congress in Chicago, were married women in wealthy or reasonably well-to-do households; by contrast, many of the women who sought admission to the bar remained unmarried and needed to engage in paid work to provide for themselves financially. As Drachman (1998: 99–100) suggested, it was "the hard realities of life, not the romantic notions of ideal womanhood, [that] determined the direction of [women lawyers'] professional careers." Even Belva Lockwood, the first woman admitted to the Supreme Court explained in her letter to the Equity Club in 1887 that she accepted "every case, no matter how difficult, occurring in civil, criminal, equitable and probate law;" indeed, although Lockwood herself was married, she was the main source of financial support for her family and was fully engaged in legal practice as well as a variety of reform efforts throughout her life (Drachman 2001: 58; Norgren 2007). Thus, while relationships between suffrage activists and women lawyers was always complex, the financial (and often unmarried) circumstances of women seeking admission to the bar may have influenced them to adopt successful legal arguments in their admission cases, even though these arguments undermined, to some extent, women's access to suffrage. Thus, Cott's argument that women lawyers were increasingly drawn to the attractions of professionalism at the end of the nineteenth century is confirmed, to some degree, in relation to suffrage; that is, in spite of reformist activities on the part of a number of individual women lawyers to provide support for the suffrage cause, women lawyers' priorities were beginning to focus on pursuit of their own professional interests. Indeed, the optimism of women lawyers that they would soon be embraced fully within the legal profession, illustrated by their comments at their conference in Chicago in 1893, seems to have erased any doubts about distancing themselves from women who were not professionals.

Thus, women lawyers at the Queen Isabella Association conference may have regarded their conference as merely a step toward the realization of their goal of becoming fully accepted as legal professionals. For them, the need for a conference of women lawyers may not have signaled the beginning of an identity of "gendered professionalism," but rather just the first step in their recognition as *lawyers* (ungendered). By accepting the ideals of professionalism based on merit and objective standards, even as they sometimes experienced the travesty of these ideals in practice (Cott 1987), they expressed fervent hopes to achieve this recognition. Yet, although *women* eventually succeeded in becoming lawyers in the late nineteenth century, they never effectively challenged the *gender* premises of the law and the legal professions (Grossberg 1990). In spite of the support and collegiality they gained in their meeting in Chicago—as *women* who were *lawyers*—it seems that they were not seeking an identity of "gendered professionalism." Drachman's conclusion (2001: vii) that "the professional and personal challenges that confront women lawyers today … reach back … to the pioneer generation of women lawyers" appears all too compelling. We may need to explore more fully the history of women's entry to the legal profession as a way of understanding "contemporary challenges of diversity and inclusion in the legal professions" (Kay 2007: 423). Clearly, it is Cott's analysis, rather than Babcock's assessment, which better reflects the relationships of feminism and professionalism on the part of women lawyers in late-nineteenth century America.

Chapter 2

An inconsistent affair

Feminism and the legal academy

Margaret Thornton

Introduction

The political pendulum that inscribes an arc from social to neoliberalism has shaped the fortunes of feminism in the Australian legal academy. The 1970s represented the high point of social liberalism when notions of the collective good and distributive justice were acknowledged in accordance with the egalitarian ideal. Although the modus operandi of any free-market society is *in*-equality, in which the values of competition, power, and hierarchy are central, under the Australian version of liberal democratic capitalism that prevailed in the 1970s and 1980s, the play of freedom was restrained by a modicum of state regulation in the interests of the common good.

Social liberalism, with its focus on collective good, not only effected some semblance of equality for women, it enabled legal feminism's emergence and short-lived tolerance. A noted product of social liberalism in Australia was the existence of a centralized wage-fixing system rather than enterprise bargaining, which benefited women as well as all low-paid workers. While there was a gender gap in terms of pay equity, it was less than in comparable countries. Neoliberal or market liberalism, generally accompanied by a neoconservative morality, has induced a general contraction of civil society and a correlative decline in distributive justice and interest in social movements. Indeed, neoliberalism, with its moral and economic conservatism, has insidiously sought to effect a re-masculinization of the academy. Neoliberal technologies of power subtly carry gendered subtexts that include regimes of depersonalized top-down authority, entrepreneurialism, and promotion of the self. In the absence of restraint on the state's exercise of power, feminism is struggling to survive within the contemporary academy.

Leaving aside the vagaries of the liberal landscape and its susceptibility to prevailing political mores, feminism will inevitably encounter resistance within the academy since it is an outsider movement. The law's singular capacity to silence feminist discourse was a familiar refrain of second-wave feminism (e.g. Smart 1989). Nevertheless, feminism has exercised a discursive effect because it is multifaceted and heteroglossic, with a marked capacity to reinvent itself. Consequently, it defies a neat definition. The tendency to use the plural form *feminisms* underscores the difficulty of setting up one theoretical framework that could offer liberatory or emancipatory possibilities for all women (Caine 1998: 419). Feminist legal theory (FLT) is similarly diverse. As an offshoot of 1970s feminism, it began by addressing the materiality of oppression against women with a platform of reforming the law but progressed to transforming fundamentally the nature of legal knowledge. These reformist and transformative dimensions roughly correspond with what used to be called liberal feminism and radical feminism (Jagger 1988). The influence of postmodernism and deconstructionism further disrupted any notion of a stable understanding of feminism, including the very idea of there being an identifiable woman at the center. FLT is concerned with the ontology and epistemology of law at a meta-level, but the phrase is loosely invoked to embrace the myriad forms of engagement between law and the feminine, broadly defined. This engagement may also include critiquing the imperialism of Western feminism from the perspective of indigenous women and those from developing countries. Nevertheless, in this chapter, I am not addressing the variegated history and philosophy of FLT so much as its dynamic relationship with the legal academy and the state.

While feminism as a social movement is not dependent on the state for its existence, FLT (with an emphasis on *legal* theory) does seem to need the state for its survival. The relationship with government is not direct but one effected indirectly through the public funding of university law schools, which is the case with most Australian law schools. Additionally, there is a high degree of control of higher education through federal government policy, which has not decreased with the state's retreat from the funding of law school places. While it is theoretically possible for feminist legal scholars to operate as *outside* the legal academy, sustained by a commitment to feminism as a "form of life" (Naffine 2002), legal scholarship in the public domain generally requires the imprimatur of an institution for legitimacy. Paradoxically, the grit associated with outsider status may be viewed positively, for the institutionalization of feminism is thought to exercise a deleterious effect on it (Jackson 2000: 2; Thornton 2004; Wiegman 2002: 19). The suggestion is that a too comfortable life may blunt the critical faculties, although residing permanently in Siberia can be chilly.

Life inside the academy undoubtedly poses difficulties for all feminist scholars, but the discipline of law creates a double jeopardy because it is ambivalent about its own academic status. Law is uncertain whether it should be classified as a humanity, a social science, or something altogether different. Women's studies, usually located within either the humanities or social sciences, originally provided a hospitable intellectual space for feminist scholarship (Jackson 2000: 4), and was not constrained by the intellectual presuppositions that beleaguer law as a professional discipline. Women's studies developed new ways of seeing by invoking the insights of a range of disciplines (e.g. Langland and

Gove 1983); whereas law was constrained by entrenched cultural and professional norms that sought to ensure its disciplinary autonomy.

A long tradition of positivist legal theory and self-referentialism has added to law's reticence about embracing feminist insights and alternative perspectives generally. Nevertheless, a short affair between feminism and the legal academy took place from the mid-1980s until approximately the turn of the century. It was inspired by and developed in tandem with initiatives from other parts of the common law world. For example, Judy Grbich and Adrian Howe participated in the Feminism and Legal Theory Project initiated by Martha Fineman, their papers appearing in *At the Boundaries of Law* (Fineman and Thomadsen 1991). Many fruitful collaborations followed in the heyday of FLT (e.g. Graycar and Morgan 1990, 2002; Naffine and Owens 1997; Thornton 1995). Pathbreaking work emerged in such traditionally masculinist areas as international law (Charlesworth et al. 1991) as well as legal theory and judicial method (Berns 1999). Additionally, the voices of indigenous women legal scholars began to be heard for the first time (Behrendt 1993). As a rich tapestry of scholarship emerged, the postmodern turn ended completely the idea of a grand narrative of feminism. Globalization, culture, whiteness, postcolonialism, lesbianism, and religion all contributed further to the diffusion of feminist scholarship (*Australian Feminist Law Journal* 1993–2009; Davies 2008; cf. Rosenbury 2003).

Despite this flurry of activity, a national report on teaching and learning claims that the influence of feminism on the Australian legal academy has been almost zero (Johnstone and Vignaendra 2003). How this conclusion was reached in view of burgeoning scholarly publishing is unclear, but it may have been based on the noticeable decline of FLT in the curriculum. The high point of legal feminism that coincided with the emergence of hardline neoliberalism may also have contributed to a desire to erase the seeming success of FLT. Moreover, a reductive view of FLT, as a static materialistic theory of women and the law, may have been hesitant to acknowledge the more diffuse and diverse manifestations as bona fide *feminist* scholarship. Finally, there is no doubt that the market discourses of consumerism and entrepreneurialism have exercised not just a depoliticizing effect on institutional feminism, but they have been accompanied by a misogynistic rhetoric averring that feminism is passé. This rhetoric is anti-feminist, racist, and homophobic. In a useful media analysis, Margaret Henderson (2008: 33) documents the way the words "feminism" and "feminist" continue to be associated with negative and often violent imagery in the media. Market discourse thereby became a convenient cloak for the reassertion of the dominance of masculinity and the heteronormative family.

Activist origins

As a corollary of social liberalism, the 1970s engendered no-fault divorce, sex discrimination, and domestic violence legislation, as well as ongoing efforts to refashion laws that impacted on women disproportionately, like those dealing with crimes of violence and sexual assault. While bringing the private sphere into the limelight for public scrutiny in accordance with the feminist aphorism "the personal is the political," unprecedented feminist activism gave rise to a sea change in the official responsiveness to issues affecting women, including the official incorporation of feminism into the polity through initiatives such as the appointment of "femocrats"—feminist bureaucrats who advised on the ramifications of government policy for women (Eisenstein 1996). Evidencing the starkness of the neoliberal turn 30 years later, the phenomenon of the femocrat has disappeared, along with a raft of other women-friendly policies (Sawer 2008).

Historically women were largely absent from the annals of the Western intellectual tradition. Dependency and subordination contributed to general representations of women in a limited range of stereotypical subject positions, such as the foolish housewife who failed to read the contract, the rape victim for whom "no" meant "yes," the sexual partner who lost her house when she acted as guarantor because she implicitly believed everything he said, etc. The frailty of these stock characters was entrenched by the vestigial causes of action of the common law, such as breach of promise, loss of consortium, and the marriage discount. Critiquing and changing such laws was a priority for feminist legal scholars.

It was one thing to repeal archaic laws but quite another to tinker with legal orthodoxy, especially when the word "feminism" carried connotations of instability and dangerousness. In the mid-1970s, the media was not averse to depicting feminism as "a whore" (Genovese 2002: 163). Thus, some feminist legal academics thought it politically wise to follow the reformist route and not to invite unnecessary scrutiny by using the provocative "F-word." When I established the Feminist Legal Action Group (FLAG) in 1978, I recall lengthy debate about whether use of the "F-word" would detract from the status of FLAG's work. Although the word "women" was perceived to be less confrontational, it was nevertheless rejected in favor of "feminist." A more theoretical bent was evinced when FLAG became FLIG (Feminist Legal Issues Group), and the focus shifted to critique and debate. FLIG was eventually superseded by F-LAW (Feminist Legal Academics Workshop), which included feminist legal academics from Australia and New Zealand who met biennially until the mid-2000s, after which F-LAW petered out. In addition to a scholarly focus, F-LAW provided a forum for discussion of issues confronting feminist scholars in the academy.

I organized the first feminist jurisprudence conference at Macquarie University in 1986. Two hundred people (mostly women) attended, and the papers formed a special issue of the *Australian Journal of Law and Society* (1986), the first devoted to feminist jurisprudence. Mary Jane Mossman from Canada, a contributor to this collection, gave the keynote address, "Feminism and Legal Method: The Difference it Makes," (1986), which was also published in the *Wisconsin Law Review* and *At the Boundaries of Law* (Fineman and Thomadsen 1991), attesting to the global reach of FLT. The paper

I contributed, "Feminist Jurisprudence: Illusion or Reality?" (1986) questioned whether feminist jurisprudence was possible or whether the concept was oxymoronic. Feminist *jurisprudence* still retains a discomforting edge, for it suggests a transformation of the entire edifice of law. Perhaps for pragmatic reasons feminist *legal theory* tends to be the preferred term, although the two are used interchangeably. Yet regardless of nomenclature, feminism in law was firmly on the agenda by the 1980s.

Formal colloquia attested to the increasing acceptance of FLT, while simultaneously underscoring its transgressive role in excavating and scrutinizing the legal landscape. Thus, the new feminist legal episteme was not confined to conventional understandings of women's rights, as determined by liberal legalism. Reflecting methodological changes in the blossoming of feminist theory more generally, FLT also became more sophisticated and diverse. It soon began to burst out of the limiting and non-threatening confines of formal gender equality to envision justice in ways that were formerly unimaginable. Poststructuralism, for example, with its disregard for orthodoxy and its focus on the way the legal subject is constituted in and by discourse, struck a chord with feminist legal scholars. A new generation of feminist legal scholars sought to invoke the insights of the humanities through semiotics, literature, and cultural studies, as illustrated by the contributions to the *Australian Feminist Law Journal*.

This new heteroglossia enriched FLT in ways that went beyond the modest beginnings of women and the law. The woman in feminist legal discourse imploded as totalizing and one dimensional. Perceived as the old-fashioned female analogue of Benchmark Man—white, Anglophonic, heterosexual, able-bodied, middle class, and favoring a right of center politics and a mainstream Christian religion—she was the standard against which Others were measured and invariably found wanting. The category "woman," which remained the subject of feminist activism, can no longer show its face in the academy without qualification and advertence to the multifaceted nature of identity. Any idea that feminism was associated with a single truth has gone out the window. However, a positivist legal system can comprehend only a single characteristic at any one time, not multiple facets of identity. The irony is that, as FLT became more sophisticated, it became less "useful" and correspondingly declined in favor with activists, mainstream theorists, media commentators, and students, which made it difficult to defend when the crunch came.

The symbiotic relationship between activist and academic legal feminism is beset with ambiguities although the material reality of women's lives has always animated feminist legal scholarship. Feminist legal activists and academics were initially committed to a common purpose, but a rift soon emerged. Martha Fineman (1991c) noted how FLT was moving away from the concrete towards abstract grand theory. This trend continued, and the relationship has become more tenuous. The very act of engaging in women's studies has been described as an act of political activism (Jackson 2000: 10), an observation that could also be made about legal feminism. However, absorption into the academy meant

that women's studies became "more bureaucratic, hierarchical and careerist …
and made central to the logic of privatization in the increasingly corporate
marketplace of higher education" (Wiegman 2002: 19). A similar observation
could be made about the status of feminism within the discipline of law.
A process of the disarticulation of women's studies in the academy from feminist
politics has been the result (Bird 2003; Shircliffe 2000; Wiegman 2002).

From women in law to feminist legal scholarship

In the early 1970s, lawyers, in conjunction with the women's movement, were in
demand to facilitate the extensive legislative changes on the political agenda.
This demand contributed to the rapid increase in the number of women
students in law schools in the 1970s and early 1980s. This was a time of growth
and, with the economy booming, the feminized or racialized identity of these
new lawyers was of secondary importance. The percentage of women law
students increased so markedly that a gendered tipping point was reached by the
early 1980s. Suddenly there were more women than men in law schools.
Nevertheless, numerosity does not necessarily equal pro-feminist politics. The
initial law school response was to "let in" more women without effecting any
curricula change. Many of the women who became legal academics had no
interest in feminist scholarship as such; they were anxious to assimilate quickly
into what remained a highly masculinized profession (Thornton 1996). They
believed that a conventional career path was the best way to promote their
careers—and they were probably right. At the same time, numerosity cannot
be discounted; it constitutes the backdrop to the legitimacy of feminism in the
legal academy, and it may embolden feminist legal scholars to persevere against
the odds.

Political as well as substantive legal issues quickly came to the fore in the legal
academy once feminist scholars had been admitted because they were loath to
accept law as it was. The influx of women students into law schools highlighted
the underrepresentation of women faculty, particularly in the professoriate
(the highest echelon of the academic hierarchy in Australia). This disjuncture,
that underscores the vexed relationship between the feminine and authority,
is ongoing despite feminist lobbying and the enactment of statutory equal
employment opportunity (EEO) and affirmative action (AA) measures (Thornton
2008). The otherness of the feminine has been entrenched in law as a result
of several thousand years of privileging masculinity in the Western intellectual
tradition, and it was not going to change overnight.

Women academics everywhere struggled against the dominant construction
of femininity in terms of reproduction, affectivity, and care, not just as an
epistemological issue but a political one. The institutional expectation was that
women should spend time nurturing students, mentoring colleagues, and promoting the interests of the institution. While feminist scholars sought to develop
an alternative model of success built on satisfaction in contrast to the masculinist

model that focused on external indicia of career achievements (Markus 1987: 101), feminist scholars faced the danger of falling victim to these pressures and becoming the public servants of academia (Aisenberg and Harrington 1988: 59), with less time for writing and the development of FLT. The absence of a critical mass of women, particularly more senior feminist scholars, imposed additional burdens on members of the first generation of feminist scholars, who had to prove their worth in the academy in conventional roles almost as a trade-off. In other words, the pursuit of feminist scholarship was not an automatic right, but a privilege beneficently bestowed after one proved to be a good university citizen.

Inspired by the women's movement in the early 1970s and a vision of what might be, I chose to attend the University of New South Wales, a new law school started with the express mission of social justice and law reform, particularly for the poor and racialized others. I do not recall that feminism was ever officially on the agenda—the human in human rights was as masculinist there as everywhere else—but the mission of the school provided a critical space, which facilitated the inclusion of feminist research.

The institutions where I spent most of my academic career—the University of New South Wales and Macquarie University Law Schools in Sydney, and La Trobe University School of Law and Legal Studies in Melbourne—were initially committed to alternative visions of the legal academy, legal education, and legal scholarships, crucial for the success of FLT. However, all these institutions succumbed to pressure to alter their orientation in favor of a more orthodox approach, particularly towards curriculum and pedagogy. Each institution experienced the rapid departure of talented and creative legal academics committed to new ways of thinking about law, following a protracted struggle. The majority of students and academics seemed to accept that conformity with the law school norm was the way to ensure acceptance by the legal profession. Paralleling the sameness/difference debate that has bedeviled feminism (e.g. Morgan 1988), alterity was equated with inferiority in the legal labor market rather than a source of strength.

More recently, the political swing rightwards has led to further turning away from distinctiveness within law schools. Conservatism, the magnetic attraction of sameness, and a desire to keep things as they are raises questions about law's ability to accommodate difference. Competition within a single market encourages a similarity of product, but it is not easy to proffer a rational explanation as to why difference is considered so threatening within supposedly liberal academic settings. The answer may reside in the psychoanalytic realm: giving voice to the other is perceived to undermine the foundational norm of benchmark masculinity.

I acknowledge the collegiality and solidarity of a group of feminist colleagues at La Trobe University where I was appointed professor of law and legal studies in 1990. The institution was unusual in its significant strengths in FLT, including criminology (e.g. Howe 1987, 1991, 1994) and critical theory (e.g. Grbich 1991, 1996). My own interests in the field were perceived as a strength. A notable factor boosting feminist scholarship was that the school was originally a school of legal studies within a faculty of social sciences, where faculty members came from a range of disciplinary backgrounds and where the focus was on under-standing law as a social phenomenon. Neither the curriculum nor the research agenda was constrained by the presuppositions of professional legal practice, for the relevant undergraduate degree did not satisfy admission requirements. There was more leeway for critique than when the school became first a School of Law and Legal Studies and then a School of Law. The strengths in FLT attracted students at undergraduate, honors, and PhD level, as well as the attainment of research grants and other indicia of excellence. However, I suggest this very success contained the seeds of the undoing of FLT, for it seemed to arouse the envy of male colleagues when the neoliberal backlash came (Thornton 2006). *Ressentiment* infuses the contemporary populist view of feminism that men are suffering because the women's movement has "gone too far" in that women have been "too successful." The emergence of men's rights groups in the context of family law is a good example of this phenomenon (Genovese 2008: 12; Henderson 2008: 31).

Pedagogical practices

I tend to favor integrating feminist perspectives throughout the curriculum rather than confining FLT to a separate course although, ideally, both approa-ches are desirable. There are downsides to both: the integrated approach depends on the good graces of colleagues who may not be sympathetic to FLT, while separatism may marginalize and disconnect FLT from mainstream curri-culum, thereby sloughing off collective responsibility. I have taught various courses around equality and discrimination from the late 1970s, which allowed the consideration of FLT, as well as race, sexuality, and intersectionality. I have also taught compulsory courses like personal injury (tort/crime), history and philosophy of law, foundation of legal studies, and equity, which provided ample scope for the seamless inclusion of FLT materials.

Rather than "preach to the converted," acquainting students with feminist perspectives is important, especially as some of them have little idea how to treat stressed clients with dignity, let alone comprehend the disproportionate impact on women of "gender-neutral" laws. For example, in a family law class role play by two students, the female "client" was hysterical due to marriage breakdown and custody problems. The male "lawyer" responded by slapping her face, and the class laughed! Incidents such as these made it essential to offer FLT to all students. Yet, only in specialist courses is it possible to develop a sophisticated theoretical approach. The core subjects of the law degree are generally accepted as a prerequisite for admission to practice in Australia without the need for a separate bar exam; within these courses the focus tends to be doctrinal and applied, while reflexivity and critique receive short shrift. This bias arises because the admitting authorities are primarily concerned with proficiency in the application of the technical rules of practice, not interrogation of those rules.

A more critical and theoretical approach to legal education was supported by a government inquiry into the law discipline in the 1980s (Pearce et al. 1987). The Pearce Report described the law degree as the new arts degree because law was increasingly regarded as a source of liberal education that would produce good citizens. Accordingly, the Pearce Report emphasized the importance of social context, theory, and critique to legal education. While no particular theoretical approach was singled out, advocating a broad liberal focus enabled the inclusion of feminist perspectives in the curriculum.

After the Pearce Report, there was a 1990s initiative by the Australian government to develop gender awareness within all compulsory subjects of the law curriculum. The gender awareness initiative followed a period of intense scrutiny of gender bias in the judiciary after it was suddenly "discovered" by the media. One of the most notorious instances in the exposé involved a remark by a judge in the course of a marital rape trial that "rougher than usual handling" may be acceptable on the part of a husband whose wife who was less than willing to engage in sexual intercourse (*R v. Johns* 1992). The ensuing public outcry demanded more attention toward the development of appropriate educative measures for prospective lawyers. The attorney-general agreed and allocated a modest sum for preparing teaching materials. For the first time there was an official injunction that gender awareness—if not FLT—should be taught in law schools. Two teams of feminist legal scholars prepared materials on three themes for incorporation into core curriculum: citizenship, work, and violence (Graycar and Morgan 1996). Copies of the materials were sent to all law schools and were made available on the Internet, but it was left to individual academics how to use them. Both the Pearce Report and the gender awareness initiative reveal clearly how the fortunes of FLT and the state are closely imbricated. Notably, both of these initiatives emanated from the federal level and therefore had Australia-wide coverage.

No sooner had these initiatives been acted upon, however, than universities were transformed by the Dawkins Reforms (Dawkins 1988). FLT had received a boost from the state with the recommendations of the Pearce Committee and the gender awareness project, but it suffered a setback with the swing to the right and the commodification of education, underscoring its sensitivity to the prevailing political climate.

The neoliberal turn

Student consumers

Within neoliberalism the market is the measure of all things; everything else is dispensable. Even though FLT really only emerged in the 1980s, the swing to the right began to induce a retreat away from it in less than two decades.

Indeed, the discourse of "post-feminism" emerged the very moment that a modicum of success could be discerned (Smart 1989: 84; Thornton 1991: 454). Henderson (2006) demonstrates how this post-feminist mentality emerged in the early 1990s through the manipulation of cultural memory. Even former conservative Australian Prime Minister, John Howard, observed in 2002 that feminism was passé (Summers 2003).

One year after the Pearce Report recommended a broad contextual approach to law, the Dawkins Reforms changed the face of higher education in Australia by restructuring and corporatizing universities and shifting to a user-pays regime. Higher education had been free since 1974, but the privatization of public goods became a notable dimension of neoliberal policy by the late 1980s (Marginson and Considine 2000). Commodification, in conjunction with the desire to be a competitive player in the global new knowledge economy, changed the arm's-length approach of the state towards universities. As Lyotard (1984) percipiently recognized, knowledge was replacing land in the struggle for power between nation states. Unsurprisingly, states have set out to harness the production of knowledge with the support of key international bodies (Organization for Economic Co-operation and Development 1996). Academic capitalism favors applied and technocratic knowledge because it has use value in the market. In contrast, there has been a notable contraction of the space afforded reflexive, critical, and theoretical perspectives because such knowledge is believed to afford little opportunity for commercialization.

Law schools have seen a curricular shift in favor of more global business, trade practices, and intellectual property courses. Thus, a decline in feminist offerings occurred. Law schools offered fewer feminist courses, often scheduled at unpopular times. The contraction of feminist perspectives in core courses also occurred. Young women quickly absorbed the neoliberal message and turned away from feminism, believing it had nothing to say to them (Dux and Simic 2008). While "free choice" was a catch cry of the so-called "second wave," it is central to the "third wave." Along with generationalism, this consumerist form of feminism has been effectively deployed by neoliberalism within popular discourse. A striking example exists in "girl power"—a form of third-wave feminism in which the lives of young women are shaped by an unrestrained commitment to individualism and free choice, particularly through popular music, cyber-technology, advertising, fashion, and sex, which synchronize with the market (Bulbeck 2006; McRobbie 2007). Within this neoliberal version of "post-feminism," the word "feminism" itself has become anathema. Interviews which I conducted in Australia, New Zealand, the UK, and Canada showed that law students no longer wanted the word "feminist" on their transcript fearing it would be a liability in the job market.

The user-pays philosophy is consistent with the observation that the more students pay for their law degree, the less tolerant of theory and critique they become. They will prefer to concentrate on the basic requirements and applied knowledge in order to secure the credentials necessary to be certified as competent practitioners. Vocationalism and consumerism have changed student attitudes towards a liberal legal education, now seen as the preserve of elite law schools.

The production of neoliberal academic subjects

The shift to applied research and the encouragement of collaborative grants with industry has been a marked result of the neoliberal embrace. One objective is to shift the cost of research from the public purse to end users, which affects knowledge transfer and facilitates the commercialization of knowledge. The emphasis on applied research also contributes to the erasure of critical and theoretical perspectives (Tombs and Whyte 2003). These new imperatives have made securing funds for feminist research more difficult because it is not deemed to have use value in the market.

Encroachment on academic options has become more pronounced with the pressure to produce research that is functional and comports with a neo-conservative morality. Unprecedented instances of direct government intervention occurred in the 2005 and 2006 rounds of Australian Research Council funding. The Council is in charge of the major government-funded research grants for humanities and social sciences, including law and legal studies. The media reported that nine internationally peer-approved projects were not ratified by the Minister for Education, Science, and Technology and therefore did not receive funding. Significantly these projects were primarily concerned with gender and sexuality, attesting to the increasingly ambivalent status of feminist research within a neoliberal climate (Jackson 2000; Wiegman 2002). While some socio-legal projects were initially targeted, they were ultimately funded. The projects that were viewed with suspicion included feminist legal research.

Political scrutiny of academics has increased globally since 9/11 (Gerstmann and Streb 2006). However, more is at stake than mere censorship. A normalization of surveillance through the emergence of an audit culture now exists; its mechanisms were originally developed for public sector employees through "risk reduction practices" introduced in the belief that employers could not be trusted to exercise independent professional judgment (Power 1997). The audit culture manifests itself in the academy by requiring that faculty provide evidence of their productivity and performance. Regular reports are filed as evidence of performativity relating to publications, competitive grants, students taught, higher degree completions, and so on. These "metrics," to invoke the voguish language of audit, are designed to render performance calculable. Journal articles, for example, are no longer evaluated according to their individual merits so much as according to the standing of the journal in which the article appears (Sauder and Espeland 2009). The prototype for law journal rankings in the Australian audit scheme, the ERA (Excellence for Research in Australia) was the Washington and Lee rankings in which generalist journals from prestigious institutions invariably received higher rankings than specialist journals. Feminist law journals suffer as specialist journals and through association with the feminine, which detractors claim to be equated with polemic rather than scholarship.

What is extraordinary about the audit culture is its rapid acceptance by academics. Foucault's concept of governmentality aptly captures the acceptance of a culture of compliance, which includes the notion of governance of the self (Foucault 1991; Rose 1999: 3). Drawing on Foucault's work, Sauder and Espeland (2009) show how technologies, such as law school rankings, are both "seductive and coercive." They are willingly absorbed into an organization at the same time as they are fiercely opposed. Individual academics, including feminist scholars, do not have to be browbeaten or cajoled into complying; they internalize the new norms and agree to self-discipline. Thus, legal scholars accept the corporate message that they should be more deferential towards authority, playing down or erasing the signs of the feminine within their scholarship and reorienting it in more acceptable applied directions. It is particularly difficult for early career researchers to resist the new technologies, attesting to the persuasiveness of the governmentality thesis.

The remasculinization of the academy

The moral conservatism that tends to accompany economic conservatism emerged as a powerful corollary of the neoliberal turn. Not only was FLT of dubious use value, it was perceived to threaten the dominant masculinist norms. FLT could be tolerated only if blanched of its radical edge. Once sufficiently sanitized and domesticated, it might even be held up as a commendable example of "diversity"—the new buzzword that replaced institutional feminism. Mary O'Brien (1984) coined the term "commatisation" to capture the submersion of gender within a list of variables taken into account by an organization: race comma gays comma gender comma class, etc. This discourse of diversity facilitates and legitimizes the erasure of feminism. Indeed, when a gendered tipping point had been reached, as in the case of law school admission, it quickly was argued that feminism was now passé. Mainstream scholars sought to discredit it as personal, political, or polemical. They claimed it lacked the objectivity, neutrality, and detachment of their own scholarship. A formalistic understanding of equality in preference to a substantive approach conveniently occludes the absence of the voice of the Other, thereby insidiously reinstantiating Benchmark Masculinity as the normative standard, as feminist legal scholars have long pointed out (e.g. Fineman 1991a).

The depersonalized technologies of audit do this very effectively by masking the culpability of male colleagues. Kenway et al. (2006: 42) capture the subtle incarnation of gender that emerges in their description of the academic subject as "*technopreneurial*," which refers to the way the favored techno-scientific knowledge is combined with business acumen. The technopreneur works alone, taking risks, and promoting the self, unconcerned about collegiality, cultural memory, or collective good. The intensification of the economic function of knowledge comes at the expense of its social function (Kenway et al. 2006). While these authors are referring to scientific and biomedical knowledge, their analysis is equally apt in light of the contemporary reversion to the privileging of techno-cratic legal knowledge with its applied, rather than critical and reflective focus.

More than the functionality of applied knowledge is at issue here in the way critique is depicted as feminized, destabilizing, and dangerous. Giroux suggests that a hatred of democracy and dissent inherent in an authoritarian neoliberal environment has given rise to a politics of "militarized masculinity," associated particularly with the war in Iraq and the domestic war on terror, which mark the return of the "warrior male":

> whose paranoia is endlessly stoked by the existence of a feminized culture of critical thinking, a gay subculture and a liberal ideology that exhibits a disrespect for top-down order and unquestioned authority and discipline.
> (Giroux 2008: 61; cf. Armitage 2005)

Viewed as "militarized knowledge factories," universities are not involved in producing conventional soldiers but graduates with a uniform habit of mind, such as well-credentialed technocratic lawyers trained to serve corporate capital and the new-knowledge economy.

The denigration of feminism coincided with populist neoconservative attacks on tertiary educated "élites" concerned about social justice, rights for indigenous people, same-sex couples, and welfare rights (Cahill 2004). This populist form of anti-feminism emerged in the United States but also appeared in other Anglophone countries, including Canada and Australia (Sawer 2004). In the attempt to reclaim "authentic manliness" through the new technocratic knowl-edge, critique as the essence of liberal academic life must be depicted as femin-ized and dispensable. Technocratic and applied knowledge, delivered as objective and neutral information, does not need to be interpreted, theorized, or critiqued, but speaks for itself. The most effective way of dispensing with critique is to contract the spaces that enable it, which spells doom for critical projects such as FLT. The evisceration of its critical space within the legal academy has enabled anti-feminism to be revived within the new-knowledge academic scripts; terms like patriarchy and sexism have become anachronistic (Lewis 2005: 11).

It is perhaps unsurprising that the gendered subtext of academic life has adapted to new circumstances and new ideologies. New knowledge is the appa-ratus that produces new forms of gender; it is not de-gendered as its technocratic veneer would have us believe. Thus, while the identity of academic subjects no longer counts as much as their productivity, the gendered subtext of the new-knowledge economy is subtly reified. Competition policy and the logic of the market necessarily produce inequality, not equality. It is notable that there has been a retreat from the language of equality and equality of opportunity in the academy, as well as in the public domain (Brodie 2008; Thornton 2001; 2008).

The legitimation of inequality tilts the scales permanently in favor of the status quo. Promotion of the self has effectively displaced a collective commitment to gender politics in the academy. The top-down, authoritarian, and over-controlled university of today has left little space for feminist voices to be heard.

Conclusion

The discourse of "post-feminism," emerging in the early 1990s and suggesting that feminism's day was done (Faludi 1991) may have been a ploy to reinstantiate masculine hegemony (McRobbie 2007). Margaret Henderson (2006) shows how post-feminism constructs the past by diluting and revising feminist experiences and their unsettling effects. As I have mentioned, "girl power" is the latest version of post-feminism. Its focus on (hetero)sex, consumerism, and fashion is designed to ensure the subordination of young women in the workplace and the erasure of feminist discourses of equality. The primary message young women lawyers are absorbing from popular culture is that they should not compete with men in ways that jeopardize their sexual desirability. Yet, they also have been imbued with the notion that they are the equals of men in the world of legal practice; feminism is passé. The girl power subtext is that how these young women look and dress is what counts in an undeniably gendered world.

However, FLT is not static, for it captures the conceptualization of the feminine at a particular epistemic moment (Thornton 2004). It may be that just as there has been a rejection of the essentialist category "woman" and a turning away from the word "feminism" itself, a new discourse will emerge. "Gender studies" and "diversity studies" represent examples of new discourses that have sought to occlude the partiality of the feminine in favor of a more neutral guise. These terms risk sloughing off the feminine altogether within a constellation of variables that play into the hands of neoliberal misogyny. The evidence based on the use of such ostensibly neutral terms in popular discourse seems to suggest that the main target of discrimination is now men not women (Henderson 2008: 34).

The dilemma for feminist legal scholars is how to respond to the market metanarrative. Small acts of resistance are inconsequential in the face of seduction by the audit culture. Nevertheless, I do not wish to end on a gloomy note. Feminist legal scholars have always been engaged in a struggle but are also animated by the hope for a better future. A new epistemic moment may well be upon us with the economic crisis of 2008–9 that gave neoliberalism a jolt. Instead of redistributive justice, nation states have paid billions of public dollars to bail out failing multinational corporations. As a result, the public's faith in neoliberalism and deregulation has been severely shaken. While there is not going to be an instantaneous abandonment of the adulation of the market—as the bail-outs reveal—nation states may be more cautious about permitting the market free rein in the future.

Australian Labor Prime Minister, Kevin Rudd (2009) argues that the neo-liberal experiment has failed; it is no more than personal greed dressed up as economic philosophy. Prime Minister Rudd exhorts a return to recognition of the central role of the state in reducing "the greater inequalities that competitive markets will inevitably generate" (29). His focus is on restraining the excesses of an unregulated market in order to preserve the social fabric of the polity. He is not proposing to decenter the market or to return to free higher education. Nevertheless, since the fortunes of the state and FLT are imbricated, it seems to me that the reclamation of some notion of the social liberal state is a predicate to a robust role for FLT in the legal academy in the future.

While I have shown that legal feminism is exceedingly sensitive to the movement of the political pendulum, the volatility induced by the global financial collapse may be just what is needed to shift the action towards the common good. In light of the depoliticizing effects of neoliberalism, which have substituted consumers for citizens, it is hoped that it is not too late. A depression is not necessary to demonstrate the worth of FLT. While it has always shown resilience and a capacity for revitalization in difficult times, my fear is that the metanarrative of the market and its varied fortunes could carry with it the seeds of feminist amnesia that will sustain the renewed masculinization of the legal academy.

Chapter 3

Have pantsuit, will travel

Patricia J. Williams

Talk about your long and winding roads. When I attended the first Feminist Legal Theory Workshop, I had big hair, a business suit with bricks for shoulder pads, and platform boots. I actually got compliments. More on suits of armor later. For now, let's just say that meeting Martha Fineman and participating in the FLT Workshop was a very important gift in allowing me to rethink the defensive armor that women of my generation wore—literally climbed into as though we were getting into a diving bell—before pioneers like Martha Fineman helped us rethink the codes inscribed in theretofore unconscious and under-theorized rituals of self-presentation.

As recently as 25 years ago, women were so rare among the legal professoriate that finding a women's restroom was a challenge. When Martha first went to Columbia Law School, faculty offices had only men's rooms—women had to take the elevator to the first floor and use the public toilets. When I came to Columbia some years later, things had improved somewhat in that there were women's rooms on every other floor. Today, thanks largely to Martha's activism (or "acting up" as some curmudgeons might recall it) there are men's and women's bathrooms on each and every floor of the law school building.

Even today, the field of law struggles to accommodate the presence of women. Perhaps the most quaintly symbolic manifestation is the requirement that the Solicitor General of the United States must wear tails—more formally known as a morning coat—when arguing the government's cases. When Elena Kagan became the first woman ever to hold that position, her very presence triggered an epiphenomenal fashion crisis that shook American socio-legal tradition to its roots.

Perhaps I overstate.

But consider the history: the tradition of the morning coat began in 1870, when the Office of Solicitor General was founded. Back then it was more or less the equivalent of what a Brooks Brothers three-piece suit might be today—elegant but not archaic. Today we associate the morning coat with arch formality, like weddings, state funerals, or an afternoon at Ascot or Henley. But in its heyday, the morning coat was a less formal version of the frock coat, literally suitable for morning rather than evening affairs. Also known as a "cutaway," the hemline commences at the waistline in front, then curves downward into two long tails in the back—thus making it suitable for horseback riding.

The persistence of this sartorial custom beyond its natural lifespan—and in the justice system of all places—is not merely a quirk of history but testament to the tenaciously and clubbishly masculinist culture that still afflicts the highest levels and most intransigently closed circles of power. Tradition, yes, but it's also the mark of a male-dominated legal profession still struggling to deal with the radical transformations of the last 30 years, during which women's numbers skyrocketed from the low single digits to approximately 50 percent of law school graduates.

From the perspective of world hunger, it's a small matter I suppose, the peculiar sartorial habits of solicitors general. Yet structurally, it's problematic. There's The Uniform for those whose endowments conform to high Victorian tradition; and then there is "something else" for those girlish "others" who'll just have to figure out a way to assimilate, accommodate, or "pass." No, it's not as insidious an affliction of gender apartheid as separate tee times for women in the PGA or the lack of women's bathrooms in the executive suite. But still the question presents: what's a gentle mistress to do when required to accessorize according to a long line of Mr. Darcy look-alikes? The cane or the whip? Balmorals or button-up boots? Bowler or bonnet? Silk stockings cum satin snood? Crinoline or calico? Seriously, now—taffeta or twill?

There is not a good deal of reassuring precedent when dealing with such dilemma. Barbara Underwood, a well-regarded public advocate, served as Acting Solicitor General for six months in 2001; and there are numbers of female assistant or deputy solicitors who have also argued before the court. Though it is not easy to find records of what any of them might have worn, there are a few legendary, perhaps apocryphal, struggles commonly shared among lawyers. My favorite is said to have occurred during the Clinton administration, when a female deputy from the Solicitor General's office wore what is variously described as a "dove-brown" or "doe-beige" business suit while arguing a case to the Supreme Court.

According to a friend who, to this day, fears being identified, Chief Justice Rehnquist "went berserk." He chastised her for inappropriate attire and followed it up with a scathing letter to the Solicitor General himself, requesting that this not occur again. Brown textiles! The scandal! (Yes, this is the same Justice Rehnquist whose love of costume led him to affix to his judicial robes a set of gold stripes he once saw adorning the fictional persona of Lord Chancellor in a production of Gilbert and Sullivan's *Iolanthe*.) In response, the Solicitor General's office thenceforth recommended that women wear what is popularly known as a "feminized" version of morning attire and/or a plain black suit. (In case you're wondering, a feminized morning suit is more or less like the men's version, only with darts at the bust line: that is, a dark jacket, often with silk trim on the lapels and those perky Scrooge McDuck tails flapping out behind. And instead of the classic striped charcoal trousers, a neo-classical striped charcoal skirt. Open question whether the same requires a Windsor-knotted tie with starched winged collar.)

In her lovely meditation, *A Room of One's Own*, Virginia Woolf ([1929]1991: 6) writes that Thackeray's "affectation of the style, with its imitation of the eighteenth century, hampers one … " She thinks about looking at his manuscript to see "whether the alterations were for the benefit of the style or of the sense. But then one would have to decide what is style and what is meaning … " (6). Here her reflection is interrupted:

> … like a guardian angel barring the way with a flutter of black gown instead of white wings, a deprecating, silvery, kindly gentleman, who regretted in a low voice as he waved me back, that ladies are only admitted to the library if accompanied by a Fellow of the College or furnished with a letter of introduction.
>
> (6)

What is style? What is meaning? Are the justices of the Supreme Court of the United States really unable to concentrate on the law of the land when female advocates wear timid-deer, bird-brown frocks rather than manly tailored frock coats? Are they really better able to engage with serious issues when twenty-first century men must gussy themselves up like nineteenth-century dandies in order to be heard? What does equality mean if the most iconic advocates in our justice system comport themselves according to nineteenth-century models of male virtue? And if it's tradition we love so much, should not the female alternative to the morning coat be that of a ruche-trimmed mini top hat with ostrich feathers and tulle silk veil; a puff-sleeved blouson over laced corset; tantalizingly ankle-grazing skirt made yet more tantalizing by a large bustle stuffed with sacks of horsehair suspended by a series of latches, collapsible armatures and springs for ease of sitting and standing?

And so I muse upon what alterations will be "for the benefit … of the sense."

"Sisterhood of the traveling pantsuits" is how Hillary Clinton put it during her speech at the Democratic National Convention in August of 2008. And with those simple words, the peculiar misery haunting a certain slice of my entire professional life flashed before my eyes.

First let me set the scene: I went to the Convention to blog my impressions. I got to the Denver Convention Center late, after getting up at four o'clock in the morning to catch the plane there. My hotel, as it turned out, was not actually in Denver but in the next suburb over; thus, I had to take a shuttle bus and light rail or a $70 cab ride while the driver tried to figure out which roads into town hadn't been blocked off. Once at the convention center, you still had to stand in line for an hour or so to get through perimeter security then walk for miles and miles on the indoor–outdoor concrete surfaces with which all of Denver is seemingly paved.

What I mean is, that if you'd worn the wrong shoes, you didn't just pop back to your room to change. And if you'd worn long pants and a snappy little power jacket with a silk lining that was slicked to your skin in the blistering heat, you didn't dare take it off, because you're middle-aged and a little worried about bra straps.

So this was the kind of stuff rattling through my brain when Hillary Clinton spoke those fateful words. I looked at her well-constructed peach pantsuit and the pantsuits of the thousands of her well-heeled contributors on the floor and thought, the night before, Michele Obama had worn a simple, single-layer sheath dress, appropriate for this weather, and a pair of low-heeled shoes. Elegant, confident, and literally cooler. This thought, this contrast, made me stop my busy blogging about unity and the future and women as astronauts. I unbuttoned my jacket, kicked off my shoes underneath the press table. Whew, I said to myself. Hillary Clinton and I are trapped in the clothes of our generation.

I suppose there's nothing like an election to turn the mind to fashion statements, so allow me this little digression upon the little-observed semiotics of what hell it has been for a woman of a certain age to dress for success. To some extent it's not exclusively woman's issue—the citizenry is often disposed to deciphering candidates' positions on serious issues, ranging from the war to the economy, from the esoterica of what they wear. Cowboy-boot politics. Italian-twill tweed. Plaid-shirt populism. Lapel-pin patriotism.

This season, however, we have been much consumed with the matter of "shoulder-pad feminism," as it was so ungraciously dubbed by pundits. The very term made me cringe, harkening back as it does to my first days out of law school some 30-odd years ago, when as a result of brand-new affirmative action policies, women entered professional life in something like numbers that mattered.

It's hard to remember how flummoxed everyone was at the prospect of women in boardrooms, women in courtrooms, women in ... power. Garden hats, tea dresses, and little white gloves simply weren't up to the task. And what a task it was. Pervasive skepticism at our presence in male geographies had to be countered with the trappings of authority, the semaphores of serious intent, the packaging of no-nonsense. Proving that we were as good as the guys thus ushered in an ugly and exaggerated anti-romanticism: no lace, no flounces, no ruffles, no pleats. No hankies as though in expectation of copious tears. No loud colors that made you sparkle or shine. No lockets, no heart-shaped objects dangling from delicate silver threads. No heaving bosoms, no bursting bras, indeed no obvious breasts. Just a uniformly square-cut suit in industrial tones, perhaps a robust rope of heavy gold for a wristwatch. We looked as though Charlotte Perkins Gilman's housewife had stepped out of her yellow wallpapered prison of sentimental virtue and bellied up to the bar.

So. The number one thing that makes me wince when I look at old photos of myself is The Power Suit. The power suit was the *de rigueur* uniform for professional women during the 1980s. It had overcompensatory shoulder pads whose width exceeded those of your average quarterback.

It is no accident that this was also the era of Big Hair—one absolutely had to have a helmet of expansively frazzled locks just to proportionalize those shoulders. "You looked like Mark Maguire," says my son as he flips through the family album, then wisely adds, "but prettier." His confusion is forgivable. In those days, women always looked steroidally bloated, pumped up to the point of near explosion.

One of *Wikipedia*'s definitions of "power suit" is "a powered exoskeleton," to wit, a machine covering the body to "assist and protect soldiers" or to "aid the survival of people in dangerous situations." That captures exactly my experience in the realm of pin-striped grey and navy-blue serge.

The second most despicable item of clothing from that era was the so-called Dressed-for-Success-Bow-at-the-Throat. This was a time, you must recall, when women and men still existed in very separate conceptual realms. In order to transgress the boundary between "women's work" and "men's work," one of the most common recommendations was that women "pass" by trading in the pearls for a tie. Not for a manly-man's tie, God forbid, but rather for a huge, flouncy, floppy, thoroughly "effeminate" and not at all "feminist," version of a bow tie. Said bow was always in red silk, like an Edwardian Christmas caroler, the better to go with the navy blue of the suit. It was like a bad gender-bending joke—us bravely liberated, big-haired, shoulder-pad feminists yoked at the throat with the mark of Little Lord Fauntleroy. Does it come as any surprise that such an ensemble might require a crisply starched Peter Pan collar?

Let me pass onto the cruelty of shoes. Heel and toe. Power and pain. There is still no such thing as a women's shoe that conveys comfort and signals power simultaneously. A serious power shoe must lend height. Height means the sadomasochistic punishment of, say, four-inch bootlets in butter-soft suede from Bloomingdale's. Despite the hard-won graduate degrees qualifying one as a professional woman of immense rationality, one nevertheless may be seduced by the ability to stand eyeball to eyeball with any man who challenges your word. It is vanity that will ensure a nightmarish escarpment of physical regret. For many moons after taking them off—and assuredly by the time you turn 50—you will hobble about at a dangerously forward-pitched slant.

What makes work "back-breaking" for many professional women is not the traditional swinging of shovel and axe, but the isometric bewilderment of balancing heavy hair, padded shoulders, and overloaded tote-bag against the angled physics of stiletto heels.

And yet I confess I love stilettos irrationally. They make me think of Andy Warhol's lovely sketches back in the days when he was an illustrator for B. Altman and I. Miller. I associate them with his beautifully inked, blotted-line pictures of ice cream cones and pink layer cakes. Stilettos are so feminine yet strong, professional yet sexy, dangerous but in control, cruel but competent. Such good lawyer garb. Such good weapons with which to crack glass ceilings.

Indeed, according to Jack Green's discussion in *The Physics Factbook*, a stiletto high heel exerts more than 15 times the pressure exerted by an elephant's foot:

> Pressure is defined as force over area. Pressure is directly proportional to the force and inversely proportional to area. This inverse relationship is an important concept when it concerns the immensity of pressure. The significance of the high heel comes into play because it has such a minute area. Due to this fact, the pressure under that high heel is extremely large. If one were to solve the aforementioned problem, the solution is deduced as follows:

$$P = \frac{F}{A} = \frac{mg}{\pi r^2} = \frac{(50kg)(9.8ms^{-2})}{\pi(0.0006m)^2} = 4,330kPa$$

> This is approximately 40 atmospheric pressures.

(Green 2003: para. 3)

If only all this rogue elephantine female power could have found its expression in an aggressively adorned tea hat or a ferociously iron-fisted velvet glove. Instead it had to be the shoe, so relentlessly jack-hammering its liberatory tattoo upwards, into the spine.

And there is no perfect antidote to such suffering. Yes, there's always the frequent if furtive resort to snub-nosed, little-girl flats. Alice-in-Wonderland shoes. Ballerina slippers. Aerosols with bouncy, innocent, rubber-ball bottoms. Such honest footgear may be gloriously, eye-rollingly more comfortable, but flats do diminish no matter how hard they try. They make you shorter to start with— even if "shorter" means "your actual height." In this, Michele Obama, at nearly six feet, enjoys a distinct advantage. Flats make me, however, feel sedate as a nun, even when they come in leopard print.

Some of this is probably because I associate flat, round-toed shoes with the boring old blood-colored Oxfords and wool knee socks I had to wear from kindergarten through middle school. School shoes. Sensible shoes—back in the day when Twiggy was iconic, an alluringly un-sensible dandelion puff in a Peter Max miniskirt. Twiggy wore Cuban heels! And patent-leather go-go boots! My mother, the breeziest of upbeat matriarchs, dismissed my complaints summarily: "Lace them up. No one's going to remember your shoes a hundred years from now."

How wrong she was. I would be a different, happier, more charitable human being if I had not had to wear those ugly red Oxfords with their unforgiving arch supports. Perhaps today I wouldn't be so easily smitten by shoes with not just elegant spindles for heels, but sharply tapered triangles for toes. Power points. I've heard that some women actually have plastic surgery to shorten their toes so as be able to squeeze into a set of narrow-nosed Manolo Blahniks. The pathetic thing is, when I walk into a meeting wearing my kick-ass Jimmy Choos,

I almost understand why. It's worth the pain! My IQ, my courage, my logic are outstanding!

But still, I wish I'd never worn them.

After Hillary finished speaking, it took me two hours and forty-five minutes to get back to my hotel. I walked miles hunting for a taxi, but outside the convention center, it was a zoo, a zoo with a shortage of cabs. I went back to the convention center, consulted a transportation guide who directed me to take a 40-minute bus ride to the Red Lion Hotel and then get a cab from there. The Red Lion was where the Texas delegation was staying; so, I rode with a lively group in gaudy cowboy hats sprinkled with red, white, and blue glitter who kept eying me with friendly suspicion and asking, "You're not from Texas, are you?" When I confessed that I was from New York it was like one of those picante sauce advertisements. "New York City!!" they said and shook their heads in unison.

I think it must have been my shoes.

Chapter 4

Grappling with equality*

One feminist journey

Martha Albertson Fineman

Introduction

In 1908, two Boston women enlisted Arthur Winfield MacLean to tutor them so they could sit for the Massachusetts bar examination. That humble but significant beginning grew into Portia Law School, later the New England School of Law. Portia was the first law school established exclusively for women, who at that time were denied entry into nearly all other schools of law (Hamilton 2008). Today women are integrated into the legal profession, making up over half of the student body at some law schools and achieving partnerships and professorships.

However, the early-twentieth century was a time of entrenched—even celebrated—gender discrimination in American society. Cloistering women away from politics and the professions was justified by assumptions about their inherent distinctiveness as human beings. Certainly women's unique role was valued, perhaps even more than that of their male counterparts, at least rhetorically. Nevertheless, the general perception of society was reflected in legal pronouncements that women's constitution and temperament meant they were ill equipped to handle the demands of public and political life. Women's divine destiny was in the nursery and kitchen. The most notorious expression of this sentiment appears in Justice Bradley's concurring opinion in *Bradwell v. Illinois* in which he opined that:

> [T]he civil law, as well as nature herself, has always recognized a wide difference in the respective spheres and destinies of man and woman. Man is, or should be, woman's protector and defender. The natural and proper timidity and delicacy which belongs to the female sex evidently unfits it for many of the occupations of civil life. The constitution of the family organization, which is founded in the divine ordinance, as well as in the nature of things, indicates the domestic sphere as that which properly belongs to the domain and functions of womanhood. The harmony, not to say identity, of interests and views which belong, or should belong, to the family institution is repugnant to the idea of a woman adopting a distinct and independent

career from that of her husband. So firmly fixed was this sentiment in the founders of the common law that it became a maxim of that system of jurisprudence that a woman had no legal existence separate from her husband, who was regarded as her head and representative in the social state ...

(*Bradwell* 1872: 141)

Bradley's perspective found its way into a variety of Supreme Court pronouncements. For example, *Muller v. Oregon* (1908), a progressive-era case upholding labor legislation that monitored women's hours in factories and laundries, cast women as different from, and weaker than, men. It is of interest because it considered legislation that separated women workers from men and found them as in need of special protection. The unanimous opinion stated:

That woman's physical structure and the performance of maternal functions place her at a disadvantage in the struggle for subsistence is obvious. This is especially true when the burdens of motherhood are upon her. Even when they are not, by abundant testimony of the medical fraternity continuance for a long time on her feet at work, repeating this from day to day, tends to injurious effects upon the body, and as healthy mothers are essential to vigorous offspring, the physical well-being of woman becomes an object of public interest and care in order to preserve the strength and vigor of the race.

(*Muller* 1908: 421)

The gender-specific approach taken by progressive reformers in *Muller* was shaped in part by the dictates of an earlier case where the court considered and rejected protective legislation. In *Lochner v. New York* (1905),[1] the court found that the police power was not sufficient to support state efforts to limit employee hours in ordinary occupations. Writing for the majority, Justice Peckham folded liberty of contract into the Due Process Clause and found that the statute interfered with "the right of contract between employer and employes [sic]" (53). The opinion also noted that the law "involve[d] neither the safety, the morals nor the welfare of the public, and that the interest of the public is not in the slightest degree affected by such an act" (57). For the advocates of progressive labor legislation, the path to securing protection must have seemed clear— make arguments that resonated with the public interest so the court would let the regulation stand.

Lochner concerned an occupation limited overwhelmingly to male workers, although the case's language does not specifically limit itself to them as a class; but, the legislation at issue in *Muller* intentionally introduced gender as a focus and limitation. When this gender-specific focus was challenged in court, arguments for upholding the legislation concentrated on asserted gender differences. Thus, the *Muller* brief devoted hundreds of pages to the proposition that the state had an interest in protecting the health of women based on the importance of their roles as mothers. It built upon prevailing beliefs about women's differences in setting out an argument that the state could limit women's liberty to contract in regard to their labor, even if it could not do so for men. Women were deemed physically and emotionally weaker than men and in need of special protection, particularly since their distinctive role in the home required that their energy not be exhausted by paid employment.

Regardless of the wording of the legislation, the proponents of *Muller* reforms were not only concerned with women workers. Organizations like the National Consumers' League and the National Women's Trade Union League supported such regulation because it was thought that women workers were more easily exploited than their male counterparts, but also because they viewed such regulations as a step toward gaining protections for all workers (Bernstein 2003). Protections for male workers were not viable until the 1930s when the court became more deferential to legislatures in the wake of the New Deal.[2] By that time, however, the notion of women needing special protections due to their domestic role and general physical and emotional sensitivities was ensconced in American jurisprudence, uprooted only in the 1960s and 1970s when the Equal Protection Clause and Title VII were used to impose gender neutrality as the preferred legal norm (Ritter 2006).

The paradox of gender equality

Muller is an interesting case from a contemporary feminist legal theory perspective because it presents a paradox of gender equality that continues to be replicated in debates. On one hand, the regulations at issue addressed the real-world circumstances of working-class women, who needed protections from oppressive and exploitative workplaces. *Muller* was greeted by some as a welcome and necessary intervention for women overwhelmed by the dual demands of work and family. Existing law precluded across-the-board protective legislation, but gender-specific reforms could be successful because women's unique reproductive and domestic roles supplied the necessary public interest in the reforms. Even if incomplete, such reforms helped the life circumstances of women who were among the most oppressed.

On the other hand, many strongly believed that it was essential to make a commitment to a more abstract and pure sense of sexual equality by requiring that women be treated the same as men, no matter how bad that treatment was. Helping some women workers by establishing "women" as a distinct and separate category of workers with different needs and circumstances justifying application of different rules solidified the general sexist tendencies of the society. Freedom from exploitation might have been the objective of such labor reform, but gaining protection in this piecemeal manner sacrificed the treatment of women as the formal equals of men in regard to the workplace and liberty of contract. Gender differences so recognized could be used against women in the future as the basis for discrimination, reinforcing women's subordination and exclusion from public life. After all, in the *Muller* era, women were still denied the right to vote based on arguments about their differences (Amendment XIX, 18 August 1920).

After *Muller*, states ushered in reforms that not only brought needed protective relief to many women, but were also used to confine some women to low-paying jobs. Protective legislation barred some women from working overtime (e.g. *Bosley v. McLaughlin* 1915; *Ex parte Hawley* 1911, aff'd *Hawley v. Walker* 1914; *Miller v. Wilson* 1915) and holding certain higher-paying jobs (Kessler-Harris 1982). These results were viewed as lessons on the fallacy of the *Muller* approach by liberal legal feminists challenging gender-specific laws in the mid-twentieth century. They urged courts to favor formal equality or equality as sameness of treatment, and this view prevailed. In *Reed v. Reed* (1971) a statutory preference for men as executors of estates was held inconsistent with the Equal Protection Clause of the US Constitution and sex-specific rules became suspect. The court held:

> To give a mandatory preference to members of either sex over members of the other, merely to accomplish the elimination of hearings on the merits, is to make the very kind of arbitrary legislative choice forbidden by the Equal Protection Clause of the Fourteenth Amendment; and whatever may be said as to the positive values of avoiding intrafamily controversy, the choice in the context may not lawfully be mandated solely on the basis of sex.
>
> (*Reed* 1971: 76–77)

Ruth Bader Ginsburg litigated *Reed* for the Women's Rights Project of the American Civil Liberties Union (ACLU) and took a lead in many other gender equality cases.

In spite of the doctrinal success of formal equality, some feminists continue to argue that there are significant limitations to this equal rights strategy. They urge recognition of differences between the social and cultural positions of women and men, as well as pluralism within the category of women. They argue for a notion of equality that is sensitive to gender differences, whether those differences arise due to biological distinctiveness or social circumstances. This approach can be described as an attempt to "put[] women into the Constitution on female rather than male terms" (Hoff 1991: 374, emphasis omitted).

Though forging a new definition of equality is at the top of my agenda, I approach things a little differently at this point in my intellectual development. We must leave the gender wars behind and address our issues in terms other than women versus men. The pressing task is how to make our sense of equality resonate with the human condition generally. In undertaking this task, there are lessons women (and men when they are caretakers) have learned while historically confined to the family, profound insights that come from confronting dependency and vulnerability on a day-to-day basis. Our aspiration for equality cannot only take the public and political aspects of life into account; we must include the roles of parents and partners as well as workers and voters in forging a new understanding of equality. The failure of the *Muller* approach was not that it recognized the need for protecting women from the exploitive workplace, but that men were not seen in need of protection from workplace exploitation and concessions to family life.

Our legal theorists have failed in overlooking what we know about humanity and the need for positive state protection, including the substantive provision of social goods. Ignoring dependency and vulnerability has meant that our legal sense of equality developed narrowly and focused on prevention of some forms of discrimination, rather than on state responsibility to respond to basic human needs. Inattention to the interdependencies inherent in the human condition has allowed us to idealize contract and individual autonomous choice in ways that mask society's role in perpetuating inequality.

One feminist journey toward understanding equality

I began my academic career arguing that equality and gender neutrality were not appropriate concepts to employ in thinking about reform of the family and family law (Fineman 1991a; see also Fineman 1983, 1986, 1987a, 1987b, 1988, 1989). I contended that the family, as our most gendered institution, was not susceptible to the imposition of a formal equality model. Ignoring gender differences and treating spouses the same could only further and deepen existing inequalities. I suggested that the family needed not formal or rule equality, but some notion of substantive or result equality that considered past circumstances and future obligations.

I identified three sites of entrenched inequality affecting most marriages. First was wage and employment inequality, which disadvantaged women in terms of compensation and conditions of employment. Next was inequality of bargaining power that persisted in family negotiations over whose individual interests should be sacrificed for the larger family good, a process that disadvantaged women due to lower earnings and culturally imposed altruism. Finally, there were inequalities in family burdens that would be carried on into the future, inequalities that arose post-divorce, with the responsibilities of custody overwhelmingly assigned to women. Maternal custody was further disadvantaging due to the difficulty of collecting child support awards.

Arguably, those inequalities have lessened in our post-egalitarian family law world, but they continue to persist in many marriages, even if to a lesser degree. While gender-neutral, equality-based reforms are firmly in the statute books and have proved successful on a rhetorical level, structural family disadvantages associated with caretaking still typically burden women more than men even after decades of feminist equality reform.

In 1991, I hoped we might fashion a more substantive or result-sensitive version of equality in the family context. The law would allow unequal or different treatment of divorcing spouses, such as unequal distribution of family assets and obligations, in order to address the existing inequalities created or exacerbated by past and future family responsibilities. This more result-sensitive version of equality would be considered "just" and appropriate because it would satisfy the need that arose from one spouse assuming primary responsibility for children within and after marriage.

My suggestion to move away from formal equality in the family context was viciously attacked by feminist legal scholars and men's groups, groups normally on different sides when it comes to family law issues. These attacks were couched in the dominant legalistic understanding of equality that demanded it be formal in nature and required sameness of treatment. Equality was about abolishing discrimination and suspicious of any difference in treatment. The feminist attacks reflected on the history of exclusion of women from public life, such as that found in *Muller*'s stigmatizing assertion of gender difference. For that reason, "special" or different treatment under law had to be rejected.

Based on these experiences I concluded that our current constitutional and statutory equality regime is inadequate. We analyze equality through the lens of discrimination, independent of, and seemingly oblivious to existing inequalities of distribution or opportunity. Our equality regime leaves unexamined existing allocations of resources and power. It assumes an equivalence in bargaining ability in assessing family, economic, and employment relationships. Unless there is some distortion introduced by impermissible bias, the state should not interfere.

While I still believe in the justness of the substantive equality outcome, my vocabulary and arguments are less focused on gender and more inclusive of those whose family or other uncounted labor is not valued in a formal equality regime. I now discuss need in terms of dependency and vulnerability. This articulation may not be any more palatable to those who buy into the rhetoric of independence and self-sufficiency, but it is more theoretically promising. Vulnerability is universal and constant. As embodied individuals, we are all just an accidental mishap, natural disaster, institutional failure, or serious illness away from descending into a dependent state. Further, dependencies are multiple and complex in form.

I have been concerned with two types of dependency. On one hand, dependency is inevitable—a part of the human condition and developmental in nature. On the other hand, those who care for dependants through essential caretaking work are themselves dependent on resources to undertake that care. Those resources must be supplied by society through its institutions. The American scheme of social responsibility relegates both dependencies to the family and, typically within that family, to women in their roles as mothers, wives, and daughters, and so on.

Observing the family through the lens of vulnerability and dependency enhances and expands beyond that institution my critique of the imposition of a formal equality regime earlier developed with marriage and divorce primarily in mind. Subsequent work in developing a theory of dependency led to the idea of universal human vulnerability, demonstrating to me that both state and market are, of necessity, implicated in situating the family within society. That work also convinced me that formal equality is also an inadequate objective in many instances beyond the realm of the family. Some of the very same reasons that formal or rule equality is inappropriate for the family illuminate why it is insufficient in addressing justice and allocation problems in the larger society. Formal equality is inevitably uneven equality because existing inequalities abound throughout society, and a concept of equality that is merely formal in nature cannot adequately address them.

Gender was an obvious entry point from which to build this larger analysis, in part because women have historically been marked as different in relationship to the state and public sphere. Their citizenship and concurrent responsibilities were anchored in the family, not in the wider polity or free-wielding market. The residues of that distinction remain in many ways to implicate the image of women as citizens. Women have secured political and civil rights, have been successful in the formal search for equality but continue to stand outside mainstream power. Equality for women remains elusive in practical and material terms, partly because they remain mired in a pre-legal notion of the family in which they are understood to have unique reproductive roles and responsibilities that define them as essentially different and necessarily subordinate in a world that values economic success and discounts domestic labor.

Of course, the distinction between the position of women in the family and that within the larger society is incoherent theoretically. The family is not a separate sphere isolated from the norms and standards applied in the larger society. Our notions about the mandates of citizenship, the appropriateness of claims to liberty and autonomy, and beliefs about relative equality resonate across societal institutions, on both an ideological and structural level.

The nature and functioning of other societal institutions profoundly affects the nature and shape of the family just as the nature and functioning of the family profoundly affects other societal institutions. Thus, the metaphor of "symbiosis"[3] seems more appropriate to describe the family in relationship to the state than does the separate spheres imagery. The family is located within the state and its institutions. Alterations in the scope or nature of one institution will correspondingly alter the scope or nature of the other. Similarly, if formal equality is inadequate or unattainable in the family, it is likely that it failed or will fail as a regime in the larger society. These are the lessons we need to learn.

Equality attained—the post-equality feminist

One way to look at our feminist equality dilemma is to realize that in the United States women have attained equality in the only way possible within our current political and legal climate. This accomplishment is a meaningful one. We guarantee equal citizenship, and we prohibit sex discrimination. Our equality regime guarantees access and opportunity to women on a par with men. We have the right to sameness of treatment and freedom from exclusion. Women's political and civil rights are formally ensured; we have access to all sorts of opportunities. We can get an education, practice a profession, earn money, own property, vote, serve on a jury, and hold office, all on a par with men. Importantly, at least on a theoretical level, this conferral of equality on women takes nothing away from men. It is apparently a win-win situation.

However, this equality is not only encompassing, it is also crude and non-discerning—a gender-blind monolith, folding all within its embrace. Men also can claim the protection of gender equality should their gender occasion different, comparatively unfavorable treatment. They can do so even if they are privileged as individuals or as members of advantaged groups. They can do so even against members of subordinated groups. An abstract notion of discriminatory treatment represents the affront to equality, not the relative position of the person seeking a remedy. Since our equality is based on anti-discrimination or sameness of treatment, different treatment is suspect unless there is some legitimate basis for distinguishing among individuals or groups. This equality rejects (at least in regard to gender) affirmative governmental measures designed to raise the unequal to a more equal position.

This vision of equality has the same problems that concerned me in the family context back in the 1980s. It operates within a configuration of existing structural, social, societal, and individual inequalities. We have equal citizenship as an abstract entitlement, but the benefits of that citizenship are unevenly distributed through existing social and cultural structures, particularly the family. In other words, there is no level playing field, and we do not have a concept of equality that will allow us to even things up a bit, except minutely, and then mostly in the context of race-based affirmative action programs. Our equality is weak and largely illusory because it fails to consider the existing inequalities of circumstances created both by inevitable and universal vulnerability inherent in the human condition and the societal institutions that have grown up around them, most notably the family and the state.

These inequalities may be beyond the ability of the state under current ideological configurations, but they are certainly not natural. The state and legal institutions confer senses of entitlement and value, including through a regime of equality that facilitates some results and protects and privileges some persons over, or instead of, others.

The future of equality

I suggest adopting two tactics to challenge the existing equality regime. Both involve relating the concept of equality to something else in order to shift our perspective and provide new questions for theoretical investigation. First, we must consider how equality has been strategically paired with and tamed by other concepts and ideals over time. Equality is only one component of citizenship, only one of the parameters that establish the ideal relationship between state and individual. Second, equality discourse must be anchored by an understanding of the human condition in which we are all vulnerable, and some of us might decline into dependency. Equality must not be built upon the false assumption that citizen capabilities are equivalent across individuals or that individual capabilities remain constant throughout a lifetime.

Equality is a dynamic concept, often placed in ideological competition with other American values such as autonomy. Equality's meaning and its relative position in this balancing can change over the course of a nation's history and response to experiences. Different aspirations and expectations for the state and individuals inform different ideological and political positions on equality, and the right to determine the nature and weight given to equality in that balancing is the battle for every generation. The balances struck will shift across history, within and among nations, as well as being complexly expressed across competing philosophies and perspectives.

In relation to reconciling and balancing values in the twenty-first century United States, citizenship is understood as conferring a guarantee of autonomy as well as equality. In recent years the promise of equality has eroded under the ascendency of a narrow and impoverished understanding of autonomy (Fineman 2004). While equality presupposes an individual seeking inclusion and consistent treatment within a group, autonomy seeks separateness and seclusion. Autonomy forms the base for the concept of self-governance and is characterized by self-sufficiency and independence, which are individual qualities considered as pre-requisites for individual freedom of will and action. They have no theoretical room for recognition of dependency and vulnerability.

Autonomy demands freedom from unnecessary or excessively constraining rules and regulations. These constraints turn out to include almost everything of a positive and progressive regulatory nature. The state's role is to stay out of the way, to facilitate competitiveness in a meritocracy that rewards individual initiative and talent. When there is a distortion, such as arises from discrimination, the state should act to correct the problem and then revert to the free market, non-intervention stance. Starting from a perspective that values individual autonomy above equality makes inequality of the status quo a given. If, however, we start with the objective of enhancing individual equality, we may see more of a need for protection from human fragility and failings than abandoning individuals to undefined crude autonomy might provide.

If we factor into the equality/autonomy mix the universality of human vulnerability and our shared possibility of becoming dependent, it is apparent that the problem the state should address is not always, nor even predominantly, that of discriminatory treatment. The problem may be in an equality that brackets off vulnerability and dependency in order to assume them and the resulting disadvantages and burdens they place on individuals. Taking vulnerability and dependency into account would reveal the inadequacies of our conception of equality as not focused on substance, but rather concerned merely with the formality of treatment. Achieving some form of substantive equality demands more from the state in terms of rules and regulations than we now condone. Substantive equality would require state intervention, even methods for the reallocation of some existing benefits and burdens. In order to have more equality for greater numbers—a collective ideal, we would have to sacrifice some adherence to the dictates of individual autonomy.

Of course, "equality" and "autonomy" are abstractions; they have no independent meaning and can be understood in conflicting ways. Their amorphous, overarching, and imprecise natures mean that both terms can be used by those holding disparate positions. Yet, neither equality nor autonomy can be understood in isolation from each other and, at least to the extent we are concerned with substantive equality, one will be emphasized at the expense of the other.

I recognize the symbolic appeal of claims for autonomy and equality and the desire to reconcile any potential conflict between them, but I argue against the current understanding of equality as the dependent value, shaped through the dominant lens of autonomy and reduced to a mere individual entitlement to be treated the same as everyone else regardless of differences in material, social, historical, or other resources. Unless confronted with the challenges presented by vulnerability and dependency, equality is nothing more than a standard for opportunity and access. It guarantees the right to strive for self-sufficiency and independence to an abstract individual shorn of limiting human characteristics and potentially debilitating social and historical inequities. Equality is not now a standard with which to assess contexts and conditions—the circumstances under which an individual competes in the markets. Nor is it used as a leveling notion, employed to even up the playing field before the games begin—a tool to ensure some degree of equality of opportunity and access. Some argue that this sense of individualized, formal equality that dominates law and culture, is all we can expect in a post-Reagan United States where we are trapped in scripts that presuppose both a meritocracy and a functioning free market in an ahistoric and context-free articulation of the American dream.

Questions we might ask about the current tradeoffs between equality and autonomy to challenge that static conclusion and open up the issue for further consideration could include

- What distortions result from viewing our aspirations through the lens of individual autonomy rather than our collective destiny of vulnerability and dependency?
- Whose interests are served by this current balance that privileges autonomy over a substantive equality frame?
- How does a preference for autonomy result in masking the reality of common vulnerability and dependency and interfere with the development of a more substantive concept of equality?
- Are there other values similarly sacrificed to autonomy when we ignore vulnerability and dependency in our political theory and policy-making?

Answering these questions would allow us to assess what harms come to our society by invoking autonomy with its complementary components of individual independence and self-sufficiency as primary aspirations for citizenship. From that assessment might come the will for political and legal change.

The second strategy to challenge the existing equality regime is to begin the hard work of constructing a viable and credible concept of substantive equality that resonates in the American context. This strategy is related to the first; for, it seeks to decenter autonomy and allow a more robust notion of equality to emerge as the guiding principle for assessing governmental action. This framing process is not only descriptive; it is also normative, a way to give a different meaning to a series of issues and help redefine them in a more progressive manner.

In accomplishing this framing, we must recognize that as a nation we are steeped in an ideology of individualism. However, it should not be forgotten that this individualism is grounded in a complementary set of beliefs about equity, access, and opportunity. Development of these concepts, particularly if they are accompanied by an appreciation of the universal and ever-present nature of our shared vulnerability and potential for becoming dependent, will be useful in redefining and repositioning both equality and autonomy.

A few years ago, I would have suggested looking to international human rights law and the constitutional processes of other industrialized democracies to go about this project of reframing. Robust notions of substantive equality are set out in international documents and cases interpreting them. For example, the Canadians realized it was simply not enough to assess equality from a formalistic perspective. The law must consider the societal context that defines groups and understand how individuals, identified and positioned in society through those groups, are advantaged or disadvantaged. Such an understanding would fulfill the Canadian courts' mandate that an interpretation of equality must be "a generous rather than a legalistic one, aimed at fulfilling the purpose of the guarantee [of substantive equality] and securing for individuals the full benefit of the Charter's protections" (*R v. Big M Drug Mart* 1985).

In other Western democracies there has been a general acceptance of the assertion that modernization and the expansion of equality mandate an obliga- tion on the part of government to guarantee fundamental social goods. This obligation has been codified, and an international consensus has emerged through international human rights documents that describe the obligations of states to citizens.

In the pantheon of international human rights, formal equality is certainly present. However, equality does not stop there, nor does the state's responsi- bility. While it is true that these documents have not been ratified by every country—certainly not by the United States—and their principles are not uniformly followed in those states that have adopted them, they do set out a full range of equal rights in aspirational terms. They stand witness to what are generally considered desirable objectives, widely accepted in many different societies, and increasingly used as the basis for articulating the need for specific laws.

However, I now believe arguments for a more expansive notion of equality are futile, at least for now. In both political and academic circles a version of American exceptionalism regarding the superiority of our laws and Constitution seems in ascendancy. Labeling human rights as "foreign fads" and proposing legislation that would lay the foundation for impeachment of judges who referred to them rather than American constitutional law indicates just how parochial our judges and politicians have become (Liptak et al. 2008: A1).

Such parochialism underscores the importance of excavating from US history and our legal and political principles the foundation for a more robust and expansive notion of equality. This would lay out the parameters for state responsibility in ensuring that access and opportunity were in fact equal, even if this meant the autonomy of some privileged individuals was of necessity somewhat crimped in the process. A formulation of state responsibility to positively guarantee access and opportunity is neither antithetical nor antagonistic to the American spirit. The guarantee of inalienable rights encompasses the idea of state obligation to ensure by positive entitlements a level playing field in the name of equality. I suggest turning our critical attention to issues of privilege and advantage, in addition to discrimination and oppression.

Of course, we must continue to consider how some individuals and groups are uniquely disadvantaged, rendered unequally and oppressively vulnerable, by the structures and ideological predispositions of our system. But we must also explore why and how some are and have been advantaged and privileged by that system.

The question then is not only who is harmed, but also who benefits by the organization of society and the structure of our institutions. We must explore the ways that state mechanisms enable and privilege some people and institutions and how that privilege may come at a cost to other people and institutions. Some are shielded by state action from the harshest implications of our shared vulnerability and the potentially resulting dependency that might arise as a result. While the privileged remain vulnerable since it is inevitable in the human condition, state provision of subsidy and support can cushion the concrete manifestations and implications of vulnerability.

When we only study the poor, the rich remain hidden and their advantages remain relatively unexamined in private spaces where there is no need to justify or explain why they deserve the privilege of state protection. Although it may be a difficult and complex undertaking, we need to excavate these privileged lives. There are certainly abundant records and instruments of privilege that can be relatively easily accessed. These archives are located in corporate boardrooms and in the rules setting up or limiting state and national regulatory regimes. They can be gleaned from tax and probate codes, history books, literature, political theories, and, of course, from the language and logic of the law.

A focus on privilege and its role in minimizing vulnerability might help to change the nature of the inquiry, away from assessing the individual characteristics of designated groups within society to see if they are the subjects of animus. The focus would not be on the identity of the disadvantaged in the sense that has been developed over the past few decades under a discrimination paradigm—gender, race, sexuality, etc.

Nor would the task be to explore the intent and purposeful nature of actions by individual employees, educators, landlords, and so on. Individual intention is not the issue, nor is discrimination. Ill will is unnecessary if everyone is operating with the same set of prejudicial assumptions and beliefs—sharing a culture that ignores the many ways in which it is organized to privilege some and not others. We are all products of our cultures, and the meta-narratives of those cultures, about what and who has value and what characteristics or actions gain entitlements, affect us all.

State structures must become the focus; the inquiry will be into how societal resources are channeled in ways that privilege and protect some while tolerating the disadvantage and vulnerability of others. It is the structures of society that need attention if we are to argue that the state has an obligation not to privilege any group of citizens over others—an affirmative obligation to structure the conditions for equality, not just prevent discrimination.

Interestingly, the same-sex marriage debates reveal the potential power of this approach. In some of those cases the plaintiffs focused on the privileges associated with marriage to develop inequality-based arguments that the state had an obligation to provide those privileges to all (Fineman 2008).

In 1999, the Supreme Court of Vermont looked into its own early American history and held that same-sex couples were entitled to receive the legal benefits and protections that were previously only afforded to married couples of opposite sexes (*Baker v. Vermont* 1999). The court focused on those benefits afforded to married couples, and there were lots of them. Marriage was the institution through which the state privileged and subsidized certain relationships. It is also the societal organization that assumes responsibility for the vulnerability of its members—the way we privatize dependency. The court's rationale in extending these benefits to same-sex couples derived, not from arguments of formal equality under the Equal Protection Clause of the US Constitution, but from a more expansive and earlier notion of equality derived from the experience of colonial America.

The Vermont Constitution's Common Benefits Clause predates the Fourteenth Amendment and is not based on a concept of discrimination. Nor does it focus only on protection for a specific category of persons. The Common Benefits Clause states:

> That government is, or ought to be, instituted for the common benefit, protection, and security of the people, nation, or community, and not for

the particular emolument or advantage of any single person, family, or set of persons, who are a part only of that community ...

(Vermont Constitution: ch. 1, art. 7)

The court distinguished federal jurisprudence from its interpretation of Vermont's Common Benefits Clause, which it characterized as a matter of concern with ends rather than merely means. It noted that federal courts had been "broadly deferential to the legislative prerogative to define and advance governmental ends, while vigorously ensuring that the means chosen bear a just and reasonable relation to the governmental objective" (*Baker* 1999: 871, emphasis omitted).

By contrast, underpinning the Common Benefits Clause was the notion that "the law uniformly afforded every Vermonter its benefit, protection, and security so that social and political preeminence would reflect differences of capacity, disposition, and virtue, rather than governmental favor and privilege" (*Baker* 1999: 876–77). The majority continued, noting that the clause prohibits "not the denial of rights to the oppressed, but rather the conferral of advantages or emoluments upon the privileged" (874). Further, the Common Benefits Clause, "at its core ... expressed a vision of government that afforded every Vermonter its benefit and protection and provided no Vermonter particular advantage" (875).

The majority was not limiting the potential classes whose interests may be protected under the Common Benefits Clause to those groups identified by the US Supreme Court. For, as the court noted, "the plaintiffs are afforded the common benefits and protections of Article 7, not because they are part of a 'suspect class,' but because they are part of the Vermont community" (*Baker* 1999: 878, note 10). This fact alone compelled the court to "police a political process whose product frequently discriminates between citizens in respect to benefits and privileges" (Friedman and Baron 2001: 152). This approach sounds like a fruitful inquiry if what we want is substantive equality, attention to the equality of outcome.

What does this mean to those of us who seek a more just and equal society? For me, gender increasingly has become the door through which I enter the discussion about equality, not the entire focus of my inquiry. Equality must escape the boundaries that have been imposed upon it by a jurisprudence of identity and discrimination and the politics surrounding it. The promise of equality cannot be conditioned upon belonging to any identity category, nor can it be confined to only certain spaces and institutions, be they in the public or the private sphere. Equality must be a universal resource, a radical guarantee that is a benefit for all.

We must not define our aspiration for equality in the shadow of autonomy in which the state is a "neutral" backdrop for a competition of presumed equals. We must begin to think first of the state's commitment to equality as one that must be rooted in an understanding of vulnerability and dependency, recognizing autonomy as a product of social policy not a naturally occurring characteristic of the human condition. Autonomy is only possible when one is positioned to share in society's benefits and burdens. Sharing in benefits and burdens can only occur when individuals have the basic resources that enable them in their particular circumstances to act in ways that are consistent with the tasks and expectations imposed upon them by their society.

The expectation that one should be able to achieve this form of autonomy— autonomy within an overarching and primary commitment to equality—should be every citizen's birthright. Autonomy in this sense concedes that all individuals share an inherent dependence on the society in which they live and that society has a responsibility to structure its institutions for the benefit of all. Recognizing this claim would fulfill our historic commitment to be a nation where the same rules apply to all, unaffected and uninfluenced by our station or status in life.

Notes

* This chapter was previously published in 43 *Western New England Law Review* 437 (2009).
1 The case involved legislation setting maximum hours for bakers.
2 *Muller* was abrogated by *Adkins v. Children's Hospital* (1923). In 1937, the Great Depression forced the court to overturn that decision; in *West Coast Hotel Co. v. Parrish* (1937), the court drew on *Muller* and overturned *Adkins* in upholding Washington's minimum wage law for women and minors. This decision paved the way for the Fair Labor Standards Act of 1938 which extended to men the wage and hours laws women had earlier won. The Act was upheld in *United States v. Darby* (1941).
3 I use this term to indicate a reciprocity or mutualism, although the term "containment" might also be appropriate. Containing family within its traditional form and function is certainly the goal of some political actors.

Engaging equality

Introduction to Section Two

This section continues the discussion of equality begun in the last section with chapters addressing the meaning of equality and the persistent dilemma for feminist legal theory presented by the recognition of differences. The chapters range from religion and gender equality, to arguments against biological and cultural determinism, to a consideration of the complexities of cultural difference.

Linda McClain considers why inequality persists, despite constitutional and human rights commitments to equality. In particular, she examines arguments against sex equality that appeal to biology, brain science, or culture. According to such arguments, differences between men and women are either biologically innate or so culturally ingrained as to be insurmountable. The chapter scrutinizes both nature and culture arguments, noting that while legal feminists are critiqued for their social engineering projects, many activists in the "marriage movement" attempt to solve "problems posed by nature" (men's inconsistent commitment to childrearing) through their own version of social engineering: the institution of marriage.

McClain argues that appeals to nature are often questionable and biased. Recent research by women achieve different findings than the traditional ones: perhaps fathers are not imperative in childrearing and non-marital social orderings based on kinship communities are biologically significant. Similarly, cultural arguments that sex equality disturbs sense of self and takes the "sexy" out of relationships are in tension with cultural findings that many women find sex equality creates better/happier relationships. The author encourages legal feminists to continue working toward equality, noting arguments proclaiming that sex equality has met its limits are refutable. She urges attention to the "politics of prehistory," or the ways in which assumptions about gender roles shape research into human evolution.

Mary Ann Case reflects on her personal journey to feminist legal theory and on the multiple generations of people who have tried to transcend the boundaries of law. Ideas of gender equity expressed in the Bible and certain Catholic teachings influenced Case's commitment to "sameness feminism," which she defines as resistance to "fixed notions concerning the roles and abilities of males and females." Splitting with her childhood Catholic faith led Case to study the lives of pre-1800 feminists, both women (often otherwise politically conservative) and radical men. She highlights two lessons gleaned from early feminists: (1) many generations of "feminists" have gone before in trying to "transcend the boundaries of the law" (this is both encouraging and discouraging); and (2) feminism and political conservatism need not necessarily be at odds (as they are now seen by both feminists and conservatives). In the political figure of Sarah Palin, a conservative who also considers herself a sameness feminist, Case finds reason to hope that feminism will tolerate greater diversity of opinion and that future generations will join its ranks.

Michèle Alexandre cautions feminists against creating their own difference-erasing biases in the search for gender equality. Her chapter addresses the frequent tension between multiculturalism and women's rights by presenting the "feminism-in-action" approach used by "grassroots" or "organic feminists." These women lack formal academic training in feminism but tackle culture-specific issues that restrict or oppress women in ways that are sensitive to their needs as women and as members of their cultures. Alexandre defines feminism-in-action as an (often successful) incrementalist approach to obtaining greater rights and freedoms for women that is rooted in the experiences and daily lives of women in diverse cultures, and she urges its use in the US abortion context. She believes it could be useful in overcoming the limits of formal/legal equality.

The chapter also attends to the problems of limited agency and "false consciousness." Although Western feminists can read the choices made by organic feminists as lacking in true agency, Alexandre encourages respect for the choices made by women in non-Western cultures. She emphasizes the importance of paying attention to the particularity and individuality of women's lives and the need for protecting women's actual choices.

Chapter 5

What's so hard about sex equality?

Nature, culture, and social engineering

Linda C. McClain

Introducing the problem

In the United States, evidence of the success of legal feminism's equality project is visible in the constitutional commitment to equal opportunity and prohibitions against legislating based on fixed notions about gender roles (Case 2009; *United States v. Virginia* 1996) and in the move toward greater sex equality in family law and other areas of private law (McClain 2006). However, sex inequality persists, and substantive equality remains elusive (Fineman 2001, 2009; McClain and Grossman 2009). Social cooperation between women and men in various domains of society is assumed to be a fundamental and necessary building block of society, but it proves hard to secure on terms of equality.

Why is sex equality so hard to achieve? One answer is that feminist quests for equality in private and public life are a form of misguided social engineering that ignores natural sex difference. I argue that equality within and among families should help guide family law and policy, supporting a more inclusive, egalitarian definition of marriage and more respect for family diversity (McClain 2006). Prominent figures in the marriage movement critique this argument for enlisting family law's channeling function for feminist equality goals but resisting marriage's channeling function of securing responsible paternal investment (Browning 2007).

This chapter examines arguments that nature and culture constrain feminist law reform. Appeals to *nature* argue that brain science and evolutionary psychology find salient differences between women and men, limiting what social engineering can achieve in fostering sex equality or reforming family law. Appeals to *culture* argue that constructions of masculinity and femininity are tenacious; challenging them threatens women's and men's sense of identity and causes resistance to equality. Contemporary society may espouse a commitment to a "gender neutral society," but men's and women's "unofficial desire" stands in the way (Mansfield 2006: 13). These contemporary claims may signal a new form of the sameness–difference debate. As such, they invite scrutiny by legal feminists.

Often at work in discussions about sex inequality is the notion of a proper equilibrium between the sexes that is upset when sex roles change or differences are minimized. However, even as critiques of feminist social engineering invoke nature and culture, problems posed by nature feature as a reason to embrace social engineering in the form of the social institution of marriage. This view of nature is distinct from the conservative religious argument that because marriage—"the natural family"—*reflects* the created order, feminist social engineering of the family is dangerous (McClain 2009).

Appeals to nature

Male and female brains and evolutionary psychology

The appeal to nature as a constraint on equality enlists brain science and evolutionary psychology, which reportedly find salient differences between women and men, linked to different reproductive biology and reproductive strategies. These differences limit what social engineering can achieve.

In the 1990s, a flurry of books, including Robert Wright's *The Moral Animal* (1995) and David Buss's *The Evolution of Desire* (1994), introduced basic concepts of evolutionary psychology and sociobiology, proposing that science shed light on sex difference, why men and women had different views about the harm of rape and sexual harassment, and why they made different choices about work–family balance (Wright 1994). Wright criticized feminist legal theorists for avoiding science. He argued that:

> [M]any of the differences between men and women are more stubborn than most feminists would like, and complicate the quest for—even the definition of—social equality between the sexes.
>
> (34)

In the early twenty-first century, brain science rivets popular attention. Once again, evolution presents limits to social engineering and affirms sex difference. Enthusing about neuropsychiatrist Louann Brizendine's work in popular science, *The Female Brain* (2006), journalist David Brooks opines, "Once radicals dreamed of new ways of living, but now happiness seems to consist of living in harmony with the patterns that nature and evolution laid down long, long ago" (2006: 14).

What are these differences and what patterns do they prescribe? Brizendine (2006: 1) declares, "more than 99 percent of male and female genetic coding is exactly the same," but the one percent difference "influences every single cell in our bodies." The inside flap of the book cover promises neurological explanations for such sex differences as:

- A woman uses about 20,000 words per day, while a man uses about 7,000.
- A woman knows what people are feeling, while a man can't spot an emotion unless somebody cries or threatens bodily harm.

- Thoughts about sex enter a woman's brain once every couple of days but enter a man's brain about once every minute.

Brizendine turns to evolutionary theory to explain the roots of brain differences. However she is not quietist about human nature. Biology need not be destiny *if* we understand how evolutionary, biological, and cultural forces shape us (2006). Social engineering *informed* by biology holds promise:

> Biology powerfully affects us but does not lock in our reality. We can alter that reality and use our intelligence and determination both to celebrate and, when necessary, to change the effects of sex hormones on brain structure, behavior, reality, creativity—and destiny.
>
> (Brizendine 2006: 6)

What does this interplay of biology and human will suggest about social cooperation on terms of equality? I focus on Brizendine's use of evolutionary theory to interpret brain difference and its implications for intimate and family life. I do not assess whether Brizendine gets the science of brain difference right, though some scientists argue she does not (Liberman 2006; Rivers and Barnett 2007). Scientists caution against letting "dubious science" give credibility to stereotypes and ignore "decades of legitimate findings" about male and female similarity (Rivers and Barnett 2007). "Inflated claims of gender differences," they warn, have costs to children, adults, and society, as they "reify stereotypes," limit opportunity, and ignore that "males and females are similar on most, but not all, psychological variables" (Hyde 2005: 581–89). These concerns echo questions about sameness, difference, and stereotypes long posed by feminist legal theory (*Mississippi University for Women v. Hogan* 1982; Littleton 1987).

"Stone Age" brains

Contemporary females, Brizendine (2006: 42) asserts, inherit the "ancient circuitry" of "our most successful foremothers." Teenage girls' drive for social connection with each other has biological and hormonal reasons. Intimacy "activates the pleasure centers in a girl's brain," triggering a near-orgasmic "major dopamine and oxytocin rush" (37). Girls are motivated "on a molecular and a neurological level" to "ease and even prevent social conflict" and to "maintaining the relationship at all costs" (40). These findings sound similar to those made by Carol Gilligan and her colleagues (1990) on how girls work to maintain connection.

Connection among females has evolutionary roots as a strategy of protection against aggressive males, evident in studies of female mammals that develop stress responses to "tend and befriend" and to form social groups "that promote safety and reduce distress for the self and offspring" (Brizendine 2006: 42). "These female networks" also share infant care, "information about where to find food," and model "maternal behavior for younger females" (42–43). Social connectedness, thus, contributes to reproductive success (43). Today's teen females, as they "reach" optimal fertility, undertake similar strategies (43).

Competition is as hardwired as cooperation. Brizendine (2006: 54) attributes the "biology of mean girls"—the harsh tactics of teen-girl cliques—to a "survival" strategy of "sexual competition" for the best male mates, a "biological imperative to compete for sexual attractiveness." Success, for both sexes, requires "some aggression," and relevant hormone levels rise during puberty (55).

Our "Stone Age brain" also shapes mate selection, sex, and motherhood (60). Brizendine repeats evolutionary psychology's familiar story of the male who chases and the female who chooses, claiming that it is "not sex stereotyping," but "the brain architecture of love, engineered by the reproductive winners in evolution" (59–60). Contemporary couples proceed "down an ancient pair-bonding path," over which they have "little control" (60).

Brizendine draws on David Buss's influential work (1994) on the different qualities women and men seek in mates. Women are "less concerned with a potential husband's visual appeal and more interested in his material resources and social status" and prefer a slightly older partner (Brizendine 2006: 61). "Scientists conclude" that these "universal" mate preferences are part of the "inherited architecture of the female brain's mate-choice system" and are "presumed to serve a purpose" (62).

What purpose? Brizendine turns to evolutionary biology scholar Robert Trivers, who explains female mate selection as a sound investment strategy stemming from their limited number of eggs and greater investment than men in bearing and raising children. A man "can impregnate a woman with one act of intercourse and walk away;" a woman is "left with nine months of pregnancy, the perils of childbirth, months of breast feeding," and "trying to ensure that child's survival" (Brizendine 2006: 62). Ancient necessities led females to seek long-term male partners to ensure reproductive success; those who "faced these challenges alone were less likely to have been successful in propagating their genes" (62). Brizendine is skeptical about whether contemporary "single motherhood … will succeed," noting that, even today, "in some primitive cultures," a father's presence enhances a child's survival rates, making a female's "safest bet" a long-term male partner to offer protection and improved access to "food, shelter and other resources" (62). In effect, women's need for protection and provision explains the so-called sex contract posited by evolutionary theorists.

Men's ancient brain circuitry, according to Buss, leads them to seek wives who are "physically attractive, between ages twenty and forty," and with "clear skin, bright eyes, full lips, shiny hair, and curvy, hourglass figures" (Brizendine 2008: 63). These traits are "strong visual markers of [female] fertility," which offers men "the biggest reproductive payoff for *their* investment" (63, emphasis in original). But "the most reproductively successful males also need to pick women who will mate only with them," ensuring their paternity (64).

Men's concern with paternity supposedly explains their concern with women's social reputation. Brizendine explains that if a woman had sex with a man on a first date or "showed off" about former bed partners, "his Stone Age brain might have judged that she would be unfaithful or had a bad reputation" (64). But male "seduction and abandonment" is an old problem (64–65). Thus, male and female reproductive strategies put them at odds. Evolution, in effect, explains the sexual double standard. High paternal investment requires men's certainty of paternity.

However, this model suggests that men have little to lose in random and casual sexual encounters. Why wouldn't they care about any potential offspring they father, if their strategy is to maximize their reproductive success? The premise implies that if men spread around enough genes, even if they do not personally invest in parental care for all offspring, some may survive due to the mother's efforts.

Male sexual jealousy, thus, has evolutionary roots and "adaptive functions"— preventing infidelity and ensuring paternity (Buss 1994: 125–29; Posner 1992: 97; Wright 2005: 66–72); it also has enormous costs, evident in domestic violence (Buss 1994). Drawing on evolutionary science, Judge Richard Posner (1992: 97, 112) argues the "biology of sex" explains men's mate-guarding behaviors such as "physical sequestration of wives, disparagement of female sexuality," and female genital mutilation. The sexes are in conflict rather than in cooperation; these male behaviors subvert female choice (Batten 1994).

Evolutionary psychology and marriage law and policy

Two ways evolutionary psychology and sociobiology feature in contemporary discussions of family law and policy are (1) arguments about why promoting "healthy marriage" and restoring a "marriage culture" are an appropriate task for government; and (2) arguments against redefining marriage to include same-sex marriage.[1] This embrace of social engineering is intriguing: because the social institution of marriage is necessary to address basic problems presented by nature, law and culture should reinforce it. Marriage is fundamental, yet fragile. Thus, marriage movement[2] authors criticize work like mine for ignoring sex difference and the purposes of marriage (Browning 2007).

These authors argue that marriage civilizes men by channeling them into socially productive roles as fathers and husbands (McClain 2006). Marriage addresses men's inclination toward procreating without taking responsibility for children and women's inclination toward procreating and rearing children, even in the absence of adequate resources and commitment by fathers (Browning et al. 2000; McClain 2006). Marriage is the social institution that *uniquely* addresses the regulation of heterosexuality and its procreative consequences, ensuring that children have a mother and a father to care for them (Blankenhorn 2007).

The marriage movement appeals to evolutionary psychology's account of men's and women's differential investment in offspring and conflicting reproductive strategies to explain society's vital interest in marriage. Marriage "closes this gap between a man's sexual and fathering capacities" (Coalition for Marriage, Families and Couples Education et al. 2000: 9). National Marriage Project Director David Popenoe (2001) testified in a congressional hearing on marriage promotion that the father–child bond is weaker than the mother–child bond and that men, naturally, tend to stray from mothers and children without the commitment of marriage.

A rationale that marriage movement authors offer for limiting marriage to one man and one woman is marriage's role in ensuring maternal *and* paternal investment in children. This argument stresses family law's channeling function (McClain 2007; Schneider 1992) and warns against altering marriage's social meaning. This argument has migrated into amici briefs and some judges' opinions in litigation over challenges by same-sex couples to state marriage laws.

One example is a dissent in *Goodridge v. Department of Public Health* (2003), where the Massachusetts Supreme Judicial Court opened the door to same-sex marriage. The *Goodridge* majority rejected the state's argument that because procreation was the central purpose of marriage excluding same-sex couples from marriage was rational. It identified "exclusive and permanent commitment," rather than procreation, as marriage's indispensable feature (*Goodridge* 2003: 961). The majority argued that the state had facilitated avenues other than marital sex for "bringing children into a family" (961–62). Dissenting, Justice Cordy contended that "the institution of marriage has systematically provided for the regulation of heterosexual behavior, brought order to the resulting procreation, and ensured a stable family structure in which children will be reared, educated, and socialized" (995). Although in contemporary society "heterosexual intercourse, procreation, and child care are not necessarily conjoined," an "orderly society requires some mechanism for coping with the fact that sexual intercourse commonly results in pregnancy and childbirth" (995).

The institution of marriage is, in effect, a form of social engineering that "fills a void" in nature: a process for "creating a relationship between the man and a woman as the parents of a particular child" (*Goodridge* 2003: 996). The marriage movement agrees that marriage resolves the "biologically based sexual asymmetry" between the sexes and "the problematic of fatherhood" by meeting the mother's and child's need for a mate and father and giving men a family role. It "helps create a greater equality between parents than nature alone can sustain" (Institute for American Values 2006: 15).

Regulating the consequences of heterosexuality also features in the majority and concurring opinions in *Hernandez v. Robles* (2006), where New York's high court upheld as constitutional excluding same-sex couples from marriage. The majority stated that the legislature could rationally conclude that same-sex couples do not need marriage as much as heterosexuals do because they are less sexually unruly, and their sexual unions do not *naturally* have procreative consequences. Moreover, the majority argued that since most children are born as a result of heterosexual relationships, which are "too often casual or temporary," the state could "choose to offer an inducement—marriage and its attendant benefits—to opposite couples making a long-term commitment to each other" (*Hernandez* 2006: 7).

By contrast, because same-sex couples must deliberately plan parenthood, they—and their children—do not need the added security and stability marriage affords because they are more likely to have family stability (*Hernandez* 2006: 7). This apparent reversal of past prejudices about homosexuals as promiscuous and irresponsible led law professor Kenji Yoshino (2006b: A19) to quip that gays and lesbians are "too good for marriage."

Marriage movement arguments about "conjugal" marriage's evolutionary significance and fragility also feature in *Lewis v. Harris* (2005), where the Appellate Division of New Jersey rejected the constitutional challenge brought by several same-sex couples.[3] Judge Parrillo, concurring, wrote that the purpose of marriage is "not to mandate procreation but to control or ameliorate its consequences" and that the "deep logic" of gender should remain as a "necessary component of marriage" (*Lewis* 2005: 276–78). Quoting marriage movement scholar Daniel Cere, Parrillo contended that *Goodridge's* characterization of the essence of marriage as a permanent and exclusive commitment misses that, historically, marriage has embraced:

> the fundamental facets of [traditional] conjugal life: the fact of sexual difference; the enormous tide of heterosexual desire in human life, the massive significance of male female bonding in human life; the procreativity of heterosexual bonding; the unique social ecology of heterosexual parenting which bonds children to their biological parents; and the rich genealogical nature of heterosexual family ties.
>
> (*Lewis* 2005: 276)

Marriage is "conjugal," not just a "close personal relationship" because of pair-bonding's evolutionary significance. Allowing same-sex couples to marry would strip marriage of this richer meaning so that it would become "non-recognizable and unable to perform its vital function" (276).

These arguments against same-sex marriage are not persuasive (McClain 2007). They rest on assumptions about sameness and difference—between men and women and between opposite-sex and same-sex couples. Allegedly, marriage ameliorates sex difference for the sake of children and has "nothing to do" with sexuality that does not have natural reproductive consequences. But courts ruling in favor of opening up civil marriage reach different conclusions about sameness and difference and eschew such a narrow focus on marriage's purposes. In *Hernandez* (2006: 32), Chief Justice Judith Kaye dissented that the state "plainly has a legitimate interest in the welfare of children" and appropriately links "tangible legal protections and economic benefits" to marriage. "The state's interest in a stable society is rationally advanced when families are established and remain intact irrespective of the gender of the spouses" (32).

Family law's channeling function is served by expanding the reach of marriage to same-sex parents.

These issues also feature in the newest wave of challenges to state marriage laws: whether the creation of a legal status alternative to marriage, such as civil unions, provides equality to same-sex couples. In *Kerrigan v. Commissioner of Public Health* (2008), the Supreme Court of Connecticut concluded that civil unions did not afford same-sex couples equal protection and that their exclusion from civil marriage lacked constitutional justification. The court determined that same-sex couples "share the same interest in a committed and loving relationship" and "in having a family and raising their children in a loving and supportive environment" as opposite-sex couples (*Kerrigan* 2008: 424). The legislature recognized these "overriding similarities" when it enacted the civil union law (424), and even though same-sex couples "cannot engage in procreative sexual conduct," the method of conceiving children is an insufficient difference to negate "fundamental and overriding similarities" (424, note 19).

Notably, the state did *not* appeal to procreation or optimal childrearing as rationales. However, the court noted that the procreation rationale raised by several amici did not satisfy an "exceedingly persuasive justification requirement": allowing same sex couples to marry "in no way undermines any interest that the state may have in regulating procreative conduct between opposite sex couples" (477, note 79). The court also argued that expanding marriage will not "diminish the validity or dignity of opposite-sex marriage," but instead reinforce "the importance of marriage to individuals and communities" (474). Citing to these amici's procreative purpose argument, dissenting Justice Zarella disagrees: "The ancient definition of marriage as the union of one man and one woman has its basis in biology, not bigotry" (*Kerrigan* 2008: 515–16).

This examination of case law and of marriage movement writings illustrates how biology, sex difference, and evolution are used to argue against expanding the definition of marriage. Because marriage is a form of social engineering that addresses problems posed by nature, it is a fundamental and fragile institution. I now turn to consideration of how some work in evolutionary science that more squarely asks "the woman question" (Bartlett 1990) may aid feminist legal theorists pondering how best to respond to these kinds of arguments. This scientific work may help with identifying different "facts" about human nature and human society.

Nature and the politics of prehistory

In this chapter, I can only sketch a few ways that feminist or female-centered work on evolutionary science may challenge the presentation of nature and evolution in popularizing accounts and in public policy arguments. Feminist legal theory should heed the politics of prehistory, or how certain gender biases or stereotypes may shape the study of human origins and impose a "paleolithic glass ceiling" (Zihlman 1997: 91). Too often, females feature only as passive participants in accounts of human origins rather than as "agents of evolutionary change" (Hager 1997: ix). As more female scientists study human origins, they have corrected this misconception and help in evaluating contemporary appeals to evolution both to oppose and to support social engineering.

For example, the marriage movement stresses the pair bond, noting female and infant dependency on male help, just as evolutionary science has asserted female dependency upon male provisioning (Hager 1997). However, the assumption of a prehistoric pair bond is "a projection back in time to a narrow Western view of marriage and mating, a formulation too rigid to account for the variation that exists cross-culturally" (Zihlman 1997: 99). The Man as Provisioner thesis assumed that to increase the human population by having a lesser interval between births, "females reduced their mobility, stayed near a home base, and became dependent upon males who provisioned their own mates and offspring," since they could be relatively certain about paternity (102). This model seems "preoccupied with questions/anxieties about male sexuality," at the expense of recognizing females' roles in human evolution (Falk 1997: 115). Female scientists have noted flaws in this model, in light of fossil evidence and studies of contemporary primate and human hunter-gatherer societies (Zihlman 1997). The pair bond may have less to do with male provisioning than with solving the problem of male mate competition, freeing a female to care for her offspring.

As primatologists put females more at the center of evolutionary study, the image of female primates has been "fleshed out to include much more than just their roles as mothers and sexual partners of males" (Fedigan 1997: 65). Scientists have studied "the significance of female bonding through matrilineal networks," "female sexual assertiveness, female long-term knowledge of the group's local environment, female social strategies, female cognitive skills, and female competition for reproductive success" (65). This "female-centered 'world view'" among primatologists makes sense: "many primate societies are female-bonded; thus kin-related females are the permanent core of the social group" (68). These facts were "not immediately recognized by primatologists," but are now "facilitating a strong focus on females as well as attracting more women to the discipline" (68).

Sarah Blaffer Hrdy's recent book, *Mothers and Others: The Evolutionary Origins of Mutual Understanding* (2009: 22) proposes that the human species is more adept at cooperation than other species because of the evolution of "cooperative breeding": the pattern of relying on "allomothers," or "alloparents," to help mothers care for their children. An "alloparent" is any non-parent who helps parents raise their young (22). While stories of human origins stress competition, Hrdy looks at cooperation.

The marriage movement ponders the male–female problematic; Hrdy (2009: 159) identifies her own "perplexing paradox":

> If men's investment in children is so important, why hasn't natural selection produced fathers as single-minded and devoted to children as

[in some species]? And given that male care is so idiosyncratically and contingently expressed, how could natural selection have favored human mothers who invariably produced offspring beyond their means to rear alone?

(162)

While the marriage movement stresses the problem of fatherlessness and looks to marriage as the solution, Hrdy looks at the way that human and nonhuman mothers enlist alloparents to assist in raising young. "These alloparental safety nets provided the conditions in which highly variable paternal commitment could evolve" (166). "Evolutionary interpretations of male behavior" have an "obsessive focus" on certainty of paternity as a prerequisite to paternal investment, but there is wide variation among men with "relatively high certainty of paternity" in terms of actually engaging in "direct care" of infants as well as instances where men who do not share a child's genes invest in childcare (167–68).

Evolutionary theory tends to project the nuclear family back in time. By contrast, Hrdy (2009: 166) describes "the typical or natural Pleistocene family" as "kin-based, child-centered, opportunistic, mobile, and very, very flexible." Like Brizendine, she would worry about single mothers but would look to the vital role of alloparents and social supports, instead of assuming male protection and provision as the best option. Indeed, "the preeminence of the man-the-hunter/sex-contract paradigm, with its accompanying stereotypes about nuclear families and maternal caregiving" have been "obstacles" to recognizing the evolution of cooperative breeding (239–40). Removing these obstacles came in part from the efforts of Hrdy and other sociobiologists ("many of us women") to "expand evolutionary theory to include selection pressures on both sexes," including postmenopausal females (258). The "grandmother hypothesis" is that "new opportunities to help kin generated selection pressures favoring longer lifespans among postmenopausal women" (255).

Assuming that hominids and early humans were patrilocal has hindered appreciation of the extent to which early residence patterns may have been matrilocal (241–43). As starting assumptions of "evolutionary-minded anthropologists" about residential patterns changed, it became possible to ask new questions about cooperative breeding and the role of alloparents (245). Studies indicate the preeminence of grandmothers among alloparents: "having a grandmother nearby has a significant impact on the childrearing success of younger kin" and may sometimes more greatly enhance child well-being than the presence of a father (253, 261). In patrilocal societies, a paternal grandmother's contribution may be more to her son's success, measured in shorter intervals between births; the presence of maternal grandmothers seems to correlate more with greater child well-being (261–64). Hrdy also refers to young human females' adeptness at communication and making friends, linking it not only to tending and befriending to obtain support, but also as a way to manufacture allomothers: "Whether consciously or not, women seek 'sisters' with whom to share care of our children" (271).

On the conflict between male and female reproductive interests, Hrdy (264–65) speaks of "patriarchal complications since the Pleistocene," suggesting earlier practices were less patriarchal. Concern with ensuring paternity and preserving the patriline leads to "practices detrimental to the well-being of mothers (and children too);" she mentions sequestering women and genital infibulations (265).

Hrdy's hypothesis about the evolution of cooperative breeding offers a corrective to evolutionary psychology's emphasis on competition and on male and female strategies. The focus on an agonistic struggle between the sexes that is bridged only through marriage detracts from a broader focus on the range of social networks and supports that contribute to successful childrearing and well-being. While the marriage movement stresses integrating sexual and parenting bonds, some feminist legal theorists (e.g. Fineman 1995, 2004) argue that focusing on the "sexual family" diverts attention from the family's important inter-generational caretaking function. It takes, Hrdy paraphrases, alloparents to raise a child. A prominent contemporary example is available: First Lady Michelle Obama's mother moved into the White House because of her crucial role caring for the Obama children (Swarns 2009). Hrdy's emphasis on the role of allo-parents could support arguments made in favor of greater family diversity—it is not the genetic tie so much as providing nurture to children that contributes to their well-being.

Culture: resisting equality

Culture is another reason often given for the difficulty of achieving sex equality. Women and men reportedly worry that sex equality pushes beyond cultural limits by requiring a kind of androgyny or sameness that denies their gendered identities. Feminist legal theorist Wendy Williams (1982) identified the problem of cultural limits decades ago, asking feminists to think "as deeply as they can about what we want the future of women and men to be"—"equality of the sexes" or "justice for two kinds of beings who are fundamentally different." In his recent book, *Manliness*, Harvey Mansfield (2006: 13) argues that there is a gap between the official commitment to a gender neutral society and men's and women's "unofficial desire." I focus briefly on two examples of cultural resistance to social cooperation on terms of sex equality: the possibility of egalitarian marriage and popular culture depictions of heterosexual romance.

Does marital happiness require inequality? Evolutionary accounts of mate selection stress men's and women's diverging criteria. More recent studies of marriage patterns suggest the growing practice of "assortative mating": rather than marrying up or down, well-educated and economically resourceful people choose to marry their peers (Paul 2006; Schwartz and Mare 2005). Meanwhile, lower-income men and women may cohabit rather than marry because they want a threshold level of economic resources before they marry (Cherlin 2009).

Egalitarian or "peer" marriage is a more just form of marriage, from a feminist or liberal perspective, than traditional marriage and more likely to be happy and stable (Schwartz 1994). Marriage equality is a factor contributing to marriage quality, particularly for women (McClain 2006). However, other scholars point out that marriages with a traditional gendered division of labor may also be quite stable so long as spouses' expectations do not change (Hetherington and Kelly 2002). Spouses may also accept an unequal division of labor even if they think it is unfair (Brinig and Nock 2002). Thus, considerable disagreement exists about whether social cooperation best takes place on terms of equality or inequality.

This debate over the desirability of egalitarian marriage surfaced recently when New York's governor Elliot Spitzer resigned after disclosure that he was a customer of a high-priced prostitution service. Spitzer apologized for his "failings" and spoke of the need to heal himself and his family as his wife, Silda Wall Spitzer, stood by his side. The image of Spitzer's wife by his side during this scandal was in stark contrast to a photo of the two of them that previously appeared on the cover of the magazine, *02138:* "Power Couples: See What Happens When Harvard Meets Harvard" (McCormack et al. 2007). Love between equals can work, and even be fun and sexy, the story and accompanying photos seemed to announce.

After the scandal, a model for happy marriage different from that of the power couple was offered by conservative self-help author, Dr. Laura Schlessinger. Stunning her host on the *Today* show, Schlessinger laid the problem of men's cheating at the door of any wife who failed to make her husband feel "like a man ... like a success ... like her hero," so that he was "very susceptible to the charm of some other woman." Schlessinger holds women "accountable" for not giving "perfectly good men" the love, kindness, respect, and attention they need, charging that "these days, women don't spend a lot of time thinking about how they can give their men what they need ... " (Armstrong 2008).[4] In Silda Wall Spitzer's case, this diagnosis seems particularly inapt, given that she put her own career aside to help her husband in his. But it does suggest cultural resistance to equality. Dr. Laura is a provocateur and her comments drew criticism; however, she is also a popular author. Her book, *The Proper Care and Feeding of Husbands* (2004: 3), indicts the women's movement as a "core destructive influence" and advises wives to treat their husbands with respect, reinforce them as head of the household, and celebrate difference. Admiration and deference will yield a wife more power and happiness than direct challenge. Mansfield (2006: 18) also speaks about admiration—"look[ing] up to someone in control"—as a proper response to manliness.

In this view, equality is a turn-off. Inequality is sexy. In the wake of recent infidelity scandals involving prominent politicians, some commentators look to evolutionary science's hypothesis that men's "philandering increases their reproductive success" (Porter 2009). The Spitzer scandal also played as a story of marital failure and a cautionary tale to wives about how to keep their marriages sexy and their men from straying. However, resistance of this diagnosis may be evident from many women finding "a catharsis" in First Lady Jenny Sanford's "hard hitting" public statements about Governor Mark Sanford's confessed infidelity—and her absence from his press conference (Kaufman 2009).

Another illustration of cultural limits concerning egalitarian marriage is the continuing issue of work–family conflict and the division of labor in the home. Laws and policies have moved us closer to a world where mothers and fathers have equal rights and responsibilities, as a legal matter, for their children and where, as a matter of social norms, women work outside the home and men play an active role in nurturing children. But the division of labor in families remains a flashpoint, as is evident from the news stories every several months about the so-called "opt-out revolution" where highly educated women are choosing to stay home rather than pursue professional success. All three generations of feminist legal theorists represented in this volume have devoted attention to these issues about care, work, and family; my focus is on what the debate suggests about cultural limits.

One cultural limit is that while workplaces have come a long way toward recognizing that workers may have caretaking responsibilities, cultural percep-tions of male workers still differ from those of female workers. Many men aspire to a more flexible balance between family life and work but may rationally perceive that they will pay a higher cost in terms of seeming committed to the job if they take advantage of employment policies designed to help parents (Jacobs and Gerson 2004).

Part of the unfinished business of feminism is that men's lives have changed to a lesser degree than women's. Some feminist theorists argue that instead of pushing the state for more public policy, wives and mothers should direct their energy toward persuading men to change (Hirschmann 2008). Legal feminist Mary Anne Case (2001) argues for directing effort toward a redistribution of responsibility from women to men rather than to employers or the state. Certainly, government is not the only relevant actor when it comes to advancing sex equality. Thus, political theorist Nancy Hirschmann (2008) raises a useful question: how can men be persuaded to change and how can women be per-suaded to insist on that change? This is a basic premise of "how to" books such as Joshua Coleman's *The Lazy Husband: How to Get Men to Do More Parenting and Housework* (2005). While Dr. Laura's book promises marital happiness by accepting role differentiation and resisting feminist ideology, Coleman's book promises to save marriages and increase marital happiness by *increasing* equality.

Mansfield proposes a different cultural limit: manliness. Manly men have a disdain for women's work, including housework. "Manliness prevents men from giving equal honor to women: this is the issue behind inequality in housework" (2006: 9, 13). If this is the case, then it suggests limits to feminist social engi-neering. On the other hand, alternative models of men's relationship to the home and to family life may suggest greater success of the feminist project. The marriage movement itself attributes women's discontent with the household division of labor as a reason why young women are less optimistic than young men about having a happy marriage and why women today are more willing to exit marriages (Popenoe and Whitehead 1999). While some marriage proponents argue that a "cultural script" of a gendered division of labor in the home is better than "endless negotiation" over roles, others support "equal rights and responsibilities" in and outside of the home (McClain 2006: 142–51).

Equality is important to marriage quality and to addressing work–life conflict. After the death of Betty Friedan, some commentators asked if feminism was a failure because women were choosing to stay home rather than juggle career and family. One response was that women were making a *choice*, and wasn't feminism, after all, about women being able to make choices? No, said feminist scholar Linda Hirshman (2005, 2006), arguing that women who were opting out were in fact making bad choices not to be celebrated as a feminist triumph. This debate about feminism's goals suggests one complication in theorizing and achieving equality. Friedan's emphasis on women getting out of the home and having careers, while paid household workers took up the slack, risked devaluing the importance of family and home life and suggested only one model of a good life to which women should aspire. However, when feminists assess the issue of choice, issues like how cultural expectations for boys and girls shape their life prospects, whether social institutions make it equally possible for women and men to pursue certain life plans, and whether problems of unequal bargaining power constrain the exercise of choice are appropriate concerns.

Popular culture offers examples of cultural resistance to sex equality even as it suggests progress toward equality. Popular books and films seem to ask, what if women don't want to have it all? What if an equilibrium between the sexes is disturbed by sex equality? What if women and men find sex inequality easier and sexier than equality?

Consider the contrast between the 2004 and 1975 films, *The Stepford Wives*, based on the best-selling novel by Ira Levin. The 1975 film, a cult classic, chronicled the marital tension arising from a suburban housewife's fledgling steps toward liberation in a photography career. Portrayed by Katherine Ross, she wonders why all the other wives in Stepford focus so blissfully and robotically on homemaking and pleasing their husbands sexually. She bonds with another wife who has dabbled with consciousness raising and "women's lib," but they cannot interest the other wives in questioning their lives. She discovers the formula for marital happiness after her friend is inexplicably transformed and just before she meets her own fate: the men's club to which the husbands belong kills the wives and replaces them with robots.

In the 2004 remake, the world is different. Women have formal equality of opportunity and are such superachievers that their husbands feel threatened. Replacing them with robots restores the gender equilibrium. The protagonist wife (Nicole Kidman) is a ruthless entertainment executive, whose proposed reality television show is a battle of the sexes show, with the premise that anything men can do, women can do better. She loses her job when a humiliated husband kills his wife and tries to assassinate her. She and her husband (Matthew Broderick) relocate to a new community where average-looking husbands have pleasant, compliant wives wearing floral dresses. Broderick is on the verge of replacing his wife with a robot because, as he puts it, she is superior to him in every way. By contrast to the original film, he cannot go through with it because, as Kidman tells him pleadingly, a robot can't say, "I love you," and mean it.

In merely three decades, the battle of the sexes has shifted from husbands made uneasy by women bristling at the constraints of the housewifely role to husbands who feel inadequate in the face of their wives' success. In each case, an equilibrium is upset by changes in gender relations. But a strange plot twist in the remake complicates the question of cultural resistance: the mastermind behind the robot scheme is a *wife* who killed her husband and replaced him with a robot when, hurt by his marital betrayal, she sought to return to a simpler, more beautiful time.

My second cultural example is Helen Fielding's wildly popular book, *Bridget Jones's Diary*, a forerunner of the "chick lit" genre. Fielding modeled her book on Jane Austen's *Pride and Prejudice*. Though separated by nearly two centuries, these books share a common theme: how does a young woman laboring under gender-based constraints negotiate the path to a happy marriage, or, at least to a successful heterosexual relationship?

Fielding's self-conscious appropriation of Austen and the frequent description of *Bridget Jones's Diary* as "post-feminist" invite feminist inquiry into how the cultural scripts of these books differ. One trajectory is from *Pride and Prejudice's* heroine, Elizabeth Bennett, an intelligent, astute critic of social conventions, to Bridget Jones, a zany diarist of and participant-observer in such conventions. A second is from the wealthy, enigmatic, and proud gentleman, Mr. Darcy to the wealthy, stiff, eminent human rights lawyer Mark Darcy.

As an Austen fan, I find the trajectory from Elizabeth to Bridget distressing. In interviews, Fielding has said that her novel is ironic. Bridget Jones is "really about trying too hard, trying to be too perfect"—to have it all; it's okay to be like Bridget, "normal" and "fun" (Penguin.com 2009). Perhaps. But another reading may be that sex equality is a bore, and sex inequality is more fun and sexier. Bridget seems too flawed to end up with the exemplary Mark Darcy. Awash in self-help books, cataloging daily her excessive intake of alcohol and cigarettes, Bridget makes foolish choice after foolish choice. She seems a much-diminished Elizabeth Bennett. In *Pride and Prejudice*, Mr. Darcy can't help his attraction to Elizabeth despite her class standing and embarrassing family; her criticism of him ultimately humbles him enough to reform his pride better to reveal his basic good character. By contrast, Bridget embarrasses herself and seems to be the only one in need of reform, even as her hapless quest for self-improvement amuses readers and film viewers.

The book inspired a popular film that further heightens the distance between Bridget and Mark by contrasting her ineptitude and inappropriateness with that of his law partner and apparent girlfriend, Natasha, his equal in education, professional achievement, and height. But Mark does not want his equal, who summons him by snapping her fingers. He wants antic, inept, and sexy Bridget, who wears a Playboy bunny costume to a costume party, accidentally shows her "bum" on television, and is a terrible public speaker. Why is Mark attracted? Bridget seems to be Mark's reward for his moral rectitude, a burst of color and chaos enlivening his steady path toward greater success. He loves Bridget, just as she is.

Trying to put a positive spin on Bridget, a feminist might argue that in *Pride and Prejudice* women and their families pay a high price in terms of social reputation and marriageability for choosing the wrong man. Lydia, Elizabeth's flirtatious younger sister, runs off with Wickham, a scoundrel to whom Elizabeth was initially attracted, and the Bennett family avoids ruin only when Mr. Darcy forces Wickham to marry Lydia. Bridget Jones, by contrast, fuses Elizabeth and Lydia: she gets to fall for and have sex with Mr. Wrong and still end up with Mr. Right. Even Bridget's mother is allowed—temporarily—to leave her husband for the wrong man and still end up all right. In both books, the hero rescues the heroine and her family, suggesting some men's superior competence and power in getting things done in the world.

Lighten up, some might say; can't feminists take a joke? Sure, but is there a take-home message about not looking for love on terms of equality?

Conclusion

Responding to assertions that "natural" differences or cultural imperatives limit the possibility of equality or necessitate particular institutional forms for the family requires that feminist theorists generate and contribute to well-informed visions of the interplay of nature and culture. We should ask what sorts of social cooperation are possible and valuable in the areas of sexuality, reproduction, and parenting. Appeals to "bridging the gender divide" in ordering human society invite feminist counter-narratives. As such narratives theorize on the proper role of social engineering and institutions, our feminist commitment to substantive equality should remain a guiding ideal.

Notes

1 Another example is the argument against moving "beyond marriage" to recognize alterative legal forms and de-emphasize the conjugal marriage model.
2 The Institute for American Values, founded by David Blankenhorn, is a central organization in the marriage movement.
3 The New Jersey Supreme Court overturned the appellate court (*Lewis v. Harris* 2006), and the legislature enacted a civil union law in response to that ruling.
4 Readers may view the show at www.msnbc.msn.com/id./235752221/.

Chapter 6

No male or female

Mary Anne Case

I take the invitation to contribute to this volume to speak very personally about how I came to feminist legal theory and what I made of it. I take my title from the New Testament, Galatians 3:28, because I came to my own radical take on sameness feminism through youthful engagement with the Catholic Church's radical past and repressive future on matters of sex equality and through engagement in college and graduate school with arguments for the equality of the sexes made from the Middle Ages through the French Revolution by otherwise conservative women defending their own right to participate in male-dominated enterprises and otherwise radical men willing to challenge all received ideas, even those concerning women's place. I brought this engagement with long history to the legal academy with me.

My chapter provides a reminder that far more than three generations have sought to transcend the boundaries of law through feminist theory; feminists, male and female, have been making their case for centuries. It is also an elegy for potential alliances lost; though many of the women who in prior centuries sought to bring their sex beyond the boundaries of the law were self-described conservatives on other matters, in my lifetime feminism and conservatism have come to be seen as antithetical, something I dealt with on a daily basis as a faculty member in two of the nation's most conservative law schools, Virginia and Chicago. Also in my lifetime, the Church that brought me to sameness feminism at first repudiated sex equality and then turned to an embrace of difference, when official guardian of doctrinal purity Joseph Ratzinger, now Pope Benedict XVI, in official pronouncements explicitly rejecting the sort of sex and gender theory to which I am committed, came close to suggesting that even souls have a sex (Ratzinger and Amato 2004).

Because the 25th Anniversary Conference at which I presented an initial version of this chapter took place close to Halloween, the prelude to the feast of All Saints, I appeared at it in something of a costume, wearing the by now somewhat moth-eaten cadet blue pantsuit I wore when I first spoke at Martha Fineman's Feminism and Legal Theory Workshop in June 1994 as a commentator on Katherine Franke's draft on the Meaning of Sex. At that time, Katherine and I and others, such as Frank Valdes, were wrestling with questions of what I have called gender discrimination, as compared and contrasted with sex discrimination. Gender discrimination, as I define it, is discrimination in favor of or against qualities coded masculine or feminine, sometimes irrespective of and at times inflected by whether the person exhibiting those qualities is male or female. Katherine and I had different analytic approaches to this topic[1] but shared normative goals, including interrogation of and resistance to what Katherine described in her draft as the "sartorial bureaucracies [which] have been [among] the institutional venues in which the struggle for sexual identity has been fought as a factual rather than a legal matter" (Franke 1994b: 13). Central to my own analysis of gender discrimination is that in the US today, sartorial and other norms are tilted sharply towards the masculine: "Women today are found in the work force, in pants, and in the outfield far more often and with far less comment than men are found in the nursery, in dresses, or in ballet class" (Case 1995a: 23, note 64). In the cocktail hour after our presentations, I made this point to Katherine by claiming that the pantsuit I was wearing was very close to what a man might wear. Katherine, who is the sort of butch who knows her way around a menswear department, correctly observed that no man would be caught dead in pants like mine, with a zipper on the side, a high waist, and flared legs. Her deconstruction of my attire did not stop there; she went on to say that, because I was wearing a high white mock turtleneck underneath a black sweater, I looked like a cleric. What's up with that, she asked? The rest of this chapter is an answer to her question.

I grew up Catholic in the immediate aftermath of Vatican II, and that, I think, says more about the kind of feminist I am than anything else. In many respects, my vision of sex equality resembles that set forth in the Equal Protection jurisprudence developed by the US Supreme Court in the last third of the twentieth century. Like the Court, I have set my face against "fixed notions concerning the roles and abilities of males and females" (*Mississippi University for Women v. Hogan* 1982: 725). Critics have suggested that this makes me no more than a product of the legal culture in which I grew up. These critics may not realize that I am just old enough to have developed an opposition to sex stereotypes before the Supreme Court did. The cultural roots of my views are in my Catholic, at least as much as in my American, upbringing.

The nuns who taught me through my 13 years of Catholic school were women who in the fancy terminology of today had rejected repronormativity. Many of them were old enough to have come to the Church, not because of a particular vocation to the religious life, but because they felt called to do something other than be wives and mothers, and the Church gave them an opportunity to be scholars and teachers. Even the priests and monks I encountered were a model for men conversing seriously with women about something other than their families and their sex life. This commingling of the sexes for purposes other than sexual or familial, and the opportunity for a woman's role beyond that of wife and mother has been part of the Church from its beginnings.

The Gospel of Luke tells the story of sisters Mary and Martha welcoming Jesus into their home. Martha, resentful that Mary was sitting at Jesus' feet listening to him preach while she was busy serving:

> stood and said: Lord, hast thou no care that my sister hath left me alone to serve? Speak to her therefore, that she help me. And the Lord answering, said to her: Martha, Martha, thou art careful, and art troubled about many things: But one thing is necessary. Mary hath chosen the best part, which shall not be taken away from her.
>
> (Luke 10:40–42, Douay-Rheims trans.)

Generations of girls like me with ambitions beyond housework took this passage to heart: their Savior had given them a choice. Among those who chose this better part were fourth-century aristocratic Roman women such as Jerome's associates Paula, Eustochium, and Melania the Elder, who "took the initiative in rejecting marriage and motherhood, fleeing the confines of the old family system and pursuing a life that offered them more autonomy and self-expression than their ancestresses had ever known" (McNamara 1984: 14). Although several did marry and bear heirs early in life, they later could "embark on a life of study, travel, charity, religious devotion and community administration that was closely akin to that enjoyed by male ascetics" (McNamara 1984: 20). Collaboration between the sexes on terms of spiritual equality not bound by fixed sex roles continued in the twelfth century Benedictine double monasteries where "[f]or the first time in history, significant numbers of women and men together studied and discussed philosophy" (Allen 1997: 408).

Among the saints I grew up with were a number of medieval women who themselves firmly rejected "fixed notions concerning the roles and abilities of males and females," including Joan of Arc who successfully led an army and, in the end, was executed for wearing male attire, and Catherine of Alexandria who according to legend was executed after besting in argument all the great scholars the Emperor had sent to persuade her out of her Christian faith. Not all of these sex-role-transgressive female saints came to a bad end, however. My personal favorite at the time, Catherine of Siena, died a natural death, honored and respected by the popes and princes with whom she corresponded. When at the age of eight, like other young Catholics, I was asked to choose for myself a confirmation name and with it a patron saint, I chose the name Catherine. I could easily have done it for Catherine of Alexandria—after all, disputing with men who might want to kill me when they lose the argument has been a favorite activity of mine from early youth. In fact, I did it for Catherine of Siena. Not for her so-called holy anorexia or other ascetic practices (Bell 1985), about which I did not know at the time and which I would have found problematic, but because she told off the Pope. She wrote the Pope a letter saying, "Here's what you do," and he did it (Catherine of Siena 1993: 37). That has always seemed to me an appropriate thing for a woman to do.

In 1970, Catherine of Siena and Teresa of Avila became the first women to be declared Doctors of the Church, authoritative teachers of Catholic doctrine. To understand the significance this had for me as a budding feminist, consider the Litany of the Saints, an extended chant of petition in which the congregation asks a long list of named saints in turn to "pray for us." These saints are grouped into categories, such as "All ye Holy Angels and Archangels" and "All ye holy Apostles and Evangelists." Before 1970, the only category in which female saints appeared by name was "All ye holy Virgins and Widows." Now, for the first time, women were included in another category, "All ye holy Doctors." Although I rarely these days have occasion to hear a litany,[2] I still invariably tear up every time I hear, "St. Ambrose, St. Augustine, St. Jerome" followed by "St. Catherine of Siena, St. Teresa, All ye holy Doctors of the Church." Yet even before the inclusion of women on non-gendered terms in a prestigious category of saints, the litany had lessons for a budding sameness feminist.[3] The default category for women was not "all ye holy Wives and Mothers," but "all ye holy Virgins and Widows," women apart from motherhood, liberated from the confines of the female role by their liberation from men.

In addition to the story of Martha and Mary, another biblical proof text for Christianity's commitment to the equality of the sexes and to the repudiation of enforced sex differences is Paul's Epistle to the Galatians 3:28: "There is no Jew or Greek, no slave or free, no male or female, for you are all one in Christ Jesus" (Douay-Rheims trans.). I have previously suggested a potential relationship between this embodiment of a Christian concept of equality and American constitutionalism, noting that, while a group or difference based vision of equality is certainly imaginable, the US legal system has moved beyond a jurisprudence of status or group rights or of equality in separate spheres to one of abstract universalism and individualism in ways important to our current constitutionalizing of women's equality and consistent with this Pauline text (Case 2002: 774). Whatever its impact on US constitutionalism, the text from Galatians certainly influenced my own development as a feminist.

My first scholarly paper as a teenager was on the question of the admission of women to the ministerial priesthood of the Catholic Church. At the time, in the early 1970s, there was a lot of talk about women's ordination and no really extensive and authoritative explanation of Catholic doctrine against it. So I did everything from having a friend whose name—Frances—could be made to look like a boy's name with the switch of a single letter from "e" to "i" write letters with alternate spellings to see which seminaries wrote her back when she said, "I'm thinking of becoming a priest" to researching the early Church and its presentation of women in leadership roles in then recently published books like Joan Morris's *The Lady Was a Bishop* (1973).

But I wept a different sort of tears than those prompted in me by the Litany's inclusion of female doctors when, late in my Catholic high school days, we visited a grade school catechism class in which children preparing a skit were casting the role of Jesus. When a little girl volunteered for the role, the catechism teacher said to her, "No, no, you can't be Jesus. You'll have to be somebody's wife or mother." Unfortunately, very shortly thereafter, this became the official position of the Catholic Church. In 1976, just when the US Supreme Court had started declaring that there should be no "fixed notions concerning the roles and abilities of males and females" embodied in law,[4] the Catholic Church did an about face and reinforced fixed notions concerning the roles and abilities of males and females. The 1965 Vatican II encyclical *Gaudium et Spes* (1965: Sec. 29) had urged, in a rather feminist way, universal acceptance of "the fundamental personal rights" of a woman "to choose a husband freely, to embrace a state of life or to acquire an education or cultural benefits equal to those recognized for men." Although it did insist that "children, especially the younger among them, need the care of their mother at home," it also stressed the need for "joint deliberation of spouses" and "active presence of fathers" before concluding, "This domestic role of [the mother] must be safely preserved, though the legitimate social progress of women should not be under-rated on that account" (Sec. 52). According to *Gaudium et Spes*, the "legitimate social progress of women" included their full and active participation in the public sphere:

> Women now work in almost all spheres. It is fitting that they are able to assume their proper role in accordance with their own nature. It will belong to all to acknowledge and favor the proper and necessary participation of women in the cultural life.
>
> (Sec. 60)

Although Vatican II argued for women's equality in the secular public sphere, a decade later, in 1976, Pope Paul VI, prompted by the ecumenical questions raised by the Episcopal Church's official acceptance of ordination without regard to sex, firmly rejected the possibility of women's equality in the hierarchy of the Church by promulgating a Declaration on the Admission of Women to the Ministerial Priesthood, for the first time in Church history marshalling extensive authoritative arguments against the possibility of women's ordination to the priesthood. The Declaration, entitled *Inter Insigniores*, went far beyond merely dashing the hopes of Catholic feminists for what they termed Equal Rites. It could be seen as denying women any place in the scheme of salvation. Although it acknowledged the authority of Galatians 3:28 as to the "equality of rights of the human person" and for the proposition "that there are no more distinctions between ... male and female," it insisted "this passage does not concern ministries" (*Inter Insigniores* 1976: Sec. 6). Instead, because the sacra-mental function of a priest was "taking the role of Christ, to the point of being his very image" and Christ was a male, it was essential that the priest, too, be male (Sec. 5). Women simply could not embody "this 'natural resemblance' which must exist between Christ and his minister ... in such a case it would be difficult to see in the minister the image of Christ" (Sec. 5). *Inter Insigniores* did have many nice things to say about women and about the opportunities Christ had opened to them, but, it insisted that, in the end, facts were facts: The "fact ... that the Incarnation of the Word took place according to the male sex ... while not implying an alleged natural superiority of man over woman, cannot be disassociated from the economy of salvation" (Sec. 5).

The difficulty with this line of argument, as Catholic supporters of women's ordination promptly pointed out, is that the "economy of salvation" also depended on Christ's being able to represent those he died to redeem: if women could not represent Christ, how could Christ represent women? And if he could not, how, then could women be said to have a place in the economy of salvation? How could they be redeemed? The St. Joan's International Alliance, a UN observer group of Catholic feminists, marked this occasion by adding to their selection of slogans for buttons the telling demand: "Ordain women or stop baptizing them."

Inter Insigniores ended whatever hope there might have been of my remaining a Catholic, but it strengthened my commitment to feminism and my interest in its history. As a Yale College student, I began looking at arguments for the equality of the sexes in Western Europe from the Middle Ages to the French Revolution, arguments that often relied on scriptural passages and saints' lives like those cited above because they were made in an environment where arguments from Christian theology were the best of all possible arguments. I learned that concern that Christ as a male might not have redeemed women and for this purpose a female Messiah might be required had arisen from time to time since the Middle Ages. Some even thought they had identified this female Messiah: the twelfth-century Guglielmites saw Guglielma of Milan as "a female incarnation of the Holy Spirit" sent to "establish a new church ruled by a female pope and female cardinals" which was the precondition for worldwide salvation (Wessley 1978: 289), and in the sixteenth century Guillaume Postel (1553) identified a Venetian woman named Jeanne as the new redeemer. I also learned that when Paul VI explained why *Inter Insigniores* was the Church's first comprehensive justification of women's exclusion from the priesthood by saying the "Magisterium has not felt the need to intervene in order to formulate a principle which was not attacked, or to defend a law which was not challenged" (*Inter Insigniores* 1976: Sec. 1), he was glossing over challenges such as those by Michel de Montaigne's covenant daughter and literary executor Marie le Jars de Gournay, who in the early seventeenth century marshaled arguments from world history, the Fathers of the Church, and Church practice in favor of women's ordination (Gournay [1641] 2002: 91).

As for broader arguments for the equality of the sexes before 1800, the people who made these arguments in the course of a centuries-long debate, often called the "*querelle des femmes*," fell largely into two groups: there were women, including Christine de Pizan around 1400, Marie Le Jars de Gournay around 1600, and Olympe de Gouges around 1800, who were by the standards of their own time by and large conservative—whether it was about issues of war and peace, monarchical politics, or the state of the French language—who wanted first of all to make their conservative voice heard in the general discourse, and then discovered that because they were women, no one was going to listen to them (Case 1993). They could be dismissed with "merely a smile or some slight shaking of [the] head [that says with] mute eloquence ... 'It's a woman speaking'" (Gournay [1641] 2002: 101). Thus, before they could make whatever point they wanted to make about whatever non-sex-specific topic they were interested in, they first had to defend the ability and the right of women to make such points, in order to be heard. They became radicalized by the fact of being women, and then started thinking more broadly in radical terms. So Christine de Pizan ([1405] 1999: 1.27.1) begins by saying, "If it were customary to send little girls to school like boys, and if they were then taught the sciences, they would learn as thoroughly and understand the subtleties of all the arts and sciences" and ends by concluding that similarly peasants, if they, too, were given the opportunity, could learn as well as the bourgeois. Similarly, Marie de Gournay ([1641] 2002: 81) concludes that the differences between men and women are no greater than those among men "according to the training they receive, according to whether they are brought up in a city or a village, or according to nationality."

The men, on the other hand, tended to be relatively radical at the outset, and then to take women's issues as an example for their radicalism. They had generally revolutionary ideas, challenging received ideas, and the most firmly entrenched received idea they could think of was the inequality of the sexes. If they could overturn this prejudice, well then everything else was up for grabs, too, because the prejudice in favor of the inequality of the sexes was the most firmly fixed and difficult to combat (Poullain de la Barre [1673] 2002: 50). While the women were clearly in earnest, for many of the men arguments in favor of sex equality seemed to have been somewhat of a game or a joke, a way of showing off their rhetorical skills by arguing a particularly difficult case (Case 1993).

After writing a senior essay on Marie de Gournay, I continued my study of the early history of feminism at the University of Munich and at Harvard Law School. I brought an engagement with long history to the legal academy with me, with a job talk on political rights for women in the French Revolution, a first published paper comparing medieval feminists with those who added sex to Title VII (Case 1993), and a tenure piece looking to the early modern period for gender-bending terminology (Case 1995a: 24–36).

Critics accused me of writing about the medieval feminists because I was interested in them and bringing in contemporary comparisons only to get tenure. I take very seriously, however, the comparison I drew between the Continental European men and women who wrote in favor of sex equality before 1800 and the Congressmen and women responsible for adding prohibitions on sex discrimination to Title VII of the 1964 Civil Rights Act (Case 1993: 124). The conventional wisdom is that the word "sex" was introduced into

Title VII as something of a joke, by the racist Chair of House Rules Committee, Virginian Howard Smith, who hoped to defeat the Civil Rights Act in its entirety. Although Smith was unquestionably a racist and would have been delighted to see Title VII as a whole fail, he was also something of a feminist, who had been a sponsor of the Equal Rights Amendment since 1946 and was known as the "Rock of Gibraltar" to the National Women's Party (Freeman 1991), a group of sameness feminists who had historically disfavored protective labor legislation for women and were seen aligned with upper middle-class business interests. The typical NWP member, like the typical female advocate for sex equality in the period before the French Revolution, was a woman quite radical on women's issues but moderate to conservative on virtually all others; one whose chief complaint with the system was simply that it excluded her and differentiated on grounds of sex.

Smith's racism interacted in important ways with his support for women's rights (Case 2002: 767). He understood quite well that, as Congresswoman Martha Griffiths put it in floor debate, "a vote against this amendment today by a white man is a vote against his wife, or his widow, or his daughter, or his sister" (110 Cong. Rec. 2580). That is to say, Smith and other legislators who supported the addition of "sex" understood what the legal academy has subsequently come to call intersectionality. For Smith, the quintessential intersectional category was not poor black lesbian but white Anglo-Saxon Christian male. As he and other conservative white Southerners saw it, unless Congress included prohibitions on sex discrimination with those on grounds of race, color, religion, and national origin, "the white woman of mostly Anglo-Saxon or Christian heritage [would be deprived of] equal opportunity before the employer" (110 Cong. Rec. 2583) compared, not only with Anglo-Saxon Christian men but also with men and women of every other race, ethnicity, and religion. Smith may have been a racist, but he did not want "his" women to take second place to men and women of other races.

Although on the House floor Smith insisted nearly half a dozen times that he was "serious" in proposing a ban on sex discrimination in employment, the joking way in which Smith introduced the word "sex" is generally seen to call his motives into question. There is, however, no basis for questioning the motives of the Congresswomen who immediately backed Smith up, the majority of whom were, like so many of the women participants in the *querelle des femmes*, moderate to conservative on issues apart from women's rights. Before she died, I had the opportunity to interview one of these women, moderate Republican Congresswoman Catherine May. "Of course we were serious," she told me. "We had been planning this all the time, and we were willing to let Smith get the credit so long as we got what we wanted."

Notably, the only woman in the House who spoke against the addition of "sex" was also the one farthest to the left on the political spectrum—New York Democrat Edith Green. Although instrumental in the passage of the Equal Pay Act a few years earlier, Green took the position that discrimination against women could not be compared with discrimination against blacks and should not be allowed to "clutter up" (110 Cong. Rec. 2581) a bill designed to remedy race discrimination. But other women in the House applied the lessons of intersectionality to point out that, without the inclusion of "sex" as a forbidden ground, Negro women as well as white women would be excluded from jobs and from protection against discrimination.

Among those who stressed intersectionality most eloquently was Martha Griffiths, the Michigan Democrat whose activism on behalf of women's rights included the successful filing of a discharge petition to get the Equal Rights Amendment onto the floor of the House, out of the Judiciary Committee where its fierce opponent Emmanuel Celler, an otherwise progressive New York Democrat who also objected to the addition of "sex" to Title VII, had kept it bottled up for years. Griffiths was not above playing to the prejudices of House Southerners by insisting that "a vote against this [sex] amendment today by a white man is a vote against his wife, or his widow, or his daughter, or his sister," (110 Cong. Rec. 2580) because, in the absence of a prohibition on sex discrimination, "white women will be last at the hiring gate" (2778) "at the bottom of the list ... with no rights at all" (2279). But she also stressed that Negro women needed a prohibition on sex discrimination were they to have any hope of equal employment opportunity, illustrating her point with examples from every class of employment, from a Negro female dishwasher seeking to move from "a greasy spoon" to a "very good restaurant which employed only ... white men" to a "a colored woman political scientist" seeking a job at a university where there "has never been a woman political scientist employed" (2579). Her final example illustrated, not only intersectionality, but the gendering of jobs:

> Supposing a little 100-pound colored woman arrives at the management's door and asks for the job of driving a haulaway truck, and he says, "Well, you are not qualified," and she says, "Oh, yes, I am. During the war I was the motorman on a streetcar in Detroit. For the last 15 years I have driven the schoolbus." Surely, Mr. Chairman, we are hiring the best drivers to drive the most precious cargo. Of course, that woman is qualified. But he has only white men drivers. Do you not know that that woman is not going to have a right under this law?
>
> (2579)

Among those who supplemented Griffiths's work on the floor of the House was Pauli Murray, who wrote a memo distributed to President Johnson and key Senators speaking from her own experience as a victim of both race and sex discrimination (Freeman 1991; Murray 1987: 356). Murray, the author, with Mary Eastwood, of "Jane Crow and the Law," and an active member of both the National Association for the Advancement of Colored People (NAACP) and the National Organization for Women (NOW), was ordained an Episcopal priest late in life and eulogized NWP founder Alice Paul in a sermon on Luke 10:42 entitled "Mary Has Chosen the Best Part" (Murray 2006:76–80).

On the House floor, Griffiths stressed the long history of cooperation between blacks and whites, men and women, in support of women's rights, noting that:

> the 19th amendment gave women the right to vote. But white women alone did not secure that right. White men voted for that right; but white people alone did not secure that right. Colored men voted for that right, and colored women were among the suffragettes. Sojourner Truth, a Detroit woman, was the greatest of all of these.
>
> (110 Cong. Rec. 2580)

This brings me to the lessons that I draw from my own past and from my study of early feminists. The first is that many more than three generations have sought to transcend the boundaries of the law through feminist theory. This is both good news and bad news. Christine de Pizan around 1400, Cornelius Agrippa of Nettesheim around 1500, Marie de Gournay around 1600, Francois Poulain de la Barre just before 1700, Olympe de Gouges just before 1800, all thought what they were arguing for was so obvious and so right that all that had to be done was to put the arguments out there and people would be persuaded and things would get better. Obviously, that didn't happen. Worse yet, one generation's arguments tended to be lost to succeeding generations, leaving them to reinvent the wheel, rather than building on the foundation of those who preceded them. But the good news here is that feminism is not a new thing under the sun, a historical oddity or a passing fad. It has a long past, and we stand with many, many generations, not only of women, but also of men.

Second, I want to highlight my disappointment at seeing how in my lifetime, feminism and conservatism have come to be seen as antithetical by both feminists and conservatives in the United States. A few examples from my personal experience may illustrate the point. When I was a student at Harvard Law School, I attended the National Conference on Women and the Law and was treated to presentations on such issues as nuclear power—not feminist approaches to nuclear power, not the effect of nuclear power on women's health, not the equivalent for nuclear reactors of the Greenham Common women's approach to nuclear weapons, but just the sort of generic opposition to building or continuing to operate more nuclear reactors common in those years following the incident at Three Mile Island. The message I took away was that Women and the Law was a left-progressive event and was therefore going to talk about everything of interest to left-progressives without even bothering to tie it into sex or gender.

I encountered the opposite problem when I began teaching at the University of Virginia Law School, which, when I taught there in the 1990s, had a more diverse array of conservative scholars than perhaps any other US law school. A mark of how established feminist legal theory had become in the legal academy was that the Virginia faculty hired me specifically because they felt the need to add a feminist theorist to the mix. Thus, I went to the University of Virginia as something of a missionary for feminism, not, at first, taking sufficient account of how often missionaries end up as martyrs, a status to which I never aspired, even in my Catholic youth. Before they knew much more about me than my commitment to feminism, some of my Virginia colleagues reflexively assumed that I must of course be on the far left-progressive side of all other issues. When she heard, for example, that I was scheduled to teach Property, my conservative colleague Lillian BeVier's reflexive response was, "I don't see why you're going to teach Property, Mary Anne, when you don't believe in it." In fact, I am not now nor have I ever been a Marxist. I even, as a Harvard Law Student, shocked those running the landlord–tenant clinic by saying that I wanted to work on the problems of small landlords.

While at Virginia, I was invited to speak at the Federalist Society conference on feminism. This was the occasion for my meeting Martha Fineman, my fellow panelist, and the first of many occasions in which Martha and I modeled disagreement among feminists: using arguments developed in her book on divorce reform, *The Illusion of Equality* (1991a), she was the only participant in the conference to challenge my call for the equality of the sexes as an unproblematically shared normative goal. Like all the panels at the conference, the one to which Martha and I were assigned was structured in a way I repudiated, as a debate between the feminists and the federalists, as if the two points of view were antithetical. As the long history of the *querelle* and the more recent history of the National Women's Party and the moderate to conservative congressional representatives' role in adding "sex" to Title VII should indicate, the mutually exclusive nature of feminism and conservatism may today be a political reality, but it is not an inevitable truth. Because I was at the University of Virginia, I was also invited in March 1996 to speak at a conference on the Legal Rights Affecting Women sponsored by the Rutherford Institute, a conservative group principally dedicated to defending religious liberty which would a year later gain notoriety for helping to represent Paula Jones against Bill Clinton. In speaking to this devoutly Christian audience, I sought to make use of my Catholic religious training to reach them on behalf of feminism by pointing out, for example, ways in which Jesus could be seen as a gender bender, embodying traditionally feminine traits such as gentleness. But, as at the Federalist Society conference a few years earlier, although there were receptive people in the audience who apologized to me for what was going on at the podium, the conference itself was structured as a fight to the finish with feminism rather than a search for common ground.

Over the course of the last decade, therefore, I had gradually been resigning myself to the fact that the idea of a feminist conservative was off the table—until, of course, 2008, when Katie Couric asked staunchly conservative

Republican vice-presidential candidate Sarah Palin the following questions, and Palin responded with the most coherent answers she gave to any questions asked of her in the course of the 2008 Presidential campaign:

COURIC: Do you consider yourself a feminist?

PALIN: I do. I'm a feminist who believes in equal rights and I believe that women certainly today have every opportunity that a man has to succeed and to try to do it all anyway. And I'm very, very thankful that I've been brought up in a family where gender hasn't been an issue. You know, I've been expected to do everything growing up that the boys were doing. We were out chopping wood and you're out hunting and fishing and filling our freezer with good wild Alaskan game to feed our family. So it kinda started with that. With just that expectation that the boys and the girls in my community were expected to do the same and accomplish the same. That's just been instilled in me.

COURIC: What is your definition of a feminist?

PALIN: Someone who believes in equal rights. Someone who would not stand for oppression against women.

(Couric 2008)

Although Palin's description of her beliefs sounds in sameness feminism, her definition is an inclusive one. It is the standard dictionary definition and one I have always personally endorsed. As I explained to the Federalist Society, attempting to persuade them that it was possible to be both a feminist and a federalist, "Dictionary definitions generally talk about a commitment to the equality of the sexes, a commitment to women's rights and the removal of restrictions that discriminate against them. I hope that there are few who, using this terminology, would not be feminists" (Case 1995b: 370).

Unfortunately, when Brian Williams asked Palin the same question ("Governor, are you a feminist?") less than a month later, she did not give the same answer. Instead, she said,

I'm not gonna label myself anything, Brian ... And I think that's what annoys a lot of Americans, especially in a political campaign, is to start trying to label different parts of America different, different backgrounds, different ... I'm not going to put a label on myself. But I do believe in women's rights, I believe in equal rights, and I am so thankful I was brought up in a family where really gender has never been an issue ...

(Erbe 2008)

I realize there are many on both the left and right who might be more comfortable with Palin's second answer. On the left are many who think Palin has no right to claim the title "feminist" if she does not hold certain substantive policy positions and act on them in her political life. For some, an organization like

"Feminists for Life," the anti-abortion group to which both Palin and the wife of Chief Justice John Roberts have ties, is a contradiction in terms. It seems to me, however, far preferable to have debates on such matters as abortion policy from within feminism than to seek to enforce a monolithic feminist orthodoxy and excommunicate from the feminist fold those who disagree. The movement will be far more vital if there is room within it for reasonable disagreement. As to matters not directly related to sex and gender, I have already expressed my view that there is room both for a diversity of opinion among people otherwise committed to feminism, and for the development of a diversity of feminist approaches. On the other hand, I find useful Palin's highlighting positions shared by feminists of otherwise diverse politics that distinguish them from the opponents of feminism. For example, Palin has repeatedly said that she is "a product of Title IX in our schools" and has praised Title IX for having "opened more than doors to just the gymnasium. It allowed us to view ourselves, and our futures, in a different way." Even today, not everyone would share Palin's enthusiasm. When a speaker at a recent University of Chicago Law and Economics workshop presented evidence that the participation in sports facilitated by Title IX had kept girls in school and in the workforce longer, at least one of my colleagues questioned why we should regard this as necessarily a good thing. I am prepared to work towards building a coalition with Palin in support of a robust interpretation of Title IX, even if it is one of the very few political issues on which the two of us may agree.

I certainly don't want to endorse Palin. I would no more support her simply because she claims to be a feminist than I would support her, as some have argued that I should, simply because she is a woman. I also agree with Palin's critics that it is important to highlight any hypocrisy or inconsistency in her politics on women's issues and to prevent her from cynically exploiting a feminist label. I don't want to get involved in labeling Palin or anyone else, but I do want to start a conversation on feminism that does not preclude any view on any other matters unrelated to sex and gender, the equality of the sexes and the oppression of women, and I hope that this will once again be possible. As my own Catholic girlhood demonstrates, inspiration for commitment to the cause of feminism can spring from the most unpredictable of sources, and, if even one young girl growing up in a conservative family can feel more comfortable calling herself a feminist because Sarah Palin has done so too, I am left more hopeful for future generations making it beyond the boundaries of the law.

Notes

1 The difference in our approaches is clear from a comparison of the titles of the law review articles we eventually published on the subject: "Disaggregating Gender from Sex and Sexual Orientation: The Effeminate Man in the Law and Feminist Jurisprudence" (Case 1995a) and "The Central Mistake of Sex-Discrimination Law: The Disaggregation of Sex from Gender" (Franke 1995).

2 "Lapsed Catholic" is far too weak a description of my distance from the Church, as I explain below.

3 What I mean by "sameness feminism," is not a claim that men and women are identical, but the repudiation of "fixed notions concerning the roles and abilities of males and females" and of sex-respecting rules (Case 1995a, 2000).

4 See e.g. *Frontiero v. Richardson* (1973) and *Weinberger v. Wiesenfeld* (1975).

Chapter 7

The new faces of feminism

Feminism-in-action and organic feminists in a post-feminist era

Michèle Alexandre

It is by no means clear ... from a feminist point of view, that minority group rights are "part of the solution." They may well exacerbate the problem. In the case of a more patriarchal minority culture in the context of a less patriarchal majority culture, no argument can be made on the basis of self-respect or freedom that the female members of the culture have an interest in its preservation. Indeed they *may* be much better off if the culture in which they were born were either to become extinct ... or encouraged to alter itself ...

(Okin: 1999: 22–23)

A true feminist call to reform in Muslim countries or among Muslim immigrants must respect their religions or cultural sentiments, while recognizing the sanctity of the first and the flexibility of the second.

(Al-Hibri: 1999: 43)

As illustrated in the above quotes, perceived tensions between multiculturalism and women's rights have often polarized social activists and academics. In the face of this tension, we, feminists, sometimes feel that we have to prioritize women's rights over cultural rights. This prioritization-style approach is faulty and dismissive. It has also proved ineffective in contexts containing complex cultural diversity. This is not to say, of course, that the women's movement has not been instrumental in achieving substantial gains over the past few decades. While the fight for true gender equality is still ongoing, it is undeniable that, progressively, feminism has had a substantial effect on the legal structure of society. As gains are made, however, the complex layers of gender biases continually unveil themselves, revealing a need to carefully create resources and craft legal arguments that can refute various forms of biases. As we, feminists, undergo this process, we, sometimes, fail to realize the ways in which we, too, can create and impose a form of dominant and excluding consciousness. One of the ways in which such consciousness manifests itself is through our disregard for the work done by grassroots, "organic" feminists throughout the world.

I use the term "organic feminists" to refer to the emergence of a feminist practice and understanding that is rooted in the concrete cultural and legal practices of a specific community. Its development is gradual and responds to experiences on the ground. Organic feminism stems neither from the imposition of force, nor from contrivances. It originates, in its practice, from women who take concrete or subtle actions, in their every-day lives, which contravene oppressive patriarchal structures. Such grassroots feminists can often indirectly help create new laws and affect women who live outside of the margins of society. That is, by resisting and/or flipping existing rules or restrictions, organic feminists bring relevant issues to the attention of the mainstream. The behavior of these feminists, on the surface, may sometimes go counter to the mainstream, particularly academic and organizational feminist views of the types of measures that are suitable for dealing with women's issues, but when explored more deeply, they share a common goal of ameliorating the lives of women. Organic feminists routinely strive to strike a fruitful balance between women's rights and cultural rights. Through their actions, they have sketched a useful blueprint for achieving a balance between these two important concerns.

Throughout the world, organic feminists are forging creative ways to battle the oppressive, intrusive, and patriarchal conditions that define women's lives. They are reasserting control over the cultural paradigm that defines them and over the trajectory of their existences. To this end, organic feminist movements take various forms. These movements often depart from the theoretical frameworks developed by many academic feminists (Collins 1991; Dworkin 1985; Myer 1994; Valverde 1987). Much of developed feminist theory, at least in law, seems to be limited to the sameness–difference and equality–inequality constructs (MacKinnon 1987, 1989).

The contrast between the rhetoric of established academic feminism and the decisions made by organic feminists throughout the world reveals a need to incorporate in our academic feminist consciousness an approach that I categorize as feminism-in-action. Feminism-in-action is exactly the sort of methodology employed by organic feminists in tackling complex problems faced by women. A feminism-in-action approach is grounded in the belief that even when women's actions are motivated by false consciousness, that choice is still to be respected and viewed as relevant in determining how to address their needs. Thus, one of the premises of feminism-in-action is that false consciousness in women's choices, real or perceived, rather than just dismissed, should be viewed as helpful to understanding and essential in addressing their situation. False consciousness can serve as a tool to identify the cultural and social obstacles that must be surmounted and removed in order for the opportunity to exercise true liberated choices by women. Ultimately, it is through understanding the details, gleaned from collecting women's narratives, that we are forced to face the reality that a discourse focused only on formal equality is no longer adequate. Instead, the details of women's lives lead us to realize that a true feminist agenda has to recognize the particularity and individuality of the lives of women and how these particulars affect their choices. This understanding must shape any methodology we use to pursue equality. Our feminist agenda must be based on the premise that equality between women (and between women and men) cannot and should not be achieved without respecting women's abstract ability to make choices as well as the actual choices they make. Consequently, this realization should lead us to lobby for legal protections for individual choice at every level.

This chapter identifies the limitations of formal equality (legal pronouncements of the equality of both genders) and the significant work done globally by organic feminists in developing an agenda based on a feminism-in-action approach. It does so by showcasing the ways in which organic feminists have overcome the limitations of the International Convention for the Elimination of all Forms of Discrimination Against Women (CEDAW) as applied to the lives of women in their regions. Throughout this chapter, I identify the ways in which feminism-in-action has quietly shaped global feminist jurisprudence balancing women's rights and cultural rights. The first part of the chapter defines in further detail the feminism-in-action approach. The second part looks at the implementation of feminism-in-action in the abortion context and organic feminists' responses to limited or nonexistent formal equality. The third part considers ways of overcoming the limitations of formal equality by using the feminism-in-action approach, and the fourth analyzes the conundrum created by the conflict of agency and false consciousness. Lastly, the chapter discusses the tools used by organic feminists around the world to implement a feminism-in-action approach in the face of the limited effects of CEDAW. The last part also proposes a blueprint, inspired by the work of these organic feminists, for the promotion of women's rights without unduly undermining the role of culture. This blueprint is also designed to help academics and mainstream activists create a common ground so as to be able to better join forces with organic feminists.

Feminism-in-action defined

A feminism-in-action approach consists of the development of measures by women, for women, based on the reality of their lives, the particularity of their locale, and the complexity of their identities. A feminism-in-action approach does not suggest that the hard-won gains of feminism be reversed. Instead, the approach builds on the overall purpose of the feminist movement: the improvement of the situation and circumstances of all women. Feminism-in-action recognizes that this goal cannot be accomplished solely by relying on formal equality. Rather, the approach recognizes that achieving true equality is a complex and progressive process; a process in which answers can only be fully known by the women directly affected.

As a result, a feminism-in-action approach requires that we create a global agenda that includes, as its primary goal, the establishment of a process for the continuing identification and re-identification of women's needs across time and place. This process would then be facilitated by the collection of narratives from women around the world (Pheterson 1989). Creating a narrative-based approach would help us better understand how to address the immediate needs of women engaged in battling patriarchy in their own way. It would provide us with the means to understand and respect the choices of these women, even when they contrast with our own established feminist ideas. We could learn how to work across our differences with other feminists toward a common objective, that of ultimately achieving both formal and substantive equality. The wisdom of this approach can be gleaned, for example, from the efforts of grassroots women fighting for the rights of sex workers (International Committee for Prostitutes' Rights 1986). By joining forces, certain academics and these organic feminists, like sex work activists, were able to bring the labor and safety concerns of sex workers to the mainstream. This process deliberately occurred independently of any judgment on these women's status as sex workers.

Measuring the effectiveness and contributions of past organic grassroots movements

Appreciation of the feminism-in-action approach has long been an undercurrent of the feminist movement. In order to attend to the disconnect often found between formal rules and lived realities, grassroots feminists historically have focused on crafting alternatives for women outside of the limited legal construct. The abortion context presents a compelling example of the power of feminism-in-action (Boston Women's Health Collective 1998). Organic feminist organizations served as the main source of support for vulnerable pregnant women before abortion was legal (Boston Women's 1998). These organic feminists helped pregnant women navigate the difficult choice and practicalities related to securing safe abortions (Blistein 2008). They were also instrumental in bringing the issues associated with abortion to the consciousness of the public and into the mainstream (Lilly 2008).

The abortion context also represents an instance where a feminist-in-action approach converged with the more formal tactics of the established feminist movement for the common goal of protecting women who risked death due to the unavailability of legal and safe abortions. This type of collaboration, that of organic grassroots activism and of a formalized feminist advocacy, is exactly the kind of collaboration that is needed to protect the interests of non-traditional women (Gordon 1990). The current, albeit fragile, protections for women in the area of abortion laws would not be possible if it were not for the efforts of organic feminists who took the theory and translated it into feminism-in-action.

Furthermore, the conflicting and complex nature of the abortion issue itself highlights the potential for ongoing coalition between organic feminists and academic and organizational feminists. The feminists who joined forces for women's right to abortion did not all share the same philosophy or conclusion as to how the right to choice should be manifested. Yet, they rallied around a right to choose in spite of varying personal assessments of what choice should mean (Gordon 1990). In this way, despite the existence of conflicting positions, a broad feminist coalition of women supported an approach to abortion that protected the interest in choice shared by most women without unduly suppressing the rights of any (Gordon 1990). The withholding of judgment in regard to any individual woman's choice in order to protect every woman's right to choose was based on the realization that, without that ability, women would be rendered even more vulnerable and their lives further endangered (Bernstein 2008). This reservation of judgment about specific outcomes allowed the formulation of a creative legal solution that allowed women to decide on issues for themselves. The emphasis on the right to individual choice must be central to any feminist approach to issues faced by non-traditional women.

Overcoming the limitations of formal equality using the feminism-in-action approach

Despite the relative gains made in the area of abortion and others, many areas of law where formal progressive reform has been accomplished have turned out to be very limiting in actuality (Banks 1989–90; Fineman 1983; Magarian 2003). Formal equality, "or equality before the law" has served to open the debate and achieve some important but restricted gains (Scales 1981; Williams 1989). However, those gains have been eroded by the development of increasingly high legal standards. When dominant groups are confronted with laws mandating that they accommodate groups they have previously subjugated, they evade such laws by creating a legal system where formal equality obscures the effects of that subjugation and perpetuates at the same time as it legitimates the historic and existing contexts of inequality. Examples of this phenomenon exist in such areas of law as employment discrimination, sexual harassment law, and rape law, which have developed gender neutrally worded barriers to women's legal recovery. In employment law, for example, while formal rules have allowed women greater access and opportunity, they have failed to address obstacles created by the real-world contexts of an unreformed workplace built around an unencumbered worker and the fact that women continue to serve as primary caretakers in most families (Bowman and Schneider 1998).

Family law is one of the areas in which the negative impacts of formal rules have been the most apparent. For example, Martha Fineman shows that in the child support context:

> Stringent state and federal provisions for the collection of child support fostered the formation of fathers' rights groups, which expressed resentment that men were not equal parents in regard to child custody. To a great extent, these groups represented a backlash to some of the successes of the feminist movement.
>
> (Fineman 1995: 82)

In addition, Fineman also points out, in regard to divorce law, that "laws governing divorce have replaced normative assessments that took conduct into account through a consideration of 'fault' with a system of default rules such as 'no-fault' divorce and preferences for joint custody, making the process more administrative than judgmental" (Fineman 1995: 159). Fineman further argues that formal equality and legal rules focusing on discrimination have systematically ignored the interests and worsened the position of the most vulnerable in society (Fineman 2008).

Fineman's vulnerability theory is, for example, particularly relevant to the legal treatment and/or neglect of non-traditional women like sex workers. As part of her vulnerability theory, Fineman argues that moving beyond, while not abandoning formal legal categories such as gender or race, will give us the tools to best address the reality of our shared, inevitable, and constant vulnerability. Fineman (2008) views the responsibility of addressing this vulnerability as being that of both the state and the private sector. Moving past rigid legal identity categories and invoking state, not only private, responsibility for addressing vulnerability will also help organic feminists in their struggle to negotiate for the protection of vulnerable women in their societies (Satz 2008). In addition, by accepting that vulnerability is universal and constant, we can effectively join with organic feminists in constructing a methodology that attempts to locate and address sites of vulnerability in all the contexts in which we operate.

The limitations of formal equality can be overcome by implementing a methodology based on feminism-in-action. In doing so, the following questions should be considered in approaching any issues affecting women: (1) are multiple and diverse narratives presented in the context in question? (2) Do patriarchal assumptions play a role in the outcomes of the conflicts that the narratives identified? (3) In what ways do the women (or sometimes men) described in these narratives try to resist and counter these assumptions? (4) What can we learn, as feminists concerned with vulnerability, from the tools and methods used by these organic feminists in their resistance? The locating of sites of specific vulnerabilities can be instrumental in helping us to understand the ways in which dependency and inequality manifest themselves in particular contexts. Understanding how vulnerabilities are created will aid us in devising ways to remove them. Organic feminists' lived narratives are a good starting point for deciphering the presence and effect of vulnerability. By studying their methods of resistance, we can honor the spirit of feminism-in-action, which roots any formulation of a feminist agenda in the realities faced by women, as well as learn from those methods.

Exploring the conundrum created by the contradictory concepts of agency and false consciousness

One of the major fears behind some feminists' reluctance to defer to individual choice lies in the belief that some of those choices, particularly those viewed as unfeminist, will be the result of false consciousness. Some versions of feminism have identified false consciousness as absolutely negative and argue that the task of feminism is to change the minds—alter the consciousness—of those women who fall victims to this state of mind (Alexander 1987). Unfortunately, the more these feminists maintain that the choices of non-traditional women are false, the more these women will distance themselves from feminism. A schism is thus created over time between groups of women who should be united around empowering all women. This pattern of judgment and distance is illustrated in both the anti-polygamy and anti-prostitution contexts (Bell 1994).

These feminists' reliance on the idea of false consciousness to dismiss individual choices with which they disagree is inappropriate and ultimately self-defeating. By doing this, they miss an important opportunity to learn about the lived realities of the women making these choices (Alexander 1987). They also risk alienating these women and, thereby, miss many opportunities to work with them on how to widen their range of choices. The universal application of an assumption of false consciousness to any decision viewed as unfeminist or even anti-woman is dangerous (Arriola 1990). The presence or absence of false consciousness can only be determined from understanding the choices available to the women at issue and why, given all possible choices, they might nonetheless choose one that appears more restricted. A judgment by the feminist who stands outside of the cultural context in which the decision was made does not negate the validity or feminist integrity of any woman's choice within that culture. Rather than viewing such decisions as a mark of being "un-feminist," we should understand that they may well be attempts by women "to do" feminism in the best way that they can given their very limited circumstances and restricted setting (hooks 1998: 929). We should therefore join forces with these women in an effort to remove the obstacles in their lives and increase the array of choices available to them.

This proposal, of course, requires that we tackle head on the question of agency and whether it can exist in restricted patriarchal contexts. Women have managed to survive and thrive in the middle of the most restricted oppressive structures, demonstrating undeniably that exercising agency under adversity is possible. Whether that agency is recorded and recognized in history may be a different matter, however. During the American civil rights movement, for example, women were instrumental in planning and implementing many of the successful projects of the movement, but the efforts of these women were not fully recognized. For instance, the stories reported about the Brown Chapel African Methodist Episcopal Church and the Edmund Pettus Bridge, sites of the Selma to Montgomery Voting Rights March of 1965, are mainly male (Tagger 1997). Each year we:

> commemorate the efforts of African Americans in Selma, Alabama and nearby rural counties to regain and secure voting rights denied to them for more than half a century. Although the efforts of the Southern Christian Leadership Conference (SCLC) and the Student Nonviolent Coordinating Committee (SNCC), under the leadership of Bernard Lee, Hosea Williams and John Lewis received more attention, local participants

and organizations, namely the Dallas County Voters League (DCVL), spearheaded the struggle.

(Tagger 1997: 18)

More particularly, little attention was called to the fact that "Amelia Boynton Robinson and Marie Foster led voter registration drives and organized their communities in a challenge that ultimately led to the passage of the Voting Rights Act of 1965" (Tagger 1997: 18). The lack of recognition does not undermine the exercise of agency by these women. Amelia Boynton and Marie Foster had worked to bring civil rights to Selma and its neighboring counties for decades and were, in fact, instrumental in convincing Dr. Martin Luther King, Jr. to come to Selma (Tagger 1997). These women, in a further exercise of their agency, decided not to fight for recognition of their roles and allowed for most of the credit to be awarded to their fellow male activists. While that decision might now be criticized and, arguably, might have helped lend a patriarchal face to the civil rights movement, it also shows how women can be effective even in the face of sexism. Black women during the civil rights movement were aware of the ingrained sexism of both black and white men. Yet, they didn't let that sexism stop their efforts, even using the lack of attention to their advantage. While black men were in the forefront politically and the apparent leaders, women were working tirelessly on implementing their vision for equality through the less publically visible organizations, such as schools, churches, and other avenues of civil society in which they dominated. While this decision to work in the less visible places might seem to be an undue deference to patriarchy, a closer look reveals it to be a shrewd strategic calculation by the women as to what was necessary to attain the larger goal that paved the way for the enactment of the Civil Rights Act. Their calculated efforts in mobilizing grassroots support ultimately benefited both people of color and women. When faced with choices by women that on the surface seem unfeminist, our first conclusion should not be a negative judgment. Rather we must look at all the circumstances and conduct an in-depth evaluation of the larger goals that these women may be attempting to achieve through their particular decisions.

Consequently, the challenge for feminists is to refrain from being wedded to a homogeneous definition of what is considered "proper feminism." Instead we must assess feminism in context, continuously trying to understand how certain decisions by women help further the interests of women in particular settings and how we can collaborate with them on their terms to broaden their options. Ultimately, when feminists disagree with the choices made by women, that fact should serve as an indicator that this is an area in great need of legal reform. Our job is not to condemn the women or their choices. Instead, our job as feminist legal scholars is to serve as rapporteurs, describing to the legal system how the law is failing to protect and enlarge women's choices, thereby exposing them to greater vulnerability.

Feminism-in-action in response to the limitation of the Convention on the Elimination of All Forms of Discrimination Against Women (CEDAW)

Organic feminists' efforts to bridge the gaps left by the formal equality issued by CEDAW are vital to advancing the international women's rights movement. The Convention codifies formal rules of equality for the protection of women around the world. For example, Article 3 of CEDAW specifies that:

> States Parties shall take in all fields, in particular in the political, social, economic and cultural fields, all appropriate measures, including legislation, to ensure the full development and advancement of women, for the purpose of guaranteeing them the exercise and enjoyment of human rights and fundamental freedoms on a basis of equality with men.
>
> (CEDAW 1981)

Still, the implementation of CEDAW has proved difficult. Allowing nation states to make reservations to CEDAW as a concession to the idea of sovereignty and as a way of attracting more signatories has placed great limitations on the formal potential of the Convention. Furthermore, CEDAW, while guaranteeing equality, has limited means of enforcement. For all these reasons, women around the world often find themselves unable to rely either on CEDAW or their domestic legal system as a means of legal protection. Consequently, when faced with oppressive constructs, these women have found creative ways to trigger progress.

The work of organic feminists illustrates that as women we all share multiple identities that, at times, lead to different choices depending on the contexts and the needs at hand. This complexity makes it difficult for outsiders to distinguish between inequities that can be addressed in absolute legal/practical terms and those that are best addressed through a more gradual process and are in need of complementary cultural and social change. That determination can be done better with the help of the women on the ground, who are directly affected by the issues at hand. The experiences and narratives that have guided their choices can also help us to identify the most immediate needs facing them and their communities. Women in the Congo, for example, exercised agency in dealing with the traumatic proliferation of rape against Congolese women. In response to this horrible reality, organic feminists in Congo organized in order to break down the cultural taboos about rape (Kimani 2007). They led the way in doing the necessary cultural work that allowed the government and international organizations to create and implement laws to punish the perpetrators and develop other efforts to protect women from rape. These actions were undertaken with the leadership of women without any reliance on a stated policy of formal gender equality. They surmounted their society's ideal characterization of a good woman (i.e. one who was not raped, since rape is a crime that stigmatizes women) by bravely talking about their own rape.

Similarly, overcoming cultural and social stigma and despite receiving threats, Kenyan ecologist, Wangari Maathai (2004), organized in conjunction with other women activists to plant a million trees. Mrs. Maathai saw the ecology movement as a springboard to improving governance. Her movement directly confronted governmental structures where pecuniary interests went counter to the environmental interests. Maathai's ecological movement is also a call for feminists to develop a framework that encompasses the environment's effects on the lives of women and recognize the limitations caused by geo-political realities. Also instructive are the organic feminists in Iran who defied the oppressive governmental regime by stalling the passing of a bill that would have allowed "temporary" marriages for men. In describing their goals, one of the women stated: "We hope we can come to agreement to legalize temporary marriage only in exceptional cases, not as a right for every man to engage it … [u]ntil then, we will try to postpone the approval of the bill as long as we can" (Mostaghim and Daragahi 2008). It is important to note that these Iranian women chose to tackle the problem gradually and incrementally rather than urging a ban on polygamy, which would not have succeeded at the time. Nor did they even fight to completely prohibit temporary marriages. This strategy is similar to the deliberate calculation used by women in the civil rights movement. While Iranian women identified banning temporary marriages as their overall goal, they strategically chose to focus on limiting and delaying the bill. These organic feminists understood, better than outsiders to their culture can, their social and legal realities. Their efforts highlight the need for deference to the desires and choices of the women most affected.

Furthermore, in Egypt, women decided to fight back against widespread sexual harassment (Arriola 1990) and to take the government to task for blaming the harassment on women's lack of modesty. Egypt is a deeply Muslim country where women and men generally practice the tenets of Islam. A Western feminist observing women in Egypt might have a hard time reconciling Muslim women's decisions to fight harassment legally by adopting a restrictive form of clothing. Many Egyptian women, however, maintain that the wearing of burkhas or other concealing clothing is a result of their own choice, independent of patriarchal compulsion. It is important to note that, after the Egyptian government's failed attempts at banning the veil in the 1990s, many Egyptian women now wear the veil in opposition to these types of infringements (Silver 1996). There exists a common thread that runs between the acts of fighting sexual harassment and the decisions to maintain a right to wear restrictive or concealing clothing. That common thread is that Egyptian women clearly intend to resist both internal and external efforts at controlling them or their bodies. Just as they do not want men harassing them or invading their privacy, they resent attempts to question their manner of dressing under the guise of women's liberation. Their ability to make choices in both contexts should be protected. If we seek to join with these women, our task as feminists must be to lend them a hand to eradicate the problems that they, as women organically connected to their society, have identified. We should not undertake to convince them to think exactly like us. If there are laws restricting dress, or cultural and social sanctions that mandate conformity, it is up to those women to assert that they desire these laws to change. We can support their efforts but must not supplant their agency.

The same issue as to the appropriate feminist response is raised when considering the choices made by women either in Egypt or other parts of the world to live in polygamy. Polygamy, as practiced traditionally, is seen by many as an extremely patriarchal and oppressive system. It is the case that many women given a choice would opt out of polygamy. However, it is also true that many other women claim they prefer a polygamous lifestyle and when given other options, whether in their country or elsewhere, they maintain that a polygamous lifestyle best suits them. While there is a possibility that such choices are motivated by false consciousness and not the result of unaffected preference, the same can be said of any choice. We all are products of our culture(s) and our culture, to some extent, shapes our preferences and guides our choices. However, as long as choices operate within restrictive cultures and social systems, it will often be impossible to assess the relationship between choice and restrictions. That relationship can better be assessed by collaborating with women operating within the culture.

Even if women's choices are affected by their culture, the results are not necessarily the product of false consciousness, but, are instead, quite often the best decision that can be made given all the circumstances. It is the woman within the particular restrictive web of her society who can enlighten the outsider to that society about her needs. A woman living in polygamous system, for example, might not be concerned with the elimination of polygamy, but might rather want to rectify the lack of legal protection faced by women in the position of second wife. Or else, she might desire that the implementation of inheritance laws be altered so that polygamous women's children, no matter the wives' rank, will have the resources necessary to access educational opportunities. Working with those women to accomplish these goals, using their stories and narratives about their needs would serve as great opportunities to implement the feminism-in-action approach.

To this end, the work and narratives of the above-mentioned organic feminists should inspire us to construct a blueprint that will help us balance cultural and gender concerns, thereby allowing us to work more closely with women from various cultures. Similar to Azziza Al-Hibri's proposal (1999) for balancing religion and culture, I propose the following blueprint to help us reconcile the tension between culture and women's rights. This blueprint, gleaned from the work of organic feminists, contains three steps for ameliorating the conditions of women without overt antagonism towards their culture: (1) separate coercion from culture by focusing on providing space and freedom for women to make decisions that at the very least minimize existing restrictions; (2) understand the usefulness of a gradual approach to the attainment of actual rights as well as that of an immediate approach; (3) promote change using tools that are integrally part of the culture. Thus, this approach, which recognizes that feminism must emerge out of the culture, views it as a mistake to consider any situation as stagnant and unchangeable.

Another difficult area, which presents an opportunity for scholars to implement this proposal, and thus practice feminism-in-action pertains to the various practices designed to promote virginity among girls and women in some societies. Assessing virginity, by most accounts, is a degrading and oppressive experience. How should we view the fact, however, that in South Africa, despite the presence of a formal rule outlawing virginity tests, young girls and women still fight to undergo the process? Virginity tests, unlike female genital mutilation, "are usually performed by elderly women, [and] involve inspecting the genitals of girls for torn hymens" (*Medical News Today* 2008). Many of the Zulu girls who decide to undergo these tests each year find the constitutional law banning the practice to be an invasion of their culture in which virginity is highly prized. Furthermore, many adult women in the Muslim diaspora have undergone plastic surgery to restore the hymen to virgin-like status. While some women who undergo the procedure do so to avoid shame upon marriage, others have done it for aesthetic reasons. How do the virginity tests advocated in Zulu culture square with the reality that many women in the West regularly scar their bodies and undergo dangerous surgery in order to attain a certain standard of beauty?

Again, the question for feminists is whether we can practice a type of feminism that honors choices, even those made within societal and cultural constraints, while protecting women. How do we want to tackle any legal hurdles that women in particular cultures consider untenable? For example, might we consider formally making virginity tests voluntary but screen for the presence of any coercive factors? Or might we focus our energy on increasing the age of consent for these types of procedures to the age of majority while simultaneously providing a multitude of educational outlets for women to be informed constantly about their options.

These suggestions might, however, still leave many feminists uncomfortable. The idea that feminism would condone a practice that has at its core the belief that the presence or absence of virginity is part of a woman's value goes against everything in which we believe. But, that is the wrong place from which to begin to think about this issue. Even if convinced that an adult woman's decision to undergo a virginity test is rooted in patriarchy, as outsiders to that specific culture we will not accomplish anything by lobbying to abolish the practice and telling adult women that they are deluded. However, in the alternative, we can work to ensure that the choices made by women are exercised safely, without coercion, and with the full protection of the law, as we have done with the very controversial issue of abortion. In addition, we can support the work of organic feminists in particular cultural settings, who are trying to make sure that women's decisions are as free and informed as possible by educating them as to the array of choices that are available to them.

As more information is made available in various cultural contexts and as cultural experiences are seen through women-centered lenses, more questions will be raised by organic feminists concerning the laws needed to provide legal protections for women. As a result, more changes and more choices will emerge. Women doing what they deem best for them, based on the context and reality of a specific time, can change that context and reality. Thus, a seemingly patriarchal choice by a woman today, with adequate information and the availability of protections and alternatives, might lead to circumstances that allow, even encourage, a completely different choice tomorrow. The important issue here is that the change of mindset should not be forced on women by either the government or feminists who purport to know best. Instead, by making sure that all legal and social resources are made available and by removing coercion, we can allow women to exercise the type of agency that is essential to everyone's self-actualization and to the flourishing of organic feminism.

Conclusion

The clash of practical or situation-based, culturally embedded solutions and abstract theoretical approaches can result in a crisis of misunderstanding among women from different societies, regions, religions, and cultures. Such misunderstanding risks stalling the unifying goal of feminism, which is to address the needs of girls and women without furthering stereotypes or doing harm. This chapter urges that when we attempt to resolve conflicting ideas about the means of providing for the needs of women, the default position should always include deference to the judgment of the women affected by the situation in question. This method also advocates a bottom-up approach that recognizes that an outsider to a situation is not the person with the best facts or understanding. Even when the immediate results do not yield the ultimate change to which feminists in different circumstances might aspire, this approach honors the realization that women are individuals with multi-layered and complex identities whose interests will not be advanced by linear analyses which ignore their multiplicity.

This chapter focused on how organic feminists (many of them non-traditional women) have helped move the cause of feminism forward. Although the voices of these women are often left out of the legal discourse, organic feminists all over the world struggle for rights using organic and grassroots devices. Feminist legal scholarship should be informed by the experiences and courage of organic feminists who often do not fit society's sexist views of womanhood. When the feminist legal community pays close attention to the lives and actions of marginalized women, it learns a great deal about the diverse needs of women and about the ways in which post-modern feminist theory can continue to interrogate the law so as to fulfill those needs.

The process of interrogating the law often entails a critical re-evaluation of traditional feminist precepts. Such re-evaluation has proved liberating for the movement. The examples above highlighted instances where organic feminism around the world has transformed legal systems and communities. There still exist a myriad of problems to be tackled by organic feminists, many as yet unaddressed by legal systems. Yet, these feminists try to maneuver within their cultural realities and multiple identities to introduce change. Non-traditional women, for example, who do not fit the express and tacit definition of appropriate womanhood sponsored by both the dominant legal system and some feminist approaches, continuously fight stereotypes and restrictive attitudes perpetuated by the legal system and, at times, by other women. One of the main challenges, in the era of post-modern feminism, is to figure out ways to include the interests of non-traditional women in a women-centric agenda for the twenty-first century. In this endeavor, we can learn a great deal from the work already begun by organic feminists around the world.

Section Three

Engaging bodies

Introduction to Section Three

The body has become increasingly important to feminist theory as scholars have rejected the liberal Enlightenment understanding of humanity. According to that model, reason and the intellect are the defining aspects of being human. The body is at best a superfluous casing for reason, at worst an impediment to reason functioning purely. By contrast, the feminist legal theorists in this section position the body as integral to our experience of being human. Their chapters emphasize the importance of material embodiment in any modern feminist legal project.

Isabel Karpin and Roxanne Mykitiuk discuss the move within feminist theory from thinking about sexual difference to thinking about embodied difference. Bodies that deviate from a constructed "normal" body are pathologized by both biological and legal discourses, which construct, reinforce, and only sometimes challenge a notion of the normative self and normative body (coded male). The authors point out that feminist legal theory has consistently and successfully challenged the notion that the self is bounded, independent, autonomous, and free to make rational decisions.

The authors offer multiple illustrations of the fluidity, contingency, and dependency of the embodied self: reproductive technologies that challenge normative notions of filial attachment, the contested line between self–other in pregnant bodies and conjoined twins, the "difference" attached to the disabled body. They argue that law should move beyond "regularizing, normalizing, and stabilizing" material bodies. Instead, following earlier feminist work, they re-imagine the self, the body, and the connection between them (an embodied self). With the primacy of the "universal, white, male, able-bodied" subject effectively challenged by feminist scholarship, the authors see an opening for the law to re-conceptualize the body as multiply different, to address needs specific to the differently abled, and to be capable of containing all embodied and vulner-able selves in its scheme of justice.

Dorothy Roberts' chapter focuses on how neoliberal policies in the US are detrimental to women's reproductive freedom. These policies discourage or punish poor, minority women's childbearing, even as they promote the child-bearing of wealthy, white women through reproductive genetic technologies.

Reprogenetics, often hailed as allowing women greater choice in selecting their children's traits, should be understood as a regulatory mechanism that pressures women to have only certain kinds of children.

Roberts argues that neoliberal policies encourage shifting responsibility for poverty and systemic social inequities from the state to the individual and create a "stratification of childbearing" in the US. Wealthy women are encouraged to take responsibility for potential disability and/or illness in their children through genetic technologies, while poor women find their reproduction punished through government refusal to provide basic aid or services aimed at addressing poverty, inequity, and health care needs.

Roberts views both these developments as policies that "obscure" the state's responsibility in addressing poverty and other social inequities. She encourages women to reject policies supporting a "reproductive hierarchy," which are harmful to the reproductive freedom of wealthy and poor women. She calls on women to support policies that will "improv[e] the social conditions that determine children's welfare."

Michael Thomson is concerned with the common construction of the male body as bounded and invulnerable in opposition to the porous, vulnerable female body. The male body is typically taken as the "benchmark" body and even equated to the "body politic." Thompson uses Fineman's work on vulnerability as a starting point for his inquiry into why the male "enfleshed, lived body" attracts so little attention in feminist legal theory. His chapter explores the political effects of the social–discursive construction of gendered bodies as "in/vulnerable," as well as attempts to move beyond the benchmark male body by challenging the normative conception and arriving at a fuller understanding of the lived male body.

Thomson wants to avoid any ensconcing of "male victimhood" in his focus on the male body. However, since it is constituted as "phallic" and "impenetrable," "bounded" and "safe," Thomson deems locating vulnerability in the male body as important. Concentrating on circumcision, he argues for a feminist exploration of the male body's vulnerability. This exploration could go beyond normativity to allow renegotiation of social relations through the explanation of shared vulnerability. This new project, Thomson hopes, will help in "re-writing" the "in/vulnerable" male body in the larger context of multiple vulnerabilities.

Chapter 8

Feminist legal theory as embodied justice

Isabel Karpin and Roxanne Mykitiuk

This chapter examines a shift within feminist legal theory from a central concern with sexual difference to one of embodied difference. The subject at the center of this theorizing is marked by bodily (as opposed to sexual) difference from the normative, self-actualizing individual of legal subjecthood. Bioethical and biotechnological inquiries too are concerned with bodily differentiation. Bodies discussed in these contexts are often anomalous or pathologized. They are brought under scrutiny, when they deviate from what is often regarded as "normal," that which is both valorized for its "species typicality" and, by extension, held out as the "natural" state of being (Buchanan et al. 2000).

Our feminist theorizing focuses on the link between biological and legal accounts of the embodied subject to interrogate the way that these meaning-making discourses reinforce and challenge each other. This approach provides opportunities for rethinking a just response to the existence of non-normatively embodied others. Thus, we examine legal responses to the bodies of non-normative selves: those classified as "disabled" or otherwise anomalous. While this shift moves away from a specific focus on women's bodies to bodily difference more generally, women's bodies remain central to our analysis because the liberal conception of the subject valorizes bodily states more easily managed by men's bodies. Women, especially through pregnancy, are destined to fail at this marker of autonomy and individuality (Karpin 1994; Mykitiuk 1994). The impetus for our interrogation originates in the work of feminist legal theorists who, along with colleagues in the humanities and social sciences, have sought over the last 25 years to (re)position material embodiment as key to feminist analysis. While difference is not always manifest along gendered lines, feminist legal theory operates as a general jurisprudential matrix within which to understand and analyze a broader ideal of embodied justice.

Here, we map out a legal feminism that invokes a commitment to the multiplicity, indeterminacy, and the contingency of the material self, at the same time as recognizing the reality of bodies and the need to live in them. While accepting instabilities as inevitable, we do not deny that we have bodies, nor do we seek to transcend them. Instead, we argue that law's repertoire of responses should move beyond regularization, normalization, and stabilization.

Deposing liberal legal feminism

As part of the deconstruction of liberal feminism, ideals such as independence, autonomy, objectivity, and disembodied abstraction have been radically interrogated (Fineman 2000; Thornton 1999; Williams 1991). For instance, Martha Fineman offers a compelling critique of liberal individualism through her thesis on the inevitability of dependency. Arguing that independence is an imaginary state that fails to account for the myriad ways in which dependency is masked or managed by familial and intimate relationships, she challenges the fundamental claim that independence is a self-evident good toward which we should all strive and around which our legal regimes should be organized. The fact that individuals almost always "exist in family or relational contexts" undermines the primacy of a claim to independence as any kind of ideal state (2000: 14).

Patricia Williams, too, challenges us to recognize our situated and embodied perspective by writing her jurisprudence autobiographically and subjectively. In *The Alchemy of Race and Rights* (1991: 3) she announces from the outset that "subject position is everything in ... analysis of the law." In doing so, she takes issue with a value system based on an unattainable abstract, the disembodied "neutral" and "objective" individual who is the subject, interpreter and enforcer of law.

Similarly, Margaret Thornton exposes the way that the liberal subject of law is a spectral abstraction denuded of its concrete reality and limitations. In her examination of Australian constitutional law she says:

> "constitutionalism" typically involves the treatment of issues at a very high level of abstraction so that distinctive private or subjective features are sloughed off. Thus, issues ostensibly located within the public domain of law can also be hidden from view, if contrary to the interests of benchmark men. In this way, the body of an individual complainant can become a mere spectre behind the text.
>
> (Thornton 1999: 754)

The traditional liberal and rationalist conception of the bounded self, identified by a controlling rationality whose integrity must be defended against invasion has thus been the subject of a sustained critique within feminist legal discourse.

The incommensurability of material limitation with the ideology of liberal legalism is an essential and motivating device in our feminist theorizing as well. It has led us to focus on the relationship among biomedical discourse, law, and feminist legal theory as fundamental. Our work is in line with what Fletcher et al. (2008: 341) describe as a "shift from more familiar notions of sexual difference to embodied differences."

While engagement with biomedical discourses and health law is a dominant organizing frame for our legal theoretical approach, our work is nevertheless overtly and determinedly within the genre of feminist legal theory. Our critical engagement with the normative legal subject is a feminist engagement regardless of whether the non-normative subject on whose behalf the critique is made is gendered female. We make this appropriative claim for feminist legal theory not because we reject the possibility of critiques of normativity from other quarters—indeed we draw heavily on the work of disability studies critiques (Davis 2002; Garland-Thomson 1997; Scully 2008; Thomas 2007), postmodern philosophies (Grosz 1994; Haraway 1991; Shildrick 1997, 2002) and other writings about the body (Bordo 2004; Frank 1995). Rather, our critique of normativity derives from and depends on our feminist legal theoretical foundations and their generational origins. The work of Finenan's feminist legal theory project, to which this book is a tribute, has been instrumental in this regard.

The ontological role of feminist legal theory does not stop when we discuss other kinds of enmbodied lives. Indeed, Shildrick describes the ontological role of feminism in the critique of a modernist discourse that devalues other others apart from women as follows:

> Since the beginning of its rejuvenation in the second half of the twentieth century, feminist theory has been marked by the recognition that many of the most fundamental tenets of modernist discourse have supported schemata in which not only women, but other others, have been systematically devalued. In response, feminism has set up alternative models of ontology, epistemology and not least ethics, which challenge both the discursive primacy of the universal, white, able-bodied, masculinist subject and the normative codes by which that subject is supposed to live.
>
> (Shildrick 2005a: 15)

She goes onto say that the attention to context and specificity that feminist scholarship offers is "a powerful challenge to what counts as the legitimate ground for bioethical inquiry" (2005a: 16). We argue that such a feminist sensibility equips us to engage in a thoroughgoing legal critique of normativity more generally and normative embodiment specifically.

Embodying justice

Our approach to embodiment wrestles with the notion that bodies have a material reality—our skin, blood, ligaments, and DNA do exist. However, "the meanings of the body are facts of culture—meanings that are provisional, multiple and ambiguous, shifting from context to context" (Sclater 2002: 5). Embodiment is a construct of shared understandings, made real by scientific/ biomedical, cultural, and legal accounts, among others. Biological accounts do not simply offer up a description of what is natural. As Sclater (2002: 5) argues, while "the body ... appears as a 'natural' entity that seems to stand outside of history, society and culture," what we see reflected in the discourse of nature or "the natural," are actually "cultural concerns embedded in the language of science; science working to negotiate the boundaries of culture."

It is necessary to unpack the unstated assumptions about the meanings (both natural and cultural) attributed to different forms of embodiment and normative embodiment in particular, in both the legal and biomedical contexts and where the two cross paths. Here, we interrogate the concepts of normal and disabled, healthy and diseased, and able-bodied and impaired. We challenge the idea of a "normal," "natural," or "pre-cultural" body as a benchmark against which other bodies are judged. "We track the way in which bodies (within medico-legal and biotechnological discourses) are regulated and managed in relation to shifting normative ideals" (Karpin and Mykitiuk 2008: 414). While for Sclater (2002: 5) "the body emerges as a contested site," we focus on law's role in adjudicating its meaning.

Before considering non-normative embodiment, we first examine two instances where the female reproductive body has confounded the "naturalization" of legal categories via biological claims. These cases illustrate the foundations of our theory of embodied justice in feminist legal theory that deconstructs the disembodied self as the pre-eminent mode of legal selfhood. We explore the crossover between biotechnological and biomedical accounts of the self and those found in law. While law often relies on biological or biomedical explanations to ground its decisions and definitions, we demonstrate how those decisions and definitions are not biologically determined. Instead, they are thoroughly legal and thus culturally circumscribed.

The filial body

Law has been instrumental in defining the filial body. As Roxanne (2002: 776) argues, "[t]he social recognition of parenthood by law is [generally] understood to follow the biological fact of procreation." Legal relationships of maternity and paternity are granted to those assumed to share an intimate biological relationship with a child based on the understanding of biology's role in the creation of parenthood. This role differs for men and women. However, the development of assisted human reproductive technologies and the consequent fragmentation of the biological and social aspects of procreation expose the social construction of the existing legal paradigm of filiation: every child is biologically related to only two legal parents, one of each sex.

The so-called "natural facts" about a child's legal mother and father actually rely on social and cultural conventions which become reified as "natural" and aligned with the biological. Moreover, wrestling with filiation in the context of reproductive technologies reveals that while "law recognizes that blood can create legal ties ... not all blood relationships are given legal recognition. Law does not always mirror nature and often it is more representative of the 'social values' it is employed to protect" (Mykitiuk 2002: 776). In light of the development and uses of assisted reproductive technologies and the multiple parties who may become involved in the reproductive context, "facts of nature" are brought into dispute:

> It becomes possible to see how the "naturalness" of heterosexuality and the nuclear family is socially constructed. Not all biological relationships are activated as [legal] ones, and law does not recognize that persons are related to one another through ties of substance and physical bonding even where such ties are not instigated through procreation.
>
> (Mykitiuk 2002: 777–78)

The pregnant body

Law's use of science to negotiate cultural boundaries in the legal treatment of the pregnant woman is another arena where a culturally circumscribed idea of the "natural" is given articulation and endorsement through legal dicta. Significant legislative, judicial, and scholarly energy has been spent debating whether a woman and her fetus should be treated as separate biological entities. If treated as separate the potential for conflict is foregrounded. If the fetus is construed as part of the woman then arguably her rights and autonomy are highlighted. Such a construction leaves the law floundering when faced with a woman who wants to assert the loss of a fetus by third-party negligence or criminal harm as a harm distinct from injury to herself. In these cases, biomedical discourses are utilized to assert a certain view. However, the construction of the fetus as a separate entity from the woman or vice versa relies not on the ascertainment of clear biological facts but on a decision to highlight either fetal differentiation from, or connection to, the woman.

For example courts in the US have been asked to adjudicate whether a woman who takes drugs while pregnant is liable for child endangerment or drug trafficking. These arguments are based on biological processes—namely, that the drugs were delivered to the child via the umbilical cord after it was born but before the cord was cut. Thus, the claim satisfies the legal requirement of biological separation at the same time as insisting on biological connection (Karpin 1994). In the Canadian abortion law case, *R v. Morgentaler* (1988) we find another example of the flexible use of biological processes in law. Madam Justice Wilson rejected one biological explanation that regards a 24-week-old fetus in utero as human life and possible legal person, in favor of another biological definition, in accord with common law, that only upon live birth does personhood begin (see also Savell 2006, for a comparison with UK and Australia). Similarly in Australia in the NSW case of *R v. King* (2003), a man was convicted of grievous bodily harm to a woman after repeatedly kicking her in the stomach and killing her fetus. At first instance the Crown failed in its argument that the death of the fetus was a form of grievous bodily harm to the mother on the grounds that the fetus was a "unique organism." However, on appeal, Chief Justice Spigelman concluded that the fetus is part of the mother and, therefore, she was the subject of grievous bodily harm. Commenting further on the question of the relationship between a woman and her fetus, the Chief Justice disavowed biological certainty, highlighting the contingent nature of that relationship in law:

> My review of the authorities indicates that there is no clear rule, applicable in all situations, as to whether the mother and foetus must be considered as one or separate. The answer will turn on the incidents of the particular legal situation under consideration including, where relevant, the scope, purpose and object of a particular statutory scheme.
>
> (490)

By setting the frame for determining whether a mother and fetus are separate as dependent on the scope and purpose of the legislation that is providing the relevant remedy, the Chief Justice tacitly acknowledged that the biological is cultural or indeed legal.

In our work on the regulation and prohibition of ex utero embryo research and development for reproductive purposes, we show how shifting definitional points based in claims to biological certainty are used to sideline women from the process of reproductive decision-making. An embryo may be classified as "unsuitable for implantation," in which case the woman will not play a role in determining whether it is implanted (Van Wagner et al. 2008). By contrast, individuality might be attributed to embryonic entities, if not legal personhood based on the asserted uniqueness of their DNA (Karpin 2006). Indeed amendments to the Australian Prohibition of Human Cloning for Reproduction Act (2002) resulted in redefining an embryo based on a precise understanding of the biological point in time when individuality is manifest. The amendments adopted "an independently developed definition of a human embryo to a slightly later stage in the fertilization process (first cell division)" (Lockhart Committee 2005: xv). First cell division was described "as determinative on the basis that the community consensus is a 'new and unique genetic entity is formed' only after the genetic material from the male and female pronuclei combine" (Karpin 2006: 606; Karpin and Ellison 2009). In fact, biologically speaking, the embryo has no capacity for individuality (in its social and cultural sense) without a woman willing to gestate it to live birth.

So far we have been using these examples to map out systematically the relationship between law and biological accounts of the self. These examples point to the capacity to deploy so-called "natural facts" to political, cultural, and legal ends. Law uses its own criteria of significance and creates its own truth. It continues to reinforce constructions of natural bodies that are in tandem with other dominant discourses of the body, particularly biomedical discourses. Law has been too ready to defer to scientific and medical expertise about bodies, sometimes opting out of addressing fundamental ethical questions and disenfranchising some citizens. However, law also "undermines its own project by its own location in culture, and by its reification of the body as something needing to be regulated" (Sclater 2002: 5). As Sclater (2002: 5) argues, "discourses and practices designed to civilise, regulate and manage the unruly, unpredictable body proliferate," legislating the body as a contested terrain. At the same time, what science knows about the body is shifting and its truth is provisional. As our major source of information and meaning about the limits of the human being, biomedical assumptions about normality affect law and what it says about normality, especially with regard to health care and disability.

Embodying justice through feminism

The legal subject in its liberal form has specific capacities that law is supposed to facilitate and protect: independence, autonomy, the freedom to make rational choices, and protection against incursion. These capacities do not stand up to feminist scrutiny. Ostensibly they are attached to a body that is held out as normative and around which fundamental values of justice, equality, harm, fault, and dignity are constructed and defined. However, this body, which is claimed to be no body in particular is, in fact, a very particular kind of body (Mykitiuk 1994). The liberal subject is still the pre-eminent mode of selfhood in law. But it is no surprise that that liberal subject is attached to a very specific body: that which has accrued sufficient social, economic, cultural, and political resources to minimize the impact of its dependency and interconnection with others. Isabel has argued elsewhere that:

> [b]odily transgressions do reside within these individuals, but they are accommodated to a point where they appear value-neutral, enabling the façade of independence to be reified in their favour. Those who demand an autonomy of self that incorporates care, responsibility, connection, dependence and even immersion with the other are seen as a definitional paradox—transgressive, messy mixed-up failures. However, it is this conception of self around which law, social, and biomedical discourses must circulate in order to ensure equality and justice.
>
> (Karpin 2005: 197)

A feminist reconfiguration of all bodies as unbounded, always dependent, and subject to the other would require a complete rethinking of the system of justice because it confounds liberalism's individuated self. This approach calls for a conception of justice based on bodily connection and dependence. Feminist theoretical critiques of liberal subjectivity and their assertion of the inevitability of dependence and vulnerability (Fineman 2000, 2008) offer an alternate way of responding to embodied relationships in the contexts in which we work, namely the crossover between biomedical discourses and law.

Take for example the broad area of the legal regulation of genetics. A feminist legal theory of otherness suggests an alternate way of thinking through the initial liberal anxiety produced by the possibility of the intimate connections and interconnections that genetics reveals. Regulating in the area of genetics offers the perfect opportunity to reconstruct the legal self in feminist terms as intimately connected with and susceptible to immersion with others. We might use genetic discourses for instance "to generate anxiety about the stability of liberal identity so that its current beneficiaries find themselves at the margins with the rest of us" (Karpin 2005: 197).

The use of genetic testing has the potential to show that "we are all in some way 'impaired' by highlighting the magnitude of human genetic variation, and by demonstrating that everyone has genetic 'abnormalities'" (Taylor and Mykitiuk 2001: 69). Moreover, the use of predictive genetic testing creates a new category of people—the "worried well" or the "not yet sick" (Lippman 2006: 18). The use of genetic technology can have the effect of identifying otherwise well individuals with genetic susceptibilities to particular disease as unhealthy or with suspect health. People who have been tested often live their lives according to strategies of health management and risk minimization to prevent the future development of the predicted disease or condition. In some cases the disease or condition never develops. Individuals, made to feel vulnerable and genetically compromised, do find themselves at the margins with the rest of us. In order to appropriate genetic discourses, however, "[l]aw in this new frame must take as its base unit a subject that is inevitably connected, vulnerable and dependent" (Karpin 2005: 197); for, genetics offers us a unique form of individuality that connects us to genetically related others. This form of individuality "disables the liberal individual premised on a distinct and separate selfhood. Instead it enables or renders able-bodied a transgressive individual whose very selfhood is already connected and vulnerable to someone else" (Karpin 2005: 198).

A central concern animating feminist critiques of law is the unsustainability of the disembodied subject of law. Female bodies, embryonic bodies, and normative bodies are given legal definition through the use of biomedical discourses; yet, that definition is not fixed in "natural facts." Rather, it is fluid and contingent. In line with the shift from gendered difference to embodied difference, highlighted at the chapter's beginning, we turn to engage broader issues of non-normative embodiment. We will look at law's regulation of conjoined twins and people with disabilities.

Conjoined embodiment

Conjoined embodiment challenges deeply rooted, internalized, and naturalized beliefs concerning the corporeal makeup of a human being. In place of a normative autonomous, stable, singular, and detached self for whom the body is often absent, conjoined embodiment (like pregnancy) offers the unsettling prospect of ambiguous and shared bodily boundaries, negotiated selfhood, and the possibility of being together in one. In contrast to the normative liberal subject, conjoined twins offer a further example of the need for embodiment to become an ontological foundation of the self. They suggest the possibility of an attachment to the corporeality of being and a conception of selfhood that is not defined and valued by its distinctiveness from the other.

Conjoined embodiment offers an opportunity to re-craft and rethink both the theoretical premises and assumptions that have been used to legitimate the normative modern subject and to engage the hegemonic imperatives which alienate, oppress, and suffocate non-conforming subject positions. The phenomenon of conjoined embodiment implicates both bodily existences that are not neatly compartmentalizable and resist classification and bodily existences which do not matter, are discounted, or are marginalized

Conjoined twins, like all other "other" bodies, exist as abject and grotesque. They provoke visceral reactions of horror, disgust, sadness, and pity. Moreover, the disciplinary regimes, including biomedicine and law, that reify corporeal boundedness and subjugate non-normative morphologies are exposed and problematized by the conjoined twin. As a medical anomaly, conjoined twins are categorized as a deformity and a birth defect predicated on the normalcy of discreteness of identity. Medical discourses attempt to account for conjointness by positing explanations of where something naturally went wrong, how a "freak" of nature occurred, and how and why the anomalies should be fixed. Biological and medical discourses provide that "siamese twins ... occur ... when ... an egg in the womb fails to divide successfully" (Clark and Myser 1998: 4). Conjoined embodiment is represented as a condition in which nature has neglected to finish its prescribed embryological work. Thus the need to "fix" conjoined bodily experiences is built into its very definition. From the outset conjoined twins are conceptually crafted as two individuals fused together whose "humanness" can only be achieved through medical intervention. The embodiment of conjoined twins is "so threatening to the order of things ... that they are almost always surgically normalized" (Garland-Thomson, 2001: 11).

This approach to embodiment and personhood is taken up in legal discourse. A compelling example is the UK case, *Re A (Conjoined twins: Medical treatment)* (2000). As was the case in *Re A*, "not infrequently one conjoined twin is 'sacrificed' to save the other from the supposed abnormality of their embodiment" (Garland-Thompson, 2003: 13). These actions are justified as preventing suffering and creating well-adjusted individuals. In *Re A*, Lord Justice Ward makes general comments about the nature of embodiment and its link to dignity and integrity to justify the separation that will kill one twin. With respect to the twin who will die if surgical separation occurs, he states:

> The only gain I can see is that the operation would, if successful, give Mary the bodily integrity and dignity which is the natural order for all of us. But this is a wholly illusory goal because she will be dead before she can enjoy her independence and she will die because, when she is independent, she has no capacity for life ... In terms of her best health interests, there are none.

(998)

Nevertheless, Lord Justice Ward ultimately decides in favor of the surgical separation, arguing that the life of the twin is so compromised by her dependence on the other twin as to be a life destined for death:

> In summary, the operation will give Jodie the prospects of a normal expectation of relatively normal life. The operation will shorten Mary's life but she remains doomed for death. Mary has a full claim to the dignity of independence which is her human entitlement. In the words of the Rabbinical scholars involved in the 1977 case in Philadelphia, Mary is "designated for death" because her capacity to live her life is fatally compromised. The prospect of a full life for Jodie is counterbalanced by an acceleration of certain death for Mary. That balance is heavily in Jodie's favour.
>
> (1010)

The fatal compromise to which Mary must succumb is evinced through her chronic incapacity for independence compared with her sister Jodie who ultimately could live independently. Lord Brooke ends his judgment with a similar response to the horror of dependency: "Finally, the doctrine of the sanctity of life respects the integrity of the human body. The proposed operation would give these children's bodies the integrity which nature denied them" (1052). Integrity, for Mary at least, is only available in death.

Re A highlights the difficulty of relying upon an idealized notion of selfhood when analyzing the rights of legal persons. The use of the phrase "the natural order" as a benchmark for determining personhood and integrity stands in stark contrast to the artificial way in which that natural order must be achieved. According to Lord Justice Ward:

> The first step is to take the scalpel and cut the skin. If it is theoretically possible to cut precisely down the mid-line separating two individual bodies, that is not surgically feasible. Then the doctors have to ascertain which of the organs belong to each child. That is impossible to do without invading Mary's body in the course of that exploration. There follow further acts of separation culminating in the clamping and then severing of the artery. Whether or not the final step is taken within Jodie's body so that Jodie's aorta and not Mary's aorta is assaulted, it seems to me to be utterly fanciful to classify this invasive treatment as an omission in contra-distinction to an act.
>
> (1003)

The use of the language "the natural" as some kind of claim to the right and the good is flawed and demonstrates the unstated assumptions and contradictions upon which this kind of judgment is made. In this instance, legal and biomedical discourses join forces to literally carve out the autonomous legal subject. Biomedicine is not just a technology, it is also an interpretive framework that reflects and shapes our attitudes to human diversity, normality, and abnormality. As Rosemarie Garland-Thomson (2002) suggests, in biomedicine there is a pervasive will to normalize the non-standard body. One could argue that these surgical separations benefit not the affected conjoined twins, "but rather they expunge the kinds of corporeal human variations that contradict ideologies the dominant order depends on to anchor truths it insists are unequivocally encoded in bodies" (Garland-Thomson 2002: 12–13). Of course, in *Re A* Jodie did benefit; she would likely not be alive if her sister had remained attached to her. Yet, in many cases the separation of conjoined twins is not driven by the imminence of death, but by the unquestioned assumption that such anomalous embodiment should be normalized. Referring to the routine consideration of separation of conjoined twins made by doctors and parents at birth, Garland-Thomson (2002: 12) argues, "So intolerable is their insult to dominant ideologies" about who we are and who we are supposed to be "that the testimonies of adults with these forms of embodiment who say they do not want to be separated [are] routinely ignored, in establishing the rational for medical treatment."

Sclater (2002: 6) claims that "[L]aw establishes regulations, institutions, and institutes expectations about what is legitimate, acceptable, natural and normal." It is this "narrative" that "gives law its authority" and the power of law "depends less on its ability to coerce and more on its ability to persuade people that the world it describes is the only available world" (Sclater 2002: 6). As seen in the case of conjoinment, law works together with medicine to literally construct the individualistic liberal citizen. Another instance where Sclater's description seems apt is law's use of biomedical discourse to regulate the production and management of disabled bodies. It is with this in mind that we turn to our final example—disability.

Disability

Typically regarded as a problem for the state, for communities, for families, and for the individual, disability is not generally understood as a feminist issue. However, the importance of feminist theoretical interrogations for discourses about disability has been highlighted by a number of disability scholars. Jackie Leach Scully states that:

> [d]isability ethics, like feminist ethics, is a form of ethical analysis consciously and conscientiously attentive to the experience of being/having a "different" embodiment. Where feminist ethics' concern is with the non-normativity introduced by gendered bodies ... disability ethics looks at the embodied effects of impairment.
>
> (Scully 2008: 11)

Bonnie G. Smith (2004: 4) also argues that "the disabled, often are seen as women are—either to be too embodied or too frail and wispy to be a real presence."

Scully, however, distinguishes between disability as a category of material difference and that of gender:

> Disability occupies an anomalous position within the typology of gender, class, ethnicity, sexuality or age, because unlike any of these it is possible for a person to exist outside the category. One can be not disabled in a way that one cannot be not gendered, or not have an age.
>
> (Scully 2008: 34)

This assertion that one can exist outside of the category (of disability) adverts to the myriad ways in which disability is claimed by medical discourse to distinguish the individual from species typicality. In fact, a view of embodiment that foregrounds its vulnerability and susceptibility to non-normative states would position all of us as variously capable and incapable, able and disabled at any given moment.

Adrienne Asch (2004: 16) suggests that we question the distinction between people who have impairments and people who do not and instead consider "which people cannot perform which activities in given environments." As Asch states:

> arguably, any person now living could, without any change in his or her physical, cognitive, sensory, and emotional make-up, be considered impaired by the same employer, government service provider, place of public accommodation or educational institution if the individual failed to meet particular standards for acceptance into a program or activity that the organisation had established.
>
> (2004: 16–17)

By arguing that we shift our perspective to the capacities of all bodies and their many limits, she suggests reconfiguring our social systems in a way that includes the largest range of individuals. All of us are limited by what our bodies are capable of doing in a particular social, cultural, and environmental context. In this sense the category of "not being able" is one outside of which we cannot, in fact, exist. Grounding our legal system and our cultural and social organizations on the concept of normative ability rather than a range of differing abilities results in an unjust and uncompromising framework. What is able bodied is actually structured by the environment.

Turning to law, Asch analyzes the concerns raised by some scholars with the use of the Americans with Disabilities Act (ADA) (1990) by people who would not normally be considered disabled. She argues that opening up disability to a multitude of forms of bodily impairment and vulnerability is, in fact, a more appropriate and just way to deal with disability. She calls this a "human variation approach to disability" (Asch 2004: 18), which shifts the balance away from a narrow range of required accommodations to a norm of accommodation for broad human variation unless (in the case of the ADA which deals with employment discrimination) the employer can prove that essential functions cannot be performed.

This approach accords with the feminist ethic of embodied justice which we support. It positions the norm as subject to variation and vulnerable to material limits. However as with conjoinment, disability is typically not seen as difference to be accommodated. Rather it is considered so disruptive of individual and community welfare that it is to be prevented, normalized, eliminated, or cured. "Solutions" to the "problem" of disability consistently locate it in the individual, not the environment or cultural constructs in which the individual operates. In the process, the disabled body/person appears as aberrant. Approaching disability as located only within the individual body is sustained by shoring up an unexamined conception of normalcy from which the disabled depart. This conception of the "normal" often relies upon biomedical discourses as authoritative about the body. Law is a key discourse that relies on biomedical understandings of bodies to regulate and resolve disputes. Nevertheless, biomedical understandings are not stable, knowable facts of nature but fluid and open to law's interpretive purposes.

O'Connell (2009: 143) argues that "[w]ithin the legal framework, a framework that elevates objectivity over subjectivity and valorizes abstractions such as justice and fairness, anti-discrimination laws occupy an unusual space as they concern themselves with questions of embodiment and materiality in often intimate detail." With this in mind we now look briefly at an Australian antidiscrimination case: *Purvis v. New South Wales* (2003), where the majority and minority judgments used the same biomedical discourse of disability to arrive at different conclusions about the meaning of disability and the determination of discrimination. In this case a boy with disabilities resulting from an illness was denied the protection of the Australian Disability Discrimination Act (1992) after school expulsion due to behavioral problems that caused him to act violently. In concluding that the school had not discriminated, the court made a decision to cordon the question of the boy's disability from the boy's violent behavior, despite the fact that disability was directly responsible for his behavioral issues. The court then chose to compare his treatment (i.e. expulsion) with a hypothetical "non-disabled child" who behaved in the same way. Belinda Smith describes the court's decision as follows:

> the factual question for the Court was: Did the school treat Daniel the same as it would treat a non-disabled student who behaved as Daniel had behaved (i.e. violently and disruptively)? The Court found that the answer was yes—Daniel was treated as he was treated because of the circumstances (i.e. his behaviour) not his disability (which was separated). Thus he was found to have been treated the same as a non-disabled comparator in these circumstances. This meant that the school had not discriminated against Daniel because of his disability.
>
> (Smith 2007: 16)

This case was dealing with a very violent boy and a school that had made significant but sometimes flawed attempts to accommodate him. Nevertheless, the majority's decision effectively disengaged the boy's disability from his embodied experience of it. Disability here is taken to a "high level of abstraction" (Thornton 1999: 756) and consequently its embodied effects are dematerialized. O'Connell (2009: 143) describes this as the fragility of anti-discrimination law which itself is vulnerable to the "very qualities that are associated with justice." She notes, "as cases are appealed to higher courts, they are increasingly abstracted and disembodied" (2009: 143).

The dissenting *Purvis* judgments of McHugh and Kirby challenged the majority's definition of Daniel's disability: "In our opinion, the behavioral manifestation of an underlying disorder or condition is itself a disability ... " (para. 27). Even the majority judgments of Justice Gummow, Justice Hayne and Justice Heydon accepted that Daniel had suffered brain damage that affected his behavior (para. 182). Furthermore, the evidence of a neurologist and a psychologist was cited to explain the condition as including "disinhibited and uninhibited behaviour" (paras. 29, 30, 182). Nevertheless, the majority of the Court decided to make the comparator an apparently non-disabled child with the same behavior. The majority was particularly swayed by the fact that there was a gap in the legislative framework. Because of this gap, had discrimination been found, the school could not have argued the exception of "unjustifiable hardship" because it was available only on admission to school, not in relation to expulsion. The dissenting judges opined that the majority should not have corrected this legislative oversight by deciding the case the way they did (see Smith 2007: 19).

Without describing the legislative framework within which the High Court was operating and the constraints posed by the legislation itself, we see that an embodied approach to justice would have shifted the focus away from the requirement for a "species typical" comparator. Embodied justice would allow a move toward inquiry into how the school could accommodate Daniel, examining the specific environmental and institutional accommodations that would need to be in place. Such an approach would recognize that Daniel's violent behavior was likely an irreducible part of him and that measures would need to be enacted and implemented to include him in the school community (with appropriate protective safeguards).

Yet, we need to be mindful that practices and policies of inclusion often send the message that to be disabled is to have a problem that limits, disrupts, or prevents the individual from participating in normal life. Brian Pronger, for example, argues that:

> The ethics of inclusion, which tries to bring otherness into a system while requiring it to manifest itself within the structure of the system, appropriates otherness, making it conform to the system. The ethics of alterity, in contrast, works not by inclusion but by openness—openness to otherness in a way that allows the other to deconstruct the system to call

into question the system's limits, particularly in its appropriation of others' otherness.

(2002: 17)

In the case of *Purvis*, an ethics of alterity, and a notion of justice as embodied, requires us to find a way to welcome Daniel into the school community while modifying that institution, its practices, and the social environment, rather than expelling the non-normative body or "fixing it" to conform to the system.

Conclusion

In our early work we investigated the way in which women were placed as problematic outsiders. We insisted on bringing women into the picture, bringing them into the body of knowledge that informs and is law, while making knowledge of and in law account for women's embodiment. To this end, we have explored the legal regulation and construction of the body, and most often the gendered body. While a part of this work has focused on the context of the use and regulation of new reproductive and genetic technologies, more recently we have explored variant corporeality in the context of conjoined twins and disability/impairment.

Our work, while aimed at re-imagining the significance of embodiment to and for women and the law, also identifies and explores the uneasy relationship between law and embodiment generally and marginalized embodiment in particular. Law does not sit in isolation but in relation to a diverse range of discourses that make up the body of law. Some of these discourses create the body of and in law, while law too shapes the body. In this sense, the body is in law, while law is also in the body, and both—law and the body—are necessarily bound up with shifting cultural discourses and practices. This matrix of relationships points to the mutually constitutive nature of both "body" and "law."

In her 1991 book, *Simians, Cyborgs and Women*, Donna Haraway proclaimed that "[l]ife is a window of vulnerability. It seems a mistake to close it. The perfection of the fully defended, 'victorious' self is a chilling fantasy ... " (224). Haraway, in writing these words, was working within a framework of the bio-politics of immunity. In biology as in law the self-actualizing fully defended, bounded, and autonomous individual is the central figure around which policy, theory, and institutions are built. Martha Fineman also challenges us to take vulnerability as a central organizing premise and to reconfigure our approach to state responsibility and to individual rights and duties around the framework of the "vulnerable self." She says:

> What should be the political and legal implications of the fact that we are born, live, and die within a fragile materiality that renders all of us constantly susceptible to destructive external forces and internal disintegration? Bodily needs and the messy dependency they carry cannot be ignored in

life, nor should they be absent in our theories about society, politics and law …

(Fineman 2008: 12)

Our situated, self-conscious, undifferentiated, and embodied selves, and our recognition of other "others," are the keys to understanding how we might begin to frame a justice system that truly is just; one that "does not defer, but engages with, alterity," one that "extends a welcome … to difference … [and] comes into play precisely where the conventional juridical and moral discourse reaches its limit" (Shildrick 2005b: 42, footnotes omitted). Our account of embodied difference provides the basis for a form of feminist legal theorizing, which, while not always identifiable in gendered terms, offers us a means to push beyond the "limit." In doing so, we afford an opening whereby law can "extend a welcome" to all kinds of difference, better respond to all forms of injustice, and embrace all embodied and vulnerable selves.

Chapter 9

Privatization and punishment in the new age of reprogenetics[1]

Dorothy E. Roberts

Introduction

My scholarship on reproduction has made me acutely aware of the stratification of childbearing in the United States. In particular, the social value placed on a woman's reproduction depends on her standing within the hierarchies of race, class, and other inequitable divisions. My research highlights the harsh dichotomy where policies punish poor black women for bearing children but advanced technologies assist mainly affluent white women not only to have genetically related children, but to have children with preferred genetic qualities. In this regard, I have worked with organizations opposing a program offering substance-abusing women in minority neighborhoods money to be sterilized and have attended many conferences where academics debate precisely which traits are acceptable to select for when testing an array of embryos for implantation. While welfare reform laws aim to deter women receiving public assistance from having even one additional healthy baby (Mink 2001), largely unregulated fertility clinics regularly implant privileged women with multiple embryos, knowing the high risk that multiple births pose for premature delivery and low birth weight (Helmerhorst 2004). The public begrudges poor mothers a meager increase in benefits for one more child but celebrates the birth of high-tech septuplets that require a fortune in publicly supported hospital care (Andrews 1999).

At the beginning of the twenty-first century, the race and class dimensions of reproduction, a chief way of creating families, are clear. My prior writing on the stratification of reproduction contrasted policies that penalize the childbearing of poor nonwhite women with policies that promote childbearing by wealthier white women (Roberts 1997). I take a different tack in this chapter. Rather than place these two categories of women in opposition, I explore how the privatization and punishment of reproduction links them together to avoid public responsibility for social inequities. Both population control programs and genetic selection technologies reinforce biological explanations for social problems and place reproductive duties on women, shifting responsibility for improving social conditions away from the state. Reproductive health policies involving both categories of women play an important role in the neoliberal state's transfer of services from the welfare state to the private realm of family and market. This chapter was completed during the last days of the Bush administration. The Obama administration promises to take the country in a very different direction, and I hope that its policies will improve the matters discussed in this chapter. However, because the policies of prior administrations, along with race and gender ideologies, have lasting legacies, the discussion that follows remains relevant today.

Viewing new reproductive technologies as a form of private regulation of women's childbearing decisions complicates the choice-versus-regulation dichotomy that typically frames discussions of these technologies' costs and benefits. Technologies that enable women to have children and to select those children's genetic traits are often viewed as entirely freedom-enhancing tools that should therefore be free from state regulation. I argue, however, that like the reproductive regulations imposed on less privileged women, use of these technologies has the potential to restrict women's control over reproduction while reinforcing social hierarchies that disadvantage women. Thus, it is possible that some state regulation will promote rather than hamper women's reproductive freedom. More importantly, recognizing the restrictive potential of reprogenetics supports greater state investment in eliminating the systemic inequities that make these technologies seem so attractive for addressing disability and illness. Rather than expand public surveillance and regulation of women's reproductive decisions, we should tackle the social conditions that limit women's options for bearing and raising healthy children who can flourish in this society.

Punishing reproduction, privatization, and social inequality

The turn of the twenty-first century ushered in an explosion of rhetoric and policies seeking to punish and regulate poor and minority women's reproductive decisions. Poor black women are especially vulnerable to proposals that punish childbearing. The view of black women as irresponsible reproducers is deeply embedded in dominant American culture and reinforced by a disparaging mythology about black mothers (Morton 1991). Negative icons of black maternity have included the sexually licentious Jezebel that legitimated white slave masters' sexual exploitation of their female slaves; the asexual Mammy, caring for her masters' children though under the supervision of her white mistress; the emasculating Matriarch held responsible for the disintegration of the black family; and the sexually irresponsible Welfare Queen breeding children just to fatten her welfare check and wasting the money recklessly on herself (Collins 2000). The most recent addition to this maternal mythology is the pregnant crack addict who is supposed to lack any maternal instinct.

Newspaper articles portray pregnant black women addicted to crack cocaine as careless and selfish women who put their love for crack above their concern for their children. Reinforcing the link between black female sexual licentiousness and maternal irresponsibility, reporters often represent them as prostitutes who become pregnant after trading sex for crack. Unlike any other drug, the chemical properties of crack cocaine are said to destroy the natural impulse to mother (Trost 1989). These women's children are also the subject of gross racial stereotyping. Some reporters claim that so-called "crack babies" not only suffer physical and emotional damage but are also more likely to become social pariahs. Noting the failure of medical research to substantiate any such condition, syndrome, or disorder, a group of researchers wrote that " 'Crack baby' is not a medical diagnosis but a media stereotype" (Frank 2003: A42).

These stereotypes of black female sexual and reproductive irresponsibility support welfare reform and law enforcement policies that severely regulate poor black women's sexual and childbearing decisions. Judges and legislators view poor black women as suitable subjects for harsh reproductive penalties because mainstream society does not view them as suitable mothers in the first place.

The rush to punish poor, substance-abusing mothers for their reproductive failures can be compared with the more temperate regulation of pregnant middle-class women who use risky pharmaceuticals to treat their mental health problems. For example, I was struck by the sympathy shown to mothers in a recent radio program discussing the dilemma of pregnant women who take Prozac and other SSRIs (Selective Serotonin Reuptake Inhibitors), which have not been approved by the FDA for use during pregnancy because there is evidence they may cause subtle neurological problems in newborns. A psychiatrist interviewed for the program explained that she tries to put the FDA warning in context: "Ultimately, when you are face-to-face with a woman struggling with depression or anxiety during or after her pregnancy, her experience of illness is, I think, the most important determinant of the right thing to do" (Aslanian 2004). This attention to the depressed mother's perspective contrasts starkly with the typical disregard of the needs and humanity of poor black women who self-medicate with crack cocaine.

By identifying procreation as the cause of deplorable social conditions, reproductive punishments divert attention away from the need for social change. Black mothers' crack use, for example, became a primary explanation for high rates of black infant mortality, a trend long predating the crack epidemic. A recent exchange in the editorial pages of the *New York Times* iterated the tension between attributing worsening rates of infant death to the deficiencies of the US health care system and to maternal substance abuse. Columnist Nicholas D. Kristof wrote that in 2002 the already abysmal infant mortality rate rose in this country to seven deaths for each 1,000 live births, placing the United States behind 41 other countries, including Cuba. Kristof (2005) noted that by slashing entitlements, especially those giving children access to health care, the government is likely to exacerbate poor maternal and infant health. In direct response to Kristof's article, Barry S. Levy, an adjunct professor at Tufts Medical School and a past president of the American Public Health Association, endorsed Kristof's diagnosis: "America's world ranking of 42nd in infant mortality, like the obesity and smoking epidemics and the recent shortage of flu vaccine, reflects the overall decline in government support for public health" (2005: A22). But Betsy McCaughey (2005), an adjunct senior fellow at the Hudson Institute, disagreed with Kristof's focus on "the shortcomings of our health system," arguing instead that "the high infant mortality rate reflects a society where young girls and women take drugs while pregnant and give birth to low-weight, drug-addicted infants."

Neither Kristof nor his respondents mentioned the contribution of reproduction-assisting technologies to the rising rate of infant deaths. The numbers of babies born with low birth weight has increased in recent years in part because of high risk multiple births to women who implant several embryos created with high-tech procedures (MacDorman et al. 2005). Affluent women who decide to take the risk of bearing unhealthy babies have not suffered the official sanctions or public vilification directed at poor women with substance abuse problems who often take steps to minimize any harm to their babies. The "Octomom" was publically castigated for having eight babies using IVF because she was unmarried and unemployed.

This diversion of attention from social causes and solutions reinforces privatization, the hallmark of the neoliberal state that pervades every aspect of public policy. In the wake of globalization, industrialized and developing states have sought to reduce the financial burden of social welfare programs while promoting the free market conditions conducive to capital accumulation. Observing this phenomenon, Canadian legal scholar Roxanne Mykitiuk, who has a chapter co-authored with Isabel Karpin in this collection (chapter 8), writes that "the public sphere embraces as its governing logic market rationales and practices" (2000: 107). Critical to this process of state restructuring is the transfer of services from the welfare state to the private realm of the market and family. At the same time, the state deliberately transforms its institutions to advance private sector interests in the market economy.

In his second term, President George W. Bush's domestic agenda explicitly revolved around promoting these neoliberal values. He called for privatization of programs traditionally provided by government as the means of establishing an "ownership society" in the United States that would replace the prevailing New Deal approach. The Cato Institute, a libertarian think-tank that champions the ownership society, describes the concept as follows:

> An ownership society values responsibility, liberty, and property. Individuals are empowered by freeing them from dependence on government handouts and making them owners instead, in control of their own lives and destinies. In the ownership society, patients control their own health care, parents control their own children's education, and workers control their retirement savings.
>
> (Boaz 2003)

President Bush's most controversial step in creating an ownership society was the restructuring of social security to allow younger workers to divert a portion of their social security taxes into private accounts that could be invested in stocks and bonds. President Bush's plans for an ownership society also included eliminating tax laws that penalize wealth accumulation and transfer, and changing class action laws to shield corporations from large tort damages awards (Hook 2005). The ownership society and the privatization philosophy it reflected demanded that individuals rely on their own wealth to meet their needs and discouraged government aid for poor mothers who face systemic hardships in caring for their children.

At the same time that the government reduced support for families, there was a parallel increase in state intervention into poor women's lives. Over the last two decades, the welfare system, prison system, and foster care system have clamped down on poor minority communities, especially inner-city black neighborhoods, thereby increasing many families' experience of insecurity and surveillance. Welfare is no longer a system of aid, but rather a system of behavior modification that attempts to regulate the sexual, marital, and childbearing decisions of poor unmarried mothers by placing conditions on the receipt of state assistance. The federal government encourages states to implement financial incentives that deter welfare recipients from having children and pressure them to get married (Personal Responsibility and Work Opportunity Reconciliation Act 1996).

The contraction of the US welfare state, culminating in the 1996 federal welfare reform legislation, paralleled the expansion of prisons that stigmatizes inner-city communities and isolates them further from the privileges of mainstream society. Radical changes in crime control and sentencing policies have led to the unprecedented buildup of the US prison population over the last 30 years. By the end of 2002, the number of inmates in the nation's jails and prisons exceeded two million. Today's imprisonment rate is five times as high as in 1972 and surpasses that of all other nations (The Sentencing Project 2006). By 2008, one in 100 Americans was behind bars (Pew Center on the States 2008: 5). The sheer scale and acceleration of US prison growth has no parallel in Western societies. African-Americans experience a uniquely astronomical rate of imprisonment, and the social effects of imprisonment are concentrated in their communities. For example, while the general imprisonment rate for men between the ages of 20 and 34 is one in 30, the rate for African-American men is one in nine (6).

Mounting social science studies on the community-level impact of mass incarceration reveal that prison has become a systemic aspect of community members' family affairs, economic prospects, political engagement, social norms, and childhood expectations for the future (Fagan et al. 2003). This social dynamic aggravates and augments the negative consequences to individual inmates when they come from and return to particular neighborhoods in concentrated numbers. Prisons break down social networks and norms needed for political solidarity and activism. Mass incarceration also destroys social citizenship at the community level through felon disenfranchisement laws that dilute neighborhood voting strength, through labor market exclusion, and by marking entire communities as criminal and undeserving of public resources.

The racial disparity in the child welfare system mirrors that of the prison system. Because child welfare policy relies heavily on the punitive removal of children from their homes, the largest group of the children awaiting adoption in the nation's public child welfare agencies is African-American (US Children's Bureau 2002). One year after Congress passed the welfare reform law, it enacted the Adoption and Safe Families Act of 1997 (ASFA). ASFA amended federal child welfare policy by prioritizing protection of children over the support of families and by promoting adoption as a means to fix the overloaded foster care system. As Mark Courtney (1998) notes, this marks the first time in US history that states have a federal mandate to protect children from abuse and neglect but no corresponding mandate to provide basic economic support to poor families. Like welfare reform, ASFA looks to a private remedy—in this case, adoption—rather than curtailing the flow of poor, minority children into foster care by providing needed resources to their families. Not only is there no guarantee that all the children awaiting adoption will be placed in adoptive homes, but adoption does nothing to address the needs of poor families who are most at risk of involvement in the child welfare system.

At times, policy regimes have emphasized the social causes of marginality and attempted to use welfare and prisons to reform and integrate socially dispossessed groups. Exclusionary regimes, such as the one we are witnessing in the United States today, paint marginalized people as undeserving and unreformable deviants to be separated from the rest of society; this is reflected in stingy public assistance and punitive anticrime policies.

There is a correlation between punishment and privatization. The decrease in state responsibility for addressing poverty and social inequality has accompanied an increase in state intervention in the lives of poor- and low-income mothers, especially women of color. In other words, economic insecurity is increasing among the most disadvantaged communities not only because of state inaction but also because of policies that affirmatively sustain, replicate, and intensify systemic political and economic subordination. And these two trends are mutually reinforcing.

Private remedies for systemic inequality and punitive state regulation of the most disadvantaged communities are two sides of the same coin. Deliberate state policies and practices work affirmatively to increase economic insecurity of these communities while obscuring the state's responsibility for causing it or government's obligation to address it. Attributing social inequities to the childbearing of poor minority women and then using this attribution to justify the regulation of reproduction is a critical component of this punitive trend away from state support for families and communities.

Reproductive genetics, privatization, and social inequality

At the other end of the reproductive caste system, new genetic technologies have generated greater surveillance of women, the ones primarily responsible for making the "right" genetic decisions. For decades, prenatal testing has provided the capacity to avoid bearing children with genetic disorders. Advances in reproduction-assisting technologies that create embryos in a laboratory have converged with advances in genetic testing to produce increasingly sophisticated methods to select for preferred genetic traits. Reproductive technologies like in vitro fertilization assist couples to have children who not only are genetically related to them but who are genetically advantaged. With preimplantation, clinicians can diagnose early embryos for their chance of having over four hundred genetic conditions and implant only the ones that probably do not have these conditions. Sperm sorting allows couples to select the sex of their children with 85 percent accuracy. Some scientists predict that reproductive cloning and genetic engineering—actually enhancing the embryo's genetic makeup—will be developed in the near future (Andrews 1999). These cutting edge procedures that enable selection of embryos for their genetic traits are part of a new kind of reproduction-assisting science called "reprogenetics."

It is important to distinguish between the ways in which genetic testing is actually implemented. On one hand, mass carrier screening programs, especially those mandated by the government and aimed at reducing the incidence of a disease in a population, have led to widespread discrimination and coercion. On the other, providing nondirective genetic counseling with informed consent to individuals who request it is unlikely to exploit women and members of minority groups. Yet genetic screening programs, even if they are supposed to be voluntary, create the expectation that women will act on the results. Communities can put pressure on parents, especially mothers, to produce genetically-screened babies for the sake of the whole.

Ashkenazi Jews in the United States have developed perhaps the most sophisticated defense and successful implementation of a community-based program of genetic screening, largely responsible for a 90 percent reduction in the incidence of Tay-Sachs disease from 1970 to 1993. Dr. Fred Rosner (2003: 81), an authority on Jewish medical ethics, defends the program as a "legitimate implementation of the biblical mandate to heal." Premarital genetic testing for Tay-Sachs has become the standard of care in some Orthodox Jewish communities where marriages are arranged. "It's now a duty, not a choice," says legal scholar Karen Rothenberg (Rosen 2003: 87).

It is increasingly routine for pregnant woman to get prenatal diagnoses for certain genetic conditions such as Down syndrome or dwarfism. Many obstetricians provide these tests without much explanation or deliberation because they consider these screenings to be a normal part of treating their pregnant patients. The director of reproductive genetics at a large Detroit hospital reported that at least half of the women referred there with an abnormal amniocentesis result were "uncertain about why they even had the test" ("The Telltale Gene" 1990: 486). A genetic counselor similarly notes:

> Patients will come in and say, "I am having the amniocentesis because my doctor told me to," but really in their hearts they are not so sure that's right

for them. Some people are relieved to find that they have a choice about having the test.

(Fenwick 1998)

Still, many pregnant women now view genetic testing as a requirement of responsible mothering. I experienced this type of shallow ethical evaluation of prenatal testing in 2000 when I was pregnant with my fourth child at age 44. My obstetrician recommended that I participate in a clinical trial by Northwestern University Medical School researchers investigating the potential for ultrasound to help detect genetic anomalies in the first trimester of pregnancy. "It's a way to get a free ultrasound," he told me. Although the researchers had an ethical obligation to reveal any significant risks entailed in the procedure, neither they nor my obstetrician discussed with me the decision I would have to make if the test results predicted that the fetus I was carrying had a high risk of Down syndrome. Instead, everyone seemed to assume that the information could only make me better off and that there was no need for serious deliberation about what I would do with it.

Like the punishment of minority women's childbearing, reprogenetics is linked to the elimination of the welfare state and support for private remedies for illness and disease. Placing responsibility for ending health disparities on individual reproductive decisions can reduce the sense of societal obligation to address systemic inequities. Reliance on eradicating illness through genetics can divert attention and resources away from the social causes of disability and disease, as well as social norms that impair social participation by sick and disabled people. Some disability rights activists argue that genetic testing may privatize disability in the sense that availability of prenatal diagnosis for a disorder may discourage government funding for research and social services for people who have the disorder (Andrews 2001).

Genetic biotechnologies also shift responsibility for addressing disease from the government to the individual by suggesting that health disparities are a result of genetic variation rather than inequitable social structures and access to health care. The FDA recently approved BiDil, the first race-based drug, to treat heart failure specifically in African-Americans. One theory supporting BiDil is that the reason for higher mortality rates among black heart patients lies in genetic differences among the races, either in the reason for getting heart disease or the reason for responding differently to various medications for it. BiDil's manufacturer discounts the importance of environmental factors in explaining differences in black and white patients' experience of heart disease to market a technological cure based on an asserted genetic difference. As law professor Jonathan Kahn (2004) has chronicled, the FDA's initial denial of approval to BiDil as a race-less drug led its creators to re-conceptualize it as a drug for blacks, enabling them not only to obtain the FDA's blessing, but also raise venture capital, receive a lucrative patent, and launch a successful marketing campaign.

At the same time, the neoliberal support for capital accumulation increasingly pervades the biotechnology industry. The initiative approved by California voters in November 2004, allocating $3 billion in tax-supported bonds to the biotechnology industry for stem cell research, illustrates the state's promotion of private investment in biotechnologies. The state-supported biotechnology industry creates a market for its genetic testing and selection products by making consumers feel obligated to use them to ensure the genetic fitness of their children.

Reprogenetics serves as a form of privatization that makes the individual the site of governance through the self-regulation of genetic risk. As Professor Mykitiuk writes:

> Is there a sense in which the new genetic technologies are being used, or are capable of being used, as a means of literally creating the responsible, autonomous, citizen of neoliberalism—that citizen who makes no legitimate claims on the state but rather, who freely exercises their capacity for choice and manages their own self care?
>
> (2000: 108)

The logic of reprogenetics could support the view that childhood illness and disability is the fault of mothers for not making the right genetic choices. Making the wrong genetic choices in turn disqualifies citizens from claiming public support. These women are, in effect, punished for their reproductive decision to have an ill or disabled child because they are denied the support they need to raise their child. In her book exploring the public consequences of private decisions about reproductive technologies, Lynda Beck Fenwick (1998: 113) asks readers to ask themselves, "Are you willing to pay higher taxes to cover costs of government benefits for babies born with genetic defects, even when the parents knew of the high likelihood or certainty such defects would occur?" As a result, the proliferation and promotion of new genetic technologies is inversely related to access to general health care.

Women bear the brunt of reprogenetics' contribution to the neoliberal restructuring of health care. Genetic technology introduces a new gendered division of reproductive labor and surveillance as women become "gatekeepers of new social order" (Mykitiuk 2000: 112) Professor Mykitiuk points out that, contrary to the deregulation that typically occurs in the service of big business, the new duties imposed on women constitute a "re-regulation intended to make possible the greater appropriation of intellectual property and its capitalization" (112).

Reprogenetics also makes eugenic thinking seem more acceptable. Sociologist Barbara Katz Rothman calls the marketing of prenatal diagnostic technologies a form of "micro-eugenics," eugenics focused on the individual (in contrast to macro-eugenics' focus on populations), that values or devalues specific characteristics believed to be inherited (2001). Some disabilities rights advocates object to preimplantation or fetal diagnoses that lead to discarding embryos and fetuses predicted to have disabilities because they devalue people who have these disabilities, implying that they should never have been born (Fenwick 1998). The quality of many disabled people's lives depends as much on social acceptance, access, and accommodation as on their physical capacities. Apart from avoiding certain fatal or severely disabling diseases, such as anencephaly or Tay-Sachs disease, reprogenetics inscribes the perceived social advantage of having or not having certain abilities or traits associated with genes. Selecting children's abilities or sex reflects the social advantages and disadvantages connected to these categories and may reinforce an unjust value system that privileges some over others. Unable to count on societal acceptance or support for children with disabilities, however, many women feel compelled to turn to genetic testing to ensure their children's welfare (Lippman 1991).

The role privileged women play in this integrated system of privatization and punishment is obscured by liberal notions of reproductive choice. Despite the potential for reprogenetics to diminish public health care and intensify regulation of women's reproductive decisions, its sponsors often defend the industry's immunity from state regulation in the name of women's reproductive freedom. Marsha Tyson Darling (2002) of the Center for African-American and Ethnic Studies at Adelphi University notes that "eugenic advocates have undertaken to infuse eugenics imperatives into the women's reproductive rights movement." They see women's ability to select the traits of their children as an aspect of reproductive choice. Concerns about the implications for women, people with disabilities, racial minorities, and other disadvantaged groups are dismissed as threats to reproductive freedom.

As I argued above, however, creating duties to use reprogenetic technologies in prescribed ways would limit women's choices. Just as important, the promotion of these technologies in the context of systemic inequalities and inadequate support for caregiving steers women to make reproductive decisions that reinforce social inequality. Thomas H. Murray (2002: 45) faults procreative liberty as the ethical framework for evaluating reproductive technology for its "difficulty summoning the ethical will to curb the indulgence of almost any parental whim." One important ethical curb on public policy as well as parental decisions that is elided by the singular focus on reproductive choice is the social harm risked by eugenic thinking.

Indeed, some clients of reprogenetics have even claimed moral superiority over women who have abortions for nonselective reasons. In an op-ed piece in the *New York Times*, Barbara Ehrenreich (2004: A21) called on women who aborted fetuses based on prenatal diagnosis to support the general right to abortion. She noted that these women sometimes distinguish themselves from women who have "ordinary" abortions. One woman who aborted a fetus with Down syndrome stated, "I don't look at it as though I had an abortion, even though that is technically what it is. There's a difference. I wanted this baby." On a website for a support group called "A Heart Breaking Choice" a mother who went to an abortion clinic complains, "I resented the fact that I had to be there with all these girls that did not want their babies" (Ehrenreich 2004: A21).

This perverse moral distinction between ordinary and so-called "medical abortion" reinforces the reproductive stratification that separates women whose childbearing is punished from those whose childbearing is technologically promoted by distinguishing even between the kinds of abortions they have. This classification of abortions is reminiscent of the historical distinction that states made between therapeutic or eugenic abortion and elective abortion. When abortion was criminalized in the United States during the second half of the nineteenth century, state laws made exceptions for cases in which pregnancy or childbirth threatened a woman's life or health (Schoen 2005). While abortions based on women's own decision not to have a child ("elective" abortions) were illegal, abortions based on physicians' judgments about the medical or social ills of pregnancy ("therapeutic" or "eugenic" abortions) were approved. Physicians' proposals for legislative reform prior to *Roe v. Wade* centered on the need for abortion to reduce either births of defective babies or births to women with psychiatric disorders. As historian Johanna Schoen (2005: 142) observes, "the debates surrounding abortion focused on specific medical conditions that might justify a therapeutic or eugenic abortion but remained hostile to elective abortion, which could extend reproductive control to women." The existence of a physical or mental impairment was more critical to the medical profession's defense of abortion than enhancing women's reproductive freedom.

States classified abortions as eugenic, therapeutic, or elective as a means of regulating women's access to them and limiting the potential of abortion to further women's emancipation. A contemporary woman who valorizes eugenic abortion while disparaging elective abortion resuscitates the nineteenth-century abortion hierarchy, a hierarchy that impedes women's reproductive self-determination. Barbara Katz Rothman (2001) distinguishes arguments for legal abortion based on "fetal defect" from feminist prochoice claims because they focus on the fetus and not on the woman. Because eugenic thinking can pressure women to abort a fetus deemed to be genetically inferior, Marsha Saxton (1998: 374) notes that the goal of the disability rights movement concerning abortion is "the right not to have to have an abortion." The incorporation of eugenic values in arguments for women's reproductive freedom neglects the history of abortion regulation as well as the potential for reprogenetics to impose restrictive expectations on women to serve as genetic screeners of children.

Conclusion

The women at opposite ends of the reproductive hierarchy are part of an interlocking system of privatization and punishment. Both the punishment of marginalized women's childbearing and the promotion of reprogenetics for privileged women place reproductive duties on women that help to privatize remedies for illness and social inequities. Instead of joining together to contest the social forces that limit their reproductive freedom, including inadequate health care and the gendered division of household labor, these women are further separated by the exclusive reprogenetics industry. Affluent women's access to high-tech solutions to infertility, disability, and illness can impede their motivation to pursue collective action against social inequities, including their own subordinated position in relation to men. The most privileged women's increasing reliance on high-tech reproductive remedies for socially caused problems thus obscures the role they share with the most disadvantaged women in the neoliberal shift from social welfare to privatization and capital accumulation. Both groups of women have an interest in halting this shift and in advocating for greater public investment in improving the social conditions that determine children's welfare.

Note

1 An earlier version of this chapter appeared as an article in volume 54 of the *Emory Law Journal* as part of the 2005 Thrower Symposium.

Chapter 10

A tale of two bodies

The male body and feminist legal theory

Michael Thomson

Introduction (or perhaps a tale of three bodies)

The male body has been strangely absent from feminist legal theory. In making this claim I distinguish concern with the male body from the established feminist interrogation of masculinity, particularly in legal theory and family law. Feminist work in the legal academy has engaged with a number of masculinities (Collier 2006). Much work has been done by feminists to understand the *masculinism* of law (Britten 1989), the *masculinity* of legal method and practice (Atkins and Hoggart 1984), and the different *men* that might populate specific areas of legal discourse and practice (Collier 1995). Whilst feminism, legal theory, and the "man question" may therefore be understood as an established nexus of enquiry, my focus here is on the male body. Specifically, I question why the male body has attracted little attention and, when it has, why the focus has been on that body's normative or "benchmark" status. In responding to this rather thin coverage, I make a case for moving beyond normativity and for feminist legal theory to engage more fully with an enfleshed and embodied male corporeality.

In arguing for a corporealization of the *man of feminism*, I am mindful of both the pitfalls and the possibilities of such a strategy. With perhaps a feminist optimism, I will start with what I see as the possibilities inherent in such a strategy. In recent work Martha Fineman (2008) has argued for a theoretical and political engagement with the concept of vulnerability. Notably, and developing from her work on the inevitability of dependence (Fineman 2005), Fineman argues that we need to conceptualize or recognize vulnerability as universal and constant. As a political project Fineman (2008: 8) asks us to "claim the term 'vulnerable' for its potential in describing a universal, inevitable, enduring aspect of the human condition that must be at the heart of our concept of social and state responsibility." In responding to this call I pick up on and recognize the connection between two aspects of Fineman's vulnerability thesis. First, I engage with the heuristic aspect of this project:

> the concept of vulnerability can act as a heuristic device, pulling us back to examine hidden assumptions and biases that shaped its original social and cultural meanings. Conceiving of vulnerability in this way renders

it valuable in constructing critical perspectives on political and societal institutions, including law.

(Fineman 2008: 9)

Second, Fineman recognizes that "[v]ulnerability initially should be understood as arising from our embodiment which carries with it the ever-present possibility of harm, injury, and misfortune" (9). In aligning these two aspects I interrogate two related ideas. Responding to the call to examine hidden assumptions and biases, I aim to explore the political effects of the social or discursive construction of (gendered) bodies as in/vulnerable. The male body is often constructed as bounded (or impermeable) and invulnerable, with the female body constructed in opposition to this. Moving on from this, both in terms of the argument I wish to make in this chapter and in my own move from work on the male body's normativity, I argue for a move to function, flesh, and fluids—a move from challenging the imaginary "benchmark" body to a greater understanding of the lived male body. Thus, I look to, and try to move forward, my own recent work with Marie Fox which has considered the law and ethics of non-therapeutic infant male genital cutting. Here I wish to foreground the vulnerability of the infant male body and its natural functioning, issues often absent or erased from circumcision discourses.

Potential pitfalls arise from the problem of talking about men and masculinity at this political moment. In his analysis of feminist or pro-feminist family law scholarship that has addressed the "man question," Richard Collier (2006: 236) expresses a hesitancy in talking about men and masculinity at a cultural moment when we are seeing the rise, and probable entrenchment, of what can be termed "male victimhood." Whilst Collier is talking specifically about developments in the field of family justice, I share his concern. Arguably there is a need for greater caution or circumspection when addressing male bodies, particularly the lived, vulnerable male body. In my conclusion I question the political consequences of such a project and suggest that the feminist gains may well outweigh the risks.

The invitation to contribute to this collection included an invitation to autobiography. And my acceptance of this challenge is, I hope, suggested in my alternative title to this introduction; there is a third body. Martha Fineman invited us to elaborate on what our own journeys have been within these projects. So, I'm going to locate my own work within this consideration of the male body in feminist legal theory. This positioning has two effects on the shape of what is to come. First, it necessarily means that the sources I am working with— which in part are markers of my academic journey—may be partial and incomplete. Second, in looking back I'm encouraged to look forward.

Autobiography (two of the three bodies)

Human Beings are neither minds nor, strictly speaking bodies ... but rather mindful and embodied social agents.

(Crossley 2001: 2–3)

I started my doctoral studies and academic career like many feminist health care lawyers with a focus on women's reproductive rights. Working in a traditional British red-brick university law school, it was originally suggested that my supervisor be the school's legal historian. He had an interest in dangerous animals, particularly badgers. After this hiccough, and after being assigned to a family and medical lawyer who has had an enduring impact on my academic work, my work resided in the reproductive ghetto, that is those substantive areas of focus (at that time) for most feminist health care lawyers. Abortion, reproductive technologies, court-ordered Cesarean sections, occupational reproductive hazards, and prosecutions for maternal prenatal behavior became the focus of my research. During this time, I delivered my first paper on the subject of fetal protection policies at a conference at the University of Manchester and received a hostile reception from an older female legal academic. She was later heard describing me as "One of those men who talk about women and can never get pregnant!" Interestingly, the hostility I experienced was, I believe, hostility to feminist analysis. This hostility was understood to be more palatable if it was refashioned as a dismissal of my work as coming from someone who was not a member of the sisterhood that she otherwise shunned. In a sense this was an experience of being a male body in feminist legal studies. With less hostility, and coming from a quite different political position, I can often read an opening hesitancy in an audience where the expectation seems to be that I will come from a father's rights, men's group, or backlash position. Again, a male body in feminist legal studies.

More recently, my work continues to occupy the terrain where health care law and feminist legal studies intersect but has shifted focus to engage with inter-disciplinary work on masculinities and health. Most recently, I have been exploring the relationship between the legal regulation of the male body in health care and ideas of masculinity (Thomson 2008). My shift to concentrate on the carnality of this body—its flesh, fluids, and processes—can perhaps be best described as part of the emergence of *legal embodiment* as an area of study (Fletcher et al. 2008). This work speaks to the wider sociological recognition that bodies are both socially constituted and material; the body operates at the intersection of discourses, institutions, and corporeality (Williams and Bendelow 1999). In this, law must be recognized as a privileged discourse and institution with particular reach and effect. As Naffine and Owens write:

> law helps to constitute and organize our very sense of the nature and activities of the body. It shapes our understanding of the body, obliging us to think of bodies in certain ways, and not in others.
>
> (Naffine and Owens 1997: 84)

Notwithstanding the shifts in my work, there has been a constant focus on technologies of the sexed and gendered body, both medical and (more directly) cultural (Thomson 2008). Within this focus, there has been an acceptance of the idea that understanding the sexed body (its physiology, structures, and processes) can only be understood in the context of gender and gender relations (Laqueur 1990). That is to say, medical/discursive technologies which address and possess the sexed body are understandable only in the context of historically specific understandings of gender (Bourdieu 2001). Finally, and opening myself up to charges of promiscuity—of being rather cavalier with my analytical tools—I have considered the bodies of the legal imagination. This emphasis can alternatively be understood as a project which seeks to *enflesh* law's imaginary anatomies but should not suggest a disregard for the material or corporeal.

A tale of two bodies

Whilst the male body has largely evaded capture within feminist legal theory, exploring masculinities has been a fertile area of enquiry. Early or first-phase feminist legal theory was often concerned with the masculinism or masculinity of legal institutions, processes, and practices. Here the claim was, in part, that there was "a persistent benchmarking and assessment of women against a normative, ideal 'benchmark' figure" (Collier 2006: 239). This benchmark "man of law" was understood as embodying a particular (authoritative, rational, unemotional, and so forth) masculinity (Atkins and Hoggart 1984). Second-phase feminist scholarship, to an extent, disembodied or dematerialized this masculinity. It became more centered on a critique of the masculine nature of law (West 1988), "one based, in contrast, on a critique of the masculine nature of legal methods and legal reasoning itself" (Collier 2000: 238).

The influence of post-modernism and post-structuralism throughout legal scholarship allowed third phase feminism to recognize not only a multiplicity of female experiences and subject positions—toppling over the (rather narrowly defined and totemic) "Woman" of much feminist thought—but it also reconsidered the *man of feminism*. Recognizing this creature as similarly heterogeneous, third-phase feminist legal theory argued against an essentialism in understanding men and women and moved us away from an attachment to the notion of a singular (oppressive) "masculinity of law" (Collier 2006: 238). Rather, women's experience of law was recognized as a result of the significant overlaps in the way both law and masculinity are constituted in discourse (Collier 2006: 239). Responding to this discursive turn and—as an earlier contributor to this volume has previously argued—in an attempt to move the lens away from women as *the problem* and from their ongoing objectification (Thornton 2004), feminist legal theory began to explore the context specific narration of particular masculinities—or perceived masculine traits—within individualized legal texts and practices (Collier 1995).

If there were corporeal or carnal preoccupations during this time, it was with women's reproductive bodies, rights, and interests. And this, of course, is understandable in the context of earlier and ongoing political struggles. The narrowness of this feminist "gaze" is understandable not only in the context of struggles to reorder the social order's understanding of women's reproductive bodies but also in the context of the place of that reproductive body in the broader project of social organization. And here it seems appropriate to quote R. W. Connell (1995) who has had such a profound impact on masculinities studies. Connell concisely observes that gender is "a way in which social practice is ordered," and continues:

> In gendering processes, the everyday conduct of life is organized in relation to a reproductive arena, defined by the bodily structures and processes of human reproduction. This arena includes sexual arousal and intercourse, childbirth and infant care, [and] bodily sex differences.
>
> (Connell 1995: 154)

But why when we recognize the place of reproduction *per se* in the ordering of social relations is it primarily the female reproductive body that has engaged feminist legal scholarship? And why the reproductive body when what we know—perhaps instinctively or physically—is that it is *the* body in its entirety that is sexed/gendered and not just the reproductive body?

The social construction of in/vulnerability

> The technique is to focus on a concept or term in common use, but also grossly under-theorized, and thus ambiguous. Even when a term is laden with negative associations, the ambiguity provides an opportunity to begin to explore and excavate the unarticulated and complex relationships inherent but latent in the term.
>
> (Fineman 2008: 9)

Whilst feminist legal theory—particularly in the health care context—has understandably mapped and remapped the reproductive ghetto, a number of feminists have embraced, explored, prodded, and picked at the male body. As Judy Grbich (1991: 69) argued in *At the Boundaries of Law*, we must explore "the ways in which legal reasoning transforms the embodied imaginings from male lives into the 'objective' form of doctrine which passes for the normative." Whilst Grbich is asking for a challenge to legal method and its masculinity/ism, it is notable that much of the work in feminist legal theory that has engaged with the male body has been in the context of the normativity of the imagined heterosexual male body. Feminist scholars have done much work to trace the effects of this body's axiomatic, normative, or benchmark position; its place as the referent for public policy and law. In these terms, and as Catherine Waldby (1995: 268) notes, the male body is frequently understood as "phallic and impenetrable." It is the bounded and safe body of the liberal individual, public policy, and law. Other bodies—permeable or penetrated—fall out with (and allow) the privileging of this hermetic imaginary body. As such, women's bodies are seen to lack integrity; they are socially constructed as partial, dependent, and lacking (Waldby 1995). Collier details the effects of these constructions and their interrelatedness:

> Th[e] masculine subject ... has been seen, in a number of respects, as a distinctively "embodied" being. Thus ... whilst the penis frequently appears within law as somehow the subject of man's rational thought and control, the vagina in contrast, has been presented as a space, as an always search-able absence. Related assumptions have been noted around the idea of there being a natural (hetero)sexual "fit" between the bodies of women and men, with notions of male (hetero)sexual activity and female passivity informing the [law].
>
> (Collier 1995: 241)

The construction of the female body as lacking integrity or completeness is also associated with dangerousness, disease and pollution (Sheldon 1999). This discursive relationship is also seen in terms of trans bodies and identities. So the male body has become an object of study in our pursuit of a better under-standing of the discursive technologies shaping our narration and construction of female and other bodies. And here it is worth turning to the heuristic element of Fineman's vulnerability project. As already noted, positioning vulnerability as a heuristic device allows us to "examine hidden assumptions and biases that shaped its original social and cultural meanings" (Fineman 2008: 9). In picking this device up here, I briefly explore the gendered construction of in/vulnerability. In focusing on gender in this analysis I do not want to suggest that in/vulnerability is not also marked along other axis, for instance those of race and class.

The construction of the hegemonic male body as invulnerable and the dis-missal or denial of bodily risks has become the hallmark of masculine status (Daniels 1997). But this cannot be disaggregated from the construction of the female body. As Cynthia Daniels notes, notions of masculinity have historically been associated with "the denial of men's physical vulnerabilities and bodily needs and the projection of these characteristics onto the maternal" (582). Recognizing the gendered construction of the in/vulnerable body and the interrelatedness of these bodily understandings allows us to challenge the systems of social organization that rely on the oppositional construction of these bodies. This is particularly the case if we accept Fineman's understanding of vulner-ability as both arising from our embodiment and as universal and constant.

A number of academics have provided a (sometimes indirect) recognition of the negative impact on some men's lived experience of their bodies which results from the social construction of the male body as bounded and invulnerable. Cynthia Daniels' observations (1997) arise from her work on male reproductive hazards and the asymmetry in our responses to gendered reproductive risks. In these instances it is clear that some men—their reproductive and other health interests, partners and any offspring—are potentially harmed by an understanding of the male body as bounded and safe and any risk projected onto the female body which is frequently constructed as the only potential vector for harm (Thomson 2007). As such, whilst Daniels' observations point to the medicalization and social regulation of the maternal body, they also provide recognition of the costs borne (at times) by the male body. More generally, Daniels' observations can feed into a broader consideration of gender and health, health promoting activities, and differences in risk taking behaviors (Courtenay 2000).

The effects on embodied masculinities have also been foregrounded by queer theoretical work that has been shaped by HIV/AIDS and the particular male body with HIV/AIDS that dominated the media in the early years of the health crisis. This work has helped us to engage with the heterosexuality of the normative male body and the effects on other masculinities. As Kane Race details in the helpful context of a broader appraisal of the masculine body and health:

> The biomedical ethics of the human subject continually conflates, defines, and privileges masculinity and the phallic body ... Within this framework, the terms "health" and "masculinity" become isomorphic. Health is understood as the ability of the body to arm itself against the world. In this respect, the female body (and the receptive male body) occupy a uniquely precarious position in modern times. The conditions of receptivity, passivity, and permeability read like an epithet for disease or disintegration.
>
> (Race 1997: 47)

Finally in the context of work that has dealt with the normative male body, I consider the contribution of Moira Gatens (1996). Her reflection on representations in and of the body politic details how the modern body politic is based on the masculine body. She describes how since the seventeenth century the masculine body has been both metaphor and metonym for the body politic. Gatens explores the limitations and violence caused when our political body is isomorphic with the masculine body. She argues that in philosophy and political theory the metaphorical use of the male body slides into metonymy, where the male body is not merely representational/heuristic but becomes that which represents all bodies and as such—perhaps circularly—is the only body represented by the body politic. So the move from metaphor to metonym affects "whose body it is that is entitled to be represented by this political corporation" (Gatens 1996: 21). This technology of exclusion affects those whose bodily specificity marks them as inappropriate analogues to the political body as this political body becomes *the* social body (Gatens 1996). And it is clear that this imagined body influences, perhaps even determines, how we manage bodies, both corporeal and social. And here I want to move back to consider the observations of Cynthia Daniels. In doing so, the thought is to marry Gatens' observations about the need for social bodies to be analogues with the masculine body and Daniels' observations about risk. The risks to which Daniels (1997) refers are primarily the risks of warfare and employment. These are routinely denied or downplayed. As Gatens notes, since ancient Greece, willingness to bodily sacrifice has been one side of a covenant that affords men fuller participation in the body politic:

> Certainly, not any human form, by virtue of its humanity, is entitled to consider itself author of or actor in the body politic. From its classical articulation in Greek philosophy, only a body deemed capable of reason and sacrifice can be admitted into the political body as an active member. Such admission always involves *forfeit*. From the original covenant between God and Abraham—which involved the forfeit of his very flesh, his foreskin—corporeal sacrifice has been a constant feature of the compact. Even the Amazons, the only female body politic that we "know" of, practiced ritual mastectomy.
>
> (Gatens 1996: 23)

An agenda beyond normativity

In feminist theory (legal and otherwise) understandings of the male body have largely followed an agenda that has sought to reveal the effects of this body's normativity. In this final section, I argue that there is a need for feminism to address the male body beyond its effects as *the* public body. I argue this in part as a challenge to our currently impoverished public discourses about the male body, an impoverishment that challenges or contradicts a number of core feminist values. In arguing this I deploy a rather *entry level* understanding of Catherine Waldby's articulation of Lacan's "imaginary anatomy":

> The particular "imaginary anatomy" of each subject is generated in relation both to its love objects, those whom it desires, and to socially generated "imaginary anatomies", to ideas about bodies which circulate in the culture.
>
> (Waldby 1995: 268)

Just as feminist work that has focused on the female reproductive body might have contributed to the degree to which the legal woman has been yoked to her over-determined body, so the focus on the normative phallic body may have acted to further entrench the normativity of this fictive physiology. Further, failure to challenge, unpack, or enflesh this normative body impoverishes conceptions of the masculine body that circulate in legal and other cultures. Arguably, this failure contributes towards the stifling of those imaginary anatomies that are available to individuals.

To flesh this out in a quite limited way I refer to the limitations imposed on my own work by a focus on this normative body. Here I make reference to a companion pair of papers from an extended project conducted with my colleague Marie Fox. This project looks at the practice and regulation of non-therapeutic male genital cutting. Given the focus of this collection it is worthwhile noting as an aside that I began working on this project whilst a Feminism and Legal Theory visitor at Cornell University in the very cold winter of 2004. The two papers I refer to here—"Sexing the Cherry: Fixing Masculinity" (Fox and Thomson 2009) and "Foreskin is a Feminist Issue" (Fox and Thomson 2009)—argue that rather than a non-issue or a politically difficult distraction from work on female genital cutting, circumcision is in fact a practice that should concern feminist scholars and activists. The papers argue that the current status of public discourse around circumcision obfuscates the role that male genital cutting has in gendering bodies and in affirming patriarchal norms. Further, in the papers (and elsewhere) we argue that the practice of male genital cutting conflicts with feminist equality objectives and commitments to values such as bodily integrity and self-determination.

One of the main arguments in "Sexing the Cherry" is that circumcision—particularly in the US—is an invasive procedure that is generally unproblematized and accepted because the cut body is in line with the normative phallic body. We argue that the foreskin is feminized; characterized as a permeable and dangerous interior space. Arguments regarding hygiene and sexually transmitted diseases have been the most enduring in the pro-cutting armory (Howe 1999). The persistence of male circumcision (following its routinization in the 1880s–1890s) can be understood in its role in distinguishing male from female and how this tapped into myths of female disease, contagion, and uncleanliness. On this reading the foreskin provides an inner sensitized world that appears incompatible with—and disrupts the aesthetic of—the phallic body; the culturally privileged model of masculine embodiment (Race 1997). The uncircumcised penis with its inner dimensions and permeability are at odds with this ideal masculine aesthetic. Further exploring the significance of this phallic ideal in explaining the persistence of circumcision, we turn to this imaginary ideal in the context of Gatens' analysis of the body politic. Actions to *perfect* the infant male body are understood in terms of how it allows the infant body to be aligned with the phallic ideal of the social and political body. To put it another way, the infant male body is cut in order to meet a normative ideal that structures expectations of both male physiology and the body politic.

As I look back on this work, and indeed on the series of papers that we have published to date on this issue, I begin to wonder where the lived body has been. Whilst we have been mindful to note the potentially significant adverse side effects that can result from the procedure (albeit that the risk of serious harm is minimal, the procedure can result in hemorrhage, scarring, partial or full amputation, and death) we have been careful not to overstate this aspect of our concern with the current legal and social responses to the procedure. At the same time, we have highlighted the very prevalent tendency to minimize the risks involved, and we would not want to undermine or erase the very real harm that the procedure can and does do to men (Fox and Thomson 2005a). And here the vulnerability of men's bodies (and their sexual and reproductive interests) can be foregrounded. If we look at the near blanket prohibition on the genital cutting of female children in most Western countries we do need to question the gendered construction of in/vulnerability. This point is underscored when it is recognized that male genital cutting often takes place without anesthetic (Waldeck 2002) and in light of this regulatory bodies still feel the need to remind medics of the necessity for effective pain relief (General Medical Council 2008). It is also notable that non-therapeutic male genital cutting is seen as an appropriate procedure through which to study neonatal pain (Lehr et al. 2007). It is inconceivable that a research ethics committee would approve such pain experiments if they were relying on female genital cutting to cause the pain to be studied. Further, in experiments to determine the effectiveness of pain relief measures for neonatal circumcision, Van Howe and Svoboda (2008) have argued that the use of placebo-controlled trials fail to meet the ethical requirements of the Helsinki Declaration which is the universally accepted standard for ethical behavior in research involving human subjects. As we have argued elsewhere, this response to the pain of male genital cutting can be understood as a product of our understanding of masculinity and the male body (Fox and Thomson 2005b).

The pain experienced by the neonate and the (minimal) risks of potentially catastrophic harm that are inherent and often ignored provide an opportunity to discuss the vulnerability of the male body. This vulnerability is arguably cloaked by our conceptions of the masculine body as invulnerable and bounded. And clearly this has an effect on how we constitute female (and trans) bodies and how we treat infant (and adult) male bodies. Accepting this as a site of vulnerability, what I want to nevertheless focus on is a less dramatic and vivid vulnerability. Here I draw attention to the vulnerability of the male body by briefly discussing male genital cutting, the foreskin, and function. In part this recognizes that in our research to date we have failed to attend to the everyday effects of male genital cutting. That is to say, turning to (physiological) function at this point brings the lived body more directly into our scholarship and contributes to a dialogue about our universal and constant vulnerability. In this I am perhaps looking forward and sketching out the next part of our project.

In October 2008 at the University of Gottingen at an international conference on the rights of children in medicine, our presentation on circumcision and the rights of older minors provoked a lot of commentary and questions. An exchange between a pediatrician and a mother of a circumcised boy (she had described holding her son as the procedure was carried out and how natural it had seemed—although she also noted how her husband had hidden upstairs in the bedroom furthest from the mother and child) ended abruptly when the pediatrician had said with the absolute conviction common to clinicians of a certain age, "It's mutilation. The tissue is functional." Whilst we have deliberately avoided using the term mutilation (in referring to both female and male genital-cutting practices), I was struck by how succinct and contained his explanation of his opposition to the procedure was. His opposition was on the basis of the child's properly (physiologically) functioning body; the foreskin's functional, sexological role.

The pediatrician's focus on function is helpful. As well as the erasure of risk in much pro-circumcision discourse, the physiological functions of the foreskin are ignored or erased so that the cultural functions can be constructed as sufficient to legitimate it as an unfettered parental choice.

It is notable that whilst our work has attempted to encourage an informed debate around male genital cutting and in that has recognized the importance and the significant history of male genital cutting to some groups, our attempts to also recognize issues such as harm, bodily integrity, children's rights, sexuality, choice, and consent have been seen as failing to recognize sufficiently the cultural function of male genital cutting. It is notable that some of this reaction has been from feminists who in other contexts would recognize bodily integrity, sexuality, choice, consent, and so forth as key feminist objectives. As regards to our continued work on this practice, in talking about function in terms of physiology I am again not dismissing the cultural function of male genital cut-ting. Rather, I am adding physiology and sexual functioning to the factors that need to be considered when we engage in a rounded and informed cost–benefit analysis of the subject which must also take into account cultural benefits and purported health benefits. Further, in highlighting the vulnerability of the infant male body and proper sexual functioning, I aim to further complicate and examine the cultural assumptions that frequently allow circumcision to be con-structed in a rather unquestioning way.

As I've noted, the exchange between the mother and the pediatrician ended abruptly, so I was not able to gauge how wide the doctor's definition of "functional" was. Was he referring only to the mechanical aspects whereby the tissue of the foreskin has a role in the mechanism of erection and allows proper movement during penetrative sex acts? Or was it functional in terms of the erogenous nature of the tissue and how it maintains the sensitivity of the head of the penis (sensitivity lost following circumcision)? Although it is unlikely, he might also (at a stretch) have been referring to the function that the foreskin can have in sex acts that are denied when this tissue is excised? Regardless of the width of his meaning, it is clear that the pediatrician was motivated by an understanding of the normal functioning of the intact penis. And in this it is perhaps enough to state bluntly that the foreskin may be characterized as "primary, erogenous tissue necessary for normal sexual functioning" (Cold and Taylor 1999: 41). Whilst serious adverse health consequences are rare, more minor adverse effects and indeed lifelong impaired sexual functioning are less rare (Cold and Taylor 1999).

In mentioning these issues in a few lines, I am asking two related sets of questions. My first set looks to the work that Marie Fox and I have done so far on this issue. Why have we been inattentive to the infant's future embodiment and embodied choices, his right to the erogenous tissue that he was born with, the right of an individual to enjoy the sexual possibilities of their "natural" body unfettered by the non-consensual actions of others? And further, in asking this, does it have greater purchase than our arguments regarding normativity? Does flesh count for more? Does this embodied argument trump just for the pediatrician of a certain age?

But here and now and looking forward, what can these practices and our critical engagement with them contribute to a wider project which seeks to reinvigorate thoughts of social justice through recognizing and theorizing our vulnerability? One aspect of an answer to this final question is to recognize how articulating and exploring the vulnerability of the male body moves us beyond normativity. It helps us to challenge a bodily ideal that is the foundation to much inequality.

Conclusions

This contribution set out to provide a tale of two bodies. It sought to engage with the place of the male body in feminist legal theory. In this effort, it detailed the focus of feminist work which has primarily explored the male body in its normativity; that is the extent to which a particular imagining of the masculine body provides the benchmark public body against which other bodies are measured, problematized, and excluded. Whilst not wanting to diminish the importance of this work and recognizing my own focus on this imaginary anatomy, this chapter has argued for a turn to flesh and fluids. It has argued for a more prominent place for the lived male body within feminist legal theory.

In arguing for an agenda beyond normativity, I have attempted to align this chapter with a broader project which seeks to renegotiate social relations and relations with the state through an exploration of our shared vulnerability. Moving away from a focus on the phallic body to bodies that are flesh and fluid—and as such vulnerable—allows us to potentially do a number of things. As detailed in the final section, looking to the vulnerability of the neonatal male body may allow us to argue more successfully for the protection of minors from genital-cutting practices. This is particularly the case when we foreground the vulnerability of normal sexual functioning and the pain and possible complications associated with this practice. As such, understanding the vulnerable (neonatal) subject may encourage a more responsive state. The focus on the vulnerable male infant also allows us to question the place of pain in the construction of masculinity and in our treatment of male children. And this leads us to the most ambitious possibility. A turn to flesh and fluids has the potential to rewrite the invulnerable male body and to suggest a reordering of our gendered construction of bodies as in/vulnerable. As Naffine (1997: 88) convincingly states, against the bounded normative male body, female bodies are constructed and regulated as "non standard or aberrant (not-male) bodies." Social relations and relations with the state are ordered around our understandings of these bodies. Enfleshing the male body of feminist legal theory, and in this process, recognizing male vulnerability may allow us to renegotiate social relations.

As such, there are considerable potential gains from the turn to male flesh and fluids that I am suggesting. In the introduction I noted that there were also potential pitfalls. Specifically, I noted that I shared Collier's hesitancy about talking about men and masculinities at this political moment, one that is seeing an entrenchment of male victimhood. Talking about men's embodied vulnerability can clearly contribute to such damaging discourses, particularly those that are anti-feminist. Yet, it is arguable that revealing male bodily vulnerabilities will provide sites where tensions and antagonisms can be resolved or at least addressed. It is clear, for example, that the asymmetry in regulatory responses to male and female genital cutting fuels an at times anti-feminist discourse from child protection and genital autonomy advocates (Farrell et al. 2008). Although I am not arguing for the criminalization of male genital cutting, a more informed response that recognized the harms done to men's embodied interests would address some of these concerns.

Whilst there is the potential for such a strategy to feed into anti-feminist backlash or victimhood discourses, it is nevertheless likely that the potential benefits outweigh these possible pitfalls. Whilst I have outlined some ambitious possibilities, talking about male embodied vulnerability will at the very least contribute to a political project which may allow us to "develop more complex subjects[s] around which to build social policy and law" (Fineman 2008: 1).

Engaging universals and engaging identities

Introduction to Section Four

The authors in this section bring feminist legal theory to basic questions of what it means to be human and how we define ourselves in relation to others. The question of identity has become increasingly controversial: some people argue that identity politics leads to counterproductive essentialism, and others maintain that identity categories are useful tools for social change. Likewise, universalizing theories have been critiqued for paying too little attention to difference, and defended as the only basis for workable ethics. The authors in this section discuss these controversies within the context of feminist legal theory.

My chapter offers the vulnerable subject as a new conception of subjectivity to replace the widely critiqued liberal subject. Vulnerability is universal to the human condition—we all get ill, injured, and eventually die. Whereas the autonomous liberal subject is expected to take care of him or herself, the vulnerable subject is understood as often, if not always, dependent on others. Because vulnerability is universal rather than specific to certain groups, it compels a more responsive state to provide everyone with the assets necessary for resilience. I argue that a vulnerability approach is more conducive to social justice than an identity-based discrimination model.

Darren Hutchinson takes a different track, challenging the idea that we are in a post-racial and post-feminist era. He uses the 2008 Democratic presidential campaign and Barack Obama's election to launch an inquiry into the continuing usefulness of identity politics. Hutchinson contends that race and gender are still important axes of discrimination. He argues that it is "dangerous and misleading" to buy into the view that we live in a post-racial or post-gender America, pointing out that nearly all sociological data draw strong links between race–sex and poverty and highlighting the continued importance of identity categories to political mobilization.

Hutchinson acknowledges the certain pitfalls associated with identity politics, such as a tendency to essentialize identity, but argues that postmodern critiques of identity provide the tools necessary to create a multidimensional approach to identity-based inequalities. According to Hutchinson, identity politics, combined with an understanding of the contingent nature of identity and its "multidimensionality," continues to be a powerful tool in working toward economic, racial, and sexual justice. Using feminist and critical race theory, liberals should work to overcome the pitfalls of identity politics rather than abandon them altogether.

Siobhán Mullaly examines the "politics of belonging," specifically in the French *Mme M* case, which involved denial of French citizenship to a Moroccan woman based on her religious practices. The case demonstrates that citizenship determinations "demarcate" insiders from outsiders and that the feminist rhetoric of gender equity is being used to forward such demarcation. Along with *Mme M*, various European headscarf cases have pitted citizenship against cultural difference, inviting feminists to question how the norms of equality and autonomy are played out. Mullally wants to use the tools of Fineman's vulnerability analysis to "interrogate the structures, concepts, and institutions that further inclusion and exclusion."

As evidenced in the recent cases, some countries are demonstrating a greater concern with "social cohesion" than "multicultural settlement." Thus, Mullally ends her chapter calling for a "dual-track approach" to citizenship and difference. She argues for a politics of multiculturalism that "combine[s] legal regulation with an expanded moral dialogue."

While legal regulation (protecting certain "constitutional essentials") is often necessary, Mullally maintains everyone has a right to participate. She suggests that antiracist and feminist theories which start from a presumption of difference, and have been instrumental in challenging the liberal feminist notion of an abject "third world woman," could help negotiate the challenge of "universality, equality, difference."

Chapter 11

The vulnerable subject*

Anchoring equality in the human condition

Martha Albertson Fineman

In this chapter I develop the concept of vulnerability in order to argue for a more responsive state and a more egalitarian society. I argue that vulnerability is universal and constant, inherent in the human condition. The vulnerability approach I propose is an alternative to traditional equal protection analysis; it moves us beyond identity-based inquiries because it focuses not only on discrimination against defined groups, but is concerned with the privileges conferred on limited segments of the population by the state through its institutions. Therefore, vulnerability analyses concentrate on our social structures and institutions established to manage our common vulnerabilities. This approach has the potential to move us beyond the confines of current discrimination-based models toward a more substantive vision of equality.

Theorizing a concept of vulnerability necessitates developing a more complex subject around which to build social policy and law; this new subject is useful in redefining and expanding current ideas about state responsibility toward individuals and institutions. In fact, I argue that the "vulnerable subject" must replace the autonomous and independent subject asserted in the liberal tradition. Far more representative of actual lived experience and the human condition, the vulnerable subject should be at the center of our political and theoretical endeavors. The vision of the state that would emerge in such an engagement would be more responsive to and responsible for the vulnerable subject, a reimagining that is essential to attaining a more equal society than currently exists in America.

Before developing the vulnerability thesis, I will address some conceptual impediments to the idea of a more responsive state. First, an impoverished sense of equality is embedded in our current legal doctrine. We understand equality in formal terms, focused on discrimination and inattentive to underlying societal inequities. Second, the view that the state's proper role is one of restraint and abstention is politically powerful. Even self-identified progressive social reformers are suspicious of the state; the rhetoric of non-intervention prevails in policy discussions, deterring positive measures designed to address inequalities. We idealize contract and correspondingly reify individual choice in ways that mask society's role in perpetuating inequality. The fact that societal institutions play a significant role in perpetrating inequality is the very reason that we need a more active and responsive state.

The limits of formal equality

For centuries, the concept of "equality" in Western thought has been associated with John Locke's philosophy of liberal individualism (and the creation of the liberal subject). "Equality" in the liberal model is the expression of the idea that all human beings are by nature free and endowed with the same inalienable rights. Although this vision of equality has inherent radical potential, in present-day America we understand "equality" narrowly as a formal anti-discrimination mandate, requiring sameness of treatment and primarily enforced through the courts. We know the protected categories under equal protection doctrine: race, sex, religion, national origin, etc. These classifications define individual legal identities and form the only axis around which claims for equal protection from the state can be made. This system of identity categories defines the organization of interest groups. These categories ultimately define the content and direction of American law.

Our understanding of equality, shaped in part by the twentieth-century history of using equal protection doctrine to fight blatant forms of discrimination, focuses on race, sex, and ethnicity. Feminist legal reformers during the latter part of the century were suspicious of any difference in treatment, even if it was designed to favor women. They demanded formal equality and rejected any "special" consideration because, in their experience, any classification based on asserted gender differences led to exclusion and subordination.

Reduced to sameness of treatment, "equality" is an inadequate tool to resist or upset persistent forms of subordination and domination. This version of equality is similarly weak in its ability to address and correct the disparities in economic and social well-being among various groups in American society where we have a growing list of material and social inequalities. We have no guarantee of basic social goods such as food, housing, and health care, and we have a network of dominant economic and political systems that tolerate and justify grossly unequal distributions of wealth, power, and opportunity. The sameness of treatment version of equality has proven resilient in the face of arguments for a more substantive, result-oriented concept of equality that takes into account past circumstances and future obligations, need, and disadvantage. Moreover, sameness of treatment has been used to argue effectively against measures like affirmative action that might generate remedies for past inequities.

The sameness of treatment model is limited in several important ways. First, it is under-inclusive. While it might be successful in addressing some situations of discrimination, it fails to protect against others, particularly discrimination on the basis of categories not receiving heightened judicial scrutiny, such as disability. Formal equality also leaves undisturbed existing institutional arrangements that privilege some and disadvantage others. It does not provide a framework for challenging existing allocations of resources and power. Unless there is some distortion introduced by impermissible bias, under the sameness of treatment model, the state should not intervene or interfere with the free market, the private individual, or the family. Thus, this model fails to account for existing inequality of circumstances.

From a political and policy perspective, the current model of equality is limited as an anti-discrimination principle; its protections do not extend to everyone. Politically, this limitedness is problematic because it can and has resulted in significant backlash. Even more significantly, the goal of confronting discrimination against certain groups has largely eclipsed the goal of eliminating material, social, and political inequalities that exist across groups. Thus, identity categories are both over- and under-inclusive. While discrimination does exist and personal characteristics can complicate any individual's experience of vulnerability, discrimination models based on identity characteristics will not produce circumstances of greater equality and may lead to less in some cases. The groups that traditional equal protection analyses recognize include some relatively privileged individuals, notwithstanding their membership in these identity groups. At the same time, disadvantage is not limited to certain groups: poverty, denial of dignity, and deprivation of basic social goods are "lack-of-opportunity categories" that the current framework does not recognize.

While race or gender may complicate and compound disadvantage, individual successes abound across these and other categories that the Equal Protection Clause demarcates. These individual successes create both theoretical and empirical pitfalls: successful individuals who belong to a suspect class can undermine the coherence and dilute the strength of critical analyses based on asserted bias against the same identity group.

The sameness of treatment framework tends to focus on individuals and individual actions, identifying the victims and the perpetuators of discrimination and defining the prohibited activities, the individual injury, and the specific intent involved in each occurrence. Systemic aspects of existing societal arrangements are left out of the picture. Existing material, cultural, and social imbalances appear to be the product of natural forces, beyond the law's ability to rectify. While it may be beyond the *will* of the law to alter, existing inequalities are not natural. They are produced and reproduced by society and its institutions. Yet inequalities and the systems that produce them are not inevitable; they can be objects of reform.

The restrained state

In American legal culture, the idea of privacy acts as a principle of restraint and abstention. We are accustomed to the assertion that it is appropriate to create barriers to keep the state out of our institutions and activities. This veneration of state non-intervention is a second major impediment to reforms intent on instituting a state that is more responsive to inequalities.

Privacy is often expressed in terms of separate spheres ideology, with the state cast as the quintessential public entity and the family cast as essentially private in its relationship with both market and state. By contrast, while the market is cast as public vis-à-vis the family, it is private when paired with the state. Current conceptions of privacy place some things and institutions presumptively beyond state regulation and control. The idea of family privacy "protects" the family and other intimate entities from state interference, while individual privacy shields certain intimate decisions from state control. Economic institutions (such as corporations) and commercial practices (like those governing wealth accumulation and distribution) are shielded by the black box of the free market as constructed in late-American capitalism.

Contributing to the sense of state restraint is the recently fashionable tendency to talk about the irrelevance—or "withering away"—of the modern state, suggesting that one effect of globalization is replacement of the state by multinational corporations; trade arrangements and treaties spanning traditional geographic boundaries render the state relatively impotent.

I propose a different interpretation. The state is not withering away but has withdrawn or been prevented by entrenched interests from fulfilling one of its traditional roles in the social compact: to act as the principal monitor or guarantor of an equal society. Nonintervention has facilitated a skewed and unequal society; thus, some form of prevailing power is essential to counter unfettered self-interest. Understood historically as the manifestation of public authority and the ultimate legitimate repository of coercive power, the state is the only realistic contender in that regard. The "state" referred to in this analysis is not necessarily the nation-state but rather an organized and official set of linked institutions, legitimated by a claim to public authority, that hold coercive power, including the ability to make and enforce mandatory legal rules. The "state" could be locally, nationally, transnationally, or internationally organized. One issue for those interested in furthering a new vision of equality must be how to modernize this conception of the state and explicitly define its appropriate relationship to institutions and individuals.

A first step toward reconception is understanding that the state manifests itself through complex institutional arrangements. The state also constitutes itself by exercising legitimate force to bring societal institutions into legal existence and regulate them under its mandate of public authority. For example, we often experience entities such as the family and the corporation as "natural" or inevitable in form and function, but such institutions are constructed; their identities are legitimated in law. They are creatures of the state, in the sense that the state's legal mechanisms bring them into existence. The state determines how family and corporation are created as coherent entities entitled to act as such in society.

This process of entity creation also establishes the state as the ultimate source of authority. Its law tells us who may join together by structuring what will constitute a legitimate institutional formation and determines the consequences of that union, be it marital or corporate. Law defines the circumstances under which a union and its actions will be considered entitled to special legal protection. Once a legal union is established, the state may also insist on participating in its termination, dictating the terms under which separation or dissolution may occur.

Many economists would respond to such observations by asserting that structuring institutions can be handled through private ordering—through contract. However, contracts as documents created and enforced by law are also dependent on the institutions of the state for interpretation, implementation, and execution. No matter how we try to isolate transactions, the state is always a residual player in "private" arrangements, fashioning the background rules that shape those agreements and maintaining the background institutions upon which parties ultimately rely. In exercising its unique role as the creator of legitimate social organizations susceptible to its ongoing coercive authority, the state should assume a corresponding responsibility to see that these organizations operate equitably.

Given the state of non-interventionist rhetoric, a brief digression on state competence is warranted. Critics of an active state often argue that state bureaucracies are inefficient and potentially corrupt. Because of the escalating sense of both the inevitability and the superiority of privatization within American political culture, we now live in an era of private schools, private prisons, even a private military—a world with corporations performing formerly public functions, displacing the state and its responsibility. It is as though the state—the public—cannot add anything distinctive. We just want to get the job done as quickly, quietly, and cheaply as possible; private entities are presumed superior to the state in this regard. Experience with Halliburton in Iraq may indicate that the private is not always the cheapest. Nor does experience support the notion that private entities are always more efficient or less corrupt than state efforts.

Concerns about efficiency and corruption must be addressed in any theory arguing for state action. While criminal and regulatory law can address corruption, we must ask whether efficiency is the appropriate measure of state success. Should we measure social goods such as education and social responsibilities or those related to criminal justice only in terms of efficiency? Economic measures may be important, but are they the only bottom line?

Should independent and public values that further the public good, such as equality, justice, and fairness, not be measured and considered when we assess the value of public action? How can public goals be articulated and established without considering how they are consistent with public norms? Public values such as equality or justice are largely unquantifiable, which may explain why they are rarely addressed in neo-classical economics or considered integral to the normative system that governs the market and other economic institutions. The state is theoretically freed from the market and profit constraints placed on individual industries and businesses; it is in a superior position to develop expertise and competence regarding the implications and implementation of .

public values. Unlike corporations, which are presumed to act only to maximize profits, the state can accomplish more ambitious, even if ultimately immeasurable and illusive, goals. If the preservation and implementation of public values are the state's responsibility, this responsibility should ensure, to the extent possible, that public goods are distributed according to those values as well.

The vulnerability thesis

In discussions of public responsibility, the concept of vulnerability often defines groups of fledgling or stigmatized subjects, designated as "populations." Public health discourse refers to "vulnerable populations," such as those who are infected with HIV–AIDS. Groups of persons living in poverty or confined in prisons are often labeled as vulnerable populations. While children or the elderly are prototypical examples of more sympathetic vulnerable populations, "vulnerability" is typically associated with victimhood, deprivation, dependency, or pathology.

In contrast, I claim the term "vulnerable" for its potential in describing a universal, inevitable, enduring aspect of the human condition that must be at the heart of our concept of social and state responsibility. Vulnerability freed from its limited and negative associations is a powerful conceptual tool with the potential to define an obligation for the state to ensure a richer, more robust guarantee of equality than is afforded under the equal protection model.

This vulnerability approach expands upon and complements my earlier work in theorizing dependency (Fineman 2004). The technique is to focus on a concept or term in common use, laden with negative associations, grossly under-theorized, and ambiguous. Ambiguity provides an opportunity to explore and excavate the unarticulated and complex relationships inherent but latent in the term. Thus reconsidered, the concept of vulnerability can act as a heuristic device, encouraging us to examine hidden assumptions and biases that shaped its original social and cultural meaning. Conceiving of vulnerability this way renders it valuable in constructing critical perspectives on political and societal institutions, including law. Vulnerability raises new issues, poses different questions, and opens up new avenues for critical exploration.

Initially, we should understand vulnerability as arising from our embodiment, which carries the ever-present possibility of harm and injury from mildly unfortunate to catastrophically devastating events. Individuals can attempt to mitigate the impact of such events, but they cannot eliminate their possibility. Understanding vulnerability begins with the realization that many such events are ultimately beyond human control.

Our embodied humanity includes the ever-constant possibility of dependency resulting from disease, epidemic, resistant viruses, or other biologically based catastrophes. Moreover, we face the constant possibility of injury by errant weather systems that produce flood, drought, famine, and fire. These are "natural" disasters beyond individual control. Our bodily vulnerability is enhanced by the realization that should we succumb to illness or injury there may be accompanying economic and institutional harms from disruption of existing relationships.

Because we are positioned differently within a web of economic and institutional relationships, our vulnerabilities range in magnitude and potential on an individual level. While undeniably universal, human vulnerability is also particular; it is experienced uniquely by each of us, and the quality and quantity of resources we possess influences this experience. The realization that no individual can avoid vulnerability entirely spurs us to look to societal institutions for assistance. Of course, society cannot eradicate vulnerability, but it can mediate, compensate, and lessen vulnerability through programs, institutions, and structures. Because vulnerability marks and shapes our personal and social lives, a vulnerability analysis must have both individual and institutional components.

The vulnerable subject

Understanding the significance, universality, and constancy of vulnerability mandates that politics, ethics, and law be fashioned around a comprehensive vision of the human experience if they are to meet the needs of real-life subjects. Currently, dominant political and legal theories are built around a universal human subject defined in the liberal tradition. These theories presume the liberal subject is a competent social actor capable of playing multiple and concurrent societal roles: the employee, the employer, the spouse, the parent, the consumer, the manufacturer, the citizen, and the taxpayer. This subject informs our economic, legal, and political principles. It is indispensable to the prevailing ideologies of autonomy, self-sufficiency, and personal responsibility, which conceive of society as constituted by self-interested individuals capable of manipulating and managing their independently acquired and overlapping resources.

The legal metaphor encapsulating this vision of societal organization is "contract." Liberal subjects have the ability to negotiate contract terms, assess their options, and make rationale choices. They consent to such agreements in the course of fulfilling society's mandate that they assume personal responsibility for themselves and their dependants. Privacy principles that restrain state institutions from interfering with the liberal subjects' entitlements to autonomy and liberty depend on this presumed competence and capability.

Vulnerability analysis questions the idea of a liberal subject, suggesting that the vulnerable subject is a more accurate and complete universal figure to place at the heart of social policy. Many critiques of the liberal subject focus on autonomy. Feminist scholars have scrutinized and criticized the empirically unrealistic ways in which dominant theory and popular politics idealize notions of independence, autonomy, and self-sufficiency. In bringing dependency and care work under discussion, feminists have offered a model of interdependence: the liberal subject enmeshed in a web of relationships and perceived as dependent upon them.

A vulnerability critique builds on these insights; however, as a more encompassing concept, vulnerability analyses are more politically potent than those based on dependency. Dependency is episodic and shifts in degree on an individual level; thus, mainstream political and social theorists often ignore it. If acknowledged at all, dependency is merely a stage that the liberal subject has left behind and is, therefore, of no theoretical interest. Moreover, society handles dependency by relegating caretaking to the zone of family privacy, beyond the scope of state concern absent extraordinary family failures, like abuse or neglect. Rendered invisible within the family, dependency is mistakenly assumed to be adequately managed for the vast majority of people. By contrast, as a state of constant possible harm, vulnerability cannot be hidden. While institutions like the family may provide some shelter, they cannot eliminate individual vulnerability and are themselves vulnerable structures susceptible to transition. Vulnerability understood as individual and institutional, as well as universal and constant, provokes a powerful critique of dominant modes of thinking about inequality.

The vulnerability perspective underscores another problematic characteristic of the liberal subject: s/he is only presented as an adult, standing outside of the passage of time and human experience. The construction of the adult liberal subject captures only one possible developmental stage—the least vulnerable—from many possible stages an actual individual passes through in a "normal" lifespan. We must confront this foundational flaw in the liberal model to develop legal and social policies that reflect the lived realities of human subjects.

The vulnerable subject embodies the fact that humans experience a wide range of differing and interdependent abilities over a lifetime. The vulnerability approach recognizes that individuals are anchored at each end of their lives by dependency and the absence of capacity. Of course, between these ends, loss of capacity and dependence may also occur, temporarily for many and permanently for some. Constant and variable throughout life, individual vulnerability encompasses not only damage that has been done in the past and speculative harms of the distant future, but also the possibility of immediate harm. Humans live with the ever-present possibility that their needs and circumstances will change. On an individual level, the concept of vulnerability captures this present potential for dependency based upon our persistent susceptibility to misfortune and catastrophe.

The vulnerable society and its institutions

The vulnerable subject presents the traditional political and legal theorist with a dilemma. What should be the political and legal implications of the fact that we live within a fragile materiality that renders us constantly susceptible to destructive external forces and internal disintegration? Bodily needs and the messy dependency they carry cannot be ignored in life, nor should they be absent in our theories about society, politics, and law. Surely the reality of our universal fragility has played some role in constructing societal institutions. Contemplating our shared vulnerability, it becomes apparent that human beings need each other and society, that we must structure our institutions in response to this fundamental human reality.

Of course, societal institutions are not foolproof shelters, even in the short term. They too can be conceptualized as vulnerable: they may fail in the wake of market fluctuations, changing international policies, institutional and political compromises, or human prejudices. Even the most established institutions viewed over time are potentially unstable and susceptible to challenges from internal and external forces. Riddled with their own vulnerabilities, society's institutions cannot eradicate, and sometimes exacerbate, our individual vulnerability. Awareness of these institutional fallibilities may intersect with the specter of our own possible dependency, making reliance on these institutions particularly frightening.

Making vulnerability theoretically central in an equality analysis redirects our attention onto the societal institutions created in response to individual vulnerability. This institutional focus enhances attention on the individual subject, placing him/her in social context. Institutions of particular interest are those created and maintained under the state's legitimating authority, since the ultimate objective of a vulnerability analysis is to argue that the state must be more responsive to and responsible for vulnerability. These institutions, in combination with the legal and governmental structures that bring them into existence and monitor their activities, constitute the state as I conceive of it.

The state-facilitated institutions that have grown up around vulnerability are interlocking and overlapping. They promise layered opportunities and support for individuals but also gaps and potential pitfalls. These institutions collectively form systems that play an important role in lessening, ameliorating, and compensating for vulnerability (Turner 2006). Together and independently they provide us with "assets"—advantages, coping mechanisms, or resources that cushion us when we are facing misfortune, disaster, and violence (Kirby 2006). These assets provide individuals with "resilience" in the face of vulnerability (Kirby 2006).

Peadar Kirby (2006: 55) identifies three types of assets provided by social organizations and institutions: physical assets, human assets, and social assets. Institutions providing physical assets impart physical or material goods through the distribution of wealth and property. These assets determine our present quality of life and provide the material basis for accumulation of additional resources—or resources that are more sustainable—in the form of savings and investments (54–55). Tax and inheritance laws impact the distribution of physical assets and are part of this system, as are banking rules and regulations and credit policies (59). Kirby notes that residential property is the single biggest asset class, accounting for 40 to 60 percent of total household wealth in Europe and around 30 percent in the United States. He warns that a crisis in the housing market could be worse than a depression, a prescient warning in view of the recent world-wide crisis generated by the sub-prime debacle (59).

Like physical assets, human assets also affect material well-being. Defined as "innate or developed abilities to make the most of a given situation" (Kirby 2006: 60), human assets provide for the accumulation of human capital or "capabilities" (Nussbaum 2006: 164) on an individual level. While reflecting some dimensions of Amartya Sen's analysis, Kirby (2006: 55) notes that Sen emphasizes capabilities and "well-being" in a way that "highlights important dimensions of what we can call the social production of resilience." Kirby's multiple asset-conferring institutional analysis seems more helpful in articulating a basis for state responsibility than Sen's focus on the development of individual capabilities. In setting out a system approach where a variety of structures confer different, complementary types of assets, Kirby reaches for robust categories that capture the complex dimensions of the idea of resilience. Kirby identifies health and education as chief among assets in this category, making the institutions governing education and health care prime candidates for a vulnerability analysis. Employment systems should be added to these examples; like education and healthcare, they develop the human being, impart assets that allow participation in the market, and facilitate the accumulation of material resources that bolster individuals' resilience in the face of vulnerability.

Finally, social assets are networks of relationships from which we gain support and strength, including the family and other cultural groupings and associations. Kirby (2006: 64–69) argues persuasively that social assets are also accumulated through political collectives in which individuals bolster their resilience by joining together to address vulnerabilities generated by the market or society. These collectives historically included trade unions and political parties, but today the welfare state and insurance are also offered as alternative, often competing, means of protection against risk. It is in this category that I would place group identification based on shared characteristics or affiliations, such as gender, race, sexual orientation, religion, etc.

Kirby's description of assets and asset-conferring institutions is analytically helpful in constructing a vulnerability analysis because it illuminates the link between asset accumulation by individuals and the creation and maintenance of societal institutions. The nature of this relationship, coupled with the fact that asset-conferring institutions initially come into legal existence through state mechanisms, places such institutions within the domain of state responsibility. As asset-conferring entities, these institutions distribute significant societal goods and should be more specifically regulated; normatively, this involvement requires that the state be vigilant in ensuring the equitable distribution of such assets.

Together with the concept of the vulnerable subject, understanding the state's relationship to asset-conferring institutions provides a vocabulary in arguing for state accountability for ensuring equality in response to individual and institutional vulnerability. Future work could broaden the idea of asset categories, perhaps distinguishing between asset-conferring, asset-preserving, and asset-enhancing systems. Also relevant to the idea of resilience are institutions that do not confer individual assets but provide some collective social good, such as maintaining order—for example, the criminal justice system and the armed services. Systems designed with institutions, not individuals, as the primary regulatory objects are also of interest; they guide capital and nation-states in accumulation and consolidation, as well as determine the range and viability of international interactions and relations. For example, international treaties and United Nations conventions are directed toward the governance of collective entities. Individuals might be benefited through such systems, but they are not the primary objective of them.

Beyond formal equality, one way to identify unfairness in asset distribution is to focus on institutions that mitigate the vulnerability of some, but not others. This approach requires that institutions justify unequal responses to shared vulnerability in a state-monitored process.

Assessing and addressing privilege and disadvantage

Within asset-conferring systems, some individuals occupy more privileged positions than others. Interactions among systems affect these inequalities. Privileges and disadvantages accumulate across systems and can combine to create effects that are more devastating or more beneficial than the weight of separate parts. Privileges conferred within certain systems can mediate or cancel out disadvantages conferred in others. A good early education may overcome poverty, particularly when coupled with a supportive family and progressive social network.

Unlike theorists who argue that an individual's multiple *identities* interact to produce webs of advantages and disadvantages, I argue that—with respect to the assets any one person possesses—systems of power and privilege interact together to create these inequalities.

A vulnerability approach addresses some of the ambiguities and anomalies evident in current models of discrimination and the identity categories these models utilize. Focusing on the interactions of asset-conferring institutions clarifies how some individuals outmaneuver disadvantages associated with existing discrimination categories of race or gender to excel, even triumph, in a "white man's world." The various systems and institutions these individuals have encountered provide them with the accumulated assets they need to succeed. Such successes sometimes cause individuals to reject group identification and deny group-associated disadvantages and the measures designed to address them by society and by successful individuals themselves. Some women CEOs reject the idea of accommodations for caretakers of small children or aging parents; some wealthy and successful African-Americans launch campaigns against affirmative action in college admissions; and some Latinos are as vocal and vicious about undocumented workers as their white counterparts.

These individuals do not disprove the existence of structural inequalities; they are the beneficiaries of institutions and systems in which privileges are conferred in more complex and particular ways than a simplistic focus on identity and discrimination would allow. Privileged within intersecting systems, these individuals escape both materially and psychologically from what are often cast as the inevitable disadvantages of their gender, race, or ethnicity. Their successes lessen identification with unmodified categories like race or gender and sometimes make them opponents of the very policies that assisted them.

Just as privilege is not tethered to identity neither is disadvantage. Vulnerability is universal and transcends historic categories of impermissible discrimination. The sub-prime mortgage crisis affected white and middle-class people as well as those in the traditional suspect categories. Welfare reform during the 1990s should have been understood as a direct attack on all vulnerable caretakers because it undermined the value of unpaid care work and demonized motherhood outside the patriarchal paradigm. The realization that disadvantage operates independently of race and gender in many instances provides an important political tool. Mobilizing around the concept of vulnerability may facilitate coalition building among those not benefiting as fully as others from current societal organization. Operating from this perspective means institutional arrangements will be the targets of protest and political mobilization, and interest groups need not be organized around differing identities. The justice inquiry will be reconfigured to focus on whether existing institutional arrangements are equally attentive across individuals and groups with shared vulnerability and whether assets are conferred in an equitable manner.

Discrimination along identity lines likely will continue, as well as an ongoing need to protest and remedy such discrimination. But, focusing on shared vulnerabilities and building a political movement around unequal institutional arrangements is a more promising and powerful approach in addressing the disadvantage that persists in society. Discrimination-based arguments have accomplished too little with respect to dismantling broad systems of disadvantage that transcend racial and gender lines, such as poverty. The vulnerability approach will take us further, for—despite progressive attempts to build strong and enduring coalitions across identity groups—such a coalition has not by and large emerged.

A vulnerability approach accomplishes several other important political objectives that illuminate why a post-identity paradigm is necessary and can powerfully address existing material and social inequalities. It allows us to celebrate the progress toward racial, ethnic, and gender equality achieved under the anti-discrimination model. Institutions historically closed to women, African-Americans, and other non-white males, are now formally open; many individuals have flourished as a result. Yet many are left behind, including some white males; anti-discrimination and formal equality have not provided them opportunities to succeed. Institutional exclusion in the formal, historic sense is not the reason these individuals are not flourishing.

Affirmative action plans are premised on the anti-discrimination model and perceived as temporary adjustments to the formal equality paradigm necessitated by past discrimination. Since they are based on historic individual identity categories, they do not focus on the institutions we must direct attention toward to address the more complicated forms of disadvantage faced in a post-equality society.

Some politicians and policymakers suggest that those left behind are suffering the just results of their individual failures and inadequacies. They rely on the assumption that unsuccessful persons fail to take advantage of the equally available opportunities afforded under existing societal systems. If we do not frame equality arguments in terms of the absence of impermissible discrimination but, rather, question whether the system provided impermissible advantage to some individuals or groups, claims that individuals are entirely responsible for their own failures become less tenable. A vulnerability inquiry proposes a more thorough and penetrating equality mandate with which to judge what is the appropriate response by the state.

This structural focus illustrates another political advantage to a vulnerability analysis; it brings institutions—not only individual actions—under scrutiny, redirecting our attention to their role in providing assets in ways that may unfairly privilege certain persons or groups, even if unintentionally. Both institutions and individuals are vulnerable to internal and external forces. They can be captured and corrupted, damaged and outgrown. They can be compromised by legacies of practices, patterns of behavior, and entrenched interests formed during periods of exclusion and discrimination but now invisible in the haze of history. Nonetheless, institutions play a vital role in addressing individual vulnerability. The resources they provide are the assets that allow us to live and aspire toward happiness despite our vulnerability. Their intentionality in discriminating either in favor of or against individuals or groups is irrelevant. The essential question is whether institutions respond unequally to the reality of our shared vulnerability in an unjustifiable way or one needing adjustment. This type of inquiry can only be mandated and monitored by the state.

The responsive state

Replacing the liberal subject with a vulnerable subject, and articulating a corresponding and compelling argument for fashioning a state more responsive to that subject, is not an easy task. Critics may argue that attacks on the liberal subject destabilize liberalism itself: if a competent, responsible adult is not at the center of social and political theory, will this not inevitably lead to less democratic modes of government and a more authoritarian state?

The answer to such questions must begin with some consideration of the history and development of our democracy and its institutions. Built upon myths of autonomy and independence, our current system fails to reflect the vulnerable as well as dependent nature of the human condition.

We must think beyond current ideological constraints and consider the possibility of an active state in non-authoritarian terms. This theoretical task—reconceptualizing the state's role—requires that we imagine responsive structures whereby state involvement actually empowers a vulnerable subject. Certainly state mechanisms that ensure a more equitable distribution of assets and privilege across society would contribute to a more robust democracy and greater public participation. The question is not one of an active versus inactive state but rather whether the state is constructed around a well-defined responsibility to implement a comprehensive and just equality regime.

Present conceptions of the state underestimate or even ignore the many ways in which the state—through law and legal institutions—shapes institutions from inception to dissolution. Currently, the state minimally supervises these institutions that provide the assets needed for resilience in the face of vulnerability. The mandate of equal protection under statutes and the Constitution prohibits discrimination and, absent the demonstration of compelling differences and/or state interest, equality of treatment is the legal norm. However, the formal equality model fails to address substantive inequalities and differential allocations of privilege produced by our institutions. By focusing on equal protection and formal equality, the current model mires us in a battle of identity politics where every gain by a minority individual becomes a justification for abandoning the pursuit of substantive equality. Moreover, when one person or group gains, other individuals and groups often perceive themselves as losing. This paradigm deflects sustained attention away from the institutional arrangements and systems that distribute disadvantage across people and groups.

Under the vulnerability approach, the mandate is the establishment of a regime of equality, but the focus is different. A vulnerability analysis magnifies state responsibility and activity. It demands that the state give equal regard to the shared vulnerability of all individuals transcending the old identity categories which limit recognition of the state's role in protecting against discrimination. A vulnerability analysis considers how the state responds to, shapes, enables, or curtails its institutions. Does it act toward those institutions in ways that are consistent with its obligation to support the implementation and maintenance of a vital and robust equality regime? This inquiry must be a fundamental mandate for the legislature, which has primary responsibility for an adequate response to vulnerability; this response in turn would be monitored by the courts.

A vulnerability analysis poses questions not restricted to a focus on discrimination against certain individuals or groups. Rather the state is required to ensure that institutions and structures within its control do not inappropriately benefit or disadvantage certain members of society. The operation and impact of those institutions and structures become the focus. The approach also addresses the argument that because some members of a group succeed, the system is functioning appropriately and needs no monitoring or transformation. The vulnerability inquiry must consider how societal resources are channeled to see if the result privileges some while tolerating the disadvantage and vulnerability of others. Focusing on the structure of societal institutions reflects the fact of the state's affirmative obligation not to privilege any group of citizens over others and to structure conditions for equality. Imagine how fruitfully political and policy discussions might proceed in this framework.

A fundamental question about our current societal arrangements that might spark controversy would begin with considering why we organize work and wealth as we do. I would like to see a discussion in state legislatures and Congress about the workings of the law itself: why do we privilege contract over status, market over family or individual? Why does law divide up the market analytically and place its various parts into competition: corporation versus workers versus consumers versus government? Why aren't all corporate constituencies represented in corporate governance and only shareholders viewed as stakeholders? Lawmakers in other countries ask such questions and respond to them in policy-making.

Premised on the idea that it is inappropriate for the state and its institutions to protect, privilege, and mediate the vulnerability of some through the creation and maintenance of societal institutions, the vulnerability approach would reveal how the state allows some to struggle with vulnerability and dependency. A focus on privilege, disadvantage, the state, and its institutions changes the nature of the legal inquiry presented for judicial determination. It moves courts away from assessing the individual characteristics of designated groups to see if they are the subjects of animus. The vulnerability paradigm asks courts to look beyond the identity of disadvantaged groups developed under a discrimination paradigm. While old identity categories should not be removed entirely from consideration, we must reframe concerns to reveal things about the organization of society that are missed otherwise.

Under this approach, exploring the intent behind the actions of individual employees, educators, or landlords is unnecessary. Neither individual intention nor discrimination are the issues. Ill will is irrelevant when all of society operates with a set of prejudicial assumptions and beliefs that our culture ignores the many ways it is organized to privilege only some. Because the shared, universal nature of vulnerability draws the whole of society—not just a defined minority—under scrutiny, the vulnerability approach provides a "post-identity" analysis of what sort of protection society owes its members.

Recognizing that privilege and disadvantage migrate across identity categories forces us to focus on individuals *and* the institutional structures and arrangements that produce or exacerbate existing inequality. The concept of vulnerability also allows us to avoid the argument that the failure is with individuals, since it is possible to point to the success of some members of protected groups. Finally, a vulnerability approach does not mean that different treatment, even the conferral of privilege or advantage, is never warranted. It means that if the state confers privilege or advantage, it has an affirmative obligation either to justify the disparate circumstances or remedy them. This political and legal culture of equality provides the backdrop against which the state, our societal institutions, and their actions must be judged.

Notes

* This chapter was previously published in 20 *Yale Journal of Law and Feminism* 1 (2008).

Chapter 12

Resistance in the afterlife of identity

Darren Lenard Hutchinson

Introduction

The election of Barack Obama as President of the United States was undeniably historic and symbolic. Obama's victory raises important questions regarding the future direction of progressive social movements, critical legal theory, and political change. Sorting through all of these complex issues requires the use of complex analytical tools. For example, the politics of sex and race (and sexuality, age, and class) framed the political contest between Obama and Hillary Clinton, because the two candidates became proxies for racial and gender advancement. Critical race theory and feminist scholarship offer methodologies, such as "multidimensionality" and "intersectionality," that could navigate the complicated identity issues presented by the 2008 Democratic primaries. Nevertheless, much of the popular discourse on Clinton versus Obama described "race or sex" as well as "progressiveness or identity politics" as mutually exclusive and competing concepts.

The Obama–Clinton political contest stoked pre-existing tensions concerning the priorities of social justice movements and white women's and blacks' claims to exceptional harm. Consequently, a significant percentage of the public and virtually all major media understood or portrayed their competition as a clash between race and sex.

Although many commentators analyzed the Obama and Clinton contest through the lens of identity politics, both candidates, particularly Obama, employed post-identity rhetoric. Even before Obama won the Democratic nomination, commentators across the ideological spectrum celebrated the demise of race and racism. Among progressives, Obama's success represented the achievement of egalitarian race blindness. Conservatives, by contrast, contended that the strength of Obama's campaign demonstrated that policies designed to ameliorate racially identifiable inequality were unnecessary and punitive to whites (e.g. Williams and Negrin 2008).

While post-identity rhetoric predated the 2008 campaign, the new post-identity discourse differs somewhat from the preceding rhetoric. In the past, liberals typically viewed the irrelevance of identity as an aspiration. During the recent campaign, however, many liberals believed that the US had finally moved beyond racial identity and race politics. Conservatives, by contrast, have preached post-racialism since the 1970s, when state actors began using race-conscious policies to remedy the effects of white supremacy.

Progressive critics who would normally question post-racial, post-gender, or post-identity rhetoric were unusually silent regarding this discourse during the presidential campaign. Analyzing these issues, however, seems essential to the work of scholars who advocate for progressive political change. Conservatives have waged a fairly successful countermovement using the themes of race neutrality that permeated progressive racial discourse during the civil rights movement. Many progressive advocates, however, have shunned post-identity talk because they believe that identity politics can mobilize social movements and serve as a useful and accurate trope for explaining material and social inequality. Furthermore, an expansive body of sociological research shows that the intersection of race and class very negatively impacts and constrains the lives of poor people of color. Poverty also correlates with gender to create (or structure) vulnerability. For these reasons, progressive theorists must critically analyze popular discourses that seek to repudiate the idea of identity or identity-based inequality.

This chapter analyzes the new post-identity rhetoric by relating it to liberal and conservative discourses that deemphasize identity. Although many commentators describe the new post-identity rhetoric as a progressive moment and criticize identity politics as a relic of a simpler, less complicated era, progressives should consider the conservative implications of this rhetoric. Postmodern theorists very persuasively contend that rhetoric is contextual and contingent, which implies that the meaning of post-identity discourse will depend largely upon the context of its use. But the pervasiveness of race- and sex-based inequality and the historical and political importance of identity-based social movements raise serious questions about the feasibility and desirability of post-identity politics, especially as a comprehensive theory of political mobilization or as an expression of a sociological truth.

Post-identity: old and new

Postmodernism challenges identity

Postmodernism has contributed greatly to identity politics and anti-subordination theories. Social constructivist accounts of identity reject biological determinism that frames and justifies the vulnerability of subordinate groups. The "one-drop" rule in the context of race and the flawed search for "real differences" to justify sex-based discrimination cannot withstand the scrutiny of contemporary scientific knowledge.

Despite the strength of postmodernist accounts of identity and the legitimizing role of "nature" in the history of group domination, many progressive theorists remain wedded to identity politics. For example, the legendary clash between critical legal studies, critical race theory, and feminism resulted from conflicting beliefs concerning the value of identity and rights. Critical legal studies scholars believed that identity politics and rights discourse were outmoded concepts of the modernist legal tradition. They viewed race and sex as social constructs that distracted progressives from the "real" or material harms caused by economic exploitation and deprivation.

Rights-based legalism received similar treatment from critical legal studies scholars. According to many of these scholars, legal actors use the promise of rights and equality to mask the injustices that the law perpetuates. Rights have value in only very discrete cases where plaintiffs seek to vindicate individualized harm. The malleability of legal discourse and the control that dominant classes exercise upon the law mean that a rights-based legal approach will never deliver substantial justice or broad progressive change (Harris 1994). Despite the credibility of legal skepticism among most progressive theorists, in the first wave of post-identity politics, the pro-identity progressives emerged victorious.

Critical race theorists responded to critical legal studies in a heavily cited issue of the *Harvard Civil Rights—Civil Liberties Law Review* billed as "Minority Critiques of Critical Legal Studies" (Symposium 1987). Critical race theorists accepted the critical legal studies movement's skepticism regarding the utility of rights, but they believed that rights could catalyze political participation by people of color in order to advance progressive political agendas (Williams 1987). Critical race theorists also believed that rights could blunt the impact of discrimination and racial hierarchy (Delgado 1987). Although conservative political activism has led to a retrenchment from the enforcement and expansion of rights, this does not mean that a rights-based approach to justice was inherently bankrupt and futile (Crenshaw 1988). Rather than abandoning rights altogether, critical race theorists sought to refashion antiracism into a more progressive or radical social movement that focused on remedying the material harms and discrimination associated with race and other forms of inequality (Crenshaw 1988: 1382–84).

Critical race theorists believed in race as forcefully and as reluctantly as they believed in rights. Even though critical race theorists agreed that race is a "social construct," they argued that it causes material harms and informs the "perspectives" through which legal analysis occurs (e.g. Lawrence 1995: 835 note 71; Powell 1997: 102). To critical race theorists, rights and race were closely linked. A recalibrated antiracist movement could use the rhetoric of rights to contest and demand remedies for racial inequality, which critical race theorists perceived as related to, but not subsumed by, economic injustice. Accepting rights, therefore, reinforced the idea of racial identity for critical race theorists. The advocacy of race-conscious legal remedies demonstrates the linkage of racial identity and rights within the critical race theory project.

Modern (or "second-wave") feminists rejected sex-based distinctions in law and advocated the "sameness" of men and women. Because law regulated sexual boundaries and structured women as subordinates, sameness became a powerful frame for contesting subjugation based on perceived difference. But during its third wave, the feminist movement would fracture, particularly due to internal critiques that questioned the "sameness" approach and that rejected the assumed universality of women (Fineman 1992: 8–13).

Some third-wave feminists began emphasizing women's inherent "differences" and unique "perspectives" and criticized policies that burdened gender-based differences. Cultural feminists argued that the law reflected a "male" view of the world, and they sought to restructure law so that it would incorporate, rather than marginalize, women's perspectives (West 1988). According to some cultural feminists, women are inherently more nurturing and collaborative than men; they view the mother-and-child relationship as a special bond that the law should value (West 1988: 15). Other feminists advanced theories that did not rest upon assumptions about sexual difference or sameness. Instead, they accepted the idea that gender is socially constructed but creates "gendered" experiences that were relevant for social policy (Fineman 1992).

While cultural feminists questioned the horizontal sameness of men and women, others asserted that vertical differences destabilized the category woman itself. Critical race and lesbian feminists were among the most vocal internal critics whose work challenged feminist essentialism. If feminists did not contextualize their research by discussing the "intersection" of race and gender, they would fail to account for the experiences of women of color, for whom patriarchy is not the exclusive source of disempowerment (Crenshaw 1991). A raceless approach does not describe the ways in which race empowers and privileges white women, which complicates the "m > f" dichotomy that characterizes much of the work by feminists (Halley 2006).

Lesbian feminists criticized feminist methodologies, such as the dominance approach developed by Catherine Mackinnon, that treated women's sexual (and other) experiences as inherently patriarchal (Franke 1994a: 555–61). They also argued that heteronormativity prevented feminists from recognizing that oppressive gender norms facilitated the subordination of lesbians and, to some extent, gay men (Eaton 1994: 187–90).

Postmodern feminists also rejected the notion of an essential woman, but they, unlike critical race and lesbian feminists, were suspicious of the category woman itself. Rather than seeking a more accurate portrayal of women's experiences, many postmodern feminists have rejected the notion that a unifying concept of gender exists. Instead, they view gender as socially constructed with contingent and shifting meanings (Higgins 1995: 1569–72).

Most feminist legal theorists, even those who employed postmodernism in their work, accepted the notion of gender identity and sex-based politics. They either believed that the law oppressed women by denying their sameness with men or that the law subordinated women by failing to account for sexual difference. Critical race feminists believed that analyzing race *and* sex could improve feminist advocacy on behalf of women. Lesbian feminists sought to deconstruct heterosexism in order to persuade feminists that GLBT rights were a feminist issue and that feminist heterosexism harmed women. And while postmodernism convinced many feminists that gender is socially constructed, many of them agreed that it nonetheless creates serious material consequences. Identity survived the rancorous third-wave feminist debates.

Renewed critiques of identity

Although antiracism, feminism, and other progressive movements survived postmodernism's assault on identity, debates over the appropriateness of identity politics did not end. Left-identified legal theorists renewed challenges to racial identity, long after critical race theorists split from critical legal studies. Furthermore, critics again contested the value of "gender identity," even though the concept survived the fractious debates during feminism's third wave.

Within racial discourse, progressively identified scholars such as Anthony Appiah, Reginald Leamon Robinson, Christi Cunningham, and Richard Ford began to question the utility of race after the clashes between critical legal scholars and critical race scholars subsided. These post-racial leftists embraced social constructivist theories of race. They also argued that because race is social, rather than biological, progressive scholars could discard it. Their work, however, differs from the earlier round of postmodern questioning of race because several of these scholars contend that race politics perpetuates the subordination of persons of color, who legitimize a history of racial oppression when they cling to race as an element of personal identity.

Robinson (2001: 1432) asserts that race consciousness causes people of color to "co-create" poverty; in other words, adhering to racial identity makes them accept the constraints that white supremacy has encoded in "colored" status. Richard Ford (2000: 1811) argues that the overuse of race causes whites to doubt blacks' claims of injustice and that linking race and culture in anti-discrimination litigation dangerously essentializes people of color and empowers courts to define a group's authentic culture. Cunningham (1999: 724) believes that material racial harm exists, but she argues that people of color should abandon race as an element of personal identity. Asserting a personal racial identity, as distinct from race-based remedies, harms people of color because they define themselves using an artificial concept rooted in domination.

Recently, some feminists have engaged in a similar inquiry as the post-racial leftists. Janet Halley, for example, has decided to take a "break" from feminism but falls short of arguing that feminism or sex should or do not exist. Instead, Halley (2006: 17–18) believes that feminist analysis is too confining because it rests on bipolar notions of gender, assumes the inherent domination of men over women, and because feminists only engage in advocacy on behalf of women. Halley has embarked upon a search for less-confining methodologies that do not emphasize identity and hierarchy but which focus on agency, particularly regarding issues of sexuality.

2008 and the political death of identity

Obama, "change," and racial transcendence

Obama's victorious presidential campaign probably did more to put the issue of post-racial identity into public discourse than any other event in contemporary US politics. Obama campaigned on a theme of "change" and "hope." Many voters believed that these concepts symbolized a break from traditional racial politics. Obama, many commentators argued, represented both the success *and conclusion* of the civil rights movement.

In February 2008 when the race between Obama and Hillary Clinton was extremely close and contentious, Peter J. Boyer published an article in the *New Yorker* entitled "The Color of Politics: A Mayor of the Post-Racial Generation." Although the article profiles Corey Booker, the black mayor of Newark, New Jersey, it also discusses Obama, comparing him with Booker. The article's description of Obama and Booker celebrates their perceived post-racial status:

> Their deeper kinship resides in their identities as breakthrough figures— African-American politicians whose appeal transcends race. Both men, reared in the post-Selma era and schooled at elite institutions, developed a political style of conciliation, rather than confrontation, which com- plemented their natural gifts, and, as it happens, nicely served their ambi- tions. The wish for a post-racial politics is a powerful force, and rewards those who seem to carry its promise.
>
> (Boyer 2008: 38)

Boyer portrays Obama and Booker as "post-racial" politicians, and he implies that attending elite universities and growing up in the post-Selma era groomed them to accommodate whites who disdain antiracist confrontation. Boyer's description of Obama and Booker as post-racial does not simply mean that he believes they individually "transcend race." Instead, Boyer uses the term to praise Obama and Booker as black politicians who appeal to whites by rejecting antiracist advocacy. Being post-racial indicates that a person of color has con- ceded to whites' belief in the social irrelevance of race (Bobo 1999: 464).

If race remains a source of vulnerability and inequality, then some measure of "confrontation" seems reasonable. Individuals who do not believe that race continues to impact economic opportunity, however, will likely embrace post- racial politics and view race-based remedies and allegations of racism with sus- picion. Boyer's celebration of post-racial politics rests on an understanding of racism and racial harms as relics of an older generation.

Senator Claire McCaskill, similarly expresses support for Obama based on her perception that he does not have anything critical to "say to white people" regarding racial injustice:

> What this man has done, Barack Obama, is, he, for the first time I think, as a black leader in America, has come to the American people not as a victim, but rather as a leader. To say to white people who have *legitimate resentments about racial politics* in this country and black people who have *understanding about bitterness and anger*, especially older black Americans who lived through some of those times where they were told that drinking fountain isn't good enough for them.
>
> (McCaskill 2008, cited in Tapper 2008, emphasis added)

Post-racialism appeals to whites who believe that racial protest has outlived its usefulness and desirability.

Another theme of the new post-racial discourse portrays racial identity as an outmoded idea that younger voters will soon retire. Older people of color are raced, while younger people of color are post-racial. *Los Angeles Times* columnist Tim Rutten, for example, argues that:

> [Obama] resonates with the young … because he personifies and articulates the post-racial America in which most of our young people now live (especially the ones in multiethnic urban centers such as Los Angeles).
>
> Anyone with children in their 20s or younger knows that they deal with race and ethnicity in ways different from their elders. Skin color is no longer a physical marker for most of them. By and large, our sons and daughters describe their friends as tall or short, funny or serious, as good students or poor athletes, but seldom—as earlier generations would have done—as a "black guy" or a "white girl." They take the sound of Spanish and the sight of Korean shop signs for granted.
>
> (Rutten 2008: A31)

Before the 2008 election, conservatives had employed the rhetoric of "color blindness" or "race neutrality" to contest affirmative action and other policies enacted to remedy discrimination or to diversify educational institutions. Obama's electoral success ushered in a new wave of conservative commentary demanding an end to race-based remedies.

Ward Connerly, a well-known foe of affirmative action, predicted that an Obama victory would delegitimize race-based remedies:

> The whole argument in favor of race preferences is that there is "institutional racism" and "institutional sexism" in American life … and you need affirmative action to level the playing field … How can you say there is

institutional racism when people in Nebraska vote for a guy who is a self-identified black man?

(cited in Williams and Negrin 2008: A1)

Following the election, Connerly, echoing McCaskill, said that Obama's victory "liberates blacks from the debilitating mindset of seeing themselves as victims in America" (cited in Williams and Negrin 2008: A1).

Ken Blackwell, a former Secretary of State of Ohio, expressed similar views regarding Obama and affirmative action:

> The fact that an African-American has been elected commander-in-chief of this country and will be the leader of the free world shows that race is not an insurmountable obstacle to success in today's America.
>
> Minorities—in fact, all Americans—should celebrate President-Elect Obama's "post-racial" vision for America. In this vision, there is no logical place for racial quotas or racial preference programs.
>
> (Blackwell 2008: paras. 7–8)

Abigail and Stephen Thernstrom opposed affirmative action and the pre-clearance requirements of the Voting Rights Act long before Obama's election victory. Once his presidential campaign became successful, they invoked Obama as evidence that these antidiscrimination measures had outlived their usefulness.

With respect to affirmative action, Abigail Thernstrom argued that Obama's success in the Democratic primaries demonstrates that "we do not need racial double standards because blacks can make it in every walk of American life" (cited in Williams and Negrin 2008:A1). She also argues that Obama's campaign "changes the conversation for the better" and "sends an important message about white racism ... and the level of white racism in this country ... if you've got a huge number of whites voting for a black man" (cited in Williams and Negrin 2008: A1).

Regarding the Voting Rights Act, the Thernstroms asserted that:

> Today, it is even clearer that race has become less of a factor in voting. The high level of white votes for Obama strongly suggests that other black candidates facing overwhelmingly white constituencies can do well ...
>
> Whites refusing to vote for black candidates has finally gone the way of segregated water fountains. Or so we hope.
>
> (Thernstrom and Thernstrom 2008: M5)

Hillary Clinton: old-school feminist or privileged white lady?

When Hillary Clinton (2008) suspended her campaign, she stated that despite the loss to Obama, she and her supporters had placed "18 million cracks" in the "highest, hardest glass ceiling." At various points during her campaign, many of Clinton's supporters and media commentators portrayed her as a victim of sexism; some even attributed her loss to sex. Although much of the negative reporting concerning Clinton was markedly gendered, many progressives passionately rejected arguments that gave feminist treatment to Clinton. Some of the commentary acknowledged the possibility of sexism but contested its role in her defeat.

Some liberal commentators believed Clinton experienced sexism during the Democratic primaries. Nevertheless, they condemned Clinton and her supporters whom they believed opportunistically paid attention to sex, overstated its significance to Clinton's loss, or operated under the assumption that sexism remained a general barrier to women's advancement.

Amy Sullivan, Senior Editor for *Time* and a liberal political commentator, has analyzed the role of gender in the Democratic primaries and described how the contest divided women voters. Sullivan (2008b: para. 6) argues that Clinton captured the pessimists among women, or those who hold a "persistent belief that women continue to face sexism and barriers in the workplace." Sullivan contends that some pessimists "may have an outmoded sense of the obstacles women face on the job" because of they are older and influenced by their prior struggle against sexism or because they have left the workplace to pursue a "work–life balance" (para. 6). According to Sullivan, these women are "more likely to place value in the symbolic power of electing a woman President" (para. 6).

Obama, by contrast, attracts "optimists" among women voters, whom Sullivan (2008b: para. 7) describes as individuals who believe that a woman (other than Clinton) "can become President ... in their lifetime." Sullivan says these women do not fear sexism because when they "look around, they see themselves making up half of business- and medical-school classes. They are law partners, CEOs and university presidents. And they don't want to rally behind a female candidate simply because she is a woman" (para. 7).

Sullivan's analysis portrays Clinton's female supporters as old-school players stuck in the vanquished past where sexism constrained women's opportunities. The post-feminist Obama supporters, by contrast, have a more realistic view of the "workplace," which Sullivan suggests is no longer a site of gender-based discrimination.

Author Lorrie Moore rejects gender-based identity politics, but she thinks that race-based identity politics remains legitimate. Moore appears far more honest than other commentators when she explicitly tosses aside gender concerns, while privileging antiracism:

> Does her being a woman make [Hillary Clinton] a special case? Does gender confer meaning on her candidacy? In my opinion, it is a little late in the day to become sentimental about a woman running for president. The political moment for feminine role models, arguably, has passed us by. The children who are suffering in this country, who are having trouble in school, and for whom the murder and suicide rates and economic dropout rates are high, are boys—especially boys of color, for whom the whole

educational system, starting in kindergarten, often feels a form of exile, a system designed by and for white girls.

(Moore 2008: D13)

Assuming that a role model—rather than fundamental economic transformation—will help "boys of color," Moore dismisses sexual politics because she believes that race is a more pressing concern. She uses this logic to validate racial, but not gender politics:

> Mr. Obama came of age as a black man in America ... He embodies, at the deepest levels, the bringing together of separate worlds. The sexes have always lived together, but the races have not. His candidacy is minted profoundly in that expropriated word "change."

(Moore 2008: D13)

"Black girls" are conspicuously absent from Moore's analysis, which allows her to avoid discussing the relevance of sex to racial justice—a topic that would undermine her wholesale dismissal of gender identity politics. Although Obama received strong support from black women, this does not render gender politics irrelevant to their social status.

Ignoring black girls, Moore narrowly defines Clinton's support as limited to "middle class white girls," and she argues that that this group does not need additional role models. To Moore (2008: D13), the need for a gender moment expired "long ago." Moore's analysis does not reserve space for gender identity politics. She conceives racial justice in male terms, and she dismisses feminism for white women as overly valued.

Conservatives watching the Democratic primaries exploited Clinton's claims of sexism in order to discredit feminism and Clinton herself. Virulently anti-feminist Phyllis Schlafly, for example, rejects the notion that sexism negatively impacted Clinton. She dismisses allegations of sexism as the product of a culture of "victimhood" among feminists:

> The bad attitude of victimhood is indoctrinated in students by bitter feminist faculty in university women's studies courses and even in some law schools. Victimhood is nurtured and exaggerated by feminist organizations using a tactic they call "consciousness raising," i.e., retelling horror stories about how badly some women have been treated until little personal annoyances grow into grievances against society.

(Schlafly 2008: para. 7)

Camile Paglia similarly bashes feminism and dismisses efforts to situate Clinton within feminist politics:

> The argument, therefore, that Hillary's candidacy marks the zenith of modern feminism is specious. Feminism is not well served by her surrogates'

constant tactic of attributing all opposition to her as a function of entrenched sexism. Well into her second term as a US Senator, Hillary lacks a
single example of major legislative achievement. Her career has consisted of
fundraising, meet-and-greets and speeches around the world expressing
support for women's rights ...

Hillary's recent remarks about politics as a "boys' club" resistant to
uppity women was sheer demagoguery ... [B]y attaching herself so blatantly
to anti-male rhetoric ... she is espousing a retrograde brand of feminism no
longer applicable to the US.

(Paglia 2008: 21)

According to Paglia, feminists condemn patriarchy because they are "paranoid."
She believes that criticizing the concentration of political power among men is
an "anti-male" and "retrograde" brand of feminism.

Finally, columnist Christopher Hitchens rails against Clinton in *Slate* for using
sexism to mask her own inadequacies. Hitchens asserts that racial distinctions are
unjustifiable, but that sex-based distinctions are legitimate due to biological determinism. He also concludes that Clinton "used the increasingly empty term *sexism* to
mask the defeat of one of the nastiest and most bigoted candidacies in modern
history" (2008: para. 8, emphasis in original). Because sexism is an "empty"
concept to Hitchens, any effort to apply a feminist analysis to Clinton is bankrupt.

The fallacies and dangers of post-identity rhetoric

Conservatives and liberals have embraced post-race and post-gender politics.
During the 2008 presidential campaign, political commentators celebrated post-
identity politics and invoked the concept in order to portray the contemporary
United States as a place where race and gender have lost much of their social
significance. The post-identity rhetoric is fallacious and dangerous. It is fallacious
because it rests on the grossly incorrect view that race and gender no longer
produce material harms for women and persons of color. This rhetoric is dangerous because if it were generally accepted, subordinate individuals would lose
the ability to explain the factors that structure their vulnerability. Acceptance of
the post-identity rhetoric would also deprive social movements of an important
instrument of political mobilization—the shared, even if varied, experience of
inequality and deprivation. The final section of this chapter elaborates the problems of post-identity politics and contends that social movements that counter
inequality on the grounds of race, gender, class, and sexuality should resist
liberal and conservative efforts to eradicate identity.

Race and sex matter

Race and sex (and other identity categories) are relevant because they continue
to produce material inequality. Additionally, race and sex were highly relevant

to Clinton and Obama during the 2008 political campaigns because identity politics made them exciting and historic candidates and ultimately helped to propel the Democrats to victory. Race, sex, and other identity categories also form the basis for social movement mobilization, without which substantial policy reform would likely not occur.

Although liberals and conservatives recently cheered post-identity politics, virtually every important social measure of well-being proves that this movement is misguided, wrongheaded, and deceitful. In this supposedly post-feminist and post-racial era, 36.5 percent of all female-headed households with children are below the poverty level. Add "of color" to the equation, and the households are mired in poverty: 43.6 percent of black women and 42.5 percent of Latina households with children live in poverty (US Census Bureau 2008, citing 2006 data). Black and Latino men are the groups most likely to be subjugated by law enforcement, and they fill the nation's prisons. Data prepared by the US Department of Justice's Bureau of Justice Statistics (2007: para. 2) finds that "[b]ased on current rates of first incarceration, an estimated 32 percent of black males will enter State or Federal prison during their lifetime, compared to 17 percent of Hispanic males and 5.9 percent of white males." Outside of prison, men of color have among the highest rates of unemployment, and in many jurisdictions, they are disproportionately interrogated, searched, and detained by police officers (see Baker 2008).

Recent studies demonstrate that women earn 80 percent of men's salaries, even after controlling for nondiscriminatory factors related to pay, such as hours, occupation, and parenthood (Dey and Hill 2007). The disparities between white men and other groups follow predictable patterns. Women of color have the lowest incomes relative to white men, but men of color and white women also have substantially lower incomes. Obama's youthful women supporters, particularly those still in college, may believe that gender no longer constrains women, but income studies do not support this optimistic view. For college graduates, the closest income parity for men and women exists immediately after graduation. After that, the pay gap widens. It might seem cliché, but the new post-feminist women may need to live longer to appreciate the reality of sexism.

Furthermore, when younger post-feminist women discount gender and identity, they exhibit the very essentialism and privilege that they condemn in Clinton's supporters. Women from secure and advantaged backgrounds face fewer burdens accessing important economic opportunities. Women of color, older women, and poor women of all ages do not have the same ability to access economic and political power. Accordingly, when young professional women dismiss sexism as insignificant, race and class privileges likely influence their perceptions—particularly if they do not perceive any significant gender-based distinctions among them and white men.

In the area of education policy, the nation's resegregated public schools look almost exactly the way they did 10 years after *Brown v. Board of Education* (1954). Every year, education policy experts document the vast inequities related to public education. Black and Latino children are more likely than any other demographic to attend racially isolated poverty schools that are marred by crime, high teacher-turnover rates, low academic performance, insufficient funding, decaying facilities, outdated books, extremely high dropout rates, low rates of college attendance, parents taxed by poverty and lack of employment, and an abundance of unrealized potential (e.g. Orfield and Lee 2006). When liberals celebrate post-racialism, they validate the racially disparate governmental policies and racial and class inequities that create these acute problems. They also legitimize court rulings that immunize these conditions from judicial invalidation and that often deem workable solutions and remedies unconstitutional. Perhaps it is not ironic that "blue" or "liberal" states are far more likely to house these schools than "red" states. Many of these states are blue only because they have large populations of Democratic-voting blacks and Latinos in the large, urban, poverty-concentrated and racially isolated cities that house these schools (Hutchinson 2008). Rather than offering these groups the fallacy of post-racialism coupled with symbolic racial advancement, upper-class progressives should use their political power to lobby for policies that address poverty, race, and substantive justice.

In addition to distorting the material inequality associated with gender and race, the post-racial and post-feminism rhetoric does not honestly portray the election campaigns in which the discourse emerged. Despite Obama's effort to remain post-racial, he invoked racial symbols frequently during his campaign. His numerous appeals to President Lincoln blatantly connected his candidacy with symbols of emancipation and progress. His references to Dr. Martin Luther King also demonstrated the historic nature of his candidacy. And while blacks have been aligned with the Democratic Party since Franklin Delano Roosevelt persuaded them to leave the Republican Party, the energy and high participation among black voters during this election cycle clearly resulted from and fueled Obama's success. Although many progressives analyzed exit polls that showed some white voters preferred Clinton to Obama due to his race, some polls also showed that a significant number of voters selected Obama due to his race (CNN 2008c). Whether these numbers influenced the outcome of the election is irrelevant. The fact that voters took race into account when selecting either Clinton or Obama demonstrates the significance of race to voter behavior. Obama exploited the relevance of race by downplaying it in order to appeal to white moderates and conservatives, but he also promoted his racial background in order to construct a progressive narrative that appealed to white liberals and to persons of color.

Clinton shied away from gender, but she also invoked it to her advantage. Women voters fueled Clinton's success, and when commentators demanded that she withdraw from the race, her supporters and Democratic strategists denounced the critiques as sexist attacks (Fouhy 2008). Later, Clinton herself mentioned the sexism she faced on the campaign trail (Romano 2008: C1). The fact that she possibly referenced sexism for political gain does not negate its reality. Nor does it make her manipulation of sex more sinister than Obama's manipulation of race. Ironically, both of the post-identity candidates advanced identity-based narratives.

Traditional racial patterns also emerged on election night. Although the mass media portrayed Obama's victory as proof of the insignificance of race, exit polls discredit the media's post-racial reporting. Since 1964, no Democrat has won a majority of white votes in a presidential election. Obama did not disturb that 44-year-old trend. In 11 of the states that Obama won, he failed to get a majority of white votes, and in five other states that he won, the vote among whites was extraordinarily close. Even in his home state of Illinois, Obama beat McCain by only three points among white voters (Hutchinson 2008).

The post-racial rhetoric also fails to appreciate the critical role that blacks and Latinos contributed to Obama's victory. Black and Latino voters helped secure his victory in almost all of the battleground states, including Pennsylvania, Nevada, Florida, Indiana, Ohio, and North Carolina (see CNN 2008a).

The "gender gap," though not as pronounced as the racial gap, also impacted the election. Obama received 56 percent of all votes cast by women. Women represented 53 percent of all votes nationwide. Women alone decided the popular vote for Obama (see CNN 2008a).

Because race, sex, sexual orientation, and other identity categories produce societal and individual harms, these categories function as instruments of organized political activity through which subordinate groups contest and resist subjugation. Social movement mobilization is essential for policy reform, and identity categories help to organize social groups around broadly shared experiences and political values. Although persons within identity groups do not have uniform experiences, the categories remain powerful methods for bringing people together ideologically and politically in order to lobby for change (Hutchinson 2002: 1467).

The post-race and post-feminism rhetoric either assumes that these categories have outlived their usefulness because they no longer produce harm or that there are more effective ways to unify people for progressive politics. The idea that race, sex, sexual orientation, and other identity categories no longer function as sources of inequality lacks empirical support. Moreover, no post-identity proponent has offered a political organizational tool that would produce as effective results as identity. Before discarding available methods of social movement organization, post-identity progressives should at least map out an alternative path. Their failure to do so suggests that post-identity movement participants have not seriously examined the political content of a world without identity.

Rules of engagement: disclaimers regarding the use of identity

The foregoing analysis contends that race and sex remain important social and political factors in the US. Although the analysis criticizes commentators who have embraced post-identity politics, identity politics is not unproblematic or beyond critique. There are several important limits related to identity politics that require elaboration. These inadequacies do not warrant the abandonment of identity politics, but they should inform decisions regarding the content of identity-based social movements.

To the extent that critics of identity politics frown upon vulgar essentialism—or simplistic identity-based voting—the criticism is compelling. Voting for a candidate simply because of "sex" or "race" does not reflect a sophisticated understanding of the political process.

Furthermore, critiquing post-racial and post-feminist discourse does not imply that inequality occurs only or primarily through the lenses of race and sex. Other factors, including class, sexuality, disability, and age are highly relevant to an analysis of material inequality. Class, however, often becomes a preferred "alternative" to discussions of race among adherents of post-racialism. But sociological data do not support this dichotomous analysis. Race and class are distinct though related concepts. The confluence of racism and poverty produces distinct social harms that might require specifically tailored solutions (Wilson 1987, 1997). By treating racial inequality as exclusively a problem of class, post-racial critics fail to appreciate the reality of racialized poverty.

Finally, condemning post-racialism and post-feminism does not preclude strategic advancement of the concepts. Political opportunities might exist if social movement actors and politicians creatively frame issues in ways that transcend race or sex. Advocating post-identity as a sociological truth or as a totalizing model of political activism, however, is unjustifiable.

Human rights or class-based frames offer some promise, but these concepts can trigger political backlash as well and can morph into traditional identity discussions. The welfare reform debates, for example, turned into discussions about race, sexuality, and the purported deviance of black women, even though the policies address economic vulnerability, not racial inequality (Roberts 1995: 2621).

Finally, the fact that much of the recent post-identity discourse took place during an election cycle might mean that many progressives who advanced the narrative did so for momentary political gain. The post-racial narrative likely allowed Obama to gain significant white votes, and his supporters advocated this trope for that purpose. The "first black president" narrative also appealed to voters wanting an historic election, and Obama's campaign and supporters marketed that idea as well.

Conclusion

For almost three decades, liberals have debated the relevance of social identity and the efficacy of identity-based politics. Despite the importance of identity-based politics to progressive social movements, during the 2008 presidential election, liberals joined conservatives and celebrated post-racial and post-feminist rhetoric. But the notion that a post-racial or post-gender society exists within the United States is misleading and dangerous.

Rather than embracing post-racial or post-gender politics, progressives should work to overcome some of the pitfalls associated with identity politics. They should also lobby for the implementation of policies that address material inequality, rather than symbolic justice. The antiracist and feminist projects have survived passionate internal dissent. But unless participants in these movements reassert the value of identity categories and cohere around a set of progressive and materialist goals, the post-identity advocates might ultimately prevail during this current wave of internal criticism.

Chapter 13

Gender equality, citizenship status, and the politics of belonging[1]

Siobhán Mullally

This chapter examines recent debates on the "politics of belonging" (Yuval-Davis 2006: 197), taking as its starting point the *Mme M* (2008) decision of the French Conseil d'État[2] on the subject of gender equality and citizenship status. In this case, the test for acquisition of citizenship became a tool with which to demarcate "insiders" and "outsiders," those who are deserving of citizenship status and those who are not. Gender, and gendered identities, played a key role in this process of demarcation, as did the negotiation of autonomy, cultural pluralism, and equality. The citizenship decision follows on the heels of a series of controversies in France and elsewhere on the wearing of the veil. These cases test the limits of religious freedom and secularism and raise challenging questions for feminism, and for the negotiation of the norms of equality and of autonomy.

The Feminism and Legal Theory Project has been engaged with questions of equality and autonomy for more than 25 years, as evidenced by the work of Martha Fineman and her many writings on questions of care, dependency, and substantive equality. Fineman's *The Autonomy Myth* and other works, have interrogated liberalism's commitment to the myth of the freely choosing subject, and with it, the presumption of an isolated, atomistic human self. In place of the paradigmatic lonely "moral geometrician" (Benhabib 1992: 52), the human self is recognized as being embedded in webs of interlocking narratives, narratives that link us with gendered identities, families, markets, and states.

Legal and other strategies to secure distributive justice and a more egalitarian society have been debated at many of the uncomfortable conversations the Feminism and Legal Theory Project has hosted over the last 25 years. More recently, the Feminism and Legal Theory Project has been engaged with the concept of vulnerability (Fineman 2008: 8–40). The vulnerability of the human condition is recognized as universal, transcending the boundaries of culture, class, gender, or race. While the condition of vulnerability is universal, however, the ability of the human person to overcome or to respond to any potential disadvantage is shaped by the resources and supports available. Vulnerability analysis has been deployed in Fineman's recent works to outline the steps that may be required to build a more responsive and supportive state (Gewirth 1996) and to analyze the institutions and structures that perpetuate group-based privilege and disadvantage.

Vulnerability may also arise from cultural or religious difference and is often linked to socio-economic disadvantages that are faced by immigrant and minority communities. Vulnerability analysis in Martha Fineman's work is presented as "post-identity," in that it moves beyond a preoccupation with group-based discrimination or status-based inequalities that retain identity categories at their core (Fredman 2007: 214–34). As such, vulnerability analysis may provide a useful set of tools to interrogate the structures, concepts, and institutions that further inclusion or exclusion. Citizenship is one such institution.

Increasingly, in Europe and elsewhere, we are witnessing the construction of new barriers to the acquisition of citizenship. Demonstrating a commitment to liberal values, including sexual equality, may require following a particular way of life or "pathway," one that fits with the dominant conception of what it means to be a member of a political community and of a nation-state. Yet such barriers, while professing a commitment to equality, may serve only to entrench further the vulnerability of an immigrant woman, who is excluded from full membership of the political community if denied citizenship. Such membership continues to have practical and normative significance. While we may have moved beyond Hannah Arendt's notion of citizenship as the "right to have rights" (1958: 297), post-national and disaggregated notions of citizenship have not yet secured for immigrant women the fuller legal protections that attach to the status of citizen.

France, citizenship, assimilation, and the headscarf debate

John Crowley (1999: 30) has defined the politics of belonging as "the dirty work of boundary maintenance." In recent years, the politicization of multicultural policies and the increasing moral panic surrounding identity politics have fuelled public concerns that group-differentiated citizenship threatens the bonds of community necessary for social cohesion. In turn, cultural symbols or signifiers of group difference, such as distinct dress codes or separate systems of religious-based personal law, have become markers both of difference and of resistance. The conflicting claims that arise between the pursuit of gender equality and the protection of collective claims raise particularly intractable questions within multicultural states (Knights 2005; McGoldrick 2006; Mullally 2006; Volpp 2001). Multicultural disputes frequently touch on the roles and status ascribed to women and children. Feminism has struggled with the politics of multiculturalism, concerned, on the one hand, to recognize the significance of religious, cultural, and other differences, and, on the other hand, reluctant to yield to claims that seek to privatize the pursuit of gender equality.

The "rifts of intercultural difference" are most keenly felt along the boundaries demarcating the public from the private sphere (Benhabib 1992: 83). These boundaries, of course, are deeply gendered. In recent years, liberal feminism has tended to dismiss multicultural politics as "bad for women" or as an "excuse for bad behaviour" (Okin 1999: 7–26). Dismissing multiculturalism as an oppositional force, however, denies the possibility of arriving at just multicultural arrangements—arrangements that both define the limits of reasonable pluralism and recognize the significance of religious and cultural differences. From a feminist perspective, collective claims have often been the "ties that bind." Collective claims are not, of course, necessarily in conflict with feminism, or as Benhabib (1999: 58) points out, "Moral autonomy and cultural pluralism need not always conflict, but when they do it is important to know where one stands."

The demarcation of gender roles has always been intertwined with debates on national identity. In nascent nation-states, gender trouble could not be countenanced. As Iris Young (2000: 252) points out, nationalist ideologies have always tended to define their groups in either–or terms. The nation is conceptualized as strictly bounded between insiders and outsiders, as nationalists struggle to define attributes of national identity or character that all members share. The task of preserving a national collectivity has been viewed as requiring intervention by the state in cultural and religious practices of immigrant communities as well as the policing of those who are allowed to enter and eventually become citizens (Yuval-Davis et al. 2005: 517). Immigration policy, in its inclusionary and exclusionary practices, acts as an initial arbiter in determining who has the possibility of belonging and becoming a future citizen (Yuval-Davis et al. 2005: 517). The demarcation between insiders and outsiders, of course, is frequently both gendered and racialized. As Stuart Hall notes, a pressing question (one that has engaged feminist legal theorists) is, "how can people live together in difference?" (cited in Yuval-Davis et al. 2006: 6). This question has become the subject of heated debate in France, following a recent decision on what it means to demonstrate belonging in contemporary French society.

In June, 2008, France's highest administrative court, the Conseil d'État, upheld a decision to deny citizenship to Mme M, aged 32, on the ground that her "radical" practice of Islam was incompatible with essential French values, specifically gender equality. She had, the Court affirmed, failed to satisfy the test of assimilation required for the grant of citizenship. Eight years previously, in 2000, Mme M (a Moroccan citizen) married a French citizen of Moroccan descent and moved to France from Morocco. She had four children, all of French nationality. She speaks fluent French. In 2004, Mme M applied for French citizenship. Her request was denied a year later because of "insufficient assimilation" into France.

The case brings to the fore the potential for conflict between the norms of autonomy, religious freedom, and the requirements of "belonging" imposed by the state. In this case, Mme M did not meet the criteria required to belong to the French state. There was, in her case, an excess of culture, an excess that went beyond defined limits. Here, "belonging" required assimilation. The Commissaire du Gouvernement, Mme Bordenave, in her *Conclusions* submitted to the Conseil d'État, stated that the refusal to grant citizenship to Mme M was not based solely on the wearing of the *niqab* but rather on her whole way of life, which displayed "*la soumission totale*" (complete submission) to the men in her family.[3] Supporting this conclusion, reference was made to her mornings spent bringing her children to school and undertaking housework and afternoons visiting her father or father-in-law. She sometimes shopped on her own, but more often, it was noted, went to the supermarket with her husband. In her favor, the Commissaire noted that she spoke French, her children attended public school, and that she was attended by a male gynecologist during her pregnancy (Conclusions de Mme Prada Bordenave 2008). (This latter reference, in particular, is strange, suggesting that if Mme M had preferred to be attended by a female gynecologist, a further failing of assimilation would have been found.)

The Commissaire noted that Mme M had maintained "*des liens très forts*" (very strong connections) with her culture of origin. Mme M, in turn, in her submissions to the Conseil d'État, argued that maintaining links with her culture of origin was not incompatible with French citizenship, and further that she had not sought to challenge or question the values of "La République," which include the protection of religious freedom. In particular, she argued that she had not contested the state's commitment to "*la laïcité*" (or secularism), which allowed her to practice her religion. Here, secularism is invoked by Mme M as a normative framework that would support a flourishing of difference, including competing conceptions of the good life. A religious life, meaning one that includes adherence to particular conceptions of Islam, for her, is a good life. In an interview, reported in the *New York Times*, Mme M, in contrast, commented on her wearing of the *niqab*:

> It is my choice. I take care of my children, and I leave the house when I please. I have my own car. I do the shopping on my own. Yes, I am a practicing Muslim, I am orthodox. But is that not my right?
>
> (Bennhold 2008: A1)

The Conseil d'État concluded, however, that she had adopted a radical religious practice, which was incompatible with the essential values of French society. It was the first time that a French court had judged someone's capacity to be assimilated into France based on private religious practice, taking *laïcité* (secularism) from the public sphere into the home.

The ruling on Mme M received almost unequivocal support across the political spectrum in France, including among many Muslims. Fadela Amara, the French Minister for Urban Affairs and former director of feminist NGO, "Ni Putes, Ni Soumises," referred to Mme M's *niqab*, as "a prison" and a "straitjacket." Rejecting appeals to liberal values of religious freedom, she argued that the *niqab* "is not a religious insignia but the insignia of a totalitarian political project that promotes inequality between the sexes and is totally lacking in democracy" (cited in Bennhold 2008: A1). As Iris Young (2000) has noted, however, the totalizing narrative always leaves a remainder. Missing from Amara's categorical rejection of the wearing of the *niqab* is any openness to Mme M's representation of the meaning and significance of her religious practice. Here, we see the error made both by strong communitarian multiculturalists and by some liberal feminists: the failure to acknowledge the possibility of difference within cultural communities. Both are working with a vision of cultures as organic and hermetically sealed wholes. In contrast, if we view cultures as internally riven and essentially contested narratives, identity then becomes, not a cultural given or an inherited attribute, but the "unique and fragile achievement of selves," weaving together conflicting narratives and allegiances (Benhabib 2002: xi, 16). This understanding of identity as dynamic, complex, and individually constituted, in turn, opens up greater possibilities for the negotiation of cultural conflicts.

Previous jurisprudence of the Conseil d'État had established that the wearing of the headscarf or veil, in itself, even in adherence to religious practice or belief, could not justify the finding of a failure to assimilate (*Mme E. Y.* 1999). What had changed since then? A hint of the changing sentiment toward cultural, and in particular, religious diversity can be seen in the Court's brief comments on Mme M's way of life. Mme M and her husband were identified as "salafistes,"[4] a group that was noted as having links with an extremist imam within the local community. Here we see the encroachment of the politics of a war on terror, used to fuel suspicions of the immigrant other and to dispel the possibility of a tolerance of difference. Difference is here equated with danger, and the recurring trope of the Muslim terrorist is conflated with Mme M's perceived excess of culture. Such equations are familiar terrain within citizenship debates. The suspicion and fear of the enemy alien, or of possible competing and disruptive allegiances, has long shaped the boundaries of belonging and membership. As Sherene Razack (2002: 4) has noted, the September 11 attacks on the World Trade Center and the Pentagon in the US greatly intensified the policing of bodies of color. This policing, most especially of minority Muslim communities, has led to increasing constraints being imposed on access to citizenship status and to the holding of dual nationality. This was occurring at a time when it had been thought that a greater acceptance of multiple and overlapping spheres of belonging was emerging, along with the decline of the significance of citizenship as a prerequisite for the assertion of rights. As Nira Yuval-Davis (2006: 213) has pointed out, "In these post-9/11 (and, in Britain, post-7/7) times, 'strangers' are seen not only as a threat to the cohesion of the political and cultural community but also as potential terrorists."

More recently, the French National Assembly has considered introducing a new legislative prohibition on the wearing of the face veil in public spaces. On 26 January 2010, the widely anticipated Parliamentary Commission Report on the wearing of the *voile intégral* (face veil) in France was published.[5] The 200-page report includes recommendations for legislative and policy initiatives to deter and limit the practice, which is described as a challenge to the French Republic and to republican values. Against those who question France's preoccupation with the veil, the report argues that the veil represents more than a piece of cloth; it reflects a system of values, a set of social and family constraints that weigh on the veiled Muslim woman. Pre-empting the presentation of the Commission's Report to Parliament, a leading figure in the governing UMP party, Jean Cope, presented proposals to Parliament for a sweeping prohibition on the wearing of the face veil in all public spaces.[6] The Commission's Report, however, recommends only that a general prohibition be considered at some time in the future, noting that it was not possible to achieve unanimity on such a recommendation.[7] Several members of the Commission, however, did support a general legislative ban, extending to all public spaces, to be justified on grounds of national security and public order. Their arguments are presented in an annexe to the main report.

The decision to recommend only a limited prohibition, restricting the wearing of the face veil in public services, was met with a heated response from Parliament, with some representatives rejecting what they referred to as a *"demi-loi."* Their response reflects broader divisions on the role of law in eliminating the practice of veiling in France and concerns arising from the compatibility of a more sweeping prohibition with constitutional and ECHR protections. Notably, however, concern as to the impact of such measures on Muslim women and girls, and on minority and immigrant communities more generally, was voiced by only a few. The Chair of the Commission, Andre Gerin (Communist MP), noted the possibility of a general prohibition on veiling being struck down by the Constitutional Court, or by the European Court of Human Rights, and the necessity of working within the limits of rights protections. These limits are pushed, however. By restricting the scope of the proposed prohibition, the Commission hopes that the requirements of proportionality, key to protections relative to the European Convention of Human Rights (ECHR) on religious freedom and freedom of expression, will be met. The concern with proportionality, and effectiveness, is evident also in the discussion on enforcement. Rather than proposing the imposition of fines or other penalties for non-compliance, the Report proposes that wearing the face veil will lead to a refusal of public services, though how this will be enforced in public transportation, for example, is unclear. The message and implications of this prohibition are clear, however. Cultural difference is to be pushed to the realms of the private; the public sphere is to remain culture free, neutral, universal. The disciplinary reach of the state is also expanded, to encompass multiple sites of contact with individuals in the public sphere. The Report's recommendation to extend the legislative prohibition on veiling follows a strangely perverse logic. As Alain Badiou notes, the face veil is viewed as a symbol of oppression, the conclusion therefore is to "banish the women who obstinately wear it. Basically put: these girls or women are oppressed. Hence they shall be punished."[8]

The veil in human rights litigation: at the limits of rights?

A series of cases on the wearing of the veil have tested the rights protected by the European Convention on Human Rights, specifically the rights to religious freedom, non-discrimination, and freedom of expression. The case of medical student Leyla Şahin (*Şahin v. Turkey* 2005) is one of these cases. It raises questions concerning the intersection of gender equality, religious freedom, and cultural identity. In 1998, Leyla Şahin was dismissed from a state university in Istanbul because she was wearing a *hijab* (Islamic headscarf) on campus, in contravention of university regulations. The European Court of Human Rights, in its final Grand Chamber Judgment of 10 November 2005, denied Leyla Şahin's claim that her right to religious freedom had been violated by the Turkish authorities' refusal to allow her to wear the *hijab* while attending a state university. The Court's rationale conceded that prohibiting the wearing of the *hijab* constitutes interference with the human right to freedom of religion, specifically Leyla Şahin's right to manifest her religion in public by observing what she perceives as an Islamic dress standard. However, interference is not always and not necessarily a violation. The ECHR was interpreted to permit states to impose restrictions on the manifestation of religion if the following requirements are met. The restriction is prescribed by law; the restriction is imposed by the state in pursuit of one or more public interest grounds, to wit: public safety, protection of public order, health or morals, or protection of the rights and freedoms of others; and the restriction is "necessary in a democratic society," i.e. it constitutes a proportionate response to a pressing social need (*Şahin v. Turkey* 2005).

A majority of 16 to 1 Grand Chamber judges found that a governmental ban in Turkey against wearing the headscarf was a necessary and proportionate response to a pressing social need. In arriving at its conclusion, the Court appealed to the doctrine of "a margin of appreciation," permitted to states, in the interpretation of the ECHR and found that the state's interference was "justified in principle and proportionate to the aim pursued" (*Şahin* 2005, para. 122). The single dissenting judge, Françoise Tulkens, rejected the appeal to the margin of appreciation doctrine, noting that no other member state of the Council of Europe had prohibited the wearing of the headscarf by Muslim students at university level. In her view, the majority's reasoning abdicated responsibility for the protection of human rights (Şahin Dissenting Opinion 2005: para. 3). The majority judgment, she concluded, applied the principles of secularism and equality so as to restrict freedom. In contrast, she argued that the principles of secularism, equality, and freedom ought to be harmonized and not applied in conflict. This possibility remained despite threats from "extremist movements," which she concluded could not be a reason to restrict the wearing of the headscarf: "Merely wearing the headscarf cannot be associated with fundamentalism and it is vital to distinguish between those who wear the headscarf and 'extremists' who seek to impose the headscarf as they do other religious symbols" (Şahin Dissenting Opinion 2005: para. 10). Judge Tulkens' concern not to conflate religious observance with violent extremism was a minority position, however. The failure of the Court to harmonize the principles of secularism, equality, and freedom, in this case, reflected a reluctance to engage with religious difference and a denial of Leyla Şahin's claim to a distinct cultural identity. The case raises challenging questions for feminists, presenting an apparent conflict between equality and autonomy.

In the *Şahin* case, the liberal discourses of equality and secularism are advanced in a salvage operation, "if not [as] salvation itself" (Bhabha 1999: 83). In the most recent headscarf case to come before the European Court, *Dogru v. France* (2008), the Court upheld a school regulation requiring the removal of headscarves during physical education classes. Relying on Article 9(2), (the right to manifest one's religious belief), the applicants complained that this regulation violated their right to manifest their religious belief. They also alleged that they had been deprived of their right to education within the meaning of Article 2 of Protocol 1 ECHR. The Court noted that the wearing of religious signs was not inherently incompatible with the principle of secularism in schools, but could become so according to the conditions in which they were worn and the consequences that the wearing of a sign might have in a particular case. In the applicants' cases, the Court considered that the conclusion reached by the national authorities, *viz,* that the wearing of the Islamic headscarf was incompatible with sports classes for reasons of health or safety, was not unreasonable. The Court accepted the state's argument that the penalty imposed was merely the consequence of the applicants' refusal to comply with the school rules and not a consequence of their manifestation of religious convictions, as they alleged. The penalty of expulsion, in the Court's view, was not disproportionate. In a summary dismissal of the right to education claims, the Court noted that the applicants had been able to continue their schooling by correspondence classes (*Dogru v. France* 2008).

Recent rulings of the UK courts under the 1998 Human Rights Act offer detailed analyses of the conflicting claims that can arise when restrictions are imposed on the display of religious symbols by educational institutions. As is revealed through law's engagement with the headscarf debate, the politics of British belonging has increasingly become concerned with defining the extent to which one may adhere to a particular culture and still "belong" to the British citizenry (Enright 2009). One of the leading cases in this field is *R (Begum) v. Head Teacher and Governors of Denbigh High School* (2007). Shabina Begum contended that the head teacher and governors of Denbigh High School excluded her from that school, unjustifiably limited her right under Article 9 of the ECHR to manifest her religion or beliefs, and violated her right not to be denied education under Article 2 of the First Protocol to the Convention. Denbigh High School's student population was overwhelmingly Muslim (79 percent). The school uniform policy permitted the wearing of the *shalwar kameeze*. Ms. Begum, however, had sought permission to wear the *jilbab* (a long coat-like garment) but was refused.

The main question for consideration by the courts was whether Ms. Begum's freedom to manifest her belief by her dress was subject to limitation or interference within the meaning of Article 9(2) ECHR and, if so, whether such limitation or interference was justified. A majority of the House of Lords concluded that Ms. Begum's Article 9 rights had not been interfered with as there was nothing to prevent her from attending a school where she was allowed to wear a *jilbab*. A minority concluded that there had been an interference with Ms. Begum's right to manifest her religious belief, noting that the ease with which an individual pupil could change schools might be overstated. However, the Lords further concluded that this interference with Article 9 rights was justified within the meaning of Article 9(2). The defining feature of the judgment was the importance the Court attached to the school's flexible uniform policy. The Court noted that the school had taken "immense pains to devise a uniform policy which respected Muslim beliefs but did so in an inclusive, unthreatening and uncompetitive way" (*Begum* 2007: para. 34). Lord Bingham noted that on a different set of facts the Court might have concluded that a student was *de facto* excluded from school, perhaps unjustifiably so. Baroness Hale noted the competing claims that can arise in such a case and stressed the exceptional position of public schools and of state education. She noted Denbigh High School, in deciding how far to go in accommodating religious requirements within its dress code, had to reconcile some complex considerations. These, she concluded, were helpfully explained by Professor Frances Radnay:

> a prohibition of veiling risks violating the liberal principle of respect for individual autonomy and cultural diversity for parents as well as students. It may also result in traditionalist families not sending their children to the state educational institutions. In this educational context, implementation of the right to equality is a complex matter, and the determination of the way it should be achieved depends upon the balance between these two conflicting policy priorities in a specific social environment.
>
> (Radnay 2003: 663)

The case of *Ms. A Azmi v. Kirklees Metropolitan Borough Council* (2007) raised the issue of religious discrimination in employment in an educational institution. Ms. Azmi, a teaching assistant in a West Yorkshire school, was asked to remove her *niqab*, a face veil worn by some Muslim women that leaves only the eyes visible, because pupils found it hard to understand her during English language lessons. The Employment Appeals Tribunal found that suspension of Ms. Azmi did not amount to discrimination on religious grounds. The Tribunal accepted that the dress code imposed by the employers potentially could constitute indirect discrimination and, therefore, it required some justification. In this case, however, the Tribunal concluded that the requirement to remove the *niqab* was a proportionate response pursuing a legitimate aim and, thus, was a permissible restriction on the Ms. Azmi's right to manifest her religious belief.

The politics of belonging underpinning these cases reflects an agenda of concern with community and social cohesion being presented as seeking to manage diverse cultural identities (United Kingdom Home Office 2004). The *Cantle Report* on community cohesion identifies "support for women's rights ... and respect for both religious differences and secular views" as common elements of nationhood (Cantle 2001: para. 5.17). The Report is also concerned, however, with the perceived dangers of excesses of culture, and the threats posed by links to "back home" politics (para. 5.1.12). This concern finds echoes in the *Mme M* case, where the wearing of the *niqab* is linked to the activities of *salafistes* and potentially subversive politics. As is evident from the *Mme M* case, where the discourse of cohesion and assimilation is linked to citizenship, the agenda of the *Cantle Report* can acquire repressive connotations (Lea 2004: 196). Kundnani (2002: 47) has noted that the appearance of the cohesion agenda has marked the end of the multicultural settlement in the UK, with the "parallel cultural bloc" now seen as part of the problem, not the solution. In recent headscarf litigation, the wearing of the veil has become a signifier of this parallel and threatening cultural bloc.

Citizenship and the politics of belonging

The *Mme M* case reinforces what Sherene Razack refers to as a familiar hierarchy of citizenship:

> on the one hand, original citizens whose values must be respected (and whose values, it goes without saying, are superior) and on the other, foreigners whose alien values have the potential to contaminate the body politic and who must be purged.
>
> (Razack 2004: 156)

Muslim women in particular, when adhering to strict Islamic dress codes, are defined as other, as "insufficiently modern." These Muslim others, are beyond reason, apparently fixed in a premodern state of abjectness. The other refuses to remain fixed, however. The universalized Western subject is constantly required to engage with difference, an engagement revealed in the law's response that is "fraught with desire, fear and anxiety" (Razack 2008: 58). Leti Volpp (2007), writing on "The Culture of Citizenship," noted that when the citizen is defined in terms of the universal, the culturally particular is defined as "other." The supposedly universalist character of liberal citizenship proves to be exclusionary, reflecting hegemonic and usually majoritarian positions (Balibar 1990: 283). The universal subject becomes again the abstract, de-particularized subject, so often critiqued by feminism. Ironically, this subject is now deployed in the pursuit of a state-sponsored feminism that stringently polices the borders of belonging. "Imperilled Muslim Women" and "Dangerous Muslim Men" are familiar tropes in citizenship discourses (Razack 2004). As noted by Purvis and

Hunt (1999: 467), the concept of nation has manifested a disturbing tendency to closure and constriction in times of crisis, with legitimate access to citizenship rights being preserved for those who meet new standards of stringency on the criteria of recognition.

The universal subject invoked to support the pursuit of gender equality masks an exclusionary particularism, however; it masks the particularism of specific histories, locations, and values. As such it risks excluding many of those who fall outside its borders. This exclusionary potential can be seen in Richard Rorty's appeal to a "solidarity" without "common humanity." Rorty (1989: 191–92) argues our sense of solidarity is strongest, "when those with whom solidarity is expressed are thought of as 'one of us', where 'us' means something smaller and more local than the human race." He concludes that "because she is a human being" is "a weak, unconvincing explanation of a generous action." A person's claim to moral consideration thereby depends on that person being one of us, being of the community. Rorty himself insists that the force of any "we"—any claim of moral community—is dependent on the contrast with a human "they," which encloses something smaller and more local than the human race. The implications of this line of reasoning can be seen in the following statement:

> I claim that the force of "us" is, typically, contrastive in the sense that it contrasts with a "they" which is also made up of human beings—the wrong sort of human beings.
>
> (Rorty 1989: 190–91)

Thus we see that the inclusionary surface of the language of community, as Nicola Lacey (1998: 134) has pointed out, often masks the exclusion of the "hated Other." The abstract, universal value of gender equality is invoked so as to exclude from its scope religious women and girls, who engage in gendered religious practices such as the wearing of the Islamic headscarf.

In the context of ever more stringent citizenship tests, ever more constraining politics of belonging, the universal subject, abstracted from context, from cultural particularity, becomes yet again an exclusionary force. But this time, it is not feminism that is on the outside, questioning the claims to universality of the citizen subject, the subject of liberal discourses of rights. Feminism appears to be on the inside. Perhaps more correctly, feminism is being instrumentalized in pursuit of this exclusionary agenda. The question for feminism is how to negotiate these apparently conflicting claims, to universality, to equality, and to difference. And what role is to be given to the value of autonomy? The headscarf debate in France and in the UK exemplifies what is widely perceived as the battle between a culture-free citizenship and a culturally laden other (Volpp 2007: 571). Citizenship and cultural difference, however, are both imagined and produced. In the *Mme M* case, the reasoning of the Conseil d'État opposes citizenship to cultural difference but does not present citizenship as neutral. Rather it is premised on particular values, specifically in this case a conception of equality of the sexes that excludes the practices of a religious Muslim woman, one who observes an "orthodox" Islam—to borrow Mme M's own words.

This denial of difference has long been a concern of feminist legal theorists. As Catharine MacKinnon (2006a: 106) notes, for example, many Polish Jews died because they only spoke Yiddish: "They could not 'pass' as not Jews." Recognition and survival depended on meeting the dominant standard. MacKinnon (2006a: 106) draws an analogy with the psychology of battered women, "keeping your head low keeps you alive." This, she says, is the equality of the Enlightenment. This, also, is the conception of equality that underpins the decision of the Conseil d'État to confirm the denial of citizenship status for Mme M. She had failed to assimilate; she had failed to demonstrate a commitment to the dominant conception of gender equality. As Habermas (1998: xxxv) has noted, however, "Equal respect for *everyone* is not limited to those who are like us; it extends to the person of the other in his or her otherness ... those who are strangers to one another and want to remain strangers" (emphasis added).

Difference feminism has been concerned to recognize the significance of difference between women, and to move away from the unitary and often exclusionary category of woman that has underpinned liberal feminist discourses on equality. Nicola Lacey (1998: 4) describes difference feminism as based on a "complex idea of equality which accommodates and values, whilst not fixing, women's specificity as women." The challenge to the unitary category "woman" has come from two main sources: the theoretical advance of post-structuralism and from black, minority ethnic, and third world women who have been ignored or rendered invisible by the false universalism that has underpinned much of liberal feminism. Black feminists and critical race feminists have taken the lead in unmasking the particular woman embodied in the unitary category "woman." This process of unmasking has required white women to recognize their own role and agency as oppressors, however unwitting. To quote Audre Lorde (1984: 117), writing more than 20 years ago: "As white women ignore their built-in privilege of whiteness and define *woman* in terms of their own experience alone, then women of Color become 'other,' the outsider whose experience and tradition is too 'alien' to comprehend." Critical race feminists have highlighted the tendency to homogenize the "third-world woman" (Kapur 2002). This tendency has lead to the creation of what Mohanty (1988: 62) terms, "a composite, singular third-world woman," a woman who is denied all agency and portrayed only as a victim. The abject woman reappears in reasoning of the Conseil d'État in the *Mme M* case, this time presented as the victim of a totalizing patriarchy, rooted in a conservative Islam. Postcolonial feminist theory has highlighted the familiar trope within European feminisms of the abject woman. As Uma Narayan (1997: 19) has noted, Victorian feminists contributed to the portrayal of the Indian woman as a dependent subject. As feminists, their own claims to political agency were supported by what they claimed as a special moral responsibility to "save" the downtrodden women of the colonies. Indian women appeared as the natural and logical "white woman's burden."

A dual-track approach

Drawing on the work of discourse ethics theorists, I would suggest that a dual-track approach to the politics of multiculturalism is required, one that combines legal regulation with an expanded moral dialogue. Legal regulation is viewed as a last resort. Its role is to define the limits of reasonable pluralism, and it does so with reference to the core moral principles of equal moral respect and egalitarian reciprocity. Legal regulation, specifying constitutional essentials that trump other legal claims, is combined with an expanded moral–political dialogue in which all have equal rights to participate. Such an expanded moral–political dialogue is necessary if we are to do justice to the "complexities of cross-cultural communication" (Benhabib 1995: 244). Such dialogues can lead to a reinterpretation of inherited traditions and recognition that religious communities may have within themselves the possibilities of more egalitarian outcomes. Difference feminism has highlighted the need to recognize such complexities.

The deliberative democratic model of multiculturalism may challenge different "ways of life" in a very fundamental sense. Voluntary self-ascription or freedom of exit and association are principles that may be incompatible with a way of life that views group membership as a given. These conditions are necessary, however, if gender equality is to be safeguarded in a multicultural society. Importantly, the dual-track approach recognizes the need to go beyond mere legal regulation of conflicting cultural claims. The denial of individual autonomy by the state in the Şahin case, and ultimately by the European Court, represents a denial of difference, a denial that goes beyond the limits of permissible regulation. The exclusion of difference is to be found also in the Mme M citizenship judgment. In both, autonomy is undermined, culture essentialized. Despite the demise of the multicultural settlement, however, the "multicultural question" has remained. How can people live together in difference, without, "either one group [the less powerful group] having to become the imitative version of the dominant one, i.e. an assimilationism/or, on the other hand, the two groups hating one another, or projecting images of degradation?" (Yuval-Davis 2006: 213). Antiracist and feminist theorists have developed ways of thinking about citizenship that are more inclusive of difference and even start from a presumption of difference. The rush to an ultimately reductionist concept of equality should not deny these ways of thinking.

Notes

1 This chapter forms part of an Irish Research Council for the Humanities and Social Sciences research project entitled *Gender Equality, Religious Diversity and Multiculturalism*.

2 The Conseil d'État is the highest quasi-judicial body in France, representing the final instance in disputes between public administration and individuals.
3 "Elle vit dans la soumission totale aux hommes de sa famille, qui se manifeste tant le port de son vêtement que dans l'organisation de sa vie quotidienne" (Conclusions de Mme Prada Bordenave 2008).
4 The term salafist is often used interchangeably with Wahabism in the West, though many adherents prefer the former. The term derives from the word *salaf* meaning to "follow" or "precede," a reference to the followers and companions of the Prophet Muhammad. Salafis generally believe that the Quran and the Prophet's practices (*hadith*) are the ultimate religious authority in Islam, rather than the subsequent commentaries produced by Islamic scholars that interpret these sources. Salafism is not a unified movement, and there exists no single Salafi sect.
5 A. Nationale, "Rapport D'Information Sur La Pratique Du Port Du Voile Intégral Sur Le Territoire National" (Paris, France 26 January 2010).
6 See full text, available at: <http://recherche2.assemblee-nationale.fr/resultats_tribun. jsp>.
7 Above note 5, p. 189.
8 See Alain Badiou, *Le Monde*, February 22, 2004.

Engaging intimacy and the family

Introduction to Section Five

Family law and intimate relations have long been central to feminist legal theory. Many first-generation feminist legal theorists wrote extensively about marriage, divorce, and child custody. Violence within intimate relationships has been a key concern for feminists inside and outside the legal discipline. The scholars in this section look to changes that have occurred in family law and continue to extend critiques of our current family law regime.

Using the trope "the houses we enter" to mean "intimate relationships, arrangements, and social practices," Robin West explores the concept of "blanket consent" in intimate relations, asking why and how women give this form of consent to intimacy without recognizing the future risks or harms they may incur. The chapter begins with a brief look at the traditional or prototypical marriage emanating from the nineteenth century into the twentieth. Under this regime, a woman who married gave blanket consent to a number of things. The concept of marital privacy supported the fiction that marriage was harmonious and that it fulfilled women's role as wife to submit to her husband sexually and to reproductivity. A woman's consent to marriage was blanket consent to all future sex, consensual or not, desired or not, and any resulting pregnancies, as well as associated maternal care.

Contemporary views of marriage or quasi-marital sexual relationships may contain traces of this prototypical marriage arrangement. West argues that contemporary women's consent to intimacy is still often seen as blanketed in or outside of marriage. In particular, West examines the contemporary college dormitory, where resident women are seen as giving "blanket consent" to sex. Sociological data show that dorms are sites of intense sexual activity, some of it nonconsensual and a good deal of it consensual but unwanted. She suggests that this happens first because sex is seen as inevitable and desirable; partners don't consult own desires but instead the cultural norms encouraging and celebrating sex as natural/healthy. Second, because of the perception of blanket consent by entering dormitories, the fact that women may not actually desire sex in a particular instance is of little consequence. West sees similarities between marriage and dorm life. Rape is illegal, but not strongly deterred or punished. If women don't desire sex, the problem is understood to be a "psychological" issue that doesn't mesh with current social norms regarding the inevitably and desirability of sex.

West admonishes feminist legal scholars to pay attention to the lives of women and commends the feminist counselors, clergy, administrators, and dormitory staff who listen to what university women are telling them about those lives. She encourages academic feminists also to listen to the women in their classrooms, to teach them about desire—that listening to one's own desires is essential, that it is both personal and political.

Laura Kessler's chapter explores the impact on family law of the de-centering of marriage as family law's central focus and tensions surrounding the displacement of marriage, and she makes predictions about the future of family law. Using the metaphor of the "frontier" allows Kessler to demonstrate how new family law scholarship is at the margins of a "developing territory," one ripe for exploration. In the new frontier scholarship, marriage is not the privileged site of intimacy; rather attention is focused on sexuality, reproduction, and caregiving. We see a shift from an older feminist preoccupation with inequality within marriage to concern about legal inequality between various forms of intimate relations.

Considering what the future holds for family law, Kessler offers some possibilities: (1) family law will disappear or substantially recede, as it is disconnected from its traditional "channeling" purpose; (2) family law will become a more general law of intimacy, which she sees has already occurred to a certain extent as evidenced by subjects taught in family law courses; (3) family law will endure, as there is resistance to its entire disappearance, especially by those committed to the patriarchal, marital family. Kessler concludes that the exploration of "alternative conceptual possibilities for studying sexual and intimate relations" will be beneficial.

Twilia Perry draws our attention to racial hierarchies that exist between women, how these hierarchies play out in family law, and some of the obstacles women face in openly talking about them. Perry contends that the existence of a racial hierarchy among woman has been "undertheorized" in feminist legal theory. Her chapter briefly considers the background of the feminist legal theory and the critical race feminism movements and their work to improve the lives of women. Perry then discusses her own entry into both of these arenas of study.

Perry forcefully argues that black women are at the bottom rung of an American racial hierarchy and that feminists must understand this hierarchy in order to better understand our cultural institutions, groups, and relationships. Gender hierarchies between men and women are often softened by the inevitable social relationships that exist between the two groups. However, far less interaction exists between blacks and whites to soften the racial hierarchy between these groups. As a consequence, talking about race across racial lines can be very difficult for women, particularly when the discussion is about issues of intimacy, family, and caretaking.

Perry offers two areas of racial hierarchy that pose problems for feminists: the theory of alimony and transracial adoption. She points out that the paradigmatic marriage at the center of most alimony cases does not exist for many non-white, lower-income women. Thus, only certain configurations of actual intimate relationships are valued in the alimony debate. Likewise, the controversy over transracial adoptions nearly always involves middle-class white families adopting children of color. Negative stereotypes of black mothers contribute to their devaluation, and as a result the problem of taking a child from its community of origin is viewed as less problematic by many. Perry warns that such insensitivity can foster resentment and generate hostilities between women that can impede our ability to work together on common issues.

She believes that the theory of alimony and the issue of transracial adoption are areas where the interests of feminist legal theorists and critical race feminist theorists could converge more productively, particularly given changing demographics which find more black women in paradigm marriages, more white women in non-paradigm intimate relationships, and more interracial family arrangements. These types of changes should change the way feminists look at women's experience of caregiving and work. Attention to racial hierarchy would also benefit feminist analysis of emerging family law issues, such as same sex marriage or reproductive technologies, promoting insights and further connections that will improve the struggle toward liberation for all women.

Adam Romero's chapter argues that family law creates privilege on two levels: it privileges the heterosexual marital family over other forms of family and privileges those with family over those living without family connections. He focuses on this second set of people, asking what justice requires for individuals with significant disabilities or dependencies who are disconnected from family. How can we reimagine law and society so all people regardless of familial status can achieve a better existence?

Romero's original demographic research on people living alone pays particular attention to adults with significant caregiving needs. As Romero emphasizes, social policies that reinforce the family as central to caregiving generate serious problems for vulnerable and dependent adults who live alone, largely rendering them invisible. His research suggests that (1) the percentage of people living alone has increased significantly in past three decades, while percentage of family households declined; (2) adults living alone compared to the general population are more likely poor, disabled, older, female, unemployed, widowed/divorced/never married; (3) disabled live-alones are more likely than the general disabled population to be poor, female, and widowed/divorced/ never married; and (4) elder adults living alone are more likely to be poor, females, and widowed/divorced/never married than elders in the general population.

After presenting the data, Romero ends the chapter with the story of three individuals who live alone with significant care needs. These stories provide "content and context" that mere data cannot show. Romero argues that the many adults living alone, barely coping physically, economically, and socially, show the "failings of the family regime." He concludes that this failure should encourage us, not to discard family entirely, but to imagine and create ways to meet the needs of these individuals.

Chapter 14

When and where they enter

Robin West

Men and women tender consent to all sorts of trades, bargains, practices, and states of affairs that affect their well-being. Some of these consensual transactions, such as on-the-spot consumer sales, are immediate, the terms are relatively clear, and the effect on well-being, fleeting. Other consensual transactions commit us to a state of affairs or a course of action that will have longer-term impact on our lives. Consent to the purchase of a home commits us to what might be a twenty or thirty year obligation to make timely mortgage payments, obligations which might become more onerous than we once thought should the value of the house decline along with our income. Consent to an "outputs contract" commits a commercial buyer to buy whatever quantity the supplier might produce—a level of obligation that might fluctuate in unexpected ways. Although common law labor contracts are "at will" on both sides, an employer and employee are free, with mutual agreement, to contractually bind themselves for longer periods.

I call this phenomenon "blanket consent." When we give "blanket consent," we consent at an early point to risks that later may come to pass. The widely shared assumption in contract law, and the various market-driven ideologies that inform it, is that should those risks occur, the entire transaction is nevertheless value enhancing; we consented to the risk and likely were compensated for it at the point of consent. Blanket consent to future risk is no different from on-the-spot consent to the terms of a sale: the giving of consent is conclusive proof of the value of the transaction to the consenting parties, even should the consensually borne and presumptively bargained-for risk come to pass. The mortgage might become far more onerous, should the value of our house go down or should our income plummet. Likewise, the outputs contract might exceed our capacity to purchase the good, should our suppliers' capacity unexpectedly rise. Our opportunity costs on a five-year labor contract might be much higher than anticipated when we first signed on. Nevertheless, even if these risks occur, we assume in both law and theory that the contract in its entirety is overall good for both parties. The harmed party agreed to assume those risks and was likely compensated for doing so. To assume otherwise would offend our assumptions regarding autonomy, liberty, self-knowledge, and self-sufficiency. We are each, after all, the best judge of our own self-interest. Who is he, she, or it—an unduly paternalistic legislator, a regulator, or a social critic—to say otherwise?

The law's rhetorical and ideological reliance on the "blanket consent" to unseen future harms, as legitimating our societal and legal inclinations to let those harms rest wherever they fall, has been plenty criticized in legal–scholarly literature. According to critical legal scholars, the anti-paternalist presumptions regarding the value of blanket consent to long-term transactions and hard-to-know risks are often misplaced, particularly in consumer and labor transactions (Kelman 1979; Kennedy 1982). We often don't understand the risks of long-term contracts, and even if we do, we're not particularly good at assessing the harms we might suffer, should a risked event transpire. Anti-paternalistic arguments, that blithely assume to the contrary, might be doing little more than legitimating a good deal of coercive behavior and masking a lot of unrelieved suffering. Over the last 25 years or so, a good number of both critical and liberal legal scholars have so argued in a range of contractual contexts.

I don't want to rehearse those now-familiar "anti-anti-paternalism" debates here. I want to extend them. Far less explored in the critical scholarship is whether there are reasons to be suspicious of the same set of anti-paternalistic or liberty-enhancing assumptions regarding women's blanket consent to the long-term relationships that define intimate life—prominently, marriage, mother-hood, and pregnancy. I think there are, for reasons that are doubly suggested by the phrase "blanket consent." Blanket consent to intimacy, when tendered by women, covers much more than meets the eye. Often women tender blanket consent to intimacy with no sense of the future harms to which they may be viewed as having consented, or of the magnitude of the risk that those harms might indeed come to pass. In this chapter, I briefly explore why that might be.

I will sometimes metaphorically refer to the intimate relationships, arrangements, and social practices to which women render blanket consent as "the houses we enter." Simply put, I urge that feminists in law should better explore the terms—legal and otherwise—of the houses women enter. Those terms can sometimes bind the women who enter, unwittingly, to rules, mores, practices, and expectations that do real harm. Excessive deference to a woman's blanket consent as a marker of value in these relationships will some-times obscure those harms in a gauze of liberty, autonomy, sexual libertarianism, individualism, and free will. We need to attend carefully to what women's blanket consent to these relationships actually covers.

The first section briefly looks at women's participation in traditional, 1950s-styled marriage, which was for much of the last century the prototype of women's experience with blanket consent. The second section looks at more contemporary examples of the phenomenon that echo the marital prototype in familiar and unfamiliar ways. The final section looks in more detail at the college or university dormitory as one house that young women now enter, with terms to which they give their blanket consent. The terms of their entrance carry a risk of attendant and un-reckoned harms. Those of us who work in the law schools of those universities should not willfully blind ourselves to that possibility by too heavy a reliance on the legitimating force of the blanket consent given on entrance.

Consent to marriage

As commonly understood and reflected in traditional vows, a woman and man both give blanket consent when they marry to all sorts of future risks: they consent to the marriage whether they become richer or poorer, whether in sickness and health, and so on. Both partners consent to a lot of risk. These are express risks, stated in the vows. Are there other risks, perhaps not so express, to which a woman, but not a man, consents? The woman consents to the "marriage," not to the terms of a private contract or even a private covenant. What is a "marriage," at law, and what does her blanket consent cover? What are the terms of the marriage, to which consent is given?

Until midway through the nineteenth century, a woman's blanket consent to marriage "covered" quite a bit more than what was expressed in any marriage ceremony. Knowingly or not, by virtue of law a woman agreed to give up her power to contract and own property, to give up the wages she earned with her labor to her husband, and to submit to her husband's authority, including the chastising violence he might use to enforce it (Siegel 1996). Her consent to these terms was blanket: she agreed at the point of marriage to whatever future risks or harms might attend her husband's exercise of these powers. It was also implied; no marriage ceremony included vows of legal nonexistence, contractual incapacity, or willful submission to physical threats and batteries. Coverture came to a slow end by virtue of mid-nineteenth century Property Act reforms, and rules granting husbands express powers of chastisement gradually died out around the same period. However, until the late *twentieth* century, by virtue of "marital rape exemptions" to the definition of rape, a woman's blanket consent to marriage covered sex-on-demand by her husband (Hasday 2000; West 1990). A wife's consent to particular acts of marital sex was not required. Her lack of consent to the act, even with all the force and resistance in the world, would not render the forced sex "rape." Her blanket consent at the altar covered it. Forced sex within marriage was fully legal.

Although rarely commented on or theorized, until the early 1970s a wife's blanket consent to marriage *also* covered the risk of forced pregnancies which might result from forced sex. Prior to *Roe*, a woman impregnated by a rape in a state that criminalized abortion had a formal right to abort a pregnancy: states that criminalized abortion made exceptions for pregnancies caused by rape. Because of marital rape exemptions, however, forced sex *within marriage* was not rape. A woman raped outside of marriage could abort a resulting pregnancy, but a woman raped *inside* marriage could not. Thus, until the early 1970s, married women were required by law to endure both nonconsensual sex within marriage *and* the nonconsensual pregnancies that might occur. By convention, they endured a good bit of unwanted maternal labor as well. Women in marriage had no right to resist nonconsensual marital sex and pregnancy, and by convention, little room to resist the ensuing nonconsensual maternal labor. That's a lot of coerced, nonconsensual sex and coerced, nonconsensual labor, spread over the entirety of adult lifetimes, endured or experienced by much of the population for most of the twentieth century.

It is not easy to explain how all the legions of explicators of contract or family law throughout the twentieth century—let alone the men and women affected—justified this coercion. By 1970, individual consent had long since emerged as the condition of legal intercourse in virtually all non-intimate fields of human endeavor. Nonconsensual, coercive labor is clearly illegal, the contracts that call for it are unenforceable, and statutes that seem to permit or require it are unconstitutional. Nonconsensual bargains are illegal; they are some form of theft. Nonconsensual touchings and intrusions into the body are assaults and batteries, and statutes that permit or require them in various contexts, such as law enforcement, are constitutionally suspect. From the late-nineteenth century on, we moved from "status" to "contract." Contractual consent rather than a status bestowed at birth determines one's legal entitlements, privileges, responsibilities, and rights. By contrast, within marriage, nonconsensual sexual penetration and nonconsensual reproductive labor, dressed up as harmonious marital sex and maternity, were both viewed as criminally and constitutionally unproblematic. Why the marital state of exception?

One answer suggested in feminist family law scholarship of the last 20 years is that twentieth-century legal regimes permitting the nonconsensual use of wives' bodies by husbands and fetuses were justified by recourse to an idealized view of marital privacy. Marriages were assumed to be harmonious; these forced intrusions into women's bodies would be presumptively to women's liking (Hasday 2000; Siegel 1996). Sexual and reproductive coercion in marriage was justified by reference to what we today call "role," or more grandly, teleological purpose. When a woman becomes a "wife," she simply becomes someone whose interests, purpose, and body will be pleasured and filled by sex and fetal life. Her "consent" to bodily intrusions therefore was not relevant, much less required. The justification for the intrusion emanated from her being, not from her will. The widespread assumption that the law had moved solidly from status to contract as a way of organizing human affairs, and had done so 150 years prior, was not true of marriage.

A somewhat different way to understand the twentieth-century justification of the law's tolerance of this coercive treatment of wives, more consistent with contemporaneous legal conceits regarding consent, is by recourse to the contractual idea of "blanket consent." The law, its official interpreters, and its subjects might have tolerated sexual and reproductive coercion within marriage because we embraced a capacious understanding of the consent women give to marriage at the altar. A woman does, after all, consent to the marriage, if not directly to the sex and pregnancies that occur within it. We might tolerate forced sex and pregnancy within marriage, but we don't tolerate forced marriage. If a woman's consent to marriage is "blanket consent," then perhaps we can understand it as covering a risk of future coercive sex, coercive pregnancy, and coercive motherhood. After all, sex, pregnancy, and motherhood are the point of the institution. Rape and unwanted pregnancies, at least within marriage, might *seem* coercive if looked at as individual acts, but they're not once we broaden the lens. When a woman married, she consented not only to the promises expressed in the vows but also to all future sex her husband might desire, wanted or not, forced or not, violent or not, resisted or not.[1] She also consented to all the pregnancies to which that forced sex might lead: wanted, unwanted, consensual, or otherwise.

These understandings—if understandings they were—were upended in the 1970s and 1980s: first through the constitutional protection of abortion rights, and second, through the state-by-state abolition of marital rape exemptions. Today, by virtue of (largely) legal abortion and (partial) repeals of the marital rape exemption, forced sex and maternity are no longer terms of a marriage contract. At least in theory, blanket consent to marriage no longer covers the risk of rape and nonconsensual pregnancy. Marriage, both in practice and theory, is a better institution because of those reforms. It is hard to imagine a large-scale national movement of marital outsiders—gay and lesbian couples—wishing to enter this particular house had these fundamental legal transformations not occurred.

Modern traces

Nevertheless, institutions don't turn on a dime; there are plenty of traces of the early regime still present in law. One trace is the still ambiguous regard in which the law holds women's consent. Marital as well as non-marital rape is a crime, and nonconsensual pregnancies within or outside marriage can be terminated, albeit within limits. Nevertheless women's consent to intimacy, in or out of marriage, is still not entirely pivotal, although it is obviously relevant, to the right to end a pregnancy or the legality of sex. In most jurisdictions rape is not defined as nonconsensual sex, in or out of marriage. Rather, and despite the efforts of scores of feminist reformers, nonconsensual sex must also be "forced" for it to be rape, and in some states must meet with resistance (Estrich 1987). Similarly, a right to an abortion is not triggered by a woman's lack of consent to the pregnancy (McDonagh 1996). Rather, a woman has only a limited right to purchase an abortion prior to viability, and even that circumscribed right is grounded in some other value—liberty, privacy, or dignity. A woman's actual consent to the use of her body is not entirely determinative, and until recently not even relevant, to the legal powers and privileges of others—men and fetuses—who benefit from the use of her body for their purposes. Our continuing refusal, in law, to think of a woman's consent or lack of consent as defining a line between the lawful and unlawful use of her body, may be a trace of the centuries-long total inconsequentiality of a wife's consent to the use of her body by her husband for sex and by fetal life for nurturance, whether she desired or took pleasure from either.

Another less obvious trace is better highlighted if we entertain the hypothesis that blanket consent, rather than teleology or marital harmony, justified the twentieth-century marital regime. To some degree, women simply may be defined, both by themselves and others, as the sort of people whose consent to intimacy in or out of marriage is *peculiarly* "blanketed." When women consent to intimacy today, just as when women consented at mid-century to marriage, their consent might cover more than meets the eye. If so, then that perception will affect how a woman's consent is interpreted, not only when consenting to a marriage but in other situations that resemble it. One effect of the former marital legal regime might be that a woman's consent to intimacy is now blanketed in a way that was once true only of her consent to marriage.

I can't prove this, but let me try to make it plausible by looking first at some familiar examples of women's blanket consent to intimacy and then at a less familiar example. First, girls or women who have sex with dates, prostitutes who have sex with their customers, or women who enter hotel rooms with men for any reason at all, notoriously find it very hard to prove that they didn't consent to the sex that followed. They not only find it hard to prove, it is difficult to find a police officer or charging district attorney who will give them the time of day. Reported date rapes rarely end in prosecutions, prostitutes virtually never successfully prove they were raped by their customers, and as Juanita Broderick learned back in the 1970s when she claimed she was raped by then Arkansas attorney general Bill Clinton in a hotel room at a convention, there's no point in trying to prove you were raped if you've consensually entered a hotel room with a powerful man. There are legitimate obstacles, mostly evidentiary, to the successful prosecution of rape charges in all these scenarios. But one reason for the difficulty so many have in even granting the *possibility* of rape in these circumstances might be, in part, that each of these scenarios—the date, the prostitution contract, and the hotel room—in some respect resembles marriage and, therefore, triggers a background assumption that the woman gave her blanket consent to the forced sex that followed. If she did, then even if sex were forced, it wasn't truly nonconsensual. Thus, the prostitution contract mimics the economic exchange of sex for support central to traditional marriage; the date mimics the sentimental bargain that is at the rhetorical heart of contemporary marriage; and the hotel encounter occurs in the site of marriage's defining act and moment, the bedroom. The ensuing sex in these exchanges might be regarded as "like" the sex in a marriage—it is something to which the girl or woman gave blanket consent. The prostitute agreed to whatever sex would follow when she struck the deal, so her consent to the actual sex is not required; the girl agreed to the date and, therefore, to the sex that might follow; and the woman in the hotel room walked into the room willingly. Like the wife in the bedroom, she impliedly consented to the room's *raison d'être*. They all consented to sex by giving prior blanket consent to intimacy at an earlier moment.

A less familiar example of blanket consent to intimacy is contemporary pregnancy post-*Roe*. One of the relatively unnoticed consequences of *Roe* is that by virtue of the choice to terminate or continue a pregnancy, the meaning of "pregnancy" has changed. Pregnancy, when women had no power to choose it, was a matter of fate; it was something that came over you. Without reliable birth control you couldn't very easily prevent it, and without legal abortion you couldn't legally terminate it. Today, pregnancy, by virtue of the power to do both, is not so much a natural change but an intimate relationship between a woman and a fetus. As such, social norms structure that relationship, as they do all others which we consensually enter. Like all relationships so structured, it has its terms. Post *Roe*, we enter it consensually: since we had the power to prevent it and the power to terminate it, we consent to the relationship of the pregnancy when we carry it to term, in a way that was not true pre-*Roe* (and pre-birth control). But what kind of consent do we give, when we consent to pregnancy? What *is* pregnancy, now that it is something we choose, rather than a condition that washes over us, without the involvement of our will? If pregnancy is a relationship to which we consent, what are its terms?

These are not questions that get asked much. I suggest that a woman's blanketed consent to pregnancy covers an awful lot. First, at least judging by particularly persistent patterns of inequitable parental labor, consent to pregnancy covers responsibility for the nurturance of the newborn and the parenting labor that follows—up to 18 years' worth, from which there is no "at will" exit allowed, by either law, sentiment, or morality. The modern phenomenon of unequal parenting might be one of the hidden terms of consensual pregnancy. We have not had or even conceived of the possibility of a legal or social revolution that would sever the connection between consent to pregnancy and consent to maternal labor that is in any way comparable to the legal and social revolutions that severed the connection between consent to a marriage and consent to marital sex, or consent to marriage and consent to relinquishment of one's earned wages. Maternal labor might be covered by the earlier blanket consent to pregnancy, as evidenced by the consensual decision not to abort as well as the conditions under which that labor is performed: no pay, reduced labor skills, no exit at will, and no or little public support. It is an echo of the consent to sex covered in an earlier age by the blanket consent to marry.

I draw two speculative conclusions from these examples. The first is that women's blanket consent to intimacy and motherhood still casts a long shadow in their lives, even if not as long a shadow as our mothers' and grandmothers' consent to marriage. From a nineteenth-century world that utterly ignored a married woman's consent to marital sex and pregnancy, we entered a twentieth-century world where, partly because of first- and second-wave feminist activism, actual consent became hugely important. We also entered a world where that consent is interpreted capaciously. Consent at the altar was read until the late-twentieth century as consent to sexual and reproductive coercion. Consent to sexual and reproductive labor mattered, but blanket consent to marriage was more than sufficient to cover it. Today, blanket consent to various forms of intimacy still brings within its sweep terms that require sexual and caregiving labor.

The somewhat metaphoric conclusion I draw is that the often unknown and unstated terms of the houses, rooms, and places we enter are highly determinative of the quality of the lives women enjoy or suffer once there. The problem is not only that these places women enter can be hard to leave but also that, by virtue of consensually entering these private rooms, a woman is assumed to have given blanket consent to whatever sexual, pregnancy, parenting, or household labor goes on there. She might not want that labor, might not have known she was bargaining for it, and it might be harmful to her. The terms of the private houses we enter—and to which we consent—can hurt.

The universities they enter

One house that women enter is the elite university or college dormitory. Women undergraduates now outnumber male undergraduates in the "top fifty" colleges and universities by a percentage that is alarming to parents, admissions officers, and high school educators. Demographically, women dominate the college scene at America's best colleges. They've entered those dormitories, of course, consensually. But do they offer a blanket consent when they enter? And if so, what does the consent cover? What are the terms of the university dormitory to which they consent? Are any of them hidden?

I believe one hidden term of entry into college intimate life is sex. An entrant's consent to the college dormitory is read as covering consent to the sexual labor that might follow, both the sex to which she gives on-the-spot consent and that to which she does not. Let me start with the nonconsensual. A consistent stream of studies and reports over the last 20 years shows that undergraduate women are subjected to an extraordinarily high level of sexual violence (Fisher et al. 2000; Rapaport and Burkhart 1984). According to studies compiled and analyzed in a recent article in the *Journal of College and University Law* by Dean Nancy Cantalupo (2009), women are *four times* as likely to be raped in college as the same age cohort outside of college (see also Sampson 2002). The rapes they are likely to suffer on college campuses tend to occur within the first few weeks of their arrival and are overwhelmingly committed by fellow students, dorm co-residents, friends, friends' friends, or dates. The victims don't report them. Surprisingly large numbers of undergraduate men in a series of now somewhat dated studies from the 1980s and 1990s self-report a willingness and desire to rape: in large percentages, they report, if they were assured that they would get away with it, they would force sex upon their dates (Sampson 2002). Rape victims, whether they report, often leave school to transfer elsewhere or drop out.

Perhaps of even greater consequence than the still serious problem of rapes on college campuses is the quality of the fully consensual sex in college dormitories—the sex to which women *do* in fact give meaningful, actual consent—not presumed, not implied, not coerced, but actual, on-the-spot consent. Does the "blanket consent" women proffer when they enter affect this sex? It might. Recent studies and a steady stream of blogs and Internet outlets make clear that, of the fully consensual opposite-sex sex that happens on campus, much of it is *unwanted*—meaning not physically desired and not physically enjoyed—by the woman (Broach 2006). Some of that unwanted consensual sex can be harmful, although in different ways than rape, to the women who suffer it. These harms have gone relatively unnoticed—perhaps just overshadowed by the last two decades of worry over the high rape rates. Consent may be absent in too much college sex and considered only marginally relevant to too many potential perpetrators. The relevance of female desire, on the other hand, as a condition for consensual sex, has disappeared entirely. This is worrisome.

Why does this happen? Why is there still not only so much sexual assault on college campuses, but also so much unwanted sex? One possibility is that the social expectation of both women and men regarding campus sex is not only of sex's presumed inevitability but also of its *desirability*. The sex will happen regardless, so you may as well consent, and as it's consensual, you may as well want it. Both partners may simply assume that consensual sex is always wanted, on both sides, equally and passionately. They consult this norm, rather than their own desires or their partner's, in deciding whether they want sex. Both the man and woman assume the woman wants sex. She acts on the basis of assumptions about what she wants, rather than on the basis of what she wants.

Another explanation, though, takes us back to blanket consent. It may be that when a woman enters the college dormitory, she gives blanket consent, and is viewed as having given blanket consent, to the unwanted sex that follows. Sometimes she and others may understand this consent as prior consent to forced sex—sex that would be rape but for the prior blanket consent. Even more often, though, the consent might be understood as prior consent not to forced sex but unwanted consensual sex. On this latter construction, what blanket consent covers is not rape—she doesn't consent to assaultive sex—but rather to unwanted sex. Then, so long as she actually consents to sex at the time of the sex—so long as it is not forced on her against her will—whether she actually desires it is of no consequence. What she blanketly consents to, in other words, upon entry, is that her desire will not be a condition of her later consent. If so, then it might not be so surprising that so much of the consensual sex that happens in dorm rooms is not desired. A woman's desire is either presumed, or its absence is presumed unimportant. She has given prior blanket consent to all of it.

If this is right then the college campus dorm room, like the hotel room, the date, or the prostitution contract, has become quasi-marital. And, there are more than a few passing family resemblances between the college dormitory and the marital abode. First, as has been true of the marital sex between husbands and wives since the late 1980s, forced sex between men and women living together in dormitories is nominally illegal, though not uniformly perceived as such and only tepidly deterred or punished. Rules against it are enforced by convention, or by sympathetic if conflicted administrators, as rules against marital rape and violence are only tepidly enforced by a sympathetic albeit conflicted state. Interest in deterring the sexual violence on campus, like the interest in deterring marital rape, waxes and wanes in the larger society with similar strategies and results: no-fault divorce provides for easy exit from violent marriages, and politically inspired civil orders of protection are designed to empower the women who hold them; voluntary departure from college and politically inspired Take Back the Night marches and Antioch Codes[2] are all designed to do likewise on campuses. None of these have been unqualified successes.

Even more striking is the family resemblance between the norms and practices surrounding consensual sex on campus, and the conventional norms governing consensual sex in conventional, patriarchal marriage. In both cases—the college coed and the conventional wife—a woman's lack of desire does not constitute a sufficient reason not to consent to sex, and the result is a lot of unwanted sex. Women in conventional marriages, particularly at mid-century, were under strong social pressure to consent to marital sex, whether or not they desired it. If they professed a lack of desire, they were labeled frigid and presumed to have an intensely personal albeit remarkably widespread psychological problem, *not* a political one. What such women should do, according to advice doled out by Ann Landers, clergy, peers, and their own mothers, about this psychological problem was basically to get over it—learn to be more desirous or just proceed regardless. Either way, the lack of desire should not be felt or perceived to be a reason not to consent. A woman learned she should consent to unwanted and undesired sex with her husband because her role demanded it, her religion demanded it, her community expected it, he had paid for it through his support, her children needed a harmonious household, he might become violent if she didn't, and so on. She could stare at the ceiling or think of the queen or disassociate from her body or make a to-do list in her head, but she was expected to and largely felt obliged to submit.

With the sexual revolution of the 1960s and 1970s, marital advice for the non-desirous wife became far more hedonic and facially equal, while its domain spread from the institution of marriage to intimate relationships across the board. The bottom line, however, did not change one whit. Self-help books, sex therapists, religious leaders, and counselors of all stripes, this time with the wind of the sexual revolution at their backs, advised that lack of female desire is a personal problem that could and should be overcome. Lack of desire is a psychological obstacle to self-actualization. The norm, against which the non-desirous wife was cast, was universal sexual desire within marriage, and the expectation, against which the resistant wife was compared, was sexual submission. A sexually liberated woman—as opposed to a politically liberated woman—would desire and submit to sex, and whether she did so in traditional monogamy, in serial monogamy, in polygamous relations, or in open marriages didn't matter. What did matter is that she submit. The bottles changed from 1950s marriage to 1970s liberation; the wine did not.

On college campuses today, a robust set of cross-cutting social norms delivers the same message to undergraduate women as was delivered to married women in the 1950s and 1960s. Consent to sex in the college dorm room might be too often assumed, but more than that, *desire* is universally, absolutely presumed. Queer theory and pro-sex feminism in high-brow culture, hot rather than cool ideals in popular culture, vaguely public dormitory sex that is openly tolerated or encouraged by administrators and staff, and of course wall-to-wall pornographic media outlets that portray sex as both boundlessly desirable and boundlessly desired by high-status women, all might have jointly created a set of behavioral expectations on campus that directly parallel the advice of Ann Landers and the clergy in the 1950s and the sex counselors, therapists, and advisers of the 1960s and 1970s. Sex will happen in the college dormitory room, as it happened in the marital bedroom, and it may or may not be mutually desired; but whether it is motivated by female desire is of no moment. It doesn't matter whether women want it on the college campus, in the same way that it didn't matter whether wives wanted it in traditional marriage. Perhaps, in both houses, mutual desire is simply assumed. Or, perhaps, in both houses, women gave their blanket consent on entering.

Some women of course find this entirely to their liking, as did plenty of mid-twentieth century wives. However, many women do not; they either go along to get along, they suffer, they move out, or they drop out. Research is scant but beginning to show that many college women find the relentlessness of unwanted sex and the pressures to engage in it traumatizing, and they suffer long-term injuries because of it (Braoch and Petretic 2006). These social and cultural terms of passage are not empowering our daughters as they consensually enter college dormitories, any more than the same terms in traditional patriarchal marriage empowered our grandmothers and mothers.

Some concluding suggestions

When I talk to feminist legal theorists, the talk is of post-feminism and post-modernism, of pro-sex feminism, of queer theory, of sex liberationist movements and sexual empowerment, and of casting off tired old ethics. I call these movements collectively "post-woman feminism," by which I mean that they have at their heart a denial that women exist, have attributes, are burdened, are subordinated, and so on. In some ways, post-woman feminism is a return to the very powerful liberal commitments that dominated American feminism for two centuries: both post-woman and liberal feminism attribute perceived differences between men and women to the purported effects of social role and stereotyping, both tend to either downplay or themselves display contempt for maternalism, and both worry that radical feminism shortchanges women by obsessing over their sexual vulnerability. Women and girls, post-woman feminist dogma goes, are "just as" strong, powerful, and as sexually driven as men. There are no differences there. While social role and sex stereotype might have created false impressions to the contrary, at heart, we are they and they us, or perhaps the former a bit more than the latter, in work, parenting, and sexual matters. Sexuality, male and female, gay and straight, unbound on college campus, is a boon for all. This claim has become a postmodern dogma, and its modality is starkly religious in the ferocity with which it is held.

There is another group of feminists on college campuses, who are decidedly pre-postmodern, who are not academics, not so steeped in "theory," and who have spent a lot of time talking to our students. They are feminist counselors, administrators, clergy, and residence hall senior staff. They tell a different story. Some undergraduate female students, they say, are traumatized, and contemporary academic feminism is not helping them. We are not attending to what is most hurtful to them in their college experiences, which is the overly sexualized social culture in which they live. Academic feminists, they note, don't want to touch that fire. Increasingly, they want to light it.

As part of the next wave of feminism, legal theorists, and scholars on campuses should aim to reconcile these two realities. As Nancy Cantalupo (2009) is now urging us to do, feminist legal theorists in particular could do this concretely in very helpful ways: we could find out what our school's procedures are for dealing with sexual assault and assault generally; find out if it is in compliance with federal law; find out if it is in accord with "best practices," and so on. That is the "take home" directive from Cantalupo's article. We can do this more generally by attending to the phenomenon of unwanted but consensual sex, not just as it appears on the pages of law reviews and as chapters in books, but as it is being practiced, and sometimes resisted, by the students we teach. We could listen more carefully to students who complain about this, as well as to the advocates who try to help them. We could teach them, if we have anything to teach them at all on this subject, to trust and follow their own hedonic instincts: to have sex that they desire and not to have the sex that they don't. We could point out to them that some research, as well as common sense, shows that failing to act on one's own hedonic desires can be injurious. Repressed sexual desire can indeed be harmful. But so too can undesired sex. We could also suggest that when women don't follow the wisdom of their pleasures and the directive of their desires, the reason they don't do so might be not only personal but also, no less than it is now and was for our mothers and grandmothers, deeply political as well.

Notes

1 Lord Hale's infamous claim—that "a husband cannot be guilty of a rape committed by himself upon his lawful wife, for by their mutual matrimonial consent and contract

the wife hath given up herself in this kind unto her husband which she cannot retreat"—was quoted in *Warren v. State* (1985) and referred to in that case as propounding a theory of "implied consent."

2 "Antioch Codes" refers to the codes of sexual conduct passed in the early 1990s by Antioch College, intended to encourage students to ensure that their sexual interactions were mutually consensual. The Codes, a public relations disaster, relied heavily on insisting that sexual partners communicate desire and consent at all stages of sexual play and were likely of only marginal utility in preventing rape. They were widely ridiculed as an excess of political correctness, as trivializing both the problem of rape and missing entirely the erotic role of silence and even resistance in fully consensual sex. For a philosophical critique of the Antioch policy, see Alan Soble (2008: 459–77), and for a rare and powerful defense of the Antioch approach, see Eva Kittay (2008: 479–87).

Chapter 15

New frontiers in family law

Laura T. Kessler

Introduction

A new discussion about families and care is unfolding in feminist legal theory and family law. Reproductive technologies, globalization, and left-of-center critiques of same-sex marriage offer an especially fertile environment for imagining sex, intimacy, care, and reproduction outside marriage and the nuclear family. These reconceptualizations continue the revisioning enabled by reproductive freedom, no-fault divorce, and women's entrance and integration into the workforce. The new family law scholarship also builds upon the vision of feminists of prior generations (Fineman 1981; Frisken 2004; Okin 1989; MacKinnon 1982; Rich 1980; Stack 1974). Earlier feminists questioned the marital family's central place in our country's law and social policy and exposed the costs of this framework to women, children, and other vulnerable people. As such, they helped us imagine sex, intimacy, care, and reproduction outside marriage and the nuclear family.

It is worth noting the extent to which this once cutting-edge vision now defines the discipline of family law. Today, a range of family relationships and sexual practices are the subjects of scholarly inquiry on the family. The implications of this trend are significant. Historically, the law of marriage, divorce, and child custody constituted the core of family law. What happens to family law when a range of relationships displaces marriage from the epicenter of scholarly inquiry on the family? Although the full effects of this diffusion are not clear, certain trends are emerging.

First, discussion has shifted from divorce and inequalities inside the marital family to inequality among families. Free from preoccupation with the domination of husbands over wives, scholars are placing renewed attention on the state, the other significant potential source of oppressive (and emancipatory) involvement in the family. The move away from marriage has also introduced more antiessentialist analysis into family law scholarship. That is, because marriage is less prevalent among low-income individuals, people of color, and same-sex couples, scholarship that is less marriage-centric is more likely to consider the life experiences of diverse individuals. Finally, with less investment in marriage as a dominant subject of scholarly interest, a perceptible shift in the disciplinary boundaries of family law is occurring. Today, constitutional law, tax law, immigration law, criminal law, and employment law—indeed, a host of areas providing background rules for families but not historically considered part of family law—are as likely to be sites of inquiry on the family as the law of marriage, divorce, and child custody.

One helpful metaphor in understanding these developments is "the frontier." In common usage, a frontier is a region that forms the margin of settled or developed territory, or a fertile area for explorative or developmental activity (*Merriam-Webster Online Dictionary* 2009). This metaphor aptly describes the recent proliferation of family law scholarship exploring sexual and intimate practices outside the settled territory of the marital family. Salient examples include multiple parenthood (Dowd 2007; Jacobs 2007; Kessler 2005); networked families (Murray 2008); polygamy (Ertman forthcoming); polyamory (Emens 2004a); unmarried fathers (Dowd 2000; Maldonado 2005, 2006); queer culture and intimacy (Franke 2004, 2008; Ruskola 2005); "marginority" sexual practices (Ertman 1995); and friendship (Franke 2008; Rosenbury 2007b; Leib 2007, 2009). A central insight of this work is that law provides the context that can facilitate or hinder unconventional intimate configurations. Some commentators therefore seek to disentangle law from sexual and intimate life (Franke 2004, 2008; Warner 2002). Others seek legal recognition (and regulation) of a wider range of intimate choices (Ertman 2001; Kessler 2005, 2007; Murray 2008).

The frontier thus provides a new metaphor, replacing older frameworks such as the "channeling" function of family law (Schneider 1992), wherein family law exists to channel sex and reproduction into marriage, the institution deemed appropriate for those activities. In the new frontiers of family law, marriage holds a less central, even disfavored, position.

In this chapter, I explore the impact on family law of de-centering marriage from its privileged position, as well as some of the tensions arising from this trend. These include not just the obvious tensions between political conservatives and liberals, but also tensions among critical left and liberal legal theorists of the family. The chapter ends with some predictions about where the new frontiers in family law may take us in the next 25 years.

New frontiers in family law

In the 1980s and early 1990s, legal feminists developed a major critique of no-fault divorce. They questioned divorce rules resulting in an equal division of marital property and little or no spousal support in most cases (Fineman 1991a; Weitzman 1985). They noted the multiple problems with this model of divorce. Most prominently, women remain responsible for a disproportionate share of housework and childcare before and after divorce, despite custody law reforms. As such, formal equality models for apportioning marital assets insufficiently provide economic security for women and children after divorce.

Legal feminists and family law scholars proposed a variety of solutions for this problem. Most developed theoretical justifications putting spousal support on firmer ground. Joan Williams (1994a, 1994b) argued that support is essentially property by another name. Stephen Sugarman (1990), Jane Rutherford (1990), Jana Singer (1989), and others conceptualized support as an expectancy interest in shared income formed at the beginning of marriage or ripening into such in marriages of long duration. Other scholars drew on private law remedies to address the economic problems of displaced homemakers, such as those available to secured creditors (Ertman 1998) or contract holders (Baker 1988; Weisbrod 1994). Still others turned to traditional economic justifications derived from human capital theory for using alimony to reallocate the financial consequences of divorce (Ellman 1989; Parkman 1992). Despite the range of perspectives, legal feminist and family law scholarship in the 1980s and 1990s was generally concerned with gender inequalities in heterosexual marriage.

This concern has largely subsided in family law scholarship for diverse and complex reasons. First, legal feminists may have made the realistic political assessment that although they have accomplished quite a bit in the divorce context,[1] the formal equality rules of divorce are not easily disrupted (Fineman 1991a). For example, the more aspirational ideals of legal feminism rooted in substantive equality have not been fully realized, particularly with regard to spousal support (American Law Institute, § 5.04, Reporter's Notes).

A set of robust internal feminist antiessentialist critiques of marriage-based solutions to women's inequality may also explain lessening scholarly interest in the disparate economic costs of divorce on women. For example, some scholars question the partnership model of marriage, because it may reinforce traditional gender roles (Rosenbury 2005; Tsoukala 2007). According to this critique, income sharing and other proposals based on a model of "equal" partnership "reinforce wifely sacrifice by rewarding women for caring for their husbands and children at the possible expense of their own tangible property acquisition or other forms of individual fulfillment" (Rosenbury 2005: 1233). This critique suggests that the partnership theory of marriage is not a good long-term solution to women's economic inequality, although it may have been a necessary interim solution to the economic destitution of women created by no-fault divorce (Rosenbury 2005; Schultz 2000).

Other feminist antiessentialist critiques show how marriage-based solutions to women's economic inequality reinforce race and sexuality essentialisms. For example, critical race feminists point out that women of color are less likely than white women to be married. If married, they are unlikely to be married to men with the kind of jobs that make generous alimony awards a path to economic independence (Perry 1994). Similarly, reviving the remedy of support in the divorce context offers little to same-sex couples denied the right of marriage or civil unions (Kessler 2008). Finally, to the extent that many of the proposals to reform divorce law were aimed at reducing the economic burdens of motherhood, they also perpetuate repronormativity (Franke 2001). These anti-essentialist critiques may explain the diminished attention in the past decade to the destitution of women post-divorce.

The national gay rights movement for marriage equality may also be responsible for decreased attention on inequality inside the marital family. Downplaying the patriarchal nature and history of marriage is one of its main political and legal strategies (Franke 2006; Polikoff 1993). For example, the traction gained by the gay rights movement for marriage equality has emerged primarily from theories of sexual privacy (Appleton 2005). In the media, advocates generally avoid the claim that prohibitions on same-sex marriage constitute sex discrimination or that allowing same-sex couples to marry will de-gender the institution of marriage in positive ways. With the exception of Hawaii (*Baehr v. Lewin* 1993), state courts have generally not gone for these arguments where raised in litigation (*Conaway v. Deane* 2007).

This rhetorical discipline is bound to impact other discourses, including academic ones. Put simply, the sanguine depictions of marriage emanating from the same-sex marriage movement render the more traditional feminist concerns that dominated family law less important. It is also probably true that gay and lesbian couples have more equal relationships, because they share sexual identity and, particularly for lesbians, a commitment to equality in relationships (Becker 1996; Blumstein and Schwartz 1983; Sullivan 2004). In sum, whether the product of a political strategy or real differences between gay and straight relationships—probably some of both—inequality inside marriage grows less important as same-sex marriage becomes a central part of the conversation in family law.

Finally, the emergence of "third-wave" and "post" feminisms may also contribute to the present shift in intellectual priorities among legal feminist and family law scholars. Third-wave and post feminism, while hard to define precisely, describe a range of critical viewpoints on previous feminist discourses, particularly "second-wave" liberal feminism. Some of the core commitments and methods of third-wave and post feminisms include attention to popular culture in ordering social life (Crawford 2007), emphasizing the fluidity and ambiguity of gender (Henry 2004), consideration of race subjectivities and a commitment to antiessentialism more generally (Henry 2004), and viewing sexuality positively, rather than primarily as a source of oppression (Wolf 1993). In this literature, legal marriage does not figure centrally as an institution or practice of concern. More generally, women are seen as controlling the nature and scope of their intimate relations, un-needing of special legal protections.

In sum, solving the problems of the heterosexual husband–wife relationship is no longer a primary project of family law scholarship. There are several possible reasons for this shift, including a sense that divorce law reform efforts have gone as far as they possibly can, the emergence of a robust set of antiessentialist critiques of marriage-based solutions to women's inequality, idealized depictions of marriage emanating from the national movement for same-sex marriage equality, and the rise of third-wave and post feminisms. The new ideas about marriage, gender, and sex circulating in these academic and political discourses serve as resources for thinking through the core questions of the family law discipline. Their impact may not be direct, but they likely serve as narrative frames that contribute to the de-privileging of heterosexual marriage in family law scholarship.

This does not mean that the traditional topics of marriage, divorce, and child custody are wholly unimportant in family law. The shifting interests of scholars away from these topics is not total nor will it ever be (Glennon 2007; Kelly 2008; Maldonado 2008). Nor is the shift away from marriage and divorce occurring in every aspect of family law scholarship or with equal force among scholars in law schools of different characteristics. There are other trends, and considerable reaction exists to the de-centering of marriage from its privileged position in family law (Blankenhorn 1995; Duncan 2001; Popenoe et al. 1996). Still, the focus of family law is undeniably shifting. What are the effects of this change? Where is the discipline going? The next section explores four potential impacts of the new frontiers in family law.

The impact of the new frontiers: four trends

More emphasis on the state

Renewed attention on the state is replacing the attention once given to husbands' domination over wives in family law. As Martha Ertman (2008) suggests, the state is always a party to every marriage. The real questions are how deeply the state is involved, how much movement there is within marriage once heterosexual marriage is de-centered, and whose interests are represented through state involvement. The lens of the new frontier allows us to see just how powerful and punitive the state's role.

There are many examples of new frontier scholarship interrogating the state's extraordinarily powerful and punitive role in families. For example, I have explored how the law systematically devalues the family care practices of African Americans, sexual minorities, men, and other "transgressive caregivers" (Kessler 2005). Indeed, one observation drawn from this research is that a central means of oppressing a disfavored group in our society is to wage war on their familyhood. Other scholars working in the new frontiers of family law are looking at topics such as how the state constructs gender through judicial custody determinations involving heterosexual and gay or lesbian parents (Rosky 2009), how the state negatively impacts the parental rights of incarcerated mothers (Kennedy 2009), and how the state influences the family organization (and dis-organization) of immigrant families (Abrams 2009). Family law has always been concerned with the legitimate bounds of state intervention in families, but the new frontiers scholarship moves beyond traditional questions of privacy between couples and with their children, to broader questions about the state's role in constituting legitimate families and intimate practices.

However, there is an interesting paradox here: with less investment in the marital family as the preferred receptacle for economic dependency, new frontiers scholarship also brings into clearer view the potentially emanicpatory role of the state in families. For example, Martha Fineman (2004) helps us imagine legal structures that put caregivers at the center of a robust system of state support. This framework works to "reconceptualize and transform our notions about the family and its relationship to the state and other social institutions" (Fineman 2004: 184). Along the same lines, Linda McClain (2006) argues that a central state function should be supporting care inside families to foster individuals' capacities for self-government. Although McClain does not abandon the normative ideal of marriage, she argues that the state has a central role in "help[ing] families engage in nurturing the capacities of family members," because "nurturing children and ensuring their moral development and education [is necessary] to prepare them to be responsible, self-governing persons" (89). In sum, in the new frontiers of family law, the state potentially plays an important role in individuals' well-being, whether as a source of oppression or economic support.

More emphasis on freedom, less on equality

The disruption of marriage as family law's central focus has also led to greater emphasis on freedom as the discipline's preferred organizing principle. Free of marriage's real and symbolic shackles—particularly the norms of stability, reciprocity, equality, partnership, commitment, and repronormativity—a new space is opened to imagine how the law might facilitate sexual and other freedoms in family life.

To be sure, this trend is overdetermined. Until the recent American economic decline and 2008 election of Barack Obama, the move from equality toward freedom was occurring as a general matter in American law and society. Neoliberalism and free market ideology, which dominated the 1980s and 1990s, emphasized freedom (Kessler 2008; McCluskey 2007). Moreover, scholars from many disciplines and perspectives have exposed the limitations of equality theory, particularly the thin conception of formal equality characterizing our liberal constitutional system (Fineman 2008; Harris 2000; McClain 2006; Nussbaum and Sen 1993; West 2003). The move toward freedom as an organizing principle of family law may also be partly due to legal feminism's move away from dominance and cultural feminism, a trend beginning largely in response to feminist efforts in the 1980s to pass anti-pornography legislation (Abrams 1995; Duggan et al. 1993; Duggan and Hunter 1995). Today, it has blossomed into a generalized critique of feminism "as it is now practiced and produced in the United States" (Halley 2004: 7).

And so perhaps the convergence of a number of left critical and right neoliberal theories of the human condition explain the move away from equality in our theorizing about the family. As critical race feminist Angela Harris (2000: 1186) observes, "some people are thinking that the rhetoric of equality has been exhausted and they're looking around for alternatives."

However, taking a somewhat more narrow view, although extremely difficult to prove, the disruption of heterosexual marriage as the central focus of family law, *by itself*, potentially has a seismic impact on the discipline. At minimum, it opens a space to think more in terms of freedom than in the past. This insight has led some to question whether a new kind of sexual liberty can find its home both inside the institution of marriage and outside of it.

For example, Katherine Franke (2008) wants to press on the difference between liberty and equality implicit in the Supreme Court's decision decriminalizing sodomy (*Lawrence v. Texas* 2003) so that arguments for opening up marriage to gay couples can be made in ways that do not re-instantiate and romanticize marriage as the "measure of all things" (2689). As a thought experiment, she suggests substituting friendship for marriage at the center of the social field in which human connection takes place. With that new frame, "our investments in marriage and marriage's investments in us are likely to yield in such a way that we can imagine making the argument for same sex couples' right to marry while also imagining and cultivating different longings … " (2687–88).

Teemu Ruskola (2005) expresses similar concerns. He asks: "With the fall of antisodomy legislation, have we finally been 'liberated'? And if so, to what?" (236). As Ruskola notes, the rhetoric and logic of *Lawrence* analogize gay relationships to marriage. For Ruskola, Franke, and other new frontiers scholars, being in a committed relationship, much less a marriage, should not be a precondition for having a constitutionally protected sex life or receiving economic benefits (Emens 2004b; Fineman 1995; Halley 1993; Kessler 2008; Polikoff 2008; Rosenbury 2007b).

More generally, new frontiers scholarship is concerned with the question of whether there is any role for the law in facilitating sexual pleasure. For example, Franke (2001) challenges legal feminists and family law scholars to think beyond the potential dangers and dependencies of intimacy to theorize sexuality positively. She asks, "Can law protect pleasure? Should it?" (182). She calls on legal feminism to build the theoretical and legal groundwork enabling conditions for sexual pleasure. Susan Appleton (2008) takes up Franke's challenge in her work on "cultural cliteracy" in family law. She notes that although family law has sex at its conceptual core, it has historically been unconcerned with sexual pleasure, particularly women's sexual pleasure. Yet, she also demonstrates the many ways that the discipline is paradoxically well-situated to take up the sex-positive project. Among other promising commitments of modern family law, sexually unfulfilled partners may leave marriage under no-fault divorce, modern family law at least aspires to treating men and women with equal respect, and procreation is no longer the formal purpose of marriage. Although Appleton questions whether a "culturally cliterate" family law could exist, by carefully thinking through the ways that family law could be reformed to take sexual pleasure more seriously, she provides a glimmer of this possibility.

In sum, de-centering marriage from its privileged position in family law creates space to imagine how the law might facilitate sexual and other freedoms in family life. More generally, in the new frontiers of the family, we see more emphasis on freedom as the organizing principle of intimate relations and less emphasis on equality.

More diversity and antiessentialist analyses

The move away from marriage also introduces more antiessentialist analysis into family law scholarship. That is, because marriage is less prevalent among low-income individuals, African Americans, and same-sex couples (Cherlin 2005), scholarship that is less marriage-centric is more likely to consider the life experiences of a diverse set of individuals.

For example, my work on "community parenting" explores parenting by more than two adults often occurring in non-marital, non-nuclear families such as divorced families, extended families, families of color, and gay and lesbian families (Kessler 2007). I argue that the law should recognize community parenting, because it is often highly functional and represents a welcome disruption to the gendered, nuclear family. Similarly, Melissa Murray's (2008) research on "networked families" reveals how much care is provided by grandparents and other extended family members, friends, au pairs, nannies, babysitters, and childcare centers. Contrary to the normative ideal of sole parental care by wives, most families are highly networked entities. Murray asks us to rethink an array of laws built on this gendered ideal, such as the Family and Medical Leave Act, Social Security Act, and employment-based health insurance programs.

Beyond these examples, a rich and diverse array of intimate configurations and practices interest scholars working in the new frontiers of family law. For example, Solangel Maldonado (2005, 2006) and Nancy Dowd (2007) explore the economic and social roles of fathers or those who act as fathers. Laura Rosenbury (2007b) raises the question of whether friendship should be the normative pinnacle of all relationships. She argues that family law's focus on marriage to the exclusion of other forms of friendship perpetuates gendered patterns of care, because extensive amounts of care by women are expected in marital relationships. Liz Emens (2004a) seeks to understand why polyamory is so widely considered undesirable, even as many people practice non-monogamous behavior. She proposes dismantling various legal burdens on polyamorists, including two-person marriage and partnership laws, adultery and bigamy laws, residential zoning laws, and custody consequences. Adam Romero (Chapter 17 in this volume) considers the legal significance of family from the perspectives of those "without a family," that is, adults in need of care who live with little or no association to family. And, of course, Martha Fineman (1991a) argued two decades ago that the parent–child relationship, not the sexual or marital relationship, should be the privileged relationship in family law.

These are but a few examples; family law is now replete with scholarship exploring a wide range of intimate relations and practices. What I hope they demonstrate is that family diversity increasingly is replacing marriage as a moral and policy foundation of family law. By diversity, I mean the idea that individuals should be able to organize their intimate relationships, care practices, and family forms in an expansive variety of ways. This emerging commitment to diversity in family law is not simply about freedom, although freedom plays a dominant role in the discussion. New frontiers scholarship includes a range of perspectives on the right balance between freedom and equality, law and culture, and public and private ordering in our legal and popular conceptions of the family. However, there is one consistent trend: disrupting the heterosexual, marital family as the main focus of the discipline leads to a consideration of a more diverse set of individuals along sex, class, and race lines, and a more diverse set of sexual and intimate relations.

Shifting disciplinary boundaries

With less investment in marriage as a dominant subject of scholarly interest, a perceptible shift in the disciplinary boundaries of family law is occurring. Today, tax law (Cain 2000; Crawford 2005; Knauer 1998), immigration law (Abrams 2009), criminal law (Kennedy 2009; Murray 2009), and discrimination law (Cossman 2009; Emens 2009; Kessler 2001), and other areas not historically considered part of family law are as likely to be sites of inquiry on the family as marriage, divorce, and child custody. Three examples illustrate this point nicely.

Kathy Abrams's work (2009) focuses on immigration law. She examines the emergence of federal workplace and residential sweeps aimed at apprehending undocumented immigrants and the emergence of the "family detention" facilities designed to house families awaiting determination of their immigration status. She argues that these policies serve to produce immigrants as less than human— "the kind of being whose deep connections with parents, children or spouses can be disregarded, indeed flagrantly violated, at will" (408). They also influence how immigrants see their future in the US, and how immigrant families are organized (or disorganized).

Bridget Crawford (2005) analyzes tax law, demonstrating how existing estate tax definitions do not recognize nonmarital associational relationships that some people consider to be family. She proposes a set of three unique family categories that would minimize complexity, help achieve statutory integrity, and bring the estate tax definitions in line with the rules' underlying policies.

A final example is Melissa Murray's (2009) exploration of the space between criminal law and family law. She argues that criminal law and family law have long had a cooperative role in constructing intimate life as either licit marital relations or illicit criminal behavior, and in channeling sexual intimacy and reproduction into marriage. She explores developments that disrupt this binary, such as the decriminalization of sodomy (*Lawrence v. Texas* 2003) and legalization of contraceptive use by unmarried persons (*Eisenstadt v. Baird* 1972). More broadly, she looks to the promise created by the potentially blurred line between family law and criminal law to imagine a space between marital sex and criminal sex, where sex can exist outside of marriage and, even possibly, outside of law.

As these examples demonstrate, legal regimes outside of family law often regulate the family much like traditional family law. Immigration law, tax law, criminal law, employment law, and other legal regimes channel care and economic support, redistribute income, define who is a legal family member, and regulate intimate, sexual, and family relations more generally. This insight generates a fundamental question: if intimate and sexual relations can be regulated by regimes far outside the law of marriage, divorce, and child custody—is the family itself, which is constituted by law, also unnatural? By making this question possible, the new frontiers of family law de-fetishizes marriage in the discipline.

Some tensions

These significant shifts in family law priorities inevitably produce a number of tensions. I classify these tensions into two categories: outside tensions and inside tensions. Outside tensions arise between those working inside family law, feminist legal theory, queer theory, and related critical legal theories to establish the new frontiers of the family and those outside these traditions who wish to contain the new frontier. Inside tensions arise between and among left critical theories and theorists of the family.

The tension between political conservatives and liberals is the most prominent outside tension resulting from the move away from marriage as *raison d'être* of family law. Political conservatives wish to preserve patriarchal marriage and the status-based organization of the family; political liberals wish to disrupt and displace this model with more fluid, egalitarian frameworks for organizing sexual and intimate relations. This disagreement is played out daily in state and national politics surrounding marriage, divorce, same-sex unions, abortion, and welfare.

More interesting, and what I would like to focus on here, are the inside tensions on the left that potentially arise with the intellectual shift away from marriage to other relationships and topics. These include tensions among liberal and critical legal feminists, and tensions among queer and straight feminist legal theorists and theories of the family.

Liberal/crit tensions

To a significant extent, the channeling model of family law is politically conservative. Legal feminists have exposed its gendered and repronormative implications (Appleton 2008; McClain 2007). Yet legal feminists and family law scholars are not universally committed to discarding marriage, whether as a practice or as an organizing principle of the discipline. Hence the development of a liberal, feminist iteration of the channeling story. In this version, the underlying ideals of protecting children and carefully defining the reach and responsibility of the state are retained, while incorporating insights about sex equality (Appleton 2007). The end goal thus becomes reconstructed, egalitarian marriage (McClain 2007).

Liberal feminist marriage reform has significantly impacted the ideals and content of family law, if not always how it plays out on the ground (Bartlett 1999). Today, family law is characterized by a commitment to formal gender equality, to women's right to exit unhappy marriages through no-fault divorce, and, at least nominally in the form of tolerance (*Lawrence v. Texas* 2003), to diversity in intimate relationships. In sum, marriage and monogamy are still the end goal of family law, just a kinder, gentler, gender-neutral version.

Why has liberal legal feminism aimed to keep the focus of family law on marriage and inequality? Partly, from the concern that as we move away from inequality inside marriage and the family, we will make a mistake. There are still lots of marriages, lots of divorces, and lots of potentially vulnerable women and children; in sum, lots of reasons to be worried about inequality inside the marital family.

Legal feminists also know very well how power simply gets reorganized under the banner of freedom. The hazards of the freedom discourse are apparent. Freedom in our political system has typically meant negative freedom from state intervention, not positive freedom facilitated through law or other resources (Harris 2000; Nussbaum and Sen 1993; West 2003). Freedom rhetoric erases vulnerability (Fineman 2008) and relieves the state of its obligation to ensure that everyone has the resources to exercise their freedom. As Angela Harris (2000: 1186) highlights, freedom stands for free-market thinking: "what's good for private corporations is good for America, free markets unhindered by inefficient social welfare programs." This impoverished version of freedom is not all there is within liberal theory, "but the thin conception does have an extremely potent political force" (1187).

Straight–queer tensions

A realpolitik take on the tensions between liberal and critical conceptions of family concerns identity politics. Once we are not focusing on marriage, we are not focusing on the interests of straight, white women. That is true; let's face it. Also, because the topic of marriage is associated with gender-based economic inequality related to women's disproportionate share of child-care and domestic labor, moving away from a focus on marriage also potentially involves de-privileging the concerns of mothers in family law. Recent scholarly debates in legal feminism between "maternalists" and "nonmaternalists"

(Kessler 2005: 50)—that is, between those who wish to value care through the law (Fineman 1995; Williams 2000) and those who fear that doing so will reinforce gender roles (Case 2001; Franke 2001; Rosenbury 2005; Schultz 2000)—exemplify this tension.

Future directions

Having described the new frontiers of family law, its landscape, and primary objections, a question arises. Where is the discipline of family law going? Although there are many possible trajectories, three potential paths seem likely. First, with the obsolescence of its core channeling purpose, family law may become so incoherent that it disappears. Second, and perhaps an interim step toward the first path, as the diffusion of the discipline's goals and subjects continues, family law may morph into something broader, such as the law of intimacy. Finally, in the face of these new developments, perhaps family law will resist transformation, remaining relatively undisturbed from its channeling priorities. In that case, the new frontiers of family law would be constructed as "not family law," that is, relegated to other "law and" subjects. I discuss these transformations from the most to least radical.

Obsolescence

As family law becomes increasingly unmoored from its historical purpose of channeling sex, care, and reproduction into marriage, one distinct possibility is that it will simply disappear. This idea is not beyond the pale when one considers that family law as we understand it has not existed for time immemorial. At common law, family law was part of the law of domestic relations, covering the master–servant, husband–wife, child–parent, and other hierarchical relationships (Blackstone 1765–69). With industrialization and the end of slavery, those categories fractured into other areas, including employment and family law. Even then, the different components of what is today understood as family law were not seen as a whole until the end of the nineteenth century, and not described as such until the mid-twentieth century (Müller-Freienfels 2003). Family law was not taught as a freestanding academic subject in law schools until the 1950s. Today, significant areas of family law are covered in virtually every other area of the law school curriculum, including constitutional law, criminal law, property law, contract law, tort law, international law, and employment law. The main point here is that disciplines are not natural; they are constructs with their own consistent sets of rules, norms, and practices. They can be made and unmade, expand and contract, fracture and morph as economic, social, and political circumstances change.

With this is mind, it may be that family law, defined as the law of marriage, divorce, and child custody, is on a natural path toward obsolescence. This has already occurred to some extent. All but the most basic exploration of the legal parameters of the parent–child relationship are now studied in a separate course known as "parent, child, and the state." Prominent family law scholars predicted this development a generation ago. For example, Mary Ann Glendon (1976) argued that the family policy of the future will be primarily concerned with practical economic and child-related problems, as the state's interest in the regulation of marriage withers away. Martha Fineman (1991a) has also argued for two decades that the parent–child relationship should be the central concern of family law.

So we are already part-way there, one might argue. As questions about the husband-wife relationship continue to decline in importance, perhaps family law will wither until it ceases to exist. I am not saying here that the legal regulation of intimate relationships will disappear, simply that the set of default rules for husbands and wives that is today largely known as "family law" will be addressed by rules traditionally associated with other disciplines. To an extent, this change is already occurring, as much of family law is now governed by at least a soft set of contract principles, if not formal contract law. Furthermore, many aspects of sexual and intimate relationships are addressed in other areas of the curriculum.

Interestingly, prominent family law scholars with very different agendas have suggested this development. Fineman (1995) recommends abolishing marriage as a legal category and, with it, the entire set of special rules attached to it, doing away with marriage and divorce laws, as well as altering those areas where "spouse" is a relevant category, such as tax law or probate and estate rules. In her vision, this change would lift the veil of privacy, allowing a more robust set of protective rules (e.g. unjust enrichment, constructive trust) to address the vulnerabilities and dependencies of intimate relationships. In contrast, Janet Halley and Brenda Cossman (2007) would dismantle family law, because they find the assumptions of vulnerability justifying the entire discipline suspect. "[F]amily law exceptionalism," as they call it, "produce[s] a vast range of disciplinary effects, running from the curriculum, the code, and case law to our understandings of sexuality, our habits of domestic architecture, our modes of distributing social security" (5). Halley (2006) argues that family law has primarily been a domain for feminist theorizing about women's subordination to men. As such, taking a break from family law is a natural corollary of her project of taking a break from (antisubordination/American) feminism. In sum, Fineman seeks to export family law's insights about dependency and vulnerability to other areas of law; Halley and Cossman seek to discard these assumptions in ways more consistent with queer theory. All reject the normative project of privileging heterosexual marriage in law and society, and with it, family law.

This could be the trajectory. Maybe. However, evidence suggests that the channeling function of family law is an extremely potent political force. Although the current national conversation around same-sex marriage has triggered a serious discussion about deregulating marriage in the US (Cornell 2004;

Coontz 2007; Fineman 1995; Polikoff 2008; Warner 2002), it is not the first one. Indeed, in family law scholarship, there is a long tradition of predicting, or arguing for, the demise of legal marriage (Glendon, 1976; Weitzman 1981). Yet marriage persists, if not as an institution with universal participation, then at least as a normative ideal (Edin and Kefalas 2005). Scholars from a broad range of political perspectives accept the channeling function of family law in some form (Duncan 2001; McClain 2007; Schneider 1992). Moreover, given capitalist commitments to privatizing dependency in the US (Fineman 1995), it is doubtful that the state will assume the support functions of marriage as it has in European countries any time soon. Given these obstacles and commitments, marriage will likely continue as a robust institution in the US, saving family law from obsolescence. A less radical transformation of the discipline is more likely, at least in the near future.

The law of intimacy

As the diffusion of its goals and topics continues, family law may morph into something broader, such as the law of intimacy. Except in name, one could argue that this change is already occurring. Recent family law scholarship considers a range intimate relations and practices that fall outside the traditional boundaries of family law, such as cohabitation, unmarried parenthood, multiple parenthood, polyamory, polygamy, self-care, and friendship. The sites of inquiry involve many areas that provide background rules for families, but which historically were not formally considered part of family law—for example, tax law, immigration law, criminal law, and employment law. The law of intimacy could potentially provide a tent to address these diverse social relations and legal domains without the disciplinary baggage of family law.

Few scholars have considered this middle ground. Given the widespread recognition of the limitations of thinking about sexual and intimate relations within the status-based construction of "the family" among nearly all stakeholders short of religious conservatives, why not formally discard the family as an organizing rubric? Marriage and divorce law could move into "law and religion" or some related topic; the rest, which is a lot, would become the law of intimacy. I suggest this only half in jest. The argument here is that liberal theories of equality are insufficient to salvage family law or "the family" from its close connection to concepts such as the sacred, private, licit, and altruistic (Halley and Suk 2009). These concepts, closely associated with traditional family law, arguably block fundamental reorganization of law and institutions governing sexual and intimate relations.

Developing a new area known as the law of intimacy may also ease the growing and perhaps unnecessary intellectual tensions between legal feminism and queer legal theory. In the legal academy, and to a certain extent in public discourses, there recently has been anxiety over who's in and who's out, whether we need to take a break from feminism (Halley 2006) or whether feminism has been misconstrued (Romero 2007), over whether we can rejuvenate "the family" into a functional concept or whether we should scrap it. Much common ground gets obscured in these conversations. Developing something like the law of intimacy might provide a framework for discussing how sex, gender, sexuality, and race work, through and with the law, without getting mired in arguments over which is the most important rubric for understanding a complex set of social processes and institutions. In the law of intimacy, equality theory would not dominate, but it would remain as an important component, and there would be more room to consider sexual and other forms of freedoms in thinking about sexual and intimate relations.

The law of intimacy may also allow us to see the plethora of new intimate configurations and practices developing in the wake of marriage's diminished importance. In political and legal discourses, intimate relations are generally assessed in relation to the married, two-parent norm promoted by traditional family law (Kessler 2007). Modern families are described as "broken," "fragmented," "divided," and "divorced" (59). These depictions of fractured, isolated parents and families are especially prominent in current political and legal discourses regarding divorce, welfare, and same-sex marriage. If we were to set aside marriage and the family as the "measure of all things" (Franke 2008: 2689), perhaps we could see the multitude of other practices, relationships, and institutions that increasingly perform the traditional functions of marriage and the family: cohabitation, cruising, masturbation, sex toys, mental health therapists, extended families, blended families, networked families (Murray 2008), daycare, nannies, schools (Rosenbury 2007a), nursing homes, prisons, the media, alternative reproduction, massage, credit cards, chat rooms, Facebook, dating services, mail-order-brides, and work (Estlund 2003; Schultz 2003), to name a few. All these practices and institutions implicate sexual and intimate relations. All are facilitated and regulated by law. Yet legal scholars have not taken on these subjects in a coherent way. The continued existence of family law, however reformed, is part of the obstacle to that project. As a descriptive matter, family law is becoming or is at least on the verge of becoming the law of intimacy. As a normative matter, much would be gained from doing the further intellectual work necessary to make it the law of intimacy.

Resistance

Finally, faced with significant resistance, family law might remain largely undisturbed from its channeling priorities. In that case, the new frontiers of family law might be constructed as "not family law," that is, relegated to other "law and" subjects. Those with a stake in the status-based organization of the family and marriage will inevitably resist the transformations described here: religious conservatives, father's rights groups, neoliberals. Even many academics and law makers committed to equality and the functional family prefer marriage as the optimal social institution for caring for and supporting children. For these constituencies, I would guess, the impulse will be to say that everything I have described here is not family law—for example, feminism, queer theory, race theory.

Ironically, in the legal academy, mainstream scholars have criticized feminism and related theories for failing to present a general theory of law applicable outside the context of a specific set of identity group interests. Yet critical theory is constructed by both its proponents and opponents; it can be a ghetto, despite its significant impact. The process by which this occurs—for example, through the organization of conferences and symposia, the writing of case books, the organization of topical sections in professional associations, the development of curricula in law schools, faculty recruitment—is a complex subject outside the scope of this chapter. However, what is clear is that the new frontiers of family law have as legitimate a claim to be family law, or the law of intimacy, as the canonical iteration of family law. Whether it will succeed in that claim is dependent on politics.

Or maybe all of the above, in certain respects

The final and most likely possibility is that all of the above trajectories will occur as a result of the new frontiers of family law—obsolescence of parts of the discipline, reorganization of the discipline into something more capacious, and resistance. I do not know from this position how it will all play out. The more interesting question is: what will be the effects on intellectual inquiries of sex, intimacy, care, and reproduction of these various developments?

Conclusion

Family law scholarship is rapidly changing. No longer primarily concerned with husbands and wives, divorce and its economic consequences, or even questions concerning the care and support of children in the wake of family dissolution or dysfunction, family law scholarship now addresses sex, intimacy, care, and reproduction in a wide range of contexts and configurations outside marriage and the nuclear family. It is more concerned with the state than in the recent past, both as a potential source of oppression and support. It incorporates more antiessentialist analysis, and its boundaries lie in legal domains far outside its traditional boundaries. Contrary to common understandings of these developments, these shifts are not generational. The new frontiers of family law are being defined by second- and third-wave, junior and senior, and tenured and untenured scholars.

Family law scholars have observed and commented on these changes for a generation (Glendon 1976; Minow 1985; Schneider 1985; Weisman 1981). The main contribution of the new frontiers of family law is not its descriptive aspect, but the questions it raises about what the discipline's current conception hides.

As this chapter illustrates, there is much to be gained by exploring alternative conceptual possibilities for studying sexual and intimate relations.

Notes

1 For example, all states have discarded rules allocating marital property according to formal title, and most states treat unvested pensions, stock options, and business goodwill as divisible marital property (Oldham 2008).

Family law, feminist legal theory, and the problem of racial hierarchy

Twila L. Perry

Introduction

Developing theoretical and doctrinal frameworks to improve women's lives is no easy task, made even more challenging by the tremendous diversity that exists among women. In recent years, a wide range of critical approaches including feminist legal theory, critical race theory, critical race feminism, lat-crit, and gay and lesbian legal theory has reflected the diversity of women's lives. Yet, these discourses encounter difficulties in bringing women together because of the multiple contexts in which the positions, interests, and priorities of various groups may diverge or conflict.

The existence of racial hierarchies among women is undertheorized in feminist legal theory and warrants much more attention than it presently receives. Reflected in popular culture and in cultural, political, and legal discourses, informal rankings of women by race and ethnicity are rooted in the histories of different groups; they persist as a consequence of continuing racial discrimination and unequal economic status.

As a central area of inquiry in feminist legal theory, family law has the potential to expose the reality of racial hierarchies through issue analysis. I begin this chapter briefly describing two of the movements in legal scholarship addressed to improving the lives of women—feminist legal theory and critical race feminism. I then describe my journey toward work in these areas, offering observations on the nature of hierarchies and the obstacles to their frank discussion. The chapter then addresses two family law issues—the search by family law scholars for a theory of alimony and the controversy over transracial adoption—to illustrate the existence of racial hierarchies among women. Finally, I comment briefly on the possible impact of recent demographic changes and suggest how attending to racial hierarchy can enrich a family law analysis.

Feminist legal theory and critical race feminism

Feminist legal theory took root in the 1970s when advocates of women's rights began using the legal system to fight sex discrimination. As the number of women in law schools, practice, and the academy grew, women began challenging the very foundation of legal rules and structures impacting women. Legal academia also witnessed the emergence of a critical legal studies movement among left-oriented scholars which emphasized approaches critiquing liberalism's focus on individual autonomy and the separation of law and politics. Critical legal studies stressed skepticism toward the value of legal rights, arguing that a focus on legal rights reinforces the status quo and keeps oppressed groups politically passive (Chamallas 2003: 66–67).

Many feminists embraced critical legal studies but also developed a separate analysis of the law that was responsive to the particulars of women's lives. While there is no one definition of feminist legal theory, as an approach it describes and analyzes the law's impact on women, particularly focusing on how law subordinates women. Feminist scholarship employs various methodologies from traditional analysis to personal narrative with the goal of improving women's circumstances.

Some scholars see feminist legal theory unfolding in three stages. The first stage in the 1970s focused on legal equality—the idea that gender should not determine legal rights and obligations. The second stage, evolving during the 1980s, emphasized the difference in women and men's lives, arguing that accounting for that difference was necessary to achieve gender justice. The third stage, which unfolded rapidly in the late 1980s and early 1990s, focused on diversity, with scholars debating issues of essentialism and attending to the differences among women rather than the differences between women and men (Chamallas 2003).

In the late 1980s, the number of law professors of color substantially increased, and critical race theory emerged as some of these professors began writing about race in new ways (Crenshaw et al. 1996; Delgado and Stefancic 1999). Critical race theory was partially an outgrowth of the critical legal studies' critique of neutrality in law. However, many race crits believed that critical legal studies failed to address adequately questions involving race (Crenshaw 2002; Valdez et al. 2002). Critical race theorists wrote about issues that were the subject of litigation in the civil rights movement, like affirmative action, voting rights, employment discrimination, and segregation in housing and education. They also wrote about the societal structures that enable racism's perpetuation. Some discussions involved cases where racial implications had been ignored, minimized, or misunderstood. Concepts of cultural domination and unconscious racism, exploration of the reasons behind persisting racial subordination and racial hierarchy, and a critique of the liberal ideal of color blindness took center stage. Some critical race theorists, notably Patricia Williams, Derrick Bell, and Richard Delgado, incorporated narratives, personal experience, and autobiography into their scholarship.

Toward the end of the 1980s, more black women entered the legal academy and began examining feminist legal theory. In two influential articles, Professors Kimberle Crenshaw (1989) and Angela Harris (1990) offered critiques of white feminist legal scholarship, advancing a new approach to legal analysis insofar as it applied to black women's lives. They argued that many white feminists articulated a feminist theory lacking in relevance for most black women. They advocated an intersectionality approach that took into account the intersection of the factors of race and gender. Race and gender were not two separate factors that complicated black women's lives, but instead they formed a complex and inextricable brew.

During the 1990s, a growing group of scholars incorporated methodological approaches including intersectionality and the use of narratives into their work; they addressed various substantive concerns ranging from reproductive rights and family life to criminal, constitutional, and employment law. The output was large, and Professor Adrien Wing's compilation, *Critical Race Feminism*, first published in 1997, is now in its second edition (Wing 2003).

I began addressing issues of race and feminism in the mid-1990s, but my thinking about the intersection of race and gender evolved gradually. Growing up in a low-income black community in New York City in the late 1950s and 1960s, it was obvious to me that, in America, race powerfully impacts on an individual's circumstances and opportunities. From my vantage point, the plight of black people seemed to be the same whether they were male or female, although I did receive one very clear message about gender as I was growing up. I knew I must take care of myself economically—I could not expect a man to care for me financially. I learned that black men had a hard time in America and were often denied work opportunities that could provide economic security. Thus I understood that, for black women, marriage, motherhood, and work would likely be combined.

Only after graduating from law school did I begin thinking more deeply about gender. As an associate in a large corporate law firm, as a law clerk to a federal judge, in law practice representing the government, and in teaching law, it became clear that being a woman, independent of race, could be a professional disadvantage. At the law firm in the mid-1970s, I was exposed to the world of all-male lunch clubs on Wall Street and the vestiges of a system that relegated many women lawyers to trusts and estates work with no meaningful partnership opportunities. In my federal clerkship and in practice at the US Attorney's office, I saw that paltry numbers of women were judges or federal lawyers. During my early years in teaching law, I saw many obstacles to success for women in the academic world, challenges likely unthinkable for their male col- leagues. Women professors who were mothers met the challenge of gaining tenure under a level of stress and exhaustion that was different than their male colleagues. As a professor of family law, I was able to consider the impact of gender in a systematic way. Many years later, I rarely think about gender without simultaneously thinking about race.

Much of my work examines intersections between feminist and critical race theory in the area of family law and resonates with the period of feminist theory that emphasized diversity among women. It draws upon much critical legal scholarship—especially feminist legal theory and critical race theory—and is inspired by the work of an earlier generation of black feminist intellectuals. These women played multiple roles as writers, scholars, and activists; their audiences were both academics and ordinary black women with a political bent. Women like Audre Lorde, whose pioneering work was at the intersection of feminism, race, and sexual orientation and women like Angela Davis and bell hooks have produced work enormously helpful to me.

The problem of racial hierarchy

The issue of racial hierarchies among women is complex and troubling. Hierarchies reflect status and power relationships in a society, and they function in both concrete and subtle ways. In terms of the concrete, those who occupy the upper levels of a hierarchy often have the power to discriminate against and stigmatize those on the lower rungs. Those at the upper level can also accrue substantial psychological benefits from their status. Not surprisingly, those on the lower rungs often suffer economic and psychological consequences. Their employment, educational, and housing opportunities are fewer than the opportunities of the dominant group. Aware of their stigmatized and devalued status, women on the lower rungs may experience frustration and resentment. Failing to engage the issue of hierarchies is like operating without an important tool for understanding institutions, groups, and interpersonal relationships.

Hierarchies of gender and race

Gender hierarchy is reflected many areas of life: in employment, in the family, in the media, and in the treatment one receives in public spaces. One of feminist legal theory's major contributions is its unmasking of the persistence of gender hierarchies even in areas where the law, on its face, is gender neutral. Gender hierarchy is a reflection of the powerful institution and ideology of patriarchy, in which dominance results from the biological status of being male.

While women occupy the lower rung of a gender hierarchy, there are also hierarchies among women. These hierarchies are based on many different factors such as class, sexual orientation, educational background, physical appearance, and immigration status. Martha Fineman (1991b) notes that society's attitudes toward women often reflect a hierarchy that judges women's worth by the standard of their relationships to men—married women at the top, widows the next rung down, divorced women another rung lower, and single mothers at the bottom. This hierarchy obviously disadvantages black women, who are disproportionately unmarried and disproportionately likely to experience marital disruption (Bramlett and Mosher 2002). Even if married, black women are more likely than white women to be widowed because black men have lower life expectancies than white men (US Census Bureau 2009: 76).

Even among women of color, there is a hierarchy. While women of color of various ethnicities are the victims of racial and ethnic stereotypes, in this country, the most degrading and vicious stereotypes are reserved for black women. Indeed, the racial hierarchy that exists among women of color may ultimately warrant an analysis as searching as the one which minority women have applied to mainstream feminism (Perry 2000).

Racial hierarchies differ from gender hierarchies. While men are dominant in the gender hierarchy, often devaluing white women and inflicting harm on them through domestic violence and workplace discrimination, white men and women are also intimates. They band together and bond to create what is perhaps society's most important social and economic unit—the family. Together they engage in what many consider life's most important enterprise—raising children. White men and women are also each others' mothers, fathers, sisters, brothers, grandparents, and cousins. Thus, despite gender hierarchy's existence, along with the issues, tensions, power struggles, and even violence that this may bring, white men and women are in many ways a team.

Although there has been a substantial increase in interracial marriages and multicultural families in recent years (US Census Bureau 2009: 52), black people and white people generally do not share family relationships. Indeed, it is rare for whites and blacks to share close, interconnected experiences where they work toward common goals with an expectation of shared rewards. The hierarchy that exists between them is generally not softened by the intimacy and interdependency often present in the gender hierarchy between white men and women.

Discussing hierarchies

Engaging men and women in a conversation about gender hierarchies can be complicated and fraught with emotion. Yet, it is often easier for women to talk about their differences with men than to talk about the differences between women—especially women of different races. Rarely do women engage in serious discussion about class differences between women of the same race. Discussing class origins and differences is a sensitive issue that can invoke a complicated range of feelings. While the self-made man is accorded a certain kind of status and admiration, a woman lifting herself up by her bootstraps doesn't elicit the same response.

Talking about race is even harder for women than talking about class. If they are honest, many people would agree that most conversations about race take place between people of the same race rather than of different races. Barack Obama's speech about race in the middle of the 2008 Democratic primary brought renewed attention to the fact that chasms in perspectives, understanding, and conversations about race run deep. When gender and the complex intersectionality of race and gender that are the core of many black women's experiences are added to the mix, the task is even more formidable.

Discussing race in the context of a legal issue that involves education or employment is one thing, but many family law issues can hit close to home emotionally. Thus, most of us, even those most committed to social justice, have to admit that we routinely take race into account in making some of our most important life decisions—who to date, who to marry, who to adopt. The relative position of people in the racial hierarchy is relevant in those determinations. Whether we will admit it, love, romantic or familial, is not blind when it comes to race.

Conversations about racial hierarchies can also be uncomfortable for those at the top of the hierarchy if they are not committed to trying to change the situation. It is difficult for those occupying the bottom rung of a hierarchy to listen to a person at the top acknowledge their advantaged position but act as if there is nothing to do about it. For the person on the lower rung, it is not pleasant to acknowledge a diminished status. All of this unease makes it easier for women to ignore the problem of racial hierarchies than to try to address it.

Race and hierarchy in family law

The search by feminist scholars for a theory of alimony and the continuing controversy over the subject of transracial adoption are examples of family law issues that have the potential to expose the existence of racial hierarchies among women. Both areas pose problems for feminist legal theory.

The search for a theory of alimony

In the late 1980s and early 1990s, family law and feminist scholars began developing a theory of alimony. This effort became necessary because developments like no-fault divorce and increased opportunities for women in the workplace caused the traditional justifications for alimony—fault and need—to lose their force. Some opponents of alimony asked, what is the theoretical basis for imposing a legal duty on one person to continue to provide financial support for another person to whom he or she no longer has a legal tie?

The need to develop a theory of alimony came about at around the same time as the emergence of the racial critique of feminist legal theory. In my own writing, I began exploring the implications of the search for a theory of alimony for those women who seemed least likely to benefit from it—black women and other women of color (Perry 1994).

The search for a theory of alimony has been largely based on a paradigm marriage. In the paradigm marriage, the wife sacrifices or slows down her career to attend to the needs and interests of her husband and children. She makes this decision believing that her marriage is for life and that in her later years she will enjoy economic security with her husband. However, if the marriage ends after she has made her sacrifice and investment but before she has "reaped her reward," the wife often finds herself in a troubling position. The husband can walk away with the most valuable asset of the marriage—a career with future earning potential. The wife finds herself with diminished economic and work-place opportunities. Family law and feminist scholars are concerned with finding ways to lessen what for many women is likely to be a hard economic fall.

Many scholars seemed to have this paradigm in mind as they developed a theory of alimony. However, the structure of marriages for most black couples often do not fit this paradigm. Most black men earn less than white men and, historically, a disproportionate number of married black women remain in the workforce compared with white women. Indeed, culturally and historically, most black women have been raised with the expectation that their future includes both mothering and working. Many black women have less of an expectation of economic compensation at the end of a marriage than a middle or upper-middle class white woman might have.

Thus, many theories proposed to justify alimony for upper-middle class white women had little relevance to the lives of most black women. Contract-based arguments premised on the concept of "expectation" that a wife's homemaker services would be rewarded over the long run seemed less relevant in a marriage where the wife was a major contributor to family finances. Theories of alimony dependent on the premise that women have "sacrificed" their careers for the well-being of their families also seemed less relevant to women who were less likely to be candidates for career trajectories leading to high status, high-paying jobs. The "law and economics" approach, justifying alimony as compensation to homemakers in marriages where spouses made the "economically rational" decision to maximize the opportunities of one spouse in the labor market, did not seem relevant to marriages where the wife worked just to make ends meet.

Moreover, alimony could be viewed as a privilege enjoyed after divorce by the most advantaged women in the society and could easily reinforce hierarchies among women based not on their own merits or achievements, but on their attachments to men. A woman economically supported by her husband was viewed as an individual deserving of financial support once she was on her own, while women without husbands whose economic needs might need to be met by the state were viewed as undeserving or even the subject of scorn. Both women may have been superb homemakers and wonderful mothers, but only one was viewed as deserving of sympathy and help. A theory of economic support for women based so closely on their attachments to men raises some troubling issues for feminist legal theory.

Many people are surprised to learn that very few divorced women are awar-ded or collect alimony. Thus, some feminists argue that alimony should be abolished because it misleads women into believing that the law will provide economic protection for them should their marriages end. They advocate, instead, that married women make decisions about work and family that will put them in a position to be economically independent in the event of divorce. This suggestion also has implications for the issue of racial hierarchies among women.

The problem this suggestion presents is who will care for the children of the upper-middle class women who enter the workforce to achieve financial independence? Their ability to work while simultaneously meeting responsibilities at home will depend upon household help, likely provided by poor women of color. The reality that the woman—employer has an interest in paying as little as possible for that help gives rise to an inherent conflict between the employer and the employee. Obviously, the hierarchal relationship between white women and African-American women in this context has historical roots reaching all the way back into slavery, and it is a context that has economic, psychological, and emotional dimensions (Rollins 1985).

Transracial adoption

In recent years, transracial and international adoption have received substantial attention. Transracial adoption has been the subject of almost continuous controversy in this country since the early 1970s. During the 1990s, the number of international adoptions in this country increased substantially, and these adoptions became the frequent focus of articles in the media and law journals. Even though issues such as poverty, the economic status of women, the nature of mothering, and the relationships between women of different classes, races and ethnicities, and nations concern many feminists, there is a lack of feminist discussion or analysis of transracial and international adoption.

Very troubling is the fact that transracial adoption is usually a one-way street. Children of black women are adopted by white women; the reverse almost never occurs. The flow of children in international adoption is also one-way—the children of women of color in poorer countries are adopted typically by white women in Western nations. Though conceptualizing these adoptions as humanitarian acts is appealing, they raise serious issues for feminist theory.

Can white families raise black children to be emotionally healthy individuals with the "survival skills" necessary to survive in an often racially hostile society? Do black communities have a legitimate political interest in social policies concerning transracial adoption? Does transracial adoption represent cultural genocide or cultural imperialism? The willingness of the social welfare system to remove black children from their families rather than focusing on family preservation efforts is a central concern. Furthermore, arguing, as some advocates do, that racial considerations in adoption undermine equality and are not in children's best interests ignores the reality that, in America, race almost always matters.

In America, black mothers have been subjected to a great deal of disparagement. They are often depicted as lazy welfare cheats or emasculating matriarchs raising a future generation of criminals and non-achievers. These negative stereotypes, which devalue black mothers and reinforce the low status of black women, are significant in the transracial adoption controversy. The images appear in books, movies, and other media outlets, as well as in legal cases where white families and black mothers are at odds.

If a society values the mothering of some women more than that of others, the separation of devalued mothers from their children is less likely to be seen as cause for concern. The children of such women may be thought to receive a lucky break if they are adopted by a higher-status family. Moreover, women who know that they are devalued will likely resent a pattern of adoption that transfers children from their group to women of higher status. They may experience feelings of resentment and hostility toward the valued group. This resentment impedes the ability of women from diverse backgrounds to form coalitions beneficial to all women.

Ironically, even as black mothers have been disparaged in their mothering of black children going all the way back to slavery, they have been viewed positively as the caretakers of white children. Black women who work as nannies, especially those employed for a long period by the same family, often serve a mothering function. The nanny's job is to provide the children in her care with physical care, discipline, and affection. In many instances, a nanny effectively may raise her employer's children. There are many black women in this country who have successfully "raised" white children without occupying the status of legal mother, but they are often denigrated in the role of mothers to their own children.

Feminist theory needs to engage the issue of racial hierarchies in the context of transracial adoption. However, it is not surprising that movement in this direction has been slow; there has been little discussion of adoption generally from a feminist perspective. Outside of the surrogacy context, feminists have expended little energy on mothers who give their children up for adoption.

Racism, patriarchy, and poverty are often reasons why so many children of color end up in the adoption system, whether coercively removed or "voluntarily" placed. Mothers of color are more likely than white, privileged women to live in circumstances where it is difficult to care for children. Some women have their children taken away. Others see adoption as the only practical solution; this reality presents a problem with complex moral dimensions that invites deeper feminist exploration.

Feminist theory could offer helpful concepts and methods for analyzing transracial adoption, but not nearly enough has been done in this area. For example, feminist theory is often considered hostile to a law and economics analysis, yet some advocates of transracial adoption employ a simplistic "supply and demand" approach to transracial adoption—refusing to take their analysis beyond the assertion that there is a large supply of black children available for adoption and a large demand for them by white families. Such an analysis leaves the mothers of these children out of the equation. Feminist themes of care and connection focus attention on the one-on-one nurturing relationship between an adoptive mother and child, but this attention can gloss over the fact that the one-way street of transracial adoption raises political and moral issues.

Autonomy and choice are important concepts for feminists when examining the decision to become a parent but are rarely used to interrogate the circumstances surrounding a poor woman's "choice" to give up her child for adoption. Arguments opposing the use of wealth as a factor in child custody decisions have not led to similar arguments in the adoption context about the unequal distribution of wealth between poor women and wealthier adopting women. The narratives of white adoptive mothers are prominent in articles supporting trans-racial adoption, but the emotional dimensions of a poor woman's decision to give her child up for adoption or the pain of women whose children have been removed through state intervention often receive short shrift.

The potential for convergences

The search for common ground

The search for a theory of alimony and the controversy over transracial adoption illustrate the failure of feminist approaches to account for the material circumstances of many black women's lives. Greater incorporation into family law of issues involving race is important, not only to head off claims that black women's concerns are marginalized or ignored. The failure of feminist theory to engage the intersection of race and gender results in lost opportunities for women from diverse backgrounds to engage more fully in collaborative thinking and action.

Feminist theory and critical race feminism have many reasons to find more common ground and become more mutually enriching. First, the goals of the two movements are similar. Both seek to promote the ability of women to sustain themselves economically, to care for their children and other depen-dent family members, and to find fulfilling personal relationships. Both move-ments seek justice and equality for groups that have known intentional discrimination and institutionalized inequality. Both focus on critiquing legal rules, examining institutional and societal structures and frameworks for bias, and unpacking concepts such as hierarchy and subordination. Both are more flexible than traditional legal methods and sometimes employ narratives, para-bles, or personal stories. Both face similar challenges in confronting questions of intersectionality, identity, essentialism, and the meaning of equality. Both have a stake in common issues such as the sustaining of affirmative action as a tool for expanding opportunities in areas where opportunities have been restricted (Perry 1994).

Exploring racial hierarchy should come naturally to feminist legal theory, since identifying and articulating harms suffered by women is an important part of that enterprise. It is not a great leap from work in the context of gender hierarchy to identifying the nature of the benefits some women receive as the consequence of a race-based hierarchy. White feminists including Peggy MacIntosh (1998) and Ruth Frankenberg (1993) have been leaders in describing the daily benefits white women receive based on their racial status, and there is more work to be done in this area.

Alimony and transracial adoption: looking toward the future

As the position of women in the society changes, the alimony analysis is likely to change. The number of married women in the workplace has increased in the last several decades (US Census Bureau 2009: 375), the earnings gap between men and women has narrowed (US Department of Labor 2008), and in a growing number of cases, women earn more than their husbands (US Department of Labor 2007: 68). Moreover, fewer men than women have been enrolling in college (Lewin 2006). The result of these changes may be that, in the future, the number of men seeking alimony upon divorce will increase. Long-held assumptions about the relationship between gender and economic dependency will invite reexamination.

Still, alimony is likely to continue as a relevant subject of feminist inquiry. Recent years have revealed a trend of some younger highly educated professional women leaving the workforce to raise their children (Belkin 2003; Stone 2007), and since the mid-1990s, the percentage of married women in the workforce has been leveling off (US Census Bureau 2009: 375). Moreover, even when women work high-paying prestigious jobs during their marriage, they still perform a disproportionate amount of caretaking responsibilities. Thus, husbands may still end up more economically advantaged than their wives after divorce, and alimony will remain an issue.

Changes in racial demographics may bring the circumstances of some women of different racial backgrounds closer together. Some growth in the black middle and upper-class has given a small number of black women the option of choosing to be full-time homemakers (Clemetson 2006). In the event of a divorce, these women will face circumstances similar to those of their upper-middle class white counterparts; they would have a stake in the search for a theory of alimony. If these women decide to remain in the workforce, they, too, will face the issue of employing other women in their homes with its inherent economic justice issues. At the same time, the number of white unmarried women giving birth has been increasing (US Census Bureau 2009: 66), giving more white women a stake in decreasing the stigmas associated with single motherhood.

Despite changing demographics that may bring the circumstances of some black women and white women together, the middle-class status of most black families is modest and insecure (Draut et al. 2008). The majority of black women continue to exist outside the traditional marriage paradigm and still struggle at the bottom of the racial hierarchy. Thus, alimony still has much less relevance to them than to the mainly white women who operate at the top of the hierarchy.

Society is also undergoing changes likely to affect the analysis of transracial adoption. More interracial marriages make obvious racial differences between children and parents appear less unusual, a factor that might facilitate the comfort of transracially adopted children. And, of course, the fact that President Barack Obama, America's first African-American President, was raised by a white mother, grandmother, and grandfather will certainly find its way into debates about whether white adoptive parents can provide black children with the "survival skills" necessary to become successful adults. Challenges by some scholars to the whole concept of racial categories will likely to play a role in discussions about transracial adoption, especially as America increasingly becomes a multiracial, multicultural society.

Yet, the issues surrounding transracial adoption that need to be addressed in feminist legal theory have not changed so dramatically. Black children continue to be removed from their homes at alarming and disproportionate rates, and many transracial adoption advocates continue to favor adoption over family preservation. Continuing patterns of housing segregation mean that most trans-racially adopted black children are still likely to grow up in white communities with the challenges of social isolation this often entails. Despite all of his success, Barack Obama's autobiography, *Dreams of My Father* (2004), makes it clear that a dominant theme in his life was the quest to define his own racial identity.

My analysis of transracial adoption has focused not on the question of whether whites can raise emotionally healthy black children but on the politics and discourse surrounding transracial adoption and on the images of black mothers in the controversy. Much of that imagery persists. Important issues that interrogate the role racial hierarchies among women play in the analysis of transracial adoption still need exploration. The transfer of children from women at the bottom of the racial hierarchy to women at the top deserves attention it has not yet received.

The first black First Lady and the racial hierarchy

While there have been improvements in the material lives of some black people during the last decades, stark economic and racial hierarchies among women still exist in this country. Black women still lag far behind white women with respect to maternal death and infant mortality, rates of incarceration, education, and life expectancy (US Census Bureau 2009: 76, 81, 145; US Department of Justice 1998: Table 5.8). Black women still occupy a lower rung on the racial hierarchy than white women in this country. Thus, the ascendance of Michelle Obama to the position of First Lady of the United States is a significant and intriguing event. What does this mean for the racial hierarchy among women?

Much attention has focused on the image of Barack Obama, a black man, as the President of the United States, but equally intriguing are the implications of Michelle Obama's image as the First Lady. Obviously, we are still at the beginning of Mrs. Obama's time in that position, and thus far, the reaction of the public to her seems favorable. In addition to her announced agendas of promoting the needs of working mothers and military families, Mrs. Obama has become something of a fashion icon. She has graced the cover of *Vogue* and has been the subject of a spread in *Vanity Fair*. These are venues in which the appearance of black women has been, to put it mildly, rare.

During the presidential campaign, however, there were a number of moments that left me concerned that the prospect of a black First Lady could hurt Barack Obama's chances of being elected President. In light of black women's position on the low rung of America's racial hierarchy, it would not be surprising if the prospect of a black First Lady was greeted by some Americans with something less than enthusiasm.

After her husband received the Democratic nomination for President, Mrs. Obama was widely criticized for stating that for the first time she was "really proud" of her country (Cooper 2008). Similar criticism may have been leveled at the wife of any nominee making such a statement, but Mrs. Obama's race was likely a factor in the attention the remark received and the reaction that ensued. This incident was soon followed by the controversial *New Yorker* cover in which Mrs. Obama was caricatured as a big-afro-wearing terrorist in fatigues and combat boots giving her husband a fist bump in a White House adorned with a picture of Osama bin Ladin above the fireplace. Despite the fact that much debate ensued as to whether the cover was acceptable satire, it is hard to recall a similar image of any other prospective First Lady as tough, angry, dangerous, and potentially murderous on the cover of a respected magazine. It seemed that Michelle Obama was beginning to be stereotyped in the press as "an angry black woman" (Nelson 2008).

After these events, Mrs. Obama kept a low profile. At the end of the summer, she was given a new and successful roll-out at the Democratic National Convention, where her prime-time speech was designed to portray her as just another American woman: a wife, a mother, and the product of a proud, hardworking, working-class American family.

The treatment Sarah Palin received during her candidacy for Vice President of the United States during the same campaign also provided an opportunity for reflection about racial hierarchies. There is no question that Palin was widely criticized for many things, including her lack of experience and knowledge, aspects of her finances, and some of her past behavior. Still, suppose, in the middle of the presidential campaign, Michelle Obama had announced that she had a teenage daughter who was pregnant, unmarried, and a high-school dropout, impregnated by another teenaged high-school dropout? It is extremely doubtful that this news would have been received by the public or press as a "private family matter." Instead, there likely would have been a barrage of commentary, stories, and statistics about black women giving birth to children outside of marriage, black women on welfare, and the issue of black children's academic achievement.

Indeed, with respect to academic achievement, it seems inconceivable that any black woman could be a candidate for such a high national office and display the low level of knowledge of economic, world, and national affairs that Sarah Palin did. And what kind of media attention would Michelle Obama have likely received if, like Cindy McCain, wife of presidential candidate John McCain, she had a history of drug addiction and stealing drugs from a charity (Kantor and

Halbfinger 2008)? As I watched the vice-presidential debate between Sarah Palin and Joe Biden, I wondered whether more aggressive questioning by the moderator, Gwen Ifill, a black woman, would have hurt Obama—some whites may not have been pleased by an image of a black woman in a commanding position in a situation where a white woman seemed to be faltering. Finally, when I heard remarks on the campaign trail by Republican nominee John McCain that Barack Obama was "measuring the drapes" for the Oval Office (*Washington Post* 2008: A16), I was even more afraid that Cindy McCain might say that Michelle Obama was measuring the drapes for the White House. In a country where black women still occupy a low rung in the racial hierarchy, some Americans might have been more comfortable with the image of Mrs. Obama cleaning the drapes.

The possibility that a black woman could be become the First Lady was an issue present during the 2008 presidential campaign, although not widely discussed in purely racial terms. Michelle Obama's status as First Lady is a major event for this nation, and how she is accepted in that role over the long term will tell a great deal about the willingness of Americans to alter long-standing prejudices and stereotypes concerning black women.

Conclusion

Notwithstanding Barack Obama's election as the first African-American President of the United States and Michelle Obama's position as the nation's first African-American First Lady, America is not rapidly transforming into a post-racial society. Michelle Obama's position does not alter the material circumstances of most black women's lives; they will continue on the bottom of the racial hierarchy as long as black people, as a group, live in unequal and diminished circumstances.

The racial hierarchies among women in this country are a function of multiple factors—the history of the various ethnic groups with which they are associated and the persistence of economic and social inequality. Can feminist legal theory make a contribution to addressing these problems?

Long-existing racial stigmas are not easily overcome. The idea that some women are deemed of lesser value than others is deeply rooted in the minds of many people. However, the persistent status of some women at the bottom of the racial hierarchy is also linked closely to their economic status. The search for a theory of alimony is less relevant to black women than to white women because of African-Americans' lower economic status. Similarly, the disproportionate numbers of black children available for adoption derives from black women's economic vulnerability. To make any contribution to the problem of racial hierarchies among women, feminist legal theory must address issues of economic justice right alongside issues of gender and racial justice.

Furthermore, understanding the lives of women at the bottom of the racial hierarchy may enrich the analysis of recently emerging issues in family law.

As the scope of family law extends beyond marriage, divorce, and the nuclear family, issues like same-sex marriage, friendship, childlessness, lifelong singleness, and the effects of reproductive technology and globalization are commanding the attention of family law scholars. This development is positive because people are structuring their lives in new ways; it is important for legal theory to keep pace with these changes.

Evaluating the lives of women with low social status can enrich family law analysis because many of these women have experience developing paradigms outside the traditional nuclear family. For example, denied the luxury of relying on the traditional family structure during slavery, black women improvised. They became "mothers" of children who were separated from their mothers. Since that time, many black women have raised children on their own, with support from communities of grandparents, neighbors, and "other mothers." Recognizing the challenges and the experiences of women who had no choice but to function outside of the traditional paradigm enhances understanding of other people living in non-traditional settings, faced with challenges of economic survival, social stigma, and other issues.

More feminist writing examines how the law subordinates women than lays out strategies for liberation (Chamallas 2003), and this problem is shared by many subordinated groups. The problem is more complex where gender intersects with race. Legal scholars who seek to confront our culture's deep-rooted patriarchy and racism must take a long-term view of the challenges they will encounter. The problem of racial hierarchies among women is sensitive and complex, but engaging it holds the potential to promote insights and further connections that can enrich us all.

Chapter 17

Living alone

New demographic research

Adam P. Romero

The development over the past two and a half decades of a discerning and diverse body of critical thought with respect to the family as a socio-legal institution is attributable in substantial part to the Feminism and Legal Theory Project, which we celebrate with this very volume. The Project's success and longevity, of course, are the result of tireless work by its founder, Martha Fineman, and many of her colleagues and students. Not only has Fineman organized an astonishing number of conferences and co-edited seven scholarly volumes, she has trained and encouraged countless students, scholars, and activists—myself included—with generosity and vigor. In addition, she has authored brilliant legal and social theory indispensable to anyone concerned for the tenacious inequalities that societies create and, in many ways, tolerate. I salute Fineman for her contributions to a more just world.

This chapter is part of a larger project that examines the importance of the concept of family in the United States, especially as related to how we collectively understand and approach human vulnerability and dependency. In particular, I am interested to consider the thorough significance of family in law and policy from the perspective of those "without family," i.e. those who live disconnected from family. What does the comprehensive relevance of family mean for and to adults who are in need of significant care but who live with little to no association to family, broadly understood, or whose families are unable to fulfill their caretaking duties? My argument is that at the same time our family regime privileges some families over others, namely via marriage, we also privilege those individuals connected to family over those who are not. Our social policy's incredible reliance on family, in conjunction with assumptions about family form and function, creates an extensive, unique, and invisible vulnerability for adults without family, particularly those who face extreme dependency. My goal for this chapter is not to fully explore this argument. Rather, framed within the context of this broader project, I present original research on the demographics of people who live alone, a growing segment of society about which we know relatively little.

When family fails: project overview

Family is constructed as critical to many, and meaningful to most, aspects of our lives in the contemporary United States. Like law, family is fundamental to the organization and operation of our society; it is central to the weave of the social fabric upon which state, economy, community, and, indeed, all of us depend for existence and sustenance. One of the most important functions of family is the provision of care and, more broadly, the management of dependencies and vulnerabilities inevitable in the human condition (Alstott 2004; Fineman 1995, 2005, 2008; Kittay 1998; Nussbaum 2002, 2006; West 1997). It is family—not the collective—that is primarily responsible for the burdens of taking care of people who cannot, for whatever reason, provide for themselves, such as children and the extremely disabled. In the execution of these responsibilities, families and especially caretakers perform the necessary task of reproducing society and populating its institutions. Thereby, caretakers work a benefit not only to the direct recipients of care but to all of society (Fineman 2005).

At the same time, family connects people to each other and to our economic, political, and cultural institutions. Family links us to and facilitates our participation in society. It is also through family relationships, especially though not exclusively through marital relationships, that the state confers a broad collection of rights and benefits. Enormous symbolic privileges and social advantages— such as public recognition and approval—also pass through family and marriage to individuals. Location within family is a position that can validate and aid claims by an individual for public accommodation or assistance. Family is crucial not only to how most of us know ourselves, but also to how each of us navigates larger society and is perceived and dealt with therein.

The centrality of family in law and policy is not natural, but rather is produced through assumptions and aspirations about the roles and duties of families and family members, as well as beliefs about the contexts in which individuals best exist and thrive. Indeed, our social policy's extensive reliance on family is possible only if we make the critical assumption that individuals are positioned within functioning families that are capable and willing to assume responsibility, to supply care and resources, to buffer misfortune and change. Certainly this assumption is informed by experience, but it is an assumption nevertheless. And while it is true that some rights, privileges, and subsidies are available to an individual qua individual, these benefits are envisioned as, and designed to be, complementary and supplementary to those buttressing the family. Individual benefits are generally intended to support, but not supplant, family responsibility for the individual.

Despite our ideals, the reality is that many families do not function well, and increasingly common patterns of behavior render ever more problematic the powerful assumption that individuals are situated within functioning families. Causal shifts in household demographics, such as the increasing number of people living alone; population traits, such as longer lifespans and the graying of the baby boom; familial and marital patterns, such as diminished fertility rates and the frequency of divorce, are trends not expected to reverse. Nor is retreat likely from the mounting demands of work and school that compete with and can inhibit the preservation of family as the primary unit of care. As a result of these and other shifts in behavior and society, a large and growing number of people fall outside of not only traditional family forms, but also familial networks altogether.

For those who effectively live alone and cannot adequately care for themselves, the centrality of family in our law and policy can have dire ramifications. Because we rely so heavily on families for the provision of care and resources to dependent persons, adult dependents without families can face extreme, sometimes perilous, adversities, many of which will go unaddressed if even acknowledged. This is the case for several different reasons, including, as I have explained, that our socio-legal approach to human vulnerability entrusts to family the care and welfare of dependent persons, thereby privatizing dependency. Further, family is constructed to play a crucial role in the management and amelioration of the risks common to living in liberal society, and in the connection of individuals to each other and to societal institutions. This means that those without family face complex and multilayered disadvantages and are more likely to be impoverished, marginalized, and abandoned.

Problems associated with living without family are played out in conjunction with class, race, gender, sexual, and national dynamics, among others. More specifically, the problem of family failure is connected to other societal patterns and contexts of disadvantage, including persistent inequalities and prejudice. Such disadvantages compound, reinforce, and even create problems associated with family failure and living without family. Above all other factors, wealth and poverty must be central to consideration of these issues. Those who are able to pay for care services are simply in a different and almost indisputably superior position vis-à-vis those who cannot. In addition, with respect to gender, we can observe that because women tend to outlive men, men partnered with women are less likely to face the dependencies of old age alone, whereas women face a greater possibility of widowhood and also poverty as they age.

A vast and vital literature exists with respect to the family as a socio-legal institution. Scholars have considered such topics as inequalities and violence within families, disparities between families, and the role of families within the broader social order. This body of thought has been affiliated with a wider political movement that rocked many of society's beliefs about family and ushered in important transformations in the law, such as no-fault divorce. Much of the critical scholarship in family law in recent years has been dedicated to examining and criticizing the range of ways in which law and policy privileges certain families over others. In particular, those families that do not or cannot access the institution of marriage have been shown to be disadvantaged legally, economically, and culturally. While some jurisdictions have begun to recognize and support non-traditional families, the marital connection between a man and woman remains the idealized family core across federal and state law. Scholarship on this subject continues to be immensely important, for many of the inequalities mapped persist, and much remains to be learned in this evolving story.

Among scholarship on the family and also care and dependency, however, there has been very little sustained attention to significantly disabled or dependent adults. Instead, the focus has been on children. Where the existence of adult dependency is identified, family is typically presumed to be in place to accept responsibility, supply resources, and administer care. No scholarship considers adults in need of substantial care but who, because of circumstance, politics, or choices made along the way, must manage their physical, emotional, and material needs without family. Accordingly, scholars have neither fully contemplated adult dependency, nor offered an adequate, let alone comprehensive, theory of family in law or liberal society. In taking adult dependents without family into account, my project complements and builds upon the existing body of critical thought. My aim is to expose and scrutinize the assumption of family that strongly informs how we as a society envision individuals and address their care needs.

Ultimately, this project asks whether family—as it is currently conceptualized and engaged in law and policy—is or is becoming obsolete in this day and age of increasing family fluidity and breakdown. And if the present concept of family is or is becoming outdated, should that concept and/or the broader societal systems in which it operates be reimagined? In other words, what does justice require with respect to a family regime that not only discriminates between families and undervalues caretaking labor, but also disadvantages and even endangers those who live disconnected from family? How might we remake society and its laws so that all people, regardless of familial status, experience improved existence, including less vulnerability, better care, and more capability? Even if family may be in the abstract the best structure for providing care and requisite resources to dependent individuals, the ability of someone to access and receive quality care simply ought not to be contingent on familial status, family form, or wealth.

New demographic research: live-alones

Many of us do not remain in families. Even those who do may not be part of a well-functioning family. Thus, the assumption that individuals are situated within functioning families is simply false for many people during periods of their lives and, for some, almost entire lifetimes. It is difficult to calculate with any precision the number of adults without family in the United States and, among those, the number who need significant care. Nevertheless, information available indicates that the number is considerable and expanding. For example, the *New York Times* reports that "hospital discharge planners and home health care agencies say they are serving more single people without an obvious person to look after them" (Gross 2005).

That more and more people are living outside of family is reflected in, and related to, various demographic shifts in the US population. These include the decreasing percentage of the population living in "family" households and the increasing percentage of the population living in "non-family" households including living alone, as discussed more fully below. During the second half of the twentieth century, the proportion of people's lives spent in marriage declined due to postponement of marriage, higher rates of divorce, and higher rates of nonmarital cohabitation (Bramlett and Mosher 2002). According to the National Center for Health Statistics (2006: Tab. A), in 2005 the national marriage rate in the United States was 7.5 per 1,000 people, and the national divorce rate was 3.6 per 1,000 people, meaning that slightly less than half of marriages end in divorce. US fertility rates have decreased over time: whereas in 1960 there were 118.0 births per 1,000 American women, in 2005 there were 66.7 births per 1,000 women (Martin et al. 2007: Tab. 1). Other relevant noteworthy trends include urbanization, which can ease life outside of family; increased school and work pressures, which can hinder family formation and family health; massive incarceration, which can disrupt and stress family relationships, even after confinement ends; and persistently widespread homelessness.

In what follows, I present original research on people who live alone using data from the US Census Bureau's 2006 American Community Survey (ACS)—an annual survey providing demographic, housing, social, and economic information about the US population and its subparts.[1] I intersperse the ACS findings with information from the decennial censuses and other surveys for trend analysis. Because the ACS is intended to replace the census long-form, comparison between them is appropriate. First, I discuss broad household trends that show the percentage of people living alone has increased dramatically over the past three-plus decades as the percentage of "family" households has declined. Second, I compare adults who live alone to the general adult population on a number of social, economic, and physical indicators. Third, I compare disabled adults living alone to the general disabled adult population. Fourth, I compare elders who live alone to the general elder population.

Because disability status and old age correlate with dependency, the latter two comparisons are perhaps the best way to get at the specific population of my broader project: significantly disabled or dependent adults without family. In this regard, it is crucial to acknowledge that people who live alone are not necessarily without family and, on the other hand, those without family do not necessarily live alone. However, no census or nationally representative survey allows me to directly assess familial status or strength of connection to family. Therefore, I use living alone as a proxy for without family. Though the proxy may not be a direct fit, the characteristics of those who live alone are apt to reflect those of people without family.

US households trends: number of people living alone increasing, "family" households decreasing

At the outset, we can observe a broad trend that single-person households are becoming increasingly common, both in sheer numbers and as percentages of total US households. In fact, people living alone became the most common specific household type in 2000, a distinction that previously belonged to spouses living with their natural and/or adopted children (Hobbs 2005: Tab. 3). The 2000 Census counted 27.2 million people living alone, constituting 26 percent of 105.5 million total households (Hobbs 2005: Tab. 2). By comparison, in the 1970 Census, 17 percent of all 63 million households were people living by themselves (Fields 2004: Tab. 1). Between 1990 and 2000, single-person households increased by more than 4.6 million households or by 21 percent (Hobbs 2005: Tab. 4). Most recent data indicate the ascendance of single-person households continues. The Current Population Survey estimated that more than 26 percent of households were single people in 2003 (Fields 2004: Fig. 2). In 2006, the ACS estimated that 30.5 million people were living alone, comprising 27 percent of all 111.6 million total households. Thus, between 1970 and 2006, single person households increased by almost 20 million or 180 percent, as documented in Table 17.1 and Graph 17.1.

Just as single-person households have grown, the proportion of "non-family" households, which includes those living alone, has consistently increased over time, rising from 19 percent in 1970 to 31 percent in 2000 and to 32 percent in 2003 (Fields 2004: Tab. 1). In 2006, there were an estimated 37 million such households, constituting 33 percent of all households. A "non-family" household is defined by the US Census Bureau as a person living alone or a householder who shares the housing unit with his or her non-relatives (Fields 2004).

Concomitant to the rise in single-person and other non-family households, the proportion of "family" households of all households has been in constant decline during the same time period, falling from 81 percent of all households in 1970 to 69 percent in 2000 and to 68 percent in 2003 (Fields 2004: Tab. 1). In 2006, there were an estimated 74.6 million family households or 67 percent of all households. A "family" household is defined by the US Census Bureau as having at least two members related by birth, marriage, or adoption, one of whom is the householder (Fields 2004). Notwithstanding the Census Bureau's limited definition of family—for example, co-habiting same-sex partners, in and of themselves, have not been counted as families—the steady rise of single-person and other non-family households and the steady decline of family households suggest that more and more people are living disconnected from family, or at least apart from family.

Characteristics of adults living alone compared to the general adult population

In this section, I compare adults living alone to the general adult population on a number of social, economic, and physical indicators using data from the 2006 ACS.[2] I begin with disability. The Census Bureau defined "disability" generally as "[a] long-lasting sensory, physical, mental, or emotional condition or conditions that make it difficult for a person to do functional or participatory

Table 17.1 Household counts and percentage of all households by type

Household type	1970[a]	1980[b]	1990[c]	2000[d]	2006[e]	Increase 1970–2006	Percent increase 1970–2006
Family	51,456,000 (0.81)	59,550,000 (0.74)	64,517,947 (0.70)	71,787,347 (0.68)	74,564,066 (0.67)	23,108,066	0.45
Non-family (including living alone)	11,945,000 (0.19)	21,226,000 (0.26)	27,429,463 (0.30)	33,692,754 (0.32)	37,053,336 (0.33)	25,108,336	2.10
Living Alone	10,842,000 (0.17)	18,255,000 (0.23)	22,580,420 (0.25)	27,230,075 (0.26)	30,496,588 (0.27)	19,654,588	1.81
Total Households	63,401,000 (1.0)	80,776,000 (1.0)	91,947,410 (1.0)	105,480,101 (1.0)	111,617,402 (1.0)	48,216,402	0.76

a Source: US Census Bureau 2004: Table HH-1.
b Source: US Census Bureau 2004: Table HH-1.
c Source: US Census Bureau 1990: Summary Tape File 1.
d Source: US Census Bureau 2000: Summary File 1.
e Source: US Census Bureau 2006b.

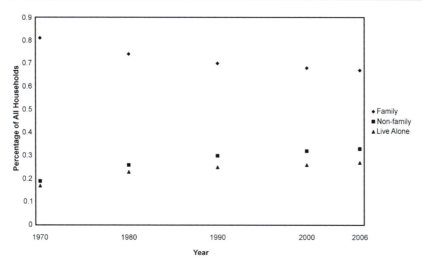

Graph 17.1 Household types as percentage of all households by year

activities such as seeing, hearing, walking, climbing stairs, learning, remembering, concentrating, dressing, bathing, going outside the home, or working at a job" (US Census Bureau 2006a: 33–34). To determine someone's disability status, the Census Bureau pursued six specific lines of inquiry related to sensory, physical, mental, self-care, mobility, and employment limitations (34). If a person aged 16 to 64 had at least one of the six limitations, she or he was considered disabled (36). Someone aged 65 or older was classified as disabled if she or he reported any one of the limitations, except employment (36).

A greater percentage of adults who lived alone were disabled than the entire adult population, as a general matter and on each of the six lines of inquiry. At the general level, 29 percent of those living alone were disabled, compared to almost 17 percent of the general adult population. As to sensory disability, which meant being blind, deaf, or having a severe vision or hearing impairment (34), 10 percent of those living alone and 5 percent of adults generally reported such disability. As for physical disabilities, respondents were asked whether they had "[a] condition that substantially limits one or more basic physical activities such as walking, climbing stairs, reaching, lifting, or carrying" (34). Twenty-one percent of people living alone reported a physical disability, compared to 11 percent of the general adult population. Third, with respect to cognitive function and mental disability, respondents were asked "if they had a physical, mental, or emotional condition lasting 6 months or more that made it difficult 'learning, remembering, or concentrating'" (34). While 10 percent of adults living alone reported such a disability, 6 percent of the broader adult population reported mental disability. Fourth, respondents were asked about limitations on self-care, specifically whether they had "a physical, mental, or emotional condition lasting 6 months or more that made it difficult 'dressing, bathing, or getting around inside the home'" (34). Six percent of those living alone and 4 percent of all adults reported a self-care disability. Fifth, the ACS questioned on mobility, specifically asking respondents "if they had a physical, mental, or emotional condition lasting 6 months or more that made it difficult 'going outside the home alone to shop or visit a doctor's office'" (35). Ten percent of adults living alone had such a mobility disability, compared to 6 percent of the general adult population. Sixth, the ACS inquired into disabilities that limit employment. Respondents were asked "if they had a physical, mental, or emotional condition lasting 6 months or more that made it difficult 'working at a job or business'" (35). Nineteen percent of those living alone, aged 16–64, and 7 percent of all adults so aged reported an employment disability. Finally, while 20 percent of people living alone had two or more of the disabilities outlined above, 10 per-cent of the general adult population did so.

In 2006, a larger proportion of those living alone were women than men: 56 percent of people living alone were women, while women constituted 51 per-cent of the general adult population. Those who lived alone were also older. While 33 percent of those living alone were aged 65 or older, this age group was 16 percent of the general adult population. Likewise, 20 percent of those living alone were aged 75 or older, while 8 percent of the general adult population was in this age range.

For those who lived alone, 76 percent were white, 6 percent were Hispanic or Latino, 13 percent were black or African-American, 3 percent were Asian, 0.6 percent were Native American or Alaska Native, 0.1 percent were Native Hawaiian or Other Pacific Islander, 0.2 percent were another race, and 1 percent were two or more races. For the general adult population, 66 percent were white, 15 percent were Hispanic or Latino, 12 percent were black or African-American, 4 percent were Asian, 0.7 percent were Native American or Alaska Native, 0.1 percent were Native Hawaiian or Other Pacific Islander, 0.3 percent were another race, and 2 percent were two or more races.

A greater percentage of live-alones were widowed, divorced, or never married. Twenty-seven percent of those living alone were widowed, 30 percent were divorced, and 35 percent had never been married. By contrast, among adults generally, 6 percent were widowed, 10 percent were divorced, and 3 percent had not been married.

Twenty-eight percent of those living alone and 25 percent of adults generally had earned a bachelor's degree or higher. Thirteen percent of those living by themselves reported being veterans of active-duty military, compared to 10 percent of the general adult population. Ninety-six percent of live-alones were US citizens, as were 93 percent of adults generally.

With respect to economic characteristics, a greater percentage of those living alone were below the federal poverty line: 18 percent of those who lived alone and 11 percent of adults generally were in poverty.[3] And where 41 percent of live-alones were below 200 percent of the federal poverty threshold, 26 percent of adults generally were in such status. Yet at the same time, a smaller percentage of people who lived alone received "public assistance," which generally included cash assistance but not Supplemental Security Income (SSI) (ACS Subject Definitions 2006: 49). One percent of single-person households received public assistance in 2006, compared to 2 percent of all households. Similarly, 7 percent of single-person households received food stamps, while 9 percent of all households received such assistance. With respect to SSI, 5 percent of those who lived alone and 4 percent of all households received the benefit.

A smaller percentage of lives-alones were employed than adults generally: 55 percent of those living alone were employed, compared to 61 percent of all adults. And while 57 percent of those living by themselves were in the labor force, 65 percent of all adults were in the labor force. The median income of those living alone was $25,000, compared to $24,287 for all adults. The mean income for those living alone was $35,788, more than $25,267 for all adults. The median earnings for people who lived alone was $12,000, less than $27,329 for adults generally. The mean earnings of people living alone was $25,182, compared to $26,358 for all adults. Finally, a smaller percentage of those living by themselves owned their homes: 54 percent of people living alone and 67 percent of adults generally reported homeownership (see Table 17.2).

Characteristics of disabled adults living alone compared to the general disabled adult population

Next, I compare disabled adults living alone to the general disabled adult population on the same social, economic, and physical indicators discussed above. According to the ACS, nearly 29 percent of adults living alone reported a disability in 2006. Thus, of the 30.5 million people living alone that year, approximately 8.8 million were disabled.

As explained above, disability status on the ACS was determined using six different inquiries. Of disabled adults living alone, 69 percent reported two or more disabilities, 33 percent reported a sensory disability, 72 percent a physical disability, 33 percent a mental disability, 20 percent a self-care disability, 34 percent a mobility disability, and 61 percent an employment disability. Of disabled adults generally, 65 percent reported two or more disabilities, 30 percent a sensory disability, 67 percent a physical disability, 37 percent a mental disability, 23 percent a self-care disability, 35 percent a mobility disability, and 60 percent an employment disability.

There were more women than men in the general disabled population, and women constituted an even greater proportion of the disabled population that lived alone. Fifty-four percent of disabled adults generally were female, as were 64 percent of disabled adults living alone. Disabled people who lived alone were older. While 55 percent of disabled people living alone were aged 65 or older, 39 percent of disabled adults generally were in the same age range. And while 38 percent of disabled live-alones were aged 75 or older, 25 percent of all disabled adults were so aged.

Table 17.2 Demographic and economic characteristics of adults living alone compared to the general adult population, 2006

Characteristic	Live alone	General adult population
Social and Physical Characteristics		
Disability (age is 16+)	28.8%	16.8%
Two or more Types of Disability (age is 16+)	19.9%	9.6%
Sensory Disability (age is 16+)	9.5%	4.9%
Physical Disability (age is 16+)	20.7%	11.0%
Mental Disability (age is 16+)	9.6%	6.0%
Self-care Disability (age is 16+)	5.8%	3.5%
Mobility Disability (age is 16+)	9.7%	5.5%
Employment Disability (age is 16-64)	19.3%	7.1%
Women (age is 15+)	55.9%	51.2%
Aged 65 or over (age is 15+)	33.4%	15.6%
Aged 75 or over (age is 15+)	20.0%	7.7%
US Citizen (age is all)	96.1%	92.7%
Widowed (age is 15+)	26.7%	6.4%
Divorced (age is 15+)	30.1%	10.5%
Never Married (age is 15+)	34.9%	3.1%
Bachelor's Degree or Higher (age is 18+)	28.2%	24.6%
Veteran (age is 18+)	12.6%	10.4%
White (age is all)	75.9%	66.2%
Hispanic or Latino (age is all)	6.4%	14.8%
Black or African American (age is all)	13.1%	12.2%
Asian (age is all)	2.7%	4.3%
Native American or Alaska Native (age is all)	0.6%	0.7%
Native Hawaiian or Other Pacific Islander (age is all)	0.1%	0.1%
Other (age is all)	0.2%	0.3%
Two or more Races (age is all)	1.1%	1.5%
Economic Characteristics		
Public Assistance Received	1.4%	2.4% of all households
Food Stamps Received	6.7%	8.8% of all households
Supplemental Security Income Received	4.7%	4.0% of all households
Below Federal Poverty Level (age is 18+)	18.2%	11.3%
Below 200% Federal Poverty Level (age is 18+)	40.9%	26.4%
Employed (Civilian and Military) (age is 16+)	54.5%	60.8%
In Labor Force (age is 16+)	57.3%	65.0%
Median Income	$25,000	$24,287
Mean Income (age is 16+)	$35,788	$25,267
Median Earnings (age is 16+)	$12,000	$27,329
Mean Earnings (age is 16+)	$25,182	$26,358
Homeowner	54%	67% of all households

Disabled adults living alone were 77 percent white, 6 percent Hispanic or Latino, 14 percent black or African-American, 1 percent Asian, 0.8 percent Native American or Alaska Native, 0.04 percent Native Hawaiian or Other Pacific Islander, 0.1 percent another race, and 1 percent two or more races. Of all disabled adults, 72 percent were white, 10 percent Hispanic or Latino, 14 percent black or African-American, 3 percent Asian, 0.9 percent Native

American or Alaska Native, 0.1 percent Native Hawaiian or Other Pacific Islander, 0.2 percent another race, and 1 percent two or more races.

Of disabled people living alone, 44 percent were widowed, 29 percent were divorced, and 19 percent were never married. Of the general disabled adult population, 19 percent were widowed, 15 percent were divorced, and 21 percent were never married.

Fourteen percent of disabled people living alone had a bachelor's degree or higher, compared to 12 percent of disabled adults in general. Fifteen percent of disabled live-alones were veterans, compared to 16 percent of all adults with a disability. Ninety-eight percent of disabled people living alone reported possessing US citizenship, as did 96 percent of all disabled adults.

A greater percentage of disabled people living alone were in poverty than disabled adults generally. Thirty-two percent of disabled live-alones were below the federal poverty level, and 66 percent were below 200 percent of the poverty line. By contrast, 21 percent of disabled adults generally were in poverty, and 46 percent fell under 200 percent of the poverty level. Three percent of disabled adults living alone received public assistance, compared to 4 percent of disabled adults in general. Fourteen percent of disabled live-alones received food stamps, compared to 16 percent of all disabled adults. Fifteen percent of disabled people living alone received SSI, compared to 13 percent of disabled adults generally.

A smaller proportion of disabled adults who lived alone were employed and/ or in the labor force. Twenty percent of disabled live-alones were employed in 2006, and 22 percent were in the labor force. Twenty-four percent of all disabled adults were employed, and 28 percent were in the labor force. The median income of disabled adults living alone was $13,700, compared to $11,700 for disabled adults generally. The mean annual income of disabled adults who lived alone was $21,209, compared to $19,157 for disabled adults in general. The median annual earnings of disabled adults living alone and all disabled adults was zero. The mean annual earnings of disabled live-alones was $6,544, compared to $7,942 for disabled adults generally. The median earnings for disabled adults living alone was zero, less than $17,720 for all disabled adults. And where 51 percent of disabled people living alone owned their homes, 68 percent of disabled adults generally were homeowners (see Table 17.3).

Characteristics of elders living alone compared to the general elder population

Finally, I compare elders living alone to the general elder population. More than 33 percent of adults who lived alone in 2006 were aged 65 or older, meaning 10.2 million people in that age bracket were living alone that year. And 20 percent of adults who lived alone in 2006 were aged 75 or older, or 6.1 million people. These numbers will of course swell as the baby-boom generation grays.[4]

Of elders living alone, 47 percent reported at least one disability, 35 percent reported two or more disabilities, 19 percent reported a sensory disability,

Table 17.3 Demographic and economic characteristics of disabled adults living alone compared to the general disabled adult population

Characteristic	Disabled adults living alone	General disabled adult population
Social and Physical Characteristics		
Disability (age is 16+)	100.0%	100.0%
Two or more Types of Disability (age is 16+)	69.2%	64.7%
Sensory Disability (age is 16+)	33.0%	29.7%
Physical Disability (age is 16+)	71.9%	66.5%
Mental Disability (age is 16+)	33.2%	37.3%
Self-care Disability (age is 16+)	20.2%	23.1%
Mobility Disability (age is 16+)	33.7%	34.9%
Employment Disability (age is 16-64)	60.9%	59.9%
Women (age is 16+)	63.8%	54.3%
Aged 65 or over	55.0%	39.4%
Aged 75 or over	38.4%	25.1%
US Citizen (age is 16+)	98.2%	95.9%
Widowed (age is 16+)	43.9%	19.1%
Divorced (age is 16+)	28.9%	15.0%
Never Married (age is 16+)	19.4%	21.1%
Bachelor's Degree or Higher (age is 18+)	13.5%	11.9%
Veteran (age is 18+)	14.9%	16.1%
White (age is 16+)	76.6%	71.6%
Hispanic or Latino (age is 16+)	5.9%	9.6%
Black or African American (age is 16+)	13.8%	13.7%
Asian (age is 16+)	1.3%	2.5%
Native American or Alaska Native (age is 16+)	0.8%	0.9%
Native Hawaiian or Other Pacific Islander (age is 16+)	0.04%	0.1%
Other (age is 16+)	0.1%	0.2%
Two or more Races (age is 16+)	1.4%	1.4%
Economic Characteristics		
Public Assistance Received	3.2%	3.6%
Food Stamps Received	13.9%	15.9%
Supplemental Security Income Received	15.1%	13.2%
Below Federal Poverty Level (age is 18+)	31.9%	20.9%
Below 200% Federal Poverty Level (age is 18+)	65.5%	46.2%
Employed (Civilian and Military) (age is 16+)	19.6%	24.1%
In Labor Force (age is 16+)	22.1%	27.7%
Median Income (age is 16+)	$13,700	$11,700
Mean Income (age is 16+)	$21,209	$19,157
Median Earnings (age is 16+)	$0	$0
Mean Earnings (age is 16+)	$6,544	$7,942
Median Earnings (Any Disability) (age is 16+)	$0	$17,720
Homeownership	51.2%	67.8%

37 percent a physical disability, 13 percent a mental disability, 10 percent a self-care disability, 20 percent a mobility disability, and 34 percent an employment disability. Of elders generally, 41 percent had at least one disability, 33 percent had two or more disabilities, 17 percent a sensory disability, 34 percent a

physical disability, 15 percent a mental disability, 14 percent a self-care disability, 21 percent a mobility disability, and 32 percent an employment disability.

Women were a larger proportion than men of the general elder population in 2006, and an even greater percentage of the elders who lived alone were women. Seventy-four percent of elders living alone were females, as were 58 percent of elders generally. While 60 percent of elders living alone were aged 75 or over, 50 percent of all elders fell into this age range.

Elders living alone were 84 percent white, 5 percent Hispanic or Latino, 9 percent black or African-American, 2 percent Asian, 0.4 percent Native American or Alaska Native, 0.03 percent Native Hawaiian or Other Pacific Islander, 0.06 percent another race, and 0.7 percent two or more races. Elders generally were 81 percent white, 6 percent Hispanic or Latino, 8 percent black or African-American, 3 percent Asian, 0.4 percent Native American or Alaska Native, 0.06 percent Native Hawaiian or Other Pacific Islander, 0.1 percent another race, and 0.6 percent two or more races.

Of elder people who lived alone in 2006, 67 percent were widowed, 20 percent were divorced, and 8 percent had never been married. Of the general elder adult population, 32 percent were widowed, 9 percent were divorced, and 5 percent had never been married.

Sixteen percent of elder people living alone had a bachelor's degree or higher, compared to 19 percent of elders in general. Seventeen percent of elder live-alones reported being a veteran, compared to 25 percent of all elders. Ninety-nine percent of elders living alone were US citizens, as were 97 percent of elders generally.

A larger percentage of elder people living alone were in poverty than elders generally in 2006. Nineteen percent of elder live-alones were below the federal poverty level, and 55 percent were below 200 percent of the poverty line. By contrast, 10 percent of elders generally were in poverty, and 33 percent fell under 200 percent of the poverty level. One percent of elders living alone received public assistance, which is the same for elders in general. Six percent of elder live-alones received food stamps, compared to 5 percent of all elders. Five percent of elder people living alone received SSI, compared to 4 percent of elders generally.

A smaller percentage of elders who lived alone were employed and/or in the labor force. Twelve percent of elder live-alones were employed, and 13 percent were in the labor force. Fourteen percent of all elders were employed, and 15 percent were in the labor force. The median income of elders living alone was $17,200 in 2006, compared to $15,900 for elders generally. The mean annual income of elders who lived alone was $25,908, compared to $26,630 for elders in general. The median annual earnings of elders living alone and all elders was zero. The mean annual earnings of elder live-alones were $3,664, compared to $5,412 for all elders. And, finally, where 67 percent of elders living alone owned their homes, 82 percent of elders generally were homeowners (see Table 17.4).

Table 17.4 Demographic and economic characteristics of elders living alone compared to the general elder adult population

Characteristic	Elders living alone	General elder population
Social and Physical Characteristics		
Disability (age is 65+)	47.4%	41.0%
Two or more Types of Disability (age is 65+)	35.2%	32.7%
Sensory Disability (age is 65+)	19.4%	17.4%
Physical Disability (age is 65+)	36.6%	33.7%
Mental Disability (age is 65+)	13.1%	14.8%
Self-care Disability (age is 65+)	10.3%	13.5%
Mobility Disability (age is 65+)	19.6%	20.9%
Employment Disability (age is 65+)	34.0%	31.9%
Women (age is 65+)	73.5%	58.0%
Age 65 or over	100%	100%
Age 75 or over	59.9%	49.2%
US Citizen (age is all)	98.5%	96.9%
Widowed (age is 65+)	67.0%	31.6%
Divorced (age is 65+)	20.2%	9.3%
Never Married (age is 65+)	8.1%	4.6%
Bachelor's Degree or Higher (age is 65+)	16.3%	18.7%
Veteran (age is 65+)	16.8%	24.5%
White (age is 65+)	83.7%	81.1%
Hispanic or Latino (age is 65+)	4.5%	6.4%
Black or African American (age is 65+)	9.2%	8.2%
Asian (age is 65+)	1.5%	3.2%
Native American or Alaska Native (age is 65+)	0.4%	0.4%
Native Hawaiian or Other Pacific Islander (age is 65+)	0.03%	0.06%
Other (age is 65+)	0.06%	0.1%
Two or more Races (age is 65+)	0.7%	0.6%
Economic Characteristics		
Public Assistance Received (age is 65+)	1.2%	1.2%
Food Stamps Received (age is 65+)	5.8%	5.3%
Supplemental Security Income Received (age is 65+)	5.4%	4.4%
Below Federal Poverty Level (age is 65+)	19.2%	9.9%
At or Below 200% Federal Poverty Level (age is 65+)	55.1%	33.1%
Employed (Civilian and Military) (age is 65+)	11.9%	14.0%
In Labor Force (age is 65+)	12.5%	14.5%
Median Income (age is 65+)	$17,200	$15,900
Mean Income (age is 65+)	$25,908	$26,630
Median Earnings (age is 65+)	$0	$0
Mean Earnings (age is 65+)	$3,664	$5,412
Homeowner	66.7%	82%

Three stories of family failure

Because real-life narratives can supply necessary content and context to more abstract data and argument, I end where I might have begun this chapter—with three stories.

Ruth Adams has lived alone most of her adult life. She managed fine until age 70 when, due to fading eyesight, she slipped on the steps to her house and smashed her knee. Ms. Adams's near blindness prevents her from doing such daily tasks as reading, cooking, filling out a growing number of medical and insurance forms, examining bills and financial documents, and writing letters and checks. Like many elderly singles without children or other family, questions never before faced now press forcefully upon her: who will she call in an emergency? Who will help her bathe? Who will chase the rodents away, sweep up a spill, take out the trash and recyclables? If hospitalized, who will advocate on her behalf? Who will refuse to accept less-than-optimal care from thinly stretched doctors and nurses and from hospital administrators facing pressures to cut costs? Who will argue with insurance companies? Inform the doctors about her allergies, medications, and dosages? Watch over the house in the event of an extended hospital stay? Burglars, Ms. Adams fears, target the elderly and in particular the frail who live alone.

Enrique Padilla was kicked out of his home at 15 because his father would not tolerate a gay son. As a homeless and fairly uneducated teen, Mr. Padilla found prostitution to be his only dependable source of food, shelter, clothes, and cash. Almost predictably, Mr. Padilla contracted HIV. Eventually, he found employment as a sales clerk, and his life stabilized. Today, at 28, Mr. Padilla lives alone in a small studio apartment in public housing. His partner was killed in a freak work accident (for which Mr. Padilla received no compensation as he was not legally tied to his partner and concomitantly did not have standing to sue for wrongful death). Recently unable to work for health reasons, Mr. Padilla lives off a complicated, inconsistent patchwork of federal, state, city, and charitable programs for poor disabled people. The anti-virals, among a whole armory of medicines, have taken their toll on Mr. Padilla's organs, especially his heart and kidneys, which are failing. Mr. Padilla undergoes dialysis four times per week at a center where he often feels disrespected and treated unfairly by staff on account of biases against Puerto Ricans and HIV-positive patients. Mr. Padilla's heart is his most immediate worry: it is swollen and bleeding; a serious operation is necessary to survive. Medicaid will cover the cost of surgery and provide some post-operative assistance, but with no one to provide the round-the-clock care needed—and incapable of caring for himself—during the long recovery period invariably following heart surgery, Mr. Padilla recently declined the operation that would save his life.

Elvira Moran has been on her own since immigrating by herself to the United States from Ecuador as a teen.[5] Now 37, Elvira suffers from amyotrophic lateral sclerosis (Lou Gehrig's disease), a progressive neurodegenerative disease that leads to loss of voluntary muscle control, muscular atrophy, and usually paralysis and death. Elvira trundles around on a walker, her speech slurs, her body is weak and wilted. She will soon need a respirator to breathe and a feeding tube for nourishment. Without relatives, and while her mother in Ecuador pleads for a visa to come help, the only person Elvira can count on is her best friend,

Christina Martinez. Christina checks in on Elvira almost every day, cooking, cleaning, and taking care of other chores. Sometimes, when Elvira's disability funds arrive late or are inadequate, Christina lends Elvira money—money Christina cannot spare. And time spent with Elvira is time away from her own family: Christina's husband, left to tend to their 3-year-old daughter, grows increasingly frustrated and angry about his wife's absences. Christina tried to move Elvira closer to her own apartment, so that it would be easier to be of service, but she was unable to find an affordable space on the ground floor or with an elevator. For a time, Elvira managed okay with weekly visits by a nurse, a social worker, a physical therapist, and an occupational therapist. An aide came for four hours per day, five days per week. But Elvira's condition is deteriorating, and when alone, she does not get along easily or very well. Once, Elvira scalded her wrist when a pot of boiling water slipped from her frail hand. She called no one and instead lectured herself aloud to "Be strong!" Another time, convulsions forced Elvira to the hospital, alone. Christina found her there the next day in a soiled hospital gown. Asked why she dedicates so much time and energy to her friend, Christina responded: "Elvira, she don't have anybody."

Life is, to a great degree, the product of ideas and ideals about family. The experiences of Ruth Adams, Enrique Padilla, and Elvira Moran, however, expose failings of the family regime in the United States. For those who require significant care and assistance, living disconnected from family can have devastating and immediate consequence. As more and more people spend more and more of their lives disaffiliated from family, we need to think long and hard about the manners in which we utilize and privilege family in law and society. Indeed, data from the US Census Bureau reveal that an increasingly large segment of US society is living alone, and that among those who live alone, many are faring less well than the general adult population on a number of social, physical, and economic factors. And while the data indicate that disabled adults living alone are similar in many ways to disabled adults generally, as are elders living alone and elders generally, we must not forget the adversities associated with living alone that can arise for such populations. In all cases, and of particular importance, a much greater percentage of those living alone were impoverished. Recognition of these points does not mean that we should turn our back on the family. We must, however, be realistic about trends in behavior if we are ever to succeed in improving the scaffolding and safety nets of society.

Notes

1 Gary Gates, Senior Fellow at the Williams Institute, UCLA School of Law, made possible the data analyses presented in this section. The analyses consider only non-institutionalized persons.
2 Because the data on the general adult population includes adults living alone, statistical analysis between the two groups is not possible. The same is true for the comparisons of disabled adults living alone to all disabled adults, and elder live-alones to elders generally.

3 For the US Census Bureau's purposes, household poverty is determined by looking at the poverty status of the householder. A householder, and thus a household, is in poverty if her or his income, combined with his co-habiting *family* members, is below the appropriate poverty threshold. Only co-habiting family members are counted in determining the householder's poverty status. Therefore, the income of a non-family member living in the household is disregarded in calculating the income of the household as well as identifying the appropriate threshold. The poverty thresholds vary depending on three criteria: size of family, number of related children, and, for one and two-person families, age of householder. For 2007, the federal poverty threshold for a single person was $10,787 (if under 65 years) or $9,944 (if 65 years and over) (US Census Bureau 2007).

4 From 1950 to 2006 the proportion of the population age 75 years and over rose from 3 to 6 percent. It is projected that by 2050, 12 percent, or about one in eight Americans, will be 75 years of age or over (National Center for Health Statistics 2008: 3, 21 Fig. 1).

5 Ms. Moran's story was told in Gross (2005).

Engaging the state

Introduction to Section Six

Over the past quarter century there has been increasing incorporation of international law and norms into feminist legal theory. The chapters in this section address the need for more intersection of the international with the feminist. International law establishes a set of principles that should be consistent with and facilitate feminist progress, yet as these authors demonstrate, much rethinking is needed to make international human rights truly feminist friendly.

Fionnuala Ní Aoláin addresses the "gendered elements" located in foundational international human rights documents and international law norms. She advises feminists to be guarded about the transformative "promises" made in transitional societies constructing new legal and social frameworks. The international human rights norms often reinforce patriarchy. In particular, instead of "dismantling" the public–private divide, the international human rights regime has reinscribed it. In international law, the "private realm is off limits for regulatory efforts," and this exclusion leads to the "shoring up of patriarchy."

Thus, in considering why women have been "structurally excluded" from the internationalized transitional process, Ní Aoláin does recognize that transitional societies are often scrutinized by human rights NGOs and others during the period of conflict/repression and that should provide some safeguards. Yet, this scrutiny cannot suffice. The international human rights norms that inform such scrutiny and have become part of the framework for addressing the society post-conflict themselves frequently reinforce problematic gender distinctions. Even as the social instability wrought by conflict tends to recede, international norms reinforce or even "impose" a public–private divide that produces legal restrictions against the advancement of women's rights.

Fiona de Londras' chapter focuses on sexual violence and how it should be dealt with in international humanitarian and criminal law, specifically addressing the "genocidal sexual violence" in the former Yugoslavia and Rwanda. Noting that both were parties to the Convention for the Elimination of Discrimination Against Women, de Londras nonetheless finds that the gendered violence during conflict emerged from deep-seated gender inequalities that existed in both societies before the genocides.

Looking at the ad hoc criminal tribunals hearing such cases, she considers whether they have been making adequate provisions in holding accountable the actors who were responsible for the sexual violence and genocide during conflict. She concludes that in spite of the positive steps taken by some tribunals to recognize violence against women as a serious crime, there has been a "systematic failure" by the tribunal prosecutors to "formulate a managed, strategic prosecutorial policy recognizing women's experience" and to assign accountability for the sexual violence committed in Rwanda and the former Yugoslavia. She provides several examples of this failure in which prosecutors have left off allegations of sexual violence from their indictments.

De Londras identifies two issues for feminists to consider in the international law context. First, there must be more effective and pervasive implementation and enforcement of CEDAW. Second, there is a need for arguments that more effectively integrate feminist approaches to violence against women into the international humanitarian and criminal law schemes. De Londras contends that addressing violence against women more accurately and effectively in this way would not only ensure greater justice for women, but would serve to protect the "integrity" of international criminal law.

Laura Spitz's chapter argues that this particular moment necessitates feminist engagement in rethinking national and constitutional approaches to equality and justice and in developing transnational institutions for this purpose. She begins by asking what Fineman means by the "state," when she calls for a "more responsive state" in formulating a vulnerability approach (chapter 11, this volume). Spitz argues that feminists could locate the "responsive state" in "transnational or supranational institutions," believing that feminist legal theorists and integration theorists could engage in a very productive conversation with one another. This chapter aims to encourage that conversation.

While many social justice activists and scholars are wary of integration, Spitz views North American integration as both *"threat"* and *"promise."* Though to date that integration has been mostly negative, Spitz argues that instead of resisting integration, feminists could push for positive, progressive modes of integration. Furthermore, although administrative law is important to organizing integration law, increasingly multilateral and multinational bodies are doing both administration and governance; yet there is real opportunity for feminists to get involved at the early stage of institutionalizing integration.

The chapter lists several ways that feminisms could be useful in an integration context: attending to problems of co-option; creating political spaces; challenging gender-neutral language (and race, class, etc.); invoking vulnerability and intersectional approaches; challenging dichotomies, fundamental concepts, the structure of knowledge, power, and privilege. Spitz concludes that (like Fineman) ordinary citizens are seeking a "more responsive state": to regulate social institutions, to protect and support them, to intervene in certain matters.

Chapter 18

Learning the lessons

What feminist legal theory teaches international human rights law and practice

Fionnuala Ní Aoláin

As the long term impact of 9/11 and the wars in Iraq and Afghanistan continue to shape and redefine international legal and political rules, this chapter reflects on the gendered elements which ground international legal norms in the contemporary international moment. As an international legal scholar I focus on how feminist legal theory can be applied in this moment, and how insights gleaned in the domestic legal context (significantly though not exclusively within Western states) are relevant to the experiences of women in multiple jurisdictional and cultural environments. Many of my observations are specifically drawn from societies emerging from war and repression and ruminate on the experiences of women in those contexts. The chapter starts from the reflection that the export of Western legal norms and ideas has often failed to engage with and address deeply entrenched gender discrimination, inequality, and violence as experienced in conflicted, post conflict, and repressive societies. Equally, there has been considerable tension between the universalism expounded by Western feminists and its reception within Southern gender discourses, as non-Western feminist scholars have cogently articulated (Gunning 1992). These strands of over-inclusivity, which are unresponsive to the local particularity of women, co-exist with the under-inclusion of a gender perspective in contexts where Western states and international institutions find themselves legally and politically embroiled in sites of conflict, repression and transition. There is often no easy co-existence between these two poles nor is negotiating a middle ground between them an easy task.

The chapter commences with an exploration of feminist theory's relevance by examining the gendered nature of the international human rights regime itself. While the reflections in this chapter have a general relevance to the international rule corpus as a whole, they are specifically aimed at the unique moments of change in societies moving towards democratization (or greater political liberty) as well as those societies moving from violent conflict to more peaceful kinds of co-existence. Human rights norms have been central in both the shaping and traversing of conversations concerning gender, as well as framing the way in which the transitional landscape, the moving from "war to peace" paradigm has been articulated (Bell 2000). These norms define the terms of the rhetorical space in which international legal and political action is born. Identifying some specific fault-lines that constrict the ability of these norms to engage fully with gender disparities, I then proceed to explore how insight from feminist legal theory may enable us to move beyond these inherited limitations. Here the chapter will focus on the significance of the public–private divide. Substantive advances in dismantling the public–private divide have been made within many Western societies. Yet, those same societies support and further entrench the operation of the public verses the private when engaged in the politics and practice of international intervention in other (transitional or conflicted) states.

The chapter subsequently explores how ideas of dependency and autonomy are equally deeply entrenched in the international legal order. The genealogy of these constructs also finds a home in the historical pedigree of international human rights law. In turn, the long-term influence of foundational documents and structures reverberate in the inter-relationship of the national and international in a transitional setting. Two evident phenomena are departure points for this foray: first, is the evidence of a sustained pattern of retrenchment or limitation on women's rights and equality in many post-conflict/ post-repressive societies. These restrictions are all the more contradictory in places where the abrogation of women's rights has been used in constituting one of the texts (or pretexts) for intervention or political change (e.g. Afghanistan). Second, a pattern of post-modern colonialism in which domestic/native practices that are more communal or group oriented in nature are relegated to the sidelines as Western autonomy-based models of legal and social responsibility are introduced by the change process. Specific examples of this are found in contexts such as gender and reparation, institutional reforms, and constitution making in transitional societies. These examples point to new forms of contemporary neo-colonialism and come with significant disadvantages and limitations for women.

History and why it matters

As the introduction suggests, despite a lofty rhetoric of universality and equality, international human rights law requires close reading to assess whether it lives up to its own stated ambition. This chapter focuses on the impact of gender inclusions and exclusions in the drafting of the Universal Declaration of Human Rights (1948) as a means to illustrate a core proposition; namely that there is a foundational bias in the body of law that has been offered up *prima facie* as an important means for redressing gender inequality across multiple jurisdictions. Examining the Declaration's drafting history reveals the character and form of the gender concept as it is rendered in the document, as well as the long-term effects this conception has had on the normative character of human rights law. Following in the footsteps of other feminist international scholars, the chapter suggests that foundational documents matter to the construction of gender relations in ways that are difficult to dislodge. They create conceptual pathways that can substantially limit theoretically open-ended visions of international human rights law. Thus, achievements typified as advances in their time may actually be better understood as generating long-term baggage that will be difficult to discard. I suggest a more skeptical view of the "gains" made for women in the Universal Declaration might contribute to the broader project of defining gender dignity, violation, and accountability in ways that consistently reflect and respond to the experiences and needs of women. This would better serve our interests than an accommodationist model, which tries to "fit" the experiences of women into an existing and constrained framework. In the broader project of feminist definition, I draw from a wide set of feminist insights into the character and operation of the legal.

In the opening paragraph of the United Nations Charter (1945: Preamble) signatory states espouse their determination to "reaffirm [their] faith in fundamental human rights, in the dignity and worth of the human person, in the equal rights of men and women." This commitment is further supported by a specific reference to the prohibition of discrimination on the basis of sex. In institutional terms, these structural commitments were followed when the Economic and Social Council established a Sub-Commission on the Status of Women which was to "submit proposals, recommendations, and reports to the Commission on Human Rights ... " (Humphrey 1983). Both Commissions played a pivotal role in the adoption of the Universal Declaration in the post-war period (Morsink 1991).

Some evaluations of the Universal Declaration laud its lack of sexism, seen as manifested in the repetition of specific phrases such as "all," "everyone," and "no-one" (Morsink 2000). Others are more circumspect in their praise. Adamantia Pollis (1982: 1) has argued that the Declaration is informed by "[t]he notion of man as an autonomous, rational, calculated being ... a notion of man but not of woman, and not even of all men but only of some." If we take seriously the claim that "[t]he structure of the international legal order reflects a male perspective and ensures its continued dominance" (Charlesworth et al. 1991: 621) then paying close attention to the words that implicate social structures is particularly important. In this view, a nod to non-discrimination may not be sufficient to identify and fully reveal the multiple ways in which women experience discrimination and exclusion. What the drafters may have understood to constitute impermissible discrimination arguably left intact (and endorsed) a social and political ordering that de facto functions to entrench the discriminations experienced by women. Three particular sections notably illustrate this implicit adoption of sex-based ordering—they include first, the Preamble and Article 1; second, Article 16; and finally, Articles 23 and 25 (Ní Aoláin forthcoming).

Specifically, in the drafting debates as to whether the term "human beings" should be substituted for "men," Bodil Begtrup (the Chair of the United Nations Council on the Status of Women (CSW)) sought an addition to be made to the Declaration's Preamble stating that "when a word indicating the masculine sex is used in the following Bill of Rights, the provision is to be considered as applying without discrimination to women" (Morsink 2000: 118). The proposal was not taken up, which meant the CSW had no choice but to seek to protect the status of women in the Declaration article by article. In addition, Articles 23 and 25 are notable in their emphasis on the male breadwinner and his right to seek remuneration "for himself and his family," as well as the affirmation of the male right to "a standard of living adequate … for himself and his family." In Article 25, motherhood is singled out for "special care and assistance." As I have explored at greater length elsewhere, the inclusion of this language was a reflected understanding of social role and social ordering at the time the Declaration was drafted (Ní Aoláin 2009). Its tone may not be surprising per se, in that the post-war human rights' treaties were conceived in a context of evident and multiple social and political inequities. However, with the passage of time and the status advancement of these foundational documents, we cannot forget that the fundamental formulae continue to have traction and shape social realities even as they promise transformation.

What do the drafting history and outcomes tell us? In thinking about their significance, it is important to pay attention to the manner in which the term "woman" or "women" can be mentioned in policy-making contexts without bringing the concept of gender into play. As feminists have long argued, we need to be cautious about whether or not the use of the term "women" or "woman" actually does real work for real women in legal contexts. We need to be clear about the entrenchment of stereotypes that the use of such terms can have and their effect in undermining, rather than advancing, the needs, priorities, and rights of women. Equally, when the term woman is entirely absent, we should not assume, as many of the Universal Declaration's drafters did, that "neutral" phrases deliver gender friendly outcomes. In fact, the opposite is likely to be true. The Declaration is not simply important on its own terms in this regard but should be understood as having had (and continuing to have) wide influence on the inclusion of human rights norms within domestic legal systems, in addition to framing the manner in which subsequent and more specific rights-based international treaties were and are agreed upon.

Foundational documents and feminism

Although passed by General Assembly resolution in 1948 with eight abstentions, there is broad agreement that the Universal Declaration constitutes a foundational document for the modern international human rights regime. Foundational documents are relatively new phenomena for the international human rights movement. The regime itself is largely a product of the post-World War II renewal, although many domestic legal systems have similar status documents (usually national constitutions or bills of rights). Foundational documents are an important conceptual and legitimating category for legal systems. They provide security and a sense of longitude to the norms they validate.

They perform important symbolic functions by giving rise to myths (and realities) of universal buy-in, validation by the body politic as a whole, and long-term legitimacy to the values they contain. The legitimacy factor allows for repeat play of the document without the need for repetitious justification; this substantiation further affirms the validity of the starting point.

There are pitfalls in reliance on these documents, of course. Foundational documents, whether domestic bills of rights or international declarations, are indisputably accompanied by gender snares as feminist scholars have long demonstrated in the domestic context. Some do better than others in this regard. The Universal Declaration makes significant attempts to engage with the pernicious effects of gender inequality. Nonetheless, I suggest that the Declaration (among other international norms) validates not only deeply problematic gender distinctions in the arena of the private (family) and the public (work), but its neutrality cloaks a deeply gendered vision of the world. Precisely because the foundational document contains, elevates, yet obscures these damaging gender dimensions an odd paradox arises. As the political worth of the document has risen, and its symbolic significance has grown, it becomes difficult to "knock down" the Universal Declaration on the grounds of its gendered failings. There is broad political and legal investment in the document by multiple constituencies. This investment is evidenced by the invocation of the Declaration as a touchstone on fundamental principles in multiple political contexts, including its use by women's advocates. It has also been imported into the domestic realm, as it affirms the validity of rights-protecting systems in the domestic contexts (whether in constitution writing, adding bills of rights, or the broader field of judicial interpretation).

Feminists find themselves reluctant to criticize the Universal Declaration, wary of the costs that such adversarial engagement might bring and cornered by a chorus of validation. Conceptually, foundational status makes an argument against the Declaration's preeminent status a difficult one to make. In many ways, the Universal Declaration presents a concise way to make a broader human rights argument. It requires much greater dissection of the Declaration to reveal its gender limitations. These "picky" arguments do better retail than wholesale. One consequence to those offering a gendered critique of the Declaration (or other human rights documents) may be to experience de-legitimization, be marked as hostile and out of the mainstream view of human rights. As a result, feminist criticism of the Universal Declaration has been subdued. This parallels (albeit imperfectly) the plight of equality feminists who seek to augment the gender equality gains for by women by utilizing imperfect constitutional instruments as a "means to the end." Here again, the compromises and implicit upholding of the status quo may be too high a price for the utilitarian gains made in such contexts, as Martha Fineman (1991a, 1995, 2004) has consistently documented over the decades. The overall containment of feminists in both circumstances, I suggest, results from the particular confluence of the silencing that a foundational document can produce along with the difficulty articulating why a gender-neutral vision fails to deliver transformational outcomes when it comes to addressing the conceptual, material, political, and social perniciousness of gender discrimination. While there have been strong feminist voices in the international legal arena articulating and asserting such structural biases, the knock-on and insidious effect that these deeply seated partialities have at the domestic level have been less well traced. As international legal norms grow in their domestic weight and authority, gaining momentum and shaping domestic legal norms, feminists need to remain attuned to the sober reality that such influence is not linear and not necessarily transformative.

Public and private

A persistent dimension of the international human rights regime is that it has functioned to buttress rather than to dismantle the public—private divide. International law scholars of the feminist hue have long articulated a notion of the way in which the "public—private" divide manifests itself in international law. As Hilary Charlesworth has noted,

> Historically, the formation of the state depended on a sexual division of labour and the regulation of women to a private, domestic, devalued sphere. Men dominated in the public sphere of citizenship and political and economic life. The state institutionalized the patriarchal family both as the qualification for citizenship and public life and also the base socio-economic group. The functions of the state were identified with men …
> (Charlesworth 1993: 9–10)

These characteristics include strong validation of the family as being at the heart of the societal contract; the articulation of work and wage as a male domain to which specific kinds of guarantees are offered; and the special status offered to motherhood. All are illustrated by the example of the Universal Declaration.

This clear-cut distinction between public and private sphere is at the heart of the traditional notion of the state. It has had a defining influence on international law and demonstrated tenacity in international legal doctrine. Accordingly, both the United Nations Charter and the Universal Declaration make the (public) province of international law distant from the (private) sphere of domestic jurisdiction. That distinction continues to maintain its hold, visible even in the Convention on the Elimination of All Forms of Discrimination Against Women (CEDAW) through the practice of states with regard to reservations, particularly in respect of Articles 2 and 16 of the Convention.

The public–private distinction perpetuates and validates women's oppression on a global level. As feminist theorists have long articulated, the most pervasive harms to women tend to occur within the inner sanctum of the private realm, within the family. As the private realm in international law has stayed effectively off limits for regulatory efforts, the message is that the private is legitimately left only to self-regulation. This ultimately translates into the shoring up of patriarchy, accomplished through the prism of supposedly transformative norms. I now turn to some of those legacies as they appear in the transitional justice context.

Complimentary national and international patriarchies

The absence of a gender dimension in the establishment, revision, and operation of new legal and political institutions in transitional societies has been acknowledged (Bell et al. 2004). The genealogy of institutional gaps for women traces back to omissions from peace-making and transitionary "deal-making." These negotiating exclusions compound the normative legal gaps, thereby facilitating further exclusions down the line. I explore here why women remain structurally excluded and why they remain excluded as the processes of transition has become increasingly internationalized.[1] Such internationalization leads us to presuppose, at least in theory, that the outcomes will be better for women. Practice to date suggests otherwise, however.

A key element in the perceived success of many transitional accountability mechanisms is the support of international organizations and other states in their establishment.[2] The "transitional moment" is usually only one point on the continuum of a protracted legal and political engagement between the transitional state and the international community. The transitional state is captured between the multiple interests of other states, their willingness to articulate views about a regime or conflict, and the moments of their formal or informal interaction with key actors at key change moments. While much could be said about this complex interaction in general, this part of my analysis will focus on two particular aspects: first, the relationship between the international community's previously articulated views on human rights compliance during a conflict or a period of authoritarian rule; and second, the complex role that the international community can play in compounding gender inequality and unaccountability once entangled with a transitional society.

First, many transitional societies have been the subject of substantial international scrutiny prior to any settlement. Transitioning societies typically have been repressive or violent (or both), and international oversight may have "named and shamed" systematic and significant human rights violations in the pre-transition phase. For example, international non-governmental organizations such as Amnesty International, Human Rights First, and Human Rights Watch may have been active through sending investigative missions, producing numerous reports, and providing a large range of supports for their domestic NGO counterparts. In the settlement phase of a conflict or a regime handover, such prior interventions are critical to framing the way in which accountability is sought, articulated, and constructed. This frame comes from intact Western conceptions of human rights hierarchies, and these conceptions are imbued with the inability of such organizations to consider the own patriarchal nature and unwillingness to recognize it at work in an exportable form (Rees 2002). Equally the frame emanates from an intact patriarchy that has been translated into the foundational documents of the international human rights regime and validated. The specific culturally exported patriarchies and an overarching legal patriarchy compliment and reinforce one another in this context. As a result, it is important to recognize that the narrative constructed about the nature and form of violations in transitional societies has as much to do with the demands for accountability at the transitional moment as it has to do with the prior narrative of violence and causality. This narrative is significantly constructed by the watchful and deeply involved international community.

International interface and influence is further compounded in the role played by such key international actors as the United Nations (UN). So, where the UN has paid particular attention to a conflicted or authoritarian society in the form of resolutions, mandated Special Rapporteurs,[3] Special Representatives, and inclusion in thematic oversight in addition to review by treaty bodies, a substantive narrative already exists in the international–national context about the form and nature of violations that have taken place. This narrative process evidences a fundamental structural problem, namely that certain kinds of bodily harms are elevated over others in terms of their perceived seriousness. Thus, violence to women often fails to "fit" the narrow legal categories that dominate general understanding of serious human rights violations (Ní Aoláin and Hamilton 2009; Radacic 2008), and "normal" pervasive sexual and physical violence against women is simply not counted in the overall narrative of conflict or regime change. Equally relevant is the importation of the public—private divide as part of the legal solutions offered by Western states and international organizations to defunct and dysfunctional legal systems in post-repressive and post-conflict societies (Ní Aoláin and Hamilton 2009). Such "neutral" devices have the quality of taking us "back to the future" in such societies. Despite being discredited or at least under considerable legal stress in the dominant legal cultures which export them, they are imposed on divided societies with little or no attention to their gendered effects. An array of cultural difference is recognized between the local and the international, but frequently overlooked are the fundamentally similar patriarchal views that internal and external elites share. These shared views operate in tandem to exclude, silence, or nullify women's needs from the transitional space. As feminist scholars of war and conflict have identified, the loosening of rigid gender roles occurring as a result of the social flux that conflict inevitably creates is not necessarily sealed off at conflict's end or transition by national male leadership. Rather this role in closing down the possibility of gender change is taken up by the male international development community, "whose own sense of patriarchy-as-normal is quite intact" (Bennett et al. 1995). This intact patriarchy has demonstrated itself as distinctly capable of reproducing the legal strictures in transitional societies that would generate significant (and likely hostile) scrutiny if suggested in their home states. Thus, this chapter highlights the essential point of the dangers of export.

Conclusion

The discussion above potently illustrates how the shape of transition for women is tremendously influenced by the role and stance of the international community and the international norms it brings to the localized situation. It also potently illustrates the extent to which human rights violations experienced by women can continue despite the claims of transition in the public—political spaces of post-conflict and post repression societies. The continuity of gender exclusion, violence, and oppression should trigger deeper questions about the quality of the transitional experience for women and the meaningfulness of accountability measures that may only scratch the surface of women's needs. It should also raise significant questions about the shortcomings and inadequacies of international legal instruments that are lauded as the means whereby to address the harms and injustices which women experience. Finally, it should encourage us to understand that despite considerable inroads on the patriarchal meta-structure in many Western states, the success or failure of patriarchy to survive and thrive is not jurisdiction dependent. Rather, globalization, as it reproduces itself and assists in the entrenchment of patriarchal norms in societies where legal transformation is promised, also works to the benefit of patriarchy, frequently in the very terms of liberal Western promise. For women, it turns out that the transformation of a society is only partial and largely exclusionary. Transformation may frequently operate to cloak their ongoing repression and inequality with the rule of law and the embrace of international legal instruments. The wise course may well be for feminists to be cautious and wary of the promises made in regard to what change will bring.

Notes

1 These exclusions remain despite UN Security Council Resolutions 1325 (2000) and 1820 (2008).
2 High Commissioner's Office in Bosnia; the International Force (IFOR) and the Stabilization Force (SFOR) in Bosnia; Interim Authority in Kosovo; UN Transitional Authority in Cambodia (UNTAC).
3 See the United Nations interface with Guatemala, where between 1982 and 1986 the Commission on Human Rights mandated a Special Rapporteur to study the human rights situation in the country, followed in 1987 by a replacement mandate—a Special Representative of the Commission to receive and evaluate information from the government on the implementation of human rights protection measures included in the new Constitution of 1985.

Chapter 19

Prosecuting sexual violence in the ad hoc International Criminal Tribunals for Rwanda and the Former Yugoslavia

Fiona de Londras

Introduction

The International Criminal Tribunal for the Former Yugoslavia (ICTY) and the International Criminal Tribunal for Rwanda (ICTR), established by the Security Council acting under Chapter VII of the Charter of the United Nations, were the first international criminal tribunals since the Nuremberg Tribunal and International Military Tribunal for the Far East established at the end of World War II. Security Council Resolutions 1503 (2003) and 1534 (2004) provide that the tribunals are to complete their proceedings by the end of 2010. These tribunals ushered in a phase in international criminal law in which *ad hoc* judicialized institutions are increasingly viable options for post-conflict societies. We now have *ad hoc* tribunals, both hybrid and completely international, for Cambodia, Sierra Leone, Lebanon, and Timor Leste as well as the permanent International Criminal Court (ICC). The age of international criminal accountability has arrived. But to what extent are these tribunals making individuals accountable for the widespread sexual violence that often occurs in times of armed conflict and genocide? This chapter considers that question in the context of the ICTY and the ICTR and assesses the extent to which the tribunals are providing justice for female victims of sexual violence.

The chapter focuses on the many doctrinal advances made by the tribunals and the less impressive operationalization of those advances. This commitment, to examine positive law and law in practice and critically appraise the dissonances that appear, is an important part of feminist legal methodology. The following analysis reveals that many difficulties relating to the prosecution of sexual violence before these tribunals are familiar to feminist legal theorists who have faced similar difficulties in domestic criminal justice systems. These difficulties lead to questions about the transfer of norms between the domestic and the international: to what extent are feminist lessons learned domestically transferred to the international sphere? What kinds of lessons about prosecuting sexual violence will transfer from international proceedings to the reconstituted justice systems in post-conflict jurisdictions?

The historical occlusion of sexual violence in international criminal law and the establishment of the ad hoc tribunals

Sexual violence against women during conflict is not a new phenomenon (Browmiller 1972). Since Henri Dunant observed the carnage of the Solferino battlefield and founded what is now the International Committee of the Red Cross and Red Crescent, armed conflict has been regulated by increasingly detailed legal codes. However, although wartime rape, indecent assault, and enforced prostitution are prohibited under Article 27 of the Fourth Geneva Convention, enforcement has been conspicuously absent. After World War II, even though criminal tribunals tried persons suspected of war crimes and atrocities, the many gender-based crimes, such as mass sterilization and rape, were scarcely addressed (Askin 1997). The International Tribunal for the Far East failed to address the position of so-called "comfort women" who were forced to act as prostitutes for Japanese soldiers, and the sexual violence perpetrated by Europe's "liberators," such as the "rape of Berlin," was swept under the proverbial carpet. Conceptualized as "letting off steam," sexual violence in conflict was not seen as a crime, or at least not one to which the liberal legal conception of accountability attached.

Seemingly, this pattern changed with the establishment of the ICTR and ICTY where crimes of sexual violence received express attention within tribunals' statutes and proceedings. The consideration of sexual violence before international, judicialized institutions is very significant. Clearly, something changed between the post-World War II proceedings and the proceedings established to address late twentieth-century atrocities. At least at the level of positive law, sexual violence was marked as unacceptable and unlawful. This sea-change is partially explicable by interim developments in international law and the profundity of the challenge posed to the international legal system by the atrocities.

From an international law perspective the ethnic cleansing and genocide in the Former Yugoslavia and Rwanda in the 1990s characterized that decade in some ways. These conflicts challenged the international community's capacity to bring about a period of international peace and security free from genocidal violence, and they forced media and international attention on the distinctly gendered experience of women and girls during conflict. The use of sexual violence including rape, sexual mutilation, forced pregnancy, forced abortion, sexual exploitation, and forced "marriage" was widespread and constituted a central part of the aggressors' genocidal mission.

During the "ethnic cleansing" in the Former Yugoslavia, Serbian soldiers and militia perpetrated sexual violence extensively, reportedly using rape systematically against Kosovar Albanian women. "Rape camps" were established; sexual humiliation and assault occurred widely. While there is evidence that sexual violence was also used against men in this conflict (Carpenter 2006), the primary victims were women. The use of sexual violence against these women was not "incidental." It was foreshadowed by propaganda portraying them as "indiscriminately fecund" (Mertus 1999: 174, 178) and was a central part of the ethnic cleansing.

Similarly, the sexualized targeting of women and girls during the Rwandan genocide resulted from a targeted propaganda effort that sexualized Tutsi women to an extreme degree. The *Interhamwe* (a Hutu paramilitary organization) were conditioned to see Tutsi women as "cockroaches": untrustworthy seductresses who wanted to undermine, feminize, and weaken Hutu men and identity (Green 2002). Tutsi women's gender intersected with their ethnicity in a way that led to the use of sexual violence against them as a tool of genocide. During the genocide hundreds of thousands of women were subjected to individual and gang rape, sexual mutilation, forced pregnancy, acts of sexual humiliation including forced sexual acts with family members, and "forced marriage." Women were forced to watch the torture and murder of their family members before being sexually abused and then killed (Human Rights Watch 1996).

The extent and nature of this sexual violence suggests two things. First, the pre-conflict state of gender equality in both counties was unsatisfactory, even though both were parties to the UN Convention on the Elimination of All Forms of Discrimination against Women (CEDAW). Escalated and extreme sexual violence during conflict does not come from nowhere; it reflects pre-existing sexual violence and conceptions of women and girls as rapeable, possessable vehicles for "hurting" men, which easily escalate in times of conflict (de Londras 2007: 113–15). Second, this sexual violence, particularly in Rwanda, was not peripheral to the conflict; it was central to the perpetrators' destructive mission. In other words, it was *genocidal* sexual violence, or sexual violence intentionally done to destroy a particular "national, ethnical, racial or religious group" as required by the Genocide Convention (de Londras 2007: 115).

International law faced real difficulties in responding to the conflicts. The widespread gender inequality in both societies forced international law to reconsider the effective implementation and enforcement of CEDAW. Furthermore, if sexual violence was not "just something that happens" but rather designed to be *part* of the conflict, then international humanitarian and international criminal law had to regulate and respond to it, not just human rights law and domestic law. Both challenges are immense, but this chapter concentrates on the latter.

Acting under Chapter VII of the UN Charter, the Security Council established the International Criminal Tribunal for the Former Yugoslavia sitting in The Hague (Security Council Resolution 827 1993) and the International Criminal Tribunal for Rwanda sitting in Arusha (Security Council Resolution 955 1994). In their statutes and jurisprudence these tribunals have pushed the boundaries of international law's conception of sexual violence during armed conflict. Nevertheless, considerable difficulties remain for addressing sexual violence against women within these tribunals; difficulties that feminist legal theorists will recognize from domestic law.

Sexual violence and the Rwandan and Yugoslav tribunals: some significant successes

This chapter is generally skeptical about the progress made by the tribunals, but it is important to acknowledge the tribunals' accomplishments, such as the inclusion and prosecution of crimes of sexual violence. However, generally speaking these accomplishments reveal themselves either at the level of positivism (i.e. in the underlying statutes of the tribunals) or as the result of extraordinary interventions by extraordinary judges and nongovernmental organizations (NGOs). The systematic operation of the *ad hoc* tribunals has not meant the full integration of women's experiences of conflict. Rather women's experiences are set out as occasional and often deeply contested occurrences.

Inclusion of crimes of sexual violence within the statutes of the tribunals

The statutes of both the ICTY and ICTR give them broadly identical jurisdictions over genocide, war crimes, crimes against humanity, and grave breaches of the Geneva Conventions (including torture). The statutes expressly mention rape as a crime against humanity (Statute of the ICTY 1993: Art. 5; Statute of the ICTR 1994: Art. 3), and the Statute of the ICTR (Art. 3(3)) provides that rape, enforced prostitution, and any kind of indecent assault can constitute a grave breach of the Geneva Conventions. While the express inclusion of rape within the statutes was noteworthy, its limitation to crimes against humanity and grave breaches of the Geneva Conventions potentially pushed sexual violence to the margins of the tribunals' work even though it was central in the conflicts. The use of rape in Rwanda, for example, formed part of the genocide perpetrated; thus, sexual violence went beyond a grave breach or a crime against humanity, but the statute's wording did not reflect this reality. The way the statutes included rape suggested that sexual violence would be taken into full account only if other prosecutable offenses were used. To some extent, this problem did arise, and both tribunals have expanded international criminal law and international humanitarian law to account more completely for women's experiences during conflict.

Notwithstanding the significance of rape's inclusion in the statutes, the tribunals' handling of sexual violence challenges its "real" significance. On one hand, the express inclusion testifies to the success of feminist organizations in the drafting process.

Janet Halley looks favorably on the organized effort of feminist organizations to include sexual violence in the statutes and the way that feminist women undertook formal roles within the tribunals. She cites this work as an example of "governance feminism," or "the incremental but by now quite noticeable installation of feminists and feminist ideas in actual legal–institutional power" (Halley et al. 2006: 340). For Halley, the inclusion of these crimes was an achievement in itself. Nevertheless, this achievement was a somewhat shallow victory. The law formally recognizes the sexual violence perpetrated during the atrocities, but the law in practice systematically minimizes the extent of the violence by under-prosecuting it. Inclusion may be significant in developing a concept of governance feminism, but mere inclusion is less significant in recognizing women's experiences of sexual violence.

This disjuncture is not a new phenomenon, nor does it present a novel difficulty for women victims, particularly of gendered crime. Feminist legal theory expresses skepticism about whether women's experiences are accurately revealed, recognized, and acted upon within a judicialized process. Too much focus on the statutes' contents sidelines questions about how the tribunals actually work, including whether they are able to provide an adequate remedy for women victims of sexual violence. We should ask if the judicial process could be designed to ensure the courtroom as a safe space for women to communicate their experiences of sexual violence. Do prosecutorial services fully appreciate and reflect in their indictments the extent to which the risk and reality of sexual violence permeated women's lives during the conflict and continues to affect them? The answer to these questions is rarely affirmative or only conditionally so. While including sexual violence crimes in the statues is an important achievement, inclusion alone signifies only a partial and distinctly positivist success.

Judicial recognition of sexual violence as the actus reus for other crimes

The express mention of sexual violence within the tribunals' statutes did not fully reflect how sexual violence can occur during armed conflict. However, the tribunals have mitigated the difficulties arising from such limited references by recognizing acts of sexual violence as the *actus reus* for other crimes. The ICTR's decision in *Prosecutor v. Akayesu* (1998) clearly demonstrates this technique: rape was held to constitute the *actus reus* for the crime of genocide. *Akayesu* concerned allegations that armed militia and/or police took hundreds of refugee Tutsi women and subjected them to repeated acts of sexual violence; that the defendant knew of, facilitated, and encouraged these acts; and was individually criminally responsible for them. Deciding that rape could form the *actus reus* for the crime of genocide required the tribunal to engage with the somewhat awkward wording of the genocide definition in Article 2 of the Statute. Like the Genocide Convention, the Statute defines genocide thus:

> [G]enocide means any of the following acts committed with intent to destroy, in whole or in part, a national, ethnical, racial or religious group, as such:
>
> (a) Killing members of the group;
> (b) Causing serious bodily or mental harm to members of the group;

(c)   Deliberately inflicting on the group conditions of life calculated to bring about its physical destruction in whole or in part;

(d)   Imposing measures intended to prevent births within the group;

(e)   Forcibly transferring children of the group to another group.

(Statute of the ICTR 1994: Art. 2)

To find that rape could be genocidal, the tribunal considered acts of sexual violence within context, accounting for the reasons and the implications of these acts on the victims and on their ethnic group. An intersectional analysis was applied by Judge Pillay when she held:

> For purposes of interpreting Article 2(2)(d) of the Statute, the Chamber holds that the measures intended to prevent births within the group, should be construed as sexual mutilation, the practice of sterilization, forced birth control, separation of the sexes and prohibition of marriages. In patriarchal societies, where membership of a group is determined by the identity of the father, an example of a measure intended to prevent births within a group is the case where, during rape, a woman of the said group is deliberately impregnated by a man of another group, with the intent to have her give birth to a child who will consequently not belong to its mother's group.
>
> (*Akayesu* 1998: para. 507)

Clearly, this case is significant, representing a ground-breaking decision on the level of positive law; however since *Akayesu* the ICTR has not repeated such progressive jurisprudential analysis on sexual violence.

Defining rape

The tribunals do not have jurisdiction over rape as a stand-alone offense; rather it comes into their jurisdiction when claimed as the *actus reus* for genocide, war crimes, crimes against humanity, or grave breaches of the Geneva Conventions. Nevertheless, the tribunals have grappled with the appropriate definition of "rape." Although rape was mentioned in their statutes, it had no pre-existing definition in international law. Developing a definition forced the tribunals to confront the same questions confronted in domestic law. These questions include what kinds of penetration should be called rape, whether non-consent must be proved as an element of the crime, and whether non-consent can ever be inferred from circumstances or must it be a matter of fact, established through examination in every individual instance?

The first case to consider the meaning of rape in international law was *Akayesu* (1998), and the ICTR declined to adopt a definition similar to those typically found in domestic law where the type of penetration and the matter of consent are material factors. Rather than defining the crime by reference to "a description of objects and body parts" (para. 597), the tribunal held that rape is "a physical invasion of a sexual nature, committed on a person under circumstances which are coercive" (para. 598). Under this definition non-consent did not need to be proved independently. Instead, if generally coercive circumstances were established, non-consent was assumed. This definition found widespread support among feminist legal theorists, with Catherine MacKinnon (2006b: 944) writing that the case was arguably the first time that "rape was defined in law as what it is in life" and Louise Chappel (2003: 6) noting that in *Akayesu* "women were recognized as individuals, as members of a group as well as having a reproductive role. For once, the woman of international law was seen as being multi-dimensional."

The ICTY's subsequent decision to draw on domestic definitions of rape severely challenged the standard laid down in *Akayesu*. In *Furundžija* (1998), a case concerning the use of rape in interrogations, the tribunal held that the apparent universal consensus of rape involved "the forcible sexual penetration of the human body by the penis or the forcible insertion of any other object into either the vagina or the anus" (para. 181). Whether oral penetration constituted rape was a matter of some dispute, although the tribunal finally did include oral penetration within its definition (para. 183). This definition was far more particularized than the conceptual one adopted by the *Akayesu* court. In *Furundžija* "the objective elements of rape" were defined as:

(i) the sexual penetration, however slight:
  (a) of the vagina or anus of the victim by the penis of the perpetrator or any other object used by the perpetrator; or
  (b) of the mouth of the victim by the penis of the perpetrator;
  ...

(ii) by coercion or force or threat of force against the victim or a third person

(para. 185)

The two cases seemingly led to divergent approaches to defining rape in international criminal law: the conceptual approach and the particularized approach. The reference to "force or the threat of force" in the *Furundžija* judgment seems particularly problematic in the context of sexual violence during armed conflict, especially when contrasted with the *Akayesu* approach that more clearly appreciates the importance of surrounding circumstances to the consideration of consent and force.

In *Kunarac* (2002: para. 438), the ICTY Appeal Chamber tried to mediate between the two standards, holding that the "force or threat of force" standard from *Furundžija* was "more narrowly stated than is required by international law" and "does not refer to other factors which would render an act of sexual penetration *non-consensual or non-voluntary* on the part of the victim." The Appeal

Chamber went on to approve the quasi-conceptual definition of rape laid down in the Trial Chamber in the same case (*Kunarac* 2001):

> [T]he actus reus of the crime of rape in international law is constituted by: the sexual penetration, however slight: (a) of the vagina or anus of the victim by the penis of the perpetrator or any other object used by the perpetrator; or (b) of the mouth of the victim by the penis of the perpetrator; where such sexual penetration occurs without the consent of the victim. Consent for this purpose must be consent given voluntarily, as a result of the victim's free will, *assessed in the context of the surrounding circumstances*. The mens rea is the intention to effect this sexual penetration, and the knowledge that it occurs without the consent of the victim.
>
> (para. 460)

The Appeal Chamber further aligned itself with *Akayesu* by holding that "the circumstances giving rise to the instant appeal and that prevail in most cases charged as either war crimes or crimes against humanity will be almost universally coercive. That is to say, true consent will not be possible" (para. 130). Under *Kunarac* then it seemed that non-consent and knowledge thereof are to be considered elements of the crime of rape (at least as a crime against humanity) in international criminal law. However, prevailing coercive circumstances could establish lack of consent. *Kunarac* therefore did not undo the divide between the "conceptual" approaches in *Akayesu* and the more particularized approach from *Furundžija*, but it did attempt to bring the approaches closer together.

Recent jurisprudence suggests that this definitional divide is being successfully breached. In *Prosecutor v. Muhimana* (2005: para. 550), the ICTR Trial Chamber found that "that the *Akayesu* definition and the *Kunarac* elements are not incompatible or substantially different in their application. Whereas *Akayesu* referred broadly to a 'physical invasion of a sexual nature', *Kunarac* went on to articulate the parameters of what would constitute a physical invasion of a sexual nature amounting to rape." Similarly, the ICTR Appeal Chamber held in *Prosecutor v. Gacumbitsi* (2006) that non-consent is an element of the crime of rape but that it can be proved by establishing that circumstances at the time of the offenses were so coercive they made meaningful consent impossible. "[T]he Trial Chamber," it was held, "is free to infer non-consent from the background circumstances, such as an ongoing genocide campaign or the detention of the victim" (para. 157).

The tribunals have made significant progress in crafting an international criminal law definition of rape that meaningfully corresponds to women's experiences of forced sexual contact, despite a few stumbles along the way. However, the definition is not perfect. Doris Buss (2002) points out that the definition tends to align itself most closely to what law generally considers the prototypical kind of rape (i.e. "stranger rape") even though rape does not always take that form.

The international criminal definition is an enormous advance on traditional, adversarial, common-law definitions of rape, which tend to state it as "the penetration of the vagina by the penis without the consent of the women where the man knew of the lack of consent" (see *DPP v. Morgan* 1976). Importantly, international criminal law accepts that coercive circumstances can make the expression of non-consent exceptionally difficult and provides for the inference of non-consent from the coercive surrounding circumstances.

Women as professional participants in the tribunals

Women's professional participation in the tribunals has been important for the recognition of sexual violence. In *Akayesu*, Navanthem Pillay, the only female judge on the bench, directed the Office of the Prosecutor (OTP) to consider amending the indictment to include charges relating to sexual violence. Women with professional positions in the tribunals have gone onto senior positions in other international legal institutions, broadening female participation in international legal and political institutions. Halley (2006: 340) identifies women's professional participation in the tribunals as a victory for governance feminism and a "newly mature engagement with power." Although women's high-level participation in international legal institutions is significant, we should not conflate *f*emale and *F*eminist. Some of the most damaging prosecutorial decisions for female victims were made by a female chief prosecutor.

Unlike the Statute of the International Criminal Court (1998: Art. 38.8.a.iii), which makes "a fair representation of female and male judges" a factor in the selection of judges, there is no requirement to ensure gender balance among the tribunals' judiciary. In fact, very limited reference is made to the gender composition of the bench in both tribunals, and in both cases this reference is limited to *ad litem* (rather than permanent) judges.

The Statute of the ICTY (1993: Art. 12.1) provides that the tribunal be staffed by 16 permanent and nine *ad litem* judges. Although the ICTY Statute (Art. 13.1.b) requires consideration of "a fair representation of female and male candidates" when proposing *ad litem* judges, it does not make such provision relating to the appointment of permanent judges.

The original text of Article 11 of the ICTR Statute provided for 14 permanent judges but did not allow for *ad litem* judges or make any reference to gender representation on the bench. Security Council Resolution 1431 (2002) changed the composition of the ICTR. It increased its permanent judiciary to 16 and provided for a pool of 18 *ad litem* judges (Statute of the ICTR: revised Art. 11). The revised Article 12 of the ICTR Statute (Art. 12.1.b) also provides that account be taken of the "importance of a fair representation of female and male candidates" when proposing *ad litem* judges.

While gender representation is considered when proposing candidates for *ad litem* appointments, such consideration does not occur in selecting permanent judges. Although, there has in fact always been female representation among the permanent judges of both tribunals, gender representation is not gender balance. For example, in early 2009, there were two female permanent judges on the

ICTY, Christine Van den Wyngaert (Belgium) and Andrésia Vaz (Senegal) and three female permanent judges on the ICTR, Khalida Rachid Khan, who is Vice President (Pakistan), Andrésia Vaz (Senegal), and Arlette Ramaroson (Madagascar).[1]

There has been significant female representation in the non-judicial staff of the tribunals. Two of the four chief prosecutors have been women (Louise Arbour and Carla del Ponte). Although feminist theorists have long doubted the extent to which women as formal participants in judicialized processes can make a real difference from a feminist perspective (Hunter 2008), women judges have been significant in both the ICTR and ICTY. Judge Pillay's intervention in the *Akayesu* case has been noted, and Judge Florence Mumba's role in crafting the *Kunarac* judgment was significant; for she insisted on recounting the testimony of woman after woman who told the tribunal about their experiences of being raped in the Foca "rape camp."

Also important is the continuing personnel transfer from the *ad hoc* tribunals to other international institutions. Through such transfers the lessons learned about sexual violence in the tribunals is horizontally transported. Two UN High Commissioners for Human Rights are women previously involved in the tribunals: Louise Arbour was the chief prosecutor, and Navanthem Pillay was on the ICTR bench. There also continues to be some transfer of judges from the tribunals to the ICC. The current Vice-President of the ICC, Judge Fatoumata Diarra (Mali), served as an ICTY *ad litem* judge. Judge Odio Benito (Costa Rica) was Vice-President of the ICTY (from 1993–95), and Judge Christine Van den Wyngaert is transitioning directly from the ICTY to the ICC.

Plus ça change, plus c'est la même chose?

The story seems positive, but underneath the positivist success remain serious concerns about whether the tribunals are providing actual remedies to women victims of sexual violence. Concern exists about whether the proceedings are being conducted in a way that appreciates and reflects the centrality of sexual violence to the atrocities. Considering the missed opportunities and the extent to which women's experiences continue to be muted during proceedings, a dimmer view of the tribunals emerges than is suggested by the positivistic success recounted above. This view is familiar to those who have followed the development of sexual violence jurisprudence in domestic jurisdictions; the tribunal difficulties, such as victim protection and prosecutorial de-prioritization of sexual violence, replicate domestic patterns.

Prosecutorial decision-making

A systematic failure exists on the part of Office of the Prosecutor (OTP) to formulate a managed, strategic prosecutorial policy recognizing women's experience and to allocate responsibility accurately by ensuring individual responsibility, including individual command responsibility, for the crimes of sexual violence committed in the Former Yugoslavia and Rwanda. This failure is reflected in the extent to which the OTP has not included charges relating to sexual violence in indictments, even when ample evidence exists that sexual violence took place. Important steps in the prosecution of sexual violence, at times, have occurred *in spite of* the efforts and strategic decision-making of the OTP. This failure is well demonstrated by the charging history of the *Akayesu* case which was the first case to hold that rape could form the *actus reus* for genocide.

Akayesu was the *bourgmestre* of the Taba commune where rape and sexual violence were widespread during the genocide. The original indictment in *Akayesu* included no charges relating to sexual violence even though there was ample witness testimony that rape and sexual violence were major elements in the genocidal strategy overseen by Akayesu. Thus, an amicus curiae brief requested the ICTR to exercise its supervisory authority and request the OTP to amend the indictment to include charges of "rape and other serious acts of sexual violence as crimes within the competence of the Tribunal" (Amicus Brief *Akayesu* 1997). The brief argued that failure to indict Akayesu on sexual violence would produce unfairness and constitute a miscarriage of justice (para. 5). During testimony before the tribunal, before the amendment of the indictment, witnesses revealed the pervasiveness of rape and sexual violence in the commune. The only female judge on the bench, Judge Pillay, then instructed the OTP to review the indictment, which was amended to include three extra charges relating to sexual violence.

The fact that it took substantial political pressure and specific judicial intervention for sexual violence charges to be added to the indictment led to defense arguments that "[t]he charges of offenses of sexual violence ... were added under the pressure of public opinion and were not credibly supported by the evidence" (para. 42). This claim called into question the credibility of the women who testified about sexual violence before the tribunal. The OTP's original failure to include sexual violence on the indictment rendered invisible the particularly gendered nature of women's experiences and formed the basis for defense attacks on witness credibility. Although *Akayesu* is rightly praised for advances in genocide and sexual violence law, it contained flaws in process. It was very nearly a lost opportunity for the OTP, and the proceeding was more traumatic than necessary for the witnesses, due to prosecutorial omissions.

Although there was a brief "*Akayesu*-effect," leading to the inclusion of sexual violence in many ICTR indictments, 2001 marked a notable reduction in such indictments (Breton-Le Goff 2002). The increasing tensions between Rwanda and the ICTR, leading to reduced cooperation (Vokes 2002), may explain this reduction in part. However, reduced sexual violence charges, the "rationalization" of the work of the OTP, and the reorientation of prosecutorial priorities clearly changed after Carla del Ponte's arrival as prosecutor in 1999. Upon taking office, she announced her intention to prosecute 153 suspects by 2005 (Sixth Annual Report of the ICTR 2000–2001). This ambitious plan required "streamlining" or "rationalization," which included dismantling the investigation unit dedicated to sexual violence crimes (Sixth Annual Report of the ICTR 2000–2001). A clear prosecutorial decision to focus on "other" crimes and to de-prioritize sexual violence occurred, possibly because of the labor-intensive nature of investigating and prosecuting such crimes. The incongruence between the OTP's marginalization of sexual violence and its centrality to the Rwandan genocide is striking and holds clear implications for the position of sexual violence before the tribunals: sexual violence is important *as long as* it does not get "in the way" of more easily prosecuted crimes.

The most recently appointed prosecutor, Serge Brammertz, appears to be willing to amend indictments issued by his predecessors to include sexual violence charges, but the tribunals' legitimate concerns of due process for defendants may prevent such amendments in some cases, particularly where evidence of sexual violence is not new but was not acted upon in the original drafting of indictments. A case currently before the ICTY, *Prosecutor v. Lukić* (2008), illustrates the problem. The defendants, Milan and Sredoje Lukić, are accused of war crimes and crimes against humanity arising from their involvement in the White Eagles paramilitary organization. Despite evidence that they perpetrated and encouraged sexual violence, their indictment did not include any counts relating to alleged sexual offenses. Given until November 2007 to amend the indictments to account for these allegations (Status Conference 2007), Prosecutor del Ponte did not make any amendments, apparently to ensure expeditious progression of the case (Prosecution Motion 2008: para. 14). In June 2008, the new prosecutor attempted to amend the indictment to include charges of rape, torture, and enslavement based on defendants' alleged involvement with a "rape camp," arguing that inclusion of these crimes was necessary "in the interests of justice." On 8 July 2008, the ICTY declined the application to amend because the unnecessary delay would prejudice the accused (Decision on Prosecution Motion 2008). The tribunal held that:

> According to the Prosecution's own submission, "the facts are not new" and many of the sources of information to which the Prosecution refers date several years back. The Chamber notes that most of the material referred to has been in the Prosecution's possession for a significant time. The Chamber further notes that on two occasions the Prosecutor herself considered to amend the indictment in this case to include new charges of sexual violence. Significantly, prior to the expiry of the deadline on 15 November 2007, the Prosecutor: "exercised her discretion not to seek an amendment ... in part, based upon her belief that amending the indictment to include new charges of sex crimes would lengthen the Prosecution's case ... " the Chamber concludes that the Prosecution has not acted with the required diligence in submitting the Motion timely in such a way as to provide adequate notice of the requested amendment to the Defence ... In view of the imminent start of the trial, the granting of the amendment

would adversely affect the Accused's right ... to be tried without undue delay.

(paras 60–61)

Prosecutorial decisions that de-prioritize sexual violence reproduce the marginalization of sexual violence from domestic criminal justice systems and distort the historical record. Furthermore, they call into question the extent to which international proceedings can transfer feminist norms to the domestic sphere when the tribunals conclude operations and allocate cases to the domestic courts. As the *Lukić* proceedings show, earlier prosecutorial decisions negatively impact the OTP's capacity to address sexual violence, even where there is a desire to do so.

The provision of a receptive theater for victim witnesses

All courts are expected to provide a remedy of some nature for civil or criminal wrongs – whether that remedy is delivered to the individual or the society. However, tribunals and other forms of post-conflict adjudication conduct their work under uniquely high, sometimes incompatible, expectations. For the ICTR and ICTY, those expectations emanated from the international community, the victims of the conflicts, and those tasked with rebuilding the rule of law. For victims of sexual violence, the tribunals held up the prospect that "truth" might win out, that the historical record might truly reflect the extent to which women and girls experienced violence in a gendered and sexualized way. For feminist legal theorists such hopes may have always seemed naïve. After all, feminism questions the capacity for *any* judicialized institutions to truly discover and reflect victims' truth, particularly given the archaic nature of many evidentiary and procedural rules.

Interestingly, the ICTY and ICTR seemed to woo feminists into believing that things would be different by instituting "rape shield" rules (Rules of Procedure and Evidence of the ICTY: Sect. 3, Rule 96; Rules of Evidence and Procedure of the ICTR: Sect. 3, Rule 96) and committing themselves to provide receptive and supportive theaters within which women's "violence stories" (Cobb 1997: 406) could be told safely and supportively. The subsequent de-prioritization of sexual violence by the OTP disabused many women of their high hopes. So adversely did some advocacy organizations respond to this retreat that several victims' organizations in Rwanda actually refuse to cooperate with the OTP. Some women in Rwanda reportedly feel a grave sense of injustice and dissatisfaction with the ICTR (Noworjee 2005). The tribunals' own handling of sexual violence testimony and interpretive methods in its judgments have significantly lowered feminist expectations.

To meet the expectation that the tribunal could record the "truth," two things were necessary. The tribunals needed to provide a safe atmosphere for women to testify, and the proceedings needed to reflect the fact that judges understood women's experience of sexual violence and that this violence resounded in multiple contexts. The contexts were those of pre-conflict society, of society during conflict, and of post-conflict society, in which many sexual violence victims were ostracized and re-victimized.

These tasks were challenging because the women were not just witnesses to what had happened but also essential instruments in reconstituting the state. Testifying before the tribunals is a performative task for the individual and a constitutive process for the state, and the international community's attempt to re-establish itself after the atrocities it failed to prevent. The process of transition and re-establishment of law is contingent upon the willingness of victims to share their story, reveal their truths, and have the law applied thereto (Humphrey 2002). Such women's stories were to be used to create a record of what had happened, to sketch the canvas on which principles of liberal legalism could be superimposed, and to form the groundwork for the re-establishment of the rule of law for the transitional and post-transitional state.

Many victims' organizations, particularly in Rwanda, complain about the questions presiding judges permit defense counsel to pose during proceedings. Although rape shield rules are in place, witnesses have been forced to answer questions such as "why did you not interrupt the act if you did not take pleasure in it?" (Crawford 2001). One attorney suggested that an individual witness could not have been raped because she had not bathed recently and did not smell very pleasant (*Nyiramasuhuko* 2001), a suggestion based on the fallacy that rape has something to do with sexual attractiveness rather than violence and power. In addition to permitting such questions and insinuations to be posed by counsel, some judges failed to conduct themselves in a manner appropriate to the seriousness of the charges and the sensitivity of witness' testimony. The testimony of Witness T. A. in *Nyiramasuhuko* has become infamous for its "laughing judges" incident in which a number of judges began to laugh as the witness was being cross-examined. The seriousness of this incident reflected the judges' biased view of the credibility of the witness and undermined the legitimacy of the tribunal process. The great cost to the witness for her participation is well captured in her comment to Binaifer Nowrojee:

> My parents, my brother and my sister were killed. I'm all alone. My relatives were killed in a horrible fashion. But I survived—to answer the strange questions that were asked by the ICTR. If you say you were raped, that is something understandable. How many times do you need to say it? When the judges laughed, they laughed like they could not stop laughing. I was angry and nervous. When I returned, everyone knew I had testified. My fiancé refused to marry me once he knew I had been raped. He said, you went to Arusha and told everyone that you were raped. Today I would not accept to testify, to be traumatized for a second time. No one apologized to me. Only Gregory Townsend [the ICTR prosecuting lawyer] congratulated me after the testimony for my courage. When you return you

get threatened. My house was attacked. My fiancé has left me. In any case, I'm already dead.

(Nowrojee 2005: 24)

Tribunal judges have significant control over how proceedings unfold, including how witnesses are questioned and cross-examined. One of the most worrying aspects of the tribunals' operation is the judges' tendency to err on the side of caution in protecting the "fair trial" rights of the accused (including the right to subject witnesses to "rigorous" cross examination). This protection has operated to the detriment of witnesses, a result also commonly seen in the prosecution of sexual violence crimes in adversarial domestic criminal justice systems.

Conclusions

International criminal tribunals exist for many reasons. Some seek to re-establish the international legal order's autonomy and legitimacy. Many involve reconstituting the state and the domestic rule of law. Through their operation they create the "true" record, the definitive politico-legal account of events. When sexual violence was central to those events, it is imperative that it be central to the tribunals' work and handled in the same sensitive and appropriate manner as other forms of violence. Only if this is accomplished can these tribunals create a remedy for the victims and construct an account reflective of how women and girls experienced events. Tribunals could also influence domestic legal structures, establishing a legal culture that addresses sexually violent crimes in ways that appreciate their seriousness, their effect on women's lives, and the law's on women who seek restitution or remedy.

Although the *ad hoc* international criminal tribunals for Rwanda and the Former Yugoslavia made significant strides in the area of sexual violence, their advances are largely positivistic and unravel easily under practice-based decisions. It is hoped that, as international criminal law develops in the ICC and elsewhere, the jurisprudence and the practice of prosecuting sexual violence will develop more positively from a feminist perspective. If that development occurs, feminist legal understandings of sexual violence will infuse the norm transfer between the international and domestic spheres. Then the legal frameworks criminalizing and punishing sexual violence will operate in ways that benefit women and bring increased integrity to international and domestic legal systems.

Note

1 Judge Vaz is a member of the Appeals Chamber of both, therefore the total female representation on the permanent judiciary of the tribunals is four.

Chapter 20

Theorizing the more responsive state

Transcending the national boundaries of law

Laura Spitz

Introduction

Martha Fineman proposes the concept of shared "vulnerability" as an alternative framework to traditional American equal protection analyses for describing, assessing, and addressing economic and social inequalities. According to Fineman (2008: 1, 19), a vulnerability analysis re-focuses social justice inquiries away from legal frameworks grounded in notions of formal equality, onto the "institutions and structures our society has and will establish to manage our common vulnerabilities," in order that we might better imagine and develop state mechanisms that ensure a more equitable distribution of assets and privileges. Within this frame, formal equality—bounded by identities and categories of discrimination—gives way to a post-identity concept of substantive equality, understood "as a universal resource, a radical guarantee that is a benefit for all" (23).

Critical to Fineman's analysis (2008: 19), and the starting point for my contribution to this book, is her assertion that a vulnerability approach to the allocation and (re)distribution of societal resources requires a more responsive state. I do not engage with the substance of her vulnerability theory here; rather, I focus on the question provoked by her call for a more responsive state: to what does she refer when she invokes the state? She does not resolve this question in her essay, except to say that the state is "the manifestation of public authority and the ultimate legitimate repository of coercive power" (6) but not necessarily the nation-state. Instead, she raises the question for others to engage. "One pressing issue for those interested in furthering a new vision of equality must be how to modernize or refine [a] conception of the state and then explicitly define its appropriate relationship to institutions and individuals within contemporary society" (6). But if not necessarily, or not only, the nation-state, where might we locate it *for the purposes* identified by Fineman?

At both a conceptual and organizational level, one answer might be transnational or supranational institutions. Literature theorizing the state typically focuses on the nation-state as the locus of state power and authority, bounded by territorial and/or geopolitical borders. Within legal scholarship, an even narrower focus is common: the state as adjudicatory apparatus. Yet it may be more productive to shift the conceptual lens to embrace a wider and less vertical conception of state power. Thus, this chapter takes Fineman's invitation to begin the task of theorizing a "more responsive state" *in* the US, by looking *beyond* the US, and putting two groups of scholars in conversation with one another: feminist legal theorists on the one hand, and integration theorists, including governance theorists, on the other. Ultimately, I suggest that feminist legal scholars might usefully begin (re)theorizing the state by engaging with the process of North American integration (and with integration theorists) to explore integration's emancipatory or progressive potential for responding to the sorts of inequalities Fineman identifies. At the same time, and just as importantly, integration theories will be made more relevant and more robust if they engage with feminism and feminist insights.

Typically, activists and social justice scholars—including feminists and critical race theorists—have been hostile to the idea of deepening continental integration in North America. Continental integration promises the annihilation of important (and knowable) cultural differences between those who live in Canada, the US, and Mexico, differences best preserved by national and local governments. These activists and scholars assert that integration is invariably a cover for American hegemony or imperialism. Finally, continental integration will exacerbate existing economic and social asymmetries between and within Canada, the US, and Mexico. I am sympathetic to these concerns, but my approach is different (Spitz 2004, 2005). Deepening continental integration potentially undermines the power, effectiveness, and legitimacy of Canada, the US, and Mexico *qua* nation-states but—and this is the crux of my thesis—this is both a *threat* and a *promise*. Transnational regional integration is potentially and simultaneously a location of domination and resistance to domination, displaying both regressive and emancipatory features (Kellner 2003; Kahn and Kellner 2007). It can be usefully explored for its potential to provide a framework for developing "state" institutions at transnational and supranational levels.

My theoretical engagement rests on four premises. First, we are in the process of something we might call "integration" in North America, and while I elaborate further below, I mean "integration" in its ordinary sense: the process of combining or integrating previously separate or differently divided groups into a new or larger whole—a sort of rebordering project (Spitz 2009: 741). In the context of North America, it is marked by simultaneous rule harmonization through deregulation and cross-pollination at the nation-state level and increasing formalization, coordination, and institutionalization at the transnational level (Spitz 2009: 755). Second, continental integration is sufficiently disruptive of our legal, political, economic, and cultural systems to present an unusual opportunity for meaningful engagement with the meaning, form, function, and constitution of the state at all levels: sub-national, national, transnational, and supranational. Third, location matters—historical, cultural, geographic, social. Therefore, general theories about the state are useful only to the extent that they accurately reflect, explain, or have predictive resonance in the context of a particularized location. Similarly, ideas developed in specific contexts may be of more or less use elsewhere. Finally, any theory of integration should potentially be, or be informed by, a theory of disintegration. "It should not only explain why countries decide to coordinate their efforts across a wider range of tasks and delegate more authority to common institutions, but *also why they do not do so* or why, having done so, they decide to defect from such arrangements" (Schmitter and Trechsel 2004: 47, emphasis added).

In the sections that follow, I sketch a preliminary definition for "integration" in the context of North America. This task is admittedly difficult because integration is a deeply contested and polysemic concept, and I do not propose to offer a comprehensive definition. Instead, I elaborate on the concept by making a series of observations aimed at moving the definitional discussion forward. I argue that there is nothing about integration *qua* integration that portends the institutionalization of a particular set of values or closes the transformative process to particular institutional actors. In this sense, integration presents an *opportunity* for feminist participation. From there, I then build on administrative law principles to argue that we reasonably can predict the increasingly autonomous development of integration institutions. Meaningful contribution to the development of North American institutions, therefore, requires engagement at the earliest stages. In this sense, it presents not only an opportunity, but an *imperative*, for feminist engagement. Finally, I offer suggestions for what feminism might contribute to integration theories and integration practices, and I conclude that theorizing the "more responsive state" requires "feminist integration theory" or "integration feminism" in North America. But before moving to the substance of my arguments, I begin with a framing exercise. I ask the reader to engage in a sort of "thought experiment" designed to disrupt reflexive resistance to my integration claim(s).

Mapping integration

Think back to eighth grade biology and your anatomy textbook where the shape of the human body was drawn in its simplest form, as nothing but an outline. In Western schools, these "simple" bodies were invariably white, male, and apparently able-bodied, but I do not intend to invoke *that* particular body here, only to use the textbook metaphor. On to that body, students could place a single transparency, designed to show one system (for example, the circulatory system). Students could add another transparency (the cardiovascular system) and then another (the lymphatic system) and so on, "building" the human body. The fun grew when students added the skeleton or organs or made it sex-specific at the same time they removed something else, "playing" with its constitution. The project was designed to show how the human body was constituted, how systems interacted, and how to identify the individual parts constituting the "whole." However, the application of each layer suggested the possibility of both normative and disruptive constitutive processes. The order of the layers, the priority of the layers, and what constituted a cognizable layer were normative and politically significant choices.

Now imagine a similar exercise involving North America. Starting with a continental outline, lay the "national borders" transparency over it. Now pick it back up (or not) and instead think of other transparencies or maps that might be laid down: maps that show trade patterns or migration patterns or electrical grids. Or families. Or the spread of disease. Try norm clusters; industrial development; legal systems; weather patterns; topography; religion; language; wealth; architecture; First Nations or Aboriginal Nations; political views; cultural preferences; and so on. Now try a transparency or set of transparencies meant to advance or highlight the "gender question/s" or the "woman question/s," such as patterns of gender violence or family law norms. Feminists might re-layer our view of an integrated space by producing a cartography of vulnerabilities (mapped by class, gender, race, et cetera). Or, to use Fineman's framework, patterns of institutional response to shared vulnerability/ies.

The point is: North America—and the social, legal, political, economic and cultural systems that constitute it—looks very different if national borders are reworked or backgrounded, depending on which (combination) of "transparencies" is foregrounded. This exercise demonstrates how the privileging of national borders obscures other patterns of human organization and development. Of course, national borders are significant. After all, law and history have made national borders our central organizing political frame. But they do not alone constitute or define the region. The fact that they remain in place does not defeat the claim that integration is deepening in politically and legally significant ways. Careful examination of the other systems and patterns that comprise the region reveals dialectical patterns and systems of deepening integration in myriad ways.

North American integration

The integration claim

"Integration" does not offer a single definition for easy summary in North America. Described broadly as "the dynamic development of political, economic, legal, and cultural ... systems and identities, *at the regional level*, pushing in the direction of new community loyalties that disrupt historical systems of political, economic, legal, and cultural ... organization" at the national level (Spitz 2009: 756, emphasis in original), it increasingly makes sense to speak about a North American political space or "shared system of rules and procedures to define who actors are, how they make sense of each other's actions and what types of actions are possible" (Sweet et al. 2001: 12). Evidence of deepening integration can be found in a variety of "places," both formal and informal. Primary among these is a series of multilateral agreements committing Canada, the US, and Mexico to a continued course of domestic deregulation and non-interference, towards the goal of harmonizing a variety of regulatory systems between the three countries. Most obvious is the North America Free Trade Agreement (NAFTA), including the NAFTA side-agreements, but others include the North American Security and Prosperity Partnership (SPP), the SPP Regulatory Cooperation Framework, the North American Forum, various tax coordination treaties, and the Council of Great Lake Governors (Spitz 2009: 757–58). Beyond formal agreements, additional examples include norm harmonization and cross-pollination; capital investment and trade patterns; im/migration patterns; transnational organizations; supranational institutions; and integration discourses. Still, the term is contested, its complexity a principle feature of the processes it seeks to capture. Though it escapes easy definition, however, it does permit for conceptual elaboration.

The first point to be emphasized is that integration is a set of *processes*, pushing in the direction of an integrated or re-bordered community, and not a discrete outcome. It is dynamic and evolving, constantly shifting and adapting (Spitz 2009: 756). In North America, it:

> has been marked and shaped by intra-continental forces we might loosely describe as neo-nationalism (particularly as a site of resistance to global hegemony and global capitalism) and regionalism (particularly as an extension of the logic of global capitalism), as well as the extra- and trans-continental forces commonly described as "globalization." It is complicated by the fact that nationalism, regionalism and globalization often push in contradictory and conflicting directions. It is further complicated by the fact that each of these—nationalism, regionalism and globalization—display progressive and emancipatory, as well as oppressive, regressive and negative, features.
>
> (Spitz 2009: 762)

Second, one of the difficulties in contemporary debates about the existence and prospect of North American integration is that important discussions of institutional priorities, cultural practices, social norms, and historical narratives tied to territorial space are frequently derailed by the invocation of imprecise and misguided claims to and about sovereignty. These claims often obscure rather than illuminate central questions about sovereignty, in part because sovereignty encompasses a wide variety of ambiguous, anachronistic, and confused meanings. Furthermore, in thinking about the "state," most legal scholarship in the US privileges centralization and/or verticalization of state functions and performances and, consequently, is imbricated with notions of sovereignty. Here, I emphasize the potential for integration to permit for focus on a more horizontal or inter-systemic conception of state-ness. So while engagement with integration presents an opportunity for (re)articulations of sovereignty in North America, sovereignty might just as usefully be bracketed for a more sustained focus on the aspirational and conceptual discussions, and then revisited when our aspirations need translating into organizational expressions and functions.

Third, to date, North American integration has been primarily *negative*—dismantling national institutions and harmonizing regulatory regimes to reduce (primarily economic) barriers between Canada, the US, and Mexico—but it need not be. A rigorous and sustained focus on the meaning of integration for Canadians, Americans, and Mexicans reveals the potential for pursuing—with broad public participation and the development and maintenance of social institutions to support political engagement—a more *positive* form of integration shaping the conditions under which markets and other forms of human activity operate. By positive, I mean the creation of state or public institutions at the North American level, explicitly designed to "govern" and provide the sorts of public social goods typically associated with Western democracies. These institutions need not replace the nation-state but instead act the role of supplement or compliment. Whether this institutionalization results from something as simple as multilateral coordination or as complex as constitutional pluralism remains an open question. So far, the regulation of transnational spaces has been more akin to administrative than constitutional law in North America. Thus, general principles of administrative law and the institutional dynamics of administrative spaces might be useful for predicting possible or plausible outcomes.

A further point to be made is that many of the actors and engines driving integration do not represent the general population, nor are they answerable to it. Yet, if each of the three North American nations takes seriously its constitutional commitments to the rule of law, representative democracy, equality, freedom, and the "common good," then they need strategies for ensuring that those values retain meaning and currency in the lives of Canadians, Americans, and Mexicans through integrative processes. Similarly, if Canadians, Americans, and Mexicans take seriously their democratic rights and responsibilities, they need strategies for ensuring their continued relevance in a world increasingly bounded and shaped by transnational, supranational, and supra-constitutional actors and forces.

Finally, continental integration is a product of, and made possible by, "the convergence of several connected developments or transformations that are usefully understood as comprising a rupture, or critical break, from certain structures and concepts endemic to modernity" (Spitz 2009: 761). These include changes in science and technology, the (re)structuring of global capital, the global turn towards neoliberalism as a hegemonic ideology and practice, and the conflation of democracy and capitalism (761). Together these developments have permitted "the market and its logic … to triumph over public goods," making "the state … subservient to economic imperatives and logic" (Kellner 2003: 5). They have worked to push in the direction of accelerating negative integration, constructing the view that legitimate resistance takes the form of national assertions of sovereignty. In all the complexities and ambiguities, an opportunity to cautiously embrace and (re)-make integration itself into an act of progressive resistance and transformation is my aim. From a critical feminist perspective that fundamentally understands the state as essential to a just society, the best chance for reconceiving a "state" that is more responsive to the requirements of social justice, social welfare, and social democracy is to use the logic and momentum of *negative* integration to push for *positive* integration at something other than the national level.

Feminist resistance to integration

Important questions remain. What forces are apt to move first to inform the substance of positive integration and thus define its normative character? How might we ensure meaningful participation in the processes of integration to the largest number of ordinary people? If integration is presently captive to, or at least responsive to, some social, political, and economic interests as opposed to others, then presumably those forces are poised to shape any new process of integration in ways that undermine the normative aims of my approach.

This critique gains particular traction because it simultaneously speaks to many different people, with a variety of viewpoints, who experience power as residing somewhere other than with them. Depending on your physical, economic, and social location in North America, you may be suspicious that whatever forces will inform the substance of integration, they are not "yours" nor will they be developed in your interest. In this view, energy and resources should be directed towards resisting integration. Nevertheless, there are few signs that the present trajectory of negative integration is slowing. On its present course, it promises to increase the democratic deficit in each of the NAFTA member states, even as it provides the framework for further dismantling domestic social welfare programs and social justice protections as barriers to trade and threats to security. Broad public participation in a more positive process offers the possibility—however slim—of improving representative democracy and safeguarding social programs and economic protections in North America.

The posture of resistance to integration might be accused of embodying a kind of naïveté of its own or, at the very least, an anachronistic view of state power. Part of what those of us committed to social justice are trying to achieve or preserve about ourselves is an approach to the world that is antithetical to the assertion of political power. Many feminists view the assertion of political power as suspect, imperialist, colonialist, universalist, and essentialist. Yet, the example of North American integration suggests that canonical left–right conceptions of verticalized state power are inadequate for describing and intervening in contemporary (re)distributions and assertions of political, economic, and social power. Power in this context appears to operate according to Foucauldian logics of micro-power, biopower, and governmentality (Foucault [2004] 2007: 108–9, 277). North American integration is best conceived as the somewhat ad hoc, localized, and horizontal constitution of networks of governmentality (Slaughter 2004). This formulation suggests that, rather than examining traditional practices of government power, we should look more closely at the evolution of administrative law in these spaces. If governmentality inheres in both apparatuses and systems of knowledge (Foucault [2004] 2007: 108) then the failure to participate in the construction of such apparatuses and systems amounts not to resistance but capitulation.

There is little doubt that a specific assertion of power is necessary to achieve the positive integration that I envision. Once we accept that power matters and inheres in a specific constitution of apparatuses and systems of knowledge, the integrationist project requires unpacking assumptions about the balance and distribution of power in North America. Mexico and Canada (and certain constituencies within the US) seemingly accept a posture of structural imbalance in negotiating with the United States. While US credentials as a regional hegemon are well established, Canada's and Mexico's acceptance of those credentials help to construct and reconstruct the US as rightfully positioned there. This acceptance also obscures the process of integration. However, Canada and Mexico (especially together with certain intra-American constituencies) possess enormous economic strength vis-à-vis the US. Canada, for example, is the United States' largest trading partner, and the largest energy supplier to the US. Positive integration with broad public participation, then, permits us to imagine transnational alliances that upset assumptions about predetermined, linear configurations of power.

Feminist resistance to state intervention

Some feminists oppose integration for some of the same reasons they oppose state intervention at any level. As with my claim for the progressive potential of transnational integration, some feminists will resist Fineman's invocation of a "more responsive state." They are at best ambivalent, more often than not antagonistic, to calls for increasing state intervention. Their arguments range from critiques of state power (Abramovitz 1986)—usually from a position that views the state as a kind of *mirror-image* of extant social distributions or as epiphenomenal of "patriarchal" or "male" power (MacKinnon 1989)—to critiques of the legal architecture and implications of "nationalism" for women and ethnic minorities. They have made important contributions to significant bodies of work challenging the progressive potential of state institutions and criticizing the effects of what has been described as American hegemony/imperialism. Their theories perform an important function, disrupting, deconstructing, and problematizing liberal and other accounts of the "state" and illuminating the myriad ways state power can be misused. Nevertheless, this work is frequently reductive, grounded in economic, sexual/gender, or technological determinism, rather than "the complex new configurations of economy, technology, polity, and culture, and attendant forces of domination and resistance" (Kellner 2004). Moreover these critiques typically rest on the view that the Westphalian nation-state is the legitimate entity within which law (and therefore critical legal activism and resistance) is organized. Even as globalization is acknowledged, it rarely leads feminist theorists to reconsider theories of the state *and its location* or to consider the potential for transnational polities to accomplish progressive change. Even attempted recourse to international law supports rather than challenges this view. The nation-state is—quite literally—the boundary and source of law.

My answer to these concerns is twofold. First, this reliance upon, and apparent acceptance of, the Westphalian system by many feminist legal theorists in the US—at least in so far as it relates to their view of the US—is complicated by forces pushing to deepen North American continental integration. Second, while these critiques have some persuasive resonance, I agree with Fineman (2008: 6, 8) that state institutions remain "the only realistic contender" to "develop expertise and competence in regard to the implications and implementation of public values [such as equality and justice]."

At the intersection of administrative law and institutionalism

Administrative law provides a useful framework for thinking about the regulation of North American integration. Administrative law is the "set of rules prescribing the proper rule-making behaviour for administrative agencies; that is, administrative law is a key set of procedures" (Shapiro 2001: 94). In North America, integration has been managed in part by domestic government agencies organized primarily under the executive branches of each national government. In the US, these include the Federal Trade Commission, the Office of the United States Trade Representative, the Federal Emergency and Management Agency, and the Transportation Security Administration. Increasingly, however, multilateral or transnational organizations are taking over this work. Examples include NAFTA tribunals, NAFTA institutions, the North American Steel Trade Committee, the dozens of committees struck under the SPP Regulatory Cooperation Framework Work Plan, the North American Energy Working Group, and the Trilateral Committee on Transborder Data.

This shift from national to transnational regulation raises interesting jurisdictional issues, including to whom are these agencies and tribunals answerable? In whose interests are they formed and developing? Who decides whose interests matter in this context? Who decides what counts as a legitimate interest? As administrative agencies, do they limit themselves to *doing* administration or are they actually *governing*? The answer to this latter question from an administrative law view, of course, is both (Shapiro 2001: 94). If they are doing administration *and* governing, then a further set of questions about democracy and domestic constitutional law is engaged, causing some scholars to focus on the democratic deficit in emerging regional polities. Such questions are worthy of inquiry but beyond the scope of this chapter. I raise the administrative law point for other reasons.

If administrative law prescribes the behavior of the administrative organs that implement integration law, then it is both reflective and *constitutive* of integration.

Furthermore, the organizational autonomy and internal logics of bureau-cratization should lead to transnational institutional practices that extend the reach of these administrative organs beyond the foundational mandates of their enabling instruments (Weber 1946), contributing to the institutionalization of this space as something other than, or extending beyond the direct control of, its constituent "parts." Finally, "[a]s [Western] polities encounter new circum-stances, they are prone to grant political executives discretion to deal with those circumstances," at the same time the urge to bring that discretion under rules is felt (Shapiro 2001: 94). This "urge" should translate into what we call "political will."

Taken together, these three observations provide both the opportunity and the case for feminist involvement at the very earliest stages of institutionalization. In other words, if we are committed to a "more responsive state" to achieve the substantive equality described by Fineman and others; "state" functions are devolving—at least in part—from the nation-state to a transnational adminis-trative space; the urge or will to regulate this space is present or may be present for the reasons described above; this transnational space is increasingly con-stituted and reconstituted by institutionalization; and institutions increasingly operate autonomously or semi-autonomously, according to their own logic, then feminists have the opportunity to help shape this space by involving themselves in these processes at every stage. Having identified this opportunity, what might feminists specifically offer the integrative processes and/or the development of integration theories in North America?

Toward a feminist theory and practice of integration

To put feminism in conversation with integration theories, one confronts a preliminary question: what does feminism mean? The standard taxonomy of feminisms includes various versions of *liberal* feminism, *radical* feminism, *post-modern* or *post-structural* feminism, *critical race* feminism, and what some authors call *critical theory* feminism (combining the insights of critical theory with a "gendered feminist politics") (Hoskyns 2004; Whitworth, 1994). This list is non-exhaustive, the categories overlap, and the lines between them are blurred, contingent, and contested. My view is that we should cast the net wide, to include as many feminisms as possible in this discussion. Not all feminisms will have something to say to all integration theories and vice versa. Some will be more adept than others for highlighting certain issues, answering others. But this conversation should be open to the largest number possible.

For the task of putting feminists into conversation with integration theorists, in order to ask the "gender question", the work of Catherine Hoskyns—developed in the context of European integration theory—provides a useful starting point:

> Gender refers to the socio-cultural meanings given to masculinity and fem-ininity and to the complex and varying relations between the two. Applying

gender perspectives, therefore, both to the rich patterns of history and to the theories constructed to order and explain them, means identifying these changing meanings and examining their causes and effects ...

The term "gender perspectives" is intended to include a spectrum of approaches and interventions. As Cynthia Weber implies, gender is not a variable that can be included or excluded at whim in theoretical constructs. Rather, it is a viewpoint that can alter not just the scope of the theory but the concepts on which it is based (Weber 2001: 89) ... [G]ender perspectives create a viewpoint rather than a theory (in the narrow scientific sense of that term) and ... without sensitivity to this viewpoint any general theory attempting to explain European integration will be partial and misleading.

(Hoskyns 2004: 217)

Gender is multivalent in its articulation with other aspects of social location. Thus, feminists might insist that gender, thus conceived, be included in the ways described by Hoskyns to "give visibility to values and situations normally ignored or marginalized, thus helping to create more inclusive and better grounded histories and theories" (217). We could start playing with the above-referenced "transparencies," although it is no easy task and will require figuring out what "adding gender" or bringing feminist theories and practices to the questions presented might look like. It will require interrogation of what counts as a "question." Thus, this section begins identifying feminist insights that might have special resonance or compelling applicability in the context of transnational integration, with the aim of encouraging broader and deeper engagement with these questions.

First, feminism/s are attuned to issues of co-optation. Feminist literatures refer to the "dangers ... of being accepted without inducing change" (Hoskyns 2004: 221). Feminists don't merely want to be "included" in the integrative processes that produce new political spaces—we want our theories and practices to "matter." Moreover, feminists are particularly adept at creating political space where none exists. Currently, North America is a kind of nascent political space; feminists might insist on room/space in order to participate in its evolution/ creation. Additionally, feminists have made important contributions to the bodies of work theorizing and demonstrating the ways in which gender-neutral (and race-neutral) rules of general application can work to disadvantage already disadvantaged people. Vigilance is required as the rules that regulate these spaces are increasingly formalized. Furthermore, feminist theory has helped identify and illuminate the ways in which law, gender, and sex interact with and exacerbate existing vulnerabilities. Feminists (largely at the insistence, at least initially, of critical race scholars) have contributed to the project of theorizing intersectionality and its consequences for identity construction (and oppression). Again, some combination of critique, participation, and vigilance is required as institutions and rules evolve.

Continental integration—particularly the institutionalization of "administrative spaces"—presents untold instances of discourses which rely on apparently knowable, inevitable, and determinative differences between form and substance, between public and private. Feminist scholars have contended with and unpacked these dichotomies. Indeed, they are especially good at challenging fundamental concepts. They are adept at theorizing the production of "knowledge" and privilege, not to mention power—all of which are implicated in the context of deepening integration. Finally, integration theories incorporate various international relations, sociological, philosophical, economic, and political science theories, including functionalism, constructivism, rationalism, and intergovernmentalism. Feminists have confronted these theories in other contexts, arguing that they simultaneously ignore gender even as they are highly gendered. Their insights promise to be instructive here.

The above suggestions are only an introduction to the myriad ways feminist expertise might be brought to bear on the contests inherent to processes of deepening integration in North America. Fionnuala Ní Aoláin makes a similar point in this volume (chapter 18) about the need for a gender dimension in the establishment, revision, and operation of new legal and political institutions in "transition societies." Indeed, we might borrow from feminist theory developed in the context of transitional or post-conflict constitutionalism. Of course, it is not a perfect analogue. There are very particular sorts of violence and disruption endemic to the "transitional" societies discussed by Professor Ní Aoláin, unique to those places/spaces. But the central insights are arguably applicable across contexts where violence and disruption take different forms. The "transition" frame is therefore a useful way for thinking about integration, especially as it focuses on the movement from former to newer forms of state institutions and governance.

There are other examples of institutional evolution in which feminists have participated, or about which there are feminist critiques. A good example is the process by which Canada's new constitution was ratified in 1982. "Very broad and comprehensive equality guarantees were entrenched in the Canadian constitution ... as a result of the largest lobbying and participatory effort ever mounted by 'ordinary Canadian citizens'" (Spitz 2005). Feminist discourse emerged as a critical component of the processes of negotiation and implementation of the Canadian constitution, especially the Charter of Rights and Freedoms. Ultimately and primarily as a result of feminist theories and feminist lawyering, the Supreme Court of Canada held that government action will be reviewed and laws struck down if they discriminate against someone on the basis of their sex (among other things), regardless of whether the laws were intended to have that effect and whether it could be proved that the discrimination had been felt by anyone else of the same sex. This principle looks something like strict scrutiny for sex/gender in the American context. But it goes even further. The Supreme Court of Canada has told Canadian courts that substantive equality must inform the interpretation and application of all other rules in Canada. At the same time, this jurisprudence is not without its critics—many of them feminist. Thus, feminists have engaged and re-engaged with Canadian constitutional law from multiple points of view at every stage of its evolution. These engagements have been constitutive of intersecting identities and produced multiple, intersecting jurisprudences. Such engagements demonstrate the value and transformative potential of feminist participation in the creation and development of state institutions *at the earliest stages*.

So far I have argued that North American integration presents an opportunity for feminists to contribute to the evolution of a "more responsive state" in the US by looking beyond its national borders to the potential for transnational and inter-systemic institutions to advance the interests of social justice and social welfare of ordinary people. Moreover, institutional theory reminds us that the institutionalization of a North American space requires our involvement at the earliest stages if we don't want to be relegated to the role of critic after-the-fact. Happily, feminisms offer integration theories a panoply of insights and methods that promise to improve their relevance and potential.

This convergence of feminist interests and expertise does not mean that there will be unambiguous (or even any) support for our involvement. In the context of Europe, Catherine Hoskyns observes:

> As far as theory is concerned, it is interesting that there has been far less engagement by feminists with integration theory than with the "parent" discipline of international relations. In that field, feminist interventions were regarded as so disruptive that a defence had to be mounted ... This involved a paternalist attempt to tell feminists what kind of theorizing was and was not acceptable. Things have not yet reached that level on the European front and indifference is still the main weapon used against any likely incursions. There are a number of possible reasons for this ... However, it should be remembered that feminists in international relations were beginning to attack the rationalist/market forces assumptions in the discipline and therefore threatening its foundations. Were this to happen in respect of integration theory then a much stronger response could be expected.
>
> (Hoskyns 2004: 234)

Of course this is true, and we would be surprised otherwise; but, it argues in the direction of more and louder involvement, not less. One of the key differences between European integration and North American integration is timing. Feminists came to the process late in Europe. By contrast, North American integration is sufficiently different and younger that feminism might "join in" at the developmental stage of integration theories' adaptation to the North American continent, and I am hopeful that feminist integration theories might emerge in North America.

The form, scope, and implications of continental integration are not well understood, presenting empirical and theoretical challenges. Feminist integration theories might examine the mechanisms by which integration and resistance to integration occurs; the processes by which economic, legal, social, cultural, and political integration(s) constrain, inform, and enable one another; the ways that integration intersects with domestic law-making; the potential for integration to improve the democratic participation and overall social welfare of North Americans *at the North American level*; a comparison with other regional integrations; and an interrogation of possible unintended consequences of strategies under consideration. My hope is that an emphasis on integration as a potentially progressive set of practices will provoke a reconsideration of national (and constitutional) approaches to equality and justice, at the same time that it presents opportunities for developing sub-national, transnational, and supranational institutions better suited than the nation-state to respond in the ways Fineman proposed.

Conclusion

Fineman is not alone in contemporary calls for a more responsive state. On the heels of recent political, economic, and cultural crises in the US, many ordinary citizens are calling on government for some combination of intervention, regulation, protection, and support. That said, at no time in history has the US been as committed by international treaties and other agreements to a continued course of domestic deregulation and non-interference. The seemingly irresolvable set of tensions presented by this impasse can be seen in President Obama's stance on the NAFTA. He assures world leaders of his intention to comply with international trade obligations, even as he assures the American public that he intends to protect American workers and America products from the harms posed by so-called free trade. His dilemma points to larger systemic fractures in the classic Westphalian system of nation-state governance in North America. We find ourselves at a place where domestic institutions have been rendered structurally incapable of providing the public goods one typically associates with a well-functioning government in Western democracies. At the same time, North American integration has uniformly failed to establish legitimate institutions with the jurisdiction and competence to fill those gaps.

Early activist responses to this impasse were largely anti-integration or anti-globalization. Bracketing for a moment the contested nature of integration and globalization, social justice and social welfare advocates in Canada, the US, and Mexico have largely argued for a reassertion of the nation-state as the bulwark against so-called free trade and attendant erosions of national safeguards and national culture. These positions depend, in part, on a conflation of transnational capitalism and transnational integration (or regionalism). Yet, nothing about integration *qua* integration portends the institutionalization of a particular set of values, nor closes the transformative process to particular institutional actors. In this opening is its radical potential. An answer to various critiques regarding the failures of public/state institutions in meeting ordinary people's needs is to create new institutions.

North American integration presents a rare and radical opportunity to rethink national and constitutional approaches to equality and justice. It also provides an opportunity to develop transnational and supranational institutions for the same purpose. This claim is compelling because it is possible and necessary. By virtue of this precise mix of conditions, the possibility for theorizing a positive architecture or framework for continental integration emerges as an opportunity for feminist intervention. In charting the way forward, feminist theorists and practitioners should be guided by a notion of engagement with the institutions of social, legal, political, and economic ordering that conceive of power as localized, dynamic, and permeable to such intervention. Beginning from such a premise permits us to imagine a "state" that might be constituted differently: more responsive, more just, and more attentive to human vulnerability.

Engaging politics

Introduction to Section Seven

Politics is a broad subject that permeates much of feminist legal theory. Feminists insisted during the 1960s that the personal was the political. The 2008 presidential campaign by Hillary Clinton illustrated that feminist thought and political strategy are often intertwined. However, as the chapters in this section show, feminist thought when it encounters political theory and discourse or political institutions often encounters deeply entrenched assumptions about gender, as well as beliefs about what is natural, normal, and desirable in politics and society. While the chapters in Section One of this book showed law's reluctance to embrace feminist theory, these last chapters show that politics and political thought may be equally resistant to fundamental change.

Holning Lau's chapter considers how gender scripting undermines the "reason-giving conversations" at the heart of deliberative democracy in three main ways. First, gender scripts create barriers to participation in democratic deliberation, so typically only women who negotiate femininity in certain ways can mount successful political campaigns. Second, the need to negotiate gender scripts can distort deliberative conversations among politicians because scripting often involves self-censorship. Finally, identity scripts distort the way communications are received by public. A woman politician who cries in public can seem weak, while a man may be seen as sensitive.

After discussing the harms gender scripting can produce, Lau suggests a redirection for feminist theory. He argues that, even though we are not in a "post-gender era," group-based identity is not necessarily useful. He contends that group-oriented approaches can actually obscure the fact that gender still matters and that power inequalities do exist. The 2008 elections showed power and disadvantage not neatly tied to group identities but associated with willingness and ability to negotiate identity scripts.

Lau ultimately uses his idea of identity scripts to argue for a "democracy reinforcement theory," wherein courts can review laws if they cause some impairment to democratic process. Laws involving gender scripts, because they impair democracy by creating barriers, distorting conversation, and misleading the public, would receive heightened scrutiny under democracy reinforcement theory. He employs the same-sex marriage debate as a specific example of how this would play out. Gender scripts are central in arguments for bans on same-sex marriage. Lau argues that removing the limitation on access to marriage for same-sex couples would thus result in also reducing the power of gender scripts.

Victoria Nourse's personal essay reflects on her role as a "minor player" in some of the major moments of late twentieth-century legal drama. We follow her from Iran Contra to Anita Hill, with an extended peak at the internal history of the passage of the Violence Against Women Act and the disappointing repeal of its civil rights remedy by the Supreme Court.

Nourse sees this world through a particular theoretical lens: one of constitutional change that views the Constitution as something that "constitutes" political life. It does so through various actors: the branches of government, the states, and the citizen.

She argues that the Constitution necessarily changes as those who constitute the nation change. In spite of the Supreme Court's repeal of the VAWA civil rights remedy for women, Nourse believes that one day the emerging constitutional consensus on women's rights will lead society to the point where a world that existed before Title VII, sexual harassment, discrimination, family leave and violence against women laws would be unimaginable.

Martha T. McCluskey argues that feminist theory is helpful in "countering the ideological and material barriers to equality amassed during the right's rule." She contends that the right's anti-egalitarian ideology is based on two assertions. The first is that some "objective" economic principles lead to the conclusion that substantive equality is really all about giving special benefits to a few at the expense of others. Second, the right's morality argument places personal responsibility with the disadvantaged and expects them to correct existing power hierarchies, not the institutions that have created or maintained those hierarchies. Seeking legal protection rather than exercising personal responsibility when you are disadvantaged is not about seeking equality but about demanding "reverse discrimination" and usurping another's rightful place. Inequality is thus necessary and natural, although the disadvantaged will get some "trickle down" crumbs from an ever-expanding pie.

McCluskey suggests essentially two strategies to resist the right's "ideological and material shadow." She argues that feminists must engage law's foundational theories and reframe the questions. An example would be to redefine the "pie" as not just dollars amassed by the wealthy in a given quarter, but as measured by the "long-term health and education of non-wealthy women and children." Deconstructing the terms "personal responsibility" and "independence" would reveal that businesses frequently rely on government support and that caretaking work is vital to society—thus government has a role to play in supporting caretaking.

McCluskey also urges feminists to engage on three fundamental levels of challenge to existing arrangements: confront the politics of law; reveal and understand the societal power of law; and recognize and engage with the complexity of identity. She argues that critical feminist theory can look at underlying policies and institutional structures that support current identity-based divisions and help us move toward crafting better ways to build coalitions.

The economic crisis and presidential election of Barack Obama may suggest the end of the right's rule, offering new opportunities for substantive equality. McCluskey encourages feminists to reach beyond the boundaries of existing law, politics, and gender identity to provide the foundation for progressive reform to take root and thrive.

Chapter 21

Gender scripting and deliberative democracy[1]

Holning Lau

Introduction

Two thousand eight was a banner year for women in politics. The presidential elections featured Hillary Clinton, whom President Obama narrowly defeated during the Democratic primaries, and Sarah Palin, the Republican nominee for Vice President. Before 2008, no woman had come as close as Clinton did to becoming a major political party's presidential nominee and only once before had a woman been the vice presidential nominee.

While 2008 marked significant progress in women's political prominence, it also illuminated gender scripting's lingering effects on American democracy. For example, members of the media treated Palin's motherhood and Clinton's tears as liabilities because they were associated with scripts for femininity. Meanwhile, parts of the media condemned John Edward's expensive haircuts as breaches of masculinity.

Legal commentators have typically focused on explicating gender scripts' harmful effects on individuals or on women as a class. In this chapter, I take a different tack, exploring gender scripts' harms to deliberative democracy. Gender scripts stifle deliberative democracy in at least three ways. First, they create barriers to participation in democratic deliberation. For example, only women who negotiate femininity in particular ways manage to mount the political stage. By unduly limiting the scope of individuals who successfully mount the political stage, gender scripts undermine the collective ideal of democratic governance. Second, pressures to negotiate gender scripts distort deliberative conversations among political actors because script negotiation often entails self-censorship. Third, deliberation is further impaired because identity scripts distort the way communications are received among political actors.

In the remainder of this chapter, I begin by elaborating on gender scripts and how they impair deliberative democracy in the three regards just highlighted. I then draw from that discussion to suggest directions for feminist theory. Examining gender scripts' effects on deliberative democracy suggests that group-oriented approaches to feminist analysis obscure some problematic power inequalities. As was the case in the 2008 elections, power and disadvantage often are not neatly tethered to group identities—such as one's biological sex—but are associated with one's ability and willingness to negotiate identity scripts. This chapter invites feminist legal scholars to focus more attention on these inequalities that do not map neatly onto group demarcations. In the last part of this chapter, I examine how gender scripts' effects on democracy should inform the debate on same-sex marriage. Specifically, I argue that gender scripts' effects on democracy buttress existing arguments for same-sex marriage.

Background on gender scripts

I use the phrase "gender script" to refer to expectations imposed on individuals based on their perceived biological sex. Although some writers use the terms "identity scripts" and "stereotypes" synonymously, I consider scripts to be the aggregation of stereotypes. Various stereotypes about women—that women carry themselves softly, possess nurturing qualities, partner with men, prioritize family over career—coalesce to form a femininity script. The notion of scripts suggests connectivity among stereotypes. In this regard, identity scripts are analogous to dramatic scripts. If someone were to turn on the television and recognize a scene from *Romeo and Juliet*, he would likely infer that the lovers on screen will tragically end their lives. Recognizing one scene in the well-known Shakespearean script triggers inferences based on the script. Psychological literature on "implicit personality theory" suggests a similar dynamic exists with regard to stereotypes (Ashmore and Del Boca 1979: 220; Schneider 2004: 194–945). For example, if a woman conforms to part of a femininity script, people whose thinking is influenced by stereotypes will infer that she stays on script by adhering to other feminine stereotypes.

Individuals negotiate identity scripts by alternatively performing and rejecting scripts. A paradigmatic example of script negotiation involves female employees in corporate settings. Consider a law firm partner who ascribes a femininity script to his female associate. To advance her career, the associate will likely negotiate that gender script by toeing a fine line—at times, rejecting the script to convey that she is assertive enough to compete in male-dominated environments and, at other times, performing the script to avoid stigma imposed on aggressive women (Yoshino 2006a: 145–54).

The negotiation of identity scripts, especially the rejection of scripts, is burdensome. Humans' cognitive biases make gender stereotypes difficult to reject. Social science research suggests that people are prone to mentally register instances where individuals conform to stereotypes, but not instances where individuals break stereotypes (Hilton and Von Hippel 1996: 251–52; Krieger 1995: 1197–98). As a result, in order for the female law associate to break feminine stereotypes of passivity, she likely would need to take extra steps to convey her assertiveness, perhaps speaking up more often and more forcefully than her male peers.

The connectivity among gender scripts' stereotypes further complicates the script negotiation process. To reject the stereotype of passivity, our hypothetical law associate would likely need to reject other aspects of femininity as well. For example, she has incentives to self-censor discussions of her children because her colleagues may be prone to inferring that women who adhere to nurturing stereotypes also adhere to passivity stereotypes (Schneider 2004: 195).

To be sure, the negotiation of gender scripts is more burdensome to some individuals than to others. For example, compared to a mother who lives with her children, a single woman who lives alone may find it more convenient to self-censor discussions of family life. Similarly, for some women, rejecting stereotypes of passivity may not pose a challenge because being especially assertive feels natural to them. These examples do not, however, detract from the fact that femininity scripts impose burdens. While men may be presumed to be relatively assertive, women often have a burden of proof; they need to demonstrate their assertiveness by disconfirming femininity scripts. Of course, that is not to say that men do not have their own gender scripts to negotiate. Power typically adheres to men who conform to a masculinity script. For many men, conforming to masculinity will feel natural. However, for the man who self-identifies with effeminate traits, such conformity will be a greater challenge.

For the remainder of this chapter, I focus on script negotiations in the political sphere, specifically in deliberative democracy. Political theorists have increasingly accepted deliberative democracy as the most desirable aspiration for American government (Dryzek 2000: 1). Deliberative democracy is a form of governance in which state actions are authorized by collective decision-making among persons engaged in free and reasoned deliberation. Conversations based on public-regarding reasons are central to deliberative democracy. That is to say, political actors are expected to provide reasons why their policy positions are desirable not just for themselves, but for the public. These reason-giving conversations promote decision-making that is collective—not only in the sense that governance is "by the people" but also "for the people." In deliberative democracy, legitimacy does not reside in sheer numbers. Instead, majority rule exists because, if a majority chooses one option over another, one generally presumes that a process of deliberation led the majority to view that option more favorably (Benhabib 1996; Gutmann and Thompson 2004). The following three sections will explore how gender scripts undermine the reason-giving conversations that are central to deliberative democracy, creating a democratic deficit. Due to space limitation, the observations below are intended only as the beginning of a larger discussion beyond these pages concerning gender scripts' effects on democratic deliberation.

Barriers to entry

Femininity scripts were a hurdle between our hypothetical lawyer and her firm's upper echelon. To overcome that barrier, the associate needed to negotiate femininity. Similarly, gender scripts create barriers to individuals' participation in democratic deliberation as elected officials. Consider the case of Sarah Palin. Some political commentators questioned how Palin could concurrently raise young children and serve as vice president, even though male candidates with young children were not similarly questioned. These critics ascribed to Palin a femininity script that portrays women as nurturing mothers who put family commitments before professional responsibilities. In many regards, Palin performed parts of a femininity script; for example, she competed in beauty pageants when she was younger, became a mother who served on the PTA, and usually opted for skirts over pantsuits. Critics seemed to connect these performances of femininity to infer that Palin would continue to adhere to the script by putting childrearing before professional duties. In this case, gender scripting became a barrier to Palin's political rise.

Gender scripts do not always become obstacles for women the way they did for Sarah Palin. For example, in a much publicized episode, Governor Ed Rendell of Pennsylvania remarked that Janet Napolitano was the perfect pick for Secretary of Homeland Security because she did not have a family. Commentators suggested that Rendell would not have made the remark if Napolitano were a man (Porter 2008; Scolforo 2008). Rendell's comments suggest that women can rise to high office only if they disconfirm the caregiver image inherent in femininity scripts.

Gender scripts have also burdened male politicians. Recall that mainstream media outlets brandished both John Edwards and John Kerry for failing to comport with masculinity scripts—Edwards because of his expensive haircuts and Kerry because of his penchant for French vacations, which were portrayed as being overly "girly" (Dery 2007). What if a hypothetical male candidate not only had concern for his hair and a penchant for French vacations, but also had an earring in his right ear and a lisp? Prejudice against this man for breaching masculinity scripts would likely limit his political career.

These cases suggest that gender scripts create barriers to individuals' participation in democratic deliberation. To be sure, each of the individuals mentioned above contributed to political discourse as candidates. Nonetheless, gender scripts formed barriers to their mounting a higher political stage that would enhance their deliberative power. To overcome these barriers, each candidate needed to negotiate the gender scripts ascribed to him or her.

The examples of Palin, Napolitano, Edwards, and Kerry illuminate inequalities in deliberative power based on individuals' negotiation of gender scripts. These inequalities are troubling because, among political theorists, a well-accepted precondition for democracy is that people have relatively equal opportunity to influence politics (Dahl 2006: ix). Inequalities of deliberative power undermine the collective nature of democracy. Inequalities of deliberative power are only acceptable if they are supported by public-regarding reasons (Lau 2010: 935–36; Sunstein 1998). Reason does not, however, support the imposition of script negotiation as a burden on political candidates. As the

Supreme Court noted in *Frontiero v. Richardson* (1973: 686), "sex characteristic[s] frequently bear[] no relation to ability to perform or contribute to society." In that vein, sex-differentiated conditions for political contribution are generally unjustified. Requiring candidates to negotiate different scripts based on their sex unduly limits the scope of individuals who can attain high political office, compromising the collective nature of democratic rule (Lau 2010: 916–20).

Distorting output

Gender scripts also distort deliberation by regulating the output of communication. Consider Hillary Clinton in the 2008 presidential primary race. Clinton had to negotiate scripts that portray women as inherently weak and, therefore, unable to lead the country as commander-in-chief. Many political commentators suspected that Clinton adopted a hawkish position on the war in Iraq to disprove assumptions of weakness (Barber 2008; CNN 2008b; Halloran 2008). Taking a policy position in order to negotiate an identity script does not itself qualify as public-regarding reasoning, which is essential to deliberative democracy (Lau 2010: 920–27).

In this regard, femininity scripts tainted deliberation on issues of national security. Recall that reason-giving conversations form the core of deliberative democracy. These conversations are supposed to have instrumental value by promoting government actions that are better informed and better thought through (Benhabib 1996). If Clinton self-censors reasons to reject the Iraq war or exaggerates reasons to support the war for the purposes of script negotiation, deliberation is tainted. The conversation becomes deprived of information that would otherwise have contributed to the instrumental value of deliberation.

Certainly, there may be reasons to support a hawkish approach to the Iraq war, and it is only speculation that Clinton strategically altered her opinions to negotiate identity scripts. It is possible that Clinton's positions felt natural and authentic to her, but we may never know for sure. As Kenji Yoshino (2006a: 149) has suggested, the relevant inquiry should not be whether any particular individual has "covered" her authentic identity, but whether there are pressures to cover in the first place. As long as there are strong incentives for women to self-censor for the purposes of script negotiation, a large question mark looms over the deliberative process. At the very least, the incentives created by gender scripts cast doubt on the deliberative process. We are left to wonder to what extent incentives to self-censor undermined reason-giving conversations.

To be clear, sex is not the only axis of identity along which harmful identity scripting stifles communicative output. Elsewhere, I have written on how identity scripts based on race and religion likely created incentives for Barack Obama to distort communications during his campaign. I have also written on how Michelle Obama possibly toned down her support of affirmative action in order to negotiate the intersectional script of the angry black woman, which is both sex-specific and race-specific (Lau 2010: 921–24).

Although this chapter has mainly focused on the deliberative power of politicians, I should note that some democratic theorists conceptualize the political sphere more broadly, acknowledging the role that the media and, indeed, ordinary citizens play in democratic deliberation (Benhabib 1996: 72). Identity scripts stymie the communicative output of journalists and ordinary citizens, just as they stymie output by politicians. Ordinary citizens negotiate identity scripts in everyday political conversations. Recall that female law firm associates have incentives to reject femininity scripts. Accordingly, a female associate who engages colleagues in political conversation over lunch has incentives to mute stereotypically feminine policy positions.

Identity scripts also distort communicative outputs of journalists. Discussions among journalists of color provide insight into the relationship between identity scripts and journalism. National Public Radio recently featured two segments on the experiences of African-American reporters. Numerous African-American journalists expressed concern that they were being held to a uniquely high standard, according to which any hint of positive reaction to Barack Obama— even clapping when Obama enters a room—would be derided as black bias inherent to black identity. Objectivity is certainly an important value in journalism. The concern of black journalists was that standards for objectivity vary from one journalist to another depending on the racial scripts ascribed to the journalist. These disparate standards generate incentives for black journalists to self-censor to a degree that is unnecessary by general standards of journalistic objectivity. One can hypothesize that gender scripts, like racial scripts, also create incentives for journalists to self-censor excessively (Mitchell 2008; NPR 2008a, 2008b; Thomas 2008).

Distorting input

Gender scripts not only cause individuals to self-censor; they also warp conversations by distorting the way messages are received. These two dynamics are closely related. Consider, again, the example of Hillary Clinton and national security. What if Clinton had rejected the Iraq war? Others likely would have dismissed her position, not on its merits, but because it was stereotypically feminine and, therefore, considered weak. The very same rejection of the war is received differently when the speaker has not been ascribed a femininity script. Interestingly, the script portraying black men as hypermasculine has typically been an unjustified burden on black men, but the ascription of black masculinity may have helped Barack Obama to speak out against the Iraq war without being dismissed as being weak (Cooper 2009; Lau 2010: 927).

During the 2008 primary race, some of the mainstream media homed in on this dynamic of distorted reception when Hillary Clinton almost shed a tear in public, after someone asked her about the travails of campaigning. Much of the country took that incident as evidence that Clinton hews to feminine identity and would be too weak to serve as president. Some commentators later noted, however, that tears are received differently when they fall from the eyes of male politicians (Freedman 2008; Scherer 2008.) In fact, male politicians have been deemed desirably sensitive for shedding tears. That was the case with Ronald Reagan (Scherer 2008). Again, this sort of biased reception stifles democratic deliberation. Conversations become stymied because ascribed identity scripts figuratively plug listeners' ears.

Directions for feminist theory and constitutional theory

Examining the relationship between gender and deliberative democracy sheds light on feminist theory and constitutional theory. The preceding sections illuminate how group-oriented approaches to feminist analysis are important, but insufficient. We are reminded to attend to harms of gender scripting that are not readily apparent by focusing on power dynamics between men and women as groups. This section elaborates on this script-oriented approach to feminist analysis and its specific implications for constitutional theory.

Leaders such as Hillary Clinton and Sarah Palin surely stand on the shoulders of feminists who paved the way for them through advocacy that focused on the rights of women as a group. As Clinton noted during her speech at the Democratic National Convention, she spoke on the 88th anniversary of women's suffrage (Faludi 2008). Such overt discrimination as denial of voting rights is unfortunately not that distant a memory. In addition, many structural inequalities continue to place specific burdens on women. Legal scholars should be mindful of these dynamics and continue working to advance the rights and well-being of women.

Focusing on men and women as groups, however, has limitations. One limitation is that it obscures inequalities within groups. A large body of antiessentialist feminist literature has criticized social understandings of women and men as monolithic entities (e.g. Cain 1994; Harris 2000; Wong 1999). Much of this writing focuses on explaining intragroup inequalities that result from the intersection of identity axes such as race and gender—for example, inequalities between white women and women of color (Crenshaw 1989, 1991). The preceding discussion of gender and deliberative democracy reminds us that inequalities also exist based on individuals' capacity for script negotiation. As the discussion of Janet Napolitano suggested, women who are mothers may often be unduly disadvantaged compared to single women who can more easily disconfirm caregiving stereotypes. Similarly, men who breach masculinity scripts are disadvantaged compared to men who adhere to masculinity scripts. The distribution of disadvantage and privilege associated with script negotiation falls along a continuum, corresponding with individuals' capacities for script negotiation. For the reasons discussed above, the inequalities that transcend the male–female binary compromise democratic deliberation.

Relatedly, while it is worth trying to identify group-based power differentials for law to remedy, attempts to identify group-based differentials are sometimes under-determinate. It is unclear what electing individual women to higher office ultimately means for the political influence of women as a group. Feminists have questioned whether Margaret Thatcher, Angela Merkel, and Sarah Palin represent women's best interests (Gould 1996; Steinem 2008). During the 2008 campaign season, some commentators suggested that Barack Obama better represented women's interests than did Hillary Clinton (Marin 2008; Sullivan 2008a). Meanwhile, other commentators have suggested that, with Clinton's and Palin's prominence in the 2008 elections, the United States is already in a post-gender era (Maese 2008). This chapter's preceding analysis demonstrates, however, that the country most certainly is not yet in a post-gender era; this reality might be obfuscated by a narrow focus on group-based assessments.

Ultimately, analysis focused on power dynamics between men and women obscures gender scripts' enduring systemic harms to democratic deliberation. For example, Hillary Clinton's political ascent has been celebrated—rightly so—as empowering women. However, focusing attention on Clinton's impact on women loses sight of potential costs to democracy associated with Clinton's rise, such as her potential self-censorship due to gender scripting on the campaign trail. Of course, self-censorship is not inherently at odds with democratic deliberation; however, self-censorship that is motivated by gender negotiation, and not by public-regarding reasons, contravenes tenets of deliberative democracy. By distorting the marketplace of ideas, such self-censorship harms democratic society at large. Gender scripting not only compromises democracy by fostering self-censorship; it also stymies democratic deliberation by distorting the reception of communications and by creating problematic barriers to entry.

By shedding light on the harmful relationship between gender scripting and democracy, this chapter buttresses the argument that gender scripts are problematic, even if they do not reinforce clear group-based subordination. Feminists such as Sylvia Law and Mary Anne Case have long argued that scripting is harmful regardless of its group-based effects. For example, reacting to laws that codify stereotypes, Law (1984: 969) argued that the government should protect "each person's ability to define herself or himself, free from sex-defined legal constraints." Similarly, Case (2002: 1472–73) has argued that ' "fixed notions concerning the roles and abilities of males and females' are problematic when embedded in law, even in law that does not in any articulable way subordinate women to men." Law and Case criticized gender scripting because it constrains individuals' self-definition. This chapter extends that critique of gender scripting: not only does gender scripting impair self-authorship; it has the aggregate effect of impairing democracy.

Acknowledging that gender scripts stifle deliberative democracy has consequences for constitutional theory—specifically for a prominent school of constitutional thought, which I will refer to as democracy reinforcement theory. Democracy reinforcement theorists argue that the Constitution should be interpreted in a manner that strengthens democracy (Ely 1998; Lau 2010;

Schacter 2004; Sunstein 1998). Merging feminist theory and democracy reinforcement theory suggests that courts should interpret the Constitution in a
manner that combats gender scripting, because combating gender scripts
strengthens democratic deliberation. It is unfeasible to rehearse here the reasons
why democracy reinforcement theory is desirable compared to competing
theories of constitutional interpretation. To be clear, I do not believe that
democracy reinforcement provides a comprehensive approach to constitutional
interpretation. As I have argued elsewhere, however, democracy reinforcement
theory is a particularly useful interpretive principle in the context of equality
jurisprudence (Lau 2010: 933–34).

According to democracy reinforcement theory, courts should have greater
power than usual to give legislation a hard second look when legislation
implicates democratic impairment (Lau 2010: 934–41; Sunstein 1998: 30, 142).
Democracy reinforcement theory reconciles the tension between judicial review
and democratic rule, which results in the so-called counter-majoritarian
difficulty. Judges' heightened review of laws that *cause* democratic impairment
reinforces democracy because doing so can improve democratic function. When
judges exercise heightened review of laws that are the *effects* of democratic
impairment, judges are not trumping democracy because the laws flowed from
flawed democratic processes in the first place. Because gender scripting impairs
deliberative democracy, laws that strongly implicate gender scripting warrant
heightened scrutiny.

The following section applies the theoretical points developed thus far to the
debate on same-sex marriage. The relationship between gender scripting and
democracy should inform the debate on same-sex marriage—both in discourse
generally and in litigation specifically.

Same-sex marriage

Except in Connecticut, the District of Columbia Iowa, Massachusetts, New
Hampshire, and Vermont, legal marriage in the United States is limited to
opposite-sex couples. This status quo implicates gender scripting in two regards.
On one hand, gender scripts are invoked to maintain bans on same-sex marriage.
On the other hand, bans on same-sex marriage entrench those very same scripts.

Deborah Widiss, Elizabeth Rosenblatt, and Douglas Nejaime recently described three ways in which gender scripts are invoked to justify bans on same-
sex marriage. First, advocates of the status quo argue that marriage should be
limited to opposite-sex couples because men and women perform opposite
and complementary roles within marriage. Second, these advocates argue that
marriage is meant to bring together men and women to create an ideal setting
for childrearing, that is to say, a setting that includes gender-complementary
male and female role models. Third, they argue that marriage is necessary
to protect vulnerable women from men who, without the stabilizing force of
marriage, would abandon the couple's children. Of course, all three of these

arguments presuppose that men and women adhere to socially constructed, complementary gender scripts (Widiss et al. 2007).

These gender scripts feed into the current understanding of marriage and are entrenched by same-sex marriage bans. Certainly, marriage laws do not explicitly require husbands and wives to perform complementary gender roles. For example, husbands are legally free to be homemakers, and wives are free to be breadwinners. Nonetheless, the above-described arguments against same-sex marriage feed into people's social understanding of marriage; therefore, many people expect opposite-sex couples who marry to adhere to complementary gender scripts. Laws that ban same-sex marriage legitimize and, therefore, entrench these gendered expectations. Moreover, social science literature suggests that merely categorizing individuals by group labels typically reifies socially constructed differences between the groups (Anastasio et al. 1997; Krieger 1995: 1191–92; Oakes 1998: 97–98; Operario and Fiske 1999: 26). In that vein, laws that define marriage as uniting "one man" with "one woman" reify social expectations of men and women as groups.

Indeed, the sociologist Steven Nock referred to marriage as a "gender factory." To clarify how marriage reproduces gender roles, Nock offered the example of unemployed men for whom being a husband means performing a masculinity script:

> [I]n a two-earner marriage, the rational husband would do more housework if he were to become unemployed. Unemployed husbands, however, do exactly the opposite. Shortly after losing their jobs, such men actually reduce their housework labor. For a married man to be unemployed is to deviate from cultural scripts of masculine identity. For such a man to assume responsibility for the "feminine" tasks of housework would be even more deviant.
>
> (Nock 2000: 1977)

Marriage laws perpetuate such gender scripting by distinguishing between men and women, implicitly endorsing the notion that men and women perform separate gender scripts. Undoing marriage laws' differentiation between men and women would abate the laws' implicit signal that women are to perform a particular role as wives while men perform a particular role as husbands (Appleton 2005: 116; Case 2002: 1488; Hunter 1991: 9; McClain 2006: 179–80). Advocates of same-sex marriage would be well served to raise public consciousness on how marriage reinforces gender stereotypes. Indeed, feminist legal scholar Susan Appleton (2005) has called for increased "gender talk" in public discourse on same-sex marriage. Such consciousness-raising conversations would be enriched by recognizing gender scripting's far-reaching effects, including its effects on democracy.

While gender talk is important to discourse on same-sex marriage generally, talking about gender's impact on deliberative democracy is particularly important to constitutional challenges against same-sex marriage bans. Specifically, script-oriented democracy reinforcement theory should inform judicial review of same-sex marriage bans. According to script-oriented democracy reinforcement theory, marriage laws' sex distinctions warrant heightened scrutiny.

Bans on same-sex marriage treat men and women differently insofar as the laws embody a sex distinction. For example, a woman who wishes to marry her female partner cannot do so because she is a woman; she would, however, be able to marry her partner if she were a man. As such, the law treats her in a particular way due to her sex. In same-sex marriage litigation, one of the couples' typical arguments is that these sex distinctions amount to disparate treatment on the basis of sex, triggering heightened scrutiny. In these cases, most state court justices have either ignored or rejected this sex discrimination argument for same-sex marriage. They typically note correctly that the sex distinctions apply equally to both men and women. That is to say, even though the law differentiates between two groups of people—men and women—both groups have their marriage options limited based on their sex. These justices then reason that equal application of the sex distinction neutralizes any disparate treatment and that equally applied sex distinctions ought not to trigger heightened scrutiny unless the distinctions were intended to entrench—or have the effect of entrenching—group-based hierarchy. Because they do not believe that marriage laws subordinate women to men, or vice versa, they refuse to review same-sex marriage bans under heightened scrutiny (Lau 2008; Williams 2007).

In essence, these justices have created a group-subordination test: equally applied sex distinctions must subordinate a particular sex to trigger heightened scrutiny. These justices distinguish same-sex marriage bans from the anti-miscegenation law in *Loving v. Virginia*, noting that the latter was enacted to reinforce white supremacy; therefore, antimiscegenation laws' equally applied race distinctions passed the judicially constructed group-subordination test (Lau 2008; Williams 2007).

Commentators have argued that rejecting the sex discrimination argument for same-sex marriage is incorrect. Some have maintained that sex distinctions in marriage laws do subordinate women and, therefore, satisfy a group-subordination test (Appleton 2005: 105; Koppelman 2002: 64–70). Others argue that justices who have rejected the sex discrimination argument have misread *Loving v. Virginia*, which did not embody a group-subordination test (Appleton 2005: 107; Koppelman 2002: 63–64; Lau 2008). In addition, commentators have argued that group subordination ought not to be a requirement for heightened scrutiny because marriage laws' sex distinctions reinforce gender scripting, which is itself problematic because scripting inhibits personal autonomy (Appleton 2005: 107).

Script-oriented democracy reinforcement theory extends this last argument. Gender scripting not only burdens individuals by limiting individuals' authority to shape their own lives; at a systemic level, gender scripts compromise political deliberation. In the interest of democracy reinforcement, courts should eschew the group-subordination test and subject marriage laws' sex distinctions to heightened scrutiny. Because bans on same-sex marriage implicate a democratic deficit associated with gender scripting, courts have good reason to subject bans on same-sex marriage to heightened scrutiny.

Traditional democracy reinforcement theory supports the group-subordination test. Theorists such as Cass Sunstein (1998: 143–44) have argued persuasively that, if a law perpetuates group-based hierarchy between sexes, the law perpetuates a democratic deficit because group-based hierarchies undermine the democratic ideal of collective governance. For this reason, courts should review laws that subordinate a particular sex with heightened scrutiny. *Script-oriented* democracy reinforcement theory reminds us, however, that laws perpetuating gender scripts also impair democracy even if they do not reify group subordination; accordingly, these laws should also trigger heightened review (Lau 2010: 938–39).

Because marriage laws are both informed by—and perpetuate—gender scripts, courts should be particularly skeptical of them. Consider the New York Court of Appeals, which held in *Hernandez v. Robles* (2006: 6) that

> the legislature could rationally proceed on the common-sense premise that children will do best with a mother and father in the home … [i]ntuition and experience suggest that a child benefits from having before his or her eyes, every day, living models of what both a man and a woman are like.

This language referring to a model man and a model woman implies that there are scripts for being a man and for being a woman. These scripts stifle democratic deliberation. It is such scripts that motivated members of the media to question whether Palin could juggle motherhood and vice presidential duties. Those gender scripts also created the incentives for Hillary Clinton to adopt policy positions to negate expectations of nurturing qualities and weakness. It was also gender scripts that caused people to view Clinton's tears differently from Reagan's.

Rather than accepting marriage laws' gender scripting in conclusory fashion—as did the New York Court of Appeals—courts should review marriage laws' sex-based entry requirement with heightened scrutiny. Doing so would be warranted from a democratic standpoint because the courts would be reinforcing democratic function. It is worth reemphasizing that commentators have already argued that, from a strictly doctrinal standpoint, marriage laws embody sex discrimination that should be reviewed under heightened scrutiny (Lau 2008; Widiss et al. 2007); alternatively, one can read doctrine to include a categorical rule against government policies that stereotype based on sex, including same-sex marriage bans (Case 2002). This essay thickens the normative support for those doctrinal arguments. It does so by developing an understanding of how marriage laws foster gender scripts that stymie democratic function. By following doctrine that supports the sex discrimination argument for same-sex marriage, courts would not be trumping democratic rule. To the contrary, courts would be ameliorating gender-based impairments to deliberative democracy.

Conclusion

At this point in history, some might wonder whether identity-based theorizing has run its course. The rise of political actors such as Barack Obama and Hillary Clinton can sometimes obfuscate the lingering effects that race and gender still have on power dynamics, including dynamics concerning deliberative power. This chapter invites readers to continue to develop identity-based theories to address those lingering effects. To that end, this chapter has adopted a feminist approach that focuses less on group-based power differentials and concentrates more on identity scripts, remaining cognizant that the privileges and disadvantages tied to gender scripting do not always map neatly along group demarcations. While this chapter has sketched some of the ways gender scripting affects power dynamics in deliberative democracy, these sketches are by no means comprehensive. These sketches highlight—and encourage continued attention to—the far-reaching effects of gender scripting.

Note

1 Parts of this chapter have been adapted from the author's *Minnesota Law Review* article, "Identity Scripts & Democratic Deliberation," which addresses this chapter's topic in greater detail.

Chapter 22

The accidental feminist

Victoria F. Nourse

Act I: Fawn Hall's Boots

The year is 1987. The place is the Senate, a room all gilt and chandelier, filled with an impossibly large crowd, flashing cameras, and a man standing tall with medals on his uniform. Colonel North's presence captivates the country. His interrogator, Arthur Liman, tough, craggy, and insistent, is viewed by the nation with suspicion.

This is the Iran–Contra investigation, the Senate's attempt to unearth how President Reagan defied the Congress's ban on aid to Central American insurgents and, secretly, sold missiles to Iran to finance the Contras. I am 20-something years old, sitting behind Arthur Liman, the head of my New York law firm, one of the most brilliant lawyers in New York, and chief counsel to the Senate Iran–Contra committee. I am hardly the center of the show: I dive under my chair for documents as my boss moves from one to the other. When I learn that someone has taken out a death threat against Liman, and the marshals have swept the room for weapons, Liman takes me aside and asks if I want to leave; I stay but dive more quickly.

My friends occasionally liken my Washington career to that of a legal Zelig or Forrest Gump: a figure appearing in unimportant roles at various moments of high legal drama during the twentieth century, from Iran–Contra to Anita Hill. There is a certain truth to this. It is a story of benevolent tokenism and accident that befits a young woman standing on the edge of a political revolution propelled by a generation of women, far more brave and revolutionary than I. I was simply the woman in the room, holding a token's burden, not of her own making, which came with an increasing sense of obligation and personal transformation.

I was in Washington for a reason. I had billed an outrageous number of hours at Paul Weiss, my New York law firm, in the belief that even if there was only one woman litigation partner out of 100, if you worked harder, someone would notice. Shortly after my plum Iran–Contra assignment was announced, I had a rude awakening. A senior associate came into my office, pounding on my desk, and yelling: "Arthur cannot take you—you have no foreign policy experience!"

What he didn't say was that my choice was not driven by the outrageous number of hours I had billed but by what he believed to be affirmative action: I was chosen because I was a young woman.

Enter Fawn Hall's boots. Oliver North's secretary, Fawn Hall, richly implicated in the Iran–Contra scandal, was rumored to have smuggled damning documents out of the White House. One senator announced that Hall, a rather striking blonde, had taken the documents out in her bra. Hall replied angrily that the statement was "sexist," (*Washington Post* 1987: A9), and the senator was forced to retract. The mention of intimate attire may have caused panic: eventually Hall would testify that she absconded with the documents in her boots (Johnson 1987: A15). The lawyers on both sides, Oliver North's lawyer Brendan Sullivan, and the Senate's Arthur Liman, had young women sit by their side, presumably as symbolic protection against charges of sexism.

So began my political education. I could not have guessed that eventually this education would force me to confront an identity and a history that I would have preferred to deny. Nor could I guess it would inspire my study of how the Constitution changes—how "An Agreement with Hell," as William Lloyd Garrison put it, could over time transcend itself. I knew little about constitutional history at the time, but I did know that at our country's founding women were generally not permitted the right to make public speeches (Amar 1995). Sitting before the TV cameras, I never spoke, but my presence signaled enormous change in the status of women that had already and would continue to happen. I did not know at the time that I would play a minor role in the future politics of women's equality.

Act II: Joe Biden's Bill

The year is 1990. I am sitting in a room off the Senate Judiciary Committee. I have been hired from the Justice Department to negotiate habeas corpus reform legislation. Eventually, my portfolio of legislative matters would cover entire crime bills. But, on that day I was so new that the then-Chairman of the Committee, Senator Biden, did not know my name. I happened to be the only woman in the room. There were other women on the staff, but none in the room that day. Thus, I was handed the task to draft "something on women" for the "crime bill." That "something" would become the Violence Against Women Act (VAWA).

Though difficult to imagine now, 15 years ago prospects for major federal legislation on rape and battering were grim; some viewed the issue as politically dangerous. Yet, history, even of the recent past, allows us the power to challenge the moral arrogance of the present. As the great historian of science Thomas Kuhn once wrote to his students: begin with the incomprehensible. Only then will one make sense of the past to the present. I undertake this personal history with some trepidation; one never writes one's own narrative accurately. But my story rests upon a helpful paradox: I am *not the point* of the story. I was but a medium between generations, between the pioneer theorists and the young and brash and ignorant lawyers (like myself) they had spawned. I was a translator between feminist theory and political power on the cusp of a mini-revolution in the politics of violence and women's inequality.

The Kuhnian historical puzzle, the incomprehensibility, is why did Congress not act earlier? Why was it such a struggle to pass VAWA? Why did presidents and judges seek to defeat the bill? Why did the chief justice take it on as his personal cause? Why, after the bill was passed, did the constitutional theory on which it was based suddenly change (Resnik 2000; Strebeigh 2009; see also House Subcommittee on Crime and Criminal Justice 1992; *Washington Post* 1992: A29)?[1]

To unravel this historical knot, we must return to the years before I reached the Senate Judiciary Committee. By the time I arrived, the country had been treated to culturally transforming events like the 1984 movie, *The Burning Bed*, which caused a sensation by portraying a woman who killed her husband after 13 years of violent abuse (Clark 1984). In 1985, Washington was shocked into self-examination when John Fedders, director of enforcement for the Securities and Exchange Commission, resigned because he had beaten his wife (*Washington Post* 1985b). By then, the surgeon general had announced a public health campaign against battering and child abuse (Office of the Surgeon General 1986). Hundreds of women's shelters had opened their doors, and rape reform laws had been enacted throughout the country.

Yet, federal legislation concerning violence against women remained politically controversial. In 1979, California Senator Alan Cranston introduced legislation to provide modest federal support ($15 million dollars for fiscal year 1981, $65 million over three years) to fund shelters (Domestic Violence Prevention and Services Act 1979). The bill passed the Senate but died in the House. In 1980, Senator Cranston tried again. By May, it was clear that the bill was controversial. Opposition senators mounted a pre-debate challenge, writing that the bill would create an "OSHA" for the family (referring to the much-maligned bureaucracy that governs workplace safety) (Mann 1980: B1). Howard Phillips, a conservative think-tank pundit, summarized the opposition: the federal government has no "business regulating the relationship between man and his wife" (Mann 1980: B1–B2). The matter should be handled, as in "the old days" by "private organizations, religious groups … *families*" (B1–B2). The question of women's injury was translated into a question of the scope of the federal government's power: "Whenever the federal government sticks its moldy fingers into an area, it tends to have a corrupting impact," said Phillips. He suggested that tax credits for charity should be the way to go, allowing the market to allocate resources "through the miracle of human diversity" (Mann 1980: B2).

By the time the Senate debated Cranston's bill, opponents were ready. Shelters, they argued, would become havens for "teenagers and others who resent family discipline" (US Senate 1980a). The bill would "dot the countryside with federally authorized hostels that double as indoctrination centers" (US Senate 1980b). Domestic violence was caused by alcohol and drug abuse, not "sexist cultural norms" (US Senate 1980c). Senators offered amendment after amendment to weaken the bill (US Senate 1980d). In the end, one proffered an amendment, limiting shelter funding to "married" couples to ensure that the bill was "family-oriented." Senator Cranston replied in exasperation: "Should women fleeing in the middle of the night from their homes be required to show their marriage licenses before being admitted?" (US Senate 1980e). At the end of the August debate, the final blow fell; an amendment was offered to eviscerate the bill's shelter funding. Debate halted (US Senate 1980f).

By the time the legislation resurfaced in September, Senator Helms led the opposition, urging that the bill would punish "domestic unhappiness," and result in federal sanctions for "spanking" and "nagging" (US Senate 1980g). Helms quoted, derisively, the opinion of the 1978 Civil Rights Commission recommending that that there were "structural factors" contributing to family violence, including the religious and legal notion "of the husband as 'head of the family'" (1980g). In his attack, Helms quoted the future chief justice of the United States—who would become a major opponent of VAWA—emphasizing the "increasing intrusion" of the federal government and the legal system into "ordinary family disputes" (1980g). According to Justice Rehnquist, the autonomy of the family was "best retained by a government which provides for no intervention except in extreme cases" (1980g).

Five years later, the political situation was not significantly improved. At an international conference, the president's daughter, Maureen Reagan, denied that shelters were "R & R centers for bored housewives," (*Washington Post* 1985a: B10) causing an apparent rift with conservative groups and her father who wanted to distance themselves from "feminist" issues. Twenty-four congressmen, describing themselves as "pro-family" complained to the Attorney General and withdrew a grant to a leading national organization on domestic violence, arguing it was "pro-lesbian, pro-abortion … and radically feminist" (*New York Times* 1985a: C4, 1985b: A14). Maureen Reagan broke ranks and criticized Attorney General Meese's position, but conservative opponents still insisted the group was full of "radical lesbians" (Kurtz 1985: A8). Ultimately, a valiant victims' rights advocate at the Justice Department had to explain that "shelters are not anti-family; *abuse* is anti-family," and the grant was restored (*Washington Post* 1985c: B6).

I knew none of this history; had I known, I might never have imagined the Violence Against Women Act. In retrospect, it was my naïveté, my privileged position as the unwitting and then ungrateful product of an earlier generation of far braver feminists, that allowed me to think what others might have thought unattainable. I suspect that the bill's champion, now Vice-President Biden, who had been in the Senate for some time, knew far better what we might face. He once told me, he never forgot the statement of Senator Denton who objected when the Judiciary Committee proposed to eliminate the marital rape exemption in federal law by saying, "Damn it, when you get married ... you kind of expect you're going to get a little sex" (Biden 2008: 240).

Nevertheless, by 1990 cultural change was afoot. With increasing media attention to the issue, the horror stories seemed to intensify. In 1988, a 6-year-old New York girl, Lisa Steinberg, was tortured to death by her lawyer-father, as his battered wife stood by (Mann 1988: D3). In 1989, Tracey Thurman's horrific story was portrayed in a popular made-for-TV movie. Thurman called the police (as she had before) warning that her husband was about to beat her but to no avail. In full view of witnesses, her husband stabbed her 13 times and broke her neck in a 27-minute attack. The policeman who arrived at the conclusion of the attack disarmed the husband but did not arrest him. Thurman, who survived partially paralyzed, sued and obtained a multi-million dollar verdict (Brennan 1989: R8; O'Connor 1989: C17). Then, in late 1989, there was the Montreal massacre: a young man moved from floor to floor in the university's engineering school, herding female students away from male companions and shooting them at close range with a hunting rifle, leaving a suicide note blaming his life's troubles on feminists (Daly 1989: A1; Pitt 1989: A9).

Political culture in the Senate lagged. May 1990 was 18 months before Anita Hill's claims that Supreme Court nominee Clarence Thomas had harassed her at the Equal Employment Opportunity Commission (EEOC), and over two years before Senator Packwood was charged with harassment by 10 women over a 20-year period (Graves and Shepard 1992: A1; *New York Times* 1991: A24). The 1992 elections, predicted to be the "year of the woman," did produce a few female senators and its first female African-American senator, but it was two years away (*New York Times* 1992b: A1). The year 1990 was still a day and age in which senators felt free to fondle interns in elevators (Morin 1992: A22; *New York Times* 1992a: A14). Yale Professor Judith Resnik once told me she had never met anyone so much in denial as me. Denial, however, is a protective mechanism, essential to hope and the willingness to proceed in the face of danger.

Why did the political culture lag so badly? Where were all the ladies in 1990? I can tell you from personal experience that they weren't in the ladies' room of the Senate. Just as Ruth Bader Ginsburg went to the ladies' room to study (Strebeigh 2009), I went to write speeches for Senator Biden in the Senate ladies' room. In 1990, there were two women in the Senate, and one had voted against Senator Cranston's bill. It was very quiet in the ladies' room.

I had been at the Senate Judiciary Committee barely months when I was assigned the task of writing something on women for the "crime bill." Coming from the Justice Department, I had argued and won cases in appellate courts. I was no feminist, much less a feminist theorist. I had never taken a course in women in the law much less feminist theory. Like many women of my generation who were told we now had it all, I feared feminism. In law school, I saw what happened to women who stood out; my only woman law professor nearly had to sue to get tenure (after she published in the *Harvard Law Review*). If I wanted to succeed, I would act like the men: ignore, deny, pretend gender did not exist.

What was this woman in denial to do when faced with the vague injunction from the chairman to write something in the crime bill for "women?" I did what I had done at the Justice Department to win cases. I did what the judge I clerked for had taught me do. That judge, named Edward Weinfeld, was the most famous trial judge in New York, a legend of a man who had been friends with the likes of Learned Hand (Nelson 2004). He was an extraordinary task master who blessed only perfection and demanded extraordinarily hard work, embracing the example of Justice Brandeis whom he revered. Weinfeld taught me to do precisely the opposite of what I had learned in law school—where concepts reign. He taught me to get the facts. Justice Brandeis was famous for the Brandeis brief, which challenged the Supreme Court's anti-labor decisions not with new doctrine, but by urging that the facts belied the doctrine. I decided to get the facts, the real world data, no holds barred, read until you drop. Little did I know that the case would make itself; even Brandeis might have smiled at the "mountain of data" (to quote Justice Souter in *United States v. Morrison* 2000: 628) that I would find as soon as I opened the books on the Library of Congress's shelves.

But first I needed some ladies. Having no real ones present, I went in search of virtual ladies. In the law library of Congress, I read the giants of women's equality law: Ruth Bader Ginsburg, Ann Freedman, Herma Hill Kay, Susan Deller Ross, Wendy Williams, Susan Estrich, Martha Fineman and, of course, Catharine MacKinnon's ground-breaking work on pornography as a civil rights violation. I held dear an article by Robin West (1990) on marital rape and equal protection as evidence that the Fourteenth Amendment did not speak of equal classification (the standard lawyerly view) but of equal *protection*.

What soon became clear was that the most important women were not on the shelves of the library of Congress. The voice of a woman had never influenced Blackstonian criminal law. No woman has ever to this day voted for it, or its modern analogs, including that great misnomer known as the "model penal code" (which no state has ever adopted in full). On the pages of the law reports of Virginia and Georgia, Massachusetts and the federal courts, were women who had been beaten and scorched and slashed and maimed, ignored and denied by the law.

Enacting legislation is not like writing a Supreme Court brief. It requires the assent of over 500 people and requires the kind of skill that most lawyers and scholars cannot fathom. Think about how hard it would be to write a brief or an article with 100 authors, now multiply that by five, and imagine that the authors all have large egos and opposing interests. Passing a bill requires skills that are not quantifiable: it requires cajoling those who are persuadable and out-maneuvering those bent on your defeat. To give one example, Chairman Biden was fond of loaning me to other senators to offer expert advice. One time, he loaned me to Senator Hatch. With my help, his staff set up a hearing, and there was gripping testimony from residents of a shelter in a small room somewhere in Salt Lake City. The hearing worked. I seem to remember that, at the end,

Senator Hatch was choked up and spontaneously hugged me, apologizing profusely afterwards. Later, he would support and even co-author VAWA.

Passing a bill requires not only the assent of over 500 powerful individuals, it also requires the concurrence of two very powerful institutions—the executive and judicial branches. Once President Clinton was elected, presidential objection disappeared. The other branch, the judiciary, would prove the most difficult to convince. In 1991, the chief justice, through the administrative body he controls (the Judicial Conference) made it clear to judges that VAWA was problematic, an example of congressional overreaching into the affairs of the states and family. Senators and congressmen were flooded with "letters from the Chief Justice ... and other Federal judges" objecting to VAWA's civil rights remedy (VAWA Hearing 1992a: 25). The chief justice set up a special sub-committee of judges within the Judicial Conference to address VAWA—a subcommittee for a single bill. I met with them on a regular basis.

If Chairman Biden was going to get VAWA, he would have to cajole the likes of Helms and "Barbed-wire" Phil Gramm (as Biden (2008: 278) called him); he would also have to take on the judiciary. On February 6, 1992, I met him at the Wilmington station, the way that staffers obtained substantial time with a senator who commuted every night to his home from Washington, D.C. On the train from Delaware, we talked about my arguments with the Judicial Conference's special committee to address the civil rights remedy in the bill. The remedy was based on two constitutional grounds: one was the Fourteenth Amendment and other civil rights remedies originally enacted after the Civil War to grant equal protection to former slaves; the other was the Commerce Clause, which the Supreme Court had used to uphold the Civil Rights Act of 1964, the law that aimed to end "separate but equal" apartheid. Both constitutional claims were well established, and there was testimony in the Senate Judiciary Committee from major constitutionalists, like Professors Cass Sunstein and Burt Neuborne, that the remedy was constitutional under then-existing standards. The Judicial Conference subcommittee was worried that the civil rights provision intruded into the rights of the states and that it would flood the federal courts with millions of cases.

On the train, I talked with the senator about the civil rights remedy and the hearing that day before then-Congressman Chuck Schumer's subcommittee on Crime and Criminal Justice. I repeated the legal arguments I'd made to the VAWA subcommittee. He asked why I'd brought *The Federalist Papers* with me if I was such a feminist; I replied that I loved legal history and always started things at the beginning. Somewhat offhandedly, I told him that I was shocked at one of the arguments made by a judge in the VAWA subcommittee: when I insisted that the remedy was based on civil rights actions available to minorities, specifically African-Americans, the judge said something like "well maybe we should not have those claims either."

Arriving at the Schumer hearing, Biden threw away my speech. (He had a habit of throwing away my speeches saying no one would believe he wrote them.

What he meant was that I wrote like a fancy intellectual, not necessarily a compliment in the world of politics.) From the moment he began, Senator Biden went on the attack: "We have got a Chief Justice who, I respectfully suggest, does not know what he is talking about, when he criticizes this legislation" (VAWA Hearing 1992b: 7). He continued:

> [The] Chief Justice and others have suggested that the bill may burden the Federal courts unnecessarily. Let me tell you something ... We have, under Title 18 of the US Code, provisions making it a Federal crime if you ... "rustle a cow," across state lines[2] ... If we can take care of cows, maybe the vaulted chambers of the Supreme Court could understand it may make sense to worry about women ...
>
> (VAWA Hearing 1992b: 8)

He went on to say:

> You cannot establish a cause of action under this bill by saying that, "I am a woman; I have a bruise; ergo, I have a civil rights claim"—as the Chief Justice would lead you to believe ... With all due respect to the Chief Justice whose repeated misstatements have generated this controversy, his speech writers have not done their homework ... they have failed to read the statute ... This country has a long tradition in which civil rights laws have been used to fight discriminatory violence ...
>
> (10–11)

He further noted that "[n]o one would say today that laws barring violent attacks motivated by race or ethnicity fall outside the Federal courts' jurisdiction" (11). He repeated what "Ms. Nourse" had told him on the train: at least one judge on the VAWA subcommittee thought that, in fact, such laws were questionable (10).

Chairman Biden went on to win the legislative battles of the VAWA war, including passage of the civil rights remedy. Frankly, when I left the Judiciary Committee staff, I did not believe it would happen. Sometime during my first semester as a law professor, I got a call at two in the morning. Demetra Lambros, who had taken my position and was nine months pregnant, was calling from the floor of the Senate to say that VAWA was about to pass; she needed my help to negotiate amendments proposed by Senator Dole. Only later did I discover that the deal I thought could not be done, and had been blocked for four years, was sealed when Senator Biden linked VAWA to other must-pass provisions in the then pending crime bill, funding them with a decrease in the size of the federal government (Biden 2008: 279).

If Biden won the great legislative battle, he ultimately lost the constitutional war created by the separation of powers. In 1995, the year after VAWA was passed, the Supreme Court decided a case that changed the rules of constitutional federal–state relations for the first time in many decades. That decision, *United States v. Lopez* (1995), would ultimately have less effect than expected—except to strike down VAWA's civil rights remedy. But the decision changed the rules of the constitutional game, well established when Congress wrote VAWA. The Supreme Court redrew the line between states and nation; under *Lopez*, legislation would only pass Commerce Clause scrutiny if the subject matter was "economic." After *Lopez*, I knew the Court would rule against VAWA on federalism grounds, if it ever reached them.

In 2000, the Supreme Court did precisely that in *United States v. Morrison*, leaving the vast majority of the VAWA intact but striking down the civil rights remedy. *Lopez* was the principal reason (*Morrison* 2000: 610), the Supreme Court reasoning that violence against women did not deal with "economic" matters, and Congress did not have the power to pass the legislation: "punishment of intrastate violence ... has always been the province of the States" (*Morrison* 2000: 618). The Commerce Clause was good enough for violent racial discrimination but not violent gender discrimination. Nor did it matter that 36 states had filed briefs in support of the remedy as consistent with states' rights. As for the Fourteenth Amendment's guarantee of equal protection, the Supreme Court relied upon two cases decided in 1883, ruling that violence against women was "private" and therefore did not constitute "state action" subject to the Fourteenth Amendment (*Morrison*, 2000: 621, citing *US v. Harris* 1883 and the *Civil Rights Cases* 1883). The decision was not without dissenters; Justice Souter (*Morrison*, 2000: 628, 634) wrote that Congress had created a "mountain of data" supporting an economic impact (women quit jobs, refused to move, and did not work because of violence), so much so that Congress's "rational basis" for its constitutional conclusions could not "seriously be questioned." In the end, Chief Justice Rehnquist won the great constitutional battle using an argument similar to that attributed to him in 1980 by opponents to Senator Cranston's bill: to accept VAWA would allow Congress to regulate "family law and other areas of traditional state regulation." (*Morrison*, 2000: 615) The judiciary, having invoked its power to "say what the Constitution is," rejected Congress's view of its constitutional power. In 2000, the VAWA civil rights remedy died in the great "marble palace" (Nourse 2008: 145) devoted outwardly to "Equal Justice Under Law."

VAWA was created not by a single man or woman but by millions of voices of men and women alike. I was the voice of the virtual woman not in the room, the millions whose voices I simply channeled from the pages of newspapers, from the insides of battered women's shelters, and the pages of the law reporters, just as Brandeis (and his sister-in-law, Josephine Goldmark) so long ago channeled the voices of working men and women (Spillenger 2005). No staffer can pass a bill. That is a fundamentally anti-democratic misunderstanding of Congress (just as it would be a radical misunderstanding to dismiss a Supreme Court opinion as the product of a Supreme Court clerk). It takes the real votes of "we the people" to make a law, voices that leaders hear and must literally *re*-present—to "make present" those who are absent.

Act III: The changing Constitution

During the 1930s, a debate raged between those who believed that we have a "living" Constitution and those who believed that the Constitution stood for "the ages," unchangeable. Justice Brandeis was on one side, President Hoover the other. The classical constitutional amendment process had failed. For decades advocates had attempted to ban child labor, and there was massive national support for the amendment. Yet, it failed. Why? As FDR said during the court-packing crisis of 1937, if he had $10,000 he could kill any constitutional amendment; the classical amendment process allows the minorities of legislatures in just a few states to block even the most widely approved amendments (Nourse 2008: 145).

Over the years, constitutionalists have debated how constitutional change happens. There is every reason for lawyers who like to follow rules to believe that, if one wants to change the Constitution, then one must follow the rules for amending it. I confess I am quite conservative about the structure of our Constitution: our nation has survived with one civil war and no real dictators, in part I believe, because that structure allows redundant means for the release of political energy—releases allowing dissenters to be heard, thus deterring violent radicalism and dictatorial ambitions. Yet, there are reasons to believe that the amendment process cannot capture fully our constitutional history; no historian believes that if one only looked at the amendments one could describe the history or constitutional life of our nation (Ackerman 2007).

In my work on the Constitution, I have always emphasized that constitutional power comes from the bottom, not the top. The Constitution is not an organizational chart of functions and offices. It is an embodiment, a constitution of the people; senators and congressmen and even presidents are the people's temporary servants under this view. More importantly, the Constitution is just what it sounds like; it "constitutes," it creates power, it exists to release and cabin political energy (Nourse 1999, 2004).

This view is hardly radical, although it is unconventional among lawyers who tend to see the text as inviting fine linguistic distinctions. Justice Holmes, perhaps the most brilliant if not the most empathic of justices once explained this view:

> [W]hen we are dealing with *words* that also are a constituent *act*, like the Constitution of the United States, we must realize that they have called into life a being the development of which could not have been foreseen completely by the most gifted of its begetters. It was enough for them to realize or to hope that they had created an organism; it has taken a century and has cost their successors much sweat and blood to prove that they created a nation.
>
> (*Missouri v. Holland* 1920: 433, emphasis added)

The Constitution constitutes, it literally constructs our political life. Its words are not merely descriptions or commands; they are, as Holmes put it, "constituent acts" calling into life persons and actions. As Austin, the philosopher of language, would explain, its words are performative. By performative, I mean the following: when one marries, the partners say "I do." The words accomplish the pact but no one thinks that a marriage can be reduced to those two words. The words are necessary, but they are not sufficient to describe the course of a marriage. So too, our constitutional life cannot be reduced to mere texts, for the Constitution performs. The most important way that the Constitution acts is by constituting the people in districts and states, so they may govern themselves. Every time a citizen votes, takes a case to court, protests, or writes a letter to Congress, they act as the Constitution commands. The Constitution's principal performers are the people.

The Constitution changes as the people participate and take control of their government, as they re-constitute themselves. Since our founding, the separation of powers has been the means by which the Constitution may change, in practice. Students of our government tend to think of the separation of powers as an impediment, but this view depends upon a conceptual mistake about the nature of constitutional power. Power is not a question of ascription or adjectival function, it is not about trying to define what is executive or legislative, but it is how these adjectives are performed by the people who act under their name. When the people converge, the branches agree. When this convergence is durable—when the institutions we know as the courts, the Congress and the presidency—approve of an action, a "constitutional convention" arises. These constitutional conventions require consensus across the branches and vast amounts of popular will sustained over time; they are what James Madison (1788: 269) once called the "liquidation" of constitutional meaning. These conventions are not embodied necessarily in formal amendments but in what Bill Eskridge (2007: 33) calls small "c" constitutionalism—framework statutes like the Americans with Disability Act and the Civil Rights Act of 1964, or landmark constitutional decisions such as *Brown v. Board of Education*, which reconstitute the people and their image of themselves, in light of the nation's most basic principles.

"Small c" constitutional change is important. Such change is constitutionally legitimate because it is carried on through the deliberate dialogue set out by the separation of powers. It is an active process: often one step forward, one step back, as the branches compete for power. The Civil Rights Act of 1964 was part of much larger constitutional story in which courts, Congress, and the president played leading roles. But as the dynamic departmental dance proceeds, oscillating between states and nation, presidents and Congress and courts, some conventions rigidify so strongly that their absence becomes unthinkable. *Brown v. Board of Education* (1954) was never written as an amendment to our Constitution but very few would repudiate it today. When Chief Justice Rehnquist was named to head the Court, it was discovered that he had once written a memo taking the position that *Brown* was wrongly decided. He knew that he had to disavow that memo if he hoped to become Chief for, by that time, *Brown* and its civil rights legacy had become a constitutional convention too strong to resist (Snyder 2000).

VAWA and its civil rights remedy were part of this constitutional dance, a drama which unfolded as Congress and the courts clashed over the question of women's equality. In part, the statute led to small "c" constitutional change: very few today make the kind of arguments made in 1980 that Congress has no role to play in this area, that VAWA will undermine the family, or reward "indoctrination" centers. Congress reestablishes its authority to act each time it reauthorizes VAWA. That the Supreme Court struck down the civil rights remedy in the law means only that the small "c" constitutional change had not become as strong as a constitutional *convention*. More work must be done for the courts and country to see the ways gender still colors our understandings of violence and how openly disavowed sex stereotypes may yet be applied in individual cases.

Coda

On my desk sits a photo of a third grader sitting at a typewriter pretending to write. She had fought hard for that typewriter, overcoming her father's resistance with the standard tactics of a third grader: whining, cajoling, stamping her foot, kissing his cheek. At the time of the photograph, in 1967, less than five percent of all law students were women; less than one percent of all law professors were women. But as this future Zelig grew up, the nation re-constituted itself. African-Americans marched, fought, and died to battle apartheid; empowered by the example, women marched and fought alongside them. Title VII may have been enacted as a joke, but it became a reality as women litigated, agencies issued regulations, and courts agreed. The Equal Rights Amendment, however popular, never reached our Constitution. In the meantime, more slowly but surely, a new constitutional convention was emerging: in Title VII and laws on sexual harassment and pregnancy discrimination, on violence and family leave. We are not yet fully there, but I cannot help but believe that one day we will no longer be able to imagine the world the way it might have looked to that third grader. This is my constitutional faith, the story of my political education.

Recently, I had lunch with President Carter, a ritual for new Emory faculty members. As one of only a few women to hold a chair on the law faculty, I relished the invitation. He wanted to talk about a new plan with a group he called "the elders" (including former South African President Nelson Mandela and former UN Secretary General Kofi Annan). The "elders" were planning a great new initiative: *eradicating the inequality of women in the world*. President Carter is not shy about small tasks. He asked me if I had received enough credit for VAWA. I said that I had received too much, and I honestly believe that. Under the theory of the Constitution that I hold dear, it is the people who govern. I will take credit for my academic work—my view of the *Federalist Papers* or the separation of powers, my theory of great constitutional cases like *Skinner v. Oklahoma* or *Lochner v. New York*. But in 1990, I was not Justice Scalia's proverbial "heady" Senate staffer (*Blanchard v. Bergeron* 1989) pushing VAWA forward. That belief is a fundamental misunderstanding of Congress and the meaning of a republican constitution, one devoted to the principle that it is the people who govern, not their temporary representatives.

Notes

1 For example, "the chief justice ... said [VAWA] ... could involve federal courts in a whole host of domestic relations disputes" (*Washington Post* 1992: A29).
2 This statute still exists, 18 USC § 2316: "Whoever transports in interstate or foreign commerce any livestock, knowing the same to have been stolen, shall be fined under this title or imprisoned not more than five years, or both."

Chapter 23

Defending and developing critical feminist theory as law leans rightward

Martha T. McCluskey

Feminist legal theory has come of age over the last quarter century; right-wing politics also has grown to cast a long shadow over law and policy, a shadow that threatens to dim feminism's visions of equality.

Critical feminist theory can be useful in countering the ideological and material barriers to equality amassed during the right's rule. By engaging both foundational theory and substantive context, critical feminism helps to resist the right-wing double binds which make policies promoting equality often appear irrational and impractical. A critical approach to legal feminism emphasizes that ideas about law, gender, and society are always constructed in relationship to a particular context of social and historical power and shaped by particular ideological perspectives, personal interests, and political agendas (Rhode 1990). Feminist critique aims not just to describe law and society or apply particular pre-given principles. It seeks to challenge fundamental assumptions and change distributions of power by understanding that knowledge always helps to create and control as well as to reveal the social world.

The right's ideological shadow

Twenty-five years ago, feminist legal critique gained momentum by challenging the double bind of formal equality (Fineman 1983; MacKinnon 1987). In the standard legal framework, the right to gender equality does not mean the right to particular substantive protections for women. Instead, it simply ensures the distribution of substantive rights in a formally neutral process without regard to gender. Formal equality grants women the right to the same legal privileges as men if women can show they really *are* the same as legally privileged men. But if gender-based disadvantages are *real* and *relevant* to women's lives, then this right to be treated the same is of little value in alleviating gendered harm (Fineman 1991a; Scales 1986). Alternatively, the formal equality framework allows women to reject equality and instead seek *different* legal treatment from men based on biological or social differences (recognizing pregnancy, child-care responsibilities, or a history of exclusion from particular opportunities) (Krieger and Cooney 1983). But any protection for unequal gender "difference" likely reinforces gender-based disadvantages by confirming and rewarding assumptions of gendered incapacity (Williams 1985).

Either way, formal equality gives women a losing choice. Feminist critique explains that this formally neutral framework is not gender neutral. If privileged men are the standard by which women are measured, women will likely seem less deserving and receive subordinate legal status regardless of whether they show they are the same as or different from men (Mackinnon 1987).

This formal idea of equality can give some men a double benefit, effectively allowing them to "have it both ways" by being both equal and different. The law can take into account the particular biological or social needs of privileged men not as special differences or costly privileges but as part of a normal or natural baseline. Many men can enjoy workplace equipment designed to fit an average male body height or work schedules designed to accommodate a stereotypical white middle-class male family role without appearing to receive special or costly accommodations. If women demand changes in workplace structure to adapt to typically female bodies or feminized social responsibilities, these changes are often interpreted as signs of those women's particular dependency or inferiority (Abrams 1989).

In the 1980s, feminist legal critique reframed this standard approach showing that formal "equal treatment" rests on substantive judgments about whose particular interests and identities to take as the norm (Minow 1990: 21–23). If underlying norms change to include the substantive interests of a broader group of women, then law reforms protecting more women's substantive interests are consistent with and necessary to legal equality. If pregnant or caretaking women are considered normal citizens and productive workers, then substantive policies, like family leave and government services supporting family responsibilities, are part of the normal vision of equal treatment, not costly accommodations for troublesome "difference" (Finley 1986). But as feminist scholars and activists developed that substantive vision of equality, the right-wing increasingly attacked it with two strands of anti-egalitarian ideology: one centering on supposedly objective economics and the other centering on morality.

In the economic version of this ideological attack, substantive equality is about giving special benefits to a few at the expense of most others; for, this vision of economics defines equality as "redistributing" slices of the economic "pie" in a zero-sum game, versus making the overall "pie" bigger to benefit everyone. This defining assumption decrees that equality fails to benefit society overall and risks *hurting* the overall good over the long run (McCluskey 2000). Equality means choosing to increase a *particular* slice of the pie, at the cost of a smaller pie on the whole.

Carried through to its logical conclusion, this view presumes that equality will hurt not just those from whom resources are taken and not just the overall pie, but also those who are the intended beneficiaries. Those with the smallest share of "pie"—those targeted for equal "redistribution"—are by definition those with the least power to compete successfully for a share of overall resources.

As the economic "pie" shrinks, those who are most unequal will lose the most as others with more resources defend their shares of a smaller pie (McCluskey 2005a: 194).

Tracking this economic logic, employment discrimination laws have been narrowly construed to offer little protection to breastfeeding women (Kessler 2001). If a woman seeks to adjust her work schedule or workspace to accommodate lactation, she risks taking money from employers who must divert resources to this "social" or "personal" need at the expense of "normal" profit-maximizing. Employers who spend money supporting breastfeeding will have less money for the investment and innovation that bring jobs or lower-priced, high-quality goods. In the longer term, the overall economy will shrink. Employers, faced with tighter resources, will be less likely to give their limited jobs to workers who may demand or need costly breastfeeding. Thus, this well-intentioned plan for substantive equality for breastfeeding women seems to end up hurting the breastfeeding women it aims to help, and risks bringing down everyone else to boot.

Note that this logic is a narrative—a rhetorical device—based on definition and metaphor, not empirical fact. This story concludes that equality is a losing policy goal in which helping those at the bottom only reinforces their subordination (McCluskey 2003; 2007a). This story asserts that the best we can do for those who are disadvantaged under existing systems is to reject equality for its proclaimed opposite: an ideal of efficiency (maximizing the pie) that accepts inequality as necessary and natural (if tragic) to promoting the overall good. Meaningful increases in equality must await increased economic growth, with the faith that this growth will somehow trickle down to those deprived of the existing pie.

The second strand of anti-egalitarian theory uses morality to attack substantive equality as a losing proposition. This strand partly accepts feminism's shift from a formal, supposedly neutral "sameness" approach to equality to the openly moral and political goal of anti-subordination—ending identity-based hierarchies. Although this right-wing moral ideology in some ways recognizes that equality means resisting powerlessness, not just establishing sameness, it puts the moral responsibility for correcting these power hierarchies on subordinated victims. This moral ideology creates a double bind in which victims of inequality are too incapacitated to be trusted with legal authority or not incapacitated enough to deserve legal protection from harm. Either way, legal rights to equality are morally suspect. Libertarian versions of this moral anti-egalitarianism assume that the primary measure of moral responsibility is the ability to defend one's own substantive interests instead of depending on legal protection from others. Communitarian versions of this moral anti-egalitarianism assume that moral responsibility is demonstrated by supporting oneself and sacrificing for others, not demanding others' support and sacrifice (McCluskey 2003: 825–29).

If women experience serious substantive harm from divorce, rape, or abortion laws, or from lack of social supports for single parenting, then women do not need stronger substantive rights or affirmative public support. Instead they need tighter discipline through self-control or control by others (parents, husbands, employers, church, or state). The failure to provide legal protection against such harms does not count as gender subordination but as "tough love" that will strengthen and teach women to better avoid, change, or accept their substantive disadvantages. If women seek legal rights to have better choices about sex, family, work, or morality, using law to make their demands proves they are not seriously victimized. Those who pursue public legal protection rather than per- sonal responsibility are seeking special treatment aimed at usurping others' rightful power. These moral arguments conclude that meaningful substantive equality must wait until victimized groups are able to accept, grow from, or mitigate the harm of any perceived or real subordination.

The right's material shadow

Along with ideological attacks, the right has countered feminism indirectly through organized efforts to direct *material* resources toward anti-egalitarian theory and practice. Over the last 25 years, the right has invested millions in providing institutional support for anti-egalitarian ideas, changing legal acade- mia particularly through support for law and economics (McCluskey 2007a). Direct ideological attacks on feminism's legitimacy as legal theory are hardly necessary because conservative institutions dominate much of the field. For most legal scholars, the easiest and fastest route to career advancement follows the methods, conversations, topics, networks, and funding opportunities promoted by conservative organizations.

Broader political and economic changes have produced new pressures in the legal profession and academy with new costs for feminist theory and practice. Substantial opportunities for feminism now exist in legal education and legal scholarship, thanks to 25 years of extensive feminist networking and mentoring, exemplified by Martha Fineman's Feminism and Legal Theory Project. But at the same time, both higher education and the legal profession have moved away from democratic ideals of public service and intellectual independence to embrace a business-like pursuit of private profit (Angel 2005). Institutional changes like the increased importance of law school rankings, declining public funding for higher education, and rising student debt levels have increased competition among law schools for high-scoring students, high-paying employ- ers, prominently publishing faculty, recognition by powerful mainstream judges and lawyers, and the favor of wealthy donors. This market context risks raising the costs to students, faculty, and institutions of pursuing feminist scholarship, teaching, and activism, particularly if that feminism embraces far-reaching critique of sociolegal power.

Despite significant increases in feminist faculty at law schools and universities, these institutions have not necessarily addressed systemic problems of gender discrimination that continue to impede feminist scholarship and action.

Women faculty often shoulder disproportionate administrative duties in the interest of gender "balance." Feminists particularly are tempted by the opportunities to change institutional structures to better support women and others traditionally disadvantaged in the profession—serving on hiring and tenure committees, designing anti-discrimination policies, or organizing publications and events to highlight marginalized work. Furthermore, the mounting institutional "domestic" labor involved in the increasing market demands for improved rankings may be distributed unequally to women, based on real or perceived gender bias shaping ideas about who is willing or able to work well with others for the good of the institution at their own expense. Feminist faculty who devote more time to teaching and institutional service may be penalized for real or perceived sacrifices in scholarship, resulting in less support for their scholarship and more pressure to serve as institutional "housekeepers" and student service providers. Feminist law faculty may find their work hindered by retaliation and harassment if their feminist involvement in institutional governance threatens those with power.

These ideological and material obstacles make critical feminist legal theory seem like an unaffordable luxury. Many legal scholars have turned away from cutting-edge critique to a more chastened approach that emphasizes pragmatism over theory, platitudes over political confrontation, raw power or pseudo-scientific positivism over law's moral subjectivity, and economic interests over gender identity (McCluskey 2007a). But the right's example provides evidence that ambitious critical theory can sometimes be *most* practical and even necessary in a context of powerful opposition. Critical feminist theory is particularly powerful in this context because it rejects the divides that have been central to the right's power: the division between ambitious theory and practical change, between rigorous reason and political passion, between public law and private market or family, between gender identity and material interests.

Resisting the right's shadow

Engaging law's foundational theory

One practical lawyering lesson is that persuasive power often depends as much on framing the questions as on providing good answers. By shifting attention from the choice between competing arguments to the underlying questions and founding assumptions, critical feminist theory challenges the right-wing ideology that makes substantive equality seem unjust. Ironically, idealistic change may be most pragmatic when the prevailing system provides bad choices.

Many scholars and policymakers respond to the prevailing economic arguments against egalitarian policies by defending limited "redistribution" as part of a policy "balance" to be weighed against economic growth (McCluskey 2007b). It may be more pragmatic and powerful to redefine what counts as the economic "pie." Economic "growth" need not be measured by dollars accumulated in a given quarter by a few rich people; it could be defined as the long-term health and education of non-wealthy women and children. For example, in the 2008 presidential campaign, John McCain challenged Obama's economic policies by suggesting Obama would be the "Redistributor in Chief." Obama responded by explaining that his policies would "grow the economy not from the top down but from the bottom up" (Bender 2008). Feminist policies such as paid family leave, public childcare, and government health insurance are no more "redistributive" than conservative-backed policies of economic development subsidies, trade regulation, or intellectual property rights. In fact feminist policies are arguably more growth-oriented than other policies (depending on what counts as growth). By rejecting a simple opposition between growing the economic pie and dividing the economic pie, feminists can refute the claims that substantive economic support for women will necessarily shrink the economic "pie" and the long-term shares available to the most disadvantaged.

Similarly, feminist critique aimed at upending the framework of moral conservatism can help strengthen standard arguments for increased substantive equality. A critical approach to feminism can unpack the double standards of "personal responsibility" and "independence" that ground the right's moral argument in which substantive equality rights seem incompatible with good citizenship or individual freedom. Conventional liberal defenses of the morality of social welfare programs tend to argue either that welfare has little effect on women's choices because welfare recipients are too disadvantaged to exercise personal responsibility, or that welfare "dependency" can be mitigated with policies designed to control recipients' irresponsibility. Critical theory pushes further into the underlying assumptions, turning the tables to consider welfare recipients as exercising responsible choices to support and sacrifice for others (McCluskey 2003). For example, Fineman (2004) argues that caretaking for dependent children is a public responsibility for which society as a whole is indebted. She explains how a myth of autonomy and self-sufficiency covers up the extent to which businesses and others depend on extensive government support and unjustly stigmatizes single mothers for seeking assistance for valuable caretaking work.

Although legal arguments often seem more threatening and less credible to the extent they resist dominant frameworks, boundary-breaking ideas may have long-term practical benefits. The right would not have spent so much money on the organized production and distribution of ideas about fundamental legal change over the last quarter century if it believed its own rhetoric that real-world power is determined not by contesting and changing ideas but by acquiescing to the limits set by fixed natural laws, interests, values, and resources. Ambitious right-wing investment in utopian theory has put previously absurd or radical policies like privatized social security, deregulated financial markets, and unchecked executive power on the table (McCluskey 2007a).

Similarly impractical and risky legal visions from a different political perspective are vital to fostering comparable energy and interest in feminism. Such visionary thinking also helps resist a rightward tilt that turns the tiniest, most incremental, or compromised steps toward equality into radical socialism. Consider John McCain's attack on raising the top marginal income tax rate from 35 to 39.6 percent. McCain portrayed this slight adjustment as "socialist," even though that change would restore the rate in place under the Clinton administration and would be far less than the top tax rate of 91 percent in 1964 (Goodman 2008).

Ideas matter—particularly ideas that reach beyond immediate practical constraint—but, they do not matter *more than* political or practical concerns. By understanding reason as inevitably grounded in, developed from, and accountable to particular human perspectives and material interests, critical feminism aims to ensure that theory is not exempt from the power of fundamental questioning that it wields.

A critical feminist perspective should engage and explore the questions of whose voices and experiences count as disinterested theory, as well as the questions of whose interests and values really are served by any particular theoretical inquiry. While feminist critique values intellectual inquiry that is not primarily directed at producing immediate policy results—rethinking the basic idea of the family, for instance—it should also engage questions about the practical and political value of any given line of intellectual argument. Questions like "what can all these abstractions *do* for a woman living in a fifth-floor cold water walk-up," are not anti-intellectual conversation stoppers as Wendy Brown and Janet Halley (2002: 2) argue in their articulation of critical theory. Such questions should be taken as important and sophisticated reminders that all theories are also practical strategies, shaped and harnessed by political and personal agendas that can and should be subject to continual scrutiny and enrichment (McCluskey 2007a).

A critical perspective that rejects the theory–practice divide can also help in challenging the silence that keeps the political economy of legal theory off limits in polite academic company. That silence helps legitimate and naturalize the dominance of right-wing ideology as powerful principle rather than patronage politics. Right-wing arguments against equality have gained substantial power not just because of ambitious questioning of foundational assumptions, but because of ambitious funding by so-called "investors" who stand to gain from decreased social spending and regulatory protection for the non-elite. From the late 1970s through the early twenty-first century, the Olin Foundation spent more than $50 million in US law schools to promote what its director termed "anti-egalitarian" theory (Simon 2004: 272). Right-wing ideas have also been successful because of right-wing material support for organizations, like the Federalist Society, that provide an intellectual and social community as well as career advancement linked to opposition to substantive equality (McCluskey 2007a).

By rethinking theory to include its material ground, especially its "housekeeping" and "mothering" needs, feminist critique can help emphasize the value of the non-intellectual work necessary to cultivate powerful theory.

Though we cannot match the right's funding, Martha Fineman's work in the Feminism and Legal Theory Project is a model of how powerful feminist theory and social change comes from smart individuals with good ideas, as well as organizing those individuals into networks and institutions that can provide mentoring, marketing, and community support—including fun and friendship.

Engaging the politics of law

A critical approach can also help resist the rightward-leaning intellectual climate that constructs support for substantive equality as unsophisticated thinking. Responding to attacks by the right, non-conservative legal scholars often adopt what William H. Simon describes as a "fear and loathing" of politics, using distance from political commitment and controversy to establish intellectual credibility (Simon 2001). Scholarship can appear most careful and constructive when it stakes out polarized abstract positions and then advocates a seemingly balanced but vague or contradictory midpoint that avoids a detailed evaluation of the competing ideas and interests supporting each side (or possible alternatives outside that polarized scheme). Alternatively, this culture often rewards scholars for presuming a world devoid of serious power contests, where justice involves rather technical problems of discovering, implementing, and articulating abstract moral principles that are mostly a matter of broad and disinterested consensus.

Feminist theory is at a disadvantage in an intellectual culture that presumes a largely conflict-free context of gender neutrality. Even cautious and "balanced" analysis of the gendered meaning and impact of particular policies can seem irresponsible or unproductive by violating this implicit taboo. Scholarship can appear reasonable and persuasive if it analyzes income tax provisions favoring breadwinner–homemaker marriage as an accidental consequence of widely accepted principles of federalism or as the natural result of institutional rigidity in the face of changing demographics. Scholarship that *links* such policies to congressional gender or race bias or to the gender, race, and economic privilege of influential interest groups is likely subject to particular scrutiny or marginalization (McCaffery 1997). Of course, the *failure* to analyze seriously such policies as a product of contested gender and racial ideologies is unlikely to be raised as a sign of intellectual bias, insignificance, or sloppiness.

If feminist theory avoids political conflict by invoking broadly accepted and seemingly gender-neutral principles in support of law reforms, then these arguments may appear credible and persuasive yet largely irrelevant. For example, scholarship defending expanded government health insurance for children on the ground that it fosters some abstract normative goal like human capacity or economic efficiency may receive little opposition from relatively conservative scholars. However, without further analysis of the political and economic interests aligned against such seemingly rational policies, and how those opposing interests might be overcome, such purely normative scholarship can seem impractical and simplistic in contrast to scholarship advancing right-wing policy goals.

The right has mobilized against substantive equality by combining arguments about disinterested principle with hard-hitting attacks on conflicting political interests. The right routinely attacks policies aimed at protecting vulnerable persons on the ground that these well-meaning policies advance elite special interests. Tort protection for "non-economic" harm (like women's reproductive injuries) is often reduced to trial lawyers' greed; support for public services like day care is criticized for enriching overpaid and incompetent unions; and environmental regulation is reduced to elite pastoralism or property value protection at the expense of working-class jobs or consumption. Such arguments reducing principled policy to partisan politics and personal gain may be contested by non-conservatives but are rarely dismissed as uncollegial or anti-intellectual. Yet, when conservatives invoke principles like "efficiency" or "market freedom" to oppose substantive feminist reforms, non-conservatives typically debate these principles at face value as coherent visions of the public interest divorced from personal or political gain (McCluskey 2003: 869–70).

Critical feminism recognizes that policy questions always involve taking sides in conflicts of partisan power and personal gain. Critical theory can show how an approach to law that openly engages this context of competing interests, identities, and ideologies is more intellectually rigorous than one that assumes politics away. If partisan power and personal gain blocks law reforms such as universal health care, then feminist analysis that combines moral and technical arguments with political strategy will be most practical.

Nevertheless, feminist theory resists the cynical disengagement and passivity of some critical perspectives that tend to reduce law entirely to narrow-minded political and economic interests. Feminist scholarship refuses a naturalized view that makes power, interest, and identity seem beyond the reach of rational analysis and moral argument. For example, Fineman (2004) analyzes the gendered vulnerability of family caretakers—like single mothers—not as an inevitable product of female weakness or maternal emotions, nor as the inevitable result of male selfishness, physical difference, or political advantage, but instead as the product of a sociolegal structure that we can imagine changing for the better.

Engaging law's societal power

Critical feminist theory is also useful in countering the right's rise by defending *law* as a tool for feminist politics. While feminist critique understands that substantive power shapes law, it also maintains a sharp focus on law's potential to shift power in society. Critical feminist theory can advance hope for substantive justice that rests neither on a strained liberal faith in formal, neutral process nor on new fundamentalisms that shift that faith from law to imagined realms of naturalized and idealized authority outside of law, such as the market, family, or divine order. Feminist critique challenges the division between public and private spheres, analyzing how law's implication in social, economic and political practices and institutions appears as natural or the product of individual choice (Olsen 1983). By changing the background rules governing the family, state, or market, new opportunities may arise to change the gendered power relationships that can impede feminist law reforms.

The right's economic and moral arguments against equality rest on the presumption that law is both too weak and too strong to protect people who lose out under the status quo (McCluskey 2007a). Thus, legal protections that try to change the presumptively natural distribution of power will inevitably fail to overcome that naturally superior authority, giving only false hope, and more dependency, for the subordinated. Workplace regulations mandating paid family or medical leave may do little to protect workers who fear employers will deny promotions or other job benefits to those who assert their rights.

Yet, this line of argument simultaneously warns that egalitarian legal protections have vast power to destroy the naturally protective authority of market or morality that supposedly offers the best hope for the powerless. Anti-statist rhetoric from both right and left often warns that even minor and well-intentioned law reforms can have complex, far-reaching, and unpredictable harmful effects on society and those they claim to help (McCluskey 2009). The hierarchical market and moral order appear too fragile to withstand even marginal adjustments designed to make current institutions a bit more responsive to the needs of those outside the elite. For example, criticisms of paid family medical leave often construe this policy as government "interference" that threatens to disrupt the market economy as a whole.

In response, some advocates of equality have adopted a minimalist approach to law, aiming to scale down legal rights and regulation to accommodate or appease the imagined authority and frailty of market, culture, family, biology, or other seemingly extra-legal spheres. For example, federal welfare reform received strong support across the political spectrum on the theory that impoverished single mothers would benefit more from the market and "traditional" morality than from legal rights to economic protection (McCluskey 2003). That new law structured punishments and benefits to induce single mothers into substituting low-wage work and marriage for government income. However, this seeming substitution of private market for public law cannot offer much power in market or family to those who lack it. The tighter the penalties on mothers who avoid formal work or marriage, the more recipients are likely to lose out on opportunities for secure and beneficial work and family. Restrictions on welfare may pressure women to engage in illegal work leading to incarceration and further economic devastation, or to rely on intimate relationships that are abusive or financially harmful in the long run, or to subject their children to inadequate care. To the extent welfare reform policies shift substantive support toward work and marriage, the more those policies will risk being challenged for disrupting prevailing market and family power. For example, meaningful public day care funding that would better support single mothers as market workers has been stymied by concerns that such funding will undermine the market through increased taxes or government debt, or that good public day care will undermine the family by discouraging parental care in two-parent families.

Feminist critique aims to debunk the imagined power of the law's outside by rejecting both market and moral fundamentalism, viewing economic and moral orders as contingent constructions of politics and law. From a critical perspective, welfare reform that replaces government benefits with work is not a shift in anti-poverty policy from government to market and family. Instead, it may be a policy mobilizing government control to regulate the labor market for business interests by increasing cheap and vulnerable labor (McCluskey 2003), to increase racial divisions (Neubeck and Cazenave 2001), and to restrict access to family privacy and intimacy (Solinger 2001).

Critical analysis digs beneath the right's anti-statist rhetoric to recognize its aggressive and successful practice of harnessing big government and systemic law reform to upend egalitarian policies. Over the last 25 years, the political and economic power of the wealthiest capital owners and businesses has expanded through regulatory institutions like the International Monetary Fund and the World Trade Organization; through increased statutory protections of laws governing welfare and technical subjects like bankruptcy; to newly expanded, non-text-based constitutional rights like corporate protection from punitive damages and restrictions on civil rights; or from centralization of government power through expansive federal preemption. Resistance to the right and rebuilding from its destructive effects requires not just reviving private political and economic power but reclaiming state power through law. It requires analyzing and engaging the interconnections between law and politics. Legal rights and institutions can protect or impede political movements and shape the available political and economic choices, their costs and benefits. For example, better legal protection of voting rights facilitated the Democratic Party's electoral victory in 2008; a restructured international currency regulation or corporate governance system could open up new options for economic change.

By rejecting an essentialized division between law and society, feminist critique helps to debunk claims that law's unintended effects are too powerful and unknowable to harness for substantive social change. Feminist critique analyzes law as always inextricably intertwined with its substantive social context. Feminist scholarship and advocacy engages legal issues as empirical problems requiring close attention to practice and interpretation on the ground. It strives to question, craft, and revise law reforms with attention to both impact and purpose. For example, feminist work on domestic violence used close connections with activists and empirical evidence to explore a variety of alternatives for using law to leverage social change, such as international human rights claims or litigation against police departments (Marcus 1994; Schneider 1994). Because knowledge of the substantive effects of law reforms can never be perfect and always risks perpetuating elitist biases, feminist critique emphasizes the need for a democratic and diverse approach to empirical analysis, subjecting claims of technical expertise and objectivity to special scrutiny.

Feminist critique rejects an anti-empirical vision that suggests law's effects are too subjective, too powerful, and too complex to be susceptible to rational design. Some postmodern or libertarian strands of the political left and right romanticize a posture of passive, detached abstention from concern with substantive justice. Feminism's commitment to gender justice seems sentimental and naïve, if not disingenuous and dangerous (Halley 2002). But critical feminism rejects the fantasy that we stand outside of law's power in some neutral space free from imperfect empirical assumptions and imperfect political and social commitments. We always live embedded in law, privileged or penalized by legal institutions; all our actions or inactions work to reinforce or change a legal regime and the assumptions about the empirical world that legal regime helps shape. Refusing to know about, care about, or respond to the injustices that pervade our daily lives is itself an action with potentially far-reaching and complex effects on others. Critical feminism can debunk such detachment from substantive justice as a political strategy likely to serve the political and economic interests of those who stand to gain from denying and acquiescing in current systems of injustice (McCluskey 2007a).

Engaging identity's complexity

Finally, a critical feminist approach can resist the right's rise by advancing ideas of substantive equality that engage and complicate current identity politics. Feminist public policy sometimes is framed as an expression of personal identity rather than as a moral and political vision. This framework echoes the double binds defining substantive equality as "special treatment," "redistribution," or dependency. If feminism is defined as protection for female identity, then it is about promoting special interests for an essentialized group in a divisive, zero-sum gain that ignores individual differences within the group identified as "female" as well as competing interests outside that group. Furthermore, if feminism is about identity rather than equality, it seems to be private and trivial, or even a lifestyle choice, rather than a rational and important public concern. For example, in the 2008 presidential Democratic primary campaign, the media often assumed that women who supported Barack Obama over Hillary Clinton did so to express their individual race or class identity, rather than to push for substantive change in public policy out of concern for the overall good. In the 1991 debate over the nomination of Supreme Court Justice Clarence Thomas, prominent commentary portrayed feminist concern about allegations of workplace sexual harassment as an expression of white professional class identity, marginal to meaningful gender justice or to Thomas's views of law (Patterson 1991).

Feminism's push for substantive equality has also been challenged by the argument that substantive protection confines women into a victim identity marked by weakness and dependency on government (Brown 1995; McElroy 1991). Despite fueling criticisms of feminist victimhood, the right has constructed and mobilized prominent victimized identities in opposition to feminist reforms. The right often portrays men, conservative Christians, homemaking mothers, or childless women as subject to oppressive feminist control (McCluskey 1997). This contest of victimized identity can make feminism seem outdated or even bullying.

To avoid such divisive and slippery identity politics, some argue for an egalitarian strategy that rejects the discursive realm of identity for greater attention to redistribution of material resources. By replacing gender with economic class, it might appear possible to mobilize a broader coalition in favor of progressive policies capable of benefiting most women and men. Policies catering to seemingly measurable individual economic gain rather than contestable identities may seem less susceptible to manipulation or elitist bias.

Yet feminist critique can help bridge the simplistic separation between cultural identity and economic "redistribution" by analyzing economic interests as socially constructed in relation to group identities (Duggan 2003). Our material interests will seem different depending on whether we see ourselves primarily as "taxpayers" who might pay for increased social services, as members of a self-sufficient and successful "middle class," as "investors" or potential lottery winners, as parents and grandparents concerned about future generations, as potentially divorced homemakers, as consumers, as workers, as community members, as global citizens, or as embodied humans vulnerable to illness and disability.

Critical feminism has rejected fixed, abstract ideas about "women," but gender as a factor in analyzing law and politics remains important. By challenging and engaging with the complicated social process of constructing identities and interests in relation to a substantive social and historical context, critical feminists have tried to open up new opportunities for political and economic coalitions capable of supporting reform. Martha Fineman's (2008) vision of substantive equality focuses on a vulnerability that is often gendered; women disproportionately assume caretaking responsibilities. Yet, this idea of vulnerability reaches beyond gender to encompass a variety of potentially fluid and intersecting interests, identities, and issues—from environmental devastation to middle-class economic insecurity. It may be an idea that can mobilize broader political and legal support for egalitarian policy in the current social context.

By viewing identity as complex and intersectional and economics as political, critical feminism understands that economic interests are steeped in identity politics. In the US, economic equality has long been feminized and racialized. For example, political commentators and policy analysts use the term "nanny state" to code progressive economics as an affront to a moral order dependent on upper-class, white male authority over women, children, and servants—especially female servants of color (McCluskey 2005b). At the 2004 Republican National Convention, California Governor Arnold Schwarzenegger used the slur "economic girlie men" against legislators supporting unions and trial lawyers in a state budget debate to suggest such positions were weak and silly (Grossman and McClain 2004). In the 2008 presidential campaign, Schwarzenegger similarly mocked Democratic candidate Obama for his "skinny legs" and "spread-the-wealth" ideas lacking "meat" in contrast to "action hero" McCain and his "pumped up" supporters, suggesting Obama was too feminine and too socialist to lead the nation (Campanile 2008). Critical feminist scholarship focuses on the continuing importance of identity politics in impeding economic equality and resists the tendency to essentialize the divide between economic class and cultural politics dealing with sex, gender, and race (McCluskey 2005). Justice Scalia, for example, defends his opposition to gay rights and abortion rights as deference to working-class culture under threat from professional elites (McCluskey 2007a: 1294 note 440). A critical approach questions *whose* interests are served by portraying gender inequality as a cultural attribute inherent to the working class, rather than as the product of policies shaped in part by elite interests. Critical analysis of the underlying policies and institutional structures that support current identity-based divisions can suggest ways of crafting policies to build new coalitions. For example, policies increasing economic support and security for diverse families might help overcome some of the "moral panic" currently directed at gay marriage (Duggan and Kim 2005).

Aftermath of the right's rule?

The formerly triumphant "free market" economy is in crisis, and newly-elected President Obama enjoys popular support for his call for major policy change. The right-wing shadow may be receding to reveal new opportunities for advancing substantive equality. Critical feminism can be useful in helping to rebuild political movements for positive change. By ambitiously questioning assumptions and thinking beyond existing boundaries, a critical approach presses us to open our imagination to the possibilities for a different, better world (Gordon 1998). Such imagination must counter the legacy of lowered expectations and complacency in the face of enormous inequalities which prevailing theories have rationalized as the inevitable or tragic consequences of maintaining economic and social order.

A critical legal approach rejects the assumption that simply redistributing money or changing political parties and individual leaders will suffice to promote major change. Critical analysis understands the current political, economic, and social institutions as legal structures designed to advance and entrench substantive power inequalities in the guise of neutral systems (McCluskey 2006). For that reason, feminist critique digs into the technical and empirical details of legal rules and political context to find the barriers to meaningful change.

Finally, *feminist* critique remains urgently important even with increased general support for policies promoting substantive equality. It is not just economic *in*equality that is tied to masculinist identity politics. Policies promoting economic *equality* are likely infused with gendered ideas and practices that reinforce and increase vulnerability and unequal burdens for many women and men. Feminist economist Randy Albelda (2008), for example, challenges a "macho" economic stimulus program that emphasizes physical infrastructure and "green jobs" focused on stereotypically male-identified construction and technology work. She argues for a "pink jobs" initiative aimed at improving the social caretaking infrastructure just as important to the nation's well-being as building roads or energy conservation. This proposal for a social caretaking stimulus program would include substantial government investment in education, health, and social services; it might expand jobs and raise salaries in areas like nursing and childcare disproportionately done by low-income women. But before such a vision of feminist reform can become reality, much feminist work reaching beyond the boundaries of existing law, politics, gender identity, and foundational theory remains to be done.

Appendix

Introduction to *At the Boundaries of the Law: Feminism and Legal Theory*

Martha Albertson Fineman

This book is the product of an increased interest in feminist scholarship as it relates to legal issues. Law is an area relatively untouched by the post-modern currents that have washed through other disciplines, but now appears to be caught within tides of critical methodologies and conclusions that threaten its very roots. This collection of papers was selected from a larger group presented over a four year period at sessions of the Feminism and Legal Theory Conference at the University of Wisconsin. They reveal that feminist legal theory represents both a subject and a methodology that are still in the process of being born. There are no "right" paths, clearly defined. This scholarship, however, can be described as sharing the objective of raising questions about women's relationships to law and legal institutions.

Theory and practice

Given the newness of the inquiry, many practitioners of feminist legal theory are more comfortable describing their work as an example of feminist "methodology" rather than an exposition of "theory." Some in fact believe that method is theory in its most (and perhaps only) relevant form.

In my opinion, the real distinction between feminist approaches to theory (legal and otherwise) and the more traditional varieties of legal theory is a belief in the desirability of the concrete. Such an emphasis also has had rather honorable nonfeminist adherents. For example, Robert Merton coined the term "theory of the middle range" to describe work that mediated between "stories" and "grand" theory. He described such scholarship as being better than mere storytelling or mindless empiricism as well as superior to vague references to the relationships between ill-defined abstractions (Merton, 1967, p. 68).

Feminist scholarship, in nonlaw areas at least, has tended to focus on specifics (Weedon, 1987, p. 11). Feminist legal scholarship, however, recently seems to be drifting toward abstract grand theory presentations. Carol Smart has warned that feminist legal theorists are in danger of creating in their writing the impression that it is possible to identify from among the various feminist legal theories that are in competition one specific form of feminist jurisprudence that will represent the "superior" (or true) version. She labels this totalizing tendency, evident in the work of many of the most well-known North American legal feminists, as the construction of a "scientific feminism," and she is explicitly critical of such grand theorizing (Smart, 1988, p. 71). The papers presented here avoid such theorizing and are connected with the material and concrete.

Grand theorizing represents the creation of a new form of positivism in a search for universal truths discoverable and ascertainable within the confines of the methodology of critical legal analysis. Middle range theory, by contrast, mediates between the material circumstances of women's lives and the grand realizations that law is gendered, that law is a manifestation of power, that law is detrimental to women. These realizations have previously been hidden or ignored in considerations of those laws that regulate women's lives. As the articles in this collection illustrate, such inequities in the legal treatment of women are best exposed by referencing and emphasizing the circumstances of their lives.

One cannot help but be aware of the difficulty of trying to do work using middle range feminist methodology within the confines of legal theory, however. Not only is there the pull toward grand theory that operates to categorize less grand scholarship as "nontheoretical," but I fear that feminist sensibilities become lost or absorbed into the morass of legal concepts and words. I, for one, am a legal scholar who has lost faith. Feminism, it seems, has not and, perhaps, cannot transform the law. Rather, the law, when it becomes the battleground, threatens to transform feminism. This is true I believe because of the obvious pull and power of the law as a "dominant discourse"—one which is self-contained (though incomplete and imperfect), self-congratulatory (though not introspective nor self-reflective) and self-fulfilling (though not inevitable nor infallible).

In order to even have a chance to be incorporated into and considered compatible with legal theory, feminist thought must adapt, even if it does not totally conform, to the words and concepts of legal discourse. Feminism may enter as a challenger, but the tools inevitably employed are those of the androphile master. And, the character of the tools determines to a large extent the shape and design of the resulting construction. It seems to me, therefore, that the task of feminists concerned with the law and legal institutions must be to create and explicate feminist methods and theories that explicitly challenge and compete with the existing totalizing nature of grand legal theory. Such a feminist strategy would set its middle range theory in opposition to law—outside of law. That is the task that has also defined the creation of this collection.

Feminist methodologies

In these articles, there are several characteristics that in various permutations and combinations provide examples for the construction of feminist legal analyses that challenge existing legal theory and paradigms. First, feminist methodology is often critical. The critical stance is gained from adopting an explicitly woman-focused perspective, a perspective informed by women's experiences. I personally believe that anything labeled feminist theory can *not* be "gender-neutral" and will often be explicitly critical of that paradigm as having historically excluded women's perspectives from legal thought. "Gender-sensitive" feminism, however, should not be viewed as lacking legitimacy because of an inappropriate bias. Rather, it is premised on the need to expose and correct *existing* bias. "Gender-sensitive" feminism seeks to correct the imbalance and unfairness in the legal system resulting from the implementation of perspectives excluding attention to the circumstances of women's gendered lives, even on issues that intimately affect those lives.

There is a tendency in traditional legal scholarship to view the status quo as unbiased or neutral. This is the logical place for feminist analysis to begin—as an explicit challenge to the notion of bias, as contrasted with the concepts of perspective and position. Feminist legal theory can demonstrate that what *is* is *not* neutral. What *is* is as "biased" as that which challenges it, and what *is* is certainly no more "correct" than that which challenges it, and there can be no refuge in the status quo. Law has developed over time in the context of theories and institutions which are controlled by men and reflect their concerns. Historically, law has been a "public" arena and its focus has been on public concerns. Traditionally, women belonged to the "private" recesses of society, in families, in relationships controlled by men, in silence.

A second characteristic of much feminist work is that it uses a methodology that critically evaluates not only outcomes but the fundamental concepts, values, and assumptions embedded in legal thought (MacKinnon, 1982, pp, 239–40). Results or outcomes in cases decided under existing legal doctrines are not irrelevant to this inquiry, but criticizing them is only a starting point. Too many legal scholars end their inquiry with a critique of results and recommendations for "tinkering"-type reforms without considering how the very conceptual structure of legal thought condemns such reforms to merely replicating injustices (Fineman, 1986). When, as is so often the case, the basic tenets of legal ideology are at odds with women's gendered lives, reforms based on those same tenets will do little more than the original rules to validate and accommodate women's experiences.

From this perspective, feminism is a political theory concerned with issues of power. It challenges the conceptual bases of the status quo by assessing the ways that power controls the production of values and standards against which specific results and rules are measured. Law represents both a discourse and a process of power. Norms created by and enshrined in law are manifestations of power relationships. These norms are coercively applied and justified in part by the perception that they are "neutral" and "objective." An appreciation of this fact has led many feminist scholars to focus on the legislative and political processes in the construction of law rather than on what judges are doing. It has also led many feminists to concentrate on social and cultural perceptions and manifestations of law and legality at least as much as on formal legal doctrinal developments.

Implicit in the assertion that feminism must be a politically rather than a legally focused method or theory is a belief about law and social change that assumes the relative powerlessness of law to transform society as compared to other ideological institutions of social constitution within our culture. Law can reflect social change, even facilitate it, but can seldom if ever initiate it. No matter what the formal legal articulation, implementation of legal rules will track and reflect the dominant conceptualizations and conclusions of the majority culture. Thus, while law can be used to highlight the social and political aspects it reflects, it is more a mirror than a catalyst when it comes to effecting enduring social change.

A third characteristic of much of feminist legal methodology is that the vision it propounds or employs seeks to present alternatives to the existing order. This may be, of course, a natural outgrowth of other characteristics of feminist legal thought, particularly when it is critical and political. I place it as separate, however, because an independent goal of much feminist work is to present oppositional values. It is often at its core radically nonassimilationist, resistant to mere inclusion in dominant social institutions as the solution to the problems in women's gendered lives. In fact, the larger social value of feminist methodology may lie in its ability to make explicit oppositional stances vis-à-vis the existing culture. The objective of feminism has to be to transform society, and it can do so only by persistently challenging dominant values and defiantly not assimilating into the status quo. The point of making women's experiences and perspective a central factor in developing social theory is to change "things," not to merely change women's perspective or their position vis-à-vis existing power relationships. To many feminist scholars, therefore, assimilation is failure, while opposition is essential for a feminist methodology applied to law.

One other characteristic of much of feminist legal theory is that it is evolutionary in nature. It does not represent doctrine carved in stone or even printed in statute books. Feminist methodology at its best represents a contribution to a series of ongoing debates and discussions which take as a given that "truth" changes over time as circumstances change and that gains and losses, along with wisdom recorded, are not immutable but part of an evolving story. Feminist legal theory referencing women's lives, then, must define and undertake the "tasks of the moment." As the tasks of the future cannot yet be defined, any particular piece of feminist legal scholarship is only a step in the long journey feminist legal scholars have begun.

Within feminist legal thought and, indeed, within the articles included in this collection, there is explicit contest and criticism as well as implicit disagreement about the wisdom of pragmatic uses of law, the effectiveness of law as an instrument of social change and, most broadly, the importance of law as a focus for feminist study. Some feminist scholarship reveals antagonist, even violent disagreement with other feminist works. Disagreements aside, however, it seems clear to me that feminist legal theory has lessons for all of society, not just for women or legal scholars. Ultimately, it is the members of our audience that will judge the effectiveness of our individual and collective voices.

Conclusion

Feminist concerns are, and must continue to be, the subject of discourses located outside of law. Law as a dominant rhetorical system has established concepts that limit and contain feminist criticisms. Feminist theory must develop free of the restraints imposed by legalized concepts of equality and neutrality or it will be defined by them. Law is too crude an instrument to be employed for the development of theory anchored in an appreciation of the differences in the social and symbolic position of women and men in our culture. Law can be and should be the *object* of feminist inquiry, but to position law and law reform as the *objective* of such theorizing is to risk having incompletely developed feminist innovations distorted and appropriated by the historically institutionalized and inextractable dictates of the "Law."

The scholarship here is critical, is political, is part of on-going debates and is concerned with methods and processes that comprise law. It is typical of the very best feminist legal scholarship in that it is about law in its broadest form, as a manifestation of power in society, and, for the most part, it recognizes that there is no division between law and power. Many of the articles recognize that law is not only found in courts and cases, in legislatures and statutes, but also in implementing institutions such as the professions of social work and law enforcement. Others reflect the fact that law is found in discourse and language used in everyday life reflecting understandings about "Law." It is evident in the beliefs and assumptions we hold about the world in which we live and in the norms and values we cherish.

I hope that the reader enjoys the excursion to the boundaries of law undertaken in this volume. A few are sure to be disturbed by some of the work presented, others, hopefully, will be inspired. Feminist legal theory has begun to expand the boundaries, redefine the borders of the law.

Madison, 1990

Bibliography

Abramovitz, M. (1986) *Regulating the Lives of Women*, Boston: South End Press.

Abrams, K. (1989) "Gender Discrimination and the Transformation of Workplace Norms," *Vanderbilt Law Review*, 42: 1183.

——(1995) "Sex Wars Redux: Agency and Coercion in Feminist Legal Theory," *Columbia Law Review*, 95: 304.

——(2009) "Family as a Vehicle for Abjection," *Utah Law Review* and *Journal of Law and Family Studies*.

Ackerman, B. (2007) "The Living Constitution," *Harvard Law Review*, 120: 1737.

Aisenberg, N. and Harrington, M. (1988) *Women of Academe: outsiders in the sacred grove*, Amherst, MA: University of Massachusetts Press.

Al-Hibri, A. (1999) "Is Western Patriarchal Feminism Good for the World and Minority Women?," in S.M. Okin, J. Cohen, J. Howard and M.C. Nussbaum (eds) *Is Multiculturalism Bad for Women?*, Princeton, NJ: Princeton University Press.

Albelda, R. (2008) "The Macho Stimulus Plan," *Boston Globe*, 28 November. Online. Available HTTP: <http://www.boston.com/bostonglobe/editorial_opinion/oped/articles/2008/11/28/the_macho_stimulus_plan/ > (accessed 26 August 2009).

Alexander, P. (1987) "Prostitution: a Difficult Issue for Feminists," in F. Delacoste and P. Alexander (eds) *Sex Work*, Pittsburgh, PA: Cleis Press; reprinted in J.G. Greenberg, D.E. Roberts, and M.L. Minow (eds) (1998) *Women and the Law*, 2nd edn, New York: Foundation Press.

Allen, P. (1997) *The Concept of Woman: volume I*, Grand Rapids, MI: W.B. Eerdmans.

Alstott, A.L. (2004) *No Exit: what parents owe their children and what society owes parents*, New York: Oxford University Press.

Amar, A.R. (1995) "Women and the Constitution," *Harvard Journal of Law and Public Policy*, 18: 465.

American Law Institute (2002) *Principles of the Law of Family Dissolution: analysis and recommendations*, Newark, NJ: LexisNexis.

Anastasio, P. et al. (1997) "Categorization, Recategorization, and Common Ingroup Identity," in R. Spears, P.J. Oaks, N. Ellmers, S.A. Haslam (eds) *Social Psychology of Stereotyping and Group Life*, Oxford: Blackwell.

Andrews, L.B. (1999) *The Clone Age: adventures in the new world of reproductive technology*, 1st edn, New York: Henry Holt.

——(2001) *Future Perfect*, 1st edn, New York: Columbia University Press.

Angel, M. (2005) "The Modern University and Its Law School: Hierarchical, Bureaucratic Structures Replace Coarchical, Collegial Ones; Women Disappear from Tenure

Track and Reemerge as Caregivers; Tenure Disappears or Becomes Unrecognizable," *Akron Law Review*, 38: 789.

Appleton, S. (2005) "Missing in Action? Searching for Gender Talk in The Same-Sex Marriage Debate," *Stanford Law and Policy Review*, 16: 97.

——(2008) "Toward a 'Culturally Cliterate' Family Law?," *Berkeley Journal of Gender, Law and Justice*, 23: 267.

Arendt, H. (1958) *The Origins of Totalitarianism*, London: George Allen and Unwin.

Armitage, J. (2005) "Beyond Hypermodern Militarized Knowledge Factories," *Review of Education, Pedagogy, and Cultural Studies*, 27: 219.

Armstrong, J. (2008) "The Sleaze-fest Continues," *Philadelphia Daily News*, 20 March: 35.

Arriola, E.R. (1990) "What's the Big Deal? Women in the New York Construction Industry and Sexual Harassment Law, 1970–85," *Columbia Human Rights Law Review*, 22: 22.

Asch, A. (2004) "Critical Race Theory, Feminism and Disability: Reflections on Social Justice and Personal Identity," in B.G. Smith and B. Hutchinson (eds) *Gendering Disability*, Piscataway, NJ: Rutgers University Press.

Ashmore, R.D. and Del Boca, F.K. (1979) "Sex Stereotypes and Implicit Personality Theory: Toward a Cognitive-Social Psychological Conceptualization," *Sex Roles*, 5: 219.

Askin, K. (1997) *War Crimes against Women: persecution in inter war crimes tribunals*, The Hague: Martinus Nijhoff.

Aslanian, S. (2004) "Suffering for Two: The Bind of Maternal Depression," *American RadioWorks*, American Public Media, August 2004. Online. Available HTTP: <http://americanradioworks.publicradio.org/features/maternaldepression/transcript.html> (accessed 6 February 2009).

Atkins, S. and Hoggart, B. (1984) *Women and the Law*, Oxford: Blackwell.

Auerbach, J. (1976) *Unequal Justice: lawyers and social change in modern America*, New York: Oxford University Press.

Babcock, B. (1998) "Book Review: Feminist Lawyers," *Stanford Law Review*, 50: 1689.

Baker, A. (2008) "Police Data Shows Increase in Street Stops," *New York Times*, 6 May: B1. Online. Available HTTP: <http://www.nytimes.com/2008/05/06/nyregion/06frisk.html> (accessed 27 August 2009).

Baker, K. (1988) "Contracting for Security: Paying Married Women What They've Earned," *Chicago Law Review*, 55: 1193.

Balibar, E. (1990) "Paradoxes of Universality," in D.T. Goldberg (ed.) *Anatomy of Racism*, Minneapolis: University of Minnesota Press.

Banks, T.L. (1989–90) "Women and Aids: Racism, Sexism and Classism," *New York University Review of Law and Social Change*, 17: 365.

Barber, A. (2008) "Hail to the Future Chief: Whoever She Is," *Newsday*, 11 June: A35.

Bartlett, K. (1990) "Feminist Legal Methods," *Harvard Law Review*, 103: 829.

——(1999) "Feminism and Family Law," *Family Law Quarterly*, 33: 475.

Batten, M. (1994) *Sexual Strategies: how females choose their mates*, New York: Tarcher/Putnam.

Becker, M. (1996) "Problems with the Privatization of Heterosexuality," *Denver University Law Review*, 73: 1169.

Behrendt, L. (1993) "Aboriginal Women and the White Lies of the Feminist Movement: Implications for Rights Discourse," *Australian Feminist Law Journal*, 1: 27.

Belkin, L. (2003) "The Opt-Out Revolution," *New York Times Magazine*, 26 October: 42. Online. Available HTTP: <http://www.nytimes.com/2003/10/26/magazine/26WOMEN.html> (accessed 26 August 2009).

Bell, C. (2000) *Peace Agreements and Human Rights*, Oxford: Oxford University Press.

Bell, C. et al. (2004) "Justice Discourses in Transition," *Journal of Social and Legal Studies*, 13: 305.

Bell, R.M. (1985) *Holy Anorexia*, Chicago: University of Chicago Press.

Bell, S. (1994) *Reading, Writing and Rewriting the Prostitute Body*, Bloomington, IN: Indiana University Press.

Bender, W. (2008) "Obama, Vowing Tax Shift, Chills in Chester," *Philadelphia Daily News*, 29 October.

Benhabib, S. (1992) *Situating the Self: gender, community and postmodernism in contemporary ethics*, Cambridge: Polity Press.

——(1995) "Cultural Complexity, Moral Interdependence, and the Global Dialogical Community," in M. Nussbaum and J. Glover (eds) *Women, Culture, and Development*, Oxford: Oxford University Press.

——(1996) "Toward a Deliberative Model of Democratic Legitimacy," in S. Benhabib (ed) *Contesting the Boundaries of the Political*, Princeton, NJ: Princeton University Press.

——(1999) "'Nous' et 'les Autres': the Politics of Complex Cultural Dialogue in a Global Civilisation," in C. Joppke and S. Lukes (eds) *Multicultural Questions*, Oxford: Oxford University Press.

——(2002), *Claims of Culture: equality and diversity in the global era*, Princeton, NJ: Princeton University Press.

Bennhold, K. (2008) "A Veil Closes France's Door to Citizenship," *New York Times*, 19 July: A1. Online. Available HTTP: <http://www.nytimes.com/2008/07/19/world/europe/19france.html> (accessed 26 August 2009).

Bennett, O. et al. (1995) *Arms to Fight, Arms to Protect: women speak out about conflict*, London: Panos.

Berns, S. (1999) *To Speak as a Judge: difference, voice and power*, Aldershot, UK: Ashgate.

Bernstein, D.E. (2003) "*Lochner's* Feminist Legacy," *Michigan Law Review*, 101: 1960.

Bernstein, J.L. (2008) "To Reproductive Freedom: Restrictive Abortion Laws and the Resulting Backlash," *Brooklyn Law Review*, 73: 1502.

Bhabha H.K. (1999) "Liberalism's Sacred Cow," in S.M. Okin, J. Cohen, M. Howard and M.C. Nussbaum (eds) *Is Multiculturalism Bad for Women?*, Princeton, NJ: Princeton University Press.

Biden, J. (2008) *Promises to Keep*, New York: Random House.

Bird, E. (2003) "The Academic Arm of the Women's Liberation Movement: Women's Studies in North America and the United Kingdom," *Women's Studies International Forum*, 25: 139.

Blackstone, W. (1765–69) *Commentaries on the Laws of England*, Oxford: Clarendon Press.

Blackwell, K. (2008) "Post-Racial *Preference* America," *The National Review Online*. Online. Available HTTP: <http://article.nationalreview.com/?q=ODNlYTM5NmYxZTljMmE2MzhmMWE1YjBlOTNhYmFhYjc=> (accessed 29 August 2009).

Blankenhorn, D. (1995). *Fatherless America*, New York: Basic Books.

——(2007) *The Future of Marriage*, New York: Encounter Books.

Bledstein, B. (1976) *The Culture of Professionalism: the middle class and the development of higher education in America*, New York: W.W. Norton.

Blistein, E. (2008) "Revisiting *Roe*: the Language of Privacy and Isolation in US and Vermont Case Law," *Vermont Bar Journal*, 34: 43.

Blumstein, P. and Schwartz, P. (1983) *American Couples*, New York: William Morrow.

Boaz, D. (2003) "Defining an Ownership Society." Online. Available HTTP: <http://www.cato.org/special/ownership_society/boaz.html > (accessed 26 August 2009).

Bobo, L.D. (1999) "Prejudice as a Group Position: Microfoundations of a Sociological Approach to Racism and Race Relations," *Journal of Social Issues*, 55: 445.

Bolt, C. (1993) *The Women's Movements in the United States and Britain from the 1790s to the 1920s*, Amherst, MA: University of Massachusetts Press.

Bordo, S. (2004) *Unbearable Weight: feminism, western culture and the body*, Berkeley, CA: University of California Press.

Boyer, P.J. (2008) "The Color of Politics: a Mayor of the Post-Racial Generation," *The New Yorker*, 4 February: 38.

Brennan, P. (1989) "A Cry for Help," *Washington Post*, 1 October: R8.

Buchanan, A. et al. (2000) *From Chance to Choice: genetics and justice*. Cambridge: Cambridge University Press.

Boston Women's Health Collective (1998) *Our Bodies Ourselves for the New Century*, New York: Touchstone.

Bourdieu, P. (2001) *Masculine Domination*, Cambridge: Polity Press.

Bowman, C.G. and Schneider, E.M. (1998) "Feminist Legal Theory, Feminist Law Making, and the Legal Profession," *Fordham Law Review*, 67: 249.

Bramlett, M.D. and Mosher, W.D. (2002) *Cohabitation, Marriage, Divorce, and Remarriage in the United States*, Washington, DC: GPO. Online. Available HTTP: <http://www.cdc.gov/nchs/data/series/sr_23/sr23_022.pdf > (accessed 3 June 2009).

Braoch, J.L. and Petretic, P. (2006) "Beyond Traditional Definitions of Assault: Expanding Our Focus to Include Sexually Coercive Experiences," *Journal of Family Violence*, 21: 477.

Breton-Le Goff, G. (2002) *Analysis of Trends in Sexual Violence Prosecutions by the International Criminal Tribunal for Rwanda from November 1995 to November 2002*, Montreal: NGO Coalition for Women's Rights in Conflict Situations.

Brinig, M. and Nock, S. (2002) "Weak Men and Disorderly Women: Divorce and the Division of Labor," in A.W. Dnes and R. Rowthorn (eds) *The Law and Economics of Marriage and Divorce*, New York: Cambridge University Press.

Britten, A. (1989) *Masculinity and Power*, Oxford: Blackwell.

Brizendine, L. (2006) *The Female Brain*, New York: Morgan Road.

Brodie, J. (2008) "We Are All Equal Now: Contemporary Gender Politics in Canada," *Feminist Theory*, 9: 145.

Brooks, D. (2006) "Is Chemistry Destiny?" [Op-Ed] *New York Times*, 17 September: D14.

Brown, W. (1995) *States of Injury: power and freedom in late modernity*, Princeton, NJ: Princeton University Press.

Brown, W. and Halley, J. (2002) *Left Legalism/Left Critique*, Durham, NC: Duke University Press.

Browning, D.S. (2007) "Linda McClain's *The Place of Families* and Contemporary Family Law: a Critique from Critical Familism," *Emory Law Journal*, 56: 1383.

Browning, D.S. et al. (2000) *From Culture Wars to Common Ground*, 2nd edn, Louisville, KY: Westminster John Knox Press.

Bulbeck, C. (2006) "Explaining the Generation Debate: Envy, History or Feminism's Victories?," *Lilith*, 15: 35.

Buss, D. (2002) "Prosecuting Mass Rape: *Prosecutor v. Dragoljub Kunarac, Radomir Kovac and Zoran Vukovic*," *Feminist Legal Studies*, 12: 92.

Buss, D.M. (1994) *The Evolution of Desire: strategies of human mating*, New York: Basic Books.

Cahill, D. (2004) "New-Class Discourse and the Construction of Left-Wing Elites," in M. Sawer and B. Hindess (eds) *Us and Them: anti-elitism in Australia*, Perth, Australia: API Network, Australia Research Institute, Curtin University of Technology.

Cain, P.A. (1991) "Same-Sex Couples and the Federal Tax Laws," *Law and Sexuality*, 1: 97.

——(1994) "Lesbian Perspective, Lesbian Experience, and the Risk of Essentialism," *Virginia Journal of Social Policy and Law*, 2: 43.

——(2000) "Heterosexual Privilege and the Internal Revenue Code," *University of South Florida Law Review*, 34: 465.

Caine, B. (1998) "Feminism," in B. Caine, M. Gatens, E. Grahame, J. Larbalestier, S. Watson, and E. Webby, *Australian Feminism: a companion*, Melbourne: Oxford University Press.

Campanile, C. (2008) "Arnold Kicks Sand in 'Skinny' Obama's Face," *New York Post*, 1 November: 7. Online. Available HTTP: <http://www.nypost.com/seven/11012008/news/politics/arnold_kicks_sand_in_skinny_obamas_face_136282.htm> (accessed 26 August 2009).

Cantalupo, N.C. (2009) "Campus Violence: Understanding the Extraordinary through the Ordinary," *Journal of College and University Law*, 35: 613.

Cantle T. (2001) *Community Cohesion: the report of the independent review team*, London: Home Office.

Carpenter, R.C. (2006) "Recognizing Gender-Based Violence against Civilian Men and Boys in Conflict Situations," *Security Dialogue*, 37: 83.

Case, M.A. (1993) "From the Mirror of Reason to the Measure of Justice," *Yale Journal of Law and the Humanities*, 5: 115.

——(1995a) "Disaggregating Gender from Sex and Sexual Orientation: the Effeminate Man in the Law and Feminist Jurisprudence," *Yale Law Journal*, 105: 1.

——(1995b) "Of Richard Epstein and Other Radical Feminists," *Harvard Journal of Law and Public Policy*, 18: 369.

——(2000) "The Very Stereotype the Law Condemns: Constitutional Sex Discrimination Law as Quest for Perfect Proxies," *Cornell Law Review*, 85: 1447.

——(2001) "How High the Apple Pie? a Few Troubling Questions about Where, Why, and How the Burden of Care for Children Should Be Shifted," *Chicago-Kent Law Review*, 76: 1753.

——(2002) "Reflections on Constitutionalizing Women's Equality," *California Law Review*, 90: 765.

——(2009) "Feminist Fundamentalism and Constitutional Citizenship," in L.C. McClain and J.L. Grossman (eds) *Gender Equality: dimensions of women's equal citizenship*, Cambridge: Cambridge University Press.

Catherine of Siena, (1993) "Come Gently Without Any Fear," L. 233; DT LXXVI, in M. O'Driscoll (ed.) *Catherine of Siena: passion for the truth, compassion for humanity: selected spiritual writings*, New Rochelle, NY: New City Press.

Chamallas, M. (2003) *Introduction to Feminist Legal Theory*, New York: Aspen.

Chappel, L. (2003) " Finding Space for Women's Interests: Developments at the UN Ad Hoc Tribunals and the International Criminal Court," paper presented at Australasian Political Studies Association Conference, University of Tasmania, Hobart, 29 September-1 October 2003. Online. Available HTTP: <http://www.utas.edu.au/government/APSA/LChappellfinal.pdf> (accessed 27 August 2009).

Charlesworth, H. (1993) "Alienating Oscar? Feminist Analysis of International Law," in D.G. Dallmeyer (ed) *Reconceiving Reality: women and international law*, Washington, DC: American Society of International Law.

Charlesworth, H. et al. (1991) "Feminist Approaches to International Law," *American Journal of International Law*, 85: 613.

Cherlin, A. (2005) "American Marriage in the Early Twenty-First Century," *The Future of Children*, 15: 33.

Chicago Legal News (1893) *Chicago Legal News*, 12 August: 435, 451.

Clark, D.L. and Myser, C. (1998) "'Fixing' Katie and Eilish: Medical Documentaries and the Subjection of Conjoined Twins," *Literature and Medicine*, 17: 45.

Clark, K.R. (1984) "Faye Dunaway Looks to Melt her Icy Image," *Chicago Tribune*, 14 December: N1.

Clemetson, L. (2006) "Work vs. Family, Complicated by Race," *New York Times*, 9 February: G1.

Clinton, H. (2008) "Transcript: Hillary Clinton Endorses Barack Obama," *New York Times*, 7 June. Online. Available HTTP: < http://www.nytimes.com/2008/06/07/us/politics/07text-clinton.html?_r=2&pagewanted=1 > (accessed 29 August 2009).

CNN (2008a) "CNN Election Center 2008: Results by State," *CNN*, 17 November. Online. Available HTTP: <http://www.cnn.com/ELECTION/2008/results/president/> (accessed 27 August 2009).

——(2008b) "Hillary Clinton to Speak at National Building Museum," [Transcript] *CNN*, 7 June. Online. Available HTTP: <http://transcripts.cnn.com/TRANSCRIPTS/0806/07/se.04.html> (accessed 27 August 2009).

——(2008c) "Obama Wins Mississippi Primary; Texas Caucus Win Estimated," *CNN*, March 11. Online. Available HTTP: <http://www.cnn.com/2008/POLITICS/03/11/miss.primary/index.html> (accessed 27 August 2009).

Coalition for Marriage, Families and Couples Education et al. (2000) *The Marriage Movement: a statement of principles*, New York: Institute for American Values. Online. Available HTTP: <http://www.americanvalues.org/pdfs/marriagemovement.pdf> (accessed 31 August 2009).

Cobb, S. (1997) "The Domestication of Violence in Mediation," *Law and Society Review*, 31: 397.

Cold, C.J. and Taylor, J.R. (1999) "The Prepuce," *British Journal of Urology International*, 83 suppl. 1: 34.

Coleman, J. (2005) *The Lazy Husband: how to get men to do more parenting and housework*, New York: St. Martin's Press.

Collier, R. (1995) *Masculinity, Law, and the Family*, London: Routledge.

——(2006) "Feminist Legal Studies and the Subject(s) of Men: Questions of Text, Terrain and Context in the Politics of Family Law and Gender," in A. Diduck and K. O'Donovan (eds) *Feminist Perspectives on Family Law*, Abingdon, UK: Routledge-Cavendish.

Collins, P.H. (1991) "Black Feminist Thought: Knowledge, Consciousness, and the Politics of Empowerment," New York: Routledge; reprinted in J.G. Greenberg, M.L. Minow, D.E. Roberts, and M.J. Frug (eds) (1998) *Women and the Law*, 2nd edn, New York: Foundation Press.

——(2000) *Black Feminist Thought: knowledge, consciousness, and the politics of empowerment*, 2nd edn, New York: Routledge.

Connell, R.W. (1995) *Masculinities*, Cambridge: Polity Press.

Coontz, S. (2007) "Taking Marriage Private," *New York Times*, 26 November: A23.

Cooper, M. (2008) "Comments Bring Wives into Fray in Wisconsin," *New York Times*, 20 February: A19.

Cooper, R.D. (2009) "Our First Unisex President? Black Masculinity and Obama's Feminine Side," *Denver University Law Review*, 86: 633.

Cornell, D. (2004) "The Public Supports of Love," in M.L. Shanley, J. Cohen, and D. Chasman (eds) *Just Marriage*, New York: Oxford University Press.

Cossman, B. (2004) "Beyond Marriage," in M.L. Shanley, J. Cohen, and D. Chasman (eds) *Just Marriage*, New York: Oxford University Press.

——(2009) "The 'Opt Out Revolution' and the Changing Narratives of Motherhood: Self Governing the Work/Family Conflict," *Utah Law Review* and *Journal of Law and Family Studies*.

Cott, N. (1987) *The Grounding of Modern Feminism*, New Haven, CT: Yale University Press.

——(1989) "Comment on Karen Offen's 'Defining Feminism,'" *Signs: a journal of women in culture and society*, 15: 203.

Couric, K. (2008) *Transcript of Interview with Sarah Palin*, CBS News, 30 September 2008. Online. Available HTTP: <http://www.cbsnews.com/stories/2008/09/30/eveningnews/main4490788.shtml> (accessed 7 June 2009).

Crossley, N. (2001) *The Social Body: habit, identity, and desire*, London: Sage.

Crawford, B. (2005) "The Profits and Penalties of Kinship: Conflicting Meanings of Family in Estate Tax Law," *Pittsburgh Tax Review*, 3: 1.

——(2007) "Toward a Third-Wave Feminist Legal Theory: Young Women, Pornography and the Praxis of Pleasure," *Michigan Journal of Gender and Law*, 14: 99.

Crawford, J. (2001) "Rwanda Tribunal's Witness Protection in Question," *Hirondelle News Agency*, 10 December.

Crenshaw, K. (1988) "Race, Reform, and Retrenchment," *Harvard Law Review*, 101: 1331.

——(1989) "Demarginalizing the Intersection of Race and Sex: a Black Feminist Critique of Antidiscrimination Doctrine, Feminist Theory, and Antiracist Politics," *University of Chicago Legal Forum*, 1989: 139.

——(1991) "Mapping the Margins: Intersectionality, Identity Politics, and Violence against Women of Color," *Stanford Law Review*, 43: 1241.

——(2002) "The First Decade: Critical Reflections, or a 'Foot in the Closing Door,'" *U.C.L.A. Law Review*, 49: 1343.

Crenshaw, K. et al. (eds) (1996) *Critical Race Theory: the key writings that formed the movement*, New York: New Press.

Crowley J. (1999) "The Politics of Belonging: Some Theoretical Considerations," in A. Geddes and A. Favell (eds) *The Politics of Belonging: migrants and minorities in contemporary Europe*, Aldershot, UK: Ashgate.

Courtenay, W.H. (2000) "Constructions of Masculinity and their Influence on Men's Well-Being: a Theory of Gender and Health," *Social Science and Medicine* 50: 1385.

Courtney, M. (1998) "The Costs of Child Protection in the Context of Welfare Reform," *The Future of Children*, 8: 23.

Cunningham, C. (1999) "The 'Racing' Cause of Action and the Identity Formally Known as Race: the Road to Tamazunchale," *Rutgers Law Review*, 30: 709.

Dahl, R. (2006) *On Political Equality*, New Haven, CT: Yale University Press.

Daly, C.B. (1989) "Montreal Women's Slayer Identified, Long Suicide Note Blames 'Feminists' for Troubles," *Washington Post*, 8 December: A1.

Daniels, C. (1997) "Between Fathers and Fetuses: the Social Construction of Male Reproduction and the Politics of Fetal Harm," *Signs: a journal of women in culture and society*, 22: 582.

Darling, M.T. (2002) "Eugenics Unbound: Race, Gender and Genetics," paper presented at Gender, Justice, and the Gene Age Conference, New York, 6–7 May 2002.

Davies, M. (2008) *Asking the Law Question: the dissolution of legal theory*, 3rd edn, Sydney: Law Book.

Davis, L.J. (2002) *Bending Over Backwards: disability, dismodernism and other difficult positions*, New York: New York University Press.

Dawkins, J.S. (1988) *Higher Education: a policy statement* (white paper), Canberra, Australia: Australian Government Publishing Service.

de Londras, F. (2007) "Telling Stories and Hearing Truths: Providing an Effective Remedy to Genocidal Sexual Violence against Women," in R. Henham and P. Behrens (eds) *The Criminal Law of Genocide: international, comparative and contextual aspects*, Aldershot, UK: Ashgate.

de Pizan, C. (1405) *Le Livre de la Cité des Dames*; trans. Rosalind Brown-Grant (1999) *The City of Ladies*, New York: Penguin.

Delgado, R. (1987) "The Ethereal Scholar: Does Critical Legal Studies Have What Minorities Want," *Harvard Civil Rights-Civil Liberties Law Review*, 22: 301.

Delgado, R. and Stefancic, J. (eds) (1994; 2nd edn 1999) *Critical Race Theory: the cutting edge*, Philadelphia: Temple University Press.

Dery, M. (2007) "Wimps, Wussies, and W.," *The Los Angeles Times*, 3 May: 23.

Dey, J.G. and Hill, C. (2007) *Behind the Pay Gap*, Washington, DC: American Association of University Women Educational Foundation. Online. Available HTTP: <http://www.aauw.org/research/behindPayGap.cfm> (accessed 27 August 2009).

Dowd, N.E. (2000) *Redefining Fatherhood*, New York: New York University Press.

——(2007) "Multiple Parents/Multiple Fathers," *Journal of Law and Family Studies*, 9: 231.

Drachman, V.G. (1984) *Hospital with a Heart: women doctors and the paradox of separatism at the New England Hospital, 1862–1969*, Ithaca, NY: Cornell University Press.

——(1993) *Women Lawyers and the Origins of Professional Identity in America: the letters of the equity club 1887–1890*, Ann Arbor: University of Michigan Press.

——(1998) *Sisters in Law: women lawyers in modern American history*, Cambridge, MA: Harvard University Press.

Draut, T. et al. (2008) *From Middle to Shaky Ground: the economic decline of America's middle class, 2000–2006*, New York: Demos.

Dryzek, J.S. (2000) *Deliberative Democracy and Beyond: liberals, critics, contestations*, Oxford, Oxford University Press.

Dubois, E.C. (1989) "Comment on Daren Offen's 'Defining Feminism,'" *Signs: a journal of women in culture and society*, 15: 195.

Duggan, L. (2003) *The Twilight of Equality? neoliberalism, cultural politics, and the attack on democracy*, Boston: Beacon Press.

Duggan, L. and Hunter, N. (1995) *Sex Wars: sexual dissent and political culture*, New York: Routledge.

Duggan, L. et al. (1993) False Promises: Feminist Anti-Pornography Legislation, *New York Law School Law Review*, 38: 133.

Duncan, W.C. (2001) "'Don't Ever Take a Fence Down': The 'Functional' Definition of Family – Displacing Marriage in Family Law," *Journal of Law and Family Studies*, 3: 57.

Dux, M. and Simic, Z. (2008) *The Great Feminist Denial*, Melbourne: Melbourne University Press.

Dworkin, A. (1985) "Against the Male Flood: Censorship, Pornography and Equality," *Harvard Women's Law Journal*, 8: 29.

Eaton, M. (1994) "At the Intersection of Gender and Sexual Orientation: Toward a Lesbian Jurisprudence," *California Review of Law and Women's Studies*, 3: 183.

Edin, K., and Kefalas, M. (2005) *Promises I Can Keep: why poor women put motherhood before marriage*, Berkeley: University of California Press.

Ehrenreich, B. (2004) "Owning Up to Abortion," *New York Times*, 22 July: A24.

Eilperin, J. (2008) "Palin Displays Her Feminist Side," *Washington Post*: 21 October. Online. Available HTTP: <http://voices.washingtonpost.com/44/2008/10/21/palin_displays_her_feminist_si.html > (accessed 7 June 2009).

Eisenstein, H. (1996) *Inside Agitators: Australian femocrats and the state*, Philadelphia: Temple University Press.

Ellman, I. (1989) "The Theory of Alimony," *California Law Review*, 77: 40.

Ely, J.H. (1980) *Democracy and Distrust: a theory of judicial review*, Cambridge, MA: Harvard University Press.

Emens, E. (2004a) "Monogamy's Law: Compulsory Monogamy and Polyamorous Existence," *New York University Review of Law and Social Change*, 29: 277.

——(2004b) "Just Monogamy?," in M.L. Shanley, J. Cohen, and D. Chasman (eds) *Just Marriage*, New York: Oxford University Press.

——(2009) "Intimate Discrimination: The State's Role in the Accidents of Sex and Love," *Harvard Law Review*, 122: 1307.

Enright, M. (2009) "Choice, Culture and the Politics of Belonging: the Emerging Law of Forced and Arranged Marriage," *Modern Law Review*, 72: 331.

Erbe, B. (2008) "Sarah Palin's Feminist Flip-Flop," *US News and World Report*, 28 October. Online. HTTP: < http://www.usnews.com/blogs/erbe/2008/10/24/sarah-palins-feminist-flip-flop.html> (accessed 7 June 2009).

Ertman, M.M. (1995) "Contractual Purgatory for Sexual Marginorities: Not Heaven, But Not Hell Either," *Denver University Law Review*, 73: 1107.

——(1998) "Commercializing Marriage: a Proposal for Valuing Women's Work through Premarital Security Agreements," *Texas Law Review*, 77: 17.

——(2001) "Marriage as a Trade: Bridging the Private/Private Distinction," *Harvard Civil Rights and Civil Liberties Law Review*, 36: 79.

——(forthcoming) "Race Treason: the Untold Story of America's Ban on Polygamy," *Columbia Journal of Gender and Law*.

Eskridge, W. (2007) "America's Statutory 'Constitution,'" *U.C. Davis Law Review*, 41: 1.

Estlund, C. (2003) *Working Together: how workplace bonds strengthen a diverse democracy*, Oxford: Oxford University Press.

Estrich, S. (1987) *Real Rape*, Cambridge, MA: Harvard University Press.

Fagan, J., West, V. and Holland, J. (2003) "Reciprocal Effects of Crime and Incarceration in New York City Neighborhoods," *Fordham Urban Law Journal*, 2003. Online. Available HTTP: <http://ssrn.com/abstract=392120> (accessed 6 February 2009).

Falk, D. (1997) "Brain Evolution in Females: an Answer to Mr. Lovejoy," in L.D. Hager (ed.) *Women in Human Evolution*, New York: Routledge.

Faludi, S. (1991) *Backlash: the undeclared war against women*, London: Chatto and Windus.

——(2008) "Think the Gender War is Over? Think Again," *New York Times*, 15 June: WK14.

Farrell, W., Sterba, J.P. and Svoboda, S. (2008) *Does Feminism Discriminate Against Men?*, New York: Oxford University Press.

Fedigan, L.M. (1997) "Is Primatology a Feminist Science?," in L.D. Hager (ed) *Women in Human Evolution*, New York: Routledge.

Fenwick, L. (1998) *Private Choices, Public Consequences: reproductive technology and the new ethics of conception, pregnancy, and family*, New York: Dutton.

Fielding, H. (1996) *Bridget Jones's Diary*, New York: Viking.

Fields, J. (2004) *America's Families and Living Arrangements: 2003*, Washington, DC: US Census Bureau. Online. Available HTTP: <http://www.census.gov/prod/2004pubs/p20–553.pdf > (accessed 3 June 2009).

Findling, J. (1994) *Chicago's Great World's Fairs*, Manchester, UK: Manchester University Press.

Fineman, M.A. (1981) "Law and Changing Patterns of Behavior: Sanctions on Nonmarital Cohabitation," *Wisconsin Law Review*, 1981: 275.

——(1983) "Implementing Equality: Ideology, Contradiction and Social Change," *Wisconsin Law Review*, 1983: 789.

——(1986) "Illusive Equality: on Weitzman's Divorce Revolution," *American Bar Foundation Research Journal*, 1986: 781.

——(1987a) "A Reply to David Chambers," *Wisconsin Law Review*: 1987: 165.

——(1987b) "Introduction to the Papers: the Origins and Purpose of the Feminism and Legal Theory Conference," *Wisconsin Women's Law Journal*, 3: 1.

——(1988) "Dominant Discourse, Professional Language, and Legal Change in Child Custody Decisionmaking," *Harvard Law Review*, 101: 727.

——(1989) "The Politics of Custody and the Transformation of American Custody Decision Making," *University of California Davis Law Review*, 22: 829.

——(1991a) *The Illusion of Equality: the rhetoric and reality of divorce reform*, Chicago: University of Chicago Press.

——(1991b) "Images of Mothers in Poverty Discourses," *Duke Law Journal*, 41: 274.

——(1991c) "Introduction," in M.A. Fineman and N.S. Thomadsen (eds) *At the Boundaries of Law: feminism and legal theory*, New York: Routledge.

——(1992) "Feminist Theory in Law: the Difference it Makes," *Columbia Journal of Gender and Law*, 2: 1.

——(1995) *The Neutered Mother, the Sexual Family and Other Twentieth Century Tragedies*, New York: Routledge.

——(2000) "Cracking the Foundational Myths: Independence, Autonomy and Self-Sufficiency," *Journal of Gender, Social Policy and the Law*, 8: 13.

——(2001) "Why Marriage?," *Virginia Journal of Social Policy and the Law*, 9: 239.

——(2004) *The Autonomy Myth: a theory of dependency*, New York: New Press.

——(2008) "The Vulnerable Subject: Anchoring Equality in the Human Condition," *Yale Journal of Law and Feminism*, 20: 1.

——(2009) "Equality: Still Illusive After All These Years," in L.C. McClain and J.L. Grossman (eds) *Gender Equality: dimensions of women's equal citizenship*, Cambridge: Cambridge University Press.

Fineman, M.A. and Thomadsen, N.S. (eds) (1991) *At the Boundaries of Law: feminism and legal theory*, New York: Routledge.

Finley, L. (1986) "Transcending Equality Theory: a Way Out of the Maternity in the Workplace Debate," *Columbia Law Review*, 86: 1118.

Fisher, B. et al. (2000) *The Sexual Victimization of College Women: findings from two national-level studies*, Washington, DC: Bureau of Justice Statistics.

Fletcher, R. et al. (2008) "Legal Embodiment: Analyzing the Body of Healthcare," *Medical Law Review*, 16: 321.

Ford, R.T. (2000) "Race as Culture? Why Not?," *U.C.L.A. Law Review*, 47: 1803.

Foucault, M. (1991) "Governmentality," in G. Burchell, C. Gordon, and P. Miller (eds) *The Foucault Effect: studies in governmentality, with two lectures by and an interview with Michel Foucault*, Chicago: University of Chicago Press.

——(2004) *Sécurité, Territoire, Population: cours au Collège de France 1977–78*; trans. G. Burchell (2007) *Security, Territory, Population: lectures at the Collège de France 1977–78*, M. Senellart, F. Elwad, A. Fontana, and A.I. Davidson (eds) New York: Palgrave Macmillan.

Fouhy, B. (2008) "Women Push Back in Support of Clinton," *FoxNews.com*, 30 March. Online. Available HTTP: <http://www.foxnews.com/wires/2008Mar30/0,4670, ClintonWomen,00.html > (accessed 27 August 2009).

Fox, M. and Thomson, M. (2005a) "A Covenant with the Status Quo? Male Circumcision and the New BMA Guidance to Doctors," *Journal of Medical Ethics*, 31: 463.

——(2005b) "Short Changed? the Law and Ethics of Male Circumcision," *International Journal of Children's Rights*, 13: 157.

——(2009) "Sexing the Cherry: Fixing Masculinity," in N. Sullivan and S. Murray (eds) *Somatechnics: Queering the Technologisation of Bodies*, Aldershot, UK: Ashgate.

——(2009) "Foreskin is a Feminist Issue," *Australian Feminist Studies*.

Frank, A.W. (1995) *The Wounded Storyteller: body, illness, and ethics*. Chicago: University of Chicago Press.

Frank, D.A. (2003) "'Crack Baby' Syndrome," [Letter to the Editor] *New York Times*, 28 November: A42.

Franke, K.M. (1994a) "Cunning Stunts: From Hegemony to Desire: A Review of Madonna's *Sex*," *New York University Review of Law and Social Change*, 20: 549.

——(1994b) "The Meaning of Sex," in *Direction and Distortion: the centrality of sexuality in the shaping of feminist legal theory* (unpublished conference papers), Atlanta: Feminism and Legal Theory Project Archives.

——(1995) "The Central Mistake of Sex-Discrimination Law: the Disaggregation of Sex from Gender," *University of Pennsylvania Law Review*, 144: 1.

——(2001) "Theorizing Yes: an Essay on Feminism, Law, and Desire," *Columbia Law Review*, 101: 181

——(2004) "The Domesticated Liberty of *Lawrence v. Texas*," *Columbia Law Review*, 104: 1399.

——(2006) "The Politics of Same-Sex Marriage Politics," *Columbia Journal of Gender and Law*, 15: 236.

——(2008) "Longing for *Loving*," *Fordham Law Review*, 76: 2685.

Frankenberg, R. (1993) *White Women, Race Matters: the social construction of whiteness*, Minneapolis: University of Minnesota Press.

Fredman S. (2007) "Recognition or Redistribution: Reconciling Inequalities," *South African Journal of Human Rights*, 23: 214.

Freedman, S. (2008) "Democrats Didn't Help Hillary," *Tampa Tribune*, 15 June: 1.

Freeman, J. (1991) "How Sex Got Into Title VII: Persistent Opportunism as a Maker of Public Policy," *Law and Inequality*, 9: 163.

Freidson, E. (1986) *Professional Powers: a study of the institutionalization of knowledge*, Chicago: University of Chicago Press.

Friedman, J.M. (1993) *America's First Woman Lawyer: the biography of Myra Bradwell*, Buffalo, NY: Prometheus Books.

Friedman, L. and Baron, C.H. (2001) "*Baker v. State* and the Promise of the New Judicial Federalism," *British Columbia Law Review*, 43: 125.

Frisken, A. (2004) *Victoria Woodhull's Sexual Revolution: political theater and the popular press in nineteenth-century America*, Philadelphia: University of Pennsylvania Press.

Garland-Thomson, R. (1997) *Extraordinary Bodies: figuring physical disability in American culture and literature*, New York: Columbia University Press.

——(2001) "Re-Shaping, Rethinking and Redefining: Feminist Disability Studies," Center for Women's Policy Studies.

——(2002) "Integrating Disability, Transforming Feminist Theory" *National Women's Studies Association Journal*, 14: 1.

Garrison, M. (1983) "Marriage: the Status of Contract," *University of Pennsylvania Law Review*, 131: 1039.

Gatens, M. (1996) *Imaginary Bodies: ethics, power and corporeality*, London: Routledge.

Gaudium Et Spes, Pastoral Constitution on the Church in the Modern World, Promulgated by his Holiness, Pope Paul VI on December 7, 1965. Online. Available HTTP: <http://www.vatican.va/archive/hist_councils/ii_vatican_council/documents/vat-ii_cons_19651207_gaudium-et-spes_en.html > (accessed 7 June 2009).

General Medical Council (2008) *Personal Beliefs and Medical Practice*, London: GMC.

Genovese, A. (2002) "Madonna and/or Whore? Feminism(s) and Public Sphere(s)," in M. Thornton (ed.) *Romancing the Tomes: popular culture, law and feminism*, London: Cavendish.

——(2008) "Poisons and Antidotes: Historicizing Feminism and Equality in an Age of Rights of Competition," *Dialogue Academy of Social Sciences in Australia*, 27: 10.

Gerstmann, E. and Streb, M.J. (eds) (2006) *Academic Freedom at the Dawn of a New Century: how terrorism, governments, and culture wars impact free speech*, Stanford, CA: Stanford University Press.

Gewirth, A. (1996) *The Community of Rights*, Chicago: University of Chicago Press.

Gidney, R.D. and Millar, W.P.J (1994) *Professional Gentlemen: the professions in nineteenth century Ontario*, Toronto: University of Toronto Press.

Gilliam, N. (1987) "A Professional Pioneer: Myra Bradwell's Fight to Practice Law," *Law and History Review*, 5: 105.

Gilligan, C. et al. (eds) (1990) *Making Connections: the relational worlds of adolescent girls at Emma Willard School*, Cambridge, MA: Harvard University Press.

Giroux, H.A. (2008) "The Militarization of US Higher Education after 9/11," *Theory, Culture, Society*, 25: 56.

Glendon, M.A. (1976) "The Withering Away of Marriage," *Virginia Law Review*, 62: 663.

Glennon, T. (2007) "Still Partners? Examining the Consequences of Post-Dissolution Parenting," *Family Law Quarterly*, 4: 105.

Goodman, A. (2008) "McCain Campaign Calls Obama a Socialist – But Why is that a Smear?" Interview with R. MacArthur, *Democracy Now*, Pacifica, 24 October 2008.

Gordon, L. (1990) *Woman's Body, Woman's Right*, New York: Penguin.

Gould, C.C. (1996) "Diversity and Democracy: Representing Differences," in S. Benhabib (ed.) *Contesting the Boundaries of the Political*, Princeton, NJ: Princeton University Press.

Gournay, M. (1641) "The Equality of Men and Women," reprinted in R. Hillman and C. Quesnel (eds; trans.) (2002) *Apology for the Woman Writing*, Chicago: University of Chicago Press.

Graves, F. and Shepard, C.E. (1992) "Packwood Accused of Sexual Advances" *Washington Post*, 22 November: A1.

Graycar, R. and Morgan, J. (1996) "Legal Categories, Women's Lives and the Law Curriculum OR: Making Gender Examinable," *Sydney Law Review*, 18: 431.

——(2002) *The Hidden Gender of Law*, Sydney: Federation Press.

Grbich, J.E. (1991) "The Body in Legal Theory," in M.A. Fineman and N.S. Thomadsen (eds) *At the Boundaries of Law: feminism and legal theory*, New York: Routledge.

——(1996) "The Taxpayer's Body: Genealogies of Exertion," in P. Cheah, D. Fraser, and J. Grbich (eds) *Thinking Through the Body of the Law*, Sydney: Allen and Unwin.

Green, J. (2003) "Pressure under High Heels," in G. Elert (ed.) *The Physics Factbook*. Online. Available HTTP: <http://hypertextbook.com/facts/2003/JackGreen.shtml> (accessed 18 June 2009).

Green, L.L. (2002) "Gender Hate Propaganda and Sexual Violence in the Rwandan Genocide: an Argument for Intersectionality in International Law," *Columbia Human Rights Law Review*, 33: 733.

Greene, M. (10 August 1891) "Letter to Louis Frank," *Papiers Frank* No. 6031 (file 2), Brussels: Bibliothèque Royale.

——(May 1895) "Letter to Louis Frank," *Papiers Frank* No. 7791–96 (envelope 1), Brussels: Bibliothèque Royale.

——(9 September 1896) "Letter to Louis Frank," *Papiers Frank* No. 6031 (file 2), Brussels: Bibliothèque Royale.

Gross, J. (2005) "Being a Patient: Alone in Illness, Seeking Steady Arm to Lean On," *New York Times*, 26 August: A1.

Grossberg, M. (1990) "Institutionalizing Masculinity: the Law as a Masculine Profession," in M.C. Carnes and C. Griffen (eds) *Meanings and Manhood: constructions of masculinity in Victorian America*, Chicago: University of Chicago Press.

Grossman, J. and McClain, L. (2004) "The 'Girlie-Man' Slur and Similar Insults: How They Show the Persistence of Sex-Role Stereotypes," Online. Available HTTP: <http://writ.news.findlaw.com/commentary/20040921_mcclain.html> (accessed 26 August 2009).

Grosz, E. (1994) *Volatile Bodies: toward a corporeal feminism*, Bloomington, IN: Indiana University Press.

Gunning, I. (1992) "Arrogant Perception, World-Travelling and Multicultural Feminism: the Case of Female Genital Surgeries," *Columbia Human Rights Law Review*, 23: 189.

Gutmann, A. and Thompson, D. (2004) *Why Deliberative Democracy?*, Princeton, NJ: Princeton University Press.

Habermas J. (1998) *The Inclusion of the Other: studies in political theory*, Cambridge, MA: MIT Press.

Hager, L.D. (ed.) (1997) *Women in Human Evolution*, London: Routledge.

Halley, I. (2004) "Queer Theory by Men," *Duke Journal of Gender, Law and Policy*, 11: 7.

Halley, J. (1993) "Reasoning about Sodomy: Act and Identity in and after *Bowers v. Hardwick*," *Virginia Law Review*, 79: 1721.

——(2002) "Sexuality Harassment," in W. Brown and J. Halley (eds) *Left Legalism/Left Critique*, Durham, NC: Duke University Press.

——(2006) *Split Decisions: how and why to take a break from feminism*, Princeton, NJ: Princeton University Press.

Halley, J. and Cossman, B. (2007) "Program," for Up Against Family Law Exceptionalism: a Conference, Harvard Law School, 2–3 February 2007. Online. Available

HTTP: <http://www.law.harvard.edu/faculty/jhalley/plst/UAFLEprogram2.07.pdf> (accessed 26 August 2009).

Halley, J. and Suk, J. (2009) *Family Law Summer Camp*, Harvard Law School, July 14–15, 2009.

Halley, J. et al. (2006) "From the International to the Local in Feminist Legal Responses to Rape, Prostitution/Sex Work and Sex Trafficking: Four Studies in Contemporary Governance Feminism," *Harvard Journal of Law and Gender*, 29: 335.

Halloran, L. (2008) "A Singular Achievement: Clinton Did Break a Glass Ceiling, Just Not the One She Hoped to," *US News and World Report*, 16 June: 25.

Hamilton, P.K. (2008) *New England School of Law*, Charleston, SC: Arcadia.

Haraway, D. (1991) *Simians, Cyborgs, and Women*, New York: Routledge.

Harris, A. (1990) "Race and Essentialism in Feminist Legal Theory," *Stanford Law Review*, 42: 581.

——(1994) "The Jurisprudence of Reconstruction," *California Law Review*, 82: 741.

——(2000) "Beyond Equality: Power and the Possibility of Freedom in the Republic of Choice," *Cornell Law Review*, 85: 1181.

Harris, B.J. (1978) *Beyond her Sphere: women and the professions in American history*, Westport, CT: Greenwood Press.

Hasday, J. (2000) "Contest and Consent: a Legal History of Marital Rape," *California Law Review*, 88: 1373.

Heath, S. (1987) "Male Feminism," in A. Jardine and P. Smith (eds) *Men in Feminism*, New York: Methuen.

Helmerhorst, F.M. et al. (2004) "Perinatal Outcome of Singletons and Twins after Assisted Conception: a Systematic Review of Controlled Studies," *BMJ*, 328: 261.

Henderson, M. (2008) "Feminism in the Hearts and Minds and Words of Men: Revisiting Men's Cultural Remembrance of Australian Feminism in the New Millennium," *Dialogue: Academy of Social Sciences in Australia*, 27: 29.

——(2006) *Marking Feminist Times: remembering the longest revolution in Australia*, Bern: Peter Lang.

Henrotin, E.M. (1893) "The Great Congresses at the World's Fair," *Cosmopolitan*, 14: 626.

Hetherington, E.M. and Kelly, J. (2002) *For Better or for Worse: divorce reconsidered*, New York: Norton.

Henry, A. (2004) *Not My Mother's Sister: generational conflict and third-wave feminism*, Bloomington, IN: Indiana University Press.

Higgins, T. (1995) "'By Reason of their Sex': Feminist Theory, Postmodernism, and Justice," *Cornell Law Review*, 80: 1536.

Hilton, J.L. and Von Hippel, W. (1996) "Stereotypes," *Annual Review of Psychology*, 47: 234.

Hirschmann, N. (2008) "Wed to the Problem? The Place of Men and State in Families," *The Good Society*, 17: 52.

Hirshman, L.R. (2005) "Homeward Bound," *The American Prospect*, 16:20.

——(2006) *Get to Work: a manifesto for women of the world*, New York: Viking.

Hitchens, C. (2008) "The First Excuse: Don't Blame Sexism for Hillary Clinton's Defeat," *Slate.com*, 16 June. Online. Available HTTP: <http://www.slate.com/id/2193684/> (accessed 27 August 2009).

Hobbs, F. (2005) *Examining American Household Composition: 1990 and 2000*, Washington, DC: US Census Bureau. Online. Available HTTP: <http://www.census.gov/prod/2005pubs/censr-24.pdf> (accessed 3 June 2009).

Hoff, J. (1991) *Law, Gender, and Injustice: a legal history of US women*, New York: New York University Press.

Hook, J. (2005) "Off to a Running Start, How Far Can GOP Go?," *Los Angeles Times*, 20 March: A1.

hooks, b. (1984) *Feminist Theory: From Margin to Center*, Boston: South End Press; reprinted in J.G. Greenberg, M.L. Minow, D.E. Roberts, and M.J. Frug (eds) (1998) *Women and the Law*, 2nd edn, New York: Foundation Press.

Hoskyns, C. (2004) "Gender Equality," in A. Wiener and T. Diez (eds) *European Integration Theory*, Oxford: Oxford University Press.

Howe, A. (1987) "'Social Injury Revisited': Towards a Feminist Theory of Social Justice," *International Journal of the Sociology of Law*, 15: 423.

——(1991) "The Problem of Privatized Injuries: Feminist Strategies for Litigation," in M.A. Fineman and N.S. Thomadsen (eds) *At the Boundaries of Law: feminism and legal theory*, New York: Routledge.

——(1994) *Punish and Critique: towards a feminist analysis of penalty*, New York: Routledge.

Hrdy, S.B. (2009) *Mothers and Others: the evolutionary origins of mutual understanding*, Cambridge, MA: Belknap Press.

Human Rights Watch (1996) *Shattered Lives: sexual violence during the Rwandan genocide and its aftermath*, New York: Human Rights Watch.

Humphrey, J. (1983) "The Memoirs of John P. Humphrey, the First Director of the United Nation's Division of Human Rights," *Human Rights Quarterly*, 5: 392.

Humphrey, M. (2002) *The Politics of Atrocity and Reconciliation: from terror to trauma*, London: Routledge.

Hunter, N. (1991) "Marriage, Law, and Gender: a Feminist Inquiry," *Law and Sexuality*, 1: 9.

Hunter, R. (2008) "Can *Feminist* Judges Make a Difference?," *International Journal of the Legal Profession*, 15: 7.

Hutchinson, D.L. (2002) "Progressive Race Blindness? Individual Identity, Group Politics, and Reform," *U.C.L.A. Law Review*, 49: 1455.

——(2008) "Reality Check: Obama's Election Victory Does not Mean that Era of Race-Based Identity Politics Has Died," *Dissenting Justice Blogspot*, 12 November. Online. Available HTTP: <http://dissentingjustice.blogspot.com/2008/11/did-election-really-mean-radical-shift.html> (accessed 27 August 2009).

Hyde, J.S. (2005) "The Gender Similarities Hypothesis," *American Psychologist*, 60: 581.

Institute for American Values (2006) *Marriage and the Law: a statement of principles*, New York: Institute for American Values.

Inter Insigniores (15 October 1976) Declaration on the Admission of Women to the Ministerial Priesthood, Sacred Congregation for the Doctrine of the Faith.

International Committee for Prostitutes' Rights (1986) *Statement on Prostitution and Human Rights*; reprinted in J.G. Greenberg, D.E. Roberts and M.L. Minow (eds) (1998) *Women and the Law*, 2d edn, New York: Foundation Press.

Jackson, S. (2000) "Networking Women: a History of Ideas, Issues and Developments in Women's Studies in Britain," *Women's Studies International Forum*, 23: 1.

Jacobs, J.A. and Gerson, K. (2004) *The Time Divide: work, family, and gender inequality*, Cambridge MA: Harvard University Press.

Jacobs, M.B. (2007) "Why Just Two? Disaggregating Traditional Parental Rights and Responsibilities to Recognize Multiple Parents," *Journal of Law and Family Studies*, 9: 309.

Johnson, H. (1987) "Self-Portrait of a Loyal Secretary who Took Risks for Boss and Cause," *Washington Post*, 9 June: A15.

Johnstone, R. and Vignaendra, S. (2003) *Learning Outcomes and Curriculum Development in Law: a Report commissioned by the Australian Universities Teaching Committee (AUTC)*, Canberra, Australia: Commonwealth of Australia.

Jordan, G.H. (2004) "Creating a Women's Culture: Women Lawyers in Illinois, 1855–1939," unpublished dissertation, University of Illinois at Chicago.

Kahn, J.D. (2004) "How a Drug Becomes 'Ethnic': Law, Commerce, and the Production of Racial Categories in Medicine," *Yale Journal of Health Policy, Law, and Ethics*, 4: 1.

Kahn, R. and Kellner, D. (2007) "Resisting Globalization," in G. Ritzer and M.A. Malden (eds) *The Blackwell Companion to Globalization*, Malden, MA: Blackwell.

Kantor, J. and Halbfinger, D.M. (2008) "Behind McCain, Washington Outsider Wanting Back In," *New York Times*, 29 October: A1.

Kapur, R. (2002) "The Tragedy of Victimization Rhetoric: Resurrecting the 'Native' Subject in International/Post-Colonial Feminist Legal Politics," *Harvard Human Rights Journal*, 15: 2.

Karpin, I. (1994) "Reimagining Maternal Selfhood: Transgressing Body Boundaries and the Law," *Australian Feminist Law Journal*, 2: 36.

——(2005) "Genetics and the Legal Conception of Selfhood," in M. Shildrick and R. Mykitiuk (eds) *Ethics of the Body: postconventional challenges*, Cambridge, MA: MIT Press.

——(2006) "The Uncanny Embryos: Legal Limits to the Human and Reproduction without Women," *Sydney Law Review*, 28: 599.

Karpin, I. and Ellison, D. (2009) "Reproduction without Women: Frankenstein and the Legal Prohibition of Human Cloning," in C. Kevin (ed.) *Feminism and the Body, Interdisciplinary Perspectives*, Cambridge: Cambridge Scholars Publishing.

Karpin, I. and Mykitiuk, R. (2008) "Going Out on a Limb: Prosthetics, Normalcy and Disputing the Therapy/Enhancement Distinction," *Medical Law Review*, 16: 413.

Kay, F. (2007) "The Social Significance of the World's First Women Lawyers," *Osgood Hall Law Journal*, 45: 398.

Kellner, D. (2003) "Globalization, Terrorism, and Democracy: 9/11 and its Aftermath," Online. Available HTTP: <http://www.gseis.ucla.edu/faculty/kellner/essays/globalizationterroraftermath.pdf> (accessed 25 July 2009).

——(2004) "Theorizing Globalization," Online. Available HTTP: <http://www.gseis.ucla.edu/faculty/kellner/essays/theorizingglobalization.pdf> (accessed 25 July 2009).

Kelly, A. (forthcoming) "Money Matters in Marriage: Unmasking Interdependence in Ongoing Spousal Economic Relations," *Louisville Law Review*, 47: 113.

Kelman, M. (1979) "Choice and Utility," *Wisconsin Law Review*, 1979: 769.

Kennedy, D. (1982) "Distributive and Paternalist Motives in Contract and Tort Law," *Maryland Law Review*, 41: 563.

——(2009) "Feminism and the Family: Incarcerated Parents, Parental Terminations and Feminist Legal Theory," paper presented at Applied Feminism Conference, University of Baltimore, 6 March 2009.

Kenway, J. et al. (2006) *Haunting the Knowledge Economy*, London: Routledge.

Kessler, L.T. (2001) "The Attachment Gap: Employment Discrimination Laws, Women's Cultural Caregiving, and the Limits of Economic and Liberal Legal Theory," *University of Michigan Journal of Law Reform*, 34: 371.

——(2005) "Transgressive Caregiving," *Florida State University Law Review*, 33: 1.

——(2007) "Community Parenting," *Washington Journal of Law and Policy*, 24: 47.

——(2008) "Getting Class," *Buffalo Law Review*, 56: 101.

Kessler-Harris, A. (1982) *Out to Work: a history of wage-earning women in the United States*, Oxford: Oxford University Press.

Kimani, Mary (2007) "Congolese Women Confront the Legacy of Rape: War and Sexual Violence Leave Survivors in Desperate Need," *Africa Renewal*, 20: 4. Online. Available HTTP: <http://www.un.org/ecosocdev/geninfo/afrec/vol20no4/204-congolese-women.html> (accessed 31 August 2009).

Kirby, P. (2006) *Vulnerability and Violence: the impact of globalization*, London: Pluto Press.

Kittay, E.F. (1998) *Love's Labor: essays on women, equality, and dependency*, New York: Routledge.

——(2008) "Ah My Foolish Heart: a Reply to Alan Soble's Antioch Sexual Offense Policy: a Philosophical Exploration" in A. Soble and N. Power (eds) *Philosophy of Sex, Contemporary Readings*, 5th edn, Lanham, MD: Rowman and Littlefield.

Knauer, N.J. (1998) "Heteronormativity and Federal Tax Policy," *West Virginia Law Review*, 101: 129.

Knights, S. (2005) "Religious Symbols in the School: Freedom of Religion, Minorities and Education," *European Human Rights Law Review*, 5: 499.

Koppelman, A. (2002) *The Gay Rights Question in Contemporary American Law*, Chicago: University of Chicago Press.

Krieger, L.H. (1995) "The Content of our Categories: a Cognitive Bias Approach to Discrimination and Equal Employment Opportunity," *Stanford Law Review*, 47: 1161.

Krieger, L.J. and Cooney, P.N. (1983) "The Miller Wohl Controversy: Equal Treatment, Positive Action, and the Meaning of Women's Equality," *Golden Gate University Law Review*, 13: 513.

Kristof, N.D. (2005) "Health Care? Ask Cuba," *New York Times*, 12 January. Online. Available HTTP: < http://www.nytimes.com/2005/01/12/opinion/12kris.html> (accessed 26 August 2009).

Kundnani, A. (2002) "The Death of Multiculturalism," *Race & Class*, 43: 41.

Kurtz, H. (1985) "Meese Delayed Grant When Conservatives Balked," *Washington Post*, 9 August: A8.

Lacey, N. (1998) *Unspeakable Subjects: feminist essays in legal and social theory*, Oxford: Hart Publishing.

Langland, E. and Gove, W. (eds) (1983) *A Feminist Perspective in the Academy: the difference it makes*, Chicago: University of Chicago Press.

Laqueur, T. (1990) *Making Sex: body and gender from the Greeks to Freud*, Cambridge, MA: Harvard University Press.

Larson, M.S. (1977) *The Rise of Professionalism: a sociological analysis*, Berkeley, CA: University of California Press.

Lau, H. (2008) "Formalism: From Racial Integration to Same-Sex Marriage," *Hastings Law Journal*, 59: 843.

——(2010) "Identity Scripts & Democratic Deliberation," 94 *Minnesota Law Review* 897.

Law, S.A. (1984) "Rethinking Sex and the Constitution," *University of Pennsylvania Law Review*, 132: 955.

Law Times (1893) *Law Times*, 5 August: 330.

Lawrence, C.R., III (1995) "Race, Multiculturalism, and the Jurisprudence of Transformation," *Stanford Law Review*, 47: 819.

Lea, J. (2003) "From Brixton to Bradford: Official Discourse on Race and Urban Violence in the UK," in G. Gilligan and J. Pratt (eds) *Crime, Truth and Justice: official inquiry, discourse, knowledge*. Cullompton, UK: Willan.

Lehr, V.T. et al. (2007) "Neonatal Facial Coding System Scores and Spectral Characteristics of Infant Crying During Newborn Circumcision," *Clinical Journal of Pain*, 5: 417.

Leib, E. (2007) "Friendship and the Law," *University of California Law Review*, 54: 631.

——(2009) "Friends as Fiduciaries," *Washington University Law Review*, 86: 665.

Levy, B.S. (2005) "Why are Infants at Risk in America?" [Letter to the Editor] *New York Times*, 14 January. Online. Available HTTP: <http://query.nytimes.com/gst/fullpage. html?res=9B0DE2DC1438F937A25752C0A9639C8B63> (accessed 26 August 2009).

Lewin, T. (2006) "The New Gender Divide: At Colleges Women are Leaving Men in Dust," *New York Times*, 6 July: A1. Online. Available HTTP: <http://www.nytimes. com/2006/07/09/education/09college.html?_r=1&scp=1&sq=The+New+Gender+ Divide&st=nyt > (accessed 26 August 2009).

Lewis, M. (2005) "More than Meets the Eye: the Under Side of the Corporate Culture of Higher Education and Possibilities for a New Feminist Critique," *Journal of Curriculum Theorizing*, 2: 7.

Liberman, M. (2006) "Neuroscience in the Service of Sexual Stereotypes." Online. Available HTTP: <http://158.130.17.5/~myl/languagelog/archives/003419.html> (accessed 31 August 2009).

Lilly, A. (2008) "Choice, Before and After," *Seven Days: Vermont's Independent Voice*, 16 January. Online. Available HTTP: <http://www.7dvt.com/2008/choice-and-after> (accessed 26 August 2009).

Lippman, A. (1991) "Prenatal Genetic Testing and Screening: Constructing Needs and Reinforcing Inequities," *American Journal of Law and Medicine*, 17: 15.

——(2006) *The Inclusion of Women in Clinical Trials: are we asking the right questions?* Toronto: Woman and Health Protection.

Liptak, A. et al. (2008) "US Court, a Longtime Beacon, Is Now Guiding Fewer Nations," *New York Times*, 18 September: A1.

Littleton, C.A. (1987) "Reconstructing Legal Equality," *California Law Review*, 75: 1279.

Lockhart Committee (2005) *Legislation Review: prohibition of Human Cloning Act 2002 and Research Involving Human Embryos Act 2002*, Canberra, Australia: Department of Health and Ageing.

Lorde A. (1984) "Age, Race, Class, and Sex: Women Redefining Difference," in A. Lorde, *Sister Outsider: essays and speeches*, Berkeley, CA: Crossing Press.

Lyotard, J.L. (1984) *The Post Modern Condition: a report on knowledge*, Manchester, UK: Manchester University Press.

McCaffery, E.J. (1997) *Taxing Women*, Chicago: University of Chicago Press.

McCaughey, B. (2005) "Why are Infants at Risk in America?" [Letter to the Editor] *New York Times*, 14 January. Online. Available HTTP: <http://query.nytimes.com/gst/ fullpage.html?res=990CE2DC1438F937A25752C0A9639C8B63> (accessed 26 August 2009).

McClain, L.C. (2006) *The Place of Families: fostering capacity, equality, and responsibility*, Cambridge, MA: Harvard University Press.

——(2007) "Love, Marriage, and the Baby Carriage: Revisiting the Channeling Function of Family Law," *Cardozo Law Review*, 28: 2133.

——(2009) "Child, Family, State, and Gender Equality in Religious Stances and Human Rights Instruments: a Preliminary Comparison," in M.A. Fineman and K. Worthington (eds) *What Is Right for Children: the competing paradigms of religion and human rights*, Farnham, England: Ashgate.

McClain, L.C. and Grossman, J.L. (2009) *Gender Equality: dimensions of women's equal citizenship*, Cambridge: Cambridge University Press.

McCluskey, M.T. (1997) *Fear of Feminism: media stories of feminist victims and victims of feminism on college campuses*, in M.A. Fineman and M.T. McCluskey (eds) *Feminism, Media and the Law*, New York: Oxford University Press.

——(2000) "Subsidized Lives and the Ideology of Efficiency," *American University Journal of Gender, Social Policy, and the Law*, 8: 115.

——(2003) "Efficiency and Social Citizenship: Challenging the Neoliberal Attack on the Welfare State," *Indiana Law Journal*, 78: 783.

——(2005a) "The Politics of Economics in Welfare Reform," in M.A. Fineman and T. Dougherty (eds) *Feminism Confronts Homo Economicus: gender, law and society*, Ithaca, NY: Cornell University Press.

——(2005b) "How Equality Became Elitist: the Cultural Politics of Economics from the Court to the 'Nanny Wars,'" *Seton Hall Law Review*, 35: 1291.

——(2006) "The Substantive Politics of Formal Corporate Power," *Buffalo Law Review*, 53: 1453.

——(2007a) "Thinking with Wolves: Left Legal Theory after the Right's Rise," *Buffalo Law Review*, 54: 1191.

——(2007b) "Changing, Not Balancing the Market: 'Economic' Politics and 'Social' Programs," in C. Dalton (ed.) *Progressive Lawyering, Globalization and Markets: rethinking ideology and strategy*, Buffalo, NY: Hein.

——(2009) "How Queer Theory Makes Neoliberalism Sexy: Economics and the Queer Challenge to Feminism," in M.A. Fineman, J.E. Jackson, and A.P. Romero (eds) *Feminist and Queer Legal Theory: intimate encounters, uncomfortable conversations*, Aldershot, UK: Ashgate.

McCormack, L. et al. (2007) "Power Couples: See What Happens when Harvard Meets Harvard," *02138*, Winter: 62.

McDonagh, E. (1996) *Breaking the Abortion Deadlock: from choice to consent*, Oxford: Oxford University Press.

MacDorman, M.F. et al. (2005) "Explaining the 2001–2 Infant Mortality Increase: Data from the Linked Birth/Infant Death Data Set," *International Journal of Health Services*, 35: 415.

McElroy, W. (ed) (1991) *Freedom, Feminism and the State*, Washington, DC: The Independent Institute.

McGoldrick, D. (2006) *Human Rights and Religion: the Islamic headscarf debate in Europe*, Oxford: Hart.

MacKinnon, C.A. (1982) "Feminism, Marxism, Method and the State: An Agenda for Theory," *Signs*, 7: 515.

——(1987) *Feminism Unmodified: discourses on life and law*, Cambridge, MA: Harvard University Press.

——(1989) *Toward a Feminist Theory of State*. Cambridge, MA: Harvard University Press.

——(2006a) *Are Women Human? And other international dialogues*, Cambridge, MA: Harvard University Press.

——(2006b) "Defining Rape Internationally: a Comment on *Akayesu*," *Columbia Journal of Transnational Law*, 44: 940.

McNamara, J. (1984) "Cornelia's Daughters: Paula and Eustochium," *Women's Studies*, 11: 9.

McNamee, G.H. (1998) *Bar None: 125 years of women lawyers in Illinois*, Chicago: Chicago Bar Association for Women.

McRobbie, A. (2007) "Top Girls?," *Cultural Studies*, 21: 718.

Maathai, W. (2004) "Land and Freedom," *The Guardian*, 11 November. Online. Available HTTP: <http://www.greenbeltmovement.org/a.php?id=26> (accessed 31 August 2009).

Madison, J. (1788) "The Federalist No. 37: Concerning the Difficulties of the Convention in Devising a Proper Form of Government," in *The Federalist; on the New Constitution* (1788). Online. Available HTTP: <http://www.constitution.org/fed/federa37.htm> (accessed 26 August 2009).

Maese, R. (2008) "Women Get Serious: 2008 Campaigns Signal Bright Future for Female Candidates," *Baltimore Sun*, 4 November: 4B.

Magarian, G.P. (2003) "Regulating Political Parties under a 'Public Rights' First Amendment," *William and Mary Law Review*, 44: 1939.

Maldonado, S. (2005) "Beyond Economic Fatherhood: Encouraging Divorced Fathers to Parent," *University of Pennsylvania Law Review*, 153: 921.

——(2006) "Deadbeat or Dead Broke: Redefining Child Support for Poor Fathers," *U.C. Davis Law Review*, 39: 991.

——(2008) "Cultivating Forgiveness: Reducing Hostility and Conflict After Divorce," *Wake Forest Law Review*, 43: 441.

Mann, J. (1980) "Help for Battered Wives Encounters Opposition," *Washington Post*, 9 May: B1.

——(1988) "A Chilling Look at Domestic Violence," *Washington Post*, 7 December: D3.

Mansfield, H.C. (2006) *Manliness*, New Haven, CT: Yale University Press.

Marcus, I. (1994) "Terrorism in the Home," in M.A. Fineman and R. Mykitiuk (eds) *The Public Nature of Private Violence: the discovery of domestic abuse*, New York: Routledge.

Marginson, S. and Considine, M. (2000) *The Enterprise University: power, governance and reinvention in Australia*, Cambridge: Cambridge University Press.

Marin, C. (2008). "Thanks to Hillary for Being a Winner at Heart," *Chicago Sun-Times*, 11 May: A17.

Markus, M. (1987) "Women, Success and Civil Society," in S. Benhabib and D. Cornell (eds) *Feminism as Critique*, Minneapolis: University of Minnesota Press.

Martin, J.A. et al. (2007) "Births: Final Data for 2005," *National Vital Statistic Reports*, 56: 6. Online. Available HTTP: <http://www.cdc.gov/nchs/data/nvsr/nvsr56/nvsr56_06.pdf > (accessed 3 June 2009).

Mather, V.M. (1993) "Evolution and Revolution in Family Law," *Saint Mary's Law Journal*, 25: 405.

Medical News Today (2008), "Virginity Testing Puts South African Government, Zulu Tribe at Odds," National Partnership for Women and Families, 30 September. Online. Available HTPP: <http://www.medicalnewstoday.com/articles/123522.php> (accessed 31 August 2009).

Merriam-Webster Online Dictionary (2009) *Merriam-Webster Online Dictionary*. Online. Available HTTP: <http://www.merriam-webster.com/dictionary/frontier> (accessed 18 June 2009).

Mertus, J. (1999) "Women in Kosovo: Contested Terrains," in S. Ramet (ed) *Gender Politics in the Western Balkans: women and society in Yugoslavia and the Yugoslav successor states*, University Park, PA: Pennsylvania State University Press.

Mink, G. (2001) "Violating Women: Rights Abuses in the Welfare Police State," *The ANNALS of the American Academy of Political and Social Science*, 577: 79.

Minow, M. (1985) "Forming Underneath Everything That Grows: Toward a History of Family Law," *Wisconsin Law Review*, 1985: 819.

——(1990) *Making All the Difference: inclusion, exclusion, and American law*, Ithaca, NY: Cornell University Press.

Mitchell, M. (2008) "No Softballs for Minority Journalists," *Chicago Sun-Times*, 28 July: 3.

Mohanty C. (1988) "Under Western Eyes: Feminist Scholarship and Colonial Discourses," *Feminist Review*, 30: 61.

Moore, L. (2008) "Last Year's Role Model," *New York Times*, 13 January: D13. Online. Available HTTP: < http://www.nytimes.com/2008/01/13/opinion/13moore.html?_r=1 > (accessed 29 August 2009).

Morgan, J. (1988) "Feminist Theory as Legal Theory," *Melbourne University Law Review*, 16: 743.

Morin, R. (1992) "Polls Find Wide Doubt of Packwood Remorse over Sexual Advances," *Washington Post*, 18 December: A22.

Morsink, J. (1991) "Women's Rights in the Universal Declaration of Human Rights," *Human Rights Quarterly*, 13: 229

——(2000) *The Universal Declaration of Human Rights: origins, drafting, and intent*, Philadelphia: University of Pennsylvania Press.

Morris, J. (1973) *The Lady was a Bishop: the hidden history of women with clerical ordination and the jurisdiction of bishops*. New York: MacMillan.

Morton, P. (1991) *Disfigured Images: the historical assault on Afro-American women*. Westport, CT: Praeger.

Mossman, M.J. (1986) "Feminism and Legal Method: the Difference it Makes," *Australian Journal of Law and Society*, 3: 30.

——(1991) "Feminism and Legal Method: the Difference it Makes," in M.A. Fineman and N.S. Thomadsen (eds) *At the Boundaries of Law: feminism and legal theory*, New York: Routledge.

——(2006) *The First Women Lawyers: a comparative study of gender, law, and the legal professions*, Oxford: Hart.

——(2008) "'Contextualizing' Bertha Wilson: Wilson as a Woman in Law in Mid-20th Century Canada," in J. Cameron (ed) *Reflections on the Legacy of Justice Bertha Wilson*, Toronto: LexisNexis.

——(forthcoming) "Bertha Wilson: 'Silences' in a Woman's Life Story," in K. Brooks (ed) *One Woman's Difference: the contributions of Justice Bertha Wilson*, Vancouver: University of British Columbia Press.

Mostaghim, R. and Daragahi, B. (2008) "Iran: Women Fight Back, and Score Rare Victory," *Los Angeles Times*, 2 September. Online. Available HTTP: <http://latimesblogs.latimes.com/babylonbeyond/2008/09/iran-women-figh.html> (accessed 31 August 2009).

Mullally, S. (2006) *Gender, Culture and Human Rights: reclaiming universalism*, Oxford: Hart.

Müller-Freienfels, R. (2003) "The Emergence of *Droit de Famille* and *Familienrecht* in Continental Europe and the Introduction of Family Law in England," *Journal of Family History*, 28: 31.

Murray, M. (2008) "The Networked Family: Reframing the Legal Understanding of Caregiving and Caregivers," *Virginia Law Review*, 94: 385.

——(2009) "Strange Bedfellows: Criminal Law, Family Law, and the Legal Construction of Intimate Life," *Iowa Law Review*, 94: 1253.

Murray, P. (1987) *Song in A Weary Throat: an American pilgrimage*, New York: Harper and Row.

———(2006) *Selected Sermons and Writings*, Maryknoll, NY: Orbis Books.

Murray, T.H. (2002) "What are Families for?" *Hastings Center Report*, 32(3): 41.

Myer, C. (1994) "Sex, Sin and Women's Liberation: Against Porn-Suppression," *Texas Law Review*, 72: 1097.

Mykitiuk, R. (1994) "Fragmenting the Body," Australian Feminist Law Journal, 2: 63.

———(2000) "The New Genetics in the Post-Keynesian State," in F. Miller, L. Weir, and R. Mykitiuk (eds) *The Gender of Genetic Futures: the Canadian biotechnology strategy: assessing its effects on women and health*, Toronto: NNEWH Working Paper Series.

———(2002) "Beyond Conception: Legal Determinations of Filiation in the Context of Assisted Reproductive Technologies," *Osgoode Hall Law Journal*, 39: 772.

Naffine, N. (1997) "The Body Bag," in N. Naffine and R. Owens (eds) *Sexing the Subject of Law*, Sydney: LBC.

———(2002) "In Praise of Legal Feminism," *Legal Studies*, 22: 71.

Naffine, N. and Owens, R.J. (eds) (1997) *Sexing the Subject of Law*, Sydney: LBC.

Narayan, U. (1997) *Dislocating Cultures: identities, traditions, and third-world feminism*, New York: Routledge.

National Center for Health Statistics (2006) "Births, Marriages, Divorces, and Deaths: Provisional Data for 2005," in *National Vital Statistics Reports*, 54: 20. Online. Available HTTP: <http://www.cdc.gov/nchs/data/nvsr/nvsr54/nvsr54_20.pdf> (accessed 3 June 2009).

———(2008) *Health, 2008, United States*. Hyattsville, MD: National Center for Health Statistics. Online. Available HTTP: <http://www.cdc.gov/nchs/data/hus/hus08.pdf> (accessed 1 August 2009).

National Public Radio (NPR) (2008a) "Covering Race on the Campaign Trail," [Transcript] *Talk of the Nation*, NPR, 6 August. Online. Available HTTP: <http://www.npr.org/templates/story/story.php?storyId=93344872&ft=1&f=1020> (accessed 27 August 2009).

———(2008b) "Journalistic Guidelines on the Campaign Trail," [Transcript] *Talk of the Nation*, NPR, 30 July. Online. Available HTTP: <http://www.npr.org/templates/story/story.php?storyId=93076313&ps=rs> (accessed 27 August 2009).

Nelson, S.A. (2008) "Black. Female. Accomplished. Attacked." *Washington Post*, 20 July: B1.

Nelson, W. (2004) *In Pursuit of Right and Justice: Edward Weinfeld as lawyer and judge*, New York: New York University Press.

Neubeck, K.J. and Cazenaven, N.A. (2001) *Welfare Racism: playing the race card against America's poor*. New York: Routledge.

New York Times (1985a) "Grant Delay: Group at Issue," *New York Times*, 17 July: C4.

———(1985b) "US Approves Grant on Domestic Violence," *New York Times*, 12 August: A14.

———(1991) "Anita Hill and the Senate's Duty," [Editorial] *New York Times*, 8 October: A24.

———(1992a) "Sexual Harassment in the Senate," [Editorial] *New York Times*, 24 November: A14.

———(1992b) "'Year of the Woman,' As Predicted," *New York Times*, 4 November: A1.

Ní Aoláin, F. (2009) "Gendering the Declaration," 24 *Maryland Journal of International Law* 335.

Ní Aoláin, F. and Hamilton, M. (2009) "Gender and the Rule of Law in Transitional Societies," 18 *Minnesota International Law Review* 380.

Nock, S.L. (2000) "Time and Gender in Marriage," *Virginia Law Review*, 86: 1971.

Norgren, J. (2007) *Belva Lockwood: the woman who would be president*, New York: New York University Press.

Nourse, V.F. (1999) "The Vertical Separation of Powers," *Duke Law Journal*, 49: 749.

——(2004) "Towards a New Constitutional Anatomy," *Stanford Law Review*, 56: 835.

——(2008) *In Reckless Hands*, New York: W.W. Norton.

Nowrojee, B. (2005) *Your Justice is Too Slow: will the ICTR fail Rwanda's rape victims?* Geneva: UN Research Institute for Social Development.

Nussbaum, M.C. (2002) "The Future of Feminist Liberalism," in E.F Kittay and E.K. Feder (eds) *The Subject of Care: feminist perspectives on dependency*, Lanham, MD: Rowman and Littlefield.

——(2006) *Frontiers of Justice: disability, nationality, species membership*, Cambridge, MA: Belknap Press.

Nussbaum, M. and Amartya, S. (1993) *The Quality of Life*, Oxford: Clarendon Press.

Oakes, P. (1998) "The Categorization Process: Cognition and the Group in the Social Psychology of Stereotyping," in W.P. Robinson (ed.) *Social Groups and Identities: developing the legacy of Henri Tajfel*, New York: Routledge.

Obama, B. (2004) *Dreams of my Father: a story of race and inheritance*, New York: Three Rivers Press.

O'Brien, M. (1984) "The Commatisation of Women: Patriarchal Fetishism in the Sociology of Education," *Interchange*, 15: 43.

O'Connor, J.J. (1989) "The Way a Battered Wife Finally Made Herself Heard," *New York Times*, 2 October: C17.

Offen, K. (1988) "Defining Feminism: A Comparative Historical Approach," *Signs: a journal of women in culture and society*, 14: 119.

Office of the Surgeon General (1986) *Surgeon General's Workshop on Violence and Public Health Report*, Washington, DC: Health Resources and Services Administration. Online. Available HTTP: <http://profiles.nlm.nih.gov/NN/B/C/F/X/> (accessed 27 August 2009).

Okin, S.M. (1989) *Justice, Gender, and the Family*, New York: Basic Books.

——(1999) "Is Multiculturalism Bad for Women?" in S.M. Okin, J. Cohen, J. Howard and M.C. Nussbaum (eds) *Is Multiculturalism Bad for Women?* Princeton, NJ: Princeton University Press.

Oldham, T. (2008) "Changes in the Economic Consequences of Divorces, 1958–2008," *Family Law Quarterly*, 42: 419.

Olsen, F.E. (1983) "The Family and the Market: a Study of Ideology and Legal Reform," *Harvard Law Review*, 96: 1497.

Operario, D. and Fiske, S.T. (1999) "Integrating Social Identity and Social Cognition: a Framework for Bridging Diverse Perspectives," in D. Abrams and M.A. Hogg (eds) *Social Identity and Social Cognition*, Malden, MA: Blackwell

Orfield, G. and Lee, C. (2006) *Racial Transformation and the Changing Nature of Segregation*, Cambridge, MA: The Civil Rights Project at Harvard University. Online. Available HTTP: <http://www.civilrightsproject.ucla.edu/research/deseg/deseg06.php> (accessed 27 August 2009).

Organization for Economic Co-operation and Development (OECD) (1996) *The Knowledge-based Economy*, Paris: OECD.

Paglia, C. (2008) "Why Women Shouldn't Vote for Hillary Clinton," *The Sunday Telegraph*, 28 April: 21. Online. Available HTTP: <http://www.telegraph.co.uk/

news/worldnews/1896080/Why-women-shouldnt-vote-for-Hillary-Clinton.html> (accessed 27 August 2009).

Parkman, A. (1992) *No-Fault Divorce: what went wrong?* Boulder, CO: Westview Press.

Patterson, O. (1991) "Race, Gender, and Liberal Fallacies," [Op-Ed] *New York Times*, 20 October: 15. Online. Available HTTP: < http://www.nytimes.com/1991/10/20/opinion/op-ed-race-gender-and-liberal-fallacies.html?scp=1&sq=Race%2C+Gender%2C+and+Liberal+Fallacies&st=nyt> (accessed 27 August 2009).

Paul, A.M. (2006) "The Real Marriage Penalty," *New York Times Magazine*, 19 November: 6.22.

Pearce, D. et al. (1987) *Australian Law Schools: a discipline assessment for the Commonwealth Tertiary Education Commission (Pearce Report)*, Canberra, Australia: Australian Government Publishing Service.

Penguin.com (2009) "Book Clubs/Reading Guides: Bridget Jones's Diary/Helen Fielding." Online. Available HTTP: <http://us.penguingroup.com/static/rguides/us/bridget_joness_diary.html > (accessed 31 August 2009).

Perry, T.L. (1994) "Alimony: Race, Privilege and Dependency in the Search for a Theory," *Georgetown Law Journal*, 82: 2481.

——(2000) "Thoughts on Identity, Choice and Coalition," *Boston College Third World Law Journal*, 20: 111.

Pew Center on the States (2008) *One in One Hundred: behind bars in America 2008*, Washington, DC: Pew Charitable Trusts. Online. Available HTTP: <http://www.pewcenteronthestates.org/report_detail.aspx?id=35904 > (accessed 31 August 2009).

Pheterson, G. (1989) *Not Repeating History, in a Vindication of the Rights of Whores*, Seattle: Seal Press.

Pitt, D.E. (1989) "Montreal Gunman Had Suicide Note," *New York Times*, 8 December: A9.

Polikoff, N. (1993) "We Will Get What We Ask For: Why Legalizing Gay And Lesbian Marriage Will Not 'Dismantle The Legal Structure of Gender In Every Marriage,'" *Virginia Law Review*, 79: 1535.

——(2008) *Beyond (Straight and Gay) Marriage: valuing all families under the law*, Boston: Beacon Press.

Pollis, A. (1982) "Liberal, Socialist and Third World Perspectives of Human Rights," in P. Schwab and A. Pollis (eds) *Towards a Human Rights Framework*, New York: Praeger.

Popenoe, D. (2001) "Testimony of David Popenoe," Hearing on Welfare and Marriage, House Ways and Means Committee, May 22.

Popenoe, D., Blankenhorn, D., and Elshtain, J.B. (1996) *Promises to Keep: the decline and renewal of marriage in America*. Lanham, MD: Rowman and Littlefield.

Popenoe, D. and Whitehead, B.D. (1999) *The State of Our Unions: the social health of marriage in America 1999*, Piscataway, NJ: The National Marriage Project, Rutgers University. Online. Available HTTP: <http://marriage.rutgers.edu/Publications/SOOU/SOOU.htm> (accessed 31 August 2009).

Porter, J. (2008) "You Can't Blame Rendell for Telling it Like it Is," *Daily News*, 5 December: 5.

Posner, R.A. (1992) *Sex and Reason*, Cambridge, MA: Harvard University Press.

Postel, G. (1553) *Les Très Merveilleuses Victoires des Femmes du Nouveau Monde*, Paris: Chez Jehan Ruelle.

Poullain de la Barre, F. (1673) "On the Equality of the Two Sexes," reprinted in M.M Welch (ed.) (2002) *Three Cartesian Feminist Treatises*; trans. Vivien Bosley, Chicago: University of Chicago Press.

Powell, J.A. (1997) "The 'Racing' of American Society: Race Functioning as a Verb before Signifying as a Noun," *Law and Inequality*, 15: 99.

Power, M. (1997) *The Audit Society: rituals of verification*, Oxford: Oxford University Press.

Pronger, B. (2002) *Body Fascism: salvation in the technology of physical fitness*, Toronto: University of Toronto Press.

Purvis, T. and Hunt, A. (1999) "Citizenship versus Identity: Transformations in the Discourses and Practices of Citizenship," *Social and Legal Studies* 8: 457.

Race, K. (1997) "The Beast with Two Backs: Bodies/Selves/Integrity," *Australian Feminist Law Journal*, 9: 24.

Radnay, F. (2003) "Culture, Religion and Gender," *International Journal of Constitutional Law*, 1: 663.

Rapaport, K. and Burkhart, B. (1984) "Personality and Attitudinal Characteristics of Sexually Coercive College Males," *Journal of Abnormal Psychology*, 93: 216.

Razack, S. (ed.) (2002) *Race, Space and the Law: unmapping a white settler society*, Toronto: Between the Lines.

——(2004) "Imperilled Muslim Women, Dangerous Muslim Men, and Civilized Europeans: Legal and Social Response to Forced Marriages," *Feminist Legal Studies*, 12: 129.

——(2008) *Casting Out: race and the eviction of Muslims from Western law and politics*, Toronto: University of Toronto Press.

Ratzinger, J. and Amato, A. (2004) *Letter to the Bishops of the Catholic Church on the Collaboration of Men and Women in the Church and in the World*, Offices of the Congregation for the Doctrine of the Faith, 31 May 2004. Online. Available HTTP: <http://www.vatican.va/roman_curia/congregations/cfaith/documents/rc_con_cfaith_doc_20040731_ collaboration_en.html > (accessed 7 June 2009).

Rees, M. (2002) "International Intervention in Bosnia-Herzegovina: the Cost of Ignoring Gender," in C. Cockburn and D. Zarkov (eds) *The Post-War Moment: militaries, masculinities and international peacekeeping*, London: Lawrence.

Resnik, J. (2000) "The Programmatic Judiciary: Lobbying, Judging, and Invalidating the Violence Against Women Act," *Southern California Law Review*, 74: 269.

Rhode, D. (1990) "Feminist Critical Theories," *Stanford Law Review*, 42: 617.

Rich, A. (1980) "Compulsory Heterosexuality and Lesbian Existence," *Signs*, 5: 631.

Ritter, G. (2006) *The Constitution as Social Design: gender and civic membership in the American constitutional order*, Palo Alto, CA: Stanford University Press.

Rivers, C. and Barnett, R.C. (2007) "The Difference Myth," *Boston Globe*, 28 October. Online. Available HTTP: <http://www.boston.com/news/globe/ideas/articles/2007/10/28/the_difference_myth/ > (accessed 31 August 2009).

Roberts, D.E. (1995) "Irrationality and Sacrifice in the Welfare Reform Debates," *Virginia Law Review*, 81: 2607.

——(1997) *Killing the Black Body: race, reproduction, and the meaning of liberty*, New York: Pantheon.

Robinson, L. (1888) Letter to Louis Frank, *Papiers Frank* No. 6031 (file 2), Brussels: Bibliothèque Royale.

——(1890) "Women Lawyers in the United States," *The Green Bag*: 2: 10.

Robinson, R.L. (2001) "The Underclass and the Role of Race Consciousness: a New Age Critique of Black Wealth/White Wealth and American Apartheid," *Indiana Law Review*, 34: 1377.

Rollins, J. (1985) *Between Women: domestics and their employers*, Philadelphia: Temple University Press.

Romano, L. (2008) "Clinton Puts up a New Fight," *Washington Post*, 20 May: C1.

Romero, A.P. (2007) "Methodological Descriptions: 'Feminist' and 'Queer' Legal Theories," *Yale Journal of Law and Feminism*, 19: 227.

——(forthcoming) "Living Alone: New Demographic Research," in M.A. Fineman (ed) *Transcending the Boundaries of Law: generations of legal feminism*. London: Routledge.

Rorty, R. (1989) *Contingency, Irony and Solidarity*, Cambridge: Cambridge University Press.

Rose, N. (1999) *Reframing Political Thought*, Cambridge: Cambridge University Press.

Rosen, C. (2003) "Eugenics – Sacred and Profane," *The New Atlantis*, 2: 79. Online. Available HTTP: <http://www.thenewatlantis.com/publications/eugenics-sacred-and-profane> (accessed 6 February 2009).

Rosenbury, L.A. (2003) "Feminist Legal Scholarship: Charting Topics and Authors, 1978–2002," *Columbia Journal of Gender and the Law*, 12: 446.

——(2005) "Two Ways to End a Marriage: Divorce or Death," *Utah Law Review*, 2005: 1227.

——(2007a) "Between Home and School," *University of Pennsylvania Law Review*, 155: 833.

——(2007b) "Friends with Benefits?," *Michigan Law Review*, 106: 189.

Rosky, C. (2009) "Like Father, Like Son: Homosexuality, Parenthood, and the Gender of Homophobia," *Yale Journal of Law and Feminism*, 20: 257.

Rothman, B.K. (2001) *The Book of Life: a personal and ethical guide to race, normality and the human gene study*, Boston: Beacon Press.

Rudd, K. (2009) "The Global Financial Crisis," *The Monthly: Australian Politics, Society and Culture*, 42: 20.

Ruskola, T. (2005) "Gay Rights versus Queer Theory: What is Left of Sodomy after *Lawrence v. Texas*?," *Social Text*, 84–85: 235.

Rutherford, J. (1990) "Duty in Divorce: Shared Income as a Path to Equality," *Fordham Law Review*, 58: 539.

Rutten, T. (2008) "The Good Generation Gap," *Los Angeles Times*, 6 February: A31. Online. Available HTTP: <http://www.latimes.com/news/opinion/la-oe-rutten6-feb06,0,776156.story > (accessed 29 August 2009).

Satz, A.B. (2008) "Disability, Vulnerability, and the Limits of Antidiscrimination, Symposium: Framing Legal and Human Rights Strategies for Change: a Case Study of Disability Rights in Asia," *Washington Law Review*, 83: 524.

Sauder, M. and Espeland, N. (2009) "The Discipline of Rankings: Tight Coupling and Organizational Change," *American Sociological Review*, 74: 63.

Savell, K. (2006) "Is the 'Born Alive' Rule Outdated and Indefensible?," *Sydney Law Review*, 28: 625.

Sawer, M. (2004) "Populism and Public Choice in Australia and Canada: Turning Equality-Seekers into 'Special Interests,'" in M. Sawer and B. Hindess (eds) *Us and Them: anti-elitism in Australia*, Perth, Australia: API Network, Australia Research Institute, Curtin University of Technology.

——(2008) "Disappearing Tricks," *Dialogue: Academy of the Social Sciences in Australia*, 27: 2.

Saxton, M. (1998) "Disability Rights and Selective Abortion," in R. Sollinger (ed) *Abortion Wars: half a century of struggle 1950–2000*, Berkeley, CA: University of California Press.

Scales, A.C. (1981) "Towards a Feminist Jurisprudence," *Indiana Law Journal*, 56: 398.

——(1986) "The Emergence of Feminist Jurisprudence: an Essay," *Yale Law Journal*, 95: 1373.

Schacter, J.S. (2004) "Ely and the Idea of Democracy," *Stanford Law Review*, 57: 737.

Scherer, M. (2008) "Hillary is from Mars, Barack is from Venus," *Salon.com*, 17 July. Online Available HTTP: <http://www.salon.com/news/feature/2007/07/12/obama_hillary/ > (accessed 27 August 2009).

Schlafly, P. (2008) "Sexism: Hillary's False Boogeyman," *World Net Daily Commentary*. Online. Available HTTP: <http://www.wnd.com/index.php?pageId=67507> (accessed 27 August 2009).

Schlessinger, L.C. (2004) *The Proper Care and Feeding of Husbands*, New York: Harper Collins.

Schmitter, P.C. and Trechsel, A.H. (2004) *The Future of Democracy in Europe: trends, analysis and reforms*, Strasbourg: Council of Europe Publications.

Schneider, C. (1985) "Moral Discourse and the Transformation of American Family Law," *Michigan Law Review*, 83: 1803.

——(1992) "The Channeling Function in Family Law," *Hofstra Law Review*, 20: 495.

Schneider, D.J. (2004) *The Psychology of Stereotyping*, New York: Guilford Press.

Schneider, E.M. (1994) "The Violence of Privacy," in M.A. Fineman and R. Mykitiuk (eds) *The Public Nature of Private Violence: the discovery of domestic abuse*, New York: Routledge.

Schoen, J. (2005) *Choice and Coercion: birth control, sterilization, and abortion in public health and welfare*, Chapel Hill, NC: University of North Carolina Press.

Schultz, V. (2000) "Life's Work," *Columbia Law Review*, 100: 1881.

——(2003) "The Sanitized Workplace," *Yale Law Journal*, 112: 2061.

Schwartz, C.R. and Mare, R.D. (2005) "Trends in Educational Assortative Marriage from 1940 to 2003," *Demography*, 42: 621.

Schwartz, P. (1994) *Love Between Equals: How Peer Marriage Really Works*, New York: Free Press.

Sclater, S.D. (2002) "Introduction," in M. Richards, A. Bainham, and S.D. Sclater (eds), *Body Lore and Laws*, Portland, OR: Hart.

Scolforo, M. (2008) "Rendell Apologizes for Comments on Napolitano," *Pittsburgh Post-Gazette*, 4 December: B5.

Scully, J.L. (2008) "Disability Bioethics: Moral Bodies, Moral Difference," Lanham, MD: Rowman and Littlefield.

Sentencing Project, The, (2006) *New Incarceration Figures: Thirty Three Consecutive Years of Growth*. Online. Available HTTP: <http://www.sentencingproject.org/doc/publications/inc_newfigures.pdf > (accessed 29 August 2009).

Shapiro, M. (2001) "Institutionalizing Administrative Space," in A.S. Sweet, W. Sandholtz, and N. Fligstein, *The Institutionalization of Europe*, Oxford: Oxford University Press.

Sheldon, S. (1999) "Reconceiving Masculinity: Imagining Men's Reproductive Bodies in Law," *Journal of Law and Society*, 26: 129.

Shildrick, M. (1997) *Leaky Bodies and Boundaries: feminism, postmodernism and (bio)ethics*, London: Routledge.

——(2002) *Embodying the Monster: encounters with the vulnerable self*, London: Sage.

——(2005a) "Beyond the Body of Bioethics: Challenging the Conventions" in M. Shildrick and R. Mykitiuk (eds) *Ethics of the Body: postconventional challenges*, Cambridge, MA: MIT Press.

——(2005b) "Transgressing the Law with Foucault and Derrida: Some Reflections on Anomalous Embodiment," *Critical Quarterly*, 47:30.

Shircliffe, B.J. (2000) "Feminist Reflections on University Activism through Women's Studies at a State University: Narratives of Promise, Compromise and Powerlessness," *Frontiers*, 21: 38.

Siegel, (1996) "'The Rule of Love': Wife Beating as Prerogative and Privacy," *Yale Law Journal*, 105: 2117.

Silver, V. (1996) "In Egypt's Schools, Fashion is Politics," *New York Times*, 30 June: A38.

Simon, W.E. (2004) *A Time for Reflection: an Autobiography*, Washington, DC: Regnery.

Simon, W.H. (2001) "Fear and Loathing of Politics in the Legal Academy," *Journal of Legal Education*, 51: 175.

Singer, J. (1989) "Divorce Reform and Gender Justice," *North Carolina Law Review*, 67: 1103.

Slaughter, A. (2004) *A New World Order*, Princeton, N.J.: Princeton University Press.

Smart, C. (1989) *Feminism and the Power of Law*, Routledge, London.

Smith, B. (2007) "From Wardley to Purvis: How Far has Australian Anti-Discrimination Law Come in 30 Years?" *Australian Journal of Labour Law*, 21: 3.

Smith, B.G. (2004) "Introduction" in B.G. Smith and B. Hutchinson (eds) *Gendering Disability*, Piscataway, NJ: Rutgers University Press.

Snyder, B. (2000) "How the Conservatives Canonized *Brown v. Board of Education*," *Rutgers Law Review*, 52: 383.

Soble, A. (2008) "Antioch's Sexual Offense Policy: a Philosophical Exploration" in A. Soble and N. Power (eds) *Philosophy of Sex: contemporary readings* (5th edn) Lanham, MD: Rowman and Littlefield.

Solinger, R. (2001) *Beggars and Choosers: how the politics of choice shapes adoption, abortion, and welfare in the United States*, New York: Hill and Wang.

Spillenger, C. (2005) "Revenge of the Triple Negative: a Note on the Brandeis Brief in *Muller v. Oregon*," *Constitutional Commentary*, 22: 5.

Spitz, L. (2004) "At the Intersection of North American Free Trade and Same-Sex Marriage," *U.C.L.A. Journal of International Law and Foreign Affairs*, 9: 163.

——(2005) "The Gift of Enron: an Opportunity to Talk About Capitalism, Equality, Globalization and the Promise of a North American Charter of Fundamental Rights," *Ohio State Law Journal*, 66: 315.

——(2009) "The Evolving Architecture of North American Integration," *University of Colorado Law Review*, 80: 735.

Stack, C.B. (1974) *All our Kin: strategies for survival in a black community*, New York: Harper and Row.

Stern, M.B. (1994) "The First Woman Admitted to Practice before the United States Supreme Court: Belva Ann Lockwood: 1879," in M.B. Stern, *We the Women: Career Firsts of Nineteenth-Century America*, Lincoln, NE: University of Nebraska Press.

Stevens, R. (1983) *Law School: legal education in America from the 1850s to the 1980s*, Chapel Hill, NC: University of North Carolina Press.

Stone, P. (2007) *Opting Out? Why women really quit career and head home*, Berkeley, CA: University of California Press.

Strebeigh, F. (2009) *Equal: women reshape American law*, New York: W.W. Norton.

Sugarman, S. (1990) "Dividing Financial Interests at Divorce," in S. Sugarman and H. Kay (eds) *Divorce Reform at the Crossroads*, New Haven, CT: Yale University Press.

Sullivan, A. (2008a) "Gender Bender," *Time*, 16 June: 36.

——(2008b) "Why Didn't More Women Vote for Hillary?" *Time*, 5 June. Online. Available HTTP: <http://www.time.com/time/magazine/article/0,9171,1812050,00. html?imw=Y > (accessed 29 August 2009).

Sullivan, M. (2004) *The Family of Woman: lesbian mothers, their children, and the undoing of gender*, Berkeley, CA: University of California Press.

Summers, A. (2003) *The End of Equality: work, babies and women's choices in 21st century Australia*, Sydney: Random House.

Sunstein, C. (1998) *The Partial Constitution*, Cambridge, MA: Harvard University Press.

Swarns, R.L. (2009) "An In-Law is Finding Washington to her Liking," *New York Times*, 4 May: A11.

Sweet, A.S. et al. (eds) (2001) *The Institutionalization of Europe*, Oxford: Oxford University Press.

Symposium (1987) "Minority Critiques of the Critical Legal Studies Movement," *Harvard Civil Rights-Civil Liberties Law Review*, 22: 297.

Tagger, B.A. (1997) "Interpreting African American Women's History through Historic Landscapes, Structures, and Commemorative Sites," *OAH Magazine of History*, 12: 17. Online. Available HTTP: <http://www.oah.org/pubs/magazine/women/tagger.htm> (accessed 27 August 2009).

Tapper, J. (2008) "McCaskill: Obama the First Black Leader to 'Come to the American People Not as a Victim but Rather as a Leader,'" Online. Available HTTP: <http://blogs.abcnews.com/politicalpunch/2008/03/mccaskill-obama.html> (accessed 29 August 2009).

Taylor, K. and Mykitiuk, R. (2001) "Genetics, Normalcy and Disability," *ISUMA: Canadian Journal of Policy Research/Revue Canadienne de Recherche sur les Politiques*, 2: 65.

"Telltale Gene, The" (1990) *Consumer Reports*, 55: 438.

Thernstrom, A. and Thernstrom, S. (2008) "Taking Race Out of the Race," *Los Angeles Times*, 2 March: M5.

Thomas, C. (2007) *Sociologies of Disability and Illness: contested ideas in disability studies and medical sociology*, New York: Palgrave Macmillan.

Thomas, W.C. (2008) "Obama Challenges Journalists' Objectivity," *Commercial Appeal*, 28 July: B1.

Thornton, M. (1986) "Feminist Jurisprudence: Illusion or Reality?" *Australian Journal of Law and Society*, 3: 5.

——(1991) "Feminism and the Contradictions of Law Reform," *International Journal of the Sociology of Law*, 19: 453.

——(ed.) (1995) *Public and Private: feminist legal debates*, Melbourne: Oxford University Press.

——(1996) *Dissonance and Distrust: women in the legal profession*, Melbourne: Oxford University Press.

——(1999) "Towards Embodied Justice: Wrestling with Legal Ethics in the Age of the New Corporatism," *Melbourne University Law Review*, 23: 749.

——(2001) "EEO in a Neo-Liberal Climate," *J Interdisciplinary Gender Studies*, 6(1): 77–104.

——(2004) "Neoliberal Melancholia: the Case of Feminist Legal Scholarship," *Australian Feminist Law Journal*, 20: 7.

——(2006) "The Dissolution of the Social in the Legal Academy," *Australian Feminist Law Journal*, 25: 3.

——(2008) "The Evisceration of Equal Employment Opportunity in Higher Education," *Australian Universities' Review*, 50: 59.

Tombs, S. and Whyte, D. (eds) (2003) *Unmasking the Crimes of the Powerful: scrutinizing states and corporations*, New York: Peter Lang.

Trost, C. (1989) "Born to Lose: Babies of Crack Users, Crowded Hospitals, Break Everybody's Heart," *Wall Street Journal*, 18 July: 1.

Tsoukala, P. (2007) "Gary Becker, Legal Feminism, and the Costs of Moralizing Care," *Columbia Journal of Gender and Law*, 16: 357.

Turner, B.S. (2006) *Vulnerability and Human Rights*, University Park, PA: Pennsylvania State University Press.

United Kingdom Home Office (2004) *The End of Parallel Lives?*, London: Home Office.

US Census Bureau (1990) *1990 Census of Population and Housing*, Summary Tape File 1. Online. Available HTTP: <http://factfinder.census.gov/metadoc/1990stf1td.pdf> (accessed 27 August 2009).

——(2000) *Census of Population and Housing*, Summary File 1. Online. Available HTTP: <http://www.census.gov/prod/cen2000/doc/sf1.pdf> (accessed 27 August 2009).

——(2004) *Households by Type: 1940 to Present*. Online. Available HTTP: <http://www.census.gov/population/socdemo/hh-fam/tabHH-1.pdf> (accessed 27 August 2009).

——(2006a) *American Community Survey, Puerto Rico Community Survey, 2006 Subject Definitions*, Washington, DC: GPO. Online. Available HTTP: <http://www.census.gov/acs/www/Downloads/2006/usedata/Subject_Definitions.pdf> (accessed 3 June 2009).

——(2006b) *2006 American Community Survey*. Online. Available HTTP <http://factfinder.census.gov/servlet/DatasetMainPageServlet?_program=ACSsubmenuId=lang=ents=> (accessed 27 August 2009).

——(2007) *Poverty Thresholds: 2007*, Washington, DC: GPO. Online. Available HTTP <http://www.census.gov/hhes/www/poverty/threshld/thresh07.html> (accessed 3 June 2009).

——(2008) *Historical Poverty Tables*. Online. Available HTTP: <http://www.census.gov/hhes/www/poverty/poverty.html> (accessed 27 August 2009).

——(2009) *Statistical Abstract of the United States: 2009*, Washington, DC: GPO.

US Children's Bureau (2002) *The AFCARS Report: interim FY 2000 estimates as of August 2002*, Washington, DC: US Department of Health and Human Services, Administration for Children and Families.

US Department of Justice, Bureau of Justice Statistics (1998) *Correctional Populations in the United States, 1998*. Online. Available HTTP: <http://www.ojp.usdoj.gov/bjs/pub/pdf/cpus9805.pdf> (accessed 27 August 2009).

——(2007) *Criminal Offenders Statistics*. Online. Available HTTP: <http://www.ojp.usdoj.gov/bjs/crimoff.htm#prevalence> (accessed 27 August 2009).

US Department of Labor, Bureau of Labor Statistics (2007) *Women in the Labor Force: a Data Book*. Online. Available HTTP: <http://www.bls.gov/cps/wlf-databook2007.htm> (accessed 27 August 2009).

——(2008) *Highlights of Women's Earnings in 2007*. Online. Available HTTP: <http://www.bls.gov/cps/cpswom2007.pdf> (accessed 27 August 2009).

Valdez, F. et al. (eds) (2002) *Crossroads, Directions and a New Critical Race Theory*, Philadelphia: Temple University Press.

Valverde, M. (1987) *Sex, Power and Pleasure*, Toronto: Women's Press; reprinted in J.G. Greenberg, D.E. Roberts, and M.L. Minow (eds) (1998) *Women and the Law*, 2nd edn, New York: Foundation Press.

Van Howe, R.S. and Svoboda, J.S. (2008) "Neonatal Pain Relief and the Helsinki Declaration," *Journal of Law, Medicine, and Ethics*, 36: 803.

Van Wagner, E. et al. (2008) "Constructing 'Health,' Defining 'Choice': Legal and Policy Perspectives on the Post-PGD Embryo in Four Jurisdictions," *Medical Law International*, 9: 45.

Vokes, R. (2002) "The Arusha Tribunal: Whose Justice?," *Anthropology Today*, 18: 1.

Volpp L. (2001) "Feminism versus Multiculturalism," *Columbia. Law Review*, 101: 1181.

——(2007) "The Culture of Citizenship," *Theoretical Inquiries in Law*, 8: 571.

Waldby, C. (1995) "Destruction: Boundary Erotics and Refiguration of the Heterosexual Male Body," in E. Grosz and E. Probyn (eds) *Sexy Bodies: the strange carnalities of feminism*, London: Routledge.

Waldeck, S. "On the Cutting Edge: Social Norm Theory and Male Circumcision," paper presented at An Uncomfortable Conversation – Sexuality and Feminist Theory: Road Blocks, Detours, and New Directions, Cornell Law School, 15–16 November 2002.

Warner, M. (2002) "Beyond Gay Marriage," in W. Brown and J. Halley (eds) *Left Legalism/Left Critique*. Durham, NC: Duke University Press.

Washington Post (1985a) "Reagan's Charge to Delegates," *Washington Post*, 11 July: B10.

——(1985b) "SEC Enforcement Chief Beat Wife Repeatedly, Court Told," *Washington Post*, 26 February.

——(1985c) "Sheltering Victims of Abuse," [Op-Ed] *Washington Post*, 14 July: B6.

——(1987) "Hall Denies Smuggling Papers in her Clothes," *Washington Post*, 16 May: A9.

——(1992) "Expanding Federal Court Role Opposed," *Washington Post*, 1 January: A29.

——(2008) "Measure those Drapes Now," [Editorial] *Washington Post*, 29 October: A16.

Wasserstrom, R.A. (1977) "Racism, Sexism, and Preferential Treatment: an Approach to the Topics," *U.C.L.A. Law Review*, 24: 581.

Weber, M. (1946) *From Max Weber: essays in sociology*, H.H. Gerth and C.W. Mills (eds) Oxford: Oxford University Press.

Weisbrod, C. (1994) "The Way We Live Now: a Discussion of Contracts and Domestic Arrangements," *Utah Law Review*, 1994: 777.

Weitzman, L.J. (1981) *The Marriage Contract: spouses, lovers, and the law*, New York: Free Press.

——(1985) *The Divorce Revolution: the unexpected social and economic consequences for women and children in America*, New York: Free Press.

Wessley, S.E. (1978) "The Thirteenth-Century Guglielmites: Salvation through Women," in D. Baker (ed.) *Medieval Women: dedicated and presented to professor Rosalind M.T. Hill on the occasion of her seventieth birthday*, Oxford: Blackwell.

Whitworth, S. (1994) *Feminism and International Relations: towards a political economy of gender in interstate and non-governmental institutions*, New York: St. Martin's Press.

Widiss, D. et al. (2007) "Exposing Sex Stereotypes in Recent Same-sex Marriage Jurisprudence," *Harvard Journal of Law and Gender*, 30: 472.

Wiegman, R. (2002) "Academic Feminism against Itself," *National Women's Studies Association Journal*, 14: 18.

Williams, J. (1994a) "Is Coverture Dead? Beyond a New Theory of Alimony," *Georgetown Law Journal*, 82: 2227.

——(1994b) "Married Women and Property," *Virginia Journal of Social Policy and Law*, 1: 383.

——(2000) *Unbending Gender: why family and work conflict and what to do about it*, New York: Oxford University Press.

Williams, J. and Negrin, M. (2008) "Affirmative Action Foes Point to Obama," *Boston Globe*, 18 March: A1. Online. Available HTTP: <http://www.boston.com/news/nation/articles/2008/03/18/affirmative_action_foes_point_to_obama/?page=1> (accessed 29 August 2009).

Williams, J.A. (2007) "The Equal Application Defense: The Equal Application Defense," *University of Pennsylvania Journal of Constitutional Law*, 9: 1207.

Williams, J.C. (1989) "Deconstructing Gender," *Michigan Law Review*, 87: 797.

Williams, P.J. (1987) "Alchemical Notes: Reconstructing Ideals from Deconstructed Rights," *Harvard Civil Rights-Civil Liberties Law Review*, 22: 401.

——(1991) *The Alchemy of Race and Rights*. Cambridge, MA: Harvard University Press.

Williams, S.J. and Bendelow, G.A. (1999), *The Lived Body: sociological themes, embodied issues*, London: Routledge.

Williams, W.W. (1982) "The Equality Crisis: Some Reflections on Culture, Courts, and Feminism," in K.T. Bartlett and R. Kennedy (eds) *Feminist Legal Theory: readings in law and gender*, New York: Westview Press.

——(1985) "Equality's Riddle: Pregnancy and the Equal Treatment/Special Treatment Debate," *New York University Review of Law and Social Change* 13: 325.

Wilson, W.J. (1987) *The Truly Disadvantaged: the inner city, the underclass, and public policy*, Chicago: University of Chicago Press.

——(1997) *When Work Disappears: the world of the new urban poor*, New York: Random House.

Wing, A.K. (1997; 2nd edn 2003) *Critical Race Feminism: a reader*, New York: New York University Press.

West, R. (1988) "Jurisprudence and Gender," *University of Chicago Law Review*, 55: 1.

——(1990) "Equality Theory, Marital Rape, and the Promise of the Fourteenth Amendment," *Florida Law Review*, 42: 45.

——(1997) *Caring for Justice*, New York: New York University Press.

——(2003) *Re-imagining Justice: progressive interpretations of formal equality, rights, and the rule of law*, Burlington, VT: Ashgate.

Wolf, N. (1993) *Fire with Fire: the new female power and how it will change the 21st century*. New York: Random House.

Woolf, V. (1991) *A Room of One's Own*, an HBJ Modern Classic, New York: Harcourt Brace Jovanovich.

Wong, J. (1999) "The Anti-Essentialism v. Essentialism Debate in Feminist Legal Theory: the Debate and Beyond," *William and Mary Journal of Law and Women*, 5: 273.

Wright, R. (1994) "Feminists, Meet Mr. Darwin," *The New Republic*, 211(22): 34.

——(1995) *The Moral Animal: why we are the way we are: the new science of evolutionary psychology*, New York: Vintage Books.

Young, I.M. (2000) *Inclusion and Democracy*, Oxford: Oxford University Press.

Yoshino, K. (2006a) *Covering: the hidden assault on our civil rights*, New York: Random House.

——(2006b) "Too Good for Marriage," *New York Times*, 14 July: A19.

Yuval-Davis, N. (2006), "Belonging and the Politics of Belonging," *Patterns of Prejudice*, 40: 197.

Yuval-Davis, N. et al. (2005) "Secure Borders and Safe Haven and the Gendered Politics of Belonging: Beyond Social Cohesion," *Ethnic and Racial Studies*, 28: 513.

Yuval-Davis, N. et al. (eds) (2006) *The Situated Politics of Belonging*, New York: Sage.

Zihlman, A. (1997) "The Paleolithic Glass Ceiling: Women in Human Evolution," in L.D. Hager (ed.) *Women in Human Evolution*, London: Routledge.

Cases

Adkins v. Children's Hospital, 261 US 525 (1923).

Azmi v. Kirklees Metropolitan Borough Council, ICR 1154, IRLR 484, UKEAT 0009_07_03 (2007).

Baehr v. Lewin, 852 P.2d 44 (Haw. 1993).

Baker v. Vermont, 744 A.2d 864 (Vt. 1999).

Blanchard v. Bergeron, 489 US 87 (1989).

Bosley v. Mclaughlin, 236 US 385 (1915).

Bradwell v. Illinois, 83 US 130 (1872).

Brown v. Board of Education, 347 US 483 (1954).

Conaway v. Deane, 932 A.2d 571(Md. 2007).

Dogru v. France, 27058/05, ECHR 1579 (2008).

DPP v. Morgan, AC 182 (1976).

Eisenstadt v. Baird, 405 US 438 (1972).

Ex parte Hawley, 22 Ohio Dec. 39 (1911).

Frontiero v. Richardson, 411 US 677(1973).

Goodridge v. Department of Public Health, 798 N.E. 2d 941 (Mass. 2003).

Hawley v. Walker, 232 US 718 (1914).

Hernandez v. Robles, 855 N.E. 2d 1 (2006).

In re French, 37 N.B.R. 359 (Can. 1905).

In re Hall, 50 Conn. 131 (Conn. 1882).

In re Ricker, 66 N.H. 207 (N.H. 1890).

Kerrigan v. Commissioner of Public Health, 957 A.2d 407 (2008).

Lawrence v. Texas, 539 US 558 (2003).

Lewis v. Harris, 875 A.2d 259 (2005).

Lewis v. Harris, 908 A.2d 196 (2006).

Lochner v. New York, 198 US 45 (1905).

Mme E.Y., 2/6 ssr, 3 février 1999, au rapport de Mme de Margerie.

Mme M, No 286798, Conseil d'État, séance du 26 mai 2008, lecture du 27 juin 2008. Online. Available HTTP: <http://www.conseil-etat.fr/ce/jurispd/index_ac_ld0820. shtml > (accessed 15 May 2009).

Miller v. Wilson, 236 US 373 (1915).

Mississippi University for Women v. Hogan, 458 US 718 (1982).

Missouri v. Holland, 252 US 416 (1920).

Muller v. Oregon, 208 US 412 (1908).

Prosecutor v. Akayesu, Case No. ICTR-96-4 (1998).

Prosecutor v. Furundžija, Case No. IT-95-17/1-T (1998).

Prosecutor v. Gacumbitsi, Case No. ICTR-2001-64-A (2006).

Prosecutor v. Lukić, Case No. IT-98-32/1-T (2009).

Prosecutor v. Kunarac, Kovač, and Vuković, Case No. IT-96-23-T and IT-96-23/1-T (2001).

Prosecutor v. Kunarac, Kovač, and Vuković, Case No. IT-96-23 and IT-96-23/1-A (2002).

Prosecutor v. Muhimana, Case No. ICTR-95-1B-T (2005).

Prosecutor v. Nyiramasuhuko et al. Transcripts, Case No. ICTR-98-42-T (2001).

Purvis v. New South Wales, HCA 62, 202 ALR 133 (2003).

R v. Big M Drug Mart, 1 S.C.R. 295 (Can. 1985).

R v. Johns, SA Supreme Court (unreported) 26 August (1992).
R v. King, 59 NSWLR 472 (2003).
R v. Morgentaler, 1 S.C.R. 30 (1988).
R (Begum) v. Head Teacher and Governors of Denbigh High School, 1 AC 100 (2007).
Reed v. Reed, 404 US 71 (1971).
Re A (Conjoined twins: Medical treatment), 4 All ER 961 (2000).
Şahin v. Turkey, application no. 44774/98, Grand Chamber Judgment of 10th
    November 2005, 19 BHRC 590 (2005).
United States v. Anthony, 24 F. Cas. 829 (CCNDNY 1873).
United States v. Darby, 312 US 100 (1941).
United States v. Lopez, 514 US 549 (1995).
United States v. Morrison, 529 US 598 (2000).
United States v. Virginia, 518 U.S. 515 (1996).
Warren v. State, 336 S.E.2d 221 (1985).
Weinberger v. Wiesenfeld, 420 US 636 (1975).
West Coast Hotel v. Parrish, 300 US 379 (1937).

Constitutions, conventions, and treaties

Charter of the United Nations, 59 Stat. 1031, T.S. 993, 3 Bevans 1153 (1945).
Convention on the Elimination of all Forms of Discrimination Against Women
    (CEDAW), G.A. res. 34/180, 34 UN GAOR Supp. (No. 46) at 193, UN Doc. A/34/
    46 (1945). Online. Available HTTP: <http://www.un.org/womenwatch/daw/cedaw/
    cedaw.htm> (accessed 26 August 2009).
Pennsylvania Constitution of 1776, Preamble. Online. Available HTTP: <http://www.
    paconstitution.duq.edu/PAC_C_1776.html > (accessed 25 August 2009).
Universal Declaration of Human Rights, G.A. Res. 217 A (III), UN Doc A/810 at
    71 (1948).
US Constitution, amendment XIX (ratified 18 August 1920).
Vermont Constitution, chap. 1, art. 7 (2002).

Judicial rules

Rules of Procedure and Evidence of the International Tribunal for Rwanda, UN Doc.
    ITR/3/Rev.1 (adopted on 29 June 1995). Online. Available HTTP: <http://www.ictr.
    org/ENGLISH/rules/080314/080314.pdf> (accessed 29 August 2009).
Rules of Procedure and Evidence of the International Tribunal for the Former Yugoslavia,
    UN Doc. IT/32/Rev. 7 (entered into force 14 March 1994). Online. Available
    HTTP: <http://www.icty.org/sections/LegalLibrary/RulesofProcedureandEvidence>
    (accessed 29 August 2009).

Legislative materials

Domestic Violence Prevention and Services Act, S. 1843, 96th Cong. (1979).
US Senate (1980a), 126 Cong. Rec. 22,797 (25 August 1980) (statement of Sen.
    Humphrey).
US Senate (1980b), 126 Cong. Rec. 22,825 (25 August 1980) (statement of Sen. Hatch).
US Senate (1980c), 126 Cong. Rec. 22, 839 (25 August 1980) (statement of the Heritage
    Foundation inserted into record by Sen. Humphrey).

US Senate (1980d), 126 Cong. Rec. 22, 821–22,846 (25 August 1980).

US Senate (1980e), 126 Cong. Rec. 22, 843 (25 August 1980).

US Senate (1980f), 126 Cong. Rec. 24,846 (25 August 1980) (statement of Sen. Cranston).

US Senate (1980g), 126 Cong. Rec. 24,120 (4 September 1980) (statement Sen. Helms).

Violence Against Women Act: Hearing on H.R. 1502 before the Subcommittee on Crime and Criminal Justice of the Committee on the Judiciary, House of Representatives, 100th Cong., 25 (1992a) (statement of Rep. Sensenbrenner).

Violence Against Women Act: Hearing on H.R. 1502 before the Subcommittee on Crime and Criminal Justice of the Committee on the Judiciary, House of Representatives, 100th Cong., 7–8, 10–11 (1992b) (statement of Sen. Biden).

Other legal documents

Amicus Brief Respecting Amendment of the Indictment and Supplementation of the Evidence to Ensure the Prosecution of Rape and Other Sexual Violence within the Competence of the Tribunal, *Prosecutor v. Akayesu*, Case No. ICTR-96–4 (1997). Online. Available HTTP: <http://www.womensrightscoalition.org/site/advocacyDossiers/rwanda/Akayesu/amicusbrief_en.php > (accessed 30 August 2009).

Conclusions de Mme Prada Bordenave (2008), Commissaire du Gouvernement, p. 4. Online. Available HTTP: <http://www.conseiletat.fr/ce/jurispd/conclusions/conclusions_286798.pdf > (accessed 15 May 2008).

Decision on Prosecution Motion Seeking Leaving to Amend the Second Indictment, *Prosecutor v. Lukić*, IT-98-32/1-PT, 8 July 2008.

Prosecution Motion, *Prosecutor v. Lukić*, IT-98–32, 12 June 2008.

Sixth Annual Report of the ICTR (2000–2001). Online. Available HTTP: <http://69.94.11.53/ENGLISH/annualreports/index.htm> (accessed 30 August 2009).

Status Conference for *Prosecutor v. Lukić*, T. 124–26, 4 September 2007.

Statutes

Fair Labor Standards Act of 1938, 29 USC §§ 201–19 (2000).

Family and Medical Leave Act of 1993, 29 USC §§2601–54 (2009).

Personal Responsibility and Work Opportunity Act of 1996, 42 USC § 601 et seq. (2009).

Rome Statute of the International Criminal Court (1998). Online. Available HTTP: <http://untreaty.un.org/cod/icc/index.html> (accessed 29 August 2009).

Social Security Act of 1935, 42 USC § 601 et seq. (2009).

Statute of the International Criminal Tribunal for Rwanda, adopted by S.C. Res. 955, UN SCOR, 49th Sess., 3453d mtg. at 3, UN Doc. S/Res/955 (1994). Online. Available HTTP: <http://www.ictr.org/ENGLISH/basicdocs/statute/2007.pdf> (accessed 29 August 2009).

Statute of the International Criminal Tribunal for the Former Yugoslavia, UN Doc. S/25704 at 36, annex, S/25704/Add.1, adopted by S.C. on 25 May 1993, UN Doc. S/Res/827 (1993). Online Available HTTP: <http://www.icty.org/sid/135> (accessed 29 August 2009).

Index